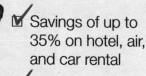

# Alabama & Florida Panhandle

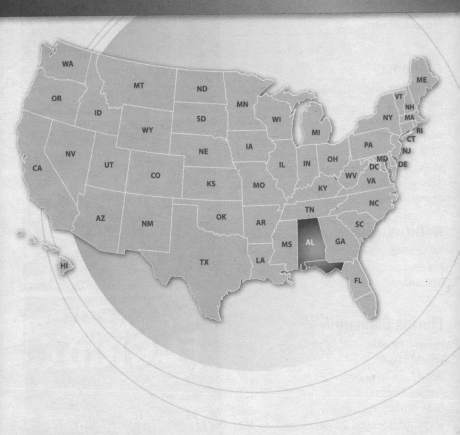

**Published by AAA Publishing**
1000 AAA Drive, Heathrow, FL 32746-5063
Copyright AAA 2014, All rights reserved

**Advertising Rate and Circulation Information: (407) 444-8280**

**Printed in the USA by Quad/Graphics**

**This book is printed on paper certified by third-party standards for sustainably managed forestry and production.**

Printed on recyclable paper.
Please recycle whenever possible.

**Stock #4662** ◆ ◆

# CONTENTS

Attractions, hotels, restaurants and other travel experience information are all grouped under the alphabetical listing of the city in which those experiences are physically located—or the nearest recognized city.

## Alabama

### ■ Birmingham ................... 42-65

## Florida Panhandle

## Featured Information

# Make the Most
## of Your *Travels*

Great vacations start long before you leave home, and
they last long after you return. Savor every moment with
TourBook resources that bring travel to life.

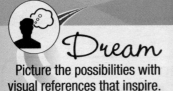

## Dream
Picture the possibilities with
visual references that inspire.

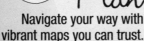

## Plan
Navigate your way with
vibrant maps you can trust.

## Experience
Explore your destination with
expert picks and itineraries.

*Turn the page to
begin your journey.*

## A to Z City Listings

Cities and places are listed alphabetically within each state or province. Attractions, hotels and restaurants are listed once — under the city in which they are physically located.

Cities that are considered part of a larger destination city or area have an expanded city header. The header identifies the larger region and cross-references pages that contain shared trip planning resources:

- Destination map – outline map of the cities that comprise a destination city or area
- Attraction spotting map – regional street map marked with attraction locations
- Hotel/restaurant spotting map and index – regional street map numbered with hotel and restaurant locations identified in an accompanying index

Cities that are not considered part of a larger destination city or area but have a significant number of listings may have these resources within the individual city section:

- Attraction spotting map
- Hotel/restaurant spotting map and index

## Location Abbreviations

Directions are from the center of town unless otherwise specified, using these highway abbreviations:

**Bus. Rte.**=business route
**CR**=county road
**FM**=farm to market
**FR**=forest road
**Hwy.**=Canadian highway
**I**=interstate highway
**LR**=legislative route
**R.R.**=rural route
**SR/PR**=state or provincial route
**US**=federal highway

## Maps

Use the navigable road maps and accompanying legend in the Atlas Section for route planning. Check the destination maps for general location reference. In select cities only, refer to the mass transit overview maps to cross-reference station names and numbers. For attraction and hotel/restaurant spotting maps, see the legend below to identify symbols and color coding.

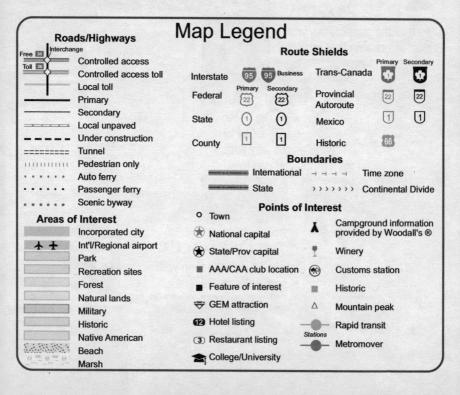

## Map Legend

### Roads/Highways

| | |
|---|---|
| Free / Interchange | |
| Toll | Controlled access |
| | Controlled access toll |
| | Local toll |
| | Primary |
| | Secondary |
| | Local unpaved |
| | Under construction |
| | Tunnel |
| | Pedestrian only |
| | Auto ferry |
| | Passenger ferry |
| | Scenic byway |

### Areas of Interest

| | |
|---|---|
| | Incorporated city |
| ✈ ✈ | Int'l/Regional airport |
| | Park |
| | Recreation sites |
| | Forest |
| | Natural lands |
| | Military |
| | Historic |
| | Native American |
| | Beach |
| | Marsh |

### Route Shields

| | Primary | Secondary |
|---|---|---|
| Interstate | 95 | 95 Business |
| Federal | 22 (Primary) | 22 (Secondary) |
| State | 1 | 1 |
| County | 1 | 1 |

| | Primary | Secondary |
|---|---|---|
| Trans-Canada | 1 | 1 |
| Provincial Autoroute | 22 | 22 |
| Mexico | 1 | 1 |
| Historic | 66 | |

### Boundaries

| | |
|---|---|
| International | Time zone |
| State | Continental Divide |

### Points of Interest

| | |
|---|---|
| ○ Town | ⚑ Campground information provided by Woodall's ® |
| ✪ National capital | ♦ Winery |
| ✪ State/Prov capital | ⊛ Customs station |
| ■ AAA/CAA club location | ■ Historic |
| ■ Feature of interest | △ Mountain peak |
| ♥ GEM attraction | ⬤ Rapid transit |
| 12 Hotel listing | ⬤ Metromover (Stations) |
| 3 Restaurant listing | |
| 🎓 College/University | |

## About Listed Establishments

AAA/CAA Approved attractions, hotels and restaurants are listed on the basis of merit alone after careful evaluation and approval by full-time, professionally trained AAA/CAA inspectors. An establishment's decision to advertise in the TourBook guide has no bearing on its evaluation or rating; nor does inclusion of advertising imply AAA endorsement of products and services.

Information in this guide was believed accurate at the time of publication. However, since changes inevitably occur between annual editions, please contact your AAA travel professional or visit AAA.com or download the AAA mobile app to confirm prices and schedules.

## Attraction Listings

> **ATTRACTION NAME,** 3 mi. n. off SR 20A (Main Ave.), consists of 250 acres with Olmsted-designed gardens, a 205-foot marble and coquina bell tower and a Mediterranean-style mansion. One of the state's oldest attractions, the tower and gardens were dedicated to the American people in 1929 by President Calvin Coolidge on behalf of their founder, a Dutch immigrant.
>
> **Hours:** Gardens daily 8-6. Last admission 1 hour before closing. Visitor center daily 9-5. Estate tours are given at noon and 2. Carillon concerts are given at 1 and 3. Phone ahead to confirm schedule. **Cost:** $10; $3 (ages 5-12). Gardens and estate $16; $8 (ages 5-12). **Phone:** (555) 555-5555.
>
> ⊟ GT ❙❙ ⊞ ⊞ Dupont Circle,13

AAA/CAA travel experts may designate an attraction of exceptional interest and quality as a AAA GEM — a *Great Experience for Members®. See GEM Attraction Index (listed on CONTENTS page) for a complete list of locations.*

Consult the online travel guides at AAA.com or visit AAA Mobile for additional things to do if you have time.

## Cost

Prices are quoted without sales tax in the local currency (U.S. or Canadian dollars). Children under the lowest age specified are admitted free when accompanied by an adult. Most establishments accept credit cards, but a small number require cash, so please call ahead to verify.

## Adventure Travel

Activities such as air tours, hiking, skiing and white-water rafting are listed to provide member information and do not imply AAA/CAA endorsement. For your safety, be aware of inherent risks and adhere to all safety instructions.

## Icons

SAVE AAA Discounts & Rewards℠ member discount

⊟ Electric vehicle charging station on premises. Domestic station information provided by the U.S. Department of Energy. Canadian station information provided by Plug'n Drive Ontario.

GT Guided Tours available

🅐 Camping facilities

❙❙ Food on premises

🔀 Recreational activities

🐾 Pets on leash allowed

⊞ Picnicking allowed

In select cities only:

🚇 Mass transit station within 1 mile. Icon is followed by station name and AAA/CAA designated station number within listing.

## Information-Only Attraction Listings

Bulleted listings, which include the following categories, are listed for informational purposes as a service to members:

- **Gambling establishments** (even if located in a AAA/CAA Approved hotel)
- **Guided food tours**
- **Participatory recreational activities** (those requiring physical exertion or special skills)
- **Wineries that offer tours and tastings**

## Mobile Tags

Scan QR codes throughout the TourBook guide to see online offers, menus, videos and more on your smartphone or tablet. If you need a QR scanner app, download one for free from your app store.

If you see a non-QR code in an ad, check the nearby text for details on which app you'll need to scan it.

# Hotel and Restaurant Listings

**1 Diamond Rating** – AAA/CAA Approved hotels and restaurants are assigned a rating of one to five Diamonds. Red Diamonds distinguish establishments that participate in the AAA/CAA logo licensing program. For details, see p. 11 or AAA.com/Diamonds.

**[fyi]** indicates hotels and restaurants that are not AAA/CAA Approved and/or Diamond Rated but are listed to provide additional choices for members:

- **Hotels** may be unrated if they are too new to rate, under construction, under major renovation or not evaluated; or if they do not meet all AAA requirements. Hotels that do not meet all AAA requirements may be included if they offer member value or are the only option; details are noted in the listing.

- **Restaurants** may be unrated if they have not yet been evaluated by AAA.

**2 Classification or Cuisine Type** – Noted after the Diamond Rating.

- **Hotel Classifications** indicate the style of operation, overall concept and service level. Subclassifications may also be added. (See p. 12 list.)

- **Restaurant Cuisine Types** identify the food concept from more than 100 categories. If applicable, a classification may also be added. (See p. 13 list.)

**3 Dollar Amounts** – Quoted without sales tax in the local currency (U.S. or Canadian dollars), rounded up to the nearest dollar. Most establishments accept credit cards, but a small number require cash, so please call ahead to verify.

- **Hotel Rates** indicate the publicly available two-person rate or rate range for a standard room, applicable all year.

- **Restaurant Prices** represent the minimum and maximum entrée cost per person. Exceptions may include one-of-a-kind or special market priced items.

**4 Spotting Symbol** – Ovals containing numbers correspond with numbered location markings on hotel and restaurant spotting maps.

**5 Parking** – Unless otherwise noted, parking is free, on-site self parking.

**6 Hotel Value Nationwide** – Blue boxes highlight member benefits available at AAA/CAA Approved locations across a hotel chain. (See Just For Members section for details.)

**7 Hotel Unit Limited Availability** – Unit types, amenities and room features preceded by "some" are available on a limited basis, potentially as few as one.

**8 Hotel Terms** – Cancellation and minimum stay policies are listed. Unless otherwise noted, most properties offer a full deposit refund with cancellations received at least 48 hours before standard check-in. Properties that require advance payment may not refund the difference for early departures. "Resort fee" indicates a charge may apply above and beyond the quoted room rate.

**9 Hotel Check-in/Check-out** – Unless otherwise noted, check-in is after 3 p.m. and check-out is before 10 a.m.

**10 Restaurant Dress Code** – Unless otherwise noted, dress is casual or dressy casual.

**11 Restaurant Menu** – Where indicated, menus may be viewed in a secure online environment at AAA.com or, if a mobile tag is provided, via the restaurant's website.

**12 Hotel Icons** – May be preceded by CALL and/or SOME UNITS.

## Member Information:

**[SAVE]** Rate guarantee: discounted standard room rate or lowest public rate available at time of booking for dates of stay.

**[ECO]** Eco-certified by government or private organization. Visit AAA.com/eco for details.

**[⊟]** Electric vehicle charging station on premises. Domestic station information provided by the U.S. Department of Energy. Canadian station information provided by Plug'n Drive Ontario.

**[X]** Smoke-free premises

In select cities only:

**[⊞]** Mass transit station within 1 mile. Icon is followed by station name and AAA/CAA designated station number within listing.

## Services:

**[←]** Airport transportation

**[🐕]** Pets allowed (Call property for restrictions.)

**[$🐕]** Pets allowed (Call property for restrictions and fees.)

**[¶¶]** Restaurant on premises

**[¶¶→]** Restaurant off premises

**[🍽]** Room service for 2 or more meals

**[⌐Y]** Full bar

## HOTEL LISTING

## RESTAURANT LISTING

🚼 Child care

**BIZ** Business area

**♿M** Accessible features (Call property for available services and amenities.)

**Activities:**

♠ Full-service casino

🏊 Pool

🏋 Health club on premises

**In-Room Amenities:**

**HS** High-speed Internet service

**sHS** High-speed Internet service (Call property for fees.)

🛜 Wireless Internet service

📶 Wireless Internet service (Call property for fees.)

🚫 No wireless Internet service

🎥 Pay movies

🧊 Refrigerator

🍱 Microwave

☕ Coffee maker

🌀 No air conditioning

📺 No TV

☎ No telephones

**13** Restaurant Icons

**SAVE** AAA Discounts & Rewards^SM member discount

**ECO** Eco-certified by government or private organization. Visit AAA.com/eco for details.

⚡ Electric vehicle charging station on premises. Domestic station information provided by the U.S. Department of Energy. Canadian station information provided by Plug'n Drive Ontario.

🌀 No air conditioning

**♿M** Accessible features (Call property for available services and amenities.)

🚬 Designated smoking section

**B** Breakfast

**L** Lunch

**D** Dinner

**24** Open 24 hours

**LATE** Open after 11 p.m.

🐾 Pet-friendly (Call property for restrictions.)

In select cities only:

🚆 Mass transit station within 1 mile. Icon is followed by station name and AAA/CAA designated station number within listing.

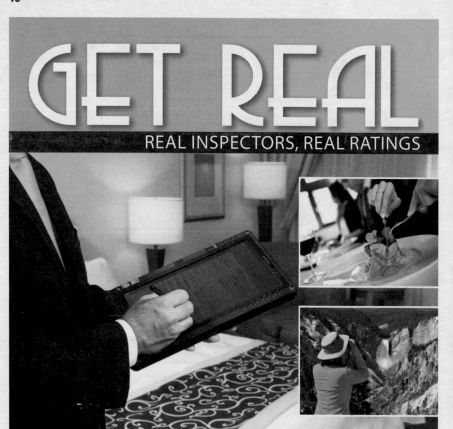

# Just For Members

## Understanding the Diamond Ratings

Hotel and restaurant evaluations are unscheduled to ensure our professionally trained inspectors encounter the same experience members do.

- When an establishment is Diamond Rated, it means members can expect a good fit with their needs. The inspector assigns a rating that indicates the type of experience to expect.
- While establishments at high levels must offer increasingly complex personalized services, establishments at every level are subject to the same basic requirements for cleanliness, comfort and hospitality. Learn more at AAA.com/Diamonds.

## Hotels

Budget-oriented, offering basic comfort and hospitality.

Affordable, with modestly enhanced facilities, décor and amenities.

Distinguished, multifaceted with enhanced physical attributes, amenities and guest comforts.

Refined, stylish with upscale physical attributes, extensive amenities and high degree of hospitality, service and attention to detail.

Ultimate luxury, sophistication and comfort with extraordinary physical attributes, meticulous personalized service, extensive amenities and impeccable standards of excellence.

## Restaurants

Simple, familiar specialty food at an economical price. Often self-service, basic surroundings.

Familiar, family-oriented experience. Home-style foods and family favorites, often cooked to order, modestly enhanced and reasonably priced. Relaxed service, casual surroundings.

Fine dining, often adult-oriented. Latest cooking trends and/or traditional cuisine, expanded beverage offerings. Professional service staff and comfortable, well-coordinated ambience.

Distinctive fine-dining, typically expensive. Highly creative chefs, imaginative presentations and fresh, top-quality ingredients. Proficient service staff, upscale surroundings. Wine steward may offer menu-specific knowledge.

Luxurious and consistently world-class. Highly acclaimed chefs, artistic and imaginative menu selections using the finest ingredients. Maitre d' and unobtrusive, expert service staff.

## What's the difference?

Red Diamonds mark establishments that participate in the AAA/CAA logo licensing program for increased visibility to members.

Black Diamonds identify all other AAA/CAA Approved and Diamond Rated establishments.

# Hotel Classifications

Quality and comfort are usually consistent across each Diamond Rating level, but décor, facilities and service levels vary by classification.

**Bed & Breakfast** — Typically owner-operated with a high degree of personal touches. Guests are encouraged to interact during evening and breakfast hours. A continental or full, hot breakfast is included in the room rate.

Berry Manor Inn, Rockland, ME

**Cabin** — Often located in wooded, rural or waterfront locations. Freestanding units are typically rustic and of basic design. As a rule, essential cleaning supplies, kitchen utensils and complete bed and bath linens are supplied.

Killarney Lodge, Algonquin Provincial Park, ON

**Condominium** — Apartment-style accommodations of varying design or décor, units often contain one or more bedrooms, a living room, full kitchen and an eating area. As a rule, essential cleaning supplies, kitchen utensils and complete bed and bath linens are supplied.

Hyatt Regency Clearwater Beach Resort & Spa, Clearwater Beach, FL

**Cottage** — Often located in wooded, rural, or waterfront locations. Freestanding units are typically home-style in design and décor. As a rule, essential cleaning supplies, kitchen utensils and complete bed and bath linens are supplied.

Montpelier Plantation and Beach, St. Kitts and Nevis

Nottoway Plantation & Resort, White Castle, LA

**Country Inn** — Although similar in definition to a bed and breakfast, country inns are usually larger in scale with spacious public areas and offer a dining facility that serves breakfast and dinner.

The Shores Resort & Spa, Daytona Beach Shores, FL

**Hotel** — Typically a multistory property with interior room entrances and a variety of guest unit styles. The magnitude of the public areas is determined by the overall theme, location and service level, but may include a variety of facilities such as a restaurant, shops, a fitness center, a spa, a business center and meeting rooms.

Alexander Holiday Homes, Kissimmee, FL

**House** — Freestanding units of varying home-style design. Typically larger scale, often containing two or more bedrooms, a living room, a full kitchen, a dining room and multiple bathrooms. As a rule, essential cleaning supplies, kitchen utensils and complete bed and bath linens are supplied.

Bryce View Lodge, Bryce Canyon City, UT

**Motel** — A one- or two-story roadside property with exterior room entrances and drive up parking. Public areas and facilities are often limited in size and/or availability.

**Ranch** — Typically a working ranch featuring an obvious rustic, Western theme, equestrian-related activities and a variety of guest unit styles.

Vista Verde Guest Ranch, Clark, CO

## Hotel Subclassifications

These additional descriptives may be added to the classification for more information:

- **Boutique** — Often thematic, typically informal yet highly personalized; may have a luxurious or quirky style that is fashionable or unique.
- **Casino** — Extensive gambling facilities are available, such as blackjack, craps, keno and slot machines.
- **Classic** — Renowned and landmark properties, older than 50 years, well known for their unique style and ambience.
- **Contemporary** — Overall theme reflects characteristics of present mainstream trends.
- **Extended Stay** — Offers a predominance of long-term accommodations with a designated full-service kitchen area within each unit.
- **Historic** — More than 75 years old with one of the following documented historical features: Maintains the integrity of the historical nature, listed on the National Register of Historic Places, designated a National Historic Landmark or located in a National Register Historic District.
- **Resort** — Extensive recreational facilities and programs may include golf, tennis, skiing, fishing, water sports, spa

treatments or professionally guided activities.

- **Retro** — Overall theme reflects a contemporary design that reinterprets styles from a past era.
- **Vacation Rental** — Typically houses, condos, cottages or cabins; these properties are "home away from home" self-catering accommodations.
- **Vintage** — Overall theme reflects upon and maintains the authentic traits and experience of a past era.

## Restaurant Classifications

If applicable, in addition to the cuisine type noted under the Diamond Rating, restaurant listings may also include one or both classifications:

- **Classic** — Renowned and landmark operation in business for 25 plus years; unique style and ambience.
- **Historic** — Meets one of the following: Listed on National Register of Historic Places, designated a National Historic Landmark or located in a National Register Historic District.

## Service Animals

Under the Americans with Disabilities Act (ADA), U.S. businesses that serve the public must allow people with disabilities to bring their service animals into all areas of the facility where customers are normally allowed to go.

Businesses may ask if an animal is a service animal and what tasks the animal has been trained to perform. Businesses may not ask about the person's disability, require special identification for the animal or request removal of the animal from the premises except in limited cases that require alternate assistance. Businesses may not charge extra fees for service animals, including standard pet fees, but may charge for damage caused by service animals if guests are normally charged for damage they cause.

Call the U.S. Department of Justice ADA Information Line: (800) 514-0301 or TTY (800) 514-0383, or visit ada.gov. Regulations may differ in Canada.

## AAA/CAA Approved Hotels

For members, AAA/CAA Approved means quality assured.

- Only properties that meet basic requirements for cleanliness, comfort and hospitality pass inspection.
- Approved hotels receive a Diamond Rating that tells members the type of experience to expect.

### Guest Safety

Inspectors view a sampling of rooms during evaluations and, therefore, AAA/CAA cannot guarantee the presence of working locks and operational fire safety equipment in every guest unit.

### Member Rates

AAA/CAA members can generally expect to pay no more than the maximum TourBook listed rate for a standard room. Member discounts apply to rates quoted within the rate range and are applicable at the time of booking. Listed rates are usually based on last standard room availability. Within the range, rates may vary by season and room type. Obtain current AAA/CAA member rates and make reservations at AAA.com.

#### Exceptions

- Rates for properties operating as concessionaires for the U.S. National Park Service are not guaranteed due to governing regulations.
- Special advertised rates and short-term promotional rates below the rate range are not subject to additional member discounts.
- During special events, hotels may temporarily increase room rates, not recognize discounts or modify pricing policies. Special events may include Mardi Gras, the Kentucky Derby (including pre-Derby events), college football games, holidays, holiday periods and state fairs. Although some special events are listed in the TourBook guides and on AAA.com, it's always wise to check in advance with AAA travel professionals for specific dates.

**If you are charged more than the maximum TourBook listed rate,** question the additional charge. If an exception is not in effect and management refuses to adhere to the published rate, pay for the room and contact AAA/CAA. The amount paid above the stated maximum will be refunded if our investigation indicates an unjustified charge.

## Reservations and Cancellations

When making your reservation, identify yourself as a AAA/CAA member and request written confirmation of your room type, rate, dates of stay, and cancellation and refund policies. At registration, show your membership card.

To cancel, contact the hotel, your AAA/CAA club office or AAA.com, depending on how you booked your reservation. Request a cancellation number or proof of cancellation.

**If your room is not as specified and you have written confirmation of your reservation for a specific room type,** you should be given the option of choosing a different room or receiving a refund. If management refuses to issue a refund, contact AAA/CAA.

### Contacting AAA/CAA About Approved Properties

If your visit to a AAA/CAA Approved attraction, hotel or restaurant doesn't meet your expectations, please tell us about it — **during your visit or within 30 days**. Be sure to save your receipts and other documentation for reference.

Use the easy online form at AAA.com/TourBookComments to send us the details.

Alternatively, you can email your comments to: memberrelations@national.aaa.com or submit them via postal mail to: AAA Member Comments, 1000 AAA Dr., Box 61, Heathrow, FL 32746.

## AAA/CAA Preferred Hotels

All AAA/CAA Approved hotels are committed to providing quality, value and member service. In addition, those designated as AAA/CAA Preferred Hotels also offer these extra values at Approved locations nationwide. Valid AAA/CAA membership required.

- **Best AAA/CAA member rates for your dates of stay**.
- **Seasonal promotions and special member offers.** Visit AAA.com to view current offers.
- **Member benefit.** See the blue boxes in hotel listings for the chains shown in the right-hand column below to find values offered at AAA/CAA Approved locations nationwide, subject to availability. Details valid at the time of publication and may change without notice.

- **Total satisfaction guarantee.** If you book your stay with AAA/CAA Travel and your stay fails to meet your expectations, you can apply for a full refund. Bring the complaint to the hotel's attention during the stay and request resolution; if the complaint is not resolved by the hotel, ask your AAA/CAA travel agent to request resolution through the AAA/CAA Assured Stay program.

| | |
|---|---|
|  | Best Western, Best Western Plus and Best Western Premier |
|  | Hilton Hotels & Resorts, Waldorf Astoria Hotels & Resorts, Conrad Hotels & Resorts, Curio - A Collection by Hilton, DoubleTree, Embassy Suites Hotels, Hilton Garden Inn, Hampton Hotels, Homewood Suites, Home2 Suites and Hilton Grand Vacations |
|  | Park Hyatt, Andaz, Grand Hyatt, Hyatt Regency, Hyatt, Hyatt Place and Hyatt House |
|  | The Ritz-Carlton, Gaylord Hotels, JW Marriott Hotels, EDITION, Autograph Collection Hotels, Renaissance Hotels, AC Hotels, Marriott Hotels & Resorts, Courtyard, SpringHill Suites, Fairfield Inn & Suites, Residence Inn, and TownePlace Suites |
| **starwood** Hotels and Resorts | Aloft, Element, Four Points, Le Meridien, Sheraton, St. Regis, Westin, W Hotels and The Luxury Collection |

# Member Discounts

Visit AAA.com/searchfordiscounts to find locations and available member discounts. Your AAA/CAA club may offer even greater discounts on theme park tickets. Amtrak and theme park discounts may be used for up to six tickets; restaurant savings may be used for up to six patrons. Other restrictions may apply. All offers subject to change. For complete restrictions, visit your AAA office or AAA.com/restrictions.

## ATTRACTIONS

### SeaWorld, Busch Gardens, Sesame Place

- Save on admission at the gate, participating AAA/CAA offices or AAA.com/SeaWorld.
- Save 10% on up-close dining; visit Guest Relations for details.

### Six Flags

- Save on admission at the gate, participating AAA/CAA offices or AAA.com/SixFlags.
- Save 10% on merchandise of $15 or more at in-park stores.

### Universal Orlando Resort and Universal Studios Hollywood

- Save on admission at participating AAA/CAA offices or AAA.com/Universal.
- Save on Blue Man Group tickets and at select food and merchandise venues in-park and at Universal CityWalk®.

The Entertainment Capital of L.A.®

## DINING

### Hard Rock Cafe

- Save 10% on food, nonalcoholic beverages and merchandise at all locations in the U.S. and Canada and select international locations.

### Landry's Seafood House, The Crab House, Chart House, Oceanaire, Saltgrass Steak House, Muer Seafood Restaurants and Aquarium Restaurants

- Save 10% on food and nonalcoholic beverages at all of the above restaurants.
- Save 10% on merchandise at Aquarium, Downtown Aquarium and Rainforest Cafe restaurants.

## SHOPPING

### Banana Republic Factory Store

- Save 10% on all purchases, including sale merchandise.

BANANA REPUBLIC
FACTORY STORE

### Gap Outlet/Gap Factory Store

- Save 10% on all purchases, including sale merchandise.

GAP OUTLET    GAP FACTORY

### Reebok/Rockport Outlet

- Save 20% on the entire purchase.

OUTLET STORES

### Tanger Outlet Centers

- Receive a free coupon book with discounts up to 20% at select merchants.

Tanger
Outlets

## TRANSPORTATION

### Amtrak

- Save 10% on rail fare booked at least three days in advance of travel date at AAA.com/Amtrak.

AMTRAK

### El Monte RV

- Save up to 10% on nightly rates booked at least 24 hours in advance of pickup at AAA.com/ElMonteRV or (800) 337-2156.

EL MONTE RV
RENTALS • SALES

### Hertz

- Save on daily, weekend, weekly and monthly rentals at AAA.com/Hertz or (800) 654-3080.

# RACK UP
## THE
# REWARDS

### Make membership an even more rewarding experience.

Here at AAA, we believe that financial rewards and benefits are what our members have come to expect. The AAA Member Rewards Visa® credit card lets you earn reward points on all of your purchases. Open an account today and let the rewards start rolling in!

✓ Earn 1 point for every $1 in purchases with your AAA Member Rewards Visa® card!*

✓ Earn double points for gas, grocery and drug store purchases!

✓ Earn triple points on qualifying AAA and travel purchases!

✓ Redeem for a AAA Voucher that gives you up to 40% more value than cash back!**

✓ Exclusive rewards to make you smile!

**VISIT** AAA.com/creditcard       **STOP BY** any AAA branch

Available at participating clubs only.

For information about rates, fees, other costs, and benefits associated with the use of this card, see your AAA Agent or visit the website provided and refer to the disclosures accompanying the online credit application.

\* Earn 1 point per dollar of new net retail purchase transactions (qualifying purchases less credits, returns, and adjustments) charged to the card each billing cycle. Earn 2 points per dollar for purchases made with the card at any eligible gas, grocery or pharmacy retail merchant categories as designated by us. Earn 3 points per dollar for purchases made with the card through any participating AAA Club when AAA is the merchant of record, or at eligible retail travel merchant categories as designated by us. Other significant terms apply. Details accompany new account materials.

\*\* 50,000 points can be redeemed for a $700 AAA Voucher compared to $500 in cash rewards. The redemption value for AAA vouchers varies based on the number of points redeemed.

This credit card program is issued and administered by Bank of America, N.A. Visa and Visa Signature are registered trademarks of Visa International Service Association, and are used by the issuer pursuant to license from Visa U.S.A. Inc. ©2014 AAA                    ARMKEDTU

Birmingham skyline

# Alabama

**The Deep South doesn't get any deeper than Alabama. This is where cotton was king, where the Confederacy was born and where Jefferson Davis' birthday is still a holiday.**

But the state is more than just a cotton-belt cliché. In addition to graceful antebellum homes, moss-draped oaks and Civil War monuments, Alabama showcases unexpected treasures, like charming covered bridges, sugar-sand beaches and a venerable Mardi Gras celebration older than the one in New Orleans.

In Montgomery you'll encounter the nation's first memorial to the persevering souls who struggled and perished during the civil rights movement. And in Huntsville you'll find NASA's Marshall Space Flight Center—where scientists developed the gee-whiz technology for sending men to the moon.

If you're like most visitors who become space cadets for a day, you'll soon realize something you might not have suspected

about this state: Alabama can really take you places. Chart a course from the sleepy South of simpler times to the scenic splendor of the state's many forests to the lively pulse of modern-day Birmingham.

## The Final Frontier

Alabama in the north is a terminus of both the Cumberland Plateau and the Blue Ridge Mountains, and what plate tectonics wrought is now a perfect place to wander. Largely wooded and riddled with rivers, the region ranges from rocky mesas to rolling hills. The resulting waterfalls, rapids, canyons and caverns are generally modest enough to be accessible to even the marginally fit, pristine enough to be paradise to all who love nature.

Boldly go east, where Cheaha Mountain's chalk-white cliffs offer sweeping views of a carpet of green and gold treetops.

Or set your coordinates to the southwest, where waves wash pure white sands and gulls scream and frolic. Just off the coast, Dauphin Island's dunes are a touchdown point for thousands of migrating birds intent on journeys of their own.

Canvass the state's mid-section and you'll surely find cotton, along with peanuts, soybeans, corn and such. But all is not flat farmland. Alien forms cover the landscape in places, courtesy of the shape-morphing effects of kudzu—the Asian import often called "the vine that ate the South" grows up to a foot a day.

Celebrate Mardi Gras in Mobile

## These are the Voyages

Kudzu's hardly the first wanderer to become attached to Alabama. At Russell Cave National Monument, near Bridgeport, evidence suggests prehistoric man made this his first home in the region—some 10,000 years ago.

Native Americans left their legacy in place names from Tuskegee to Tuscaloosa. And fierce struggles for territorial control among Spanish, French and British settlers shaped the state's history, culture, architecture and people.

A zest for friendlier competition lives on. While allegiance to church and family may nourish an Alabamian's soul, it is college football that warms the heart of the state. Visit in the fall and you just might find yourself transported to a modern-day battlefield where flags and first downs have replaced muskets and mortar.

Hospitality is another tradition residents proudly perpetuate, serving up a sampling of "the Deep South" with a smile. To see some traditional Southern imagery, tour Mobile's Oakleigh neighborhood of varied historic homes.

More than anything, you'll find Alabama is proud of its progress. For proof, visit the Birmingham Civil Rights Institute, where you can step into settings that unflinchingly recreate past conflicts, then access archives and educational programs dedicated to protecting future human rights. After dark, trek to Birmingham's Five Points South district, which draws an eclectic mix of the pierced and the professional with its restaurants, nightclubs and modern boutiques.

## Recreation

From Conecuh's soggy bottomlands in the south to William B. Bankhead's unspoiled Sipsey Wilderness in the northwest, Alabama's national forests alone offer enough preserved habitats to soothe any hiker's soul.

Walk in the footsteps of the Native Americans who for centuries worshipped, played, hunted and fought here. Along Indian House Trail, at Buck's Pocket State Park north of Grove Oak, you'll find jagged rock overhangs that once sheltered Cherokees. At Cheaha State Park, near Anniston, Bald Rock Nature Trail delivers you to an awesome overlook with views of foothills once claimed by the Creek Indians. And about 15 miles outside of Tuscaloosa, 320-acre Moundville Archaeological Park formerly was the center of the formidable Moundville Indian civilization.

Golfers will want to follow footsteps of a different kind on the state's renowned Robert Trent Jones Golf Trail, which counts Auburn/Opelika's Grand National—a PGA championship course—among its 26 stops at 11 locations.

Prefer fishing to fairways? Off the coast of Orange Beach, ships and tanks left over from World War II, Korea and Vietnam have become artificial reefs and now shelter plentiful populations of red snapper, grouper, amberjack and triggerfish.

To get out to where they're biting, look for saltwater fishing charters at Orange Beach. Or head to Dauphin Island where a deepwater fishing pier extends more than 800 feet into the Gulf.

If you're after freshwater fishing, keep this in mind: They don't call Weiss Lake in Cherokee County "Crappie Capital of the World" for nothing. The 30,200-acre lake also offers plenty of bass and catfish as well as opportunities for boating, water skiing and swimming.

Still more adventure can be found underground. Caves formed in the limestone and sandstone landscape of northeastern Alabama are a mecca for spelunking enthusiasts—in fact, Huntsville is home to the National Speleological Society.

Dexter Avenue King Memorial Baptist Church, Montgomery

# Historic Timeline

|  |  |
|------|-------|
| 1519 | Explorer Alonso Álvarez de Pineda sails into Mobile Bay. |
| 1763 | The Treaty of Paris ending the French and Indian War gives Mobile to Britain. |
| 1819 | Alabama is admitted as the 22nd state. |
| 1861 | Montgomery becomes the first capital of the Confederacy. |
| 1915 | The boll weevil devastates the state's one-crop cotton economy and forces a diversification in agriculture. |
| **1955** | Rosa Parks' arrest after refusing to surrender her bus seat to a white passenger sparks the Montgomery Bus Boycott. |
| 1960 | The George C. Marshall Space Flight Center is established in Huntsville. |
| **1965** | Despite violent opposition, Dr. Martin Luther King Jr. leads a march from Selma to Montgomery to protest voting inequities. |
| 1989 | The nation's first memorial to the civil rights movement and those who died during the struggle is dedicated in Montgomery. |
| 2002 | Birmingham native Vonetta Flowers is the first African-American to win a gold medal in a Winter Olympic Games sport. |
| 2005 | Hurricane Katrina, the nation's most extensive and costly natural disaster, strikes the Gulf Coast. |

# What To Pack

| Temperature Averages Maximum/Minimum | JANUARY | FEBRUARY | MARCH | APRIL | MAY | JUNE | JULY | AUGUST | SEPTEMBER | OCTOBER | NOVEMBER | DECEMBER |
|---|---|---|---|---|---|---|---|---|---|---|---|---|
| Birmingham | 54/34 | 59/37 | 67/44 | 74/51 | 82/60 | 88/68 | 91/72 | 91/71 | 85/64 | 75/53 | 65/44 | 56/36 |
| Dothan | 59/38 | 64/41 | 71/48 | 78/54 | 86/63 | 91/70 | 92/72 | 92/70 | 88/65 | 79/55 | 70/47 | 61/40 |
| Florence | 51/31 | 56/35 | 65/42 | 73/50 | 81/59 | 88/66 | 91/70 | 91/69 | 85/62 | 74/50 | 63/41 | 53/34 |
| Huntsville | 51/32 | 56/36 | 65/42 | 74/50 | 81/59 | 88/67 | 91/71 | 91/69 | 85/63 | 75/51 | 64/42 | 54/34 |
| Mobile | 61/40 | 65/43 | 71/49 | 78/55 | 85/64 | 89/70 | 91/73 | 91/73 | 87/68 | 79/58 | 71/49 | 63/42 |
| Montgomery | 57/36 | 62/39 | 70/45 | 77/52 | 84/61 | 90/68 | 92/72 | 92/71 | 87/65 | 78/54 | 69/44 | 60/37 |

**From the records of The Weather Channel Interactive, Inc.**

# Good Facts To Know

## ABOUT THE STATE

**POPULATION:** 4,779,736.

**AREA:** 52,420 square miles; ranks 30th.

**CAPITAL:** Montgomery.

**HIGHEST POINT:** 2,407 ft., Cheaha Mountain.

**LOWEST POINT:** Sea level, Gulf of Mexico.

**TIME ZONE(S):** Central. DST.

## GAMBLING

**MINIMUM AGE FOR GAMBLING:** Most games of chance are illegal in Alabama, so no minimum age has been established. Bingo is permitted for charitable purposes in certain counties (the minimum age is 19).

## REGULATIONS

**TEEN DRIVING LAWS:** No more than one passenger (unless accompanied by family members or licensed driver 21 or over) is permitted. Driving is not permitted midnight-6 a.m. The minimum age for an unrestricted driver's license is 17. Phone (334) 242-4400 for more information about Alabama driver's license regulations.

**SEAT BELT/CHILD RESTRAINT LAWS:** Seat belts are required for driver and front-seat passengers ages 15 and over. Children ages 6-14 are required to use a seat belt; child restraints are required for children under age 6. AAA recommends the use of seat belts and appropriate child restraints for the driver and all passengers.

**CELL PHONE RESTRICTIONS:** Drivers under 18 who have held an intermediate license for less than 6 months are banned from using cell phones and text messaging while driving. Texting while driving is prohibited for all drivers. In Montgomery, the use of a handheld cell phone while driving is prohibited.

**HELMETS FOR MOTORCYCLISTS:** Required for all riders and passengers.

**RADAR DETECTORS:** Permitted for non-commercial vehicles.

**MOVE OVER LAW:** Driver is required to slow down and vacate the lane nearest stopped police, fire and rescue vehicles using audible or flashing signals. The law also requires drivers to move over for tow truck drivers assisting motorists.

**FIREARMS LAWS:** Vary by state and/or county. Contact Alabama Department of Public Safety, 301 S. Ripley St., Montgomery, AL 36104; phone (334) 242-4445.

## HOLIDAYS

**HOLIDAYS:** Jan. 1 ▪ Martin Luther King Jr. Day and Robert E. Lee's Birthday, Jan. (3rd Mon.) ▪ Washington's Birthday/Presidents Day, Feb. (3rd Mon.) ▪ Confederate Memorial Day, Apr. (4th Mon.) ▪ Memorial Day, May (last Mon.) ▪ Jefferson Davis' Birthday, June (1st Mon.) ▪ July 4 ▪ Labor Day, Sept. (1st Mon.) ▪ Columbus Day, Oct. (2nd Mon.) ▪ Veterans Day, Nov. 11 ▪ Thanksgiving ▪ Christmas, Dec. 25.

## MONEY

**TAXES:** Alabama's statewide sales tax is 4 percent with local options to impose additional increments. There also is an occupancy tax on lodgings.

## VISITOR INFORMATION

**INFORMATION CENTERS:** State welcome centers are on I-65 southbound, about 3 mi. s. of the Tennessee border south of Ardmore ▪ I-10 westbound, 1 mi. w. of the Florida border north of Seminole ▪ I-10 eastbound, 1 mi. e. of the Mississippi border west of Grand Bay ▪ I-85 southbound, 1 mi. w. of the Georgia border near Lanett ▪ I-59 southbound, at the Georgia border northeast of Hammondville ▪ I-59 northbound and I-20 eastbound, at the Mississippi border near Cuba ▪ US 231 northbound, 1 mi. n. of the Florida border south of Madrid ▪ and I-20 westbound, near the Georgia border east of Heflin. Restrooms are open 24 hours. Travel and routing information is dispensed 8-5.

**FURTHER INFORMATION FOR VISITORS:**
Bureau of Tourism and Travel
401 Adams Ave., Suite 126
Montgomery, AL 36104
(800) 252-2262

**NATIONAL FOREST INFORMATION:**
National Forest Service
2946 Chestnut St.
Montgomery, AL 36107
(334) 832-4470

**FISHING AND HUNTING REGULATIONS:**
Division of Wildlife and Freshwater Fisheries
Department of Conservation and Natural Resources
64 N. Union St., Suite 567
Montgomery, AL 36104
(334) 242-3465
(888) 848-6887 (licenses)

**RECREATION INFORMATION:**
Division of State Parks
Department of Conservation and Natural Resources
64 N. Union St., Suite 468
Montgomery, AL 36130
(800) 252-7275 (reservations and information)

# Alabama Annual Events

Please call ahead to confirm event details.

## JANUARY

- Alabama Horse Fair
  Montgomery
  800-945-8033
- Birmingham Bowl
  Birmingham
  205-733-3776
- GoDaddy Bowl / Mobile
  251-635-0011

## FEBRUARY

- Black Heritage Tours
  Montgomery
  334-240-4617
- Black Heritage Festival
  Anniston
  256-237-6766
- Mercedes-Benz Marathon
  Weekend / Birmingham
  205-870-7771

## MARCH

- Bridge Crossing Jubilee
  Selma / 334-526-2626
- World Championship
  Rodeo and Southeastern
  Livestock Exposition
  Montgomery
  334-265-1867
- Cottontail's Village Arts and
  Crafts Festival
  Birmingham
  205-836-7178

## APRIL

- Alabama Chicken and Egg
  Festival / Moulton
  256-905-0700
- Honda Indy Grand Prix of
  Alabama / Birmingham
  205-699-9609
- Auburn CityFest / Auburn
  334-501-2936

## MAY

- George Washington Carver
  Commemorative Festival
  Tuskegee
  334-727-6619
- WhistleStop Weekend and
  Rocket City BBQ Festival
  Huntsville
  256-564-8100
- Alabama Jubilee Hot Air
  Balloon Classic / Decatur
  800-232-5449

## JUNE

- Gadsden RiverFest
  Gadsden
  256-543-3472
- Gulf Coast Hot Air Balloon
  Festival / Foley
  251-943-3291
- Helen Keller Festival
  Tuscumbia
  256-383-0783

## JULY

- W.C. Handy Music Festival
  Florence
  256-766-7642
- Spirit of America Festival
  Decatur
  256-350-2028
- Independence Day 1776
  Montevallo
  205-665-3535

## AUGUST

- Gulf Coast Ethnic and
  Heritage Jazz Festival
  Mobile
  251-432-8343
- Franklin County Watermelon
  Festival / Russellville
  256-332-1760
- Sidewalk Moving Picture
  Festival / Birmingham
  888-767-9338

## SEPTEMBER

- Alabama State
  Championship Races
  Phenix City
  334-297-2594
- Leeds Fall Festival & John
  Henry Celebration / Leeds
  205-699-5001
- Riverfest / Decatur
  800-524-6181

## OCTOBER

- Kentuck Festival of the Arts
  Northport
  205-758-1257
- Alabama Renaissance Faire
  Florence
  256-768-3031
- National Shrimp Festival
  Gulf Shores
  251-968-4327

## NOVEMBER

- Frank Brown International
  Songwriters Festival
  Orange Beach
  850-492-7664
- National Peanut Festival
  Dothan
  334-793-4323
- Greater Gulf State Fair
  Mobile
  251-344-4573

## DECEMBER

- Christmas on the River
  Demopolis
  334-289-0270
- Victorian Front Porch Tour
  Opelika
  334-887-8747
- Christmas Tour of Homes
  Eufaula
  334-687-6664

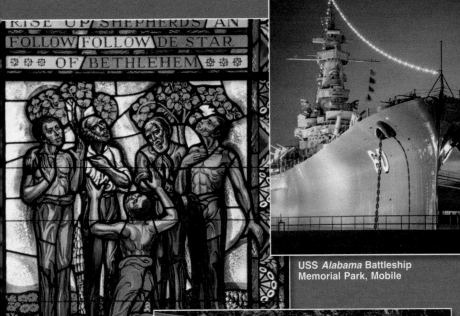

RISE UP SHEPHERDS AN
FOLLOW FOLLOW DE STAR
✿✿✿ OF BETHLEHEM ✿✿✿

USS *Alabama* Battleship
Memorial Park, Mobile

Tuskegee University
Chapel, Tuskegee

Hank Williams statue,
Montgomery

Huntsville Botanical Garden, Huntsville

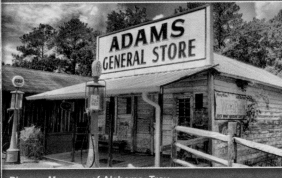

Pioneer Museum of Alabama, Troy

# Index: Great Experience for Members

## AAA editor's picks of exceptional note

Anniston Museum of Natural History

The American Village

Birmingham Museum of Art

Shrine of the Most Blessed Sacrament

See Orientation map on p. 30 for corresponding grid coordinates, if applicable.

# Alabama Atlas Section

## ROADS/HIGHWAYS

- INTERSTATE
- CONTROLLED ACCESS
- CONTROLLED ACCESS TOLL
- TOLL ROAD
- PRIMARY DIVIDED
- PRIMARY UNDIVIDED
- SECONDARY DIVIDED
- SECONDARY UNDIVIDED
- LOCAL DIVIDED
- LOCAL UNDIVIDED
- UNPAVED ROAD
- UNDER CONSTRUCTION
- TUNNEL
- PEDESTRIAN ONLY
- AUTO FERRY
- PASSENGER FERRY
- SCENIC BYWAY
- 10 DISTANCE BETWEEN MARKERS
- EXIT NUMBER–FREE/TOLL
- INTERCHANGE FULL/PARTIAL
- WELCOME CENTER
- REST AREA/ SERVICE CENTER

## BOUNDARIES

- INTERNATIONAL
- STATE
- COUNTY
- TIME ZONE
- CONTINENTAL DIVIDE

## ROAD SHIELDS

- 95 INTERSTATE/BUSINESS
- 22 U.S./STATE/COUNTY
- 27 FOREST/INDIAN
- TRANS- CANADA
- 1 PROVINCIAL AUTOROUTE
- 1 MEXICO
- HISTORIC ROUTE 66
- VT 41 REFERENCE PAGE INDICATOR

## AREAS OF INTEREST

- INDIAN
- MILITARY
- PARK
- FOREST
- GRASSLANDS
- HISTORIC
- INT'L/REGIONAL AIRPORT
- INCORPORATED CITY

## POINTS OF INTEREST

- TOWN
- NATIONAL CAPITAL
- STATE/PROVINCIAL CAPITAL
- AAA/CAA CLUB LOCATION
- FEATURE OF INTEREST
- COLLEGE/UNIVERSITY
- CAMPGROUND INFORMATION PROVIDED BY WOODALL'S®
- CUSTOMS STATION
- HISTORIC
- LIGHTHOUSE
- MONUMENT/MEMORIAL
- STATE/PROVINCIAL PARK
- NATIONAL WILDLIFE REFUGE
- SKI AREA
- SPORTS COMPLEX
- DAM

## CITIES/TOWNS

are color-coded by size, showing where to find AAA Approved and Diamond rated lodgings or restaurants listed in the AAA TourBook guides and on AAA.com.

- Red - major destinations and capitals; many listings
- Black - destinations; some listings
- Grey - no listings

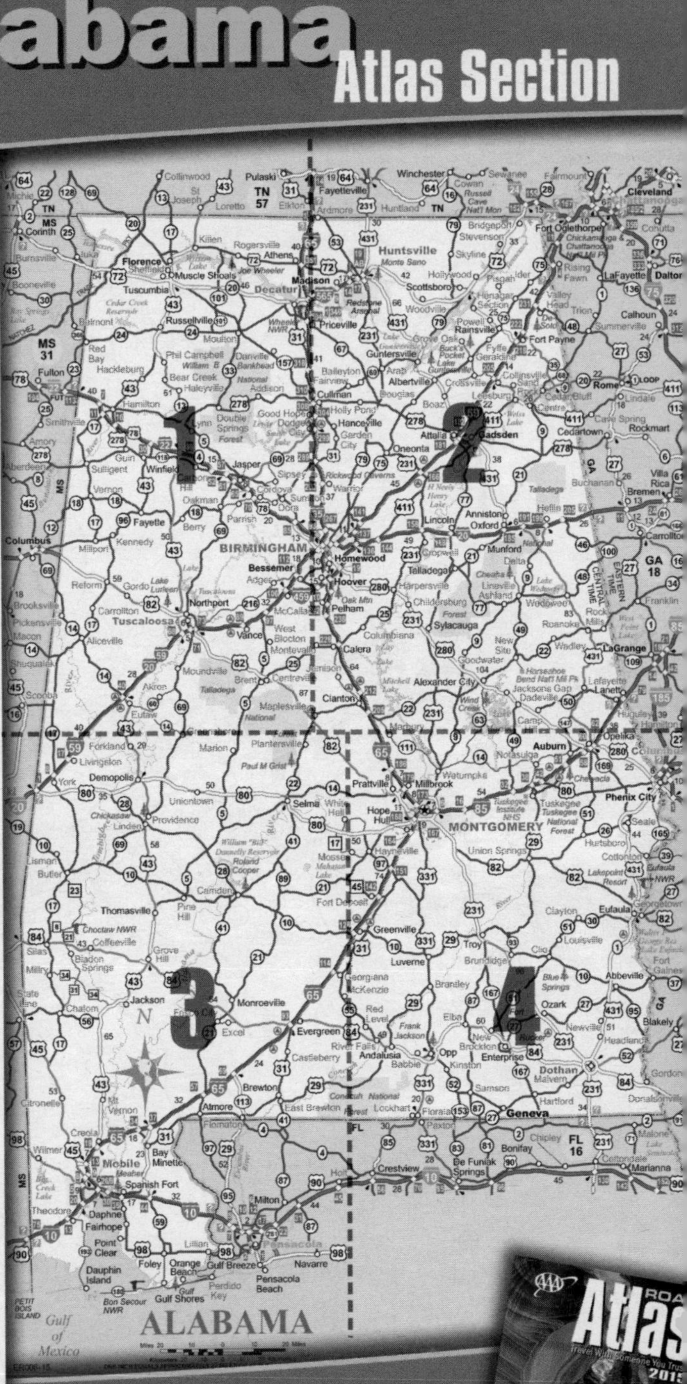

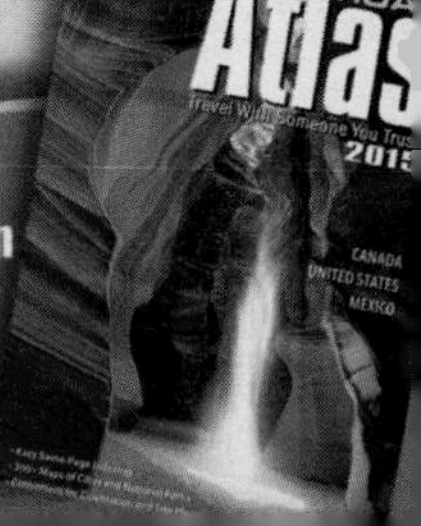

**ALABAMA**

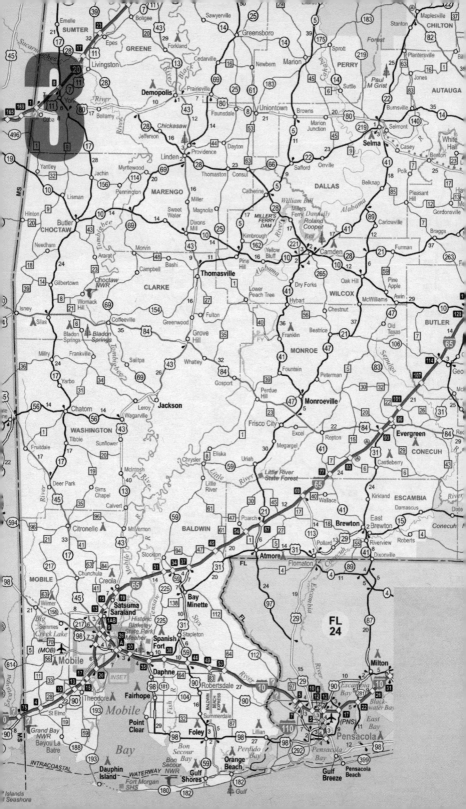

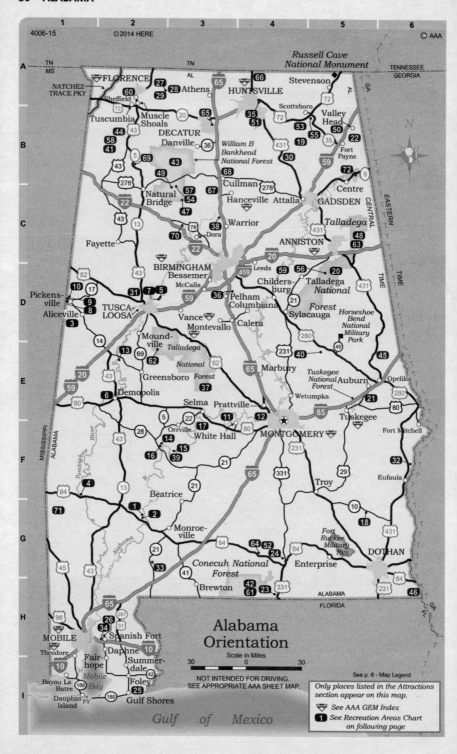

Alabama
Orientation

Scale in Miles
30                                    30

NOT INTENDED FOR DRIVING.
SEE APPROPRIATE AAA SHEET MAP.

See p. 6 - Map Legend

Only places listed in the Attractions
section appear on this map.

⏣ See AAA GEM Index
**1** See Recreation Areas Chart
   on following page

# Recreation Areas Chart
The map location numerals in column 2 show an area's location on the preceding map.

| | MAP LOCATION | CAMPING | PICNICKING | HIKING TRAILS | BOATING | BOAT RAMP | BOAT RENTAL | FISHING | SWIMMING | PETS ON LEASH | BICYCLE TRAILS | NATURE PROGS. | VISITOR CENTER | LODGE/CABINS | FOOD SERVICE |
|---|---|---|---|---|---|---|---|---|---|---|---|---|---|---|---|
| **NATIONAL FORESTS** *(See place listings.)* | | | | | | | | | | | | | | | |
| **Conecuh (G-3)** 84,000 acres on the Alabama-Florida border. | | • | • | • | • | • | | • | • | • | • | | | | |
| **Talladega (C-5)** 389,000 acres. Central Alabama. | | • | • | • | • | • | | • | • | • | | | | | |
| **Tuskegee (E-5)** 11,054 acres n.e. of Tuskegee. | | • | • | • | | | | • | | • | • | • | | | |
| **William B. Bankhead (B-3)** 180,000 acres. Northwestern Alabama. | | • | • | • | • | • | | • | • | • | • | | | | |
| **NATIONAL MILITARY PARKS** *(See place listings.)* | | | | | | | | | | | | | | | |
| **Horseshoe Bend (D-5)** 2,040 acres 12 mi. n. of Dadeville on SR 49. | | | • | • | • | • | | • | • | • | | | • | | |
| **ARMY CORPS OF ENGINEERS** | | | | | | | | | | | | | | | |
| **Claiborne Lake (G-2)** 5,930 acres 20 mi. n.w. of Monroeville via SR 41 to Claiborne Lock and Dam on the Alabama River. | **1** | • | • | • | • | • | | • | | • | • | | | | |
| **Isaac Creek (G-2)** 713 acres 20 mi. n.w. of Monroeville off SR 41 and CR 17 at Claiborne Lock and Dam. | **2** | • | • | • | • | • | | • | | • | • | | | | |
| **Cochrane Recreation Area (D-1)** 327 acres 10 mi. s. of Aliceville via SR 17 on the Tennessee-Tombigbee Waterway. | **3** | • | • | • | • | • | | • | | • | | | | | |
| **Coffeeville Lake (F-1)** 8,300 acres 3.5 mi. w. of Coffeeville on US 84. | **4** | • | • | | • | • | | • | | • | | | | | |
| **Deerlick Creek Recreation Area (D-2)** 300 acres 12 mi. n.e. of Tuscaloosa on US 82 and Rice Mine Rd. | **5** | • | • | • | • | • | | • | • | • | | | | | |
| **Demopolis (E-2)** 10,000 acres 6 mi. w. of Demopolis on US 80 to Lock and Dam Rd. | **6** | • | • | • | • | • | | • | • | • | | | • | | |
| **Holt Lake (D-2)** 2,300 acres 10 mi. n. of Tuscaloosa on SR 216 to Lock and Dam Rd. | **7** | • | • | • | • | • | | • | • | | | | • | | |
| **Pickensville Recreation Area (D-1)** 325 acres in Pickensville, 1 mi. w. of jct. SRs 14 and 86. | **8** | • | • | • | • | • | | • | • | • | | | | | |
| **Pickensville Campground (D-1)** 310 acres 1 mi. w. of Pickensville via SR 86 on the Tennessee-Tombigbee Waterway. | **9** | • | • | • | • | • | | • | • | • | | | | | |
| **Pickensville Day Use Area (D-1)** 15 acres in Pickensville, 1 mi. w. of jct. SRs 14 and 86. | **10** | | • | • | • | • | | • | • | • | | | • | | |
| **R.E. "Bob" Woodruff Lake (E-3)** 12,510 acres 25 mi. w. of Montgomery via US 80 to Robert F. Henry Lock and Dam on the Alabama River. | **11** | • | • | • | • | • | | • | • | • | | | • | • | |
| **Gunter Hill (E-4)** 422 acres 9 mi. w. of Montgomery on Booth Rd. | **12** | • | | • | • | • | | • | | • | | | | | |
| **Warrior Lake (E-2)** 9,200 acres 3 mi. e. of Eutaw on SR 14 to Lock and Dam Rd. | **13** | • | • | • | • | • | | • | | | | | | | |
| **William "Bill" Dannelly Reservoir (F-3)** 17,000 acres 45 mi. s.w. of Selma on the Alabama River via SR 28. | **14** | • | • | • | • | • | • | • | • | • | • | | • | • | |
| **Chilatchee Creek (F-3)** 552 acres 9 mi. e. of Alberta off CR 29. | **15** | • | | • | • | • | | • | • | • | | | | | |
| **Millers Ferry Campground (F-2)** 60 acres 12 mi. n.w. of Camden on SR 28. | **16** | • | | • | • | • | | • | • | • | | | | | |
| **Six Mile Creek (F-3)** 95 acres 6 mi. s. of Selma via SR 41 and CR 152. | **17** | • | • | | • | • | | • | | • | | | | | |
| **STATE** | | | | | | | | | | | | | | | |
| **Blue Springs (G-5)** 103 acres 6 mi. e. of Clio off SR 10. Tennis; playground. | **18** | • | • | | | | | • | • | • | | | | | |
| **Buck's Pocket (B-4)** 2,000 acres 2 mi. n. of Grove Oak off SR 227. Playground. | **19** | • | • | • | • | • | • | • | | • | • | | | | |
| **Cheaha (D-5)** 2,799 acres 29 mi. s. of Oxford off Hwy. 431. Museum, playground. No pets permitted in swimming area or lodging facilities. *(See Anniston p. 35.)* | **20** | • | • | • | • | | | • | • | • | • | • | • | • | • |
| **Chewacla (E-5)** 696 acres 4 mi. s. off US 29. Playground. *(See Auburn p. 37.)* | **21** | • | • | • | | | | • | • | • | • | | | • | • |
| **Desoto (B-5)** 3,502 acres. Scenic. Tennis; playground, pool. *(See Fort Payne p. 81.)* | **22** | • | • | • | • | • | | • | • | • | • | • | • | • | • |

# Recreation Areas Chart

The map location numerals in column 2 show an area's location on the preceding map.

| | MAP LOCATION | CAMPING | PICNICKING | HIKING TRAILS | BOATING | BOAT RAMP | BOAT RENTAL | FISHING | SWIMMING | PETS ON LEASH | BICYCLE TRAILS | NATURE PROGS. | VISITOR CENTER | LODGE/CABINS | FOOD SERVICE |
|---|---|---|---|---|---|---|---|---|---|---|---|---|---|---|---|
| **Florala (H-4)** 40 acres off US 331 in Florala. Playground. | 23 | • | • | • | • | • | • | • | • | • | • | • | | | • |
| **Frank Jackson (G-4)** 2,050 acres 3 mi. n. of Opp off US 331. Playground. | 24 | • | • | • | • | • | | • | • | • | | | • | | |
| **Gulf (I-2)** 6,150 acres 10 mi. s. of Foley off SR 59. Golf (18 holes). | 25 | • | • | • | • | • | • | • | • | • | • | • | • | • | • |
| **Historic Blakeley (H-2)** 3,800 acres just w. of SR 225 in Spanish Fort. Historic. Horseback riding; nature trails. *(See Spanish Fort p. 142.)* | 26 | • | | • | | | | • | | | | • | | | |
| **Joe Wheeler (A-2)** 2,550 acres 2 mi. w. of Rogersville off US 72. Golf (18 holes); marina, multiuse trails. | 27 | • | • | • | • | • | • | • | • | • | | • | | • | • |
| **First Creek (A-3)** 1,800 acres 2 mi. w. of Rogersville via US 72. Golf (18 holes); tennis; playground. | 28 | • | • | • | • | • | • | • | • | • | | | | | |
| **Joe Wheeler Dam (A-2)** 420 acres 9 mi. n. of Town Creek off SR 101. Tennis; playground. | 29 | | • | • | • | • | | • | • | • | | • | | | |
| **Lake Guntersville (B-4)** 5,559 acres 6 mi. n.e. of Guntersville off SR 227. Golf (18 holes); tennis; horse trails, playground. | 30 | • | • | • | • | • | • | • | • | • | • | • | | • | • |
| **Lake Lurleen (D-2)** 1,625 acres 12 mi. n.w. of Tuscaloosa off US 82. Playground. | 31 | • | • | • | • | • | • | • | • | • | | • | • | | |
| **Lakepoint Resort (F-6)** 1,220 acres 7 mi. n. of Eufaula off SR 431. Golf (18 holes); playground. | 32 | • | • | • | • | • | • | • | • | • | | • | | • | • |
| **Little River (G-2)** 2,100 acres 11 mi. n. of Atmore on SR 21. Playground. | 33 | • | • | • | • | • | • | • | • | • | | | | • | |
| **Meaher (H-2)** 1,327 acres 2 mi. w. of Spanish Fort on US 90. *(See Spanish Fort p. 142.)* | 34 | • | • | • | • | • | | • | | • | | | | | |
| **Monte Sano (B-4)** 2,140 acres 4 mi. e. of Huntsville. Playground. | 35 | • | • | • | | | | | | • | • | • | | • | • |
| **Oak Mountain (D-3)** 9,940 acres 3 mi. e. of US 31 from Pelham off I-65 exit 246. Scenic. Golf, tennis; horse rental, playground. *(See Pelham p. 135.)* | 36 | • | • | • | • | • | • | • | • | • | • | • | | • | • |
| **Paul M. Grist (E-3)** 1,080 acres 15 mi. n. of Selma off SR 22. Playground. | 37 | • | • | • | • | • | | • | • | • | | • | | | |
| **Rickwood Caverns (C-3)** 380 acres off I-65 exit 284 (northbound) or exit 289 (southbound) in Warrior. Horse rental, playground. *(See Warrior p. 152.)* | 38 | • | • | | | | | | • | • | | • | | | |
| **Roland Cooper (F-3)** 236 acres 6 mi. n.e. of Camden off SR 41. Golf (nine holes); playground. | 39 | • | • | • | • | • | • | • | | | | | | • | |
| **Wind Creek (E-4)** 1,445 acres 7 mi. s.e. of Alexander City off SR 63. Playground. | 40 | • | • | • | • | • | • | • | • | • | | • | | | • |
| **OTHER** | | | | | | | | | | | | | | | |
| **Bear Creek (B-2)** 670 acres 30 mi. s.w. of Russellville via US 43 and SR 172. | 41 | • | • | • | • | • | | • | • | • | | • | • | • | • |
| **Blue Lake (H-4)** 11 acres 13 mi. s.w. of Andalusia on SR 137. | 42 | | • | • | • | | | • | • | • | | | | | |
| **Brushy Lake (B-3)** 150 acres 12 mi. s. of Moulton on FR 245. | 43 | • | • | • | • | • | | • | | • | | • | | | |
| **Cedar Creek (B-2)** 4,300 acres 10 mi. w. of Russellville via SR 24 and CR 41. | 44 | • | • | | • | • | • | • | | | | | | • | • |
| **Chambers County Lake (E-6)** 183 acres 5 mi. s.e. of Lafayette on CR 83. | 45 | | • | | • | • | • | • | | • | • | • | | | • |
| **Chattahoochee Park (H-6)** 596 acres 11 mi. s.e. of Gordon via SR 95. | 46 | • | • | • | • | • | | • | • | • | • | • | | • | |
| **Clear Creek (C-3)** 600 acres 5 mi. n. of Jasper via SR 195 to Manchester, then n. on CR 27. | 47 | • | • | • | • | • | | • | • | • | | • | | | |
| **Coleman Lake (C-5)** 250 acres 10 mi. n. of Heflin via US 78, CR 61 and FRs 553 and 500. | 48 | • | • | | • | | | • | • | • | | | | | |
| **Corinth (B-2)** 500 acres 7 mi. e. of Double Springs via US 278, CR 33 and FR 113. | 49 | • | • | | | • | | • | • | • | | | | | |
| **Dekalb County Lake (B-5)** 120 acres off SR 75 at Sylvania. | 50 | • | • | • | • | • | • | • | | | | • | | | • |
| **Ditto's Landing (B-4)** 214 acres 12 mi. s. of Huntsville via US 231 on Hobbs Island Rd. Softball field. | 51 | • | • | • | • | • | | • | | • | | • | | | |

# Recreation Areas Chart

The map location numerals in column 2 show an area's location on the preceding map.

| | MAP LOCATION | CAMPING | PICNICKING | HIKING TRAILS | BOATING | BOAT RAMP | BOAT RENTAL | FISHING | SWIMMING | PETS ON LEASH | BICYCLE TRAILS | NATURE PROGS. | VISITOR CENTER | LODGE/CABINS | FOOD SERVICE |
|---|---|---|---|---|---|---|---|---|---|---|---|---|---|---|---|
| Gantt Lake (G-4) 2,747 acres 11 mi. n. of Andalusia on US 29. Water skiing. | 52 | | | | • | • | | • | • | • | | | | | |
| Goose Pond Colony (B-4) 365 acres 6 mi. s. of Scottsboro via SR 79. Golf (36 holes); amphitheater. | 53 | • | • | • | • | • | • | • | • | • | | | • | • | • |
| Houston (C-3) 1,000 acres 6 mi. s.e. of Double Springs via US 278, CRs 33 and 63 and FR 118. | 54 | • | • | • | • | • | | • | • | • | | | | | |
| Jackson County Park (B-5) 63 acres 2 mi. s. of Scottsboro on County Park Rd. Playground. | 55 | • | • | • | • | • | | • | • | | | | | | |
| Lake Chinnabee (D-4) 250 acres 13 mi. n.e. of Talladega on SR 42. | 56 | • | • | • | • | | | • | | • | | | | | |
| Lewis Smith Lake (C-3) 21,200 acres 7 mi. s.w. of Cullman on CR 22. | 57 | • | • | • | • | • | • | • | • | • | | | • | • | • |
| Little Bear (B-2) 1,680 acres 12 mi. w. of Russellville via SR 24. | 58 | • | • | • | • | | | • | • | • | | | | | |
| Logan Martin Lake (D-4) 18,000 acres w. of Talladega on the Coosa River. | 59 | • | • | | • | • | • | • | • | • | | | | • | • |
| McFarland (A-2) 325 acres in Florence on SR 20 below O'Neal Bridge. | 60 | • | • | | • | • | | • | • | • | | | | | • |
| Open Pond (H-4) 150 acres 15 mi. s.w. of Andalusia via US 29 and SR 137. | 61 | • | • | • | • | | | • | | • | | | | | |
| Payne Lake (E-2) 800 acres 16 mi. n.e. of Greensboro on SR 25. | 62 | • | • | • | • | | | • | • | • | | | | | |
| Pine Glen (C-5) 5 acres 6 mi. n. of Heflin via US 78 and FR 500. | 63 | • | • | | | | | • | | • | | | | | |
| Point A Lake (G-4) 700 acres 5 mi. n.w. of Andalusia off US 29. | 64 | • | • | | • | • | • | • | | | | | | | |
| Point Mallard Park (B-3) 750 acres at the e. end of 8th St. S.E. in Decatur. Golf (18 holes); ice rink. *(See Decatur p. 70.)* | 65 | • | • | | | | | • | • | • | • | | | | |
| Sharon Johnston (A-4) 250 acres 12 mi. n.e. of Huntsville on Coleman Rd. Horse arena, pool, shooting range. | 66 | • | • | | | | | • | • | • | | | | | |
| Smith Lake Park (C-3) 172 acres s.w. of Cullman via SR 69 and CR 222. Miniature golf, playground. | 67 | • | • | • | • | • | | • | • | • | | | • | | |
| Sportsman Lake Park (B-3) 160 acres 1 mi. s. on US 31 in Cullman. Paddleboat rental. No motor boats. | 68 | • | • | • | • | | | • | • | • | | • | | | • |
| Upper Bear (B-2) 1,860 acres 16 mi. s. of Russellville via US 43, near Bear Creek. | 69 | • | • | • | • | | | • | • | • | | | | | |
| Walker County Lake (C-3) 163 acres 3 mi. s.e. of Jasper off Old US 78. | 70 | | • | • | • | | | • | | • | | | | | • |
| Washington County Lake (G-1) 84 acres 2 mi. w. of Millry off CR 34. | 71 | • | • | | • | • | | • | | • | | | | | • |
| Weiss Lake (B-5) 30,200 acres just n.e. of Centre on SR 9 along the Coosa River. | 72 | • | • | • | • | • | • | • | • | • | | | • | • | • |

## ABBEVILLE pop. 2,688

**GUESTHOUSE INN ABBEVILLE**                              334/585-5060

▽▽ ▽▽ **Motel. Rates not provided. Address:** 1237 US Hwy 431 S 36310 **Location:** Jct SR 27. **Facility:** 40 units. 2 stories (no elevator), exterior corridors. **Pool(s):** outdoor.

⚓ HS 🛜 🛗 🖥 🖥 / SOME UNITS 🛒

## ALABASTER pop. 30,352
• **Part of Birmingham area — see map p. 43**

**CANDLEWOOD SUITES ALABASTER**                          205/620-0188

▽▽ ▽▽ **Extended Stay Hotel. Rates not provided. Address:** 1004 Balmoral Dr 35007 **Location:** I-65 exit 238, just e. **Facility:** 88 efficiencies. 4 stories, interior corridors. **Activities:** exercise room. **Guest Services:** complimentary and valet laundry.

🍴 CALL 🅚 BIZ HS 🛜 📹 🛗 🖥 🖥 / SOME UNITS 🛒

## ALBERTVILLE pop. 21,160

**MICROTEL INN & SUITES BY WYNDHAM ALBERTVILLE**
(256)894-4000

▽▽ ▽▽
Hotel
$69-$89

**Address:** 220 Hwy 75 N 35951 **Location:** Jct US 431 and SR 75, just ne. Located in a busy commercial area. **Facility:** 58 units. 3 stories, interior corridors. **Pool(s):** outdoor. **Guest Services:** coin laundry. **Featured Amenity:** continental breakfast.

SAVE 🍴 ⚓ HS 🛜 / SOME UNITS 🛒 🛗 🖥 🖥

### WHERE TO EAT

**SEBASTIEN'S ON MAIN**                                  256/660-1222

▽▽ ▽▽ American. Fine Dining. $8-$27 **AAA Inspector Notes:** An eclectic variety of hanging chandeliers, along with a multitude of twinkling lights against a black ceiling, create a starry night atmosphere at this restaurant. Touches of brick, iron, wood and draped fabric give a Bohemian flavor to this café. **Features:** full bar. **Address:** 330 Hwy 75 N 35951 **Location:** Jct US 431 and SR 75, just ne. D CALL 🅚

## ALEXANDER CITY pop. 14,875

**BAYMONT INN & SUITES ALEXANDER CITY**                  (256)234-7099

▽▽ ▽ Hotel $49-$89 **Address:** 4335 US Hwy 280 35010 **Location:** US 280, just s of jct SR 22; just nw of jct SR 63. **Facility:** 60 units. 2 stories (no elevator), exterior corridors. **Terms:** cancellation fee imposed. **Pool(s):** outdoor. **Activities:** exercise room. **Guest Services:** valet laundry.

⚓ BIZ 🛜 🛗 🖥 🖥 / SOME UNITS 🛒

**DAYS INN**                                             (256)234-6311

▽▽ ▽ **Motel** $69-$100 **Address:** 3146 US Hwy 280 35010 **Location:** Jct US 280 and SR 22. **Facility:** 62 units. 1-2 stories (no elevator), exterior corridors. **Pool(s):** outdoor.

🍴 ⚓ BIZ 🛜 🛗 🖥 🖥 / SOME UNITS 🛒 HS

**HAMPTON INN**                                          (256)234-2244

▽▽ ▽▽ Hotel $109-$119 **Address:** 1551 Elkahatchee Rd 35010 **Location:** Just s of jct US 280 and SR 22, just w. **Facility:** 61 units. 3 stories, interior corridors. **Terms:** 1-7 night minimum stay, cancellation fee imposed. **Pool(s):** outdoor. **Activities:** exercise room.

| **AAA Benefit:** Members save 5% or more! |

CALL 🅚 ⚓ BIZ HS 🛜 ❌ 🖥 / SOME UNITS 🛗 🖥

## ALICEVILLE (D-1) pop. 2,486, elev. 190'

SAVE **ALICEVILLE POW MUSEUM** is at 104 Broad St. N.E. Photos, artifacts, documents, drawings, uniforms, weapons and helmets fill the museum and tell the story of German POWs once held in Aliceville. During World War II, the city was one of 511 camps in the United States. A 15-minute video presentation provides insight into life as a prisoner in the camp. A second building houses exhibits honoring the U.S. military. **Time:** Allow 1 hour minimum. **Hours:** Tues.-Sat. 10-noon and 1-4. Closed major holidays. **Cost:** $10; $7 (ages 51+ and military with ID); $5 (ages 6-18). **Phone:** (205) 373-2363.

## ANDALUSIA pop. 9,015

**BEST WESTERN ANDALUSIA INN**                           (334)222-9999

▽▽ ▽▽
Motel
$75

**AAA Benefit:** Members save up to 20%!

**Address:** 305 W Bypass 36420 **Location:** Jct US 84 and SR 55, 0.5 mi s. **Facility:** 41 units. 2 stories (no elevator), exterior corridors. **Pool(s):** outdoor.

SAVE 🍴 CALL 🅚 ⚓ ♿ HS 🛜 🛗 🖥 🖥

**COMFORT INN**                                          (334)222-8891

▽▽ ▽▽ **Motel** $70-$131 **Address:** 1311 Dr MLK Jr Expwy 36420 **Location:** On US 84 Bypass, just e of jct US 29. **Facility:** 48 units. 2 stories (no elevator), exterior corridors. **Pool(s):** outdoor. **Activities:** exercise room. **Guest Services:** coin laundry.

🍴 ⚓ HS 🛜 🛗 🖥 🖥

**ECONO LODGE**                                          (334)222-7511

▽▽ ▽▽
Motel
$55

**Address:** 1421 Dr MLK Jr Expwy 36420 **Location:** On US 84 Bypass. **Facility:** 56 units. 2 stories (no elevator), exterior corridors. **Pool(s):** outdoor. **Guest Services:** coin laundry.

SAVE 🍴 CALL 🅚 ⚓ 🛜 🛗 🖥 🖥 / SOME UNITS 🛒

**HOLIDAY INN EXPRESS & SUITES**                         334/427-2740

▽▽▽ ▽ **Hotel. Rates not provided. Address:** 16727 US Hwy 84 36421 **Location:** Jct CR 57. **Facility:** 68 units. 3 stories, interior corridors. **Pool(s):** outdoor. **Activities:** exercise room. **Guest Services:** complimentary and valet laundry.

CALL 🅚 ⚓ BIZ HS 🛜 ❌ 🛗 🖥 🖥

## WHERE TO EAT

**CHEN'S GARDEN**      334/222-5300

▼ Chinese. Casual Dining. $5-$10 **AAA Inspector Notes:** This restaurant's daily buffet offers a multitude of items. Patrons can sample chicken broccoli, sesame chicken, teriyaki beef, peel-and-eat shrimp and crab legs, in addition to offerings from the salad bar, plus soups and desserts. **Address:** 1217 Dr MLK Jr Expwy 36420 **Location:** On US 84 Bypass, just e of jct US 29. [L] [D]

**DAVID'S CATFISH HOUSE**      334/222-3127

▼▼ Southern Seafood. Casual Dining. $6-$15 **AAA Inspector Notes:** Best known for its all-you-can-eat-catfish and cheddar grits, this eatery also offers plates of crab, shrimp, chicken, steak and burgers. Check out the giant rocking chair on the front porch. **Features:** beer only. **Address:** 1842 E Three Notch St 36421 **Location:** Jct US 84, 0.5 mi n on US 29. [L] [D] CALL [M]

**HOOK'S BAR-B-Q**      334/428-2278

▼ Barbecue. Quick Serve. $6-$14 **AAA Inspector Notes:** Diners will be hooked on this rib joint's wood-smoked ribs. A complimentary slice of luscious pound cake is included with every platter meal ordered. **Address:** 605 Dr MLK Jr Expwy 36420 **Location:** Jct US 84/SR 55 and US 29/84, 1.2 mi e; corner of 6th Ave. [L] [D]

**LARRY'S REAL PIT BAR-B-Q**      334/427-0140

▼ Barbecue. Family Dining. $7-$12 **AAA Inspector Notes:** Slow-cooked barbecue ribs, pork, chicken and beef are the staples of this laid-back, informal eatery. **Address:** 1309 Dr MLK Jr Expwy 36420 **Location:** On US 84 Bypass. [L] [D] CALL [M]

**OFELIA'S ITALIAN RESTAURANT**      334/427-1400

▼▼ Italian. Casual Dining. $7-$17 **AAA Inspector Notes:** A hidden treasure, this quaint bistro is situated in a former residential house with homey décor. The menu offers delectable authentic Italian fare with daily specials. Whether diners choose spaghetti, lasagna, chicken or veal parmigiana, ravioli or fettuccine Alfredo, it is all homemade and delicious. **Features:** full bar. **Address:** 401 River Falls St 36420 **Location:** Jct US 84 and SR 55, 0.6 mi e. [L] [D]

# ANNISTON (C-5) pop. 23,106, elev. 745'

Samuel Noble and Daniel Tyler established textile mills and blast furnaces in Anniston to help launch the South into the mainstream of the Industrial Revolution after the devastating effects of the Civil War. In 1879 the owners hired several Eastern architects to build a modern company town, which opened to the public in 1883. Many historic structures from this model city remain.

West of town is Anniston Army Depot, one of the nation's largest ordnance and reclamation depots. The highest point in the state, 2,407-foot Cheaha Mountain, is south of town in Cheaha State Park *(see Recreation Areas Chart).*

**Calhoun County Convention and Visitors Bureau:** 1330 Quintard Ave., Anniston, AL 36201. **Phone:** (256) 237-3536.

[GEM] [SAVE] **ANNISTON MUSEUM OF NATURAL HISTORY** is at 800 Museum Dr., at jct. SR 21 and US 431 in Lagarde Park. The Birds of the Americas Exhibit Hall features more than 400 specimens of North American birds, including extinct and endangered species collected by 19th-century naturalist William Werner.

Other highlights are the Environments of Africa Hall, containing more than 100 African animals displayed in simulated natural settings; a walk-through

re-creation of an Alabama cave; Egyptian mummies; and a temporary exhibit gallery. The Dynamic Earth depicts the planet's formation and includes minerals, fossils, gemstones and dinosaurs. Nature Space offers a large learning area with hands-on activities. Nature trails and gardens are on the grounds.

**Time:** Allow 2 hours minimum. **Hours:** Mon.-Sat. 10-5, Sun. 1-5, Memorial Day-Labor Day; Tues.-Sat. 10-5, Sun. 1-5, rest of year. Closed Jan. 1, Easter, Thanksgiving, Christmas Eve and Christmas. **Cost:** $6; $5.50 (ages 60+ and active military with ID); $5 (ages 4-17). Rates may increase for special exhibits. **Phone:** (256) 237-6766. [♿]

[SAVE] **BERMAN MUSEUM OF WORLD HISTORY,** jct. US 431 and SR 21 at 840 Museum Dr. in Lagarde Park, contains more than 3,000 objects, including an array of rare weapons and armor, and an art collection with bronzes by Frederic Remington. Many of the items belonged to historical figures such as Napoleon I and Jefferson Davis. A jeweled royal Persian scimitar and Asian art are other highlights.

**Time:** Allow 1 hour minimum. **Hours:** Mon.-Sat. 10-5, Sun. 1-5, Memorial Day-Labor Day; Tues.-Sat. 10-5, Sun. 1-5, rest of year. Closed Jan. 1, Thanksgiving, Christmas Eve and Christmas. **Cost:** $5; $4.50 (ages 61+ and military with ID); $4 (ages 4-17). Rates may increase for special exhibits. **Phone:** (256) 237-6261.

**CHURCH OF ST. MICHAEL AND ALL ANGELS** is at 1000 W. 18th St. at jct. Cobb Ave. The 1888 church, built in the Norman style, has a 95-foot tower housing 12 bells. The interior is noteworthy for its 12-foot-long white Carrara marble altar, alabaster reredos, stained-glass windows and hand-carved woodwork. **Hours:** Mon.-Fri. 8-11:30 and 12:30-4. **Cost:** Free. **Phone:** (256) 237-4011.

**DAMN YANKEES STEAK/FISH & OYSTER BAR**    256/236-7000

▼▼ Seafood. Casual Dining. $9-$29 **AAA Inspector Notes:** Located in the heart of town, this restaurant/bar has served the community for more than a decade serving an eclectic menu using the freshest ingredients. A five-percent discount is available for cash customers. **Features:** full bar, happy hour. **Address:** 919 Noble St 36201 **Location:** Between 9th and 10th sts; downtown. **Parking:** street only. [L] [D]

**TOP O' THE RIVER**      256/238-0097

▼▼ Regional Seafood. Family Dining. $11-$20 **AAA Inspector Notes:** Down-home hospitality is apparent as complimentary coleslaw in an aluminum measuring cup, cornbread in a cast-iron skillet and pickled onions, are all presented before you even place your order. The house specialty of catfish is served in heaping measures, and you'll also find shrimp, chicken, ribs and steak lining the menu. **Features:** full bar, Sunday brunch. **Address:** 3330 McClellan Blvd 36201 **Location:** I-20 exit 185, 6 mi n on US 431/SR 21. [D] CALL [M]

# ATHENS (A-3) pop. 21,897, elev. 720'
• Hotels p. 36 • Restaurants p. 36

Athens State University hosts ▼ Tennessee Valley Old Time Fiddlers Convention in early October. The 2-day event features performances in

18 music and dance categories as well as country cooking and 150 arts and crafts vendors.

**ALABAMA VETERANS MUSEUM AND ARCHIVES** is at 100 W. Pryor St. in the old L&N Freight Depot. This museum relates the stories of local military personnel from the Civil War to the present through the display of uniforms and other military artifacts. **Time:** Allow 1 hour minimum. **Hours:** Mon.-Sat. 9-3. Closed Jan. 1, Thanksgiving and Christmas. **Cost:** Donations. **Phone:** (256) 771-7578.

### BEST WESTERN ATHENS INN          (256)233-4030

Hotel
$95-$120

**AAA Benefit:**
Members save up to 20%!

**Address:** 1329 US 72 35611 **Location:** I-65 exit 351, just w. **Facility:** 83 units. 2 stories (no elevator), exterior corridors. **Terms:** 3 day cancellation notice. **Pool(s):** outdoor. **Activities:** limited exercise equipment. **Guest Services:** coin laundry.

### HAMPTON INN & SUITES          (256)232-2377

**Hotel** $99-$149 **Address:** 1222 Kelli Dr 35613 **Location:** I-65 exit 351, just e on US 72, then just s. **Facility:** 88 units. 4 stories, interior corridors. **Terms:** 1-7 night minimum stay, cancellation fee imposed. **Pool(s):** heated indoor. **Activities:** exercise room. **Guest Services:** valet and coin laundry.

**AAA Benefit:**
Members save 5% or more!

### HOLIDAY INN EXPRESS          256/232-7931

**Hotel.** Rates not provided. **Address:** 16074 Athens-Limestone Blvd 35613 **Location:** I-65 exit 351, just w. **Facility:** 71 units. 3 stories, interior corridors. **Pool(s):** heated indoor. **Activities:** hot tub, exercise room. **Guest Services:** valet and coin laundry.

### QUALITY INN ATHENS          (256)232-0030

**Hotel** $63-$80 **Address:** 1488 Thrasher Blvd 35611 **Location:** I-65 exit 351, just e, then just n. **Facility:** 56 units. 2 stories (no elevator), exterior corridors. **Pool(s):** outdoor. **Guest Services:** valet and coin laundry.

### SLEEP INN ATHENS          (256)232-4700

**Hotel** $67-$82 **Address:** 1115 Audubon Ln 35611 **Location:** I-65 exit 351, just nw. **Facility:** 60 units. 3 stories, interior corridors. **Pool(s):** outdoor. **Guest Services:** valet and coin laundry.

---

**WHERE TO EAT**

### CLARK'S RESTAURANT          256/771-7700

**American. Casual Dining.** $7-$19 **AAA Inspector Notes:** It is common to see local folks warmly greeting one another at this popular eatery. Well-prepared meals at an economical price in a down-home atmosphere is what can be found here. Although there is typically a wait for a table, it is well worth it. **Features:** Sunday brunch. **Address:** 1221-D Kelli Dr 35613 **Location:** I-65 exit 351, just e on US 72, then just s.

### LAWLERS BARBECUE          256/233-1818

**Southern Barbecue. Quick Serve.** $4-$20 **AAA Inspector Notes:** Whether dining in, taking out or driving through, this spot is plain and simple. Enjoy the original recipe barbecue sauce, original recipe potato salad and original recipe cherry cheesecake. **Address:** 1506 Hwy 72 E 35611 **Location:** I-65 exit 351, just e.

### LUVICI'S          256/233-5550

**Southern Comfort Food. Casual Dining.** $6-$22 **AAA Inspector Notes:** In the heart of historic downtown, and adjoining an 1800s-style mercantile store, this nostalgic small town restaurant is noted for its hearty country breakfasts and lunches. The lunch menu offers Southern favorites such as meatloaf, pot roast, fried chicken and catfish. Open for dinner until 8:30 pm Thursday through Saturday. **Address:** 105 N Jefferson St 35611 **Location:** Between W Market and W Hobbs sts; downtown. **Parking:** street only.

### MAC'S SPORTS BAR & STEAKHOUSE          256/232-6161

**American. Casual Dining.** $8-$21 **AAA Inspector Notes:** This casual restaurant features a simple meat-and-potato-style menu. The bar is in the rear of the building with its own entrance. Rotating hot entrée lunch specials are offered daily. **Features:** full bar. **Address:** 1733 S Jefferson St 35611 **Location:** I-65 exit 351, 1.8 mi w on US 72, then just s.

### PICASSO'S GRILL          256/262-9064

**American. Casual Dining.** $8-$19 **AAA Inspector Notes:** Enjoy fresh and flavorful entrées with American and Italian influences in a contemporary casual setting. This eatery is a welcome addition to Athens' dining-out options. The friendly, cordial staff will not disappoint. **Features:** full bar, happy hour. **Address:** 1260 US 72 E, Suite G 35611 **Location:** I-65 exit 351, 0.5 mi w.

### VILLAGE PIZZA          256/262-8654

**Pizza. Quick Serve.** $7-$20 **AAA Inspector Notes:** On the town square, across the street from the county courthouse, is this quaint pizzeria. Upon entering, the focal point is the arched brick oven from which the scent of baking pizza emanates. A small bar is located to the left and to the right is the L-shaped dining area with tables and chairs as well as wall booths. In addition to the house specialty, subs, salads, wings and a few pasta dishes are on the menu. Only lunch is served on Sunday. **Features:** full bar. **Address:** 222 W Market St 35611 **Location:** Corner of Jefferson St; downtown. **Parking:** street only.

### WILDWOOD DELI          256/206-9384

**Deli. Quick Serve.** $6-$10 **AAA Inspector Notes:** Frequented mostly by downtown professionals and shoppers, this cozy deli predominantly does a brisk take-out business. There is limited seating for indoor dining as well as some tables and chairs on the sidewalk out front. Sandwiches, subs and hot dogs are the staples of the simple menu. **Features:** patio dining. **Address:** 113 W Market St 35611 **Location:** Between Marion and Clinton sts; downtown. **Parking:** street only.

---

# ATMORE pop. 10,194

### HAMPTON INN          (251)368-9090

**Hotel** $99-$124 **Address:** 45 W Rivercane Blvd 36502 **Location:** I-65 exit 57, just s. **Facility:** 81 units. 4 stories, interior corridors. **Terms:** 1-7 night minimum stay, cancellation fee imposed. **Pool(s):** outdoor. **Activities:** exercise room. **Guest Services:** coin laundry, area transportation.

**AAA Benefit:**
Members save 5% or more!

### HOLIDAY INN EXPRESS          251/368-1585

**Hotel.** Rates not provided. **Address:** 111 Lakeview Cir 36504 **Location:** I-65 exit 57, just s. **Facility:** 80 units. 3 stories, interior corridors. **Pool(s):** outdoor. **Activities:** exercise room. **Guest Services:** coin laundry, area transportation.

## WIND CREEK CASINO & HOTEL (866)946-3360

▼▼▼ ▼▼▼
Contemporary
Hotel
$99-$399

**Address:** 303 Poarch Rd 36502 **Location:** I-65 exit 57, 0.6 mi s on SR 21, then just nw. **Facility:** This contemporary, high-rise structure, with its distinctive sloping roof, is easily identified off the interstate. The full-service property has a casino, multiple restaurants and a night club. 236 units. 17 stories, interior corridors. **Parking:** on-site and valet. **Terms:** check-in 4 pm, cancellation fee imposed. **Amenities:** safes. **Dining:** 5 restaurants, also, FIRE Steakhouse, Taste Buffet, see separate listings, nightclub. **Pool(s):** outdoor. **Activities:** hot tub, exercise room, spa. **Guest Services:** valet laundry, area transportation.

 (SAVE) 🏊 🍴 📶 🍽 CALL &M ⛵ 🛜 🐾 🔒 🅿

---

### WHERE TO EAT

**DAVID'S CATFISH HOUSE** 251/368-3063

▼▼ ▼ Southern Comfort Food. Casual Dining. $6-$17 **AAA Inspector Notes:** This casual, down-home restaurant can be found in a rustic wood building 1.5 miles from the center of town. It is fun to check out the numerous antique toys, tools and memorabilia displayed throughout the multiple dining areas. All-you-can-eat catfish or shrimp menu selections are available. As a keepsake, take a picture of the kids seated on the 8-foot rocking chair situated out front. **Address:** 1804 S Main St 36502 **Location:** I-65 exit 57, 7.8 mi s on SR 21. [L] [D] CALL &M

---

### FIRE STEAKHOUSE 251/368-8007

▼▼▼ ▼▼▼
Steak
Seafood
Fine Dining
$18-$48

**AAA Inspector Notes:** Entering into this stylish, contemporary restaurant you will see the elegantly set tables which preview the special dining experience in store. Friendly, attentive staff provide personalized service. Multiple chef surprises are incorporated throughout your meal. The presentation of a beautiful long stemmed rose is the crowning touch to an elegant evening. **Features:** full bar. **Reservations:** suggested. **Address:** 303 Poarch Rd 36502 **Location:** I-65 exit 57, 0.6 mi s on SR 21, then just nw; in Wind Creek Casino & Hotel. **Parking:** valet and street only.

[D] CALL &M

**Specializing in prime steaks
and seafood**

---

**TASTE BUFFET** 251/368-8007

▼ American. Quick Serve. $12-$14 **AAA Inspector Notes:** This all-you-can-eat café offers a salad bar, meat carving station, pizza, Asian favorites and Southern comfort foods. Check the schedule, as some evenings offer designated specials such as steak or ribs. Desserts are plentiful, even offering some sugar-free selections. **Address:** 303 Poarch Rd 36502 **Location:** I-65 exit 57, 0.6 mi s on SR 21, then just nw; in Wind Creek Casino & Hotel. **Parking:** valet and street only. [L] [D] CALL &M

---

## ATTALLA (C-4) pop. 6,048, elev. 548'

**TIGERS FOR TOMORROW AT UNTAMED MOUNTAIN,** 708 CR 345, is a 140-acre wildlife preserve that is home to more than 160 rescued animals, including bears, foxes, black leopards, African lions, mountain lions, panthers, tigers and wolves. Visitors can follow the dirt paths to see the animals in their spacious fenced-in areas. Youngsters can interact with barnyard animals at the contact yard. In addition, educational programs are offered.

**Note:** Visitors must wear closed-toe shoes. Photography is not permitted. Guided tours are available by appointment. **Time:** Allow 1 hour minimum. **Hours:** Wed.-Sun. 9-5, Mar.-Nov.; Sat.-Sun. 9-5, rest of year. Closed Jan. 1, Thanksgiving and Christmas. Phone ahead to confirm schedule. **Cost:** $12; $6 (ages 3-11). Guided 2-hour tour (includes general admission) $25. Cash only. **Phone:** (256) 524-4150. GT 🎟

## AUBURN (E-5) pop. 53,380, elev. 698'
**• Hotels p. 38 • Restaurants p. 39**

Auburn is the home of Auburn University, which was established in 1856 and is now the largest university in Alabama; its enrollment exceeds 25,000. During football season nearly 90,000 people pack Jordan-Hare Stadium to watch the Auburn Tigers. The Old Main, Church Street and Auburn University historic districts encompass many buildings dating from 1847 to 1927. Of interest is the Auburn University Chapel, an 1850 Gothic Revival structure at Thach Avenue and S. College Street.

Four miles south of town off US 29 is Chewacla State Park, comprising 696 acres that include a 23-acre fishing and swimming lake, walking trails and waterfalls. Other amenities include vacation cabins, campsites, hiking and bicycle trails, picnic areas and a playground; phone (334) 887-5621 or (800) 252-7275. *See Recreation Areas Chart.*

**Auburn-Opelika Tourism Bureau:** 714 E. Glenn Ave., Auburn, AL 36830. **Phone:** (334) 887-8747 or (866) 880-8747.

**AUBURN UNIVERSITY,** 100 S. College St., was founded in 1856 by the Methodist Church and envisioned as a religious, educational and cultural center for men. The institution is now a state-supported, land-grant university. A walking tour of campus can be arranged through the Office of Admissions; maps are available in the student center. **Hours:** Mon.-Fri. 7:45-4:45. Closed major holidays. **Cost:** Free. **Phone:** (334) 844-4244. GT

**Jonathan B. Lovelace Hall of Honor** is at 250 Beard-Eaves Ct. in Auburn Arena on the Auburn University campus. The museum honors Auburn University's athletic programs, players and coaches with film clips, photos, jerseys and equipment. Seventeen interactive displays showcase each sport at the university. The school's athletic championship trophies along with Bo Jackson's Heisman trophy are on display. The Auburn Spirit Theater shows 25 brief film clips highlighting memorable moments from the university's long sports history.

**Time:** Allow 30 minutes minimum. **Hours:** Mon.-Fri. 8-5. The attraction closes early when there is a home basketball game or gymnastics event. Closed major holidays. Phone ahead to confirm schedule. **Cost:** Free. **Phone:** (334) 844-4750.

**Jule Collins Smith Museum of Fine Arts** is off I-85 exit 51, then 2 mi. n. on US 29/SR 147 to 901 S. College St., on the Auburn University campus. American and European art from the 19th- and 20th centuries is displayed in eight galleries. The permanent collection includes works by Marc Chagall, Salvador Dalí, Henri Matisse, Joan Miró, Pablo Picasso and Pierre-Auguste Renoir. Traveling exhibits also are featured. The modernistic building is on manicured grounds.

**Time:** Allow 1 hour minimum. **Hours:** Mon.-Fri. 8:30-4:45, Sat. 10-4:45. Closed Jan. 1, July 4, Thanksgiving and Christmas. **Cost:** Donations. **Phone:** (334) 844-1484. GT ⊞

### CLARION INN & SUITES UNIVERSITY CENTER
(334)821-7001

Hotel
$75-$200

**Address:** 1577 S College St 36832 **Location:** I-85 exit 51, 1.4 mi w on US 29/SR 147. **Facility:** 119 units. 2-3 stories (no elevator), exterior corridors. **Pool(s):** outdoor. **Activities:** limited exercise equipment. **Guest Services:** coin laundry. **Featured Amenity:** full hot breakfast.

SAVE ⊞ 🛏 BIZ 🛜 ⊟ 🖨
🖳 / SOME UNITS 🅢

### THE CRENSHAW GUEST HOUSE
334/821-1131

▼▼▼ **Historic Bed & Breakfast.** Rates not provided. **Address:** 371 N College St 36830 **Location:** Just w of downtown; in historic district. **Facility:** Located just north of Auburn University campus, this Victorian home offers well-appointed rooms with many original features, including claw-foot tubs, tiled fireplaces (inoperable), and bead board ceilings. 7 units, some two bedrooms and cottages. 1 story, interior/exterior corridors. **Activities:** picnic facilities. **Guest Services:** complimentary and valet laundry.

🛜 ✕ 🗯 / SOME UNITS 🐾 ⊟ 🖨 🖳

### HAMPTON INN
(334)821-4111

▼▼▼▼ **Hotel** $99-$249 **Address:** 2430 S College St 36832 **Location:** I-85 exit 51, 0.4 mi se. **Facility:** 102 units. 3 stories, interior corridors. **Terms:** 1-7 night minimum stay, cancellation fee imposed. **Pool(s):** outdoor. **Activities:** exercise room. **Guest Services:** valet and coin laundry.

> **AAA Benefit:** Members save 5% or more!

CALL 🈺 🛏 🛜 🖳 / SOME UNITS ⊟ 🖨

### HOLIDAY INN EXPRESS HOTEL & SUITES AUBURN
334/502-1090

▼▼▼▼ **Hotel.** Rates not provided. **Address:** 2013 S College St 36832 **Location:** I-85 exit 51, 0.6 mi n on US 29/SR 147. **Facility:** 82 units. 3 stories, interior corridors. **Pool(s):** outdoor. **Activities:** hot tub, exercise room. **Guest Services:** valet and coin laundry.

⊞ CALL 🈺 🛏 BIZ 🛜 ✕ ⊟ 🖳 / SOME UNITS 🖨

### QUALITY INN
(334)502-5020

▼▼ **Motel** $74-$199 **Address:** 1212 Mall Pkwy 36831 **Location:** Located behind Village Mall. **Facility:** 42 units. 2 stories (no elevator), exterior corridors. **Pool(s):** outdoor. **Activities:** exercise room. *(See ad this page.)*

⊞ 🛏 BIZ 🛜 ⊟ 🖨 🖳 / SOME UNITS 🅢

### SLEEP INN & SUITES
(334)501-7171

Hotel
$79-$155

**Address:** 135 Spirit Dr 36832 **Location:** I-85 exit 51, just w on S College St, then just n. **Facility:** 72 units. 4 stories, interior corridors. **Pool(s):** heated indoor. **Activities:** limited exercise equipment. **Guest Services:** coin laundry. **Featured Amenity:** breakfast buffet.

SAVE ⊞ CALL 🈺 🛏 BIZ 🛜
⊟ 🖨 🖳 / SOME UNITS 🅗🅢

───── ▼ See AAA listing this page ▼ ─────

AAA Vacations® packages ... unforgettable experiences and unrivaled value

**WHERE TO EAT**

### AMSTERDAM CAFE
334/826-8181

▼▼ American. Casual Dining. $12-$33 **AAA Inspector Notes:** Don't let the bar-like appearance through the windows deceive you at this local favorite. In a comfortable, warm setting, a casual, yet refined and attentive staff is more than happy to make suggestions from the unique Southern menu. The delectable crab cake and avocado sandwich has been voted to Alabama's list of "Top 100 Things to Eat Before You Die." Other favorites include apple-brined pork chop with collard greens, or lamb shank ravioli. Finish that off with pumpkin crème brûlée. **Features:** full bar, patio dining. **Address:** 410 S Gay St 36830 **Location:** Jct S Gay St and Samford Dr, just e. **Parking:** on-site and street. [L] [D] CALL [&M]

### ARICCIA ITALIAN TRATTORIA & BAR
334/844-5140

▼▼▼ Italian. Fine Dining. $10-$30 **AAA Inspector Notes:** Romantic and intimate yet surprisingly spacious, this modern trattoria-style restaurant presents fresh, delicious, traditional dinners. A somewhat open-style kitchen doesn't detract from the atmosphere: Cozy, round booths are available in addition to typical table seating. Whether visiting the area for an event or staying in the hotel, a meal here should be on your list. **Features:** full bar, patio dining, Sunday brunch, happy hour. **Reservations:** suggested. **Address:** 241 S College St 36830 **Location:** Just e of downtown; just n of AU campus; in The Hotel at Auburn University & Dixon Conference Center.

[B] [L] [D] [LATE] CALL [&M]

### BIG BLUE BAGEL
334/501-2245

▼ Deli Sandwiches. Quick Serve. $5-$8 **AAA Inspector Notes:** Predominately frequented by students from the nearby university, this is a great place for a quick sub or bagelwich. **Features:** beer only. **Address:** 120 N College St 36830 **Location:** Between Glenn and Magnolia aves; downtown. **Parking:** street only.

[B] [L] [D]

### COUNTRY'S BARBECUE
334/821-8711

▼ Barbecue. Casual Dining. $2-$10 **AAA Inspector Notes:** Friendly servers dish up such barbecue favorites as chicken, pork, beef and ribs at this rustic, country-themed restaurant. Try the buttermilk fried chicken, it is a crowd pleaser. **Features:** beer only. **Address:** 1021 Opelika Rd 36830 **Location:** Jct Dean Rd, 0.6 mi n.

[L] [D]

### FUJI SUSHI BAR & JAPANESE CUISINE
334/887-7766

▼▼ Japanese Sushi. Casual Dining. $7-$12 **AAA Inspector Notes:** This bustling establishment, offering a varied sushi menu and teriyaki plates at affordable prices, is very popular with the college crowd. **Features:** full bar. **Address:** 1499 S College St 36832 **Location:** I-85 exit 51, 1.5 mi ne on SR 147. [L] [D] CALL [&M]

### GOOD OL' BOYS
334/826-3900

▼▼ American. Family Dining. $7-$15 **AAA Inspector Notes:** Fried catfish is king at this rustic, down-home restaurant. **Features:** Sunday brunch. **Address:** 1843 Sandhill Rd 36830 **Location:** I-85 exit 51, 1.2 mi e to Sandhill Rd, then 1.8 mi n on CR 10.

[D] CALL [&M]

### HAMILTON'S ON MAGNOLIA
334/887-2677

▼▼▼ American. Fine Dining. $7-$35 **AAA Inspector Notes:** Some inventive and tasty creations at this popular downtown spot include Buffalo shrimp chips, Korean barbecue rack of lamb and halibut and shrimp sauté. Specialty martinis include the lemon drop and hocus pocus. For dessert, try the Irish crème brûlée. **Features:** full bar, patio dining. **Address:** 174 E Magnolia Ave 36830 **Location:** Jct E Magnolia Ave and Gay St; downtown. **Parking:** street only.

[L] [D] CALL [&M]

### MAESTRO 2300
334/821-4448

▼▼▼ New Mediterranean. Fine Dining. $24-$31 **AAA Inspector Notes:** Enter into this intimate bistro and be enveloped by the Mediterranean-influenced décor. A variety of dining areas are enclosed with intricate, swirling wrought iron dividers, deep-wood panels are suspended from the ceiling and sheer hanging fabrics add a soft touch. Using the freshest regional ingredients mandates a frequently changing menu. **Features:** full bar, patio dining. **Reservations:** suggested. **Address:** 2300 Moores Mill Rd 36830 **Location:** Jct CR 109 and 146, just w; in Ogletree Village. [D] CALL [&M]

### MIKE & ED'S BAR-B-Q OF AUBURN
334/501-1866

▼ Barbecue. Casual Dining. $4-$12 **AAA Inspector Notes:** Everyone seems to enjoy this popular eatery, whether it's for a sit-down meal or if sharing a tailgate take-away. Try the tasty barbecue pork, ribs, or chicken dinners, or you can opt for a hickory-smoked ham or turkey. Whether you decide to dine in or take away, you'll enjoy the friendly service. **Features:** patio dining. **Address:** 307 N College St 36830 **Location:** Between Braggs Ave and Warrior Ct; downtown. [L] [D]

### NIFFER'S PLACE
334/821-3118

▼▼ Burgers Wings. Casual Dining. $7-$15 **AAA Inspector Notes:** Whimsical décor adds to the relaxed atmosphere at this popular college hangout. **Features:** full bar, patio dining. **Address:** 1151 Opelika Rd 36830 **Location:** I-85 exit 58, 1.5 mi n on US 280, then 3 mi w on SR 14. [L] [D] CALL [&M]

### PANNIE-GEORGE'S KITCHEN
334/821-4142

▼ Comfort Food Soul Food. Family Dining. $7-$12 **AAA Inspector Notes:** Guests are welcomed like members of the family at this popular homestyle kitchen. Serving up Southern-style favorites for years, the kitchen's most popular items are the fried chicken and macaroni and cheese. Other menu items change daily. If you're hoping for dinner, be sure to visit on Wednesday, Thursday or Friday; otherwise enjoy a hearty lunch every day except Saturday, when they are closed. **Features:** patio dining, Sunday brunch. **Address:** 2328 S College St, Suite 6 36832 **Location:** I-85 exit 51, just n. [L]

### VEGGIES TO GO
334/821-1660

▼ Southern. Quick Serve. $4-$8 **AAA Inspector Notes:** Expect simple and straightforward Southern homestyle cooking at this eatery. Order and pick up your food at the counter. The menu offers meat-and-two, meat-and-three, or three-veggie or four-veggie plates. Don't pass up a sip of the sweet tea. **Features:** Sunday brunch. **Address:** 1650 S College St, Suite 2 36830 **Location:** I-85 exit 51, 1.2 mi w on US 29/SR 147. [L] [D] CALL [&M]

### ZAZU GASTROPUB
334/887-0206

▼▼▼ American. Casual Dining. $8-$26 **AAA Inspector Notes:** Take a break from the activities at Auburn and enjoy a delicious and artistic meal, beautifully presented, served by a knowledgeable and attentive staff. Creative selections include sweet & spicy scallops, Creole andouille sausage and Gulf rock shrimp flatbread, and the very popular cornbread waffles and buttermilk-fried chicken. **Features:** full bar, happy hour. **Reservations:** suggested, weekends. **Address:** 149 E Magnolia Ave 36830 **Location:** Between N College and N Gay sts; downtown. **Parking:** on-site (fee) and street. [L] [D]

## BAY MINETTE pop. 8,044

### SHRIMP BASKET
251/937-3655

▼▼ Seafood. Casual Dining. $7-$14 **AAA Inspector Notes:** A casual, nautical atmosphere can be found in this spot where seafood abounds. Shrimp, oysters and fish can be steamed, grilled or fried. Burgers and chicken are available for meat lovers. Rotating nightly all-you-can-eat specials are offered. **Features:** full bar, patio dining. **Address:** 1111 Hwy 31 S 36507 **Location:** 1.5 mi s on SR 59/US 31; center. [L] [D] CALL [&M] [◪]

## BAYOU LA BATRE (I-1) pop. 2,558, elev. 7'

Although the Maubilla Indians were the first people to settle in the area, Bayou La Batre was officially founded by Joseph Bosarge in 1786 as part of a Spanish land grant. The city's main street is the bayou where trawlers are often three or four abreast on both sides of the tributary as it enters the Mississippi Sound. Bayou La Batre's boatbuilding, seafood and petroleum industries are among the largest on the Gulf Coast.

**Bayou La Batre Area Chamber of Commerce:** 13640 N. Wintzell Ave., P.O. Box 486, Bayou La Batre, AL 36509. **Phone:** (251) 824-4088.

## BEATRICE (G-3) pop. 301, elev. 269'

**RIKARD'S MILL HISTORICAL PARK** is at 4116 SR 265N. The highlight in the piney woods along Flat Creek is the restored 1845 water-powered gristmill that grinds corn into meal and grits. Blacksmithing and cane syrup making demonstrations also are presented. A cane syrup making day is held the second Saturday in November.

**Time:** Allow 1 hour minimum. **Hours:** Fri.-Sat. 9-5, mid-Apr. to mid-Nov. **Cost:** $4; $3 (ages 0-11 and 65+). Special events admission $5; $3 (ages 0-11 and 65+). **Phone:** (251) 789-2781. GT

## BESSEMER (D-3) pop. 27,456, elev. 515'

• Hotels & Restaurants map & index p. 54
• Part of Birmingham area — see map p. 43

**BESSEMER HALL OF HISTORY MUSEUM,** 1905 Alabama Ave., is in the restored 1916 Southern Railroad Depot. Native American artifacts, pioneer items, Civil War memorabilia and a collection of old telephones and business machines—including a typewriter from Adolf Hitler's hideaway, The Eagle's Nest—are among the items displayed. Changing exhibits include pieces pertinent to the industrial history of Jefferson County. Also on display is the one-millionth Pullman Standard boxcar built in Bessemer. **Time:** Allow 30 minutes minimum. **Hours:** Tues.-Sat. 9-3. Closed major holidays. **Cost:** Donations. **Phone:** (205) 426-1633.

SAVE **SPLASH ADVENTURE WATERPARK,** 4599 Alabama Adventure Pkwy., features a 27,000-square-foot wave pool, a giant wet play structure with a huge dump bucket, a lazy river, a children's activity pool and a variety of water-tubing slides and flumes as well as Wipeout Adventure Course, Space Bowl, Up Surge and Water Maze. A zipline also is offered.

**Time:** Allow 3 hours minimum. **Hours:** Open daily at 10:30, mid-May to mid-Sept. Closing times vary. Phone ahead to confirm schedule. **Cost:** $28.99; $21.99 (ages 4-9 and 55+). **Parking:** $7. **Phone:** (205) 481-4750. [T]

### BEST WESTERN PLUS BESSEMER HOTEL & SUITES
(205)481-1950 **61**

Hotel
$90-$100

**AAA Benefit:** Members save up to 20%!

**Address:** 5041 Academy Ln 35022 **Location:** I-20/59 exit 108, just sw. **Facility:** 70 units. 3 stories, interior corridors. **Pool(s):** outdoor. **Activities:** exercise room. **Guest Services:** coin laundry. **Featured Amenity:** full hot breakfast.

### COMFORT INN
(205)428-3999 **62**

Hotel $85-$200 **Address:** 5051 Academy Ln 35022 **Location:** I-20/59 exit 108, just sw. **Facility:** 59 units. 3 stories, interior corridors. **Amenities:** safes. **Pool(s):** outdoor. **Activities:** exercise room. **Guest Services:** coin laundry.

▼ See AAA listing p. 41 ▼

(See map & index p. 54.)

### COUNTRY INN & SUITES BY CARLSON  (205)481-0007  57

▼▼▼ Hotel $75-$220 **Address:** 4985 Academy Ct 35022 **Location:** I-20/59 exit 108, just sw. **Facility:** 66 units. 3 stories, interior corridors. **Terms:** cancellation fee imposed. **Pool(s):** heated indoor. **Activities:** hot tub, exercise room. **Guest Services:** coin laundry.

### FAIRFIELD INN & SUITES BY MARRIOTT BIRMINGHAM BESSEMER  (205)277-1700  58

▼▼▼ Hotel $120-$131 **Address:** 4980 Academy Ln 35022 **Location:** I-20/59 exit 108, just sw. **Facility:** 76 units. 4 stories, interior corridors. **Pool(s):** heated indoor. **Activities:** hot tub, exercise room. **Guest Services:** valet and coin laundry.

**AAA Benefit:** Members save 5% or more!

### HAMPTON INN  (205)425-2010  56

▼▼▼ Hotel $109-$149 **Address:** 4910 Civic Ln 35022 **Location:** I-20/59 exit 108, 0.5 mi ne. **Facility:** 84 units. 4 stories, interior corridors. **Terms:** 1-7 night minimum stay, cancellation fee imposed. **Pool(s):** outdoor. **Activities:** exercise room. **Guest Services:** coin laundry.

**AAA Benefit:** Members save 5% or more!

### HOLIDAY INN EXPRESS & SUITES  205/424-2600  59

▼▼▼ Hotel. Rates not provided. **Address:** 5001 Academy Ln 35022 **Location:** I-20/59 exit 108, just sw. **Facility:** 63 units. 3 stories, interior corridors. **Pool(s):** heated indoor. **Activities:** exercise room. **Guest Services:** valet and coin laundry.

### QUALITY INN  (205)428-3194  60

▼▼ Motel $60-$200 **Address:** 5021 Academy Ln 35022 **Location:** I-20/59 exit 108, just sw. Located in a light commercial area. **Facility:** 60 units. 2 stories (no elevator), exterior corridors. **Pool(s):** outdoor. **Activities:** picnic facilities, exercise room. **(See ad p. 40.)**

### SLEEP INN  (205)424-0000  63

▼▼ Hotel $70-$150 **Address:** 1259 Greenmor Dr 35022 **Location:** I-459 exit 6, just s, then just w. **Facility:** 71 units. 3 stories, interior corridors. **Amenities:** safes. **Pool(s):** outdoor. **Activities:** exercise room.

---

## WHERE TO EAT

### BOB SYKES BAR-B-Q  205/426-1400  77

◆ Barbecue. Family Dining. $9-$17 **AAA Inspector Notes:** In the family since 1957, this restaurant builds on its fine tradition of treating guests to succulent ribs and pulled pork, as well as barbecue chicken and burgers. A number of sides complement the offerings. Also good here are the pies. **Address:** 1724 9th Ave 35020 **Location:** I-20/59 exit 112 (18th St/19th St), 0.7 mi e, then just s.

### THE BRIGHT STAR  205/426-1861  78

▼▼ Southern Greek. Casual Dining. $8-$30 **AAA Inspector Notes:** *Historic.* Specializing in Greek cuisine with some American fare offered, this family-owned restaurant has been in operation since 1914. Memorabilia of the local area is on display. **Features:** full bar. **Address:** 304 19th St N 35020 **Location:** I-20/59 exit 112 (18th St/19th St), 1 mi e; downtown. **Parking:** valet and street only.

### EZELL'S CATFISH CABIN  205/424-5860  79

▼▼ Seafood. Casual Dining. $8-$21 **AAA Inspector Notes:** Sit right down in this cozy Southern-style fishing cabin and enjoy some freshly fried catfish, trout or Gulf shrimp. Oysters are also available in season. **Features:** beer & wine. **Address:** 5060 Academy Ln 35022 **Location:** I-20/59 exit 108, just sw.

### RAILROAD CAFE  205/424-1073  80

▼▼ Southern American. Family Dining. $3-$14 **AAA Inspector Notes:** Simple, Southern-style cooking is what you'll find here. Comfort foods include fried chicken, chicken and dumplings as well as sandwiches, steaks, fish, hamburgers and hot dogs. Lunch specials are offered daily. While you dine enjoy the nostalgia—cookie tins, lunch boxes, railroad knickknacks, and yesteryear toys...many of which are original— are on full display floor to ceiling and wall to wall. Occasionally, trains click-clack past the back door. **Features:** Sunday brunch. **Address:** 1205 Lake Dr SE, Suite 111 35022 **Location:** I-459 exit 6, just s; in Morgan Village Plaza.

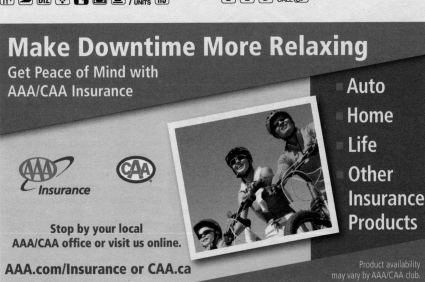

# Birmingham

## Then & Now

Alabama's largest city also is one of its youngest. Since its founding in 1871, Birmingham has transformed itself from empty farmland in the foothills of the Appalachian Mountains to steel boomtown to major commercial and service center. Despite the bustle found in any metropolitan center, traditional Southern hospitality is still characteristic of the city's residents.

The Jones Valley's rare abundance of the essential ingredients for steel production—iron ore, coal and limestone—was known as early as the 1850s, contributing to the settlement's early growth. Small furnaces were erected in the area during the Civil War to produce munitions for the Confederate Army.

However, the lack of rail lines to move iron and steel products thwarted any major industrial effort. In 1871, when two railroad lines converged, plans for a larger settlement were drawn and capitalists from around the state rushed in to exploit the new city's resources. The fledgling city was named, fittingly enough, after England's major industrial hub, Birmingham. Within decades Birmingham was established as a major manufacturing center. The speed with which it grew and prospered earned it the nickname "Magic City."

This initial vigor paled after World War II. Cheaper and higher quality iron ore imported from abroad as well as diminished steel orders combined to close several factories, resulting in widespread unemployment. The smog and smoke accumulated from years of heavy industry further dimmed prospects for the "Pittsburgh of the South."

In the 1960s an even darker cloud formed over the city when the racial unrest that had been building across the South erupted in violence. In 1963 civil rights movement leaders sponsored sit-ins, marches and pickets to protest segregation and force local businesses to employ more African-Americans. Kelly Ingram Park (formerly West Park), occupying a square block, was the assembly point for participants in the Christian Leadership Conference's sit-ins, boycotts and marches.

The police response to the civil unrest during this period was swift and sometimes brutal, including the use of high-pressure water hoses and police dogs. Thousands were arrested, including Dr. Martin Luther King Jr. It was during his incarceration that King wrote his widely read essay, "Letter from a Birmingham Jail." In June 1963 business and civil rights leaders reached an agreement, and Birmingham residents soon rallied around the common goal of peaceful resolution.

The Birmingham of the 21st century is strikingly different from the city of the

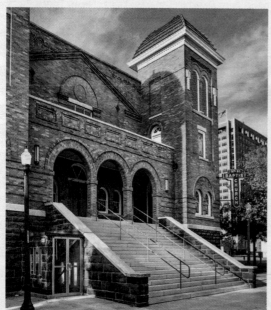

Sixteenth Street Baptist Church

(Continued on p. 44.)

# Destination Birmingham

This map shows cities in the Birmingham vicinity where you will find attractions, hotels and restaurants. Cities are listed alphabetically in this book on the following pages.

# Fast Facts

## ABOUT THE CITY

**POP:** 212,237 ▪ **ELEV:** 1,200 ft.

## MONEY

**SALES TAX:** State, county and city sales taxes total 10 percent in Birmingham. A lodging tax of 16 percent also is levied.

## WHOM TO CALL

**EMERGENCY:** 911

**POLICE (non-emergency):** (205) 328-9311

**HOSPITALS:** Princeton Baptist Medical Center, (205) 783-3000 ▪ St. Vincent's Birmingham, (205) 939-7000 ▪ St. Vincent's East, (205) 838-3000 ▪ Trinity Medical Center, (205) 592-1000 ▪ UAB (University of Alabama at Birmingham) Hospital, (205) 934-4011 ▪ UAB Hospital-Highlands, (205) 930-7000.

## WHERE TO LOOK AND LISTEN

**NEWSPAPERS:** Birmingham has one major newspaper, *The Birmingham News.* Smaller daily and weekly papers cater to the suburbs and special interests.

**RADIO:** Birmingham radio station WERC (105.5 FM) is an all-news/weather station ▪ WBHM (90.3 FM) is a member of National Public Radio.

## VISITOR INFORMATION

**Greater Birmingham Convention and Visitors Bureau:** 2200 Ninth Ave. N., Birmingham, AL 35203. **Phone:** (205) 458-8000 or (800) 458-8085.

**Birmingham Business Alliance:** 505 N. 20th St., Suite 200, Birmingham, AL 35203. **Phone:** (205) 324-2100.

## TRANSPORTATION

**AIR TRAVEL:** Birmingham-Shuttlesworth International Airport (BHM) is served by major domestic carriers and regional commuter lines. Most major hotels provide shuttle service, usually free, to and from the airport. Taxi fare from the airport to downtown is about $20 one way.

**RENTAL CARS:** One of the largest car rental agencies in the city, Hertz, (205) 591-6090 or (800) 654-3080, offers discounts to AAA members.

**RAIL SERVICE:** Amtrak trains destined for New York and New Orleans depart from the station at 1819 Morris Ave.; phone (205) 324-3033.

**BUSES:** Greyhound Lines Inc., at 618 19th St. N., provides commercial bus service to and from the city; phone (205) 252-7190 or (800) 231-2222.

**TAXIS:** Taxis are on the meter system. The typical charge is $4.50 initially and $2 for each additional mile. The two largest companies are American Cab Co., (205) 322-2222 ▪ and Yellow, (205) 252-1131.

**PUBLIC TRANSPORTATION:** Birmingham-Jefferson County Transit Authority provides bus service around town and into the outlying suburbs. Basic bus fare is $1.25. The authority also manages DART, a system of vintage trolleys serving the downtown area; the fare is 25c. Exact change is required for both buses and DART. Phone (205) 521-0101 for schedule and route information.

(Continued from p. 42.)

past generation. Gone are the pollution-spewing smokestacks of manufacturers; the city's renovated central business district boasts a smog-free skyline.

Racial tensions have likewise dissipated, due in large part to the opening of the Birmingham Civil Rights Institute, across from Kelly Ingram Park. The facility, which has given the city an outlet to tell its own story, has helped mend the injustices of the past and promote human relations not just in Birmingham but throughout America.

Having experienced the pitfalls of a single-industry economy, Birmingham has diversified to include medical, engineering, educational, financial and technological industries among its top resources. Medicine and medical research figure prominently in its future; the city has 21 hospitals.

While the largest single employer is the University of Alabama at Birmingham, one out of every 10 people in the workforce is involved in health care. The university's medical center specializes in open-heart surgery and diabetes treatment. The Kirklin Clinic at the University of Alabama at Birmingham, 2000 6th Ave. S., is a 430,000-square-foot health-care clinic designed by I.M. Pei.

Samford University is Alabama's largest private college and includes the Howard College of Arts and Sciences, the Cumberland School of Law and professional schools of pharmacy, nursing, business, music, education and divinity.

Birmingham's extensive public park system provides a wealth of opportunities for recreation and relaxation. Lovers of art and history will find the murals and Rucker Agee map collection at the Linn-Henley Research Library, 2100 Park Pl., worth their while; phone (205) 226-3665. The city's lively arts groups and wide variety of cultural offerings add to the enjoyment this modern metropolis provides residents and visitors alike.

# Must Do: AAA Editor's Picks

- Revisit Birmingham's age of heavy industry at the **Sloss Furnaces National Historic Landmark**—one of the last places to see a blast furnace in America. The factories and the availability of materials for iron production within a 30-mile radius made Birmingham the South's industrial center for nearly 90 years. Though Birmingham's economy eventually diversified, the city's moniker seems a fitting tribute, as it was named after the United Kingdom's industrial center. Along the way, it's also been called "The Pittsburgh of the South" and "The Magic City."

- Experience the antebellum South at the **Arlington Antebellum Home and Gardens,** which was built by Judge William S. Mudd, one of the 10 founders of the city. Birmingham's lone plantation includes beautifully manicured grounds and a Greek Revival home that was occupied by Union troops during the Civil War.

- Head to the revitalized **Ruffner Mountain Nature Preserve** for a nature-lover's retreat. Once containing mines and quarries, the grounds now feature a boardwalk and trails traversing the Red Mountain ridge. The LEED-certified nature center is the source for answers to all your environmental questions, and you can learn about turtles, owls and other native wildlife on-site.

- Brake for **Barber Vintage Motorsports Museum** to admire early to modern motorcycles, Lotus race cars and everything involved in motorsports entertainment. The world-renowned collection is housed in a 740-acre park with a 2.38-mile racetrack.

- Take in the views of the city with Vulcan, the god of fire and smithery, who continues to watch over Birmingham. Located on Red Mountain, the **Vulcan Park and Museum** showcases the prominent statue first unveiled at the 1904 St. Louis World's Fair and provides a great place to practice your photography skills.

- March in the footsteps of legends when you visit the six-block Civil Rights District. Powerful landmarks such as **Sixteenth Street Baptist Church, Birmingham Civil Rights Institute** and **Kelly Ingram Park** bear witness to the problems and progress of the city.

- Stop by **Pepper Place** in the **Lakeview Design District** to experience how a once-industrial part of town transitioned to a shopper's paradise. Trendy stores put Birmingham's style on the map with attention-grabbing architectural details, antiques and colorful displays. But the farmers market is the main draw on Saturdays; it boasts a variety of products grown within 100 miles.

- Take note: Birmingham is increasingly cited as a must-visit foodie destination due to its fresh and flavorful cuisine. Over the past few years, the James Beard Foundation—aka the Oscars of the food world—has hailed the **Hot and Hot Fish Club's** chef as the best in the South and has recognized **Highlands Bar & Grill** as a finalist for outstanding restaurant in the country.

  - Try at least one down-home dish during your visit. Despite the availability of creative and cosmopolitan fare, the South is just as renowned for its biscuits, grits and typical "Southern" fare. A good place to start would be **John's City Diner,** open since 1944 and home to one-of-a-kind coleslaw.

  - Jam to a concert or go to a free fitness class at **Railroad Park,** a 19-acre green space that connects the downtown with Southside and the campus of University of Alabama at Birmingham. The site mixes industrial touches—recycled bricks and cobblestone—with water features, open lawns and more than 600 trees.

  - Spend hours at the **Birmingham Museum of Art** with its numerous themed rooms. Reputedly one of the best regional museums in the nation, there are more than 24,000 paintings, sculptures, prints, drawings and pre-Columbian artifacts that visitors can see for free. The museum even has hands-on exhibits for children.

Enjoy the farmers market at Pepper Place

# Birmingham 1-day Itinerary

AAA editors suggest these activities for a great short vacation experience.

## Morning

- To prepare for a busy day in Birmingham, eat a hearty breakfast with the locals at **Niki's Restaurant** on 2nd Avenue. The generous, down-home selections should keep visitors well-fueled during a walking tour of the nearby **Civil Rights District**.

- Designated in 1992, the six-block area commemorates the African-American struggle for equality. A historic turning point occurred at the **Sixteenth Street Baptist Church** on Sept. 15, 1963. On that day, four African-American girls died in a racially motivated bombing that eventually swayed public support toward the landmark Civil Rights Act of 1964.

- A short distance away is the ⚜**Birmingham Civil Rights Institute**, which provides a sobering yet hopeful reflection on race relations within the city and elsewhere. Highlights include the jail cell where the Rev. Martin Luther King Jr. wrote his "Letter from Birmingham Jail," and statues of civil rights leaders that stand in the adjacent **Kelly Ingram Park.**

- Make an upbeat stop at the **Alabama Jazz Hall of Fame.** Located within **Carver Theatre,** which opened in 1935 as a segregated spot for African-Americans to watch first-run movies, the hall of fame traces the music style's origins and showcases priceless memorabilia. Personal effects of jazz and blues greats like Duke Ellington, Ella Fitzgerald and W.C. Handy remind visitors of those bygone days. Call ahead for the performance schedule so you can round off your jazz education with a live performance or two.

## Afternoon

- A couple blocks away you'll encounter kid-friendly **McWane Science Center** and **John W. Woods IMAX Dome Theater.** Test hands-on exhibits, enjoy one of the many IMAX film offerings available or buy a combination ticket to experience the best of both.

- Did you build up an appetite in the meantime? Head downtown where Southern hospitality is on the menu at the atmospheric **Café Dupont.** Housed in a renovated storefront, this restaurant uses local ingredients in its fusion of soul food and contemporary flavors.

- A few blocks northwest is the renowned ⚜**Birmingham Museum of Art.** Regional to international artists display their objets d'art in this free museum. Only have an hour to spare? Download a best-of list from the museum's website, and make the most of your time.

- Next up is the **Alabama Sports Hall of Fame Museum.** If you're a sports enthusiast, this stop is a home run with more than 5,000 items, including Heisman trophies, dioramas,

Alabama Sports Hall of Fame

equipment and uniforms. Inductees such as Hank Aaron, Willie Mays, Carl Lewis and Paul "Bear" Bryant make up the more than 200 honorees.

## Evening

- You'll think a wrong turn landed you in New Orleans after heading south for supper at **Veranda on Highland.** The fine-dining restaurant offers creative Southern, Creole and Cajun cuisine. Cocktails with names like "Bless Her Heart" and "I Do Declare" add flair to the menu.

- After satisfying your appetite, it's time to decide: Should you revel or relax? Party people should kick up their heels at either **Five Points South** or the **Lakeview Design District** to sample Birmingham nightlife. You'll find live music venues, dive bars, dance floors and everything in between.

- Fans of peace and quiet should drive south toward **Red Mountain** to forge a picture-perfect ending to their evening. There, nature lovers can take a relaxing stroll, or they can head somewhere with an even better view.

- ⚜**Vulcan Park and Museum** tops Red Mountain—and indeed Birmingham—with a 124-foot-tall Vulcan. Created for the 1904 St. Louis World's Fair, the world's largest cast-iron statue of the god remains the main draw, but you can learn area history as well as explore the vast park complex if you arrive early enough. Come later to view the twinkling lights below, and you'll see why some call Birmingham "The Magic City."

## Arriving

### By Car

Several major highways intersect in Birmingham, providing easy access from all directions. North-south I-65 cuts straight through the city, affording direct routes from Montgomery and Nashville, Tenn. From Chattanooga, Tenn., and other points northeast, I-59 runs through the Appalachian foothills before merging with I-20, intersecting I-65 near the city center and continuing southwest into Mississippi.

I-459 branches off from I-59 just east of the city limits and loops southward to bypass downtown traffic, rejoining I-20/59 near McCalla. Approaching from due east, I-20 meets the I-459 bypass before merging with I-59 downtown.

## Getting Around

### Street System

Laid out in an orderly grid pattern, Birmingham is fairly easy to navigate. The downtown area is bounded by I-20/59 to the north, I-65 to the west and US 31, the Red Mountain Expressway, to the east. North-south thoroughfares are designated as streets, while east-west routes are avenues. Both streets and avenues are numbered, although some also have names, such as University Boulevard (Eighth Avenue South).

Unless otherwise posted, a right turn on red is permitted after a complete stop.

### Parking

With numerous public and private lots, parking is not a problem in Birmingham. Garages generally charge from $5 to $10 per day; on-street metered parking is available downtown.

## Shopping

Downtown warehouses that once produced America's oldest soft drink, Dr Pepper, now comprise the upscale **Pepper Place,** which is one of the region's better-known interior design centers. Other retail centers include **Colonial Brookwood Village,** US 280E and Lakeshore Drive, with anchor stores Belk and Macy's; and **The Summit,** at US 280E and I-459, which has Belk and Saks Fifth Avenue as well as many upscale specialty shops. Window-shoppers and novelty hunters will want to visit the antique shops and trendy boutiques of **Five Points South,** off 20th Street S. and Highland Avenue.

Twelve miles south in Hoover, at I-459 and US 31S, is **Riverchase Galleria;** it is *the* place to shop while you're in the Birmingham area. Topped by one of the largest glass skylights in the Western Hemisphere, the Galleria includes Belk, JCPenney, Macy's, Sears, more than 200 specialty stores, an office tower and a sizable hotel.

## Big Events

Ring in the new year with the ⬙ **BBVA Compass Bowl.** Held during the first week in January at **Legion Field,** the football event is a match-up between teams from the Big East and Southeastern conferences.

Birmingham heralds spring in late April or early May with the ⬙ **ONB Magic City Art Connection,** an outdoor art show and festival held in **Linn Park.** Food, wine, music and workshops accompany the art exhibits.

Barber Motorsports Park holds three automotive events. In late April the 3-day **Honda Indy Grand Prix of Alabama,** an IZOD IndyCar Series event, takes place. In late June the 2-day **Triumph Superbike Classic** features an air show, vintage road racing and a parts swap meet. The **Barber Vintage Festival** is a 3-day event held in mid-October and offers a rally, motorcycle auction, swap meet and more vintage racing.

Other city events include an **Oktoberfest** in mid-September and the **Greek Food Festival** in late September.

The **Southern Women's Show** at **Birmingham-Jefferson Convention Complex** in early October is a 4-day event focused on women's issues—from topics as important as health and fitness to lighter subjects like fashion and makeovers.

Beginning in mid-December and lasting a little more than 2 weeks is the **Zoolight Safari** at **Birmingham Zoo.**

## Sports & Rec

Alabama's unofficial status as "Football Capital of the South" is largely the legacy of University of Alabama coach Paul "Bear" Bryant, who led his **Crimson Tide football** team to more than 300 victories. For Crimson Tide sports tickets phone (205) 348-2262.

Watch vintage road racing at the Triumph Superbike Classic

Relive the memories of music legends at the Alabama Jazz Hall of Fame

The **University of Alabama at Birmingham,** (205) 975-8221; **Samford University,** (205) 726-2966; **Miles College,** (205) 929-1615; and **Birmingham-Southern College,** (205) 226-4935, also have competitive sports teams. The **Birmingham Barons,** AA **baseball** affiliates of the Chicago White Sox, play their home games at **Regions Field;** phone (205) 988-3200.

Free self-guiding tours of the restored 1910 **Rickwood Field,** 1137 2nd Ave. W., are offered when the park is open (typically Mon.-Fri. 8-4:30 and some weekends). Baseball greats Ty Cobb, Babe Ruth, Satchel Paige and Willie Mays played here. Visitors can pick up a brochure leading them on a route to see the highlights; a walk on the field is sure to be a thrill for dedicated baseball fans. Guided tours with additional access to the locker room and press box are available by appointment; phone (205) 458-8161.

**Auto racing** attracts legions of fans to the **Talladega Superspeedway** *(see Talladega p. 144).* The raceway holds two **NASCAR Sprint Cup** events as well as the **NASCAR Nationwide Series** and **ARCA** events. The **Birmingham Race Course,** 1000 John Rogers Dr., offers on-site greyhound **dog racing;** phone (205) 838-7500.

**Note:** Policies concerning admittance of children to pari-mutuel betting facilities vary. Phone for information.

**Tennis** courts can be found at most city parks, along with facilities for **hiking** and **bicycling.** City **golf** courses include **Highland Park,** 3300 Highland Ave. S., and **Roebuck,** 8920 Roebuck Blvd. For information about other public golf courses and tennis courts, phone the convention and visitors bureau, (205) 458-8000 or (800) 458-8085.

## Performing Arts

The **University of Alabama at Birmingham Department of Theatre** presents dramatic productions, special concerts, big-name entertainment and shows in the **Alys Robinson Stephens Performing Arts Center** late September through May; phone (205) 975-2787 or (877) 278-8457. **The Terrific New Theatre,** open year-round, features off-Broadway shows; phone (205) 328-0868. The **Birmingham Children's Theatre,** one of the largest professional children's theaters in the country, presents nine different shows throughout the year; phone (205) 458-8181.

Contemporary and experimental dramas are hallmarks of the **Birmingham Festival Theatre,** which features new playwrights and local talent; phone (205) 933-2383.

The **Alabama Ballet** stages most of its performances at the Samford University **Wright Center;** phone (205) 322-4300. **Opera Birmingham** sponsors performances throughout the year; phone (205) 322-6737.

## ⚑ ATTRACTIONS

**ALABAMA JAZZ HALL OF FAME** is at 1631 Fourth Ave. N. at jct. 17th St. The museum, in the 1935 Carver Theatre for the Performing Arts, spotlights jazz greats who have links to Alabama. Photographs, instruments, costumes and other artifacts belonging to such legends as Nat King Cole, Duke Ellington, Ella Fitzgerald and Lionel Hampton are exhibited. Jazz performances and theatrical productions are presented.

**Time:** Allow 1 hour minimum. **Hours:** Tues.-Sat. 10-5. Guided tours are available Tues.-Wed. and Fri. 10-2, Sat. 2-5. Closed major holidays. **Cost:** Self-guiding tour $2. Guided tour $5. Reservations are recommended for tours. **Phone:** (205) 327-9424. [GT]

**ALABAMA MUSEUM OF THE HEALTH SCIENCES** is on the campus of the University of Alabama at Birmingham, on the 3rd floor of the Lister Hill Library at 1700 University Blvd. The museum has collections of equipment and instruments relating to medicine, nursing, ophthalmology and dentistry from the past seven centuries. **Time:** Allow 45 minutes minimum. **Hours:** Mon.-Fri. 9-5. Closed major holidays. Phone ahead to confirm schedule. **Cost:** Free. **Phone:** (205) 934-4475.

[SAVE] **ALABAMA SPORTS HALL OF FAME MUSEUM** is at 2150 Richard Arrington Jr. Blvd. N., next to the Birmingham-Jefferson Convention Complex. In addition to various sports-related displays, films highlight memorable sports moments and the athletic achievements of Alabama sports champions. **Hours:** Mon.-Fri. 9-5. Closed major holidays. **Cost:** $5; $4 (ages 60+); $3 (students with ID); free (ages 0-5); $14 (family). **Phone:** (205) 323-6665.

**ARLINGTON ANTEBELLUM HOME AND GARDENS,** 331 Cotton Ave. S.W. in Old Elyton, dates from the 1840s and is Birmingham's only remaining Greek Revival structure. The wonderfully preserved two-story house—with spacious porches and balconies in the front and back—was built by Judge William S. Mudd, one of the 10 founders of the city. It sits on a 6-acre estate with beautifully landscaped gardens and large magnolia trees. Brochures provide details of the house and describe structural changes that have been made to the property over the years.

The wide entry hall once served as a formal reception area for guests. The rest of the downstairs includes a sitting room, formal dining room and a parlor. Upstairs are four bedrooms. The rooms are furnished with 19th-century furniture, artwork and crafts. While the decor is not original to the house, it reveals how the wealthy lived in this era.

**Time:** Allow 30 minutes minimum. **Hours:** Tues.-Sat. 10-4, Sun. 1-4. Last tour begins 1 hour before closing. Closed major holidays. **Cost:** $5; $4.50 (ages 55+); $3 (ages 6-18). Cash only. **Phone:** (205) 780-5656. GT

**BARBER VINTAGE MOTORSPORTS MUSEUM** is off I-20E exit 140, e. on US 78, s. on Rex Lake Rd., then w. to 6030 Barber Motorsports Pkwy. Possessing what is considered to be the world's largest collection of motorcycles, the museum presents about 750 of its more than 1,400 machines; the earliest example dates to 1902. More than 60 Lotus race cars also are showcased. **Time:** Allow 1 hour minimum. **Hours:** Mon.-Sat. 10-5, Sun. noon-5. Closed major holidays. **Cost:** $15; $10 (ages 4-12). **Phone:** (205) 699-7275.

**BIRMINGHAM BOTANICAL GARDENS,** 2612 Lane Park Rd., comprises nearly 68 acres of flowers, trees and shrubs. More than 230 species of

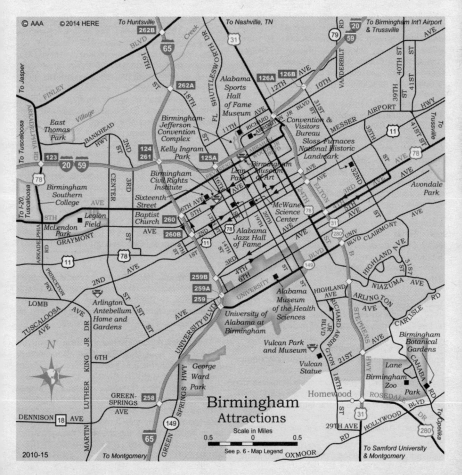

Birmingham
Attractions

2010-15

birds can be observed. The grounds also contain a conservatory and a Japanese garden as well as 27 landscaped gardens and plant collections. A horticultural lending library contains gardening books, magazines, CDs and DVDs.

Picnicking is permitted in designated locations. Pets are not permitted. **Time:** Allow 2 hours minimum. **Hours:** Garden daily dawn-dusk. Garden center daily 9-5. **Cost:** Free. **Phone:** (205) 414-3900. ⓘ 🌲

**BIRMINGHAM CIVIL RIGHTS INSTITUTE,** 520 16th St. N., is a museum and a research and education facility that contains permanent exhibits describing the Birmingham Civil Rights Movement and worldwide human rights struggles. An 8-minute introductory movie details class struggles and violent labor strikes occurring in the early 20th century between wealthy Birmingham steel industrialists and coal miners. Touch-screen monitors in the Arrington Resource Gallery offer access to an audiovisual history library.

**Time:** Allow 2 hours minimum. **Hours:** Tues.-Sat. 10-5, Sun. 1-5. Last admission 30 minutes before closing. Closed major holidays. **Cost:** $12; $6 (college students with ID); $5 (ages 65+); $3 (non-Jefferson County students in grades 4-12); free (non-Jefferson County students in grades K-3, Jefferson County residents ages 0-17 and to all Sun.). **Phone:** (205) 328-9696 or (866) 328-9696.

**Kelly Ingram Park,** part of the Birmingham Civil Rights Institute, is bordered by 16th and 17th sts. N. and 5th and 6th aves. N. Statues depict the struggles encountered by demonstrators at this 4-acre site where major civil rights demonstrations occurred in the 1960s. Statues include "Four Spirits," "The Children's March" and "Praying Ministers." A self-guiding audio tour is available; wands may be rented at the Birmingham Civil Rights Institute ticket booth.

Guided walking tours are available by appointment. **Time:** Allow 30 minutes minimum. **Hours:** Daily dawn-dusk. **Cost:** Free. **Phone:** (205) 328-9696, (205) 328-1850 for walking tour appointments, or (866) 328-9696, ext. 204, for information. ⓖⓣ

**BIRMINGHAM MUSEUM OF ART,** 2000 Rev. Abraham Woods Jr. Blvd., features a permanent collection of more than 25,000 paintings, sculptures, drawings and decorative arts representing a rich panorama of cultures dating from ancient to modern times, including African, American, Asian, European, Native American and Pre-Columbian art. Highlights include Renaissance paintings, 18th-century French furniture and English ceramics, featuring one of the largest Wedgwood collections in the world. The museum is home to one of the finest Asian art collections in the Southeast.

The facility includes a large sculpture garden as well as a library containing more than 25,000 items, including rare books, art reference books and exhibition catalogues. **Time:** Allow 1 hour minimum. **Hours:** Museum Tues.-Sat. 10-5, Sun. noon-5. Library Wed. noon-4 and by appointment. Closed city holidays. **Cost:** Free. Fees may be charged for special exhibits. **Phone:** (205) 254-2565, or (205) 254-2982 for the library.

**BIRMINGHAM ZOO,** 2630 Cahaba Rd. in Lane Park, is one of the South's largest zoos. Birds, reptiles and mammals from around the world dwell in simulated natural settings. Visitors can feed giraffes at the Kiwanis Giraffe Encounter or watch the African bull elephant herd roam the Trails of Africa. A children's zoo and a predator display are featured along with daily interactive programs. A train and carousel also are available.

**Hours:** Daily 9-5 (also Tues. and Fri.-Sun. 5-7, Memorial Day weekend-Labor Day). Holiday hours may vary; phone ahead. **Cost:** Zoo Wed.-Mon. $14; $9 (ages 2-12 and 65+). Zoo Tues. $7; $4.50 (ages 2-12 and 65+). Train or carousel ride $2.50. **Phone:** (205) 879-0409. ⓘ

**McWANE SCIENCE CENTER,** downtown at 200 19th St. N. at jct. 2nd Ave. N., offers four levels of science adventures and interactive exhibits. Children under 6 can explore Just Mice Size, where everything appears 10 times larger than normal. ScienceQuest has hands-on exhibits about motion, energy, light and sound, while World of Water takes a look at aquatic life from around the globe. A dinosaur exhibit features fossils and interactive games. Films at the John W. Woods IMAX Dome Theater surround visitors with action.

**Time:** Allow 2 hours minimum. **Hours:** Science center Mon.-Sat. 10-6, Sun. noon-6, June-Aug.; Mon.-Fri. 9-5, Sat. 10-6, Sun. noon-6, rest of year. Closed Jan. 1, Easter, Thanksgiving, Christmas Eve and Christmas. **Cost:** Science center $13; $12 (ages 65+); $9 (ages 2-12). Combination ticket with John W. Woods IMAX Dome Theater (excludes feature-length films) $18; $16 (ages 65+); $13 (ages 2-12). **Parking:** $5. **Phone:** (205) 714-8300 or (877) 462-9263. ⓘ

**John W. Woods IMAX Dome Theater** is downtown in the McWane Science Center at 200 19th St. N. at jct. 2nd Ave. N. The theater is five stories high and presents large-format science and nature films as well as feature-length Hollywood movies.

**Time:** Allow 1 hour minimum. **Hours:** Shows are given on the hour Mon.-Sat. 10-6, Sun. noon-6, June-Aug.; Mon.-Fri. 9-5, Sat. 10-5, Sun. 1-5, rest of year. Closed Jan. 1, Easter, Thanksgiving, Christmas Eve and Christmas. **Cost:** Educational film $9; $8 (ages 2-12 and 65+). Feature-length film $10; $9 (ages 2-12 and 65+). Combination ticket with McWane Science Center (excludes feature-length films) $18; $16 (ages 65+); $13 (ages 2-12). **Parking:** $5. **Phone:** (205) 714-8300 or (877) 462-9263.

**RUFFNER MOUNTAIN NATURE PRESERVE** is at 1214 81st St. S. The nature center of this 1,036-acre forest and wildlife sanctuary focuses on Ruffner Mountain's biology, geology and history and features the Tree Top Visitor Center with animal exhibits and the Mountainside Pavilion, used for picnics and events. There are 12 miles of hiking trails; one trail ends at an overlook with a panoramic view of the city. A wetland with a boardwalk also is on the grounds.

Street parking is available for visitors wanting trail access when visitor center gate is closed. **Time:** Allow 2 hours minimum. **Hours:** Trails daily dawn-dusk. Tree Top Visitor Center & Mountainside Pavilion Tues.-Sat. 9-5, Sun. 1-5; closed Jan. 1, Thanksgiving, Christmas Eve and Christmas. Phone ahead to confirm schedule. **Cost:** Donations. Program prices vary. **Phone:** (205) 833-8264. 🎦 🎟

**SIXTEENTH STREET BAPTIST CHURCH,** downtown at 1530 6th Ave. N. at jct. 16th St., is where four young girls died in a 1963 Sunday morning bombing that became a pivotal event in the civil rights movement. A 45-minute video program recounts the event and the role this African-American church played in shaping local and national history. A stained-glass window donated by the people of Wales commemorates the tragedy. **Hours:** Tues.-Fri. 10-3, Sat. by appointment 10-1. **Cost:** $5. **Phone:** (205) 251-9402.

**SLOSS FURNACES NATIONAL HISTORIC LANDMARK** is at 20 32nd St. N. Built in 1882 to produce pig iron, these blast furnaces were the backbone of the city's industrial economy until the 1970s. Now converted into a museum of history and industry, it is the only such preservation project in the nation. A 32-acre park surrounds the site. A self-guiding tour brochure interprets history and describes the furnaces' operations.

**Time:** Allow 30 minutes minimum. **Hours:** Tues.-Sat. 10-4, Sun. noon-4. Guided tours are offered Sat.-Sun. at 1, 2 and 3. Closed city holidays. Phone ahead to confirm schedule. **Cost:** Free. **Phone:** (205) 324-1911. 🆖

**SOUTHERN MUSEUM OF FLIGHT/ALABAMA AVIATION HALL OF FAME,** 4343 73rd St. N., presents 8 decades of aviation history. The hall of fame honors aviators with ties to the state, including the Wright brothers, who flew from an airfield that became part of Maxwell Air Force Base in Montgomery. Military, commercial, experimental and Cold War-era aircraft are displayed. Other exhibit areas highlight the Tuskegee Airmen and women in aviation.

**Time:** Allow 1 hour minimum. **Hours:** Tues.-Sat. 9:30-4:30. Closed major holidays. **Cost:** $7; $6 (students with ID and senior citizens); free (ages 0-3 and military with ID). **Phone:** (205) 833-8226.

▽GEM **VULCAN PARK AND MUSEUM** is at the top of Red Mountain at 1701 Valley View Dr. The showpiece of this 10-acre urban park is the 60-ton, 56-foot-high Vulcan Statue, depicting the mythological Roman god for which the park is named. It is seated on a 124-foot-high pedestal. Giuseppe Moretti designed the statue, which is one of the world's largest cast-iron figures. It was cast in Birmingham for the 1904 Louisiana Purchase Exposition in St. Louis, Mo. Vulcan, the Roman god of fire and the inventor of metalwork, pays tribute to the city's iron industry. The open-air balcony of the observation tower allows for an up-close look.

Inside the interpretive Vulcan Center, Birmingham's past, present and future come to life through static and interactive exhibits about the region's geology, history and industrial growth. A visitor information center also is available. The park grounds and the observation tower offer spectacular views of the city. **Time:** Allow 1 hour minimum. **Hours:** Park grounds daily 7 a.m.-10 p.m. (open Jan. 1 and Thanksgiving 1-10). Vulcan Center Museum Mon.-Sat. 10-6, Sun. 1-6. Observation tower Mon.-Sat. 10-10, Sun. 1-10 (weather permitting). Closed Christmas Eve and Christmas. Phone ahead to confirm schedule.

**Cost:** Park grounds free before 6 p.m. Admission before 6 p.m. (includes Vulcan Center/Museum and observation tower) $6; $5 (ages 65+ and military with ID); $4 (ages 5-12). Admission after 6 p.m. (includes park grounds and observation tower) $4; free (ages 0-4). **Phone:** (205) 933-1409. 🆖 🎦 🎟

## Sightseeing
### Walking Tours

Brochures detailing self-guiding tours of the **Birmingham Downtown Historic District** are available from the Greater Birmingham Convention and Visitors Bureau, 2200 Ninth Ave. N.; phone (205) 458-8000 or (800) 458-8085.

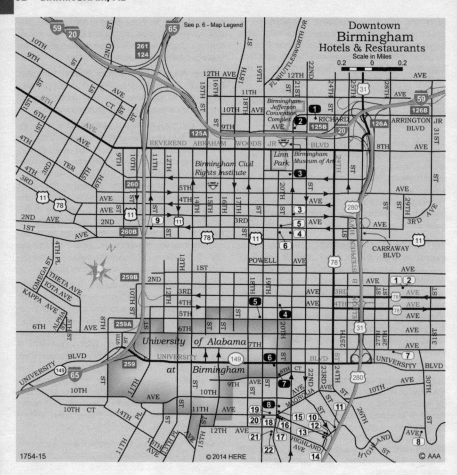

# Downtown Birmingham

This index helps you "spot" where approved hotels and restaurants are located on the corresponding detailed maps. Hotel daily rate range is for comparison only. Restaurant price range is a combination of lunch and/or dinner. Turn to the listing page for more detailed rate and price information and consult display ads for special promotions.

## DOWNTOWN BIRMINGHAM

| Map Page | Hotels | Diamond Rated | Rate Range | Page |
|---|---|---|---|---|
| **1** this page | **The Westin Birmingham** | ◈◈◈◈ | $149-$359 SAVE | 61 |
| **2** this page | **Sheraton Birmingham Hotel** | ◈◈◈ | $129-$299 SAVE | 61 |
| **3** this page | The Tutwiler - Hampton Inn & Suites | ◈◈◈ | $119-$229 | 61 |
| **4** this page | SpringHill Suites by Marriott Birmingham Downtown at UAB | ◈◈◈ | $99-$169 | 61 |
| **5** this page | **Courtyard by Marriott Birmingham Downtown UAB** | ◈◈◈ | $119-$299 SAVE | 60 |
| **6** this page | DoubleTree by Hilton Hotel Birmingham | ◈◈◈ | Rates not provided | 60 |
| **7** this page | **Residence Inn by Marriott Birmingham Downtown @ UAB** (See ad p. 61.) | ◈◈◈ | $103-$179 SAVE | 60 |
| **8** this page | The Hotel Highland at Five Points South, an Ascend Collection Hotel Member | ◈◈◈ | $127-$205 | 60 |

| Map Page | Restaurants | Diamond Rated | Cuisine | Price Range | Page |
|----------|-------------|---------------|---------|-------------|------|
| ① p. 52 | Bettola | ▽▽▽ | Italian Pizza | $9-$20 | 62 |
| ② p. 52 | Cantina Tortilla Grill | ▽ | Mexican | $4-$11 | 62 |
| ③ p. 52 | Surin & Company | ▽▽ | Thai | $6-$14 | 63 |
| ④ p. 52 | John's City Diner | ▽▽ | American | $10-$23 | 63 |
| ⑤ p. 52 | Pita Loco | ▽ | Mediterranean | $5-$15 | 63 |
| ⑥ p. 52 | Cafe Dupont | ▽▽▽▽ | Regional American | $14-$40 | 62 |
| ⑦ p. 52 | Sol y Luna | ▽▽▽ | Southwestern | $10-$16 | 63 |
| ⑧ p. 52 | Rojo | ▽ | Mexican | $7-$15 | 63 |
| ⑨ p. 52 | Niki's Restaurant | ▽ | American | $8-$13 | 63 |
| ⑩ p. 52 | Bottega Cafe | ▽▽▽ | Italian | $11-$39 | 62 |
| ⑪ p. 52 | Bottega Restaurant | ▽▽▽▽ | Italian | $25-$39 | 62 |
| ⑫ p. 52 | Taj India | ▽▽ | Indian | $9-$20 | 63 |
| ⑬ p. 52 | Hot and Hot Fish Club | ▽▽▽▽ | New World | $25-$38 | 62 |
| ⑭ p. 52 | Veranda on Highland | ▽▽▽ | American | $25-$42 | 63 |
| ⑮ p. 52 | Cosmo's Pizza | ▽▽ | Pizza | $3-$24 | 62 |
| ⑯ p. 52 | Highlands Bar & Grill | ▽▽▽▽ | French | $27-$36 | 62 |
| ⑰ p. 52 | Chez Fon Fon | ▽▽▽ | French | $10-$23 | 62 |
| ⑱ p. 52 | Fuego Cantina and Saloon | ▽▽ | Tex-Mex | $8-$18 | 62 |
| ⑲ p. 52 | Surin West | ▽▽ | Thai | $8-$24 | 63 |
| ⑳ p. 52 | Golden Temple Vegetarian Cafe | ▽▽ | American | $6-$11 | 62 |
| ㉑ p. 52 | **26** | ▽▽▽ | New American | $9-$24 | 62 |
| ㉒ p. 52 | **Ocean** | ▽▽▽▽ | Seafood | $30-$50 | 63 |

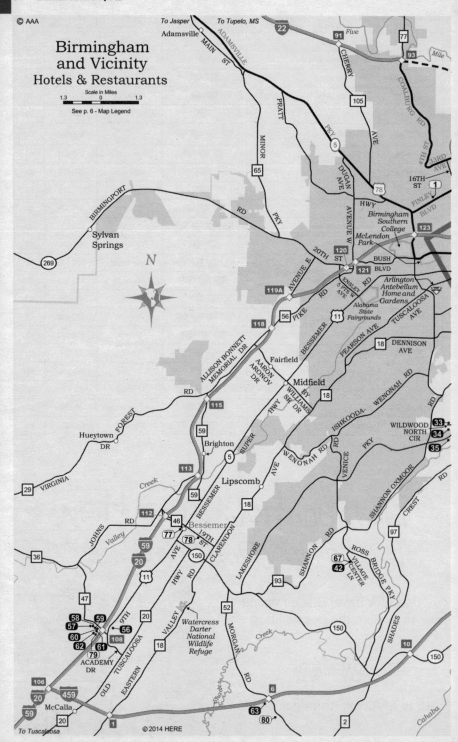

# Birmingham
## and Vicinity
### Hotels & Restaurants

Scale in Miles
1.3   0   1.3

See p. 6 - Map Legend

© 2014 HERE

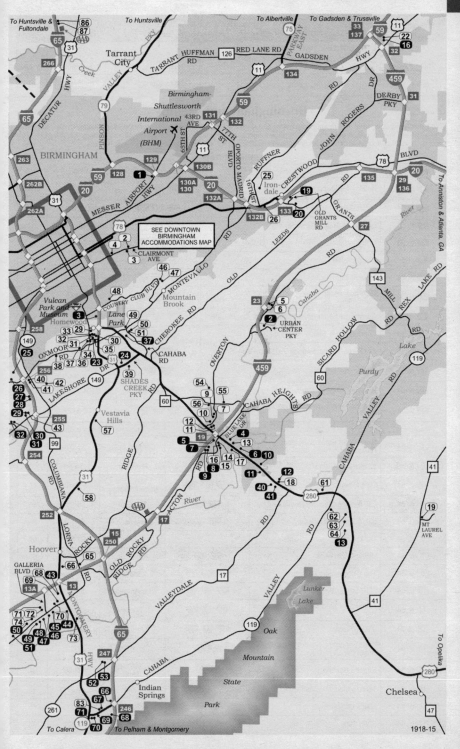

1918-15

| ✈ Airport Hotels | | | | |
|---|---|---|---|---|
| **BIRMINGHAM INTERNATIONAL** (Maximum driving distance from airport: 1.6 mi) | | | | |
| Map Page | | Diamond Rated | Rate Range | Page |
| **1** p. 54 | Holiday Inn-Airport, 1.6 mi | ▼▼▼ | Rates not provided | 64 |

# Birmingham and Vicinity

This index helps you "spot" where approved hotels and restaurants are located on the corresponding detailed maps. Hotel daily rate range is for comparison only. Restaurant price range is a combination of lunch and/or dinner. Turn to the listing page for more detailed rate and price information and consult display ads for special promotions.

## BIRMINGHAM

| Map Page | Hotels | Diamond Rated | Rate Range | Page |
|---|---|---|---|---|
| **1** p. 54 | Holiday Inn-Airport | ▼▼▼ | Rates not provided | 64 |
| **2** p. 54 | Hilton Garden Inn Birmingham SE/Liberty Park | ▼▼▼ | $99-$199 | 64 |
| **3** p. 54 | **Embassy Suites Birmingham** | ▼▼▼ | $129-$209 SAVE | 63 |
| **4** p. 54 | Drury Inn & Suites-Birmingham Southeast | ▼▼▼ | $110-$189 | 63 |
| **5** p. 54 | Hampton Inn-Colonnade | ▼▼▼ | $99-$159 | 64 |
| **6** p. 54 | Marriott Birmingham | ▼▼▼ | $171-$181 | 64 |
| **7** p. 54 | SpringHill Suites by Marriott Birmingham Colonnade | ▼▼▼ | $89-$169 | 64 |
| **8** p. 54 | **Courtyard by Marriott Birmingham Colonnade** | ▼▼▼ | $89-$159 SAVE | 63 |
| **9** p. 54 | Comfort Inn & Suites - Colonnade | ▼▼▼ | $80-$149 | 63 |
| **10** p. 54 | La Quinta Inn Birmingham / Cahaba Park South | ▼▼ | $65-$214 | 64 |
| **11** p. 54 | Quality Inn & Suites | ▼▼ | Rates not provided | 64 |
| **12** p. 54 | Residence Inn by Marriott Birmingham | ▼▼▼ | $104-$169 | 64 |
| **13** p. 54 | Hampton Inn & Suites Birmingham 280E-Eagle Point | ▼▼▼ | $109-$129 | 64 |

| Map Page | Restaurants | Diamond Rated | Cuisine | Price Range | Page |
|---|---|---|---|---|---|
| ① p. 54 | Niki's West Steak & Seafood Restaurant | ▼ | Comfort Food | $5-$26 | 65 |
| ② p. 54 | V. Richards Cafe | ▼ | American | $5-$9 | 65 |
| ③ p. 54 | Little Savannah | ▼▼▼ | Southern Natural/Organic | $13-$38 | 65 |
| ④ p. 54 | Los Amigos Mexican Restaurant | ▼▼ | Mexican | $6-$14 | 65 |
| ⑤ p. 54 | Billy's Sports Grill | ▼▼ | American | $6-$20 | 64 |
| ⑥ p. 54 | Taziki's Mediterranean Cafe | ▼ | Greek | $7-$13 | 65 |
| ⑦ p. 54 | Urban Cookhouse | ▼▼ | American | $7-$10 | 65 |
| ⑨ p. 54 | The Cheesecake Factory | ▼▼▼ | International | $9-$30 | 64 |
| ⑩ p. 54 | FLIP burger Boutique | ▼▼▼ | New American | $7-$21 | 64 |
| ⑪ p. 54 | Fleming's Prime Steakhouse & Wine Bar | ▼▼▼ | Steak | $40-$80 | 64 |
| ⑫ p. 54 | Village Tavern | ▼▼▼ | American | $10-$31 | 65 |
| ⑬ p. 54 | Kobe Japanese Steak House & Sushi Bar | ▼▼ | Japanese | $7-$21 | 65 |
| ⑭ p. 54 | Edgar's Bakery | ▼ | Breads/Pastries Deli | $5-$8 | 64 |
| ⑮ p. 54 | Taziki's Mediterranean Cafe | ▼ | Greek | $7-$13 | 65 |
| ⑯ p. 54 | Max's Delicatessen | ▼▼ | Jewish Deli | $8-$15 | 65 |
| ⑰ p. 54 | Surin 280 | ▼▼ | Thai | $8-$24 | 65 |

| Map Page | Restaurants (cont'd) | Diamond Rated | Cuisine | Price Range | Page |
|---|---|---|---|---|---|
| ⑱ p. 54 | Superior Grill | ▽▽ | Tex-Mex | $7-$26 | 65 |
| ⑲ p. 54 | Stones Throw Bar & Grill | ▽▽▽ | Regional American | $8-$37 | 65 |

### TRUSSVILLE

| Map Page | Hotel | Diamond Rated | Rate Range | Page |
|---|---|---|---|---|
| ⑯ p. 54 | Hampton Inn Birmingham/Trussville | ▽▽▽ | $104-$109 | 146 |

| Map Page | Restaurant | Diamond Rated | Cuisine | Price Range | Page |
|---|---|---|---|---|---|
| ㉒ p. 54 | El Cazador Mexican Restaurant | ▽▽ | Mexican | $5-$13 | 146 |

### IRONDALE

| Map Page | Hotels | Diamond Rated | Rate Range | Page |
|---|---|---|---|---|
| ⑲ p. 54 | Holiday Inn Express Hotel & Suites Birmingham East | ▽▽▽ | Rates not provided | 100 |
| ⑳ p. 54 | Hampton Inn & Suites Birmingham Airport Area | ▽▽▽ | $109-$159 | 100 |

| Map Page | Restaurants | Diamond Rated | Cuisine | Price Range | Page |
|---|---|---|---|---|---|
| ㉕ p. 54 | Irondale Cafe | ▽ | American | $7-$9 | 100 |
| ㉖ p. 54 | Hamburger Heaven | ▽ | Burgers | $2-$7 | 100 |

### HOMEWOOD

| Map Page | Hotels | Diamond Rated | Rate Range | Page |
|---|---|---|---|---|
| ㉓ p. 54 | **Aloft Birmingham Soho Square** | ▽▽▽ | $129-$199 [SAVE] | 87 |
| ㉔ p. 54 | **Courtyard by Marriott Birmingham Homewood** | ▽▽▽ | $109-$169 [SAVE] | 88 |
| ㉕ p. 54 | Super 8 | ▽▽ | $55-$63 | 88 |
| ㉖ p. 54 | Comfort Inn | ▽▽▽ | $79-$124 | 87 |
| ㉗ p. 54 | Hampton Inn-Lakeshore | ▽▽▽ | $99-$129 | 88 |
| ㉘ p. 54 | Residence Inn by Marriott Birmingham Homewood | ▽▽▽ | $109-$179 | 88 |
| ㉙ p. 54 | **BEST WESTERN PLUS Carlton Suites** | ▽▽▽ | $119-$169 [SAVE] | 87 |
| ㉚ p. 54 | Drury Inn & Suites-Birmingham Southwest | ▽▽▽ | $125-$189 | 88 |
| ㉛ p. 54 | Hilton Garden Inn Birmingham-Lakeshore | ▽▽▽ | $119-$159 | 88 |
| ㉜ p. 54 | TownePlace Suites by Marriott Birmingham Homewood | ▽▽▽ | $125-$153 | 88 |
| ㉝ p. 54 | Holiday Inn Hotel Birmingham/Homewood | ▽▽▽ | Rates not provided | 88 |
| ㉞ p. 54 | **Country Inn & Suites By Carlson** | ▽▽▽ | $99-$129 [SAVE] | 88 |
| ㉟ p. 54 | Candlewood Suites Birmingham-Homewood | ▽▽▽ | Rates not provided | 87 |

| Map Page | Restaurants | Diamond Rated | Cuisine | Price Range | Page |
|---|---|---|---|---|---|
| ㉙ p. 54 | De Vinci's | ▽▽ | Italian | $8-$16 | 89 |
| ㉚ p. 54 | Homewood Gourmet | ▽ | Deli | $7-$14 | 89 |
| ㉛ p. 54 | Demetri's B.B.Q. | ▽ | Barbecue | $5-$14 | 88 |
| ㉜ p. 54 | DoDiYo's | ▽▽▽ | Mediterranean | $8-$26 | 89 |
| ㉝ p. 54 | Jackson's Bar & Bistro | ▽▽ | American | $7-$19 | 89 |
| ㉞ p. 54 | Dave's Pizza | ▽ | Pizza | $8-$35 | 88 |
| ㉟ p. 54 | Michael's Restaurant | ▽▽▽ | Steak Seafood | $10-$55 | 89 |
| ㊱ p. 54 | O' Carr's Restaurant | ▽▽ | Deli Sandwiches | $6-$10 | 89 |
| ㊲ p. 54 | Nabeel's Cafe and Market | ▽▽ | Greek | $7-$19 | 89 |

| Map Page | Restaurants (cont'd) | Diamond Rated | Cuisine | Price Range | Page |
|---|---|---|---|---|---|
| ㊳ p. 54 | New York Pizza | ◆◆ | Pizza | $5-$29 | 89 |
| ㊴ p. 54 | Brio Tuscan Grille | ◆◆◆ | Italian | $12-$28 | 88 |
| ㊵ p. 54 | Paw Paw Patch | ◆ | Southern American | $6-$7 | 89 |
| ㊶ p. 54 | Pho Que Huong | ◆◆ | Vietnamese | $6-$18 | 89 |
| ㊷ p. 54 | Gian Marco's Restaurant | ◆◆◆ | Italian | $12-$40 | 89 |
| ㊸ p. 54 | Landry's Seafood House | ◆◆ | Seafood | $9-$44 SAVE | 89 |

**MOUNTAIN BROOK**

| Map Page | Hotel | Diamond Rated | Rate Range | Page |
|---|---|---|---|---|
| ㊲ p. 54 | Hampton Inn-Mountain Brook | ◆◆◆ | $99-$159 | 128 |

| Map Page | Restaurants | Diamond Rated | Cuisine | Price Range | Page |
|---|---|---|---|---|---|
| ㊻ p. 54 | La Paz Restaurant | ◆◆ | Mexican | $7-$17 | 129 |
| ㊼ p. 54 | Surin of Thailand | ◆◆ | Thai Sushi | $7-$22 | 129 |
| ㊽ p. 54 | Chez Lulu & Continental Bakery | ◆◆ | French | $10-$35 | 128 |
| ㊾ p. 54 | Avo | ◆◆◆ | Northern American | $9-$38 | 128 |
| ㊿ p. 54 | daniel george restaurant & bar | ◆◆◆ | American | $10-$36 | 129 |
| (51) p. 54 | Olexa's | ◆◆ | American | $8-$14 | 129 |

**HOOVER**

| Map Page | Hotels | Diamond Rated | Rate Range | Page |
|---|---|---|---|---|
| ㊵ p. 54 | **Hyatt Place Birmingham/Inverness** | ◆◆◆ | $84-$209 SAVE | 90 |
| ㊶ p. 54 | Homewood Suites by Hilton | ◆◆◆ | $109-$169 | 90 |
| ㊷ p. 54 | **Renaissance Birmingham Ross Bridge Golf Resort & Spa** | ◆◆◆◆ | $252-$362 SAVE | 91 |
| ㊸ p. 54 | **Hyatt Regency Birmingham-The Wynfrey Hotel** | ◆◆◆ | $99-$329 SAVE | 90 |
| ㊹ p. 54 | **Courtyard by Marriott Birmingham Hoover** | ◆◆◆ | $94-$159 SAVE | 89 |
| ㊺ p. 54 | Days Inn at the Galleria | ◆◆ | $69-$109 | 89 |
| ㊻ p. 54 | Hampton Inn & Suites Hoover | ◆◆◆ | $99-$175 | 90 |
| ㊼ p. 54 | **Hyatt Place Birmingham/Hoover** | ◆◆◆ | $79-$169 SAVE | 90 |
| ㊽ p. 54 | Embassy Suites Birmingham/Hoover | ◆◆◆ | $149-$369 | 90 |
| ㊾ p. 54 | Microtel Inn & Suites by Wyndham Hoover/ Birmingham | ◆◆ | $79-$200 | 90 |
| ㊿ p. 54 | Holiday Inn Hoover | ◆◆◆ | $119-$129 | 90 |
| (51) p. 54 | Residence Inn by Marriott Birmingham/Hoover | ◆◆◆ | $139-$299 | 91 |
| (52) p. 54 | Homewood Suites Birmingham-SW/Riverchase Galleria | ◆◆◆ | $99-$279 | 90 |
| (53) p. 54 | La Quinta Inn & Suites Birmingham Hoover | ◆◆ | $69-$234 | 90 |

| Map Page | Restaurants | Diamond Rated | Cuisine | Price Range | Page |
|---|---|---|---|---|---|
| (61) p. 54 | Lloyd's Restaurant | ◆◆ | American | $5-$24 | 92 |
| (62) p. 54 | Bellinis Ristorante & Bar | ◆◆◆ | Italian | $8-$36 | 91 |
| (63) p. 54 | Don Pepe | ◆◆ | Mexican | $6-$18 | 91 |
| (64) p. 54 | Bella Cucina | ◆◆ | European | $10-$22 | 91 |
| (65) p. 54 | Costa's Mediterranean Cafe | ◆◆ | Mediterranean | $7-$21 | 91 |
| (66) p. 54 | The Fish Market Restaurant | ◆ | Seafood | $8-$23 | 91 |

| Map Page | Restaurants (cont'd) | Diamond Rated | Cuisine | Price Range | Page |
|----------|---------------------|---------------|---------|-------------|------|
| 67 p. 54 | Brock's | ▽▽▽ | Mediterranean | $8-$38 | 91 |
| 68 p. 54 | Shula's America's Steak House | ▽▽▽ | Steak | $11-$86 | 92 |
| 69 p. 54 | J. Alexander's Restaurant | ▽▽▽ | American | $10-$29 | 92 |
| 70 p. 54 | STIX | ▽▽ | Asian Sushi | $7-$32 | 92 |
| 71 p. 54 | Firebirds Wood Fired Grill | ▽▽▽ | American | $11-$40 | 91 |
| 72 p. 54 | Edgar's Bakery | ▽ | Breads/Pastries Deli | $7-$8 | 91 |
| 73 p. 54 | La Dolce Vita | ▽▽▽ | Italian | $10-$35 | 92 |
| 74 p. 54 | Southern Legacy BBQ & Brew | ▽▽ | Barbecue | $5-$22 | 92 |

**BESSEMER**

| Map Page | Hotels | Diamond Rated | Rate Range | Page |
|----------|--------|---------------|------------|------|
| 56 p. 54 | Hampton Inn | ▽▽▽ | $109-$149 | 41 |
| 57 p. 54 | Country Inn & Suites By Carlson | ▽▽▽ | $75-$220 | 41 |
| 58 p. 54 | Fairfield Inn & Suites by Marriott Birmingham Bessemer | ▽▽▽ | $120-$131 | 41 |
| 59 p. 54 | Holiday Inn Express & Suites | ▽▽▽ | Rates not provided | 41 |
| 60 p. 54 | Quality Inn (See ad p. 40.) | ▽▽ | $60-$200 | 41 |
| 61 p. 54 | **BEST WESTERN PLUS Bessemer Hotel & Suites** | ▽▽▽ | $90-$100 [SAVE] | 40 |
| 62 p. 54 | Comfort Inn | ▽▽▽ | $85-$200 | 40 |
| 63 p. 54 | Sleep Inn | ▽▽ | $70-$150 | 41 |

| Map Page | Restaurants | Diamond Rated | Cuisine | Price Range | Page |
|----------|-------------|---------------|---------|-------------|------|
| 77 p. 54 | Bob Sykes Bar-B-Q | ▽ | Barbecue | $9-$17 | 41 |
| 78 p. 54 | The Bright Star | ▽▽ | Southern Greek | $8-$30 | 41 |
| 79 p. 54 | Ezell's Catfish Cabin | ▽▽ | Seafood | $8-$21 | 41 |
| 80 p. 54 | Railroad Cafe | ▽▽ | Southern American | $3-$14 | 41 |

**PELHAM**

| Map Page | Hotels | Diamond Rated | Rate Range | Page |
|----------|--------|---------------|------------|------|
| 66 p. 54 | Ramada Inn | ▽▽ | $60-$236 | 135 |
| 67 p. 54 | Sleep Inn | ▽▽ | $75-$276 | 135 |
| 68 p. 54 | **BEST WESTERN PLUS Oak Mountain Inn** | ▽▽▽ | $100-$200 [SAVE] | 135 |
| 69 p. 54 | Holiday Inn Express | ▽▽▽ | Rates not provided | 135 |
| 70 p. 54 | Hampton Inn & Suites Pelham | ▽▽▽ | $89-$175 | 135 |
| 71 p. 54 | Fairfield Inn & Suites by Marriott Birmingham Pelham/I-65 | ▽▽▽ | $104-$175 | 135 |

| Map Page | Restaurant | Diamond Rated | Cuisine | Price Range | Page |
|----------|-----------|---------------|---------|-------------|------|
| 83 p. 54 | 2 Pesos Mexican Cafe | ▽▽ | Mexican | $6-$21 | 135 |

**VESTAVIA HILLS**

| Map Page | Restaurants | Diamond Rated | Cuisine | Price Range | Page |
|----------|-------------|---------------|---------|-------------|------|
| 54 p. 54 | Mudtown Eat & Drink | ▽▽ | American | $9-$29 | 151 |
| 55 p. 54 | Miss Myra's Pit Bar-B-Q | ▽ | Southern Barbecue | $5-$12 | 151 |
| 56 p. 54 | Satterfield's | ▽▽▽ | Continental | $26-$40 | 152 |

**VESTAVIA HILLS (cont'd)**

| | | | | | |
|---|---|---|---|---|---|
| ⑤⑦ p. 54 | Klingler's European Bakery and Cafe | ◈◈ | German | $6-$21 | 151 |
| ⑤⑧ p. 54 | Diplomat Deli | ◈◈ | Sandwiches Deli | $6-$20 | 151 |

**FULTONDALE**

| Map Page | Restaurants | Diamond Rated | Cuisine | Price Range | Page |
|---|---|---|---|---|---|
| ⑧⑥ p. 54 | Casa Fiesta | ◈◈ | Mexican | $7-$25 | 82 |
| ⑧⑦ p. 54 | Stix | ◈◈ | Asian | $8-$33 | 82 |

## DOWNTOWN BIRMINGHAM
• Restaurants p. 62
• Hotels & Restaurants map & index p. 52

### COURTYARD BY MARRIOTT BIRMINGHAM DOWNTOWN UAB
(205)254-0004  **5**

◈◈◈
Hotel
$119-$299

COURTYARD® Marriott.

**AAA Benefit:** Members save 5% or more!

**Address:** 1820 5th Ave S 35233 **Location:** I-65 exit 259B, 0.6 mi e. Next to UAB Medical Center. **Facility:** 122 units. 6 stories, interior corridors. **Parking:** on-site (fee). **Activities:** exercise room. **Guest Services:** valet and coin laundry, boarding pass kiosk.

(SAVE) (icons) CALL (icons) BIZ HS (icons) / SOME UNITS (icons)

### DOUBLETREE BY HILTON HOTEL BIRMINGHAM
205/933-9000  **6**

◈◈◈ **Hotel.** Rates not provided. **Address:** 808 20th St S 35205 **Location:** Jct University Blvd, 0.8 mi s. **Facility:** 298 units, some two bedrooms. 14 stories, interior corridors. **Parking:** on-site (fee). **Pool(s):** outdoor. **Activities:** exercise room. **Guest Services:** valet laundry, area transportation.

**AAA Benefit:** Members save 5% or more!

(icons)

### THE HOTEL HIGHLAND AT FIVE POINTS SOUTH, AN ASCEND COLLECTION HOTEL MEMBER
(205)933-9555  **8**

◈◈◈ **Hotel** $127-$205 **Address:** 1023 20th St S 35205 **Location:** Jct University Blvd and 20th St S, 0.3 mi s. **Facility:** 63 units. 8 stories, interior corridors. **Parking:** on-site (fee) and valet. **Amenities:** safes. **Activities:** exercise room. **Guest Services:** valet laundry.

(icons) / SOME UNITS (icons)

### RESIDENCE INN BY MARRIOTT BIRMINGHAM DOWNTOWN @ UAB
(205)731-9595  **7**

◈◈◈
Extended Stay Hotel
$103-$179

Residence Inn® Marriott.

**AAA Benefit:** Members save 5% or more!

**Address:** 821 20th St S 35205 **Location:** Jct University Blvd, just s; corner of 8th Ct S. **Facility:** 129 units, some two bedrooms and efficiencies. 7 stories, interior corridors. **Parking:** on-site (fee). **Pool(s):** outdoor. **Activities:** exercise room. **Guest Services:** valet and coin laundry. **Featured Amenity:** full hot breakfast. (See ad p. 61.)

(SAVE) (icons) CALL (icons) (icons) BIZ HS (icons) / SOME UNITS (icons)

(See map & index p. 52.)

## SHERATON BIRMINGHAM HOTEL    (205)324-5000

Hotel
$129-$299

Sheraton
HOTELS & RESORTS

**AAA Benefit:** Members save up to 15%, plus Starwood Preferred Guest® benefits!

**Address:** 2101 Richard Arrington Jr Blvd N 35203 **Location:** I-20/59 exit 22nd St. Adjacent to Birmingham Jefferson Convention Complex. **Facility:** 757 units. 17 stories, interior corridors. **Parking:** on-site (fee) and valet. **Terms:** cancellation fee imposed. **Amenities:** video games. **Pool(s):** heated indoor. **Activities:** sauna, game room, exercise room. **Guest Services:** valet and coin laundry, area transportation.

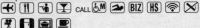 / SOME UNITS

## SPRINGHILL SUITES BY MARRIOTT BIRMINGHAM DOWNTOWN AT UAB    (205)322-8600

 Hotel $99-$169 **Address:** 2024 4th Ave S 35233 **Location:** Between 20th St S and Richard Arrington Jr Blvd. **Facility:** 150 units. 6 stories, interior corridors. **Parking:** on-site (fee).

**AAA Benefit:** Members save 5% or more!

**Pool(s):** heated indoor. **Activities:** exercise room. **Guest Services:** complimentary and valet laundry, luggage security pick-up, area transportation.

## THE TUTWILER - HAMPTON INN & SUITES    (205)322-2100

 Historic Hotel $119-$229 **Address:** 2021 Park Pl 35203 **Location:** Between Richard Arrington Jr Blvd and 20th St, just s of Woodrow Wilson Park. **Facility:** This restored historic hotel features elegant public areas and many large rooms. 149 units. 8 stories, interior corridors. **Parking:** valet only. **Terms:** 1-7 night minimum stay, cancellation fee imposed. **Activities:** exercise room. **Guest Services:** valet laundry, area transportation.

**AAA Benefit:** Members save 5% or more!

 / SOME UNITS

## THE WESTIN BIRMINGHAM    (205)307-3600

Hotel
$149-$359

**WESTIN®**
HOTELS & RESORTS

**AAA Benefit:** Members save up to 15%, plus Starwood Preferred Guest® benefits!

**Address:** 2221 Richard Arrington Jr Blvd N 35203 **Location:** I-20/59 exit 125 westbound; exit 125A eastbound. **Facility:** Nestled in the heart of downtown, this hotel is chic and modern in décor. Visitors are welcomed into a spacious, luxurious lobby that adds a new realm of high-end hospitality. 294 units, some two bedrooms. 9 stories, interior corridors. **Terms:** cancellation fee imposed. **Amenities:** safes. **Pool(s):** heated outdoor. **Activities:** hot tub, exercise room, massage. **Guest Services:** valet laundry, area transportation.

 / SOME UNITS

▼ See AAA listing p. 60 ▼

Upgrade to Plus or Premier membership

for *more* of the benefits you need most

**(See map & index p. 52.)**

### WHERE TO EAT

**26**                                              205/918-0726  (21)

▼▼▼

New
American
Casual Dining
$9-$24

**AAA Inspector Notes:** This stylish, contemporary bistro offers an eclectic variety of delectable items to please a wide range of tastes. In warm weather, the glass storefront garage doors open to create a sidewalk cafe atmosphere. **Features:** full bar, patio dining, happy hour. **Address:** 1210 20th St S 35205 **Location:** Between 12th (Highland Ave) and 13th aves S; in Five Points South. **Parking:** valet and street only.
L  D

**BETTOLA**                                        205/731-6499  (1)

▼▼▼ Italian Pizza. Casual Dining. $9-$20 **AAA Inspector Notes:** Chic yet casual, the long and narrow loft-style dining room features tightly spaced tables lined up along a continuous banquette that runs from one end of the dining room to the other. The design makes the open kitchen, with its brick oven imported from Naples, Italy, the centerpiece of the dining experience. Appropriately, Neopolitan pizzas are the signature specialty of the house. Crusts are thin in the middle with a delicious bubble of crust around the outer edge, and toppings are simple. **Features:** full bar, patio dining. **Address:** 2901 2nd Ave S 35233 **Location:** Jct 2nd Ave and 29th St S; in Martin Biscuit Building.   L  D  CALL  &M

**BOTTEGA CAFE**                                   205/939-1000  (10)

▼▼▼ Italian. Casual Dining. $11-$39 **AAA Inspector Notes:** This popular trattoria sustains a casual atmosphere without compromising quality. Community tables and a frenetic pace make for an enjoyable dining experience. On the seasonal menu are fresh Gulf seafood, organic vegetables and flatbreads and pizza cooked over a wood fire. Weeknight specials deserve a look. **Features:** full bar, patio dining. **Address:** 2240 Highland Ave S 35205 **Location:** Just w of US 31/SR 3; in Five Points South. **Parking:** valet and street only.
L  D  CALL  &M

**BOTTEGA RESTAURANT**                             205/939-1000  (11)

▼▼▼ Italian. Fine Dining. $25-$39 **AAA Inspector Notes:** Here you'll find gourmet dishes served in a tasteful atmosphere. A friendly, attentive staff makes for a very pleasant experience as you sample creative meat, fowl and seafood dishes, a wide selection of appetizers and many tasty desserts. **Features:** full bar, patio dining. **Reservations:** suggested. **Address:** 2240 Highland Ave S 35205 **Location:** Just w of US 31/SR 3; in Five Points South. **Parking:** valet and street only.  D

**CAFE DUPONT**                                    205/322-1282  (6)

▼▼▼ ▼▼▼ Regional American. Fine Dining. $14-$40 **AAA Inspector Notes:** The chef combines his special touches with foods from around the region, such as Georgia quail and Gulf shrimp. He also dabbles in other meat and seafood preparations. The dining room offers a warm and soothing atmosphere in which to enjoy the nicely presented creations. **Features:** full bar, patio dining. **Reservations:** suggested. **Address:** 113 20th St N 35203 **Location:** Between 1st and 2nd aves N. **Parking:** valet only.
L  D  CALL  &M

**CANTINA TORTILLA GRILL**                         205/323-6980  (2)

▼▼ Mexican. Casual Dining. $4-$11 **AAA Inspector Notes:** This grill sustains a casual, laid-back atmosphere. Customers order and pay at the counter, then find a table and wait for their food to be delivered. While the menu is limited, each flavorful item is prepared with care. **Features:** full bar, happy hour. **Address:** 2901 2nd Ave S 35233 **Location:** Jct 2nd Ave and 29th St S; in Martin Biscuit Building.  L  D

**CHEZ FON FON**                                   205/939-3221  (17)

▼▼▼ French. Casual Dining. $10-$23 **AAA Inspector Notes:** Delicious food is served in a wonderful atmosphere that is upscale in every way. French-style infuses all aspects of the food and design at the amazing local favorite. **Features:** full bar, patio dining. **Address:** 2007 11th Ave S 35205 **Location:** I-65 exit 259 (University Blvd), 1 mi e to 20th St, then just s; in Five Points South. **Parking:** valet and street only.  L  D  ◣

**COSMO'S PIZZA**                                  205/930-9971  (15)

▼▼ ▼▼ Pizza. Casual Dining. $3-$24 **AAA Inspector Notes:** For more than 25 years, this groovy neighborhood café/bar has been kneading fresh dough and making such breads as ciabatta, focaccia and hoagies. For a starter, try antipasto, alligator sausage or a zesty spinach salad. Diners enjoy salads, calzones, and, of course, pizza, either by the slice or a whole pie. More than 35 standard and gourmet toppings allow for a myriad of combinations. A variety of beers complement the customized thin-crust pies. Weekend brunch is pretty amazing, too. **Features:** full bar, patio dining, Sunday brunch, happy hour. **Address:** 2012 Magnolia Ave 35205 **Location:** Corner of 20th St S and Magnolia Ave; across from Highlands United Methodist Church; in Five Points South. **Parking:** on-site (fee) and street.  L  D  ◣

**DREAMLAND BAR-B-QUE**                            205/933-2133

▼▼ Barbecue. Casual Dining. $8-$20 **AAA Inspector Notes:** "Ain't nothing like 'em nowhere" is the motto at this barbecue cafe. The menu is small, but that is okay because everybody comes for one thing: the ribs. Barbecue dishes come with white bread and a kicking sauce. Friendly Southern hospitality and a casual backdrop help make this place a favorite. **Features:** beer only. **Address:** 1427 14th Ave S 35205 **Location:** I-65 exit 259 (University Blvd), 0.7 mi e, then s on 15th St S.  L  D  CALL  &M

**FUEGO CANTINA AND SALOON**                       205/933-1544  (18)

▼▼ ▼▼ Tex-Mex. Casual Dining. $8-$18 **AAA Inspector Notes:** In the heart of Five Points South and just blocks from the university, stop here for vibrant, delicious dishes and live entertainment. Spice up your meal with varying levels of "fuego" (fire) or cool down with a margarita, mojito, martini, 16 beers on tap, or one of more than 30 wines by the glass. Sit inside, enjoy the 'saloon' with live music, pool and darts, or relax on the patio when the weather is agreeable. **Features:** full bar, patio dining, happy hour. **Address:** 1101 20th St S 35205 **Location:** Jct 20th St S and 11th Ave S; just se of University Blvd; in Five Points South. **Parking:** street only.
L  D  LATE  CALL  &M  ◥  ◣

**GOLDEN TEMPLE VEGETARIAN CAFE**                  205/933-8933  (20)

▼▼ American. Quick Serve. $6-$11 **AAA Inspector Notes:** Serving Magic City for some 32 years, this cafe lets vegetarians and non-vegetarians alike load up on sandwiches, salads, chips, guacamole, quesadillas (particularly the delicious spinach), smoothies, juices, teas and many tofu offerings. A health food store adjoins the cafe. **Address:** 1901 11th Ave S 35205 **Location:** Just s of jct University Blvd/20th St; in Five Points South.  B  L

**HIGHLANDS BAR & GRILL**                          205/939-1400  (16)

▼▼▼ ▼▼ French. Fine Dining. $27-$36 **AAA Inspector Notes:** A refined, yet unstuffy, atmosphere makes this place popular with local professionals and businesspeople. Its daily changing menu always offers fresh, in-season dishes, a fine wine selection and impeccably prepared desserts. Popular with the faculty of the nearby university and more affluent local citizenry, the restaurant attracts a pleasant, well-dressed clientèle. The menu focuses on local, seasonal foods. **Features:** full bar. **Reservations:** required. **Address:** 2011 11th Ave S 35205 **Location:** Just se of jct University Blvd/20th St; in Five Points South. **Parking:** valet and street only.  D

**HOT AND HOT FISH CLUB**                          205/933-5474  (13)

▼▼▼ ▼▼ New World. Fine Dining. $25-$38 **AAA Inspector Notes:** A classic exhibition kitchen embellishes this bistro's cozy, intimate setting. Fascinating to watch, the well-trained staff creates imaginative works of culinary art. Owner and "Iron Chef" winner Chris Hastings's daily changing menu guarantees the freshest items available from regional vendors as well an interesting experience for your palate. I believe you will depart, as I did, having experienced a memorable dining event. **Features:** full bar, patio dining. **Reservations:** suggested. **Address:** 2180 11th Ct S 35205 **Location:** Just off US 31. **Parking:** valet and street only.  D

**JIM 'N NICK'S BAR-B-Q**                          205/320-1060

▼▼ Barbecue. Casual Dining. $9-$24 **AAA Inspector Notes:** Southern hospitality reigns at Jim 'N Nick's, where diners get neighborly treatment as they dig into huge portions of tasty lean sausage, fresh chili, juicy smoked beef and pork. A slice of sublime homemade pie ends the meal on a high note. **Features:** full bar. **Address:** 1908 11th Ave S 35209 **Location:** I-65 exit 259 (University Blvd), 1 mi e, then just s on 20th St; in Five Points South. **Parking:** street only.
L  D

**(See map & index p. 52.)**

### JOHN'S CITY DINER    205/322-6014   (4)

▽▽ ▽▽ American. Casual Dining. $10-$23 **AAA Inspector Notes:** *Classic.* This has been a popular down-home eatery in the Birmingham historic district since 1944. The décor is retro and nostalgic. The menu offers many fresh seafood dishes and country-style vegetables, as well as their famous coleslaw. **Features:** full bar. **Address:** 112 Richard Arrington Jr Blvd 35203 **Location:** Between 1st and 2nd aves N. (L) (D)

### NIKI'S RESTAURANT    205/251-1972   (9)

▽ American. Cafeteria. $8-$13 **AAA Inspector Notes:** *Classic.* A city landmark, this restaurant serves delicious home-cooked meals in a relaxed setting. Police officers, lawyers, professionals and locals have been mingling here for more than 50 years. Daily offerings include 13 meats and 32 vegetables, along with traditional Greek dishes. Despite its nondescript appearance, this place is a hot spot. **Address:** 1101 2nd Ave N 35203 **Location:** I-65 exit 260B (3rd Ave N), just n, just e on 12th St N, then just s. (B) (L) (D) (⊠)

### OCEAN    205/933-0999   (22)

Seafood
Fine Dining
$30-$50

**AAA Inspector Notes:** This award-winning restaurant focuses on fresh seafood from around the world, a raw bar with an array of oyster species and sushi rolls. Lending excitement to the contemporary atmosphere are many textures, designs and accent lighting. The seafood tower for two is popular, as are fresh catches prepared any of eight ways. **Features:** full bar, patio dining. **Reservations:** required. **Address:** 1218 20th St S 35205 **Location:** Between 12th (Highland Ave) and 13th aves S; in Five Points South. **Parking:** valet only. (D) CALL(⌖M)

### PITA LOCO    205/252-4899   (5)

▽ Mediterranean. Quick Serve. $5-$15 **AAA Inspector Notes:** This small restaurant specializes in Middle Eastern cuisine and treats patrons to the best hummus around. Those whose tastes are less adventurous can opt for American staples, such as burgers and sandwiches. **Features:** patio dining. **Address:** 2000 2nd Ave N 35203 **Location:** Between 20th and 21st sts; in lobby of Frank Nelson Building. **Parking:** street only. (B) (L) (D)

### ROJO    205/328-4733   (8)

▽ Mexican. Casual Dining. $7-$15 **AAA Inspector Notes:** Upon entering this hot spot, guests walk to the counter to order their favorite Latin, Mexican or American dish, such as sizzling fajitas, burritos filled with steak or chicken or cheese-smothered nacho platter. Minutes later, it is brought to the table. No one leaves here hungry. **Features:** full bar, patio dining, Sunday brunch, happy hour. **Address:** 2921 Highland Ave S 35205 **Location:** Jct 30th St S and Highland Ave S. **Parking:** street only. (L) (D)

### SOL Y LUNA    205/322-1186   (7)

▽▽ ▽ Southwestern. Casual Dining. $10-$16 **AAA Inspector Notes:** This place serves up very authentic Mexican and Southwestern cuisine. The décor puts you in a Taos or Santa Fe state of mind, and the food does, too. A soft lobster tomatillo is an example of the succulent food options. Servers are very knowledgeable. Find a nice selection of premium tequilas—more than 30 varieties are available. **Features:** full bar, patio dining, Sunday brunch. **Reservations:** suggested, weekends. **Address:** 2811 7th Ave S 35233 **Location:** Between 28th and 29th sts; in Lakeview District. (D)

### SURIN & COMPANY    205/297-0996   (3)

▽▽ Thai. Casual Dining. $6-$14 **AAA Inspector Notes:** Enjoy an Asian lunch—including stir fry meals, sushi and noodle bowls—at this attractive and contemporary downtown eatery exhibiting artwork by local artisans. **Address:** 2100 3rd Ave N, Suite 100 35203 **Location:** I-65 exit 260B (3rd Ave N), 1 mi n. **Parking:** street only. (L) CALL(⌖M)

### SURIN WEST    205/324-1928   (19)

▽▽ ▽ Thai. Casual Dining. $8-$24 **AAA Inspector Notes:** Located in the eccentric Five Points area, this restaurant offers Thai dishes, lunch specials and sushi all served in a dark atmosphere. **Features:** full bar. **Address:** 1918 11th Ave S 35205 **Location:** I-65 exit 259 (University Blvd), 1 mi n, then just s on 20th St S; in Five Points South. **Parking:** street only. (L) (D) CALL(⌖M)

### TAJ INDIA    205/939-3805   (12)

▽▽ ▽ Indian. Casual Dining. $9-$20 **AAA Inspector Notes:** Enjoy authentic Indian cuisine amid bona fide Indian-style décor. An enormous number of choices includes tandoori dishes to curries to vegetarian options. Servers are informed and attentive. **Features:** full bar, Sunday brunch. **Address:** 2226 Highland Ave S 35205 **Location:** Jct 22nd St S; just e of Five Points South. (L) (D)

### VERANDA ON HIGHLAND    205/939-5551   (14)

▽▽ ▽ American. Casual Dining. $25-$42 **AAA Inspector Notes:** This sophisticated restaurant affords a luscious dining experience for the discriminating palate. Gracious servers bring out flavorful menu selections created from fresh, locally grown ingredients. **Features:** full bar, Sunday brunch. **Reservations:** suggested. **Address:** 2220 Highland Ave S 35205 **Location:** Just w of US 31/SR 3; in Five Points South. **Parking:** valet and street only. (D)

# BIRMINGHAM (B-3)

- **Restaurants p. 64**
- **Hotels & Restaurants map & index p. 54**

### COMFORT INN & SUITES - COLONNADE    (205)968-3700   (9)

▽▽ ▽▽ Hotel $80-$149 **Address:** 4400 Colonnade Pkwy 35243 **Location:** I-459 exit 19 (US 280), 1.6 mi w on Southwest Frontage Rd. **Facility:** 66 units. 2 stories, interior corridors. **Pool(s):** outdoor. **Guest Services:** coin laundry. 🛰 📶 🖥 🖨 🖵

### COURTYARD BY MARRIOTT BIRMINGHAM COLONNADE    (205)967-4466   (8)

▽▽ ▽▽ Hotel $89-$159

**COURTYARD** *Marriott.*

**AAA Benefit:** Members save 5% or more!

**Address:** 4300 Colonnade Pkwy 35243 **Location:** I-459 exit 19 (US 280), 1.6 mi w on Southwest Frontage Rd. **Facility:** 122 units. 4 stories, interior corridors. **Pool(s):** heated indoor. **Activities:** hot tub, exercise room. **Guest Services:** valet and coin laundry. (SAVE) 🍽 CALL(⌖M) 🛰 (BIZ) 📶 ✕ 🖵 /SOME UNITS 🖨 🖥

### DRURY INN & SUITES-BIRMINGHAM SOUTHEAST    (205)967-2450   (4)

▽▽ ▽▽ Hotel $110-$189 **Address:** 3510 Grandview Pkwy 35243 **Location:** I-459 exit 19 (US 280 E), just e. Located in Grandview Business Park. **Facility:** 149 units. 6 stories, interior corridors. **Terms:** cancellation fee imposed. **Pool(s):** heated outdoor, heated indoor. **Activities:** hot tub, exercise room. **Guest Services:** valet and coin laundry. 🍽 🛰 (BIZ) (HS) 📶 ✕ 🖨 🖥 🖵 /SOME UNITS 🐾

### EMBASSY SUITES BIRMINGHAM    (205)879-7400   (3)

▽▽ ▽▽ Hotel $129-$209

EMBASSY SUITES HOTELS.

**AAA Benefit:** Members save 5% or more!

**Address:** 2300 Woodcrest Pl 35209 **Location:** Just n of jct US 31 and 280 exit 21st Ave southbound, 0.3 mi s. Located on Red Mountain. **Facility:** 242 units, some two bedrooms. 8 stories, interior corridors. **Terms:** 1-7 night minimum stay, cancellation fee imposed. **Pool(s):** heated indoor. **Activities:** hot tub, exercise room. **Guest Services:** valet and coin laundry, area transportation. **Featured Amenity:** breakfast buffet. (SAVE) 🛄 🍽 🍴 🍸 CALL(⌖M) 🛰 (BIZ) (SHS) 📶  🖨 🖥 🖵 /SOME UNITS 🐾

(See map & index p. 54.)

## HAMPTON INN & SUITES BIRMINGHAM 280E-EAGLE POINT
(205)981-0024  **13**

▼▼▼▼ **Hotel** $109-$129 **Address:** 6220 Farley Ct 35242 **Location:** I-459 exit 19 (US 280), 4.6 mi s, just s on Doug Baker Blvd, then 0.5 mi e; in The Village at Lee Branch Plaza. **Facility:** 106 units. 4 stories, interior corridors. **Terms:** check-in 4 pm, 1-7 night minimum stay, cancellation fee imposed. **Pool(s):** outdoor. **Activities:** exercise room. **Guest Services:** valet and coin laundry.

**AAA Benefit:** Members save 5% or more!

## HAMPTON INN-COLONNADE
(205)967-0002  **5**

▼▼▼ **Hotel** $99-$159 **Address:** 3400 Colonnade Pkwy 35243 **Location:** I-459 exit 19 (US 280), 0.5 mi w on South Frontage Rd. **Facility:** 133 units. 5 stories, interior corridors. **Terms:** 1-7 night minimum stay, cancellation fee imposed. **Pool(s):** outdoor. **Activities:** limited exercise equipment. **Guest Services:** valet laundry, area transportation.

**AAA Benefit:** Members save 5% or more!

## HILTON GARDEN INN BIRMINGHAM SE/LIBERTY PARK
(205)503-5220  **2**

▼▼▼ **Hotel** $99-$199 **Address:** 2090 Urban Center Pkwy 35242 **Location:** I-459 exit 23, just e on Liberty Pkwy, 0.6 mi s on Overton Rd, then just n. Located in a quiet area. **Facility:** 130 units. 6 stories, interior corridors. **Terms:** 1-7 night minimum stay, cancellation fee imposed. **Pool(s):** heated indoor. **Activities:** hot tub, exercise room. **Guest Services:** valet and coin laundry, area transportation.

**AAA Benefit:** Members save 5% or more!

## HOLIDAY INN-AIRPORT
205/591-6900  **1**

▼▼▼ **Hotel.** Rates not provided. **Address:** 5000 Richard Arrington Jr Blvd N 35212 **Location:** I-20/59 exit 129, just s. **Facility:** 220 units. 9 stories, interior corridors. **Pool(s):** outdoor. **Activities:** exercise room. **Guest Services:** valet laundry, boarding pass kiosk, area transportation.

## LA QUINTA INN BIRMINGHAM / CAHABA PARK SOUTH
(205)995-9990  **10**

▼▼ **Hotel** $65-$214 **Address:** 513 Cahaba Park Cir 35242 **Location:** I-459 exit 19 (US 280), 1.2 mi e. **Facility:** 99 units. 3 stories, interior corridors. **Activities:** exercise room.

## MARRIOTT BIRMINGHAM
(205)968-3775  **6**

▼▼▼ **Hotel** $171-$181 **Address:** 3590 Grandview Pkwy 35243 **Location:** I-459 exit 19 (US 280), 0.6 mi e. Located in Grandview Business Park. **Facility:** 295 units. 8 stories, interior corridors. **Pool(s):** heated indoor. **Activities:** exercise room. **Guest Services:** complimentary laundry, boarding pass kiosk, area transportation.

**AAA Benefit:** Members save 5% or more!

## QUALITY INN & SUITES
205/991-1055  **11**

▼▼ **Hotel.** Rates not provided. **Address:** 707 Key Dr 35242 **Location:** I-459 exit 19 (US 280), 1.3 mi e. **Facility:** 63 units. 3 stories, interior corridors. **Pool(s):** heated indoor. **Activities:** exercise room. **Guest Services:** valet laundry.

## RESIDENCE INN BY MARRIOTT BIRMINGHAM
(205)991-8686  **12**

▼▼▼ **Extended Stay Hotel** $104-$169 **Address:** 3 Greenhill Pkwy 35242 **Location:** I-459 exit 19 (US 280), 2 mi e. Located in a modern commercial area. **Facility:** 128 units, some two bedrooms, efficiencies and kitchens. 2 stories (no elevator), exterior corridors. **Pool(s):** outdoor. **Activities:** tennis, exercise room. **Guest Services:** valet and coin laundry.

**AAA Benefit:** Members save 5% or more!

## SPRINGHILL SUITES BY MARRIOTT BIRMINGHAM COLONNADE
(205)969-8099  **7**

▼▼▼ **Hotel** $89-$169 **Address:** 3950 Colonnade Pkwy 35243 **Location:** I-459 exit 19 (US 280), 0.8 mi w on South Frontage Rd. **Facility:** 120 units. 4 stories, interior corridors. **Pool(s):** outdoor. **Activities:** exercise room. **Guest Services:** valet and coin laundry.

**AAA Benefit:** Members save 5% or more!

## WHERE TO EAT

## BILLY'S SPORTS GRILL
205/956-2323  **5**

▼▼ American. Casual Dining. $6-$20 **AAA Inspector Notes:** With easy access off the interstate, this rustic café makes for a quick stop when traveling. Occasionally live bands are presented, so check the website for the schedule. **Features:** full bar, patio dining, Sunday brunch. **Address:** 4520 Overton Rd, Suite 104 35210 **Location:** I-459 exit 23, just ne.

## THE CHEESECAKE FACTORY
205/262-1800  **9**

▼▼▼ International. Casual Dining. $9-$30 **AAA Inspector Notes:** What started as a small bakery in Los Angeles in the 1970s has since blossomed into one of the most recognizable restaurant chains today. Known for their large portion sizes and seemingly never-ending menu, this restaurant features over 200 selections to choose from! The "SkinnyLicious" menu options may appeal to those counting calories. **Features:** full bar, patio dining, Sunday brunch, happy hour. **Address:** 236 Summit Blvd 35243 **Location:** I-459 exit 19 (US 280), just n; in The Summit shopping center, upper level.

## EDGAR'S BAKERY
205/968-4031  **14**

▼ Breads/Pastries Deli. Quick Serve. $5-$8 **AAA Inspector Notes:** The aroma of delightful desserts is sure to grab everyone's attention upon entering. The menu focuses on light lunches, with wraps, salads and quiches. **Address:** 3407 Colonnade Pkwy 35243 **Location:** I-459 exit 19 (US 280), 0.5 mi w on S Frontage Rd; in The Shops of Colonnade.

## FLEMING'S PRIME STEAKHOUSE & WINE BAR
205/262-9463  **11**

▼▼▼ Steak. Fine Dining. $40-$80 **AAA Inspector Notes:** The warm, clubby atmosphere is the ideal setting for perfectly grilled steaks and seafood. Side dishes come in hearty portions, and salads are fresh and crisp. More than 100 wine selections are available. **Features:** full bar. **Address:** 103 Summit Blvd 35243 **Location:** I-459 exit 19 (US 280), just n; in The Summit shopping center. **Parking:** on-site and valet.

## FLIP BURGER BOUTIQUE
205/968-2000  **10**

▼▼▼ New American. Casual Dining. $7-$21 **AAA Inspector Notes:** You know you are not in a typical burger joint when you see the sterile white décor with its swirling psychedelic patterned ceiling, 10 ft. high vinyl tufted dining cubicles and servers passing by with smoking drinks. An imaginative concept comes to fruition by Top Chef winner Richard Blais who achieves his goal to "redefine the burger category." Menu selections between the buns are not limited strictly to beef. **Features:** full bar, patio dining, happy hour. **Address:** 220 Summit Blvd, Suite 140 35243 **Location:** Just n of jct US 280 and I-459; in The Summit shopping center.

**(See map & index p. 54.)**

### FULL MOON BAR-B-QUE
205/991-7328

▼ Barbecue. Quick Serve. $6-$20 **AAA Inspector Notes:** A Birmingham-area chain, this much-loved pork house is known for its half-moon cookies. Patrons savor barbecue ribs, pork and chicken, which are slow-cooked over real hickory wood in brick fire pits. **Features:** beer only. **Address:** 4635 Hwy 280 E 35242 **Location:** Between Key Dr and Inverness Pkwy. [L] [D]

### KOBE JAPANESE STEAK HOUSE & SUSHI BAR
205/298-0200  (13)

▼▼ Japanese. Casual Dining. $7-$21 **AAA Inspector Notes:** Watch as food is prepared right before the many diners' eyes. Cooks have several tricks up their sleeves as they prepare an assortment of Japanese dishes as well as hand-rolled sushi. **Features:** full bar. **Address:** 3501 Grandview Pkwy 35243 **Location:** I-459 exit 19 (US 280), just e. [L] [D]

### LITTLE SAVANNAH
205/591-1119  (3)

▼▼▼ Southern Natural/Organic. Casual Dining. $13-$38 **AAA Inspector Notes:** In a historic neighborhood, the restaurant allows for cozy, intimate dining. The menu changes frequently to take advantage of the availability of seasonal ingredients. Tantalizing starters range from fried blue crab dumplings to black tiger shrimp over creamy polenta. Hearty entrees run the gamut from house-smoked duck to wild boar. Such seafood as Nantucket scallops and Hawaiian prawns is always on the menu. Tempting dessert selections and varied wines round out a fine meal. **Features:** full bar, patio dining, Sunday brunch, happy hour. **Reservations:** suggested. **Address:** 3811 Clairmont Ave 35222 **Location:** Between 38th and 39th sts S; near Highland Golf Course. **Parking:** street only. [D] 🐾

### LOS AMIGOS MEXICAN RESTAURANT
205/324-5896  (4)

▼▼ Mexican. Casual Dining. $6-$14 **AAA Inspector Notes:** There is always a fiesta here, where the service is quick and friendly and the traditional Mexican favorites are tasty. Choices include burritos, tacos and enchiladas. **Features:** full bar. **Address:** 3324 Clairmont Ave 35222 **Location:** US 31 exit 8th Ave S, 8.7 mi ne; jct Clairmont and University aves; in Piggly Wiggly Shopping Center. [L] [D]

### MAX'S DELICATESSEN
205/968-7600  (16)

▼▼ Jewish Deli. Quick Serve. $8-$15 **AAA Inspector Notes:** Here is the authentic Jewish delicatessen you have been searching for, complete with homemade chicken and matzo ball soup, chopped liver, brisket and even bagels and lox. **Address:** 3431 Colonnade Pkwy, Suite 400 35243 **Location:** I-459 exit 19 (US 280), 0.5 mi w on S Frontage Rd; in The Shops of Colonnade. [L] [D] CALL 🛒M

### NIKI'S WEST STEAK & SEAFOOD RESTAURANT
205/252-5751  (1)

▼ Comfort Food. Cafeteria. $5-$26 **AAA Inspector Notes:** The rustic dining room of this popular eatery is often packed with locals seeking a great meal of Southern favorites at a reasonable price. Run by the same family since 1957, a trip through the cafeteria line will have diners' trays filled with generous portions of catfish, breaded veal chops and Greek broiled chicken along with a choice of side dishes. House specialties include steak, seafood and breakfast selections. **Address:** 233 Finley Ave W 35204 **Location:** I-65 exit 262B, 1 mi w. [B] [L] [D]

### STONES THROW BAR & GRILL
205/995-0512  (19)

▼▼▼ Regional American. Casual Dining. $8-$37 **AAA Inspector Notes:** Serving contemporary Southern cuisine, this restaurant features an open dining room and a casually comfortable atmosphere. The menu is comprised of organic vegetables and free-range meats, fowl and lamb. Favorites include a half-pound all-natural burger, shrimp and grits and a selection of grilled seafood. **Features:** full bar, patio dining. **Address:** 3 Mt. Laurel Ave 35242 **Location:** Jct US 280/CR 41 (Dunnavant Valley Rd), 3.3 mi ne on CR 41 (Dunnavant Valley Rd). **Parking:** street only. [L] [D] CALL 🛒M

### SUPERIOR GRILL
205/991-5112  (18)

▼▼ Tex-Mex. Casual Dining. $7-$26 **AAA Inspector Notes:** Sizzling fajitas are a popular menu item here: Served with fresh tortillas and a heaping platter of meat, the dish offers a lot to make guests happy. Try the queso, a mix of spicy, rich cheese and pepper. **Features:** full bar, patio dining, happy hour. **Address:** 4701 Hwy 280 35242 **Location:** I-459 exit 19 (US 280), 2 mi e. [L] [D]

### SURIN 280
205/968-8161  (17)

▼▼▼ Thai. Casual Dining. $8-$24 **AAA Inspector Notes:** A long, lean gilded Buddha statue greets you as you enter this contemporary-style establishment. The expanded menu offers diners a wide variety of ethnic Thai dishes as well as sushi. **Features:** full bar. **Address:** 16 Perimeter Park S 35243 **Location:** I-459 exit 19 (US 280), 0.5 mi s. [L] [D] CALL 🛒M

### TAZIKI'S MEDITERRANEAN CAFE
205/968-6622  (15)

▼ Greek. Quick Serve. $7-$13 **AAA Inspector Notes:** Quick, flavorful Greek cuisine is offered here where both indoor and outdoor patio seating is available. **Features:** beer & wine, patio dining. **Address:** 3439 Colonnade Pkwy, Suite 1000 35243 **Location:** I-459 exit 19 (US 280), 0.5 mi w on S Frontage Rd; in The Shops of Colonnade. [L] [D]

### TAZIKI'S MEDITERRANEAN CAFE
205/956-1300  (6)

▼ Greek. Quick Serve. $7-$13 **AAA Inspector Notes:** This café is a great alternative to greasy fast food when on the go. Meals are prepared in a flash for take out or in-house dining. A relaxed, laid-back atmosphere prevails for those who wish to leisurely enjoy the cuisine. **Features:** beer & wine. **Address:** 4520 Overton Rd, Suite 100 35242 **Location:** I-459 exit 23, just ne. [L] [D] CALL 🛒M

### URBAN COOKHOUSE
205/969-6700  (7)

▼▼ American. Casual Dining. $7-$10 **AAA Inspector Notes:** Eat nutritiously at this informal café where the motto is buy local, eat urban. Purchasing produce from regional farmers guarantees the freshest ingredients. Meats are prepared to tender perfection in ceramic kamado-style cookers. Guests can order take-home dinners for four to go. **Features:** beer & wine, patio dining. **Address:** 250 Summit Blvd, Suite 102 35243 **Location:** Just n of jct US 280 and I-459; in The Summit shopping center. [L] [D] CALL 🛒M

### VILLAGE TAVERN
205/970-1640  (12)

▼▼▼ American. Casual Dining. $10-$31 **AAA Inspector Notes:** Attentive, personable servers bring out fresh entrees of steak, seafood, chicken, wood-oven pizzas, sandwiches, soups, salads and some downright tasty made-in-house potato chips. The comprehensive offerings, including a children's menu, ensure there is something for everyone. **Features:** full bar, Sunday brunch, happy hour. **Reservations:** suggested. **Address:** 101 Summit Blvd 35243 **Location:** I-459 exit 19 (US 280), just n; in The Summit shopping center, lower level. **Parking:** on-site and valet. [L] [D] CALL 🛒M

### V. RICHARDS CAFE
205/591-7000  (2)

▼ American. Casual Dining. $5-$9 **AAA Inspector Notes:** A recent offshoot of a gourmet market, this quaint cafe prepares fresh and delicious food, including soups, salads and sandwiches. **Features:** wine only, Sunday brunch. **Address:** 3916 Clairmont Ave 35222 **Location:** US 31 exit 8th Ave, 1 mi e. [B] [L]

## BREWTON (H-3) pop. 5,408, elev. 84'

**THOMAS E. MCMILLAN MUSEUM** is at 220 Alco Dr. in the Fine Arts Center at Jefferson Davis Community College, just w. off US 31, following signs. This small museum offers archeological artifacts and historical exhibits. Permanent displays include prehistoric Native American and Early American military and civilian items; other exhibits interpret the heritage of the southwestern Alabama region. Temporary exhibits also are presented. **Hours:** Tues.

and Thurs. 9-3, Fri.-Mon. and Wed. by appointment. **Cost:** Free. **Phone:** (251) 809-1528.

## CALERA (D-3) pop. 11,620, elev. 497'
• Part of Birmingham area — see map p. 43

**HEART OF DIXIE RAILROAD MUSEUM** is at 1919 Ninth St. This museum features an operating railroad; two restored depots; a collection of railroad artifacts and memorabilia; and an outdoor collection of railroad locomotives, cars and cabooses and a signal garden. A 1-hour ride aboard a standard-gauge train is offered.

**Time:** Allow 1 hour minimum. **Hours:** Museum Sat. 9-4, mid-Mar. to mid-Dec.; otherwise by appointment. Train rides depart at 11 and 2, mid-Mar. to mid-Nov.; schedule varies for special events. Closed major holidays. Phone ahead to confirm schedule. **Cost:** Museum admission by donation. Standard 1-hour train trip $12.84; $9.17 (ages 2-11). One-hour train trip in locomotive $32.11. One-hour train trip in caboose $22.94. **Phone:** (205) 668-3435. 🎢

HAMPTON INN CALERA (205)668-6565
◆◆◆ **Hotel** $109-$129 **Address:** 93 Metro Dr 35040 **Location:** I-65 exit 231, 0.6 mi n on US 31, then just w. **Facility:** 91 units. 4 stories, interior corridors. **Terms:** 1-7 night minimum stay, cancellation fee imposed. **Pool(s):** outdoor. **Activities:** exercise room. **Guest Services:** valet and coin laundry.

**AAA Benefit:** Members save 5% or more!

QUALITY INN (205)668-3641
◆◆ **Hotel** $86-$96 **Address:** 357 Hwy 304 35040 **Location:** I-65 exit 231, just se. **Facility:** 65 units. 2 stories (no elevator), exterior corridors. **Pool(s):** outdoor. **Guest Services:** coin laundry.

## CENTRE (B-5) pop. 3,489, elev. 663'

**CHEROKEE HISTORICAL MUSEUM** is at 101 E. Main St. An eclectic mix of more than 7,000 artifacts fills this 1919 three-story former department store, which itself provides an interesting glimpse into the past. Offerings include vintage cars and tractors, photographs, housewares and cowboy bathtubs. **Time:** Allow 1 hour minimum. **Hours:** Tues.-Fri. 9-4, first Sat. of the month 9-1. Closed major holidays. **Cost:** $3; $2 (ages 64+ and students with ID); $1 (ages 7-12). **Phone:** (256) 927-7835. 🍴

## CHILDERSBURG (D-4) pop. 5,175, elev. 412'

On this site in 1540 Hernando de Soto discovered Coosa, a Creek Indian capital and sacred peace town. Since European settlement in the early 19th century, Childersburg has evolved into a lumber and farm community with paper manufacturing and recycling as its major industry. Just north is Kymulga Grist Mill Park and the 105-foot Kymulga Covered Bridge, which was built in the 1860s and spans Talladega Creek.

**Childersburg Chamber of Commerce:** 805 Third St. S.W., P.O. Box 527, Childersburg, AL 35044. **Phone:** (256) 378-5482.

**DESOTO CAVERNS PARK,** 5 mi. e. on SR 76 to 5181 DeSoto Caverns Pkwy., covers 80 acres surrounding the historic onyx-marble caverns named for Hernando de Soto. Hour-long guided tours include a laser light and water show in the Great Onyx Chamber, which is larger than a football field and higher than a 12-story building. The park also offers more than 25 outdoor attractions and a playground.

During the Civil War the Confederates mined saltpeter in the caverns to make gunpowder; during Prohibition the caverns became a popular speakeasy and square dance hall. Centuries earlier, the Creek Indians considered the caves to be a hallowed place from which their forefathers emerged to establish the Creek nation.

**Hours:** Mon.-Sat. 9-6:30, Sun. 1-6:30, in July; Mon.-Sat. 9-5:30, Sun. 1-5:30, Mar.-June and Aug.-Oct.; Mon.-Sat. 10-4:30, Sun. 1-4:30, rest of year. Closed Thanksgiving and Christmas. **Cost:** Park free. Cave tour $20.99; $17.99 (ages 3-11). Tickets for individual activities $5.99 each. **Phone:** (256) 378-7252 or (800) 933-2283. 

## CLANTON pop. 8,619, elev. 600'

BEST WESTERN INN (205)280-1006
◆◆ Hotel $76-$100

**AAA Benefit:** Members save up to 20%!

**Address:** 801 Bradberry Ln 35046 **Location:** I-65 exit 205, 0.5 mi e. Located on hilltop. **Facility:** 53 units. 2 stories (no elevator), exterior corridors. **Terms:** 3 day cancellation notice. **Pool(s):** outdoor.

HOLIDAY INN EXPRESS CLANTON (205)280-1880
◆◆◆ Hotel $99-$130

**Address:** 815 Bradberry Ln 35046 **Location:** I-65 exit 205, 0.5 mi e. **Facility:** 63 units. 3 stories, interior corridors. **Terms:** cancellation fee imposed. **Pool(s):** heated indoor. **Activities:** exercise room. **Guest Services:** coin laundry. **Featured Amenity:** full hot breakfast.

## COLUMBIANA (D-4) pop. 4,197, elev. 524'
• Part of Birmingham area — see map p. 43

**KARL C. HARRISON MUSEUM OF GEORGE WASHINGTON** is at 50 Lester St. The museum, encouraged by a sixth-generation granddaughter of Martha Washington, contains letters, china, 18th- and 19th-century wooden furniture, books and other personal effects of the first family and their descendants. **Time:** Allow 1 hour minimum. **Hours:** Mon.-Fri. 10-3. Closed major holidays. **Cost:** Free. **Phone:** (205) 669-8767.

## CONECUH NATIONAL FOREST (G-3)

Elevations in the forest range from 200 ft. in the swamp areas to 320 ft. at Open Pond Tower. Refer to AAA maps for additional elevation information.

On the Alabama-Florida border, Conecuh National Forest covers almost 84,000 acres. Backpacking is permitted along the 20-mile Conecuh Trail, which offers 5- and 13.5-mile loops through the forest and a 1.5-mile loop around Open Pond. Deer, squirrels, rabbits and quails are commonly sighted; alligators and wild turkeys also can be seen. The trail offers five different starting points, including Open Pond Recreation Area, which has year-round facilities for camping, fishing, boating, hiking and picnicking.

Bicycling is permitted on the north loop of the Conecuh Trail and the 1.5-mile loop around Open Pond. Blue Lake Recreation Area, 13 miles southwest of Andalusia via US 29 and SR 137, offers hiking, picnicking, swimming, fishing and boating Apr.-Oct. Trail maps can be purchased from the district ranger's office in Andalusia. Open Pond Recreation Area open daily 7 a.m.-10 p.m., year-round. Blue Lake Recreation Area open daily 6 a.m.-10 p.m., Apr.-Oct. Day-use fee $3. For more information contact the District Rangers Office, 24481 SR 55, Andalusia, AL 36420; phone (334) 222-2555. *See Recreation Areas Chart.*

## CULLMAN (B-3) pop. 14,775, elev. 802'
• Restaurants p. 68

Cullman was the vision of John G. Cullmann, a German immigrant who bought a tract of land in 1872, upon which he hoped to establish a self-sustaining colony of his countrymen. Beginning with only five German families, the project was so successful that 6 years later the Alabama legislature designated Cullman the seat of the newly created county, also named for its founder.

An abundance of timber and coal created such prosperity that Queen Wilhelmina of the Netherlands gave her backing to the Dutch company organized to develop the community's resources. World War I prevented the full materialization of the project, and the town's economic base shifted to electrical equipment production and poultry processing.

Clarkson Covered Bridge—7 miles west of I-65 on US 278, then 2 miles north following signs—is one of Alabama's largest. The surrounding wooded area is home to Clarkson Bridge Park, which contains picnic facilities, hiking paths and a non-operating gristmill.

Arts and crafts are the focus of the 2-day Bloomin' Festival, a juried arts event that takes place in early April on the St. Bernard Abbey and preparatory school campus at 1600 St. Bernard Dr. S.E. In addition to more than 140 artists' booths, festivalgoers enjoy live music and children's activities.

**Cullman Area Chamber of Commerce & Visitor Center:** 301 2nd Ave. S.W., Cullman, AL 35055. **Phone:** (256) 734-0454 or (800) 313-5114.

**AVE MARIA GROTTO** is off I-65 exit 308, then 4 mi. e. on US 278 to 1600 St. Bernard Dr. S.E., on the grounds of St. Bernard Abbey and its preparatory school. Over a 50-year period, Benedictine monk Brother Joseph Zoettl used pictures as his guide to create a beautifully landscaped 4-acre park with 125 miniatures of famous churches, buildings and shrines from many parts of the world. Construction materials range from bits of discarded glass and jewelry to native stone and marble.

Brother Joseph was 80 years old when he created his final miniature in 1958. The grotto is in an old quarry, its landscape accentuated by gently sloping paths. **Time:** Allow 1 hour minimum. **Hours:** Daily 9-5. Closed Jan. 1 and Christmas. **Cost:** $7; $5 (ages 60+); $4.50 (ages 6-12). **Phone:** (256) 734-4110.

**CULLMAN COUNTY MUSEUM,** 211 2nd Ave. N.E., is in a replica of the home of town founder John Cullmann. Displays representative of the town's rural past and its German heritage include antique clothing, interior scene with various historical items showcased in storefront windows. Also presented are Native American artifacts, a Civil War exhibit and a life-size bronze statue of Cullmann. **Hours:** Mon.-Fri. 9-4, Sun. 1:30-4:30. Closed major holidays. **Cost:** $5; $4 (ages 65+); $3 (ages 0-11). **Phone:** (256) 739-1258 or (800) 533-1258.

**BEST WESTERN FAIRWINDS INN**          (256)737-5009

Motel
$77-$135

**AAA Benefit:** Members save up to 20%!

**Address:** 1917 Commerce Ave NW 35055 **Location:** I-65 exit 310, just e. **Facility:** 50 units. 2 stories (no elevator), exterior corridors. **Pool(s):** outdoor. **Activities:** picnic facilities, limited exercise equipment. **Guest Services:** coin laundry.

**COMFORT SUITES**          (256)255-5999

Hotel $99-$149 **Address:** 2048 St Joseph Dr NW 35058 **Location:** I-65 exit 310, just e, then just n. **Facility:** 68 units. 3 stories, interior corridors. **Pool(s):** outdoor. **Activities:** exercise room. **Guest Services:** valet and coin laundry.

**HAMPTON INN**          (256)739-4444

Hotel $98-$169 **Address:** 6100 Alabama Hwy 157 35058 **Location:** I-65 exit 310, just e. **Facility:** 86 units. 3 stories, interior corridors. **Terms:** 1-7 night minimum stay, cancellation fee imposed. **Pool(s):** outdoor. **Activities:** exercise room. **Guest Services:** valet and coin laundry.

**AAA Benefit:** Members save 5% or more!

Use travel time to share driving tips and rules of the road with your teens

**HOLIDAY INN EXPRESS HOTEL & SUITES** (256)736-1906

▼▼▼ **Hotel** $99-$189 **Address:** 2052 Hayes Dr NW 35058 **Location:** I-65 exit 310, just ne. **Facility:** 78 units. 3 stories, interior corridors. **Pool(s):** heated indoor. **Activities:** exercise room. **Guest Services:** valet and coin laundry.

`[¶+] CALL [&M] [🚲] [BIZ] [HS] [📶] [🍴] [🖥] [☕]`

**QUALITY INN** (256)734-1240

▼▼ **Hotel** $80-$85 **Address:** 5917 SR 157 NW 35058 **Location:** I-65 exit 310, just e. **Facility:** 50 units. 2 stories (no elevator), exterior corridors. **Pool(s):** outdoor. **Guest Services:** coin laundry.

`[¶+] [🚲] [BIZ] [📶] [🍴] [🖥] [☕]`

**SLEEP INN & SUITES** (256)734-6166

▼▼ **Hotel** $75-$120 **Address:** 2050 Old Hwy 157 35057 **Location:** I-65 exit 310, just ne. **Facility:** 54 units. 3 stories, interior corridors. **Pool(s):** outdoor. **Activities:** limited exercise equipment. **Guest Services:** coin laundry.

`[¶+] [🚲] [BIZ] [HS] [📶] [🍴] [🖥] [☕] /SOME UNITS [🕭]`

**WHERE TO EAT**

**AJ'S STEAKHOUSE** 256/775-1653

▼▼ **Steak.** Casual Dining. $5-$16 **AAA Inspector Notes:** Enjoy a no-frills steak dinner at this steakhouse where choices include a variety of cuts and sizes. For those not in a beefy mood, choose from chicken, pork, shrimp and catfish dishes. **Features:** senior menu. **Address:** 917 2nd Ave SW 35055 **Location:** I-65 exit 310, 0.9 mi e on SR 157, then 1.4 mi s on US 31. `[D] CALL [&M]`

**THE ALL STEAK RESTAURANT** 256/734-4322

▼▼▼ **Steak.** Casual Dining. $8-$26 **AAA Inspector Notes:** This local favorite has a new downtown location, a move which offers spacious dining rooms, plus a cozy little bar in the back, featuring, quite possibly, Alabama's most entertaining bartender. Steak purists will appreciate the "no steak sauce" approach. The famous little orange roll is a delightfully sticky conclusion to your evening. **Features:** full bar, Sunday brunch, happy hour. **Reservations:** suggested. **Address:** 323 3rd Ave SE 35055 **Location:** Corner of 4th St SE; downtown. **Parking:** on-site and street. `[B] [L] [D] CALL [&M]`

**BUENA VISTA MEXICAN RESTAURANT** 256/737-5050

▼▼ **Mexican.** Casual Dining. $5-$12 **AAA Inspector Notes:** The brightly colored fiesta decor and the scent of fajitas on the grill make for a celebratory atmosphere at this Mexican eatery. **Address:** 1644 Brantley Ave 35055 **Location:** I-65 exit 310, 1 mi e on SR 157, 0.8 mi s on US 31, then just e. `[L] [D] CALL [&M]`

**CARLTON'S ITALIAN** 256/739-9050

▼▼ **Italian.** Casual Dining. $5-$19 **AAA Inspector Notes:** For more than 20 years, this intimate downtown bistro has been family owned and operated. The standard menu is expanded on weekend evenings to offer additional ethnic fare. **Features:** beer & wine, patio dining. **Address:** 208 3rd Ave SE 35055 **Location:** Between 2nd and 3rd sts; downtown. **Parking:** street only. `[L] [D]`

**GRUMPY'S ITALIAN GRILL** 256/734-2544

▼ **Pizza.** Casual Dining. $5-$14 **AAA Inspector Notes:** Pizza is what most customers return for at this downtown eatery but calzones, sandwiches, salads, wings and some pasta dishes also are available on the menu. **Features:** full bar, happy hour. **Address:** 402 5th St SW 35055 **Location:** Between 4th and 5th aves SW; downtown. **Parking:** street only. `[L] [D]`

**JOHNNY'S BAR-B-Q** 256/734-8539

▼▼▼

Barbecue
Casual Dining
$6-$19

**AAA Inspector Notes:** Celebrating 50 years of smoking-good pork, chicken, catfish and hush puppies, this is where the locals go for a guaranteed delicious meal. Simple, straightforward and laid back, the fresh barbecue aroma greets you in the parking lot. Save room for homemade cheesecake; daily flavors are posted at the front door. **Address:** 1401 4th St SW 35055 **Location:** I-65 exit 308 (US 278), 1.2 mi e. `[L] [D]`

**PASQUALE'S PIZZA & PASTA** 256/734-4599

▼ **Italian Pizza.** Casual Dining. $6-$19 **AAA Inspector Notes:** Specializing in pizza, this ristorante also prepares spaghetti, ravioli, lasagna, calzones, sandwiches and salads. An all-you-can-eat buffet is offered for lunch and dinner on weekdays. **Features:** beer only. **Address:** 915 2nd Ave NW 35055 **Location:** I-65 exit 310, 0.9 mi e on SR 157, then 1.5 mi s on US 31. `[L] [D]`

**RUMORS DELI & COFFEE HOUSE** 256/737-0911

▼ **Sandwiches.** Quick Serve. $5-$9 **AAA Inspector Notes:** While perusing the many specialty shops and boutiques in the restored warehouse district, stop by this eclectic spot for a quick coffee break or a made-to-order sandwich. The whimsical decor of this coffee house/deli offers a visual diversion and possibly a conversation stimulus. **Features:** patio dining. **Address:** 105 1st Ave NE 35055 **Location:** Across from Clark St NE; downtown.

`[B] [L] [🖐]`

## DANVILLE (B-3) elev. 600'

**JESSE OWENS MEMORIAL PARK AND MUSEUM** is at 7019 CR 203. At the 1936 Olympic games in Nazi-era Berlin, this African-American track star won four gold medals. The museum depicts Owens' athletic and humanitarian achievements through interactive video exhibits, rare film footage and memorabilia. The park features a replica of Owens' Alabama boyhood home, an 8-foot bronze sculpture of the Olympian, a replica of the 1936 broad jump pit, a 1936 Olympic torch, two baseball fields and a playground.

**Time:** Allow 1 hour minimum. **Hours:** Mon.-Sat. 10-4, Sun. 1-4. Closed Jan. 1, Thanksgiving and Christmas. **Cost:** Free. **Phone:** (256) 974-3636. `[⛩]`

## DAPHNE (H-2) pop. 21,570, elev. 157'

Daphne had its beginnings in the early 18th century when it served as a gathering spot for European fur traders. A popular legend claims that Gen. Andrew Jackson directed his troops during the War of 1812 from a fork in one of Daphne's live oaks.

Owing to a prime location on the Eastern Shore, Daphne is sometimes called "Jubilee City." The name refers to the harvesting and celebrating in which the residents indulge when a natural convergence of summer tidal and weather conditions forces multitudes of fish and crustaceans into shallow shoreline waters, where they easily become the catch-of-the-day. The city also is home to the United States Sports Academy, 1 mile east on US 98, an undergraduate and graduate school devoted to sports education.

Bayfront Park, on Bayfront Drive, and May Day Park, on the west side of College Street, are pleasant places to picnic and enjoy views of the water. A boat launch is available at May Day Park.

**Eastern Shore Chamber of Commerce & Visitor Center:** 29750 Larry Dee Cawyer Dr., P.O. Drawer 310, Daphne, AL 36526-0310. **Phone:** (251) 621-8222.

**AMERICAN SPORT ART MUSEUM AND ARCHIVES** is on the campus of the United States Sports Academy, 1 mi. e. on US 98 at One Academy Dr. The museum celebrates the world of sports through artistic interpretation. A large collection of sculpture, paintings and works in other media is complemented by an archive of sports history. **Time:** Allow 30 minutes minimum. **Hours:** Mon.-Fri. 8-4. Closed major holidays. **Cost:** Donations. **Phone:** (251) 626-3303.

**MALBIS MEMORIAL CHURCH** (Greek Orthodox), 29300 SR 181, is a copy of a Byzantine church in Athens, Greece. The mosaic-adorned church contains several striking murals and a hand-carved, white marble wall. The freestanding wall serves as a backdrop for the altar, marble pulpit and bishop's throne, all of which were imported from Greece. **Hours:** Daily 9-4. Closed Christmas. **Cost:** Free. **Phone:** (251) 626-3050.

**BEST WESTERN PLUS DAPHNE INN & SUITES**
(251)625-6260

Hotel
$89-$129

**AAA Benefit:** Members save up to 20%!

**Address:** 8931 Sawwood St 36526 **Location:** I-10 exit 38, just nw. **Facility:** 65 units. 3 stories, interior corridors. **Pool(s):** outdoor. **Activities:** exercise room. **Guest Services:** valet and coin laundry.

**COMFORT SUITES OF DAPHNE** (251)626-1113
Hotel $89-$129 **Address:** 29450 N Main St 36526 **Location:** I-10 exit 35A eastbound; exit 35 westbound, just s. **Facility:** 77 units. 3 stories, interior corridors. **Pool(s):** outdoor. **Activities:** exercise room. **Guest Services:** valet and coin laundry.

**HAMPTON INN MOBILE-EAST BAY DAPHNE** (251)626-2220
Hotel $99-$139 **Address:** 29451 US Hwy 98 36526 **Location:** I-10 exit 35A eastbound; exit 35 westbound, just s. **Facility:** 132 units. 6 stories, interior corridors. **Terms:** 1-7 night minimum stay, cancellation fee imposed. **Pool(s):** outdoor. **Activities:** exercise room. **Guest Services:** valet and coin laundry.

**AAA Benefit:** Members save 5% or more!

**HILTON GARDEN INN** (251)625-0020
Hotel $109-$139 **Address:** 29546 N Main St 36526 **Location:** I-10 exit 35B eastbound; exit 35 westbound, just s. **Facility:** 124 units. 5 stories, interior corridors. **Terms:** 1-7 night minimum stay, cancellation fee imposed. **Pool(s):** heated indoor. **Activities:** hot tub, exercise room. **Guest Services:** valet and coin laundry.

**AAA Benefit:** Members save 5% or more!

**HOLIDAY INN EXPRESS & SUITES** (251)621-1223
Hotel $99-$149 **Address:** 29725 Woodrow Ln 36526 **Location:** I-10 exit 38, just nw. **Facility:** 83 units. 3 stories, interior corridors. **Pool(s):** outdoor. **Activities:** exercise room.

**HOMEWOOD SUITES BY HILTON MOBILE EAST BAY/DAPHNE** (251)621-0100
Extended Stay Hotel $159-$259 **Address:** 29474 N Main St 36526 **Location:** I-10 exit 35A eastbound; exit 35 westbound, just s. **Facility:** 104 efficiencies, some two bedrooms. 7 stories, interior corridors. **Terms:** 1-7 night minimum stay, cancellation fee imposed. **Pool(s):** outdoor. **Activities:** exercise room. **Guest Services:** valet and coin laundry.

**AAA Benefit:** Members save 5% or more!

**MICROTEL INN & SUITES BY WYNDHAM DAPHNE/MOBILE** (251)621-7807
Hotel $60-$109 **Address:** 29050 US 98 36526 **Location:** I-10 exit 35A eastbound; exit 35 westbound, 0.5 mi s. **Facility:** 71 units. 4 stories, interior corridors. **Terms:** cancellation fee imposed. **Guest Services:** coin laundry.

### WHERE TO EAT

**BANGKOK THAI CUISINE** 251/626-5286
Thai. Casual Dining. $8-$13 **AAA Inspector Notes:** This award-winning Thai restaurant offers not only a palatable but visual taste of Thai culture. Intricately carved wood furniture and adornment fill the dining room along with ethnic artwork and crafts. A wide variety of Thai, Asian and sushi dishes is offered. The food is prepared with no additives or preservatives. **Address:** 28600 US 98 36526 **Location:** I-10 exit 35A eastbound; exit 35 westbound, 1 mi s; in Jubilee Point Plaza.

**ROSIE'S GRILL** 251/626-2440
American. Casual Dining. $8-$16 **AAA Inspector Notes:** This cozy roadside café is noted for its "garbage" burgers (where guests create their own custom burger with numerous variety of fixings), a T-Bird sandwich and fresh tacos. **Features:** full bar, patio dining, Sunday brunch, happy hour. **Address:** 1203 US 98, Suite 3D 36526 **Location:** I-10 exit 35A eastbound; exit 35 westbound, 4.2 mi s; in Market Place strip mall.

**TEAK HOUSE THAI CUISINE** 251/625-8680
Thai. Casual Dining. $8-$15 **AAA Inspector Notes:** Diners can choose from an extensive selection of ethnic dishes prepared to their level of spicy tolerance at this casual Thai spot. Lunch specials are offered daily from 11 am to 3 pm. **Features:** beer & wine. **Address:** 1703 US Hwy 98 36526 **Location:** I-10 exit 35A eastbound; exit 35 westbound, 3.7 mi s.

## DAUPHIN ISLAND (I-1) pop. 1,238, elev. 6'
• Restaurants p. 70

Early in the 1700s the French established the first European settlement in the Louisiana Territory on Dauphin (DOFF-in) Island, which they originally named Massacre because of the many human skeletons they found. When the group realized the island's potential as a defense post, the name was changed to Dauphin, the title of the eldest son of Louis XIV, and the settlement was moved to the mainland. For 2 centuries the island served military purposes only.

Today much of the island is a bird sanctuary. The Dauphin Island Park and Beach Board, in partnership with the National Audubon Society and the Dauphin Island Bird Sanctuary Inc., maintains 160 acres with interpretive walking trails that are free and open to the public.

A bridge that forms part of SR 193 provides an especially scenic entrance to the island, which also is accessible by ferry from the Fort Morgan Peninsula, near Orange Beach and Gulf Shores; phone (251) 861-3000 for ferry rates and schedule. The Gulf Shores and a large freshwater lake provide many opportunities for recreation. Chartered fishing trips may be arranged at Dauphin Isle Marina. A nearby fishing pier and a boat ramp also are available.

**Dauphin Island Chamber of Commerce:** P.O. Box 5, Dauphin Island, AL 36528. **Phone:** (251) 861-5524 or (877) 532-8744.

**THE ESTUARIUM AT THE DAUPHIN ISLAND SEA LAB,** just past the ferry landing at 102A Bienville Blvd., is a public aquarium focusing on the four key ecosystems of coastal Alabama—the swamps of the Mobile-Tensaw River delta, Mobile Bay, the barrier islands and the Gulf of Mexico. A boardwalk can be followed through a salt marsh; descriptive panels identify local vegetation and wildlife. Interactive exhibits, aquariums and touch tanks depict one of the country's largest estuary systems.

An American alligator, crabs, eels, jellyfish, lobsters, an octopus, oysters, sharks, shrimp, turtles and various types of fish are some of the marine life that can be seen. **Hours:** Mon.-Sat. 9-6, Sun. noon-6, Mar.-Aug.; Mon.-Sat. 9-5, Sun. 1-5, rest of year. Closed Jan. 1, Easter, Thanksgiving, Christmas Eve, Christmas and Dec. 31. **Cost:** $10; $8 (senior citizens); $6 (ages 5-18 and students with ID). **Phone:** (251) 861-7500 or (866) 403-4409.

**FORT GAINES HISTORIC SITE,** 51 Bienville Blvd., was one of two fortifications guarding Mobile Bay during the Civil War. Directly opposite on Mobile Point, Fort Morgan (see Gulf Shores p. 85) guarded the eastern entrance to the bay. The two forts overlook the site of the Battle of Mobile Bay.

Fort Gaines, completed by the Confederacy in 1861, is a five-sided brick rampart with bastions. The site includes cannons, kitchens and blacksmith shops as well as a museum displaying Civil War artifacts. **Time:** Allow 30 minutes minimum. **Hours:** Daily 9-5. Closed Thanksgiving, Christmas Eve and Christmas. **Cost:** $6; $4 (ages 5-12). **Phone:** (251) 861-6992.

LIGHTHOUSE BAKERY                                251/861-2253

▼ Breads/Pastries Sandwiches. Quick Serve. $3-$9 **AAA Inspector Notes:** Patrons can start off their day with a great cup of coffee and a freshly baked cinnamon roll or cheese Danish or come in around midday for a light lunch centered on a great-tasting sandwich. Everything here is made from scratch. **Address:** 919 Chaumont Ave 36528 **Location:** Just e of SR 193. [B] [L]

**DECATUR** (B-3) pop. 55,683, elev. 573'
• Restaurants p. 72

Reduced to four buildings by the end of the Civil War and blighted by a yellow fever epidemic in 1888, Decatur survived and then prospered when chemical companies were established in the 1950s.

Wheeler Lake, one of the Tennessee Valley Authority reservoirs spread across northern Alabama, is just northwest. The city's waterfront supports both industry and recreation.

One of the best-preserved Victorian-era neighborhoods in Alabama, the Old Decatur District between the Tennessee River and Lee Street is most easily explored on a walking tour. This historic district occupies the original townsite settled in 1820. The tree-lined neighborhood contains late 19th-century houses, shops and the restored 1833 Old State Bank (see attraction listing), which survived the Civil War.

Equally interesting is the Albany Heritage District north of Delano Park on US 31. Once known as the new Chicago of the South because of its development by Northern industrialists, this Victorian neighborhood enjoyed a boom period prior to the yellow fever epidemic. Fine examples of Queen Anne, Shingle and Eastlake architectural styles are concentrated along Gordon Drive and Sherman and Jackson streets. Several of the houses in both historic districts are open during the Christmas Tour of Homes in early December.

**Decatur/Morgan County Convention and Visitors Bureau:** 719 6th Ave. S.E., P.O. Box 2349, Decatur, AL 35602. **Phone:** (256) 350-2028 or (800) 232-5449.

**Self-guiding tours:** Maps outlining walking tours through the Old Decatur District and the Albany Heritage District are distributed by the convention and visitors bureau. Also available is a brochure for a 13-block Civil War walking tour through the Old Decatur district, which includes important sites from the 1864 battle for Decatur.

**COOK'S NATURAL SCIENCE MUSEUM,** 412 13th St. S.E., contains displays of mounted wildlife, an extensive insect exhibit, live snakes, shells, coral, and a rock and mineral collection. **Time:** Allow 1 hour minimum. **Hours:** Mon.-Sat. 9-noon and 1-5, Sun. 2-5. Closed Jan. 1, Thanksgiving, Christmas Eve and Christmas. **Cost:** Free. **Phone:** (256) 350-9347.

**THE OLD STATE BANK,** 925 Bank St. N.E., opened in 1833 as a branch of the Alabama state bank system. During the Civil War the building served as a military hospital and guardhouse. **Time:** Allow 30 minutes minimum. **Hours:** Mon.-Fri. 9:30-noon and 1-4:30. Closed major holidays. Phone ahead to confirm schedule. **Cost:** Free. **Phone:** (256) 341-4818. [GT]

**POINT MALLARD PARK,** 2901 Point Mallard Dr. S.E., is a 750-acre recreation park on the Tennessee River featuring an aquatic center with a wave pool, an Olympic-size pool, waterslides, a children's duck pond and a beach. Other facilities include a lighted tennis complex with an indoor bubble dome, a playground, a recreation center, soccer and baseball fields, nature and bicycle trails, an 18-hole championship golf course, a driving range, batting cages and a year-round ice-skating complex. *See Recreation Areas Chart.*

**Hours:** Grounds daily 6 a.m.-10 p.m. Aquatic center daily 10-6 (also Tues. and Thurs. 6-8 p.m.), Memorial Day weekend to mid-Aug.; Sat.-Sun. 10-6, mid-Aug. through Labor Day. **Cost:** Park free. Aquatic center Tues. and Thurs.-Sun. $20; $15 (ages 5-11 and 62+). Aquatic center Mon. and Wed. (also Tues. and Thurs. 5-8 p.m.) $10; $7.50 (ages 5-11 and 62+). Holiday prices may vary; phone ahead. **Phone:** (256) 341-4900.

**WHEELER NATIONAL WILDLIFE REFUGE** occupies approximately 35,000 acres surrounding the middle third of Wheeler Reservoir, between the cities of Decatur and Huntsville; the visitor center is at 3121 Visitors Center Rd. The refuge, one of Alabama's largest and oldest, attracts a variety of migratory waterfowl. Thousands of sandhill cranes and dozens of endangered whooping cranes spend the winter here. Habitats include pine uplands, mud flats, tupelo swamps, bottomland hardwoods and agricultural fields. The visitor center offers displays about conservation and the Tennessee River. Nature trails are available.

Boating, fishing and hunting are permitted. Hunting permits are available at the visitor center. **Hours:** Daily 9-5, Oct.-Feb.; Tues.-Sat. 9-4, rest of year. **Cost:** Free. **Phone:** (256) 350-6639.

**AMBERLEY SUITE HOTEL**　256/355-6800
▼▼▼ **Hotel.** Rates not provided. **Address:** 807 Bank St NE 35601 **Location:** US 31 to Church St, just w; in downtown historic district. **Facility:** 110 units. 3 stories, interior corridors. **Pool(s):** outdoor. **Activities:** exercise room. **Guest Services:** coin laundry.

**BEST WESTERN RIVER CITY HOTEL**　(256)301-1388

Hotel
$72-$80

**AAA Benefit:** Members save up to 20%!

**Address:** 1305 Front Ave SW 35603 **Location:** I-65 exit 334, 8 mi n. **Facility:** 59 units. 3 stories, interior corridors. **Pool(s):** outdoor. **Guest Services:** coin laundry. **Featured Amenity:** breakfast buffet.

**HAMPTON INN DECATUR**　(256)355-5888
▼▼▼ **Hotel** $109-$159 **Address:** 2041 Beltline Rd SW (SR 67) 35601 **Location:** Jct US 31/SR 67, 3.6 mi w. Located in a busy commercial district. **Facility:** 90 units. 4 stories, interior corridors. **Terms:** 1-7 night minimum stay, cancellation fee imposed. **Pool(s):** outdoor. **Activities:** exercise room. **Guest Services:** valet laundry.

**AAA Benefit:** Members save 5% or more!

**MICROTEL INN & SUITES BY WYNDHAM**　(256)301-9995
▼▼ **Hotel** $59-$79 **Address:** 2226 Beltline Rd SW (SR 67) 35601 **Location:** SR 67, 4 mi w of jct US 31. **Facility:** 76 units. 3 stories, interior corridors. **Terms:** 3 day cancellation notice. **Pool(s):** outdoor. **Activities:** exercise room. **Guest Services:** coin laundry.

**QUALITY INN**　(256)355-2229
▼▼ **Hotel** $67-$79 **Address:** 2120 Jameson Pl SW 35603 **Location:** SR 67, 1.6 mi s of jct US 72A; 3.9 mi n of jct US 31. **Facility:** 60 units. 2 stories (no elevator), exterior corridors. **Pool(s):** outdoor. **Activities:** exercise room. **Guest Services:** valet laundry. *(See ad this page.)*

**ASIAN BUFFET & GRILL**  256/353-1555

▼ Asian. Quick Serve. $7-$12 **AAA Inspector Notes:** The numerous buffet tables are continuously replenished with piping hot dishes. Fresh sushi rolls and made-to-order grilled selections are also available. **Address:** 1702 Beltline Rd SW 35601 **Location:** Jct Danville Rd SW and SR 67, just s. L D

**BIG BOB GIBSON'S BAR-B-Q**  256/350-6969

Southern Barbecue Casual Dining $4-$20

**AAA Inspector Notes:** Classic. Family owned since 1925, this place is heaven for barbecue lovers, and its food has been praised in countless magazines and reviews. One bite of the delicious smoked barbecue coated in tangy sauce, and guests understand what the fuss is all about. **Address:** 1715 6th Ave SE 35601 **Location:** On US 31; 1.2 mi n of jct SR 67. L D

**THE BRICK DELI & TAVERN**  256/355-8318

▼▼ Sandwiches. Casual Dining. $6-$8 **AAA Inspector Notes:** Established in 1998, this restaurant offers a wide variety of specialty sandwiches or they can make one to your specifications. Twenty-five domestic and imported beers are available on tap. Enjoy live music Wednesday through Saturday, or challenge friends on the available pool tables, dart boards and video games. **Features:** full bar, patio dining, happy hour. **Address:** 112 Moulton St E 35601 **Location:** Between 1st and 2nd aves NE; downtown. L D LATE ✎

**CAFE 113**  256/351-1400

▼▼▼ Continental. Fine Dining. $20-$40 **AAA Inspector Notes:** In a commercial district downtown, this café has an eclectic decor that is as interesting as the food is good. A varied selection of red meat, fish and fowl is offered. The friendly waitstaff provides professional service. **Features:** full bar, happy hour. **Address:** 113 Grant St 35601 **Location:** Between 1st and 2nd aves SE; center. **Parking:** street only. D

**FULIN'S ASIAN CUISINE**  256/355-3588

▼▼ Asian. Casual Dining. $8-$23 **AAA Inspector Notes:** This eatery offers a full array of Asian cuisine including Chinese, Japanese and Thai all served in a simple but stylish atmosphere. **Features:** full bar. **Address:** 1241 Point Mallard Pkwy SE, Suite 406 35601 **Location:** Jct US 31 and SR 67, just e; in Crossings of Decatur Shopping Plaza; across from Target. L D CALL ⚫M

**GOLDEN PHOENIX CHINESE RESTAURANT**  256/350-7688

▼ Chinese. Casual Dining. $7-$18 **AAA Inspector Notes:** Vivid colors of the Oriental wall murals add to the ambience at this spot where dining on numerous items is offered at the buffet. A poll conducted by the local newspaper found that this place serves the city's best Chinese food. **Features:** beer & wine, happy hour. **Address:** 2219 Danville Rd 35601 **Location:** SR 67; jct Beltline Rd SW, just e. L D CALL ⚫M

**KYOTO JAPANESE STEAKHOUSE**  256/309-0220

▼▼ Japanese. Casual Dining. $7-$30 **AAA Inspector Notes:** Energetic hibachi chefs will delight and entertain you here; or, dine at the sushi bar, if you'd rather. Whichever you choose, rest assured that your taste buds will be more than satisfied. Large portions leave something to look forward to tomorrow. Dining late? Don't miss the after-dinner happy hour. **Features:** full bar, happy hour. **Address:** 1605 Beltline Rd, Suite D-1 35603 **Location:** Jct US 31, 2.2 mi ne on SR 67; in Decatur Commons Plaza. L D

**Visit AAA.com/searchfordiscounts to save**

**on dining, attractions, hotels and more**

**SIMP MCGHEE'S**  256/353-6284

▼▼ American. Casual Dining. $18-$36 **AAA Inspector Notes:** Antiques abound in this converted 1890s dry goods building. Cajun and seafood specialties are found here, alongside beef, pork and fowl. Metal ceilings, hardwood floors and old-time pictures help guests step back in time more than 100 years. Casual dining on the first floor with a more formal setting on the second. **Features:** full bar, patio dining. **Address:** 725 Bank St 35601 **Location:** Between Vine and Lafayette sts NE; in historic downtown. **Parking:** street only. D 🛒

**TASTE OF CHINA**  256/340-3443

▼ Chinese. Casual Dining. $5-$11 **AAA Inspector Notes:** This compact restaurant serves up big taste and ample portions for a small price. **Address:** 2941 Point Mallard Pkwy, Unit J 35603 **Location:** I-65 exit 334, 1 mi w; in Mallard Shopping Plaza. L D

# DEMOPOLIS (E-2) pop. 7,483, elev. 117'

A small band of Napoleonic exiles founded Demopolis (dem-AH-po-lis), "city of the people," in 1817. They optimistically attempted to establish vineyards and olive groves, but being unaccustomed to farming, the French Emigrants for the Cultivation of the Vine and Olive soon deserted the four townships Congress had granted them.

In the 1820s American planters settled on the banks of the Tombigbee River and launched the era of the Black Belt's cotton prosperity. Although cotton continues its reign, the products of cattle ranches, dairy farms and soybean fields also contribute to the area's economy.

Christmas on the River, a 4-day event in early December, features candlelight antebellum home tours, an arts and crafts show, a championship barbecue cook-off, and a nighttime nautical parade with fireworks and festively lit boats.

**Demopolis Area Chamber of Commerce:** 102 E. Washington St., P.O. Box 667, Demopolis, AL 36732. **Phone:** (334) 289-0270.

**BLUFF HALL,** overlooking the Tombigbee River at 405 Commissioners Ave., exemplifies two major architectural trends in the antebellum South. Built in 1832 as a Federal townhouse, the brick structure was later remodeled in Greek Revival style when a colonnaded portico, a large rear wing and a louvered gallery were added.

The restored house contains period clothing, Empire and Victorian furniture, and local history displays. **Hours:** Tours Tues.-Sat. 10-5, Sun. 2-5. Closed Jan. 1, Easter, July 4, Thanksgiving and Christmas. **Cost:** $5; $4 (students with ID); $3 (ages 6-18). **Phone:** (334) 289-9644. GT

SAVE **GAINESWOOD,** at 805 S. Cedar Ave., is a historic mansion featuring original furnishings, domed ceilings and fluted columns. Built in 1821 as a dogtrot cabin, the house gradually grew to more than 6,200 square feet as Gaineswood became the center of a cotton plantation in the mid-1800s. Altered and modified in the century following the Civil War, the property has been restored to its 1860s appearance by the Alabama Historical Commission.

**Time:** Allow 45 minutes minimum. **Hours:** Tues.-Fri. 10-4, first Sat. of the month 10-2, otherwise by appointment. Closed state holidays. Phone ahead to confirm schedule. **Cost:** $7; $5 (college students and military with ID and senior citizens); $3 (ages 6-18). Cash only. **Phone:** (334) 289-4846.

**BEST WESTERN PLUS TWO RIVERS HOTEL & SUITES**
(334)289-2611

Hotel
$110-$120

**AAA Benefit:**
Members save up to 20%!

**Address:** 662 US Hwy 80 W 36732 **Location:** Jct US 43, 0.8 mi w. **Facility:** 43 units, some kitchens. 2 stories, interior corridors. **Pool(s):** outdoor. **Activities:** exercise room. **Guest Services:** valet and coin laundry.

ECONO LODGE INN & SUITES  (334)287-0300
Hotel $70-$90 **Address:** 1035 Hwy 80 W 36732 **Location:** Jct US 43, 1 mi w. Located in a commercial area. **Facility:** 45 units. 2 stories, interior corridors. **Guest Services:** valet laundry.

## DORA (C-3) pop. 2,025, elev. 394'

**ALABAMA MINING MUSEUM** is 2.8 mi. s. of jct. CR 81 and US 78 at 120 East St. Through exhibits about mining technology and the lifestyle of the coal miner, the museum demonstrates how Alabama became one of the most important coal-mining regions in the country 1890-1940. A 1900s train, mining cars, a post office and a one-room schoolhouse are included. **Time:** Allow 1 hour minimum. **Hours:** Tues.-Sat. 10-4. Closed Jan. 1, July 4 and Christmas. **Cost:** Free. **Phone:** (205) 648-2442.

## DOTHAN (G-6) pop. 65,496, elev. 355'
• Restaurants p. 74

When the railroad came to Dothan (DO-thin) in 1889, the rustic settlement was populated only by rowdy lumberjacks and turpentine workers. By 1910 mechanized farming brought new economic vigor to the rolling terrain of Wiregrass country.

Almost equidistant from Atlanta, Birmingham, Mobile and Tallahassee, Fla., modern Dothan is a natural marketing center involved in the cultivation of peanuts.

Part of Alabama's Robert Trent Jones Golf Trail, Highland Oaks Golf Course, 800 Royal Pkwy., offers a choice of four nine-hole courses.

Noteworthy historic attractions in town include the Dothan Opera House, built as a city auditorium in 1915. A series of 14 murals painted on buildings in the city's historic downtown spotlights people, places and events prominent in Dothan's history.

**Dothan Area Convention & Visitors Bureau:** 3311 Ross Clark Cir., P.O. Box 8765, Dothan, AL 36304. **Phone:** (334) 794-6622 or (888) 449-0212.

**Shopping areas:** Wiregrass Commons, with Belk, Dillard's, and JCPenney, is a major mall in the Ross Clark Circle area off US 231.

**LANDMARK PARK** is at 430 Landmark Dr. This 135-acre living-history park includes a restored 1895 house and a late 19th-century farm complete with farm animals, a sugar cane mill and a smokehouse. Also featured are a 1908 church, a schoolhouse, a general store, a drugstore, nature trails, a boardwalk and a marsh containing native wildlife. An interpretive center offers planetarium shows, nature displays and art exhibits.

Special events are held throughout the year. Pets are not permitted. **Hours:** Mon.-Sat. 9-5, Sun. noon-6. Planetarium shows are offered Sat. at 11, 1 and 3, Sun. at 1 and 3. Closed Jan. 1, Thanksgiving and Christmas. **Cost:** Park $4; $3 (ages 3-12). Planetarium $2. Shows are not recommended for ages 0-3. **Phone:** (334) 794-3452.

**WATER WORLD,** 1 blk. w. of Ross Clark Cir. in Westgate Park at 401 Recreation Rd., has a wave pool, a triple flume slide, the Great White Slide, a children's pool and a play area. **Note:** Only persons wearing swimsuits are permitted in the water.

**Hours:** Mon.-Fri. 10-5 (also Tues. and Thurs. 5-9), Sat. 10-6, Sun. 1-6, Memorial Day weekend-first weekend in Aug.; schedule varies May 1-day before Memorial Day weekend and day after first weekend in Aug.-Sept. 30. **Cost:** $12 (ages 13-59); $9 (ages 3-12); free (ages 60+). Tues. and Thurs. 5-9 p.m. $6; $4.50 (ages 3-12); free (ages 60+). Tube rental $3. **Phone:** (334) 615-3750.

**WIREGRASS MUSEUM OF ART** is just n. off US 84 Bus. Rte. at 126 Museum Ave., just e. of the civic center. The museum features five galleries dedicated to contemporary and regional art as well as a fountain garden area. Housed in a century-old historical building that once served as the city's water and power plant, the museum also offers an interactive children's art gallery, art programs and changing exhibitions. Information outlining the Wiregrass Murals Walking Tour can be obtained here. **Time:** Allow 1 hour minimum. **Hours:** Tues.-Sat. 10-5. Closed major holidays. **Cost:** Donations. **Phone:** (334) 794-3871.

**BEST WESTERN DOTHAN INN & SUITES**
(334)793-4376

Motel
$79

**AAA Benefit:**
Members save up to 20%!

**Address:** 3285 Montgomery Hwy 36303 **Location:** 0.3 mi n of Ross Clark Cir. **Facility:** 150 units, some efficiencies. 2 stories (no elevator), interior/exterior corridors. **Pool(s):** outdoor. **Guest Services:** valet and coin laundry. **Featured Amenity: full hot breakfast.**

## COMFORT SUITES (334)792-9000

WWWW Hotel $74-$129 **Address:** 1650 Westgate Pkwy 36303 **Location:** 0.7 mi n of jct US 231 and 431, just e. **Facility:** 75 units. 3 stories, interior corridors. **Pool(s):** outdoor. **Activities:** exercise room. **Guest Services:** valet and coin laundry.

CALL ⓢⓂ ➋ (BIZ) (HS) 🛜 ✕ 🛢 🖼 🖵 /SOME UNITS 🔌🛏

## COUNTRY INN & SUITES BY CARLSON (334)479-8900

WWWW Hotel $89-$109 **Address:** 3465 Ross Clark Cir 36303 **Location:** Just w of jct US 231; northwest part of town. **Facility:** 64 units. 3 stories, interior corridors. **Terms:** cancellation fee imposed. **Pool(s):** heated indoor. **Activities:** hot tub, exercise room. **Guest Services:** coin laundry.

(¶↑) CALL ⓢⓂ ➋ (BIZ) (HS) 🛜 ✕ 🛢 🖼 🖵

## COURTYARD BY MARRIOTT DOTHAN (334)671-3000

WWWW Hotel $99-$126 **Address:** 3040 Ross Clark Cir 36303 **Location:** Just s of jct US 84; west end of town; behind Shoney's. **Facility:** 78 units. 3 stories, interior corridors. **Pool(s):** indoor. **Activities:** exercise room. **Guest Services:** valet and coin laundry, boarding pass kiosk.

**AAA Benefit:** Members save 5% or more!

(¶) (Ⓨ) CALL ⓢⓂ ➋ (BIZ) 🛜 ✕ 🛢 🖼 🖵

## FAIRFIELD INN BY MARRIOTT DOTHAN (334)671-0100

WWWW Hotel $80-$95 **Address:** 3038 Ross Clark Cir 36301 **Location:** Just s of jct US 84; west end of town. **Facility:** 63 units. 3 stories, interior corridors. **Pool(s):** indoor. **Guest Services:** valet laundry.

**AAA Benefit:** Members save 5% or more!

(¶↑) CALL ⓢⓂ ➋ 🛜 ✕ 🖵 /SOME UNITS 🛢 🖼

## HOLIDAY INN DOTHAN (334)699-1400

WWWW Hotel $111-$123 **Address:** 2740 Ross Clark Cir SW 36301 **Location:** Jct US 231 and 431, 2 mi nw. **Facility:** 100 units. 4 stories, interior corridors. **Pool(s):** outdoor. **Activities:** hot tub, exercise room. **Guest Services:** valet and coin laundry.

(✈) (¶) (🍴) (Ⓨ) CALL ⓢⓂ ➋ (BIZ) (HS) 🛜 ✕ 🛢 🖼 🖵

## LA QUINTA INN & SUITES-DOTHAN (334)793-9090

WWWW Hotel $79-$174 **Address:** 3593 Ross Clark Cir 36303 **Location:** Just w of jct US 231; northwest end of town. **Facility:** 122 units. 5 stories, interior corridors. **Pool(s):** outdoor. **Guest Services:** valet and coin laundry, boarding pass kiosk, area transportation.

(✈) (¶↑) CALL ⓢⓂ ➋ (👨‍👩‍👧) (BIZ) 🛜 🛢 🖼 🖵 /SOME UNITS 🐾

## SLEEP INN & SUITES (334)671-2086

WWW Hotel $70-$95 **Address:** 4654 Montgomery Hwy 36303 **Location:** On US 231, 1.7 mi n of Ross Clark Cir Bypass. **Facility:** 67 units. 3 stories, interior corridors. **Pool(s):** outdoor. **Activities:** exercise room. **Guest Services:** valet and coin laundry.

(¶↑) CALL ⓢⓂ ➋ (HS) 🛜 ✕ 🛢 🖼 🖵

## SUPER 8 (334)792-3232

WW Motel $55-$125 **Address:** 2215 Ross Clark Cir 36301 **Location:** Just w of US 231; south end of town. **Facility:** 44 units, some kitchens. 2 stories (no elevator), exterior corridors. **Pool(s):** outdoor.

(¶↑) ➋ (HS) 🛜 🛢 🖼 🖵

---

Recommend places you'd like us to

inspect at AAA.com/TourBookComments

---

## BASKETCASE CAFE 334/671-1117

WW Sandwiches. Casual Dining. $5-$11 **AAA Inspector Notes:** This casual downtown luncheonette offers a variety of sandwiches, salads and pasta dishes. Be sure to order the yummy signature homemade soup du jour. **Features:** full bar. **Address:** 228 S Oates St 36301 **Location:** Between Crawford and Washington sts; downtown. (L)

## BELLA'S 334/699-3449

WWWW Italian. Fine Dining. $15-$32 **AAA Inspector Notes:** The multilevel dining areas, brick archways and stucco walls create a Tuscan villa ambience, which enhances the classic menu selections. Try lasagna, chicken Marsala or fettuccine Alfredo, and finish your meal with luscious, homemade tiramisu. **Features:** full bar. **Reservations:** suggested. **Address:** 111 W Troy St 36303 **Location:** Between N Foster and N Oates sts; downtown. **Parking:** street only. (D)

## CONESTOGA STEAK HOUSE 334/794-4445

WW Steak. Casual Dining. $10-$21 **AAA Inspector Notes:** A small white residential-style structure houses this no-frills diner. The menu is limited to the house specialty offering a variety of steak cuts cooked to diners' specifications. Friday and Saturday evenings usually draw a crowd, so be prepared to wait. **Features:** beer & wine. **Address:** 3549 Montgomery Hwy 36303 **Location:** 0.8 mi n of Ross Clark Cir. (D)

## CRYSTAL RIVER SEAFOOD 334/794-4153

WW Seafood. Casual Dining. $8-$27 **AAA Inspector Notes:** For generous portions, good service and reasonably priced fresh seafood, this restaurant does not disappoint. **Features:** beer & wine. **Address:** 3460 Ross Clark Cir 36303 **Location:** Just w of jct US 231; northwest part of town. (L) (D)

## DISTRICT RESTAURANT & ULTRA LOUNGE 334/673-2623

WW Burgers. Gastropub. $6-$15 **AAA Inspector Notes:** Geared for the young, mature professional, this upscale establishment offers a variety of entertainment along with a limited menu of specialty burgers, sandwiches and finger foods which are available all night. Weekends are filled with music including frequent battle of the band competitions, upbeat tunes for the dancing crowd and even karaoke night. A dress code and cover charge may apply. **Features:** full bar, patio dining, happy hour. **Address:** 158 N Foster St 36301 **Location:** Between W Main and Troy sts; downtown. **Parking:** street only. (D) (LATE) CALL ⓢⓂ 🐾

## FIRE STONE WOOD FIRED PIZZA & GRILL 334/446-1234

WW Pizza. Casual Dining. $6-$20 **AAA Inspector Notes:** Originally built in the 1930s, this Art Deco building has been fully renovated. Two wood-fired ovens are constantly aglow waiting to bake scrumptious gourmet pizza. Whether dining indoors or out on the patio, guests can enjoy an adult beverage from a wide selection of more than 30 beer brands and 20 wine-by-the-glass offerings. **Features:** full bar, patio dining, happy hour. **Address:** 250 S Oates St 36301 **Location:** Between Crawford and Washington sts; downtown. (L) (D) CALL ⓢⓂ

## HUNT'S SEAFOOD RESTAURANT 334/794-5193

WW Seafood. Casual Dining. $7-$27 **AAA Inspector Notes:** Since 1956, this bustling local favorite has continued its tradition of specializing in seafood prepared in a variety of ways. Chicken, steak and ribs also are available for meat lovers. The casual atmosphere makes for a relaxed dining experience. **Features:** full bar. **Address:** 177 Campbellton Hwy 36301 **Location:** Just s of jct US 231 and 84. (L) (D)

## LA BAMBA MEXICAN CAFE 334/712-4574

W Mexican. Casual Dining. $5-$12 **AAA Inspector Notes:** A taste of old Mexico can be experienced at this colorful and festive eatery. Patrons try burritos or enchiladas with a margarita while viewing the ethnic decor and listening to traditional music. **Features:** full bar. **Address:** 3039 Ross Clark Cir 36301 **Location:** Just s of jct US 84; west end of town. (L) (D)

## LARRY'S REAL PIT BAR-B-Q
334/792-5211

 Barbecue. Casual Dining. $6-$14 **AAA Inspector Notes:** Prompt and friendly service complement large portions of tasty barbecue at this eatery. **Address:** 3115 Ross Clark Cir 36301 **Location:** Just n of jct US 84; west end of town. [L] [D]

## MIA'S ITALIAN RESTAURANT
334/793-6868

Italian. Casual Dining. $6-$15 **AAA Inspector Notes:** Near the intersection of two busy highways sits this simple, locally operated restaurant. Its limited menu features pizzas in various sizes, including a small personal size. Also find some standard pasta dishes and hot or cold subs. **Features:** beer only. **Address:** 2695 S Oates St 36301 **Location:** Jct US 231 and 431, just s. [L] [D] CALL

## MOM'S KITCHEN
334/792-7257

American. Casual Dining. $4-$17 **AAA Inspector Notes:** Simple and basic is what you'll find here, from the rustic log cabin structure to the menu consisting of staple meals that moms make. Breakfast is available all day long. If stopping by midday, be sure to review the extensive weekday lunch specials posted on the wall. The friendly service, hearty portions, good variety and economical prices ensure a return visit. **Address:** 2413 Ross Clark Cir 36301 **Location:** Jct US 431 and 231, 0.8 mi nw; corner of S Park Ave.

[B] [L] [D] CALL

## OLD MEXICO
334/712-1434

Mexican. Casual Dining. $7-$14 **AAA Inspector Notes:** The eatery offers authentic Mexican cuisine in a festive atmosphere. Start with tortilla chips and salsa served on arrival, then mix and match choices from an excellent selection of your favorite entrées. Guests will find a full bar and an attentive staff. **Features:** full bar. **Address:** 2920 Ross Clark Cir 36301 **Location:** 0.8 mi s of jct US 84; west end of town. [L] [D]

## OLD MILL RESTAURANT
334/794-8530

Steak Seafood. Casual Dining. $8-$25 **AAA Inspector Notes:** The upscale establishment specializes in steak and seafood. Fish selections are filleted on the premises and include grouper and salmon along with Gulf shrimp and scallops. The beef is cut in house and marinated in the restaurant's signature sauce. **Features:** full bar, early bird specials. **Address:** 2557 Murphy Mill Rd 36303 **Location:** Jct Ross Clark Cir Bypass, 1.4 mi n on US 231, then just w.

[L] [D] CALL

## THE RED ELEPHANT PIZZA AND GRILL
334/673-7492

Pizza. Family Dining. $7-$13 **AAA Inspector Notes:** When everyone likes different toppings, you can order individual-size pizzas here as well as family-size to please the crowd. Burgers, sandwiches and some pasta and grilled dishes are also on the menu. This is a great place to take the kids, as it has a small arcade. **Features:** full bar. **Address:** 3108 Ross Clark Cir, Suite 4 36303 **Location:** Jct US 84 and 231; in Circle West Shopping Center. [L] [D] CALL

## SUPER CANTON CHINESE RESTAURANT
334/677-6966

Chinese. Quick Serve. $6-$8 **AAA Inspector Notes:** Just the place for a quick and hot meal, this eatery prepares standard Chinese fare for dine-in or take-out. A drive-through window facilitates easy pick-up. **Features:** patio dining. **Address:** 2200 Ross Clark Cir 36301 **Location:** Just w of US 231. [L] [D]

## THAI HOUSE
334/699-2064

Thai. Fine Dining. $9-$24 **AAA Inspector Notes:** This intimate bistro, with fabulous authentic Thai cuisine, offers an upscale contemporary atmosphere. Traditional dishes are custom prepared to adjust for each person's spicy tolerance-ranging from mild to Thai spicy. **Features:** full bar. **Reservations:** suggested. **Address:** 4177 Montgomery Hwy, Suite 10 36303 **Location:** Jct SR 210, 1.2 mi nw on US 231; in Sycamore Place Plaza. [L] [D] CALL

## ZAKI'S MEDITERRANEAN GRILL
334/792-8300

Mediterranean. Casual Dining. $6-$9 **AAA Inspector Notes:** Located on the corner of the southeast entrance to the Wiregrass Commons Mall, this cozy eatery offers a limited menu of well-prepared healthy dishes, such as gyros, greek salad, falafel, dolmades and a nice selection of vegetarian options. The all-inclusive meals for four are a great deal. **Features:** patio dining. **Address:** 109 Anchor Dr 36303 **Location:** Jct US 231 and 431, just e.

[L] [D] CALL

# ENTERPRISE (G-5) pop. 26,562, elev. 349'
• Restaurants p. 76

Enterprise's economy was at a standstill in 1915 after the voracious, snouted boll weevil arrived in Coffee County from Mexico. The half-inch beetle systematically began destroying the area's cotton crop, the sole base of Coffee County's economy. Though farmers bombarded the insect with chemicals and poisons, it succeeded in reducing the crop to one-tenth its usual size.

Out of necessity farmers planted a number of cash crops. Included among them were peanuts, which flourished. The transition to diversified farming was so successful that the town is credited with playing a significant role in the agricultural revolution of the South. The gate city to Fort Rucker Military Reservation (see place listing p. 82), Enterprise today is a blend of agriculture, industry and military interests.

**Enterprise Chamber of Commerce:** 553 Glover Ave., P.O. Box 310577, Enterprise, AL 36331. **Phone:** (334) 347-0581 or (800) 235-4730.

**Self-guiding tours:** The chamber of commerce offers information about a walking tour of Enterprise; the route features historical buildings and a variety of architectural styles.

**BOLL WEEVIL MONUMENT,** in the center of town at jct. Main and College sts., may well be the country's only tribute to an insect. Erected in 1919, it memorializes the destructive beetle that crippled cotton farming throughout the South. The resulting economic shift from agriculture to industry ushered in a new era. An inscription on the statue reads, "In profound appreciation of the Boll Weevil and what it has done as the herald of prosperity." **Hours:** Daily 24 hours. **Cost:** Free. **Phone:** (334) 347-0581 for the chamber of commerce.

## AMERICAS BEST VALUE INN & SUITES
(334)348-2378

Motel $60-$70 **Address:** 101 Access Dr 36330 **Location:** Jct US 84 and SR 167, 0.5 mi w. **Facility:** 45 units. 1 story, exterior corridors. **Pool(s):** outdoor. **Guest Services:** coin laundry.

## BEST WESTERN PLUS CIRCLE INN
(334)393-5248

 Hotel $76-$105

**AAA Benefit:** Members save up to 20%!

**Address:** 715 Boll Weevil Cir 36330 **Location:** Jct US 84 and SR 27, just se. **Facility:** 50 units. 2 stories, interior corridors. **Terms:** cancellation fee imposed. **Pool(s):** outdoor. **Guest Services:** valet and coin laundry.

## QUALITY INN
(334)393-2304

Motel $78-$98 **Address:** 615 Boll Weevil Cir 36330 **Location:** On US 84 Bypass. **Facility:** 78 units, some kitchens. 2 stories (no elevator), exterior corridors. **Pool(s):** outdoor. **Guest Services:** valet and coin laundry.

## WHERE TO EAT

**BRASAS BRAZIL**    334/393-6500

◆◆ Brazilian. Casual Dining. $8-$24 **AAA Inspector Notes:** Dinner at this casual eatery includes the traditional Brazilian Rodizzio, which offers a sampling of roasted meats, carved table side by dashing gauchos. **Features:** beer & wine. **Address:** 8 N Pointe Pkwy 36330 **Location:** Jct US 84 and SR 167, just e, just n.

L  D  CALL ᏜM

**JIN JIN CHINESE RESTAURANT**    334/393-5600

◆ Chinese. Quick Serve. $5-$11 **AAA Inspector Notes:** Although a majority of patrons take out their orders, booths, tables and chairs are available for dining in. All of your favorite dishes are available and quickly prepared to your specifications. Daily luncheon specials are offered. **Address:** 4201 US 84 Bypass, just s of jct SR 248; in West Gate Shopping Center. L  D

**LA LEYENDA 3**    334/347-3336

◆◆ Mexican. Casual Dining. $6-$13 **AAA Inspector Notes:** Tucked away in the rear corner of a shopping center, this spacious restaurant offers quick and friendly service. A wide range of menu options are available, with some creative variations on typical dishes. **Features:** full bar. **Address:** 621 Boll Weevil Cir, Suite 14 36330 **Location:** On US 84 Bypass, just s of jct SR 248; in West Gate Shopping Center. L  D  CALL ᏜM

**MILANO RISTORANTE**    334/308-3238

◆◆ Italian. Family Dining. $6-$25 **AAA Inspector Notes:** This casual, intimate bistro claims to have the best Italian food in town. It offers an array of flavorful pasta dishes, subs and, of course, pizza. No Italian meal is complete without a traditional cannoli or luscious tiramisu. **Features:** beer & wine. **Address:** 5 N Pointe Pkwy 36330 **Location:** Jct US 84 and SR 167, just e, just n.

L  D  CALL ᏜM

## EUFAULA  (F-6) pop. 13,137, elev. 200'

Antebellum houses are the hallmark of Eufaula, named after a tribe of the Creek Confederacy that lived in the region. The Seth Lore Historic District contains 19th-century structures embodying Greek Revival, Italianate and Victorian styles. Many can be seen during the Pilgrimage of Homes held every spring.

Fishing, boating and water skiing are enjoyed on Lake Eufaula, formed by the Walter F. George Lock and Dam on the Chattahoochee River.

**Eufaula-Barbour County Chamber of Commerce:** 333 E. Broad St., Eufaula, AL 36027. **Phone:** (334) 687-6664 or (800) 524-7529.

**Self-guiding tours:** Driving-tour maps that highlight Eufaula's outstanding antebellum houses as well as information about the Pilgrimage of Homes are available at the Shorter Mansion (see attraction listing) and the chamber of commerce.

**EUFAULA NATIONAL WILDLIFE REFUGE,** 7 mi. n. on US 431, then 2 mi. e. to 367 SR 165, is an 11,184-acre refuge on the Chattahoochee River that provides a feeding and resting habitat for migratory waterfowl. It houses more than 280 species of birds, including ducks, geese, egrets and herons, as well as such woodland mammals as beavers, foxes, deer and bobcats. The refuge has nature displays in the administrative office, a nature trail and two observation towers. **Hours:** Refuge daily dawn-dusk. Office Mon.-Fri. 8-4:30. Closed major holidays. **Cost:** Free. **Phone:** (334) 687-4065.

SAVE  **FENDALL HALL** is 1 mi. w. off US 431 at 917 W. Barbour St. Built around 1860, the Italianate-style Fendall Hall was home to five generations of the Young family. Now a house museum, the structure has been restored to depict the second generation's residency (1880-1917). Highlights include hand-painted murals in three of the first-floor rooms, a black and white marble entrance floor and Italian marble fireplaces. The house is furnished with period pieces, including some family items; the primary furnishing styles are Empire and Eastlake.

**Time:** Allow 30 minutes minimum. **Hours:** Mon.-Fri. and first Sat. of the month 10-4. Closed state

▼ See AAA listing p. 77 ▼

holidays. **Cost:** $5; $4 (ages 65+); $3 (ages 6-18). **Phone:** (334) 687-8469. ⟨GT⟩

⟨SAVE⟩ **SHORTER MANSION,** on US 431 at 340 N. Eufaula Ave., is an outstanding example of neo-classic architecture. Built in 1884 by wealthy cotton planter Eli Sims Shorter II, the mansion was enlarged and completed in 1906. The restored house is furnished with antiques. **Hours:** Mon.-Sat. 10-4. Closed Jan. 1, Memorial Day, July 4, Labor Day, Thanksgiving, Christmas Eve and Christmas. Phone ahead to confirm schedule. **Cost:** $5; $3 (ages 5-12). **Phone:** (334) 687-3793 or (888) 383-2852.

**BAYMONT INN & SUITES EUFAULA**     (334)687-7747
◈◈ **Motel** $59-$99 **Address:** 136 Towne Center Blvd 36027 **Location:** On US 431, 1 mi s of US 82 E. **Facility:** 40 units. 2 stories (no elevator), exterior corridors. **Pool(s):** outdoor. **Activities:** exercise room. *(See ad p. 76.)*

⟨🛎⟩ ⟨🍽⟩ ⟨📶⟩ ⟨🛗⟩ ⟨📷⟩ ⟨🖥⟩ / SOME UNITS ⟨🐾⟩

**EUFAULA COMFORT SUITES**     (334)616-0114
◈◈◈ **Hotel** $105-$140 **Address:** 12 Paul Lee Pkwy 36027 **Location:** 1.7 mi s on US 431 from jct US 82 E, just e. **Facility:** 54 units. 2 stories, interior corridors. **Pool(s):** heated indoor. **Activities:** sauna, hot tub, exercise room.

CALL ⟨🖥⟩ ⟨🛎⟩ ⟨BIZ⟩ ⟨📶⟩ ⟨✕⟩ ⟨🛗⟩ ⟨📷⟩ ⟨🖥⟩ / SOME UNITS ⟨🐾⟩

### WHERE TO EAT

**THE CAJUN CORNER**     334/616-0816
◈◈ Cajun. Casual Dining. $8-$23 **AAA Inspector Notes:** This downtown eatery, in the historic Bluff City Inn, offers a bit of New Orleans in both décor and menu. Decorated in a Mardi Gras theme, this cafe offers such Cajun dishes as seafood gumbo, crawfish etouffée and red beans and rice. **Features:** full bar, patio dining. **Address:** 114 N Eufaula Ave 36027 **Location:** Corner of W Broad St and US 431; in historic downtown area. **Parking:** street only.

⟨L⟩ ⟨D⟩ ⟨🐾⟩

**RIVER CITY GRILL**     334/616-6550
◈◈◈ American. Casual Dining. $7-$27 **AAA Inspector Notes:** Located across the street from the town green gazebo, this locally-owned restaurant and lounge offers small-town charm. On Saturday they are open only for dinner. **Features:** full bar. **Address:** 209 E Broad St 36027 **Location:** Just e of N Randolph Ave; downtown. **Parking:** street only. ⟨L⟩ ⟨D⟩ CALL ⟨🖥⟩

## EVERGREEN pop. 3,944

**ECONO LODGE INN & SUITES**     (251)578-2100
◈◈ **Motel** $65-$80 **Address:** 215 Hwy 83 36401 **Location:** I-65 exit 96, just w. **Facility:** 40 units. 2 stories (no elevator), exterior corridors.

⟨🛎⟩ ⟨HS⟩ ⟨📶⟩ ⟨🛗⟩ ⟨📷⟩ ⟨🖥⟩ / SOME UNITS ⟨🐾⟩

**SLEEP INN & SUITES**     (251)578-9590
◈◈◈ **Hotel** $99-$110 **Address:** 78 Liberty Hill Pl 36401 **Location:** I-65 exit 96, just ne. **Facility:** 56 units. 3 stories, interior corridors. **Pool(s):** outdoor. **Activities:** exercise room. **Guest Services:** coin laundry.

CALL ⟨🖥⟩ ⟨🛎⟩ ⟨📶⟩ ⟨🛗⟩ ⟨📷⟩ ⟨🖥⟩ / SOME UNITS ⟨🐾⟩

### WHERE TO EAT

**BLACK ANGUS RESTAURANT**     251/578-5777
◈◈◈ Steak. Casual Dining. $8-$26 **AAA Inspector Notes:** This locally-owned-and-operated restaurant proudly identifies itself as the only steakhouse in the region. Its location right off the interstate makes it a good dining option while traveling through the area. **Features:** full bar. **Address:** 1545 Ted Bates Rd 36401 **Location:** I-65 exit 96, just w. ⟨L⟩ ⟨D⟩ CALL ⟨🖥⟩

**BUBBA'S BBQ**     251/578-4770
◈ Barbecue. Quick Serve. $5-$16 **AAA Inspector Notes:** Not far off the interstate, this corrugated metal rib shack is set back slightly off the road and can be easily bypassed. Slow-cooked barbecue of pork, beef or chicken is ready to be served for a quick, hearty meal. Inside and out, the place is covered with vintage metal signs of a simpler time. **Address:** 281 Hwy 83 36401 **Location:** I-65 exit 96, 1 mi s. ⟨L⟩ ⟨D⟩

**SHRIMP BASKET**     251/216-3223
◈◈ Seafood. Casual Dining. $6-$14 **AAA Inspector Notes:** Seafood abounds in this casual, nautical atmosphere. Shrimp, oysters and fish can be steamed, grilled or fried. Burgers and chicken are available for meat lovers. Rotating nightly all-you-can-eat specials are offered. **Features:** full bar, patio dining. **Address:** 64 Liberty Hill Pl 36401 **Location:** I-65 exit 96, just e. ⟨L⟩ ⟨D⟩ CALL ⟨🖥⟩

## FAIRHOPE (I-2) pop. 15,326, elev. 125'
**• Hotels p. 78 • Restaurants p. 78**

Founded upon utopian ideals, Fairhope was established in 1894 by Henry George and several families who funded the colony with a Single Tax System. Under the plan, residents hold a renewable 99-year lease on their land and own all improvements. The single tax colony pays all taxes. Civic pride and idealism still prevail as evidenced by the city's attractively landscaped streets and profusion of flowering gardens. An artistic migration accounts for the resort's many unusual downtown shops, galleries and restaurants. Every year in March, the artistic theme is carried over into the ◈ Arts and Crafts Festival of Fairhope that is held downtown and spans 3 days.

On a bluff above Mobile Bay, Fairhope's 2 miles of beach are the setting for local yachting competitions in the summer. Flounder, crab and shrimp can be caught easily during Jubilee, Mobile Bay's natural late-summer phenomenon in which bottom-dwelling marine life, delirious because of a sudden lack of oxygen in the water, head toward the shore. When alarms sound, every available bucket, cooking pot and washbasin is enlisted to harvest this seafood bonanza.

At the marina, the Fairhope Pier extends a quarter of a mile into the bay, providing good fishing and panoramic views of the surrounding area.

**Eastern Shore Chamber of Commerce & Visitor Center:** 327 Fairhope Ave., Fairhope, AL 36532. **Phone:** (251) 928-6387 or (251) 621-8222.

**Shopping areas:** Downtown Fairhope features art galleries and numerous antique, book, craft, clothing and gift shops.

**EASTERN SHORE ART CENTER,** 401 Oak St., has four galleries presenting exhibits that change monthly. Displays include paintings, photographs, sculpture, pottery, baskets and canvas art. Visitors also can view artists working in the center's fine arts academy classes. **Time:** Allow 30 minutes minimum. **Hours:** Tues.-Fri. 10-4, Sat. 10-2. Closed major holidays. **Cost:** Free. **Phone:** (251) 928-2228.

**WEEKS BAY NATIONAL ESTUARINE RESEARCH RESERVE,** 14 mi. e. to 11300 US 98, is a 6,525-acre reserve focusing on the Weeks Bay estuary that provides a rich, diverse habitat for a variety of fish and crustaceans. Its broad, shallow waters are fed by tributaries branching off from the Fish and Magnolia Rivers.

A visitor center displays a collection of regional plants and live animals. Self-guiding nature trails and boardwalks wind through wetlands, marshes and forests. **Time:** Allow 1 hour minimum. **Hours:** Mon.-Sat. 9-5. Visitor center closed state and federal holidays. **Cost:** Free. **Phone:** (251) 928-9792.

---

HAMPTON INN FAIRHOPE-MOBILE BAY          (251)928-0956

▼▼▼▼ Hotel $99-$179 **Address:** 23 N Section St 36532 **Location:** Just n of jct CR 48 (Fairhope Ave); in historic downtown. **Facility:** 89 units. 4 stories, interior corridors. **Terms:** 1-7 night minimum stay, cancellation fee imposed. **Pool(s):** outdoor. **Activities:** exercise room. **Guest Services:** valet and coin laundry.

**AAA Benefit:** Members save 5% or more!

---

KEY WEST INN          (251)990-7373

▼▼ Motel $54-$119 **Address:** 231 S Greeno Rd 36532 **Location:** On US 98, 1.9 mi s of jct SR 104. **Facility:** 54 units. 2 stories (no elevator), exterior corridors. **Terms:** cancellation fee imposed. **Pool(s):** outdoor. **Guest Services:** coin laundry.

---

## WHERE TO EAT

THE FAIRHOPE INN & RESTAURANT          251/928-6226

▼▼▼ Regional American. Casual Dining. $12-$36 **AAA Inspector Notes:** A Louisiana influence flavors contemporary preparations of seafood, beef, pork, veal, chicken and duck. The restaurant's attractive bed-and-breakfast-style setting includes an enclosed veranda and decor featuring gilded mirrors and antiques. **Features:** full bar, patio dining, Sunday brunch. **Reservations:** suggested. **Address:** 63 S Church St 36532 **Location:** Just s of Fairhope Ave; center. L D

---

JULWIN'S SOUTHERN COUNTRY RESTAURANT
251/990-9372

▼▼ Southern Comfort Food. Casual Dining. $6-$10 **AAA Inspector Notes:** *Classic.* Located in the heart of the retail district, Baldwin County's oldest restaurant has been serving up country-style breakfasts and lunches since 1945. **Address:** 411 Fairhope Ave 36532 **Location:** Between Bancroft and Section sts; downtown. **Parking:** street only. B L

---

MARKET BY THE BAY CAFE          251/929-7203

▼ Seafood. Quick Serve. $8-$18 **AAA Inspector Notes:** Shrimp, oysters and fish are the staple of this popular no-frills roadside café where you can either eat in or take out. On Sunday and Monday only lunch is served. **Features:** full bar. **Address:** 365 S Greeno Rd 36532 **Location:** On US 98, 2 mi s of jct SR 104. B L D

---

MARY ANN'S          251/928-3663

▼ Deli. Casual Dining. $6-$17 **AAA Inspector Notes:** This cheerful, bustling place has been a fixture in the heart of Fairhope since 1984. To add a personal touch, Mary Ann is often wandering around greeting her guests. The breakfast menu offers a pre-made egg casserole, French toast and muffins. Quiche of the day and custom-made sandwiches are available all day. The lunch selection also includes soups and salads. **Features:** beer & wine, patio dining. **Address:** 85 N Bancroft St 36532 **Location:** Corner of Equality St; downtown; in Windmill Market. **Parking:** street only. L

---

MASTER JOE'S          251/928-8668

▼▼ Asian Sushi. Casual Dining. $11-$36 **AAA Inspector Notes:** The popularity of this Asian bistro is a testament to the quality of its delicious and distinctive menu selections. Sushi Master Xian Joe Ou, a China native, studied his craft for 10 years in Japan before bringing his talents to the United States. **Time:** Allow 1 hour minimum. **Address:** 21 N Section St 36532 **Location:** Jct CR 48 (Fairhope Ave) and 3 (N Section St), just n; in historic downtown. **Parking:** street only. L D CALL

---

## FAYETTE (C-2) pop. 4,619, elev. 364'

**FAYETTE ART MUSEUM** is 1 mi. n. of CR 18 at 530 N. Temple Ave. Boasting a 3,500-piece collection, the museum features fine art and six folk art galleries with works by such artists as Sybil Gibson; the Rev. Benjamin Perkins; Mose Tolliver; and Jimmy Lee Sudduth, who used mud, sand, grass and berries in his art. **Time:** Allow 1 hour minimum. **Hours:** Mon.-Fri. 9-noon and 1-4. Closed major holidays. **Cost:** Free. **Phone:** (205) 932-8727.

---

ROSE HOUSE INN          (205)932-4744

▼▼▼ Historic Bed & Breakfast $79-$109 **Address:** 325 2nd Ave NW 35555 **Location:** 0.3 mi w on SR 18, 0.3 mi n. Located in a residential area. **Facility:** This restored historic home—and the adjacent, more modern guest house—is set back from the street, centered in a nicely landscaped yard of mature oak trees. Relax on a wrap-around porch or under a shady gazebo. 10 units, some two bedrooms. 2 stories (no elevator), interior corridors. *Bath:* some shared. **Terms:** 7 day cancellation notice-fee imposed.

---

## FLORENCE (A-2) pop. 39,319, elev. 580'

• Restaurants p. 80

Florence is the largest of the four cities in the Muscle Shoals Area *(see place listing p. 129).* Incorporated in 1818—a year before Alabama became a state—Florence began as a trading post on a westbound stagecoach route.

Ferdinand Sannoner, an Italian engineer commissioned to design the new city, named it after his birthplace in Italy. Florence's parks and plazas express Sannoner's vision while accommodating an expanding industrial base. Major electrometallurgical and aluminum-, rubber- and steel-fabricating plants are in the area.

Wilson Dam, east of Florence on SR 133, possesses one of the world's highest single-lift navigation locks, which lift commercial and pleasure boats up to 100 feet in a single operation. Under Tennessee Valley Authority (TVA) control since 1933, the dam, 4,541 feet long and 137 feet high, also boasts the largest hydroelectric generating capacity of all the TVA dams.

Oscar DePriest, the first African-American man to serve in Congress, and William Christopher "W.C." Handy, famed blues composer, were born in Florence. Handy earned the title "Father of the Blues" through such compositions as "St. Louis Blues" and "Memphis Blues." Handy is honored by jazz and blues artists during the 10-day long W.C. Handy Festival, held in late July. In Florence, the Fourth of July is synonymous with the ⚑ Spirit of Freedom Celebration, when thousands gather in McFarland Park along the Tennessee River to enjoy food, music, fireworks and family activities. The ⚑ Alabama Renaissance Faire is a 2-day event featuring magicians, knights on horseback, sword fighting, arts and crafts, and food. The fair takes place in Wilson Park in late October.

**Florence/Lauderdale Tourism Office:** One Hightower Pl., Florence, AL 35630. **Phone:** (256) 740-4141 or (888) 356-8687.

**Shopping areas:** Florence's leading retail center is Regency Square Mall, 1.25 miles west of US 43. It has Belk, Dillard's, JCPenney and Sears.

**CHILDREN'S MUSEUM OF THE SHOALS** is at 2810 Darby Dr. at the entrance to Diebert Park. The hands-on exhibits, mainly about the local area, encourage young visitors to learn using their imaginations and creativity. In the adjacent park are a playground and walking trails. **Time:** Allow 2 hours minimum. **Hours:** Thurs.-Sat. 10-4:30. Closed major holidays. **Cost:** $5; free (ages 0-1). **Phone:** (256) 765-0500. 🅰️

**FRANK LLOYD WRIGHT ROSENBAUM HOUSE MUSEUM** is at 601 Riverview Dr., off Dr. Hicks Blvd. Houses in Frank Lloyd Wright's Usonian genre were designed to provide low-cost yet elegant suburban homes for individual middle income families, homes that would grow and evolve as the family grew and evolved. The flat, multilevel roof and overhanging eaves, the board-and-batten walls, the expanses of glass, the flowing space and the hot-water heating system embedded in the concrete floor are Usonian hallmarks.

Originally 1,540 square feet, the cypress, glass and brick Rosenbaum residence was completed in 1940; two Wright-designed wings, totaling 1,080 square feet, were added in 1948. The Rosenbaums lived in the house until 1999, when the city purchased the home and its Wright-designed furniture and began a meticulous restoration.

**Time:** Allow 1 hour minimum. **Hours:** Guided tours Tues.-Sat. 10-4, Sun. 1-4. Last tour begins 30 minutes before closing. Closed major holidays. **Cost:** $8; $5 (ages 62+ and students with ID). **Phone:** (256) 740-8899. 🄶🅣

**INDIAN MOUND AND MUSEUM,** 1028 S. Court St., is one of the largest domiciliary Native American mounds in the Tennessee Valley. The pre-Columbian mound measures 43 feet high with a summit that is 145 feet by 94 feet. A museum features 10,000-year-old artifacts. **Hours:** Tues.-Sat. 10-4. Closed major holidays. **Cost:** $2; 50c (students with ID). **Phone:** (256) 760-6427. 🄶🅣

**POPE'S TAVERN MUSEUM,** 203 Hermitage Dr., was a stagecoach stop and inn during the early 1800s and later a hospital for Confederate and Union soldiers during the Civil War. The museum has Civil War memorabilia and rare antiques. **Time:** Allow 30 minutes minimum. **Hours:** Tues.-Sat. 10-4. Closed major holidays. **Cost:** $2; 50c (students with ID). **Phone:** (256) 760-6439. 🄶🅣

**W.C. HANDY HOME AND MUSEUM,** 620 W. College St. at jct. Marengo St., is the birthplace of composer and musician William C. Handy. Known as "Father of the Blues," Handy was born in the log cabin Nov. 16, 1873. The house contains his piano, trumpet, memorabilia and tributes from renowned people. **Time:** Allow 30 minutes minimum. **Hours:** Tues.-Sat. 10-4. Closed major holidays. **Cost:** $2; 50c (students with ID). **Phone:** (256) 760-6434. 🄶🅣

---

COMFORT SUITES FLORENCE                256/246-2300
▽▽▽ **Hotel. Rates not provided. Address:** 140 Matthew Paul Ct 35630 **Location:** Jct SR 133 (Cox Creek Pkwy), just ne on US 43/72, just n. **Facility:** 68 units. 4 stories, interior corridors. **Pool(s):** heated indoor. **Activities:** hot tub, exercise room. **Guest Services:** valet and coin laundry.
🅟 CALL 🄻Ⓜ 🛆 BIZ HS 📶 ✕ 🛏 🖥 🍺

---

HAMPTON INN & SUITES - DOWNTOWN FLORENCE
                                        (256)767-8282
▽▽▽ **Hotel** $104-$134 **Address:** 505 S Court St 35630 **Location:** On US 43/72; jct SR 17 and 157. **Facility:** 88 units. 5 stories, interior corridors. **Terms:** check-in 4 pm, 1-7 night minimum stay, cancellation fee imposed. **Pool(s):** heated indoor. **Activities:** hot tub, exercise room. **Guest Services:** valet and coin laundry.

> **AAA Benefit:** Members save 5% or more!

CALL 🄻Ⓜ 🛆 BIZ HS 📶 🛏 🖥 🍺

---

HAMPTON INN FLORENCE MIDTOWN           (256)764-8888
▽▽▽ **Hotel** $99-$109 **Address:** 2281 Florence Blvd 35630 **Location:** On US 43/72, 0.4 mi nw of jct SR 133 (Cox Creek Pkwy). Located in a busy commercial area. **Facility:** 90 units. 4 stories, interior corridors. **Terms:** 1-7 night minimum stay, cancellation fee imposed. **Pool(s):** outdoor. **Activities:** exercise room. **Guest Services:** valet and coin laundry.

> **AAA Benefit:** Members save 5% or more!

🅟 🛆 BIZ 📶 🛏 🖥 🍺

---

## MARRIOTT SHOALS HOTEL & SPA  (256)246-3600

Hotel
$159-$245

MARRIOTT

**AAA Benefit:**
Members save 5% or more!

**Address:** 10 Hightower Pl 35630 **Location:** Waterfront. Jct US 43/72 and SR 133 (Cox Creek Pkwy S), 1.5 mi s; just n of Wilson Dam. Located in a quiet area. **Facility:** Overlooking the Tennessee River, this upscale hotel offers the finest accommodations in North Alabama. Relax in the on-site spa or resort-style outdoor pool, or enjoy an evening meal around outdoor fire pits. 199 units. 6 stories, interior corridors. **Parking:** on-site and valet, winter plug-ins. **Terms:** check-in 4 pm. **Amenities:** safes. **Dining:** 360 Grille, see separate listing, entertainment. **Pool(s):** outdoor, heated indoor. **Activities:** sauna, hot tub, steamroom, fishing, playground, game room, trails, exercise room, spa. **Guest Services:** valet and coin laundry, area transportation.

---

### WHERE TO EAT

## 360 GRILLE  256/246-3660

Regional
American
Fine Dining
$20-$70

**AAA Inspector Notes:** While rotating in the circular restaurant, twenty-two stories high above the Tennessee Valley, diners can expect stunning views and creatively prepared dry-aged steaks, chops and fresh fish. Using ingredients supplied by local organic farms and hydroponic greenhouses, the seasonal menu changes four times a year. A three-course chefs tasting menu is available with wine pairings from the exceptional list of more than 115 stocked bottles. **Features:** full bar, happy hour. **Reservations:** suggested. **Address:** 10 Hightower Pl 35630 **Location:** Jct US 43/72 and SR 133 (Cox Creek Pkwy S), 1.5 mi s; just n of Wilson Dam; in Marriott Shoals Hotel & Spa.

### RICATONI'S ITALIAN GRILL  256/718-1002

Italian. Casual Dining. $10-$25 **AAA Inspector Notes:** Since 1996, this ristorante has served up numerous wood-oven baked pizza and Old World pasta entrées. The friendly atmosphere and service brings the customers back often. **Features:** beer & wine. **Address:** 107 N Court St 35630 **Location:** Between Tennessee and W Mobile sts; downtown. **Parking:** street only.

### UMI JAPANESE STEAKHOUSE  256/718-6868

Japanese Sushi. Casual Dining. $7-$30 **AAA Inspector Notes:** Sushi, hibachi and other Asian dishes await you at this attractive, contemporary Asian-themed restaurant. **Features:** full bar. **Address:** 201 N Cox Creek Pkwy 35630 **Location:** Jct US 43/72 and SR 133 (Cox Creek Pkwy).

Keep Your Hands, Eyes and Mind on the Road

AAA.com/distraction

## FOLEY (I-2) pop. 14,618

**Shopping areas:** More than 120 factory outlet stores, including Banana Republic, Brooks Brothers, Gap Outlet, Polo Ralph Lauren, Seiko and Tommy Hilfiger, comprise [SAVE] Tanger Outlet Stores, 2601 S. McKenzie St. (SR 59).

## BEST WESTERN RIVIERA INN  (251)943-8600

Motel
$75-$140

Best Western

**AAA Benefit:**
Members save up to 20%!

**Address:** 1504 S McKenzie St 36535 **Location:** On SR 59, 1.1 mi s of jct US 98. **Facility:** 42 units. 2 stories (no elevator), exterior corridors. **Terms:** cancellation fee imposed. **Pool(s):** outdoor. **Activities:** exercise room. **Guest Services:** coin laundry.

### COMFORT SUITES  (251)923-2610

Hotel $85-$190 **Address:** 150 W Riviera Blvd 36535 **Location:** 1.8 mi s of jct US 98 and SR 59, just w. **Facility:** 62 units. 3 stories, interior corridors. **Terms:** check-in 4 pm. **Pool(s):** heated indoor. **Activities:** exercise room. **Guest Services:** coin laundry.

### ECONO LODGE & SUITES  (251)943-9100

Hotel
$55-$109

**Address:** 2682 S McKenzie St 36535 **Location:** On SR 59, 1.9 mi s of jct US 98. **Facility:** 82 units. 3 stories, exterior corridors. **Terms:** check-in 4 pm. **Pool(s):** outdoor. **Activities:** hot tub, exercise room. **Guest Services:** coin laundry.

### WHERE TO EAT

### THE GIFT HORSE RESTAURANT  251/943-3663

Southern. Casual Dining. $11-$16 **AAA Inspector Notes:** Historic. Experience true Southern hospitality and cuisine at this 1912 landmark restaurant, with its "groaning" 28-foot mahogany table from 1840. Diners help themselves to seafood gumbo, praline sweet potatoes and, perhaps, fried chicken. The buffet table provides a daily changing menu. Your server will ensure your glass is full and empty plates are taken away promptly. **Address:** 209 W Laurel Ave 36535 **Location:** On US 98, just w of jct SR 59. **Parking:** street only.

### LAMBERT'S CAFE  251/943-7655

Comfort Food. Family Dining. $12-$22 **AAA Inspector Notes:** Tired of the same old approach to serving dinner rolls? Then perhaps the "home of throwed rolls" is for you! With its rural American decor, home-cooking menu and bread literally thrown to you from across the room, this eatery definitely is a novelty. **Address:** 2981 S McKenzie St 36535 **Location:** SR 59, 2.4 mi s of jct US 98.

### SHRIMP BASKET  251/943-6643

Seafood. Family Dining. $7-$14 **AAA Inspector Notes:** Seafood abounds in this casual, nautical atmosphere. Shrimp, oysters and fish can be steamed, grilled or fried. Burgers and chicken are available for meat lovers. Changing nightly all-you-can-eat specials are offered. **Features:** full bar. **Address:** 1500 S McKenzie St 36535 **Location:** On SR 59, 1.1 mi s of jct US 98.

WOLF BAY LODGE                                251/987-5129

WWW Seafood. Casual Dining. $6-$30 **AAA Inspector Notes:** Founded in 1973, this establishment has risen from the ashes twice. In 2004, Hurricane Ivan destroyed it, and again in 2008, it burned to the ground. You can't keep this family-owned-and-operated enterprise down, though, as it's once again serving the community. The rustic hunting lodge atmosphere is complete with mounted game heads and fish on the knotty pine walls. A fieldstone fireplace helps keep the clientèle warm. **Features:** full bar. **Address:** 20801 Miflin Rd 36535 **Location:** Jct SR 59 and CR 20, 0.8 mi e.

L   D   CALL 🅰M

## FORT MITCHELL (F-6) elev. 354'

**FORT MITCHELL NATIONAL CEMETERY,** 6 mi. s. of US 431 at 553 SR 165, contains the graves of military personnel from World War I to Operation Desert Storm. Five archeological sites, including prehistoric upland campsites, historic Creek settlements, the Fort Mitchell Military Post area, a Creek trading house and a log school building, are in and around the cemetery. **Hours:** Cemetery daily dawn-dusk. Office Mon.-Fri. 8-4:30. **Cost:** Free. **Phone:** (334) 855-4731.

## FORT PAYNE (B-5) pop. 14,012, elev. 897'

Fort Payne is associated with interesting geological formations and Native American history, the latter embodied in the nearby Cherokee town of Willston, established in 1779. The town of Fort Payne was established in the late 19th century around the stockade that held the Cherokees prior to their forced westward migration on the Trail of Tears.

Fort Payne's Opera House, in the center of town, was built in 1889 and is the oldest active theater in Alabama. Restored as a cultural arts center, the opera house can be toured by appointment; phone (256) 845-6888.

South of town, Little River Canyon National Preserve's 14,000 acres offer recreational opportunities to suit most any taste. Kayaking, picnicking, rock climbing, bird-watching, mountain biking, hiking, swimming and canoeing are among the outdoor pursuits to be enjoyed. The Little River, which flows atop Lookout Mountain, has created waterfalls, canyons and sandstone cliffs, all of which can be appreciated from numerous overlooks along a scenic rim drive. DeSoto State Park *(see attraction listing and Recreation Areas Chart)* is within the preserve. For additional information contact the preserve's headquarters at 4322 Little River Trail N.E., Suite 100; phone (256) 845-9605.

**DeKalb Tourism:** 1503 Glenn Blvd. S.W., P.O. Box 681165, Fort Payne, AL 35968. **Phone:** (256) 845-3957 or (888) 805-4740.

**ALABAMA FAN CLUB AND MUSEUM,** 101 Glenn Blvd., is at jct. SR 35 and US 11, 1 mi. e. of I-59 exit 218. The museum traces the career of the country music band Alabama and displays costumes, musical instruments and awards, including the group's gold and platinum records. **Time:** Allow 30 minutes minimum. **Hours:** Wed.-Sat. 9-5, Sun. 1-5. **Cost:** $3; $2 (ages 56+); $1.50 (ages 0-11). **Phone:** (256) 845-1646.

**DEPOT MUSEUM,** just s.e. off US 11 at 105 5th St. N.E., is in an 1891 Richardsonian Romanesque-style railroad depot. Exhibits include Native American artifacts, 19th-century farm and office equipment, photographs and household items from the late 1800s and early 1900s, a caboose, and more than 90 dioramas depicting nursery rhymes and historic events. **Time:** Allow 30 minutes minimum. **Hours:** Wed.-Fri. 10-3, Sun. 2-3:45. Last admission 30 minutes before closing. Closed major holidays. **Cost:** $3; $1 (ages 7-18). **Phone:** (256) 845-5714.

**DESOTO STATE PARK** is at 7104 DeSoto Pkwy. N.E. The range known as Lookout Mountain runs through the park, which is situated along the west fork of the Little River. The river flows into Little Canyon National Preserve. Also within the park is DeSoto Falls, which drops 100 feet.

Hiking and biking trails extend throughout the park. A swimming pool operates Memorial Day through Labor Day. Lookout Mountain Parkway, a scenic road, passes through the park. *See Recreation Areas Chart.* **Hours:** Daily dawn-dusk. **Cost:** Park free. Picnic area $1 per person. Swimming pool $3. **Phone:** (256) 845-5380 or (800) 568-8840.

🅰 🍴 ✖ 🏕

DAYS INN                                      (256)845-2085

WW◆ Motel $66-$76 **Address:** 1416 Glenn Blvd SW 35968 **Location:** I-59 exit 218, just w. **Facility:** 65 units. 2 stories (no elevator), exterior corridors. **Terms:** 3 day cancellation notice. **Pool(s):** outdoor. **Guest Services:** valet and coin laundry.

🍴 ⊳ 📶 🔲 ▭ ▱ / SOME UNITS 🔲

HAMPTON INN                                  (256)304-2600

WWW◆ Hotel $109-$159 **Address:** 1201 Jordan Rd SW 35968 **Location:** I-59 exit 218, just w. **Facility:** 58 units. 4 stories, interior corridors. **Terms:** 1-7 night minimum stay, cancellation fee imposed. **Pool(s):** heated indoor. **Activities:** exercise room. **Guest Services:** valet and coin laundry.

**AAA Benefit:** Members save 5% or more!

🍴 CALL 🅰M ⊳ BIZ HS 📶 🔲 ▭ ▱

HOLIDAY INN EXPRESS & SUITES        (256)997-1020

▽▽▽▽
Hotel
$99-$199

**Address:** 112 Airport Rd W 35968 **Location:** I-59 exit 218, just w. **Facility:** 60 units. 3 stories, interior corridors. **Terms:** cancellation fee imposed. **Pool(s):** heated outdoor. **Activities:** limited exercise equipment. **Guest Services:** valet and coin laundry. **Featured Amenity:** full hot breakfast.

 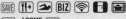
SAVE 🍴 ⊳ BIZ 📶 🔲 ▭

▱ / SOME UNITS HS

## FORT RUCKER MILITARY RESERVATION (G-5)

**U.S. ARMY AVIATION MUSEUM** is on SR 249, 10 mi. s. of US 231, at the Fort Rucker Army Post, Building 6000. The museum contains an extensive collection of U.S. Army aircraft, with emphasis on the evolution of the helicopter. Many one-of-a-kind planes are displayed.

Exhibits include an R4-B, the first military production helicopter; an AH-64 Apache combat helicopter; and several World War I aircraft. **Note:** Visitors ages 16 and older must have photo ID. Vehicle registration and proof of insurance must also be presented. **Time:** Allow 1 hour, 30 minutes minimum. **Hours:** Mon.-Sat. 9-4, Sun. noon-4. Closed Jan. 1, Thanksgiving, Christmas Eve, Christmas and Dec. 31. **Cost:** Free. **Phone:** (334) 255-3036 or (888) 276-9286.

## FULTONDALE pop. 8,380
- **Hotels & Restaurants map & index p. 54**
- **Part of Birmingham area — see map p. 43**

**COMFORT SUITES**　　　　　　　(205)259-2160
▼▼▼ Hotel $95-$114 **Address:** 1325 Old Walker Chapel Rd 35068 **Location:** I-65 exit 267, just e to Park St, then just s. **Facility:** 70 units. 3 stories, interior corridors. **Pool(s):** heated indoor. **Activities:** hot tub, exercise room. **Guest Services:** valet and coin laundry.

**FAIRFIELD INN & SUITES BY MARRIOTT BIRMINGHAM FULTONDALE/I-65**　　　　(205)849-8484
▼▼▼▼ Hotel $104-$175 **Address:** 1795 Morris Ave 35068 **Location:** I-65 exit 267, 0.7 mi e. **Facility:** 75 units. 3 stories, interior corridors. **Pool(s):** heated indoor. **Activities:** hot tub, exercise room. **Guest Services:** valet and coin laundry.

**AAA Benefit:** Members save 5% or more!

**HAMPTON INN**　　　　　　　(205)439-6700
▼▼▼ Hotel $99-$144 **Address:** 1716 Fulton Rd 35068 **Location:** I-65 exit 267, just e. **Facility:** 64 units. 4 stories, interior corridors. **Terms:** 1-7 night minimum stay, cancellation fee imposed. **Pool(s):** outdoor. **Activities:** exercise room. **Guest Services:** valet laundry.

**AAA Benefit:** Members save 5% or more!

**HOLIDAY INN EXPRESS & SUITES BIRMINGHAM-FULTONDALE**　　(205)439-6300
▼▼▼ Hotel $89-$169 **Address:** 1733 Fulton Rd 35068 **Location:** I-65 exit 267, just e. **Facility:** 67 units. 3 stories, interior corridors. **Pool(s):** outdoor. **Activities:** limited exercise equipment. **Guest Services:** valet and coin laundry.

Ask about on-the-go vehicle

battery testing and replacement

### WHERE TO EAT

**CASA FIESTA**　　　　　　205/849-0062　(86)
▼▼ Mexican. Casual Dining. $7-$25 **AAA Inspector Notes:** Expect generous portions of favorite South of the Border foods at this festive cantina along with fast and friendly service. **Features:** full bar. **Address:** 3417 Lowery Pkwy, Suite 103 35068 **Location:** I-65 exit 267, just e, then just s; in shopping plaza next to Books-A-Million.

**STIX**　　　　　　　　205/849-9677　(87)
▼▼ Asian. Casual Dining. $8-$33 **AAA Inspector Notes:** It's like three restaurants in one location, as you can dine on sushi, hibachi or Chinese/Japanese cuisine. Expect a feast for your eyes as well as your appetite thanks to an entertaining presentation by the grill chefs and the colorful, whimsical dishes created by the sushi masters. **Features:** full bar. **Address:** 3405 Lowery Pkwy 35068 **Location:** I-65 exit 267, just e, then 0.5 mi s on Frontage Rd.

## GADSDEN (C-5) pop. 36,856, elev. 558'
- **Restaurants p. 84**

This town in the foothills of Lookout Mountain is one of Alabama's largest industrial centers. Industry began to flourish in Gadsden as early as 1895, not long after William P. Lay built an electrical plant in hopes of enticing investors into the area. Today local industries produce steel, rubber, fabricated metal, electrical equipment and electronic devices.

But the town is not all work and no play: Gadsden Riverfest provides 2 days of arts and crafts, shopping, music, food and children's activities in mid-June. The festival is held in Moragne Park on SR 411. Gadsden also is along the corridor of the World's Longest Yardsale. Beginning on the first Thursday in August, the annual event runs for 4 days and spans five states including Georgia, Kentucky, Ohio and Tennessee. ⟫ Christmas at the Falls is an annual event held late November through late December in Noccalula Falls Park *(see attraction listing)*. The event features millions of twinkling lights, the Children's Fantasy Land, a tour through the Pioneer Village and a train ride.

**Gadsden Chamber of Commerce:** One Commerce Sq., P.O. Box 185, Gadsden, AL 35902. **Phone:** (256) 543-3472.

**Shopping areas:** Gadsden Mall, on US 411, contains Belk, Sears and many smaller stores. Nineteen miles north of town on US 431 is the Boaz Outlet complex, a factory outlet mall with stores selling Gap, Polo Ralph Lauren, Tommy Hilfiger, Vanity Fair and other name-brand products at discounted prices.

**EMMA SANSOM MONUMENT,** 90 Broad St. at jct. First St., is a memorial to the 15-year-old Alabama girl who guided Confederate Gen. Nathan Bedford Forrest as he pursued 2,000 Federal troops. The statue depicts Emma pointing to a shortcut across Black Creek, which enabled Forrest to capture the Union forces. The night of his victory Forrest sent his "highest regards to Emma Sansom for her gallant conduct" and asked for a lock of her hair as a keepsake. **Hours:** Daily 24 hrs. **Cost:** Free. **Phone:** (256) 543-3472 (for Gadsden Chamber of Commerce).

**GADSDEN MUSEUM OF ART,** 515 Broad St., displays a permanent collection of paintings, sculpture, decorative arts and historical artifacts as well as changing exhibits. **Time:** Allow 30 minutes minimum. **Hours:** Tues.-Sat. 10-5 (also Thurs. and first Fri. of the month 5-7). Closed major holidays. Phone ahead to confirm schedule. **Cost:** Free. **Phone:** (256) 546-7365.

**MARY G. HARDIN CENTER FOR CULTURAL ARTS,** 501 Broad St., features exhibits by local and national artists. The Imagination Place Children's Museum has hands-on exhibits as well as a child-size city complete with a grocery store, a bank and a doctor's office. The center has a working 72-foot model railroad depicting 1940s Gadsden. Concerts are presented summer weekends.

   **Time:** Allow 1 hour minimum. **Hours:** Mon.-Sat. 10-5, Sun. 1-5. Closed Jan. 1, Easter, Thanksgiving and Christmas (children's museum also closed first Mon. of the month). **Cost:** $6; $5 (ages 2-12). **Phone:** (256) 543-2787.

**NOCCALULA FALLS PARK** is 2.5 mi. n. of the business district at 1500 Noccalula Rd. Creek waters plummet 95 feet from a limestone ledge within the park, which also includes a covered bridge, a war memorial and botanical gardens. An indoor/outdoor animal habitat is home to barnyard animals, birds, llamas, deer and rescued exotic species. A 1-mile train ride departs from the park's train station, passing the falls en route to an on-site pioneer village containing split-log buildings.

   **Hours:** Daily 9-5, Mar. 1 to mid-Oct. (also 5-7, early June-late Aug.); 10-4, mid- to late Oct. **Cost:** (includes park and amenities) $6; $4 (ages 55+); $3 (ages 4-12). **Phone:** (256) 549-4663.

COMFORT SUITES OF GADSDEN          (256)538-5770

 **Hotel** $86-$190 **Address:** 96 Walker St 35904 **Location:** I-59 exit 181, just n. **Facility:** 84 units. 3 stories, interior corridors. **Pool(s):** outdoor. **Activities:** limited exercise equipment. **Guest Services:** coin laundry.

FAIRFIELD INN & SUITES BY MARRIOTT GADSDEN
                                         (256)538-2100

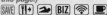 **Hotel** $109-$120 **Address:** 116 Walker St 35904 **Location:** I-59 exit 181, just w. **Facility:** 91 units. 4 stories, interior corridors. **Pool(s):** heated outdoor. **Activities:** hot tub, exercise room. **Guest Services:** valet and coin laundry.

| | |
|---|---|
| | **AAA Benefit:** Members save 5% or more! |

**HAMPTON INN GADSDEN**          (256)546-2337

**Hotel** $89-$200

| | |
|---|---|
| *Hampton Inn* | **AAA Benefit:** Members save 5% or more! |

**Address:** 129 River Rd 35901 **Location:** I-759 exit 4B, just n on US 411. **Facility:** 100 units. 3 stories, interior corridors. **Terms:** 1-7 night minimum stay, cancellation fee imposed. **Pool(s):** outdoor. **Guest Services:** valet laundry. *(See ad this page.)*

**HAMPTON INN GADSDEN/ATTALLA I-59**   (256)538-5222

**Hotel** $89-$139

| | |
|---|---|
| *Hampton Inn* | **AAA Benefit:** Members save 5% or more! |

**Address:** 206 Walker St 35904 **Location:** I-59 exit 181, just w. **Facility:** 82 units. 4 stories, interior corridors. **Terms:** 1-7 night minimum stay, cancellation fee imposed. **Pool(s):** outdoor. **Activities:** exercise room. **Guest Services:** valet and coin laundry. *(See ad this page.)*

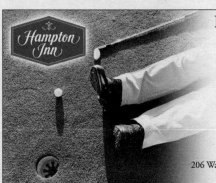

## HOLIDAY INN EXPRESS & SUITES    (256)691-0225

  **Hotel** $99-$159 **Address:** 106 Walker St 35904 **Location:** I-59 exit 181, just n. **Facility:** 70 units. 3 stories, interior corridors. **Pool(s):** outdoor. **Activities:** hot tub, exercise room. **Guest Services:** coin laundry.

---

### WHERE TO EAT

THE FISH MARKET GADSDEN    256/547-4141

 Seafood. Casual Dining. $10-$30 **AAA Inspector Notes:** A wide variety of fresh seafood at inexpensive prices awaits you at this casual restaurant. A small retail area offers a selection of hard to find condiments. Only lunch is served on Sunday. **Features:** full bar, patio dining, happy hour. **Address:** 1504-B Rainbow Dr 35901 **Location:** I-759 exit 4B, 0.8 mi n on US 411. [L] [D] CALL

LAS BRISAS    256/546-8408

Mexican. Casual Dining. $5-$14 **AAA Inspector Notes:** This very casual and friendly restaurant offers all the expected appetizers, entrées and desserts. Plus it's open every day of the year. **Features:** beer & wine. **Address:** 202 Albert Rains Blvd/US 411 35901 **Location:** Just s of jct US 278/411 and 431. [L] [D]

MATER'S PIZZA AND PASTA EMPORIUM    256/547-2556

Pizza Seafood. Casual Dining. $6-$24 **AAA Inspector Notes:** This long-time establishment, open since 1978, is situated in a sprawling one-story red brick building with green striped awnings on the fringes of the center of town. Its maze of small, attached rooms includes an oyster bar and game room equipped with a pool table. The pizza is so memorable that, by popular demand, it can be shipped anywhere in the country. **Features:** full bar, patio dining. **Address:** 329 Locust St 35901 **Location:** Corner of N 4th St; downtown. **Parking:** street only. [L] [D]

TOP O' THE RIVER    256/547-9817

Seafood. Family Dining. $12-$21 **AAA Inspector Notes:** From near and far, people line up to get into this restaurant, which features catfish, chicken, shrimp and steak. The fresh-baked cornbread, still warm in its own mini iron skillet, is a real treat. Also worth a try are the unusual fried dill pickles. The decor is simple, with booth seating and windows along one wall that afford a river view. Service is casual and friendly, yet knowledgeable. **Features:** full bar, patio dining. **Address:** 1606 Rainbow Dr 35901 **Location:** I-759 exit 4A, 0.8 mi s on US 411. [D] CALL

## GARDENDALE pop. 13,893

• **Part of Birmingham area — see map p. 43**

### BEST WESTERN PLUS GARDENDALE    (205)631-1181

**Hotel** $99-$125    **AAA Benefit:** Members save up to 20%!

**Address:** 842 Thompson St 35071 **Location:** I-65 exit 271, 0.6 mi w, then just s. **Facility:** 59 units. 3 stories, interior corridors. **Pool(s):** outdoor. **Activities:** exercise room. **Featured Amenity:** full hot breakfast.

## GENEVA pop. 4,452

BRIARWOOD INN OF GENEVA    (334)684-7715

  **Motel** $79-$108 **Address:** 1503 W Magnolia Ave 36340 **Location:** On SR 52, 0.3 mi w of jct SR 196. **Facility:** 27 units, some kitchens. 1 story, exterior corridors. **Terms:** cancellation fee imposed. **Pool(s):** outdoor.

## GREENSBORO (E-2) pop. 2,497, elev. 220'

**MAGNOLIA GROVE HISTORIC HOUSE MUSEUM** is at 1002 Hobson St., at the w. end of Greensboro's historic district at jct. Main St. and US 14. This two-story Greek Revival structure was built about 1840 by the wealthy planter Col. Isaac Croom and later was the boyhood home of Croom's great-nephew, Richmond Pearson Hobson, a hero of the Spanish-American War. The house is furnished with original pieces belonging to the Croom and Hobson families.

**Time:** Allow 45 minutes minimum. **Hours:** Tues.-Fri. 10-4, first Sat. of the month 10-2; other times by appointment. Closed state holidays. **Cost:** $5; $4 (students and military with ID and senior citizens); $3 (ages 6-18). **Phone:** (334) 624-8618.

## GREENVILLE pop. 8,135

### BEST WESTERN INN    (334)382-9200

 **Motel** $60-$90     **AAA Benefit:** Members save up to 20%!

**Address:** 56 Cahaba Rd 36037 **Location:** I-65 exit 130, just n on SR 185. **Facility:** 45 units. 2 stories (no elevator), exterior corridors. **Pool(s):** outdoor. **Guest Services:** valet laundry.

### COMFORT INN    (334)383-9595

 **Hotel** $68-$104

**Address:** 1029 Fort Dale Rd 36037 **Location:** I-65 exit 130, just n on SR 185. **Facility:** 54 units. 3 stories, interior corridors. **Pool(s):** outdoor. **Activities:** limited exercise equipment. **Featured Amenity:** continental breakfast.

### HAMPTON INN-GREENVILLE    (334)382-9631

**Hotel** $89-$129     **AAA Benefit:** Members save 5% or more!

**Address:** 219 Interstate Dr 36037 **Location:** I-65 exit 130, just n on SR 185. **Facility:** 69 units. 3 stories, interior corridors. **Terms:** 1-7 night minimum stay, cancellation fee imposed. **Pool(s):** outdoor. **Activities:** exercise room. **Guest Services:** coin laundry. **Featured Amenity:** full hot breakfast.

---

Add AAA or CAA Associate Members to bring home the benefits of membership

**HOLIDAY INN EXPRESS & SUITES**          (334)382-2444

Hotel
$84-$124

**Address:** 100 Paul Stabler Dr 36037 **Location:** I-65 exit 130, just n on SR 185, then just w on Cahaba Rd. **Facility:** 67 units. 3 stories, interior corridors. **Pool(s):** outdoor. **Activities:** exercise room. **Guest Services:** complimentary and valet laundry.

SAVE [Y↑] CALL [&M] [≈] [BIZ] [HS]
[≈] [X] [🔒] [📷] [💻]

**WHERE TO EAT**

BATES HOUSE OF TURKEY RESTAURANT          334/382-6123
American. Family Dining. $6-$8 **AAA Inspector Notes:** Turkey and all the fixings are served up just like a Thanksgiving feast at this family-owned restaurant. Patrons can even take home one of the eatery's organic birds. **Address:** 1001 Fort Dale Rd 36037 **Location:** I-65 exit 130, just w. [L]

OLD MEXICO          334/383-9950
Mexican. Casual Dining. $6-$14 **AAA Inspector Notes:** Standard, well-prepared Mexican cuisine makes up the menu at this place, which draws charm from its vibrant decor. Locals come for the fajitas and delicious half-price margaritas on Wednesday night. **Features:** full bar. **Address:** 941 Fort Dale Rd 36037 **Location:** I-65 exit 130, just s on SR 185. [L] [D] [◥]

# GULF SHORES (I-2) pop. 9,741, elev. 2'
• Hotels p. 86 • Restaurants p. 86

Gulf Shores has attracted vacationers with its Gulf of Mexico beaches, excellent fishing and scenic golf courses since the 1930s. It boasts resort facilities as well as sailing, parasailing, swimming, snorkeling, scuba diving and fishing opportunities in Gulf waters. Charter boat fishing can be arranged at Orange Beach. Among the offerings at the National Shrimp Festival, a 4-day event held in October, are arts and crafts, children's activities, music, a boat show and a sandcastle contest.

**Gulf Shores & Orange Beach Tourism:** 3150 Gulf Shores Pkwy., P.O. Box 457, Gulf Shores, AL 36542. **Note:** The office will have a new location in early 2015; phone for details. **Phone:** (251) 974-1510 or (800) 745-7263.

**ALABAMA GULF COAST ZOO,** 1204 Gulf Shores Pkwy., is the residence of more than 500 animals, including lions, Bengal and Siberian tigers, primates, leopards, wolves, wallabies and American black bears. A petting zoo, reptile house and aviary are on the grounds. Seasonal animal encounters are offered as well as educational animal shows. The zoo was the subject of the Animal Planet show, "The Little Zoo that Could," which focused on its struggle to rebuild after it was struck by numerous hurricanes in 2004.

**Time:** Allow 1 hour minimum. **Hours:** Daily 9-4. Closed Jan. 1, Thanksgiving and Christmas. **Cost:** $11; $9 (ages 55+); $8 (ages 3-12). **Phone:** (251) 968-5731.

**BON SECOUR NATIONAL WILDLIFE REFUGE,** 12295 SR 180, consists of 7,000 acres of coastal land with geographic features ranging from sand dunes to woodlands. Many types of wildlife, including some endangered species, can be seen. Nature and hiking trails are on-site. Pets are not permitted. **Hours:** Daily dawn-dusk. Office Mon.-Fri. 7-3:30. Closed major holidays. **Cost:** Free. **Phone:** (251) 540-7720.

**FORT MORGAN STATE HISTORIC SITE** is 21 mi. w. to 110 SR 180W, at the entrance to Mobile Bay; the fort shared strategic importance with Fort Gaines *(see Dauphin Island p. 70)* during the Civil War. After a 14-day siege in 1864, this Confederate stronghold surrendered following the Battle of Mobile Bay. The fort was reactivated during the Spanish-American War and World Wars I and II. A museum and artillery pieces also are featured.

Ferry service links Fort Morgan to Dauphin Island. Brochures for walking tours are available. **Time:** Allow 1 hour minimum. **Hours:** Fort daily 8-5. Museum daily 9-4:30. Closed Jan. 1, Thanksgiving and Christmas. **Cost:** $7; $5 (ages 65+); $4 (ages 6-18). **Phone:** (251) 540-7127.

**GULF SHORES MUSEUM** is at 244 W. 19th Ave. Exhibits cover such topics as hurricanes, local industries and maritime history. **Time:** Allow 1 hour minimum. **Hours:** Tues.-Fri. 10-noon and 1-5, Sat. 10-2. Closed major holidays. **Cost:** Free. **Phone:** (251) 968-1473.

**WATERVILLE USA** is at 906 Gulf Shores Pkwy. The water park includes ten body and tube slides (including a six-lane mat racer slide), a wave pool, lazy river, a separate area for children, and a water playground known as Shrimp Boat Village. Flowrider is a boogie board/surf machine that creates an endless wave. Other park attractions include go-carts, a roller coaster, miniature golf, children's rides, a trampoline and the House of Bounce.

**Time:** Allow 2 hours minimum. **Hours:** Water park daily 10-6, Memorial Day weekend to mid-Aug.; Sat.-Sun. 10-6, in late May and mid-Aug. through Labor Day. Amusement park daily 10-10, first Sat. in Mar. to mid-Aug.; phone for schedule of limited days and hours rest of year. **Cost:** Water park $29.95; $24.95 (military with ID); $20.95 (ages 60+ and under 42 inches tall); free (ages 0-2). Amusement park $24.95; $19.95 (military with ID); $15.95 (ages 60+ and under 42 inches tall); free (ages 0-2). Prices may vary. **Phone:** (251) 948-2106. [Y↑]

Keep a current

AAA/CAA Road Atlas

in every vehicle

## BEST WESTERN ON THE BEACH    (251)948-2711

Hotel
$79-$499

**AAA Benefit:**
Members save up to 20%!

**Address:** 337 E Beach Blvd 36542 **Location:** Oceanfront. On SR 182, just e of jct SR 59. **Facility:** 101 units, some efficiencies and kitchens. 3-6 stories, interior/exterior corridors. **Terms:** 2-4 night minimum stay - seasonal and/or weekends, cancellation fee imposed. **Pool(s):** outdoor, heated indoor. **Activities:** hot tub, fishing.

[SAVE] [📶] [🏊] [BIZ] [📶] [🖥] [🖨]
/ SOME UNITS [HS] [📷]

## COURTYARD BY MARRIOTT GULF SHORES CRAFT FARMS
(251)968-1113

Hotel $89-$259 **Address:** 3750 Gulf Shores Pkwy 36542 **Location:** On SR 59, 2.4 mi n of jct SR 180. **Facility:** 90 units. 3 stories, interior corridors. **Pool(s):** outdoor. **Activities:** exercise room. **Guest Services:** coin laundry, boarding pass kiosk.

**AAA Benefit:**
Members save 5%
or more!

[📶] [🛎] CALL [⚴M] [🏊] [BIZ] [HS] [📶] [✕] [🖥] [📷]
/ SOME UNITS [📷]

## STAYBRIDGE SUITES-GULF SHORES    251/975-1030

Extended Stay Hotel. Rates not provided. **Address:** 3947 Hwy 59 36542 **Location:** On SR 59, 3.1 mi n of jct SR 180. **Facility:** 88 efficiencies, some two bedrooms. 4 stories, interior corridors. **Pool(s):** outdoor. **Activities:** exercise room. **Guest Services:** valet and coin laundry.

[📶] CALL [⚴M] [🏊] [BIZ] [HS] [📶] [🖥] [📷] [📷]
/ SOME UNITS [🍸]

### WHERE TO EAT

## KING NEPTUNE'S SEAFOOD RESTAURANT    251/968-5464

Seafood. Casual Dining. $5-$38 **AAA Inspector Notes:** This small, unassuming establishment is a local favorite which remains busy throughout the year. Well-prepared meals at reasonable prices keep the clientele steady. The menu features a wide variety of selections as well as daily specials. **Features:** full bar, patio dining. **Address:** 1137 Gulf Shores Pkwy 36542 **Location:** Jct SR 180, just s on SR 59. [L] [D]

## LUCY BUFFETT'S LULU'S AT HOMEPORT MARINA
251/967-5858

Seafood. Family Dining. $9-$20 **AAA Inspector Notes:** The open-air waterfront restaurant has a fun Caribbean resort feel to it and serves very simple, local seafood such as fried crab claws, fried oysters or peel-and-eat shrimp. They also feature live music every night, a sand dune playground area for children and boat dockage. This place is all about fun. **Features:** full bar, patio dining. **Address:** 200 E 25th Ave 36542 **Location:** From north end of Intracoastal Waterway Bridge, just e on E 29th Ave, just s. [L] [D] [AC]

## NOLAN'S RESTAURANT AND LOUNGE    251/948-2111

Seafood Steak. Fine Dining. $18-$49 **AAA Inspector Notes:** The deep rich wood, candles and curved brick partitions create an intimate setting for a romantic dinner at this restaurant. Bring your dancing shoes as the party starts at 7:30 pm with live dance music in the adjoining lounge. **Features:** full bar, happy hour. **Address:** 1140 Gulf Shores Pkwy 36542 **Location:** Jct SR 59 and 180, just s; in Sawgrass Landing; next to Alabama Gulf Coast Zoo.
[D] CALL [⚴M]

---

Choose real ratings you can trust from
professional inspectors who've been there

## ORIGINAL OYSTER HOUSE    251/948-2445

Seafood. Casual Dining. $7-$29 **AAA Inspector Notes:** This family-oriented restaurant is popular with locals and visitors alike, and it is easy to see why. Friendly staffers serve fresh seafood in generous portions, and the salad bar is loaded with healthy greens. **Features:** full bar. **Address:** 701 Gulf Shores Pkwy 36542 **Location:** On SR 59, 0.7 mi s of SR 180; in Bayou Village.
[L] [D] CALL [⚴M]

# GUNTERSVILLE    pop. 8,197

## HAMPTON INN LAKE GUNTERSVILLE    (256)582-4176

Hotel $119-$149 **Address:** 14451 US Hwy 431 S 35976 **Location:** Waterfront. Jct Gunter Ave (US 431) and SR 69, 1.9 mi s. **Facility:** 79 units. 4 stories, interior corridors. **Terms:** 1-7 night minimum stay, cancellation fee imposed. **Pool(s):** heated outdoor. **Activities:** marina, fishing, picnic facilities, exercise room. **Guest Services:** valet and coin laundry.

**AAA Benefit:**
Members save 5%
or more!

[📶] [🏊] [BIZ] [📶] [✕] [🖥] [📷] [📷]

## WYNDHAM GARDEN LAKE GUNTERSVILLE    (256)582-2220

Hotel $90-$142 **Address:** 2140 Gunter Ave 35976 **Location:** Waterfront. Jct US 431 (Gunter Ave) and SR 79. **Facility:** 99 units. 3 stories, exterior corridors. **Dining:** nightclub, entertainment. **Pool(s):** heated outdoor. **Activities:** boat dock, fishing, playground, picnic facilities, limited exercise equipment. **Guest Services:** valet and coin laundry.

[📶] [🍴] [🍸] CALL [⚴M] [🏊] [BIZ] [HS] [📶] [✕] [🖥]
[📷] [📷] / SOME UNITS [🍸]

### WHERE TO EAT

## CRAWMAMA'S    256/582-0484

Southern Seafood. Casual Dining. $10-$27 **AAA Inspector Notes:** The focus is on food and fun at this no-frills dining shack. A plethora of seafood is available—steamed, grilled or fried. Various sampler platters can get a bit pricey, but portions are abundant. The bucket on your table is for the empty shells. Leave your mark, as hundreds of patrons in the past, by posting a signed dollar bill. Lunch service is available on Saturdays beginning at 11:30 a.m. Fridays and Saturdays feature live music. **Features:** full bar. **Address:** 5002 Web Villa 35976 **Location:** Jct US 431 (Gunter Ave) and SR 69, 2.1 mi s; behind The Venue. [D] [✕]

## OUTLAW STEAKHOUSE    256/582-4653

Steak. Casual Dining. $6-$20 **AAA Inspector Notes:** This casual mess hall will rustle up some juicy steaks for all of the cowpokes who visit. Bring the kids because they also offer tender vittles for the little buckaroos. **Features:** full bar, Sunday brunch, happy hour. **Address:** 4641 Wyeth Dr 35976 **Location:** Jct SR 69, 1.9 mi s, just e. [B] [L] [D] [✕]

## ROCK HOUSE EATERY    256/505-4699

Southern American. Casual Dining. $8-$27 **AAA Inspector Notes:** An ivy covered stone and glass exterior indicates the welcoming, relaxed atmosphere inside. A cozy fire warms on a chilly day and outdoor patio seating is available for warmer ones. Closed evenings Sunday through Tuesday. **Features:** full bar, Sunday brunch. **Address:** 1201 Gunter Ave 35976 **Location:** Corner of Loveless St; downtown. **Parking:** street only. [L] [D] CALL [⚴M]

## TOP O' THE RIVER    256/582-4567

Seafood. Family Dining. $12-$21 **AAA Inspector Notes:** This popular family-style restaurant can welcome and serve more than 700 people at a time. The place is well known for its excellent catfish, delicious homemade cornbread, coleslaw and hushpuppies, but coming in a close second are the fried dill pickles and mustard greens. Lakeview tables are a hot commodity, so ask for one specifically if you'd like a view to enjoy, too. **Features:** beer & wine, Sunday brunch. **Address:** 7004 Val Monte Dr 35976 **Location:** Jct US 431 (Gunter Ave), 1.1 mi e on Wyeth Dr, follow signs to waterfront.
[D] CALL [⚴M]

# HANCEVILLE (C-3) pop. 2,982, elev. 541'

**THE EVELYN BURROW MUSEUM** is at 801 Main St. N.W. on the Wallace State Community College campus. The eclectic objects displayed are part of the personal collection amassed by a local couple over a 65-year period. They include historical Biblical scenes depicted on fine china, Tiffany lamps, Fabergé plates, Dresden porcelain and an impressive set of horse sculptures.

**Time:** Allow 1 hour minimum. **Hours:** Tues.-Fri. 9-5, Sat. 10-2. Closed major holidays and college holidays. Phone ahead to confirm schedule. **Cost:** Free. **Phone:** (256) 352-8457 or (866) 350-9722.

**SHRINE OF THE MOST BLESSED SACRAMENT**, 3222 CR 548, sits on 400 acres of beautiful, tranquil countryside. Mother Angelica, founder of EWTN (Eternal Word Television Network), was inspired to build the temple during a trip to Bogotá, Colombia, in 1995. The architecture of the upper church, which was completed in 1999, is representative of 13th-century Italian Romanesque-Gothic Franciscan churches and monasteries in Assisi and Umbria. The structure is truly an international work of art thanks to materials, craftspeople and artisans from Alabama and around the world. For instance, marble came from Brazil, Finland, Italy, South Africa and Spain; red jasper came from Turkey; stained-glass windows were made in Germany; exterior limestone composite bricks were made in Canada; and the clay roof tiles were produced in Colombia.

The lower church's small devotional chapel houses images of the Shroud of Turin as well as a crèche carved out of a hillside. This life-size nativity scene is meant to be a year-round reminder of the wonder of Christmas. Nearby is Castle San Miguel, similar to the temple in architectural style. It is intended to inspire visitors to model the honorable and courageous behavior of historic saints and knights. Suits of armor, tapestries, medieval manuscripts, and statues of Saint Joan of Arc and Saint Michael are displayed. Also on the grounds are Stations of the Cross, a 110-foot campanile with a 14-bell carillon and a replica of the Lourdes Grotto.

**Note:** Modest attire is requested; sleeveless shirts, tank tops, shorts and miniskirts/dresses are not permitted. Silence is required inside the temple. Photography inside the shrine is not permitted. **Time:** Allow 1 hour minimum. **Hours:** Mon.-Sat. 6 a.m.-9 p.m., Sun. 6-6. Mass is celebrated at 7 and noon. The rosary is said at 8:20 a.m. **Cost:** Donations. **Phone:** (256) 352-6267. 🍴 ⛱

QUALITY INN HANCEVILLE                    (256)352-0151
🔻🔻 **Hotel** $77-$110 **Address:** 810 Main St NE 35077 **Location:** I-65 exit 287, 16 mi n on US 31. **Facility:** 42 units. 2 stories (no elevator), interior corridors. **Pool(s):** outdoor. **Activities:** limited exercise equipment. **Guest Services:** coin laundry.
🍴 🛍 🛜 💻 / SOME UNITS 🔌 🖨

# HOMEWOOD pop. 25,167

- **Restaurants p. 88**
- **Hotels & Restaurants map & index p. 54**
- **Part of Birmingham area — see map p. 43**

---

**ALOFT BIRMINGHAM SOHO SQUARE**
(205)874-8055  **23**

Hotel
$129-$199

**AAA Benefit:** Members save up to 15%, plus Starwood Preferred Guest® benefits!

**Address:** 1903 29th Ave S 35209 **Location:** I-59 exit 126A, 3.5 mi s on US 31, then just w; corner of 19th St S; downtown. **Facility:** 111 units. 5 stories, interior corridors. *Bath:* shower only. **Amenities:** safes. **Dining:** Michael's Restaurant, see separate listing. **Pool(s):** heated indoor. **Activities:** exercise room. **Guest Services:** valet and coin laundry.

SAVE 🍴 🍸 CALL 🛗M 🛍 BIZ HS 🛜 ✕ 🎦 🔌 💻 / SOME UNITS 🐾

**Close to Downtown Birmingham, UAB & Samford University! Walk to Homewood shops and restaurants.**

---

**BEST WESTERN PLUS CARLTON SUITES**
(205)940-9990  **29**

🔻🔻🔻
Hotel
$119-$169

Best Western PLUS

**AAA Benefit:** Members save up to 20%!

**Address:** 140 State Farm Pkwy 35209 **Location:** I-65 exit 255, just w to Wildwood Pkwy, then just n. **Facility:** 103 units. 4 stories, interior corridors. **Pool(s):** heated indoor. **Activities:** exercise room. **Guest Services:** valet and coin laundry.

SAVE 🍴 CALL 🛗M 🛍 BIZ HS 🛜 🔌 🖨 💻 / SOME UNITS 🔌

---

CANDLEWOOD SUITES BIRMINGHAM-HOMEWOOD
205/769-9777  **35**
🔻🔻🔻 Extended Stay Hotel. Rates not provided. **Address:** 400 Commons Dr 35209 **Location:** I-65 exit 255, 0.7 mi w, then just s. **Facility:** 81 kitchen units. 4 stories, interior corridors. **Activities:** picnic facilities, exercise room. **Guest Services:** complimentary and valet laundry.
🍴 BIZ HS 🛜 ✕ 🔌 🖨 💻 / SOME UNITS 🔌

COMFORT INN                    (205)916-0464  **26**
🔻🔻🔻 Hotel $79-$124 **Address:** 226 Summit Pkwy 35209 **Location:** I-65 exit 256 northbound; exit 256A southbound, just w. **Facility:** 115 units. 5 stories, interior corridors. **Pool(s):** outdoor. **Activities:** exercise room. **Guest Services:** valet and coin laundry.
🍴 🛍 BIZ 🛜 🔌 🖨 💻

---

(See map & index p. 54.)

## COUNTRY INN & SUITES BY CARLSON
(205)451-4000 **34**

Hotel
$99-$129

**Address:** 485 Wildwood N Cir 35209 **Location:** I-65 exit 255, just w, then just n. **Facility:** 70 units. 4 stories, interior corridors. **Pool(s):** outdoor. **Activities:** hot tub, exercise room. **Guest Services:** coin laundry. **Featured Amenity:** continental breakfast.

## COURTYARD BY MARRIOTT BIRMINGHAM HOMEWOOD
(205)879-0400 **24**

COURTYARD® Marriott.

**AAA Benefit:** Members save 5% or more!

**Address:** 500 Shades Creek Pkwy 35209 **Location:** On SR 149, just e of jct US 31. Across from Brookwood Village Mall. **Facility:** 140 units. 3 stories, interior corridors. **Terms:** check-in 4 pm. **Pool(s):** outdoor. **Activities:** exercise room. **Guest Services:** valet and coin laundry, boarding pass kiosk.

/ SOME UNITS

## DRURY INN & SUITES-BIRMINGHAM SOUTHWEST
(205)940-9500 **30**

Hotel $125-$189 **Address:** 160 State Farm Pkwy 35209 **Location:** I-65 exit 255, 0.5 mi on northwest frontage road. **Facility:** 138 units. 5 stories, interior corridors. **Terms:** cancellation fee imposed. **Pool(s):** heated outdoor, heated indoor. **Activities:** hot tub, exercise room. **Guest Services:** valet and coin laundry.

/ SOME UNITS

## HAMPTON INN-LAKESHORE
(205)313-2060 **27**

Hotel $99-$129 **Address:** 30 State Farm Pkwy 35209 **Location:** I-65 exit 255, just e on Lakeshore Pkwy, just n on Wildwood Pkwy, then 0.8 mi w. **Facility:** 97 units. 6 stories, interior corridors. **Terms:** 1-7 night minimum stay, cancellation fee imposed. **Pool(s):** outdoor. **Activities:** exercise room. **Guest Services:** valet and coin laundry.

**AAA Benefit:** Members save 5% or more!

## HILTON GARDEN INN BIRMINGHAM-LAKESHORE
(205)314-0274 **31**

Hotel $119-$159 **Address:** 520 Wildwood Cir N 35209 **Location:** I-65 exit 255, just w, then just n. **Facility:** 95 units. 6 stories, interior corridors. **Terms:** 1-7 night minimum stay, cancellation fee imposed. **Pool(s):** heated indoor. **Activities:** hot tub, exercise room. **Guest Services:** valet and coin laundry.

**AAA Benefit:** Members save 5% or more!

## HOLIDAY INN HOTEL BIRMINGHAM/HOMEWOOD
(205)942-6070 **33**

Hotel. Rates not provided. **Address:** 492 Wildwood Cir N 35209 **Location:** I-65 exit 255, just w, then just n. **Facility:** 108 units. 5 stories, interior corridors. **Pool(s):** heated indoor. **Activities:** exercise room. **Guest Services:** valet and coin laundry.

## RESIDENCE INN BY MARRIOTT BIRMINGHAM HOMEWOOD
(205)943-0044 **28**

Extended Stay Hotel $109-$179 **Address:** 50 State Farm Pkwy 35209 **Location:** I-65 exit 255, 1 mi nw on northwest frontage road. **Facility:** 120 units, some two bedrooms, efficiencies and kitchens. 3 stories, interior corridors. **Pool(s):** outdoor. **Activities:** hot tub, exercise room. **Guest Services:** valet and coin laundry.

**AAA Benefit:** Members save 5% or more!

/ SOME UNITS

## SUPER 8
(205)945-9888 **25**

Hotel $55-$63 **Address:** 140 Vulcan Rd 35209 **Location:** I-65 exit 256 northbound; exit 256A southbound, just nw. **Facility:** 95 units. 2-3 stories (no elevator), interior corridors. **Terms:** 3 day cancellation notice. **Activities:** exercise room. **Guest Services:** coin laundry.

/ SOME UNITS

## TOWNEPLACE SUITES BY MARRIOTT BIRMINGHAM HOMEWOOD
(205)943-0114 **32**

Extended Stay Hotel $125-$153 **Address:** 500 Wildwood Cir N 35209 **Location:** I-65 exit 255, 0.6 mi w, then just n. Adjacent to Lowe's. **Facility:** 127 kitchen units, some two bedrooms. 4 stories, interior corridors. **Pool(s):** outdoor. **Activities:** exercise room. **Guest Services:** valet and coin laundry.

**AAA Benefit:** Members save 5% or more!

/ SOME UNITS

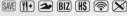 WHERE TO EAT

## BRIO TUSCAN GRILLE
205/879-9177 **39**

Italian. Fine Dining. $12-$28 **AAA Inspector Notes:** While the atmosphere is casual, upscale Tuscan villa-style decor lends a sophisticated touch to the dining experience. Both lunch and dinner offer all the attentiveness a diner expects. From the garlic, spinach and artichoke dip starter to beef, chicken, veal, seafood and homemade pasta entrees, there is a selection to satisfy all tastes. Among specialties are home-made mozzarella, crisp flatbreads and wood-fired oven-baked pizza, in addition to a selection of steak. **Features:** full bar, Sunday brunch, happy hour. **Address:** 591 Brookwood Village 35209 **Location:** US 280, w on Shades Creek Pkwy, just s; in Brookwood Village Mall. **Parking:** on-site and valet.

## DAVE'S PIZZA
205/871-3283 **34**

Pizza. Casual Dining. $8-$35 **AAA Inspector Notes:** Gourmet pizza and sandwiches make up the menu at the family-friendly hot spot, a local favorite. During colder months, the dining room is enclosed and heated, but it becomes an open-air spot in the summer. Heaters and warmed blankets allow for year-round al fresco dining on the patio. **Features:** full bar, patio dining, happy hour. **Address:** 1819 29th Ave S 35209 **Location:** Jct US 31, just w. **Parking:** street only.

## DEMETRI'S B.B.Q.
205/871-1581 **31**

Barbecue. Quick Serve. $5-$14 **AAA Inspector Notes:** Known for great barbecue pulled pork, chicken and tender and moist spare ribs, this place also serves a wonderful breakfast of omelets, hot cakes and French toast that the staff describes as unimaginably great. Completing the menu are numerous salads and homemade pies. **Address:** 1901 28th Ave S 35209 **Location:** Jct US 31 and 28th Ave S, just w.

**(See map & index p. 54.)**

## DE VINCI'S
205/879-1455 (29)

▼▼ ▼▼ Italian. Casual Dining. $8-$16 **AAA Inspector Notes:** Calzones, pizza, pasta and traditional Italian specialties are the bill of fare at this family-operated eatery, where small dining rooms have a comfy, homelike feel. Stuffed olives are a good starter, and any of the well-prepared main courses are a great choice. **Features:** full bar, patio dining, Sunday brunch. **Address:** 2707 18th St S 35209 **Location:** Jct US 31 and Rosedale Dr, just w, just s.

[B] [L] [D] CALL &M

## DODIYO'S
205/453-9300 (32)

▼▼ ▼▼ Mediterranean. Casual Dining. $8-$26 **AAA Inspector Notes:** Dark, rich wood, colorful handwoven textiles and an interesting display of ancient artifacts from throughout the Mediterranean basin reflect the wide range of culinary influences incorporated in the menu. **Features:** full bar, patio dining, happy hour. **Address:** 1831 28th Ave S, Suite 110 35209 **Location:** Between 18th and 19th sts; downtown; in SoHo Square, behind City Hall. **Parking:** on-site and valet. [L] [D] CALL &M 🐾

## GIAN MARCO'S RESTAURANT
205/871-9622 (42)

▼▼ ▼▼ Italian. Fine Dining. $12-$40 **AAA Inspector Notes:** Tuscan influences weave throughout the menu at the lively and ever-so-popular neighborhood restaurant. This is the place to be for those who can secure a reservation. **Features:** full bar, patio dining. **Reservations:** suggested. **Address:** 721 Broadway St 35209 **Location:** I-65 exit 256B, just s to Green Springs Hwy, just e to Carr Ave, then 0.4 mi e. [L] [D]

## HOMEWOOD GOURMET
205/871-1620 (30)

▼▼ Deli. Quick Serve. $7-$14 **AAA Inspector Notes:** Owner/chefs Chris and Laura Zapalowski carry on former owner Chef Franklin Biggs' tradition by bringing gourmet style to specialty deli style sandwiches as well as pasta, poultry, seafood and meat dishes. Signature items include the baby blue salad (or Carlene's plate, which adds barbecue salmon to this salad). Try roll-ups of turkey and cranberry, Santa Fe beef with pepper jack, pesto chicken salad, or the beef and blue sandwich. **Features:** patio dining. **Address:** 1919 28th Ave S 35209 **Location:** Jct US 31 and 28th Ave S, just w.

[L] [D] CALL &M

## JACKSON'S BAR & BISTRO
205/870-9669 (33)

▼▼ ▼▼ American. Casual Dining. $7-$19 **AAA Inspector Notes:** Located in the heart of town, this contemporary watering hole offers a range of food selections including small plates, full entrées, personal pizza, salads and burgers as well as more than 30 beers and 20 wines. **Features:** full bar, Sunday brunch. **Address:** 1831 28th Ave S 35209 **Location:** Between 18th and 19th sts; next to City Hall; downtown. **Parking:** street only. [L] [D] CALL &M

## LANDRY'S SEAFOOD HOUSE
205/916-0777 (43)

▼▼ ▼▼ Seafood. Casual Dining. $9-$44 **AAA Inspector Notes:** An ideal spot for healthy seafood dinners and special occasions, the restaurant produces a wonderful clam chowder. Menu selections come from all the world's oceans. **Features:** full bar, happy hour. **Address:** 139 State Farm Pkwy 35209 **Location:** I-65 exit 255, just w to Wildwood Pkwy, then just n.

SAVE [L] [D]

## MICHAEL'S RESTAURANT
205/871-9525 (35)

▼▼ ▼▼ Steak Seafood. Casual Dining. $10-$55 **AAA Inspector Notes:** Gaze at the skyscraper photograph mural of Birmingham while dining on succulent steak and seafood at this stylish, contemporary restaurant. Lunch is not served on Saturday. **Features:** full bar, patio dining, Sunday brunch, happy hour. **Address:** 1903 29th Ave S 35209 **Location:** I-59 exit 126A, 3.5 mi s on US 31, then just w; corner of 19th St S; downtown; in Aloft Birmingham Soho Square. **Parking:** on-site and street.

[L] [D] CALL &M

## NABEEL'S CAFE AND MARKET
205/879-9292 (37)

▼▼ ▼▼ Greek. Casual Dining. $7-$19 **AAA Inspector Notes:** Greek food—including pita sandwiches, cold plates and salads—is the primary focus at this cafe, which has a full bar and grocery mart on site. The strong entrée selection lists moussaka, pastitsio and spanakopita. Rounding out the menu are baklava and kataifi. **Features:** full bar, patio dining. **Address:** 1706 Oxmoor Rd 35209 **Location:** Jct Central Ave and Oxmoor Rd. **Parking:** street only.

[L] [D] 🐾

## NEW YORK PIZZA
205/871-4000 (38)

▼▼ ▼▼ Pizza. Family Dining. $5-$29 **AAA Inspector Notes:** This local (and very popular) pizzeria celebrates the Big Apple with pizzas named after city landmarks, calzones and sandwiches, all made to order, for dine-in or take-out. A large dining room ensures that parties of all sizes can relax and share a meal. Families can expect casual, friendly service at a reasonable price. **Features:** beer & wine. **Address:** 1010 Oxmoor Rd 35209 **Location:** I-65 exit 256A, 1 mi ne; in Edgewood shopping area. **Parking:** on-site and street.

[L] [D]

## O' CARR'S RESTAURANT
205/879-2196 (36)

▼▼ ▼▼ Deli Sandwiches. Quick Serve. $6-$10 **AAA Inspector Notes:** Patrons will find a lengthy list of salads and sandwiches at this popular lunch spot where more than two thousand pounds of their signature chicken salad is sold each week. Homemade cheesecake is a must. **Address:** 2909 18th St S 35209 **Location:** US 31, just w on 29th Ave S, just s. [L]

## PAW PAW PATCH
205/941-1117 (40)

▼▼ Southern American. Quick Serve. $6-$7 **AAA Inspector Notes:** The fare centers on basic country cooking: meatloaf, fried chicken, string beans, black-eyed peas, cheesy macaroni and cheese and desserts of cobbler or warm banana pudding. Portions are large, and tasty rolls are part of the tastes-like-home food. **Address:** 410 Green Springs Hwy 35209 **Location:** I-65 exit 256A, just e. [L] [D]

## PHO QUE HUONG
205/942-5400 (41)

▼▼ ▼▼ Vietnamese. Casual Dining. $6-$18 **AAA Inspector Notes:** The Vietnamese eatery specializes in pho, a chicken or beef based broth with accompanying meat, bean sprouts, basil, jalapeños and lime. It is very aromatic, healthy and satisfying. Many other options abound. The décor here is rather nondescript. **Features:** beer only. **Address:** 430 Green Springs Hwy, Suite 15 35209 **Location:** I-65 exit 255, 0.3 mi e to Green Springs Hwy, then just s.

[L] [D]

# HOOVER pop. 81,619

- **Restaurants p. 91**
- **Hotels & Restaurants map & index p. 54**
- **Part of Birmingham area — see map p. 43**

## COURTYARD BY MARRIOTT BIRMINGHAM HOOVER
(205)988-5000 (44)

▼▼ ▼▼ ▼▼
Hotel
$94-$159

COURTYARD® Marriott

**AAA Benefit:** Members save 5% or more!

**Address:** 1824 Montgomery Hwy S 35244 **Location:** I-459 exit 13B, 1 mi s on US 31. **Facility:** 153 units. 3 stories, interior corridors. **Pool(s):** outdoor. **Activities:** exercise room. **Guest Services:** valet and coin laundry, boarding pass kiosk.

SAVE ⫬❚ CALL &M 🏊 BIZ 📶
✕ ❚ ▣ / SOME UNITS ▦

## DAYS INN AT THE GALLERIA
(205)985-7500 (45)

▼▼ ▼▼ Hotel $69-$109 **Address:** 1800 Riverchase Dr 35244 **Location:** I-459 exit 13, 0.5 mi s on US 31, then 0.4 mi w on SR 150. Across from Galleria Mall. **Facility:** 132 units. 2 stories (no elevator), exterior corridors. **Pool(s):** outdoor. **Activities:** limited exercise equipment. **Guest Services:** coin laundry.

⫬❚+ 🏊 BIZ 📶 ▣ / SOME UNITS 🛏 ❚ ▦

(See map & index p. 54.)

## EMBASSY SUITES BIRMINGHAM/HOOVER    (205)985-9994 **48**

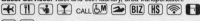

**Hotel** $149-$369 **Address:** 2960 John Hawkins Pkwy 35244 **Location:** I-459 exit 13, 0.5 mi s on US 31, then 0.9 mi w on SR 150. **Facility:** 208 units, some two bedrooms. 9 stories, interior corridors. **Terms:** 1-7 night minimum stay, cancellation fee imposed. **Pool(s):** heated indoor. **Activities:** hot tub, exercise room. **Guest Services:** valet and coin laundry, area transportation.

> **AAA Benefit:**
> Members save 5% or more!

[icons]

## HAMPTON INN & SUITES HOOVER    (205)380-3300 **46**

**Hotel** $99-$175 **Address:** 4520 Galleria Blvd 35244 **Location:** I-459 exit 13, 0.5 mi s on US 31, then 0.6 mi w on SR 150. **Facility:** 102 units. 5 stories, interior corridors. **Terms:** 1-7 night minimum stay, cancellation fee imposed. **Pool(s):** heated indoor. **Activities:** hot tub, exercise room. **Guest Services:** valet and coin laundry, area transportation.

> **AAA Benefit:**
> Members save 5% or more!

[icons]

## HOLIDAY INN HOOVER    (205)682-2901 **50**

**Hotel** $119-$129 **Address:** 2901 John Hawkins Pkwy 35244 **Location:** I-459 exit 10 northbound, 2.2 mi ne; exit 13A (Galleria Blvd) southbound, just sw. **Facility:** 112 units. 5 stories, interior corridors. **Terms:** cancellation fee imposed. **Pool(s):** heated indoor. **Activities:** exercise room. **Guest Services:** valet and coin laundry.

[icons]

## HOMEWOOD SUITES BIRMINGHAM-SW/RIVERCHASE GALLERIA    (205)637-2900 **52**

**Extended Stay Hotel** $99-$279 **Address:** 121 Riverchase Pkwy E 35244 **Location:** I-65 exit 247, just sw on Valleydale Rd, then just n. **Facility:** 113 efficiencies, some two bedrooms. 6 stories, interior corridors. **Terms:** 1-7 night minimum stay, cancellation fee imposed. **Pool(s):** outdoor. **Activities:** exercise room. **Guest Services:** valet and coin laundry.

> **AAA Benefit:**
> Members save 5% or more!

[icons]

## HOMEWOOD SUITES BY HILTON    (205)995-9823 **41**

**Extended Stay Hotel** $109-$169 **Address:** 215 Inverness Center Dr 35242 **Location:** I-459 exit 19 (US 280), 1.8 mi e, then just s. **Facility:** 95 efficiencies, some two bedrooms. 4 stories, interior corridors. **Terms:** 1-7 night minimum stay, cancellation fee imposed. **Pool(s):** outdoor. **Activities:** exercise room. **Guest Services:** valet and coin laundry.

> **AAA Benefit:**
> Members save 5% or more!

[icons]

## HYATT PLACE BIRMINGHAM/HOOVER    (205)988-8444 **47**

**Hotel** $79-$169

**HYATT PLACE**

**AAA Benefit:** Members save 10%!

**Address:** 2980 John Hawkins Pkwy 35244 **Location:** I-459 exit 13, 0.5 mi s on US 31, then 0.8 mi w on SR 150. Located in a busy commercial area. **Facility:** 126 units. 6 stories, interior corridors. **Terms:** cancellation fee imposed. **Pool(s):** outdoor. **Activities:** exercise room. **Guest Services:** valet laundry, area transportation. **Featured Amenity:** breakfast buffet.

[icons] / SOME UNITS

## HYATT PLACE BIRMINGHAM/INVERNESS    (205)995-9242 **40**

**Hotel** $84-$209

**HYATT PLACE**

**AAA Benefit:** Members save 10%!

**Address:** 4686 Hwy 280 E 35242 **Location:** I-459 exit 19 (US 280), 1.7 mi e, then just s to Inverness Pkwy. **Facility:** 126 units. 6 stories, interior corridors. **Terms:** cancellation fee imposed. **Pool(s):** heated outdoor. **Activities:** exercise room. **Guest Services:** valet laundry, area transportation. **Featured Amenity:** breakfast buffet.

[icons] / SOME UNITS

## HYATT REGENCY BIRMINGHAM-THE WYNFREY HOTEL    (205)705-1234 **43**

**Hotel** $99-$329

**HYATT REGENCY**

**AAA Benefit:** Members save 10%!

**Address:** 1000 Riverchase Galleria 35244 **Location:** I-459 exit 13. Adjacent to Riverchase Galleria. **Facility:** 329 units. 14 stories, interior corridors. **Parking:** on-site (fee) and valet. **Terms:** check-in 4 pm, cancellation fee imposed. **Amenities:** safes. **Dining:** Shula's America's Steak House, see separate listing, entertainment. **Pool(s):** outdoor. **Activities:** hot tub, exercise room. **Guest Services:** valet laundry, area transportation.

[icons] / SOME UNITS

## LA QUINTA INN & SUITES BIRMINGHAM HOOVER    (205)403-0096 **53**

**Hotel** $69-$234 **Address:** 120 Riverchase Pkwy E 35244 **Location:** I-65 exit 247, just sw on Valleydale Rd, then just n. **Facility:** 133 units. 4 stories, interior corridors. **Pool(s):** outdoor. **Activities:** hot tub, exercise room. **Guest Services:** valet and coin laundry.

[icons] / SOME UNITS

## MICROTEL INN & SUITES BY WYNDHAM HOOVER/BIRMINGHAM    (205)444-3033 **49**

**Hotel** $79-$200 **Address:** 500 Jackson Dr 35244 **Location:** I-459 exit 10 northbound, 2.2 mi ne; exit 13A (Galleria Blvd) southbound, just sw. **Facility:** 59 units. 4 stories, interior corridors. **Activities:** limited exercise equipment.

[icons]

(See map & index p. 54.)

## RENAISSANCE BIRMINGHAM ROSS BRIDGE GOLF RESORT & SPA

(205)916-7677 **42**

Resort Hotel
$252-$362

**AAA Benefit:**
Members save 5% or more!

**Address:** 4000 Grand Ave 35226 **Location:** I-459 exit 10, 1.6 mi w on SR 150, 4 mi n on Ross Bridge Pkwy, then just w. **Facility:** Escape the hustle and bustle of the city and retreat in luxury to the rolling hills of Alabama at this unique Scottish castle setting. Don't miss the resident bagpiper who performs at sunset. 259 units. 6 stories, interior corridors. **Parking:** on-site and valet. **Terms:** check-in 4 pm. **Amenities:** video games, safes. **Dining:** 2 restaurants, also, Brock's, see separate listing. **Pool(s):** heated outdoor, heated indoor. **Activities:** hot tub, steamroom, regulation golf, tennis, recreation programs in summer, bicycles, game room, exercise room, spa. **Guest Services:** valet laundry, area transportation.

⟨SAVE⟩ ⟨⟩ ⟨⟩ ⟨⟩ ⟨⟩ CALL ⟨&M⟩ ⟨⟩ ⟨BIZ⟩ ⟨$HS⟩ ⟨⟩ ⟨⟩ ⟨⟩ ⟨⟩ ⟨⟩

### R RENAISSANCE®
BIRMINGHAM ROSS BRIDGE GOLF RESORT & SPA

**Retreat to beautiful rolling hills and the casual elegance of a royal retreat.**

## RESIDENCE INN BY MARRIOTT BIRMINGHAM/HOOVER

(205)733-1655 **51**

▼▼▼ **Extended Stay Hotel** $139-$299 **Address:** 2725 John Hawkins Pkwy 35244 **Location:** I-459 exit 13A (Galleria Blvd/SR 150), 0.5 mi se to SR 150, then 1.5 mi s. **Facility:** 118 units, some two bedrooms, efficiencies and kitchens. 5 stories, interior corridors. **Pool(s):** outdoor. **Activities:** exercise room. **Guest Services:** valet and coin laundry.

**AAA Benefit:**
Members save 5% or more!

⟨⟩ CALL ⟨⟩ ⟨⟩ ⟨BIZ⟩ ⟨HS⟩ ⟨⟩ ⟨⟩ ⟨⟩ ⟨⟩ ⟨⟩ / SOME UNITS ⟨⟩

## WHERE TO EAT

### BELLA CUCINA
205/995-1770 **64**

▼▼ European. Casual Dining. $10-$22 **AAA Inspector Notes:** This charming bistro is tucked away in the corner, partially hidden by a mound of greenery but can be found under The Melting Pot. The European cuisine features French, German, Italian and American dishes as well as sandwiches, salad, fruit plates and fondue, plus entrée and dessert crepes. **Features:** beer & wine, patio dining. **Address:** 611 Doug Baker Blvd, Suite 103 35242 **Location:** I-459 exit 19 (US 280), 4.6 mi s, then just s; in The Village at Lee Branch Plaza. ⟨L⟩ ⟨D⟩ CALL ⟨&M⟩

### BELLINIS RISTORANTE & BAR
205/981-5380 **62**

▼▼▼ Italian. Fine Dining. $8-$36 **AAA Inspector Notes:** This quaint bistro offers a rustic villa-style atmosphere with its brick and stucco walls and archways. The pulled-back drapes hanging throughout can be closed to create an intimate, secluded area while dining on the superbly-prepared cuisine. Lunch is served only on weekdays. **Features:** full bar, patio dining, happy hour. **Reservations:** suggested. **Address:** 6801 Cahaba Valley Rd, Suite 106 35242 **Location:** I-459 exit 19 (US 280), 3.7 mi e, then just s on SR 119; in Cadence Center Plaza. ⟨L⟩ ⟨D⟩ CALL ⟨&M⟩

Show you care with AAA/CAA Gift
Membership, perfect for any occasion

### BROCK'S
205/949-3051 **67**

▼▼▼ Mediterranean. Fine Dining. $8-$38 **AAA Inspector Notes:** Seafood, beef and poultry are prepared with Mediterranean flair in the subdued, romantic atmosphere. **Features:** full bar, patio dining, Sunday brunch. **Reservations:** suggested. **Address:** 4000 Grand Ave 35226 **Location:** I-459 exit 10, 1.6 mi w on SR 150, 4 mi n on Ross Bridge Pkwy, then just w; in Renaissance Birmingham Ross Bridge Golf Resort & Spa. **Parking:** on-site and valet. ⟨B⟩ ⟨D⟩ CALL ⟨&M⟩

### CAJUN STEAMER - BAR & GRILL
205/985-7785

▼▼ Cajun. Casual Dining. $9-$26 **AAA Inspector Notes:** Have a seat on the patio or inside the cool air-conditioned dining room. Either way, you'll feel as though you're visiting the Big Easy. Here you'll find Crescent City food with Magic City style. **Features:** full bar, patio dining, happy hour. **Address:** 180 Main St, Suite 200 35244 **Location:** I-459 exit 13A (Galleria Blvd/SR 150), just e; in Patton Creek Shopping Center. ⟨L⟩ ⟨D⟩

### COSTA'S MEDITERRANEAN CAFE
205/978-1603 **65**

▼▼ Mediterranean. Casual Dining. $7-$21 **AAA Inspector Notes:** This popular Greek and Italian restaurant dishes up Mediterranean standards in huge portions. Fresh, warm garlic loaves accompany each entrée. Among Italian offerings are baked ziti, baked lasagna and veal parmigiana. Greek selections range from moussaka and pastitsio to preparations of lamb, chicken and pork. Homemade sauces are incomparable. **Features:** full bar. **Address:** 3443 Lorna Rd 35216 **Location:** I-65 exit 252, just s to Lorna Rd, then 1.5 mi se. ⟨L⟩ ⟨D⟩ CALL ⟨&M⟩

### DON PEPE
205/408-3880 **63**

▼▼ Mexican. Casual Dining. $6-$18 **AAA Inspector Notes:** This rustic cantina atmosphere makes you feel like you are dining South of the border. **Features:** full bar, happy hour. **Address:** 230 Doug Baker Blvd, Suite 300 35242 **Location:** I-459 exit 19, 4.6 mi e on US 280; in Publix Plaza. ⟨L⟩ ⟨D⟩ CALL ⟨&M⟩

### EDGAR'S BAKERY
205/444-1220 **72**

▼ Breads/Pastries Deli. Quick Serve. $7-$8 **AAA Inspector Notes:** Delicious bread and light lunches are affordable and fast at this local bakery chain. Choose from a wide assortment of luscious pastries. **Features:** patio dining. **Address:** 180 W Main St, Suite 240 35244 **Location:** I-459 exit 13A (Galleria Blvd/SR 150), just e; in Patton Creek Shopping Center. ⟨B⟩ ⟨L⟩ CALL ⟨&M⟩

### FIREBIRDS WOOD FIRED GRILL
205/733-2002 **71**

▼▼▼ American. Casual Dining. $11-$40 **AAA Inspector Notes:** The restaurant re-creates the atmosphere of a mountain lodge. Hand-cut steaks and seafood dominate the menu, which also lists a few pork and chicken entrees, as well as elk tenderloin medallions and buffalo meatloaf. The kitchen uses wood grilling, and pizzas bake in a wood-burning oven. Flavorful food, enhanced presentations and a skilled, knowledgeable and attentive staff, together with distinctive physical elements, make this place appealing. **Features:** full bar. **Reservations:** suggested. **Address:** 191 Main St 35244 **Location:** I-459 exit 13A (Galleria Blvd/SR 150), just s; in Patton Creek Shopping Center. ⟨L⟩ ⟨D⟩

### THE FISH MARKET RESTAURANT
205/823-3474 **66**

▼ Seafood. Family Dining. $8-$23 **AAA Inspector Notes:** Fresh fish is the promise at this spot. The walls in the large dining room display an ocean mural and some mounted fish. Fish selections are plentiful, but those who prefer land-based fare also have a range of choices. **Features:** full bar. **Address:** 1681 Montgomery Hwy 35216 **Location:** I-65 exit 252, 1.4 mi s. ⟨L⟩ ⟨D⟩ CALL ⟨&M⟩

### FULL MOON BAR-B-QUE
205/822-6666

▼ Barbecue. Quick Serve. $6-$20 **AAA Inspector Notes:** Known as Alabama's best little pork house and famous for its half-moon cookies, this chain found throughout the Birmingham area offers barbecue ribs, pork and chicken, slow-cooked over real hickory wood in brick fire pits. **Features:** beer only. **Address:** 2000 Patton Chapel Rd 35216 **Location:** I-65 exit 252, 1.2 mi s on US 31 S. ⟨L⟩ ⟨D⟩

(See map & index p. 54.)

### J. ALEXANDER'S RESTAURANT          205/733-9995  69
▼▼▼▼ American. Casual Dining. $10-$29 **AAA Inspector Notes:** The busy and casual restaurant prepares classic fare—including steak, grilled fish and prime rib—in the open kitchen. The dessert menu is excellent. **Features:** full bar. **Address:** 3320 Galleria Cir 35244 **Location:** I-459 exit 13 (US 31), just sw on Riverchase Galleria perimeter road. 〔L〕 〔D〕 CALL 〔&M〕

### LA DOLCE VITA          205/985-2909  73
▼▼▼▼ Italian. Casual Dining. $10-$35 **AAA Inspector Notes:** This popular local restaurant serves such traditional Italian favorites as rigatoni Bolognese, veal Toscana and fried calamari. Sunday dinners vary each week. An intimate atmosphere makes this a memorable experience. Give yourself permission to enjoy a dessert! **Features:** full bar, happy hour. **Reservations:** suggested. **Address:** 1851 Montgomery Hwy, Suite 107 35244 **Location:** I-459 exit 13B, 1 mi s on US 31; in Riverchase Plaza. 〔L〕 〔D〕

### LLOYD'S RESTAURANT          205/991-5530  61
▼▼ American. Family Dining. $5-$24 **AAA Inspector Notes:** This menu offers plenty if you're hungry. Locals swear by the hamburger steak with gravy. Choose from St. Louis-style ribs, chicken or fried catfish, available whole or filets. The atmosphere is friendly and casual. **Address:** 5301 Hwy 280 S 35242 **Location:** I-459 exit 19 (US 280 S), 4 mi s. 〔L〕 〔D〕 CALL 〔&M〕

### SHULA'S AMERICA'S STEAK HOUSE          205/444-5750  68
▼▼▼ Steak. Fine Dining. $11-$86 **AAA Inspector Notes:** Comfortable and club-like, the dining room is decorated with Dolphins football memorabilia. Finish off the 48-ounce porterhouse steak and be recognized on a plaque. The lamb chops and seafood are good, too, as is the to-die-for seven-layer chocolate cake. **Features:** full bar. **Reservations:** suggested. **Address:** 1000 Riverchase Galleria 35244 **Location:** I-459 exit 13; in Hyatt Regency Birmingham-The Wynfrey Hotel. **Parking:** on-site and valet. 〔L〕 〔D〕

### SOUTHERN LEGACY BBQ & BREW          205/988-0744  74
▼▼ Barbecue. Casual Dining. $5-$22 **AAA Inspector Notes:** Tender, fall-off-the-bone ribs are the draw to this sports bar-style establishment. A huge communal table is the focal point surrounded by 23 flat-screen TVs and some 20 cold beers on tap. **Features:** full bar. **Address:** 2943 John Hawkins Pkwy 35244 **Location:** I-459 exit 13, 0.5 mi s on US 31, then 0.9 mi w on SR 150.
〔L〕 〔D〕 CALL 〔&M〕

### STIX          205/982-3070  70
▼▼ Asian Sushi. Casual Dining. $7-$32 **AAA Inspector Notes:** Diners have the option of sampling from the sushi bar, full of fresh fish; the traditional Asian menu, full of unique twists on classic dishes; or the teppanyaki grills, full of excitement and entertainment. **Features:** full bar, happy hour. **Address:** 3250 Galleria Cir 35244 **Location:** I-459 exit 13 (US 31); adjacent to Riverchase Galleria Shopping Mall. 〔L〕 〔D〕 CALL 〔&M〕

## HOPE HULL

### FAIRFIELD INN & SUITES BY MARRIOTT MONTGOMERY AIRPORT          (334)281-6882
▼▼▼▼ Hotel $79-$139 **Address:** 7560 Mobile Hwy 36105 **Location:** I-65 exit 164, just e. **Facility:** 87 units. 4 stories, interior corridors. **Pool(s):** heated indoor. **Activities:** exercise room. **Guest Services:** valet and coin laundry, area transportation.

| **AAA Benefit:** Members save 5% or more! |
|---|

〔✈〕 CALL 〔&M〕 〔🚐〕 〔BIZ〕 〔HS〕 〔📶〕 〔✕〕 〔🛢〕 〔🖥〕 〔🖳〕

### HAMPTON INN AIRPORT          (334)280-9592
▼▼▼▼ Hotel $89-$139 **Address:** 60 Wasden Rd 36043 **Location:** I-65 exit 164, just w. **Facility:** 78 units. 3 stories, interior corridors. **Terms:** 1-7 night minimum stay, cancellation fee imposed.

| **AAA Benefit:** Members save 5% or more! |
|---|

**Pool(s):** outdoor. **Activities:** exercise room. **Guest Services:** valet and coin laundry, area transportation.
〔✈〕 CALL 〔&M〕 〔🚐〕 〔BIZ〕 〔HS〕 〔📶〕 〔🖳〕

/ SOME UNITS 〔S🛢〕 〔🛢〕 〔🖳〕

## HORSESHOE BEND NATIONAL MILITARY PARK (D-5)

Twelve miles north of Dadeville on SR 49, the 2,040-acre Horseshoe Bend National Military Park preserves the site of Andrew Jackson's decisive victory over the Red Stick Creeks, a faction of the Creek Nation. The battle was the last military action of the Creek War of 1813-14 and resulted in the Treaty of Fort Jackson, which ceded 23 million acres of land to the United States.

In August 1813 hostilities between the Red Sticks and frontiersmen erupted with a massacre at Fort Mims in which 250 men, women and children died. On March 27, 1814, Jackson's force of Tennessee Militia, Regular U.S. Infantry and Lower Creek and Cherokee allies destroyed Chief Menawa's Red Stick warriors gathered in the "horseshoe bend" of the Tallapoosa River. The victory opened much of central Alabama and southern Georgia to settlement and gave Jackson national fame.

The park visitor center contains a museum featuring exhibits of Creek and military history as well as a 20-minute film presentation about the battle. Six stops along a 3-mile road through the battlefield interpret the encounter. A 2.8-mile nature trail also offers views of the battlefield. Museum daily 9-4:30. Battlefield road daily 8-5. Closed Jan. 1, Thanksgiving and Christmas. Free. Phone (256) 234-7111. *See Recreation Areas Chart.*

## HUNTSVILLE (B-4) pop. 180,105, elev. 750'
• Hotels p. 95 • Restaurants p. 97

Huntsville was the site of the first English-speaking settlement in Alabama. In 1819 the first constitutional convention and state legislature met in Huntsville, and Alabama became the 22nd state of the Union.

The nation's space program began in Huntsville in 1950. Spearheaded by the development of the *Saturn V* moon rocket by Dr. Wernher von Braun and his team of German scientists, space technology and exploration have gained increasing momentum through the advances made at the NASA George C. Marshall Space Flight Center, established in 1960.

Originally created to design NASA's rocket propulsion systems, the Marshall Center later became involved in all aspects of the space program, including research in microgravity as well as spacecraft and experimental research and development. The Marshall Center developed the engines and rockets used to launch the space shuttle.

The Tennessee River and its many adjoining lakes provide a variety of recreational opportunities, including water skiing and fishing. A number of parks beautify downtown and the environs.

Big Spring International Park, west of Courthouse Square, is on the site where John Hunt founded the city in 1805. It also is the location of the Fearn Canal, which was used in the 19th century to transport cotton to the river. Throughout the park are gifts from foreign countries; of special interest is a sculptured bridge from Japan. Various festivals are held in the park throughout the year. From late November to early January the park offers an ice rink that is open daily; for Skating in the Park details phone (256) 535-4350.

The Madison County Nature Trail, 12 miles from downtown on Green Mountain, includes a 16-acre lake, a covered bridge and a wildlife sanctuary.

The Twickenham Historic District, downtown and south and east of Courthouse Square, is one of Alabama's largest antebellum residential districts. Descendants of the original owners live in many of the houses. Free guided walking tours of the historic district, a living museum of 19th-century architecture, are provided by the convention and visitors bureau select Saturdays during spring.

The Old Town Historic District, east and north of Courthouse Square, contains 19th- and early 20th-century houses, some still in the process of restoration. Restored bungalows dominate the Five Points Historic District.

Galaxy of Lights Drive-Through Nights is held late November through late December in the Huntsville Botanical Garden. The event is a light extravaganza featuring large animated displays.

**Huntsville/Madison County Convention and Visitors Bureau:** 500 Church St., Huntsville, AL 35801. **Phone:** (256) 551-2370 or (800) 772-2348.

**Self-guiding tours:** Maps outlining tours of three of Huntsville's historic areas as well as brochures and CDs detailing points of interest in the city and county are available from the convention and visitors bureau.

**Shopping areas:** More than 100 stores, including Belk, JCPenney and Sears, offer opportunities for browsing and bargain hunting at Madison Square Mall, US 72W at Research Park Boulevard. Parkway Place, at Bob Wallace and Drake avenues, includes Belk and Dillard's. Bridge Street Town Centre, at Research Park Boulevard and Old Madison Pike, offers outdoor specialty shopping and restaurants.

In high-tech Huntsville the Historic Huntsville Foundation operates Harrison Brothers Hardware at 124 South Side Sq. Established in 1879 and moved to this site in 1897, clerks at this old-fashioned hardware store ring sales of vintage tools, housewares and other items on a hand-cranked cash register.

Lowe Mill Arts & Entertainment, located in an old textile mill at 2211 Seminole Dr., supports a diverse community of local artisans. The arts center, open Wednesday through Saturday, houses locally owned shops promoting artists. Across town, the Five Points Historic District offers an eclectic mix of distinctive boutiques.

**ALABAMA CONSTITUTION VILLAGE,** 109 Gates Ave., marks the site of the 1819 constitutional convention by which Alabama entered the Union. Eight reconstructed buildings depict Southern life in the early 1800s. Costumed guides demonstrate crafts and domestic skills typical of 19th-century Alabama. Santa's Village is set up during the holiday season; lights adorn the historic houses, snow machines make fresh snow nightly, and visitors can make crafts and decorate gingerbread cookies.

**Time:** Allow 1 hour minimum. **Hours:** Tues.-Sat. 10-4, Mar.-Oct. Santa's Village open daily 5-9, day after Thanksgiving-late Dec. **Cost:** $12; $10 (ages 4-17 and 55+); $5 (ages 1-3). Combination ticket with EarlyWorks Children's Museum or Historic Huntsville Depot $20; $15 (ages 4-17 and 55+); $5 (ages 1-3). Combination ticket with EarlyWorks Children's Museum and Historic Huntsville Depot $25; $20 (ages 4-17 and 55+); $5 (ages 1-3). **Phone:** (256) 564-8100.

**BURRITT ON THE MOUNTAIN,** atop Round Top Mountain at 3101 Burritt Dr., features an 11-room mansion containing antique furnishings and exhibits about local history. A historic park contains restored 19th-century rural homes furnished in period. Nature trails also are on the grounds.

**Time:** Allow 1 hour minimum. **Hours:** Tues.-Sat. 9-5, Sun. noon-5, Apr.-Oct.; Tues.-Sat. 10-4, Sun. noon-4, rest of year. Last admission 30 minutes before closing. Closed Jan. 1, Thanksgiving, Christmas Eve and Christmas. **Cost:** $10; $9 (ages 60+ and military with ID); $8 (ages 3-17). Additional fees may apply during special events. **Phone:** (256) 536-2882.

**EARLYWORKS CHILDREN'S MUSEUM** is downtown at 404 Madison St. A film, narrated by native Alabamian Bo Jackson, serves as an introduction to this interactive museum. Visitors learn about the people, agriculture, mining, politics and history of the South. Children can hear stories from a talking tree, try on 19th-century clothing, explore a 46-foot keel boat and turn the handle on a cotton gin to separate seeds from the bolls.

**Time:** Allow 1 hour minimum. **Hours:** Tues.-Sat. 9-4. Closed Jan. 1, Thanksgiving, Christmas Eve and Christmas. **Cost:** $12; $10 (ages 4-17 and 55+); $5 (ages 1-3). Combination ticket with Alabama Constitution Village or Historic Huntsville Depot $20; $15 (ages 4-17 and 55+); $5 (ages 1-3). Combination ticket with Alabama Constitution Village and Historic Huntsville Depot $25; $20 (ages 4-17 and 55+); $5 (ages 1-3). **Phone:** (256) 564-8100.

**HISTORIC HUNTSVILLE DEPOT** is at 320 Church St. Highlights include an extensive collection of locomotives and railway cars, a multimedia presentation about railroad history, a vintage fire truck exhibit and an HO model train exhibit. After Union forces captured the building in 1862, it served as a military prison. Graffiti scratched into the building's walls by Confederate and Union soldiers is still visible. Life-size robotic figures talk about 1912 railroad operations.

**Hours:** Tues.-Sat. 10-4, Mar.-Dec. Closed first 2 weeks in May, Thanksgiving, Christmas Eve and Christmas. **Cost:** $12; $10 (ages 4-17 and ages 55+); $5 (ages 1-3). Combination ticket with Alabama Constitution Village or EarlyWorks Children's Museum $20; $15 (ages 4-17 and 55+); $5 (ages 1-3). Combination ticket with Alabama Constitution Village and EarlyWorks Children's Museum $25; $20 (ages 4-17 and 55+); $5 (ages 1-3). **Phone:** (256) 564-8100.

**HUNTSVILLE BOTANICAL GARDEN,** off I-565 exit 15 then .5 mi. e. to 4747 Bob Wallace Ave., comprises 112 acres of gardens featuring day lilies, ferns, trilliums, herbs, vegetables and aquatic plants. In the Garden Railway, a miniature train chugs through a landscaped European village. The Garden of Hope is a peaceful respite planted by and benefiting those with cancer.

Native northern Alabama wildflowers embellish a nature trail. Also on the grounds is the 9,000-square-foot open-air Butterfly House, open May through September. In addition there are eight children's gardens, including a storybook garden, a bamboo garden and a space garden. Seasonal festivals are held throughout the year.

**Time:** Allow 1 hour minimum. **Hours:** Mon.-Sat. 9-6 (also Thurs. 6-8 p.m.), Sun. noon-6, Apr.-Sept.; Mon.-Sat. 9-5, Sun. noon-5, rest of year. Closed Jan. 1, Thanksgiving and Christmas. **Cost:** $12; $10 (ages 55+ and military with ID); $8 (ages 3-18). Additional fees may apply during special events. **Phone:** (256) 830-4447. ⓘ ⓐ

**HUNTSVILLE MUSEUM OF ART,** downtown at 300 Church St. S.W. in Big Spring Park, features major traveling exhibitions and works by nationally and regionally acclaimed artists and a gallery of works by local children. **Time:** Allow 1 hour minimum. **Hours:** Tues.-Sat. 11-4 (also Thurs. 4-8), Sun. 1-4. Closed major holidays. **Cost:** $10; $8 (ages 60+ and students, educators and military with ID); $5 (ages 6-11 and to all Thurs. 5-8 p.m.). **Phone:** (256) 535-4350 or (800) 786-9095. ⓘ

**SCI-QUEST** is at 1435 Paramount Dr. This hands-on learning experience explores the mysteries of science in seven themed galleries. Visitors can learn about electricity, light and sound; experience an earthquake; or enter a tornado chamber. **Time:** Allow 1 hour minimum. **Hours:** Mon.-Sat. 9-5 (also Sat. 5-6), Sun. noon-5. Last admission 1 hour before closing. Closed major holidays. Phone ahead to confirm schedule. **Cost:** $10; $9 (ages 3-18 and 65+). Additional fees may apply during special events. **Phone:** (256) 837-0606.

**STATE BLACK ARCHIVES, RESEARCH CENTER AND MUSEUM** is at 4900 Meridian St. N., in the James Hembray Wilson Building on the campus of Alabama A&M University. Along with African-American research materials, the center houses a museum with exhibits relating to African-American history and culture. Permanent exhibits focus on Buffalo soldiers, African-American women and an art collection featuring prominent artists such as Romare Bearden and Jacob Lawrence.

**Hours:** Mon.-Fri. 8-5. Last tour begins 1 hour before closing. Closed university holidays. **Cost:** $5; $4 (ages 60+); $3 (ages 5-11). **Phone:** (256) 372-5846. ⓖⓣ

**U.S. SPACE AND ROCKET CENTER,** One Tranquility Base just off I-565, is an exposition center featuring one of the world's largest collections of space and rocket hardware. Interactive exhibits simulate the experience of space flight, including travel aboard the space shuttle.

Attractions include the restored *Saturn V* moon rocket, Mission to Mars climbing wall, MARS motion-based simulator, Spacewalk, Space Shot, Kids' Cosmos, Davidson Center 3D Digital Theater, G-Force accelerator and Spacedome IMAX Theater. The Rocket Park displays NASA rockets and Army defense missiles, including a full-scale shuttle exhibit. On display in Shuttle Park is the orbiter *Pathfinder*, which includes two solid rocket boosters, main engine nozzles and an external tank. The U.S. Space Camp and Aviation Challenge program facilities adjoin the museum property.

**Hours:** Center daily 9-5. 3-D theater daily 10-4. IMAX theater daily 11-3; phone ahead to confirm schedule. Closed Jan. 1, Thanksgiving, Christmas Eve, Christmas and Dec. 31. **Cost:** $20; $15 (ages 6-12). Museum and one movie $25; $20 (ages 6-12). Museum and two movies $30; $25 (ages 6-12). 3-D theater $8; $7 (ages 6-12). IMAX theater $8; $7 (ages 6-12). Feature-length films $10; $9 (ages 4-12). **Phone:** (256) 837-3400 or (800) 637-7223. ⓘ ⓐ

**Spacedome IMAX Theater** is at One Tranquility Base just off I-565 in the U.S. Space and Rocket Center. The theater presents space and science films projected on a 67-foot dome screen that surrounds viewers.

**Time:** Allow 1 hour minimum. **Hours:** Daily 11-3. Closed Jan. 1, Thanksgiving, Christmas Eve, Christmas and Dec. 31. Phone ahead to confirm schedule. **Cost:** $8; $7 (ages 6-12). One movie and U.S. Space and Rocket Center $25; $20 (ages 6-12). Two movies and U.S. Space and Rocket Center $30; $25 (ages 6-12). Feature-length films $10; $9 (ages 4-12). **Phone:** (256) 837-3400 or (800) 637-7223.

**VETERANS MEMORIAL MUSEUM** is at 2060A Airport Rd. Visitors may see some 30 military vehicles from 20th-century wars as well as modern vehicles, including one of the oldest surviving military jeeps. Other highlights include Alabama's Merci Boxcar, one of 49 boxcars presented by France in 1950, along with an M42 Duster, a World War II M36 Tank Destroyer and Harley and Indian motorcycles. Artifacts from as far back as the Revolutionary War are on display. A reference library is available.

**Hours:** Wed.-Sat. 10-5, Memorial Day-Labor Day; 10-4, rest of year. Closed Jan. 1, Thanksgiving and Christmas. **Cost:** $5; $4 (ages 65+); $3 (ages 0-17). **Phone:** (256) 883-3737.

**WEEDEN HOUSE MUSEUM,** 300 Gates Ave. S.E., preserves furniture and architecture of the Federal period. The 1819 house is the birthplace of artist-poet Maria Howard Weeden who became famous in the 1890s for her watercolor portraits of former slaves and poems that captured their personalities and stories. Features include hand-carved mantels and a leaded-glass fanlight as well as her 19th-century watercolors. Weeden's poems are read during guided tours. **Time:** Allow 1 hour minimum. **Hours:** Tours Thurs.-Sat. 10-3:30. **Cost:** $5; $4 (ages 60+ and military with ID); $2.50 (ages 5-11). **Phone:** (256) 536-7718. GT

**WHEELER NATIONAL WILDLIFE REFUGE**—see Decatur p. 71.

### BEST WESTERN PLUS ROCKET CITY INN & SUITES
(256)837-7412

Hotel
$70-$85

**AAA Benefit:** Members save up to 20%!

**Address:** 6200 Torok Cir 35806 **Location:** I-565 exit 14B, 2.6 mi n on SR 255 (Research Park Blvd), then 0.6 mi w on US 72. **Facility:** 62 units, some efficiencies. 3 stories, interior corridors. **Pool(s):** outdoor. **Activities:** exercise room. **Guest Services:** coin laundry.

### COMFORT INN HUNTSVILLE
(256)562-2525

Hotel $79-$97 **Address:** 4725 University Dr NW 35816 **Location:** I-565 exit 14B, 1.5 mi e. **Facility:** 70 units. 4 stories, interior corridors. **Pool(s):** heated indoor. **Activities:** hot tub, exercise room. **Guest Services:** coin laundry.

### COMFORT SUITES
(256)562-2400

Hotel $85-$92 **Address:** 6224 Torok Cir 35806 **Location:** I-565 exit 14B, 2.6 mi n on SR 255 (Research Park Blvd), then 0.6 mi w on US 72. **Facility:** 70 units. 4 stories, interior corridors. **Pool(s):** heated indoor. **Activities:** exercise room. **Guest Services:** valet and coin laundry.

  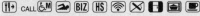

### COUNTRY INN & SUITES BY CARLSON
(256)837-4070

Hotel $95-$135 **Address:** 4880 University Dr 35816 **Location:** I-565 exit 14B, 2.6 mi n on SR 255 (Research Park Blvd), then 1 mi e on US 72. **Facility:** 170 units. 3 stories, interior corridors. **Amenities:** Some: safes. **Pool(s):** outdoor. **Activities:** hot tub, exercise room. **Guest Services:** valet and coin laundry, area transportation.

### COURTYARD BY MARRIOTT-HUNTSVILLE
(256)837-1400

Hotel
$79-$139

COURTYARD Marriott.

**AAA Benefit:** Members save 5% or more!

**Address:** 4804 University Dr 35816 **Location:** I-565 exit 14B, 1.5 mi e. **Facility:** 149 units. 3 stories, interior corridors. **Pool(s):** outdoor. **Activities:** exercise room. **Guest Services:** valet and coin laundry, boarding pass kiosk.

### DAYS INN & SUITES
(256)971-0208

Hotel $60-$100 **Address:** 1145 McMurtrie St 35806 **Location:** I-565 exit 14B, 2.6 mi n on SR 255 (Research Park Blvd), 0.8 mi w on US 72, then just s. Adjacent to Westside Shopping Center. **Facility:** 44 units. 2 stories, interior corridors. **Terms:** cancellation fee imposed. **Pool(s):** outdoor. **Guest Services:** coin laundry.

### DOUBLETREE SUITES BY HILTON HUNTSVILLE SOUTH
(256)882-9400

Hotel $109-$169 **Address:** 6000 S Memorial Pkwy 35802 **Location:** I-565 exit 19A, 5 mi sw on US 231. **Facility:** 149 units. 3 stories, interior corridors. **Terms:** 1-7 night minimum stay, cancellation fee imposed. **Amenities:** safes. **Pool(s):** heated outdoor. **Activities:** exercise room. **Guest Services:** valet and coin laundry.

**AAA Benefit:** Members save 5% or more!

### EMBASSY SUITES HUNTSVILLE HOTEL & SPA
256/539-7373

Hotel. Rates not provided. **Address:** 800 Monroe St SW 35801 **Location:** I-565 exit 19C; downtown; connected to Von Braun Center. **Facility:** 295 units. 10 stories, interior corridors. **Parking:** on-site (fee). **Amenities:** safes. **Dining:** Ruth's Chris Steak House, see separate listing. **Pool(s):** heated indoor. **Activities:** hot tub, exercise room, spa. **Guest Services:** valet and coin laundry, area transportation.

**AAA Benefit:** Members save 5% or more!

### EXTENDED STAY AMERICA HUNTSVILLE-U.S. SPACE AND ROCKET CENTER
(256)830-9110

Extended Stay Hotel $69-$89 **Address:** 4751 Governors House Dr 35805 **Location:** I-565 exit 17A, just s, then 0.5 mi w. **Facility:** 108 efficiencies. 3 stories, exterior corridors. **Terms:** cancellation fee imposed. **Guest Services:** coin laundry.

### FAIRFIELD INN BY MARRIOTT HUNTSVILLE
(256)971-0921

Hotel $84-$299 **Address:** 1385 Enterprise Way 35806 **Location:** I-565 exit 14B, 0.4 mi w of jct SR 255 (Research Park Blvd). **Facility:** 79 units. 3 stories, interior corridors. **Pool(s):** heated indoor. **Activities:** hot tub, exercise room. **Guest Services:** valet laundry.

**AAA Benefit:** Members save 5% or more!

## FOUR POINTS BY SHERATON (256)772-9661

FOUR POINTS BY SHERATON
Hotel
$89-$189

**AAA Benefit:** Members save up to 15%, plus Starwood Preferred Guest® benefits!

**Address:** 1000 Glenn Hearn Blvd 35824 **Location:** I-565 exit 8, 1.3 mi s; in Huntsville International Airport. **Facility:** 146 units. 4 stories, interior corridors. **Activities:** exercise room. **Guest Services:** valet laundry, boarding pass kiosk, rental car service. **Featured Amenity:** breakfast buffet.

`SAVE` `❘❘` `🐾` `Y` CALL `&M` `BIZ` `HS` `🛜` `✕` `🖶` `🖵` / `SOME UNITS` `🖶` `🖼`

## HAMPTON INN & SUITES HUNTSVILLE-SOUTHEAST/HAMPTON COVE, AL (256)532-2110

Hotel $89-$94 **Address:** 6205 Hwy 431 S 35763 **Location:** I-565 exit 19A to Governors Dr, 7.5 mi s on US 431; jct Caldwell Ln. **Facility:** 95 units. 4 stories, interior corridors. **Terms:** 1-7 night minimum stay, cancellation fee imposed. **Activities:** exercise room. **Guest Services:** valet and coin laundry.

**AAA Benefit:** Members save 5% or more!

CALL `&M` `🏊` `BIZ` `HS` `🛜` `✕` `🖶` `🖼` `🖵`

## HAMPTON INN-ARSENAL/SOUTH PARKWAY (256)882-2228

Hotel $99-$159 **Address:** 501 Boulevard South SW 35802 **Location:** I-565 exit 19A, 5 mi s on US 231, then just w. **Facility:** 90 units. 5 stories, interior corridors. **Terms:** 1-7 night minimum stay, cancellation fee imposed. **Pool(s):** outdoor. **Activities:** exercise room. **Guest Services:** valet laundry.

**AAA Benefit:** Members save 5% or more!

`❘❘` CALL `&M` `🏊` `BIZ` `🛜` `🖶` `🖼` `🖵`

## HAMPTON INN HUNTSVILLE (256)830-9400

Hotel $79-$109 **Address:** 4815 University Dr 35816 **Location:** I-565 exit 14B, 2.6 mi n on SR 255 (Research Park Blvd), then 1 mi e on US 72. **Facility:** 156 units. 3 stories, interior/exterior corridors. **Terms:** 1-7 night minimum stay, cancellation fee imposed. **Activities:** exercise room. **Guest Services:** valet laundry.

**AAA Benefit:** Members save 5% or more!

`❘❘` CALL `&M` `🏊` `BIZ` `HS` `🛜` `🖶` `🖼` `🖵`

## HILTON GARDEN INN HUNTSVILLE SOUTH/REDSTONE ARSENAL (256)881-4170

Hotel $89-$159 **Address:** 301 Boulevard South SW 35802 **Location:** I-565 exit 19A, 5 mi s, then just w. **Facility:** 102 units. 5 stories, interior corridors. **Terms:** 1-7 night minimum stay, cancellation fee imposed. **Pool(s):** heated indoor. **Activities:** hot tub, playground, exercise room. **Guest Services:** valet and coin laundry.

**AAA Benefit:** Members save 5% or more!

`❘❘` `Y` `🏊` `BIZ` `HS` `🛜` `✕` `🖶` `🖼` `🖵`

## HILTON GARDEN INN HUNTSVILLE/SPACE CENTER 256/430-1778

Hotel. Rates not provided. **Address:** 4801 Governors House Dr 35805 **Location:** I-565 exit 15, just e, then just ne on access road. **Facility:** 101 units. 4 stories, interior corridors. **Pool(s):** outdoor. **Activities:** hot tub, picnic facilities, exercise room. **Guest Services:** coin laundry, boarding pass kiosk.

**AAA Benefit:** Members save 5% or more!

`❘❘` `Y` CALL `&M` `🏊` `BIZ` `SHS` `🛜` `🖶` `🖼` `🖵`

## HOLIDAY INN EXPRESS HOTEL & SUITES 256/721-1000

Hotel. Rates not provided. **Address:** 3808 University Dr 35816 **Location:** I-565 exit 17A, just e. **Facility:** 146 units. 2 stories (no elevator), interior corridors. **Pool(s):** outdoor. **Activities:** picnic facilities, exercise room. **Guest Services:** valet and coin laundry, area transportation.

`✈` `❘❘` `🐾` `🏊` `BIZ` `🛜` `🖵` / `SOME UNITS` `S` `🖶` `🖼`

## HOLIDAY INN RESEARCH PARK (256)830-0600

Hotel $89-$149 **Address:** 5903 University Dr 35806 **Location:** I-565 exit 14B, 2.6 mi n on SR 255 (Research Park Blvd), then just e on US 72. Located at Madison Square Mall. **Facility:** 200 units. 5 stories, interior corridors. **Terms:** check-in 4 pm. **Dining:** entertainment. **Pool(s):** outdoor, heated indoor. **Activities:** sauna, hot tub, exercise room. **Guest Services:** valet and coin laundry, area transportation.

`✈` `❘❘` `🐾` `Y` CALL `&M` `🏊` `BIZ` `🛜` `🎥` `🖶` `🖼`

## HOMEWOOD SUITES BY HILTON VILLAGE OF PROVIDENCE (256)895-9511

Extended Stay Hotel $109-$164 **Address:** 15 Town Center Dr 35806 **Location:** I-565 exit 14B, 2.6 mi n on SR 255 (Research Park Blvd), 1.4 mi nw on US 72, just n on Providence Main St, then just w. **Facility:** 107 efficiencies, some two bedrooms. 4 stories, interior corridors. **Terms:** 1-7 night minimum stay, cancellation fee imposed. **Pool(s):** outdoor. **Activities:** exercise room. **Guest Services:** valet and coin laundry.

**AAA Benefit:** Members save 5% or more!

`❘❘` CALL `&M` `🏊` `BIZ` `HS` `🛜` `🖶` `🖼` `🖵`

## HUNTSVILLE HOTEL & SUITES 256/837-8907

Extended Stay Hotel. Rates not provided. **Address:** 4020 Independence Dr 35816 **Location:** I-565 exit 17A, 1.1 mi n on SR 53 (Jordan Ln), just w on US 72, then just n. **Facility:** 112 kitchen units. 2 stories (no elevator), exterior corridors. **Terms:** check-in 4 pm. **Pool(s):** outdoor. **Guest Services:** valet and coin laundry.

`❘❘` `🏊` `🛜` `🖶` `🖼` `🖵` / `SOME UNITS` `S`

## LA QUINTA INN & SUITES HUNTSVILLE MADISON SQUARE MALL (256)830-8999

Hotel $69-$169 **Address:** 4890 University Dr NW 35816 **Location:** I-565 exit 14B, 1.3 mi n on SR 255 (Research Park Blvd) to US 72, then 0.9 mi e. **Facility:** 98 units, some two bedrooms. 3 stories, interior corridors. **Pool(s):** outdoor. **Activities:** limited exercise equipment. **Guest Services:** valet laundry.

`❘❘` CALL `&M` `🏊` `BIZ` `🛜` `🖵` / `SOME UNITS` `🐾` `🖶` `🖼`

## LA QUINTA INN HUNTSVILLE (RESEARCH PARK) (256)830-2070

Hotel $65-$139 **Address:** 4870 University Dr NW 35816 **Location:** I-565 exit 14B, 2.6 mi n on SR 255 (Research Park Blvd), then 1.1 mi e on US 72. **Facility:** 130 units. 2 stories (no elevator), exterior corridors. **Pool(s):** outdoor. **Guest Services:** valet and coin laundry.

`❘❘` `🏊` `🛜` `🖵` / `SOME UNITS` `🐾` `HS` `🖶` `🖼`

## LA QUINTA INN HUNTSVILLE (SPACE CENTER) (256)533-0756

Hotel $55-$162 **Address:** 3141 University Dr NW 35816 **Location:** I-565 exit 17A, 1.1 mi n on SR 53 (Jordan Ln), then 0.6 mi e on US 72. **Facility:** 130 units. 2 stories (no elevator), exterior corridors. **Pool(s):** outdoor.

`❘❘` `🏊` `🛜` `🖵` / `SOME UNITS` `🐾` `🖶` `🖼`

Pick up vibrant, top-quality travel guides and atlases at AAA/CAA offices

## MARRIOTT HUNTSVILLE

(256)830-2222

▼▼▼▼ Hotel $99-$349 **Address:** 5 Tranquility Base 35805 **Location:** I-565 exit 15, just sw. Adjacent to U.S. Space and Rocket Center. **Facility:** 290 units. 7 stories, interior corridors. **Amenities:** video games, safes. **Dining:** Porter's Steakhouse, see separate listing. **Pool(s):** heated outdoor, heated indoor. **Activities:** exercise room. **Guest Services:** valet and coin laundry, boarding pass kiosk.

> **AAA Benefit:**
> Members save 5% or more!

## MICROTEL INN & SUITES BY WYNDHAM HUNTSVILLE

(256)859-6655

▼▼ Hotel $59-$79 **Address:** 1820 Chase Creek Row 35811 **Location:** Jct US 72 and Shields Rd, just n, then just w. **Facility:** 62 units. 3 stories, interior corridors. **Pool(s):** outdoor. **Activities:** exercise room.

## SLEEP INN & SUITES

(256)382-2583

▼▼ Hotel $81-$95 **Address:** 4727 University Dr NW 35816 **Location:** I-565 exit 14B, 1.5 mi e on US 72. **Facility:** 66 units. 4 stories, interior corridors. **Activities:** exercise room. **Guest Services:** valet and coin laundry.

## SPRINGHILL SUITES BY MARRIOTT DOWNTOWN

(256)512-0188

▼▼▼▼ Hotel $109-$186 **Address:** 745 Constellation Place Dr 35801 **Location:** I-565 exit 19A (US 231 S), 0.6 mi s to Clinton Ave exit, then just s. **Facility:** 149 units. 6 stories, interior corridors. **Amenities:** safes. **Pool(s):** heated outdoor. **Activities:** exercise room. **Guest Services:** valet and coin laundry.

> **AAA Benefit:**
> Members save 5% or more!

## SPRINGHILL SUITES BY MARRIOTT HUNTSVILLE WEST/RESEARCH PARK

(256)430-1485

▼▼▼ Hotel $119-$134 **Address:** 320 Providence Main St 35806 **Location:** I-565 exit 14B, 2.6 mi n on SR 255 (Research Park Blvd), then 0.8 mi w on US 72. **Facility:** 88 units. 4 stories, interior corridors. **Pool(s):** outdoor. **Activities:** exercise room. **Guest Services:** valet and coin laundry.

> **AAA Benefit:**
> Members save 5% or more!

## TOWNEPLACE SUITES BY MARRIOTT HUNTSVILLE

(256)971-5277

▼▼▼ Extended Stay Hotel $89-$299 **Address:** 1125 McMurtrie Dr 35806 **Location:** I-565 exit 14B, 2.6 mi n on SR 255 (Research Park Blvd), 0.8 mi w on US 72, then just s. Adjacent to Westside Centre Shopping Plaza. **Facility:** 86 units, some two bedrooms, efficiencies and kitchens. 3 stories, interior corridors. **Pool(s):** outdoor. **Activities:** picnic facilities, exercise room. **Guest Services:** valet and coin laundry.

> **AAA Benefit:**
> Members save 5% or more!

## THE WESTIN HUNTSVILLE

(256)428-2000

▼▼▼▼ Hotel $99-$239

**WESTIN** HOTELS & RESORTS

> **AAA Benefit:**
> Members save up to 15%, plus Starwood Preferred Guest® benefits!

**Address:** 6800 Governors West NW 35806 **Location:** I-565 exit 14A, 0.5 mi n on SR 255 (Research Park Blvd), just w on Madison Pike, then 0.5 mi n. **Facility:** This full-service property is the keystone of the Bridge Street Town Centre, which is near Cummings Research Park and within walking distance of many restaurants, shops and entertainment options. 210 units, some two bedrooms. 11 stories, interior corridors. **Parking:** on-site and valet. **Terms:** cancellation fee imposed. **Amenities:** safes. **Dining:** Sage Grille, see separate listing. **Pool(s):** heated outdoor, heated indoor. **Activities:** hot tub, exercise room, spa. **Guest Services:** valet laundry, luggage security pick-up, area transportation.

---

### WHERE TO EAT

## ANOTHER BROKEN EGG CAFE

256/883-2915

▼▼ Breakfast Sandwiches. Casual Dining. $5-$14 **AAA Inspector Notes:** Enjoy a breakfast experience you will not soon forget; huge cinnamon buns, Popeye's omelet and fruit and nut pancakes or french toast are some of the menu specialties. **Features:** full bar, patio dining, Sunday brunch. **Address:** 2722 Carl T. Jones Dr SE 35802 **Location:** Jct US 231 and Airport Rd, 1.2 mi e, then 1.2 mi se; in Valley Bend Shopping Center.

## CAFE BERLIN

256/880-9920

▼▼ European. Casual Dining. $8-$19 **AAA Inspector Notes:** The small, pleasantly decorated restaurant with its light lime walls, warm woods and bistro-style chairs and tables offers an interesting selection of European-inspired cuisine. The smartly attired waitstaff, in ruffled tuxedo shirts and long black aprons, add to the modern, Euro look. **Features:** full bar, Sunday brunch, happy hour. **Address:** 964 Airport Rd 35802 **Location:** I-565 exit 19A, 3.4 mi s on US 231 exit Airport Rd, then 0.3 mi e; in Piedmont Station Plaza.

---

Check DrivingLaws.AAA.com for local motor vehicle laws when traveling

---

## CONNORS STEAK & SEAFOOD  256-327-8425

Steak
Seafood
Fine Dining
$9-$31

**AAA Inspector Notes:** Steaks and seafood abound in this rustic, country-lodge atmosphere. Dark wood and a fieldstone fireplace add a warm touch. **Features:** full bar, patio dining, happy hour. **Reservations:** suggested. **Address:** 345 The Bridge St NW, Suite 101 35806 **Location:** I-565 exit 14A, 0.5 mi n on SR 255 (Research Park Blvd), then just w on Old Madison Pike; in Bridge Street Town Centre. L D CALL M

### Fresh seafood, premium aged steaks, pastas and more

---

### COTTON ROW RESTAURANT  256/382-9500

American
Fine Dining
$10-$36

**AAA Inspector Notes:** Exposed brick walls and rich dark wood along with granite and wrought iron touches convey an earthy tone to this intimate bistro. Wall-length sliding glass doors open to expand the dining area onto the sidewalk for outdoor seating. Lunch is offered Wednesday through Friday. **Features:** full bar, patio dining. **Reservations:** suggested. **Address:** 100 Southside Square 35801 **Location:** Corner of Madison St; downtown; across from courthouse. **Parking:** valet and street only. D CALL M

---

### GRILLE 29  256/489-9470

Steak Seafood. Fine Dining. $11-$39 **AAA Inspector Notes:** Specializing in steaks and seafood, the chef here prepares each dish to perfection, with sides and sauces to complement the selections. Lighter portions of some dinner entrées are offered for lunch, as well as overstuffed sandwiches and crisp, fresh salads. **Features:** full bar, patio dining, Sunday brunch. **Reservations:** suggested. **Address:** 445 Providence Main St, Suite 101 35806 **Location:** I-565 exit 14B, 2.6 mi n on SR 255 (Research Park Blvd), 1.4 mi nw on US 72, then just n; corner of Town Center Dr. **Parking:** street only. L D CALL M

---

### LANDRY'S SEAFOOD HOUSE  256/864-0000

Seafood. Casual Dining. $12-$28 **AAA Inspector Notes:** An ideal spot for healthy seafood dinners and special occasions, the restaurant produces a wonderful clam chowder. Menu selections come from all the world's oceans. **Features:** full bar, happy hour. **Address:** 5101 Governor's House Dr 35805 **Location:** I-565 exit 15, just s on Bob Wallace Rd, then just e. SAVE L D

---

### LITTLE PAUL'S BARBECUE  256/536-7227

Barbecue. Quick Serve. $4-$18 **AAA Inspector Notes:** Delicious home-style barbecue and friendly service keeps loyal customers coming back to this popular, family-owned restaurant. Their homemade pies (whole or by the slice) are heavenly. **Address:** 815 Madison St 35801 **Location:** Downtown; across from Huntsville Hospital. L D

---

### MAIN ST CAFE & BAKERY  256/881-0044

Sandwiches Desserts. Quick Serve. $6-$8 **AAA Inspector Notes:** All sandwiches are made using freshly-baked bread, but don't overlook the homemade cakes, soups and salads (the pasta salad is a favorite). The pies, available whole or by the slice, are made from scratch. With its yellow-striped awning, checkered floor and desserts on display, it feels like Main Street USA. **Features:** patio dining. **Address:** 7500 S Memorial Pkwy 35802 **Location:** I-565 exit 19A, 5 mi s on US 231/431/Memorial Pkwy. **Parking:** street only. B L

---

### NICK'S RISTORANTE  256/489-8280

Italian. Fine Dining. $20-$40 **AAA Inspector Notes:** Located in a small shopping center, this corner storefront will surprise you upon entering. The cigar lounge features rich wood accents and plush leather sofas, and casual chatter fills the air. A lighter bar menu is offered until 7 pm. The non-smoking enclosed dining room is stylishly enhanced with dark red walls, wrought-iron adornments, a built-in wooden wine case and pre-set, cloth-covered tables. Scrumptious food and friendly, excellent service is the norm. **Features:** full bar, happy hour. **Reservations:** suggested. **Address:** 10300 Bailey Cove Rd, Suite 1 35803 **Location:** I-565 exit 19A, 6.2 mi s on US 231/431, 1.5 mi e on Weatherly Rd, then just s; in Creek Side Corners Shopping Plaza. D CALL M

---

### NOTHING BUT NOODLES  256/922-1650

Noodles. Casual Dining. $6-$11 **AAA Inspector Notes:** As the name implies, this quick-serve café offers a variety of noodles and pasta, including American, Cajun, Italian and Asian. Made fresh and bursting with flavor, there's something here for everyone. Appetizers, soups and salads also are available. Leave room for the homemade dessert. **Features:** beer & wine. **Address:** 6125 University Dr, Suite E-2 35806 **Location:** I-565 exit 14B, 2.6 mi on SR 255 (Research Park Blvd), then 0.3 mi w on US 72; in University Place Shopping Center. L D CALL M

---

### OL' HEIDELBERG CAFE  256/922-0556

German. Casual Dining. $9-$20 **AAA Inspector Notes:** From the traditionally-costumed staff to the cuckoo clocks on the wall, this restaurant is true to its traditions. Authentic German dishes are offered using good, quality ingredients. Generous portions and simple preparations are the standards of a menu that features wiener schnitzel (veal, pork or chicken). Other German favorites include spaetzle, sausage specialties, German salads, sandwiches and seafood. **Features:** beer & wine. **Address:** 6125 University Dr, Suite E14 35806 **Location:** I-565 exit 14B, 2.6 mi n on SR 255 (Research Park Blvd), then 0.3 mi w on US 72; in University Place Shopping Center. L D CALL M

---

### PANE E VINO PIZZERIA  256/533-1180

Italian
Pizza
Casual Dining
$7-$15

**AAA Inspector Notes:** This popular bistro at Huntsville's Big Spring Park Lake is just behind the downtown Museum of Art. Meet with friends before a concert at the Von Braun Center. Make it a very special date and dine inside, or order something to go and picnic under one of the park's many gazebos. Pizzas are named after famous artists: The Jackson Pollock, a personal favorite, is topped with chicken pesto. Others include the Michelangelo, Monet and van Gogh. Pasta, calzones and panini round out the menu. **Features:** full bar, patio dining, happy hour. **Address:** 300 Church St 35801 **Location:** Corner of Williams Ave; downtown; in Huntsville Museum of Art. **Parking:** street only. L D

---

### PAPOU'S GREEK CUISINE  256/534-5553

Greek. Casual Dining. $8-$23 **AAA Inspector Notes:** On a quaint, tree-lined city square, a narrow entryway leads to a taste of Greece. A wall mural of a Mediterranean seascape creates the right ambience for your mind and palate. This cozy café is open weekdays for lunch, and Wednesday through Saturday for dinner. **Features:** beer & wine. **Address:** 110 South Side Square 35801 **Location:** Between Madison and Franklin sts; downtown. **Parking:** street only. L D

---

### P.F. CHANG'S CHINA BISTRO  256/327-8320

Chinese. Fine Dining. $8-$25 **AAA Inspector Notes:** Trendy, upscale decor provides a pleasant backdrop for New Age Chinese dining. Appetizers, soups and salads are a meal by themselves. Vegetarian plates and sides, noodles, chow meins, chicken and meat dishes are created from exotic, fresh ingredients. **Features:** full bar. **Reservations:** suggested. **Address:** 305 The Bridge St 35806 **Location:** I-565 exit 14A, 0.5 mi n on SR 255 (Research Park Blvd), then just w on Old Madison Pike; in Bridge Street Town Centre. L D CALL M

---

**PHIL SANDOVAL'S MEXICAN RESTAURANTE**  256/489-5711

▼▼▼ Mexican. Casual Dining. $7-$13 **AAA Inspector Notes:** The constant chatter heard here indicates the popularity of this establishment. The colorful, rustic décor of unfinished wood, bright ceramics and twinkle lights adds to the festive atmosphere. **Features:** full bar. **Address:** 6125 University Dr 35816 **Location:** I-565 exit 14B, 2.6 mi n on SR 255 (Research Park Blvd), then 0.3 mi w on US 72; in University Place Shopping Center. Ⓛ Ⓓ CALL Ⓖ Ⓜ

**PHUKET EXTRAORDINARY THAI EXPERIENCE**  256/489-1612

▼▼ Thai Sushi. Casual Dining. $8-$22 **AAA Inspector Notes:** Tasty Thai cuisine, as well as sushi, can be enjoyed in the bright, contemporary dining room of this casual eatery. Outdoor sidewalk seating also is available. **Features:** full bar, patio dining, happy hour. **Address:** 475 Providence Main St, Suite 102 35806 **Location:** I-565 exit 14B, 2.6 mi n on SR 255 (Research Park Blvd), 1.4 mi nw on US 72, then just n. **Parking:** street only. Ⓛ Ⓓ CALL Ⓖ Ⓜ

**PORTER'S STEAKHOUSE**  256/830-2222

▼▼▼ Steak. Fine Dining. $15-$31 **AAA Inspector Notes:** This intimate, upscale bistro features antique adornments and dark wood encasements—all reminiscent of a home library. **Features:** full bar. **Address:** 5 Tranquility Base 35805 **Location:** I-565 exit 15, just sw; in Marriott Huntsville. Ⓓ CALL Ⓖ Ⓜ

**ROSIE'S MEXICAN CANTINA**  256/922-1001

▼▼ Mexican. Casual Dining. $7-$17 **AAA Inspector Notes:** Drive up to this cantina, where you'll find a lively atmosphere, cheerful staff and a Mexican fiesta attitude any day of the year. Feast on generous portions of south-of-the-border cuisine, including fajitas, chiles rellenos and Mexican lasagna. Service is friendly, knowledgeable and efficient. **Features:** full bar, happy hour. **Address:** 6196 University Dr 35816 **Location:** I-565 exit 14B, 2.6 mi n on SR 255 (Research Park Blvd), then 0.3 mi w on US 72. Ⓛ Ⓓ

**RUTH'S CHRIS STEAK HOUSE**  256/539-3930

▼▼▼ Steak. Fine Dining. $20-$83 **AAA Inspector Notes:** The main fare is steak, which is prepared from several cuts of Prime beef and cooked to perfection, but the menu also lists lamb, chicken and seafood dishes. Guests should come hungry because the side dishes, which are among the a la carte offerings, could make a meal in themselves. **Features:** full bar. **Reservations:** suggested. **Address:** 800 Monroe St SW 35801 **Location:** I-565 exit 19C; downtown; connected to Von Braun Center; in Embassy Suites Huntsville Hotel & Spa. **Parking:** on-site and valet. Ⓛ Ⓓ CALL Ⓖ Ⓜ

**SAGE GRILLE**  256/428-2000

▼▼▼▼ Mediterranean. Fine Dining. $9-$30 **AAA Inspector Notes:** Inside the Westin at Bridge Street Town Centre, this contemporary restaurant serves a tasteful range of steak, seafood, ribs, burgers and sandwiches. Celebrate a special occasion in an intimate booth, or enjoy a beer and watch the game on the bar TV. Professional and friendly staff deliver an attentive evening. **Features:** full bar, patio dining, senior menu. **Address:** 6800 Governors West NW 35806 **Location:** I-565 exit 14A, 0.5 mi n on SR 255 (Research Park Blvd), just w on Old Madison Pike, then 0.5 mi n; in The Westin Huntsville. **Parking:** on-site and valet. Ⓑ Ⓛ Ⓓ CALL Ⓖ Ⓜ

**SAM & GREG'S PIZZERIA - GELATERIA**  256/533-9030

▼▼ Pizza. Casual Dining. $6-$23 **AAA Inspector Notes:** Located in a renovated brownstone-like storefront, this charming bistro offers made-to-order crispy, thin-crust pizza and luscious homemade gelato. It's also reputed to be haunted! **Features:** beer & wine, patio dining. **Address:** 119 North Side Square 35801 **Location:** Between Jefferson and Washington sts; downtown; across from courthouse. **Parking:** street only. Ⓛ Ⓓ

**SHAGGYS BURGERS & TACOS**  256/270-9999

▼▼ Burgers. Quick Serve. $3-$9 **AAA Inspector Notes:** Colorful wall-mounted surfboards and kites hung from the ceiling suggest the laid-back atmosphere of this casual burger joint with a Mexican twist. Can't decide between sweet potato fries or standard french fries? Order both, they'll mix it. The breakfast menu also offers Mexican influences. Along with a variety of bottled beers, adults will enjoy frosty, frozen margaritas. **Features:** beer only, patio dining. **Address:** 1267-E Enterprise Way 35806 **Location:** I-565 exit 14B, 0.4 mi w of jct SR 255 (Research Park Blvd), then just s. Ⓑ Ⓛ Ⓓ CALL Ⓖ Ⓜ

**SHEA'S EXPRESS**  256/532-5282

▼▼ Breakfast Sandwiches. Quick Serve. $6-$13 **AAA Inspector Notes:** On the fringes of downtown, turn into the driveway where a bright red caboose sits and straight ahead is this charming café. The focal point of the contemporary décor is the wall covered with crosses from around the world, which were gifts from appreciative customers. The highlight of the week is Saturday brunch when live jazz music is presented. Enjoy the music while sipping a mimosa or fuzzy navel and munching on the likes of crab cakes Benedict or cranberry-orange French toast. **Features:** beer & wine, patio dining. **Address:** 415 Church St, Suite E-5 35801 **Location:** I-565 exit 19C, just s on Jefferson St, just w on Monroe St, then just n. Ⓑ Ⓛ CALL Ⓖ Ⓜ

**SUN CAFE**  256/585-1422

▼▼ Asian. Casual Dining. $8-$23 **AAA Inspector Notes:** This cozy, intimate restaurant offers a stylish, contemporary décor. The expansive menu offers varied sushi options, as well as Chinese, Thai and vegetarian dishes. Pesticide-free produce is used in their preparation. **Features:** full bar. **Address:** 930 Old Monrovia Rd, Suite 3 35806 **Location:** I-565 exit 14B, 2.6 mi n on SR 255 (Research Park Blvd), 0.5 mi e on US 72, then just n; in HH Gregg Shopping Center. Ⓛ Ⓓ CALL Ⓖ Ⓜ

**TERRANOVA'S ITALIAN RESTAURANT**  256/489-8883

▼▼ Italian. Casual Dining. $8-$18 **AAA Inspector Notes:** Authentic Italian dishes inspired by the owner's many trips to Italy line this restaurant's classic menu. Guests can savor eggplant parmigiana, manicotti, penne alla vodka, lasagna, spaghetti, chicken cannelloni, fettuccine Alfredo, and, of course, tiramisu and spumoni. Buon appetito! **Features:** full bar, patio dining. **Reservations:** required. **Address:** 1420 Paramount Dr, Suite 1 35806 **Location:** I-565 exit 14B, 2.6 mi n on SR 255 (Research Park Blvd), 1.7 mi n on US 72, then just n; at Paramount Place Plaza. Ⓛ Ⓓ CALL Ⓖ Ⓜ

**WEST END GRILL**  256/722-8040

▼▼ American. Casual Dining. $8-$13 **AAA Inspector Notes:** This local watering hole likens itself to a modern day "Cheers" atmosphere. The basic home-style cooking is what draws many. Heaping portions are enough to satisfy the heartiest of appetites at prices to please all. Menu favorites include homemade meatloaf, Southern fried chicken and slow-cooked pot roast which is so tender a knife is not needed to cut it. Save room for the yummy peach or blackberry cobbler. **Features:** full bar, patio dining, happy hour. **Address:** 6610 Old Madison Pike 35806 **Location:** I-565 exit 14A, 0.5 mi n on SR 255 (Research Park Blvd), then just e. Ⓛ Ⓓ LATE

**WINTZELL'S OYSTER HOUSE**  256/726-0511

▼▼ Southern Seafood. Casual Dining. $9-$24 **AAA Inspector Notes:** Diners can request their oysters fried, stewed or nude at this eatery, which has been preparing them 10 different ways since 1938. The menu also lists an exceptional variety of seafood. **Features:** full bar. **Address:** 5100 Sanderson St 35805 **Location:** I-565 exit 14B, 2.6 mi n on SR 255 (Research Park Blvd), 1 mi e on US 72, then just s. Ⓛ Ⓓ CALL Ⓖ Ⓜ

**Remember, car seats, booster seats and seat belts save lives**

## IRONDALE pop. 12,349

- Hotels & Restaurants map & index p. 54
- Part of Birmingham area — see map p. 43

### HAMPTON INN & SUITES BIRMINGHAM AIRPORT AREA
(205)933-0444 20

 Hotel $109-$159 Address: 3930 Old Grants Mill Rd 35210 Location: I-20 exit 133, just e. Facility: 99 units. 4 stories, interior corridors. Terms: 1-7 night minimum stay, cancellation fee imposed. Pool(s): heated indoor. Activities: exercise room. Guest Services: valet laundry, area transportation.

**AAA Benefit:** Members save 5% or more!

 CALL 🆎M 🛏 🖼 BIZ HS 🛜 ✖ 🖥
/ SOME UNITS 🍳 🖼

### HOLIDAY INN EXPRESS HOTEL & SUITES BIRMINGHAM EAST
19

 Hotel. Rates not provided. Address: 811 Old Grants Mill Rd 35210 Location: I-20 exit 133, just sw on Crescent Blvd, then just s. Facility: 100 units. 4 stories, interior corridors. Activities: exercise room. Guest Services: valet and coin laundry, area transportation.

🆎 🛏 BIZ HS 🛜 🖥 / SOME UNITS 🍳 🖥 🖼

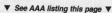
### WHERE TO EAT

### HAMBURGER HEAVEN
205/951-3570 26

🦅 Burgers. Quick Serve. $2-$7 AAA Inspector Notes: This restaurant's name says it all. Birmingham loves this burger joint, and newcomers will, too. Features: patio dining. Address: 1703 Crestwood Blvd 35210 Location: I-20 exit 132B, just s on Montevallo Rd, then 0.5 mi e. L D CALL 🆎M 🐕

### IRONDALE CAFE
205/956-5258 25

🦅 American. Cafeteria. $7-$9 AAA Inspector Notes: The original whistle stop cafe gained renown for its inspirational part in the book and movie, "Fried Green Tomatoes." Good home cooking is as Southern as it gets, and the prices are right. Address: 1906 1st Ave N 35210 Location: I-20 exit 133, 0.7 mi nw on 20th St S.
L D CALL 🆎M

## JACKSON pop. 5,228

### BEST WESTERN SUITES
(251)246-6030

Motel
$90-$96

**AAA Benefit:** Members save up to 20%!

Address: 3218 College Ave 36545 Location: Jct US 43 and SR 69, 2 mi n. Facility: 24 units. 1 story, exterior corridors. Pool(s): outdoor. Activities: exercise room. Guest Services: valet laundry.

SAVE 🛏 HS 🛜 ✖ 🖥 🖼 🖥

### HAMPTON INN JACKSON AL
(251)246-7300

 Hotel $99-$134 Address: 4150 N College Ave 36545 Location: Jct US 43 and SR 69, 2.6 mi n. Facility: 70 units. 3 stories, interior corridors. Terms: 1-7 night minimum stay, cancellation fee imposed. Pool(s): outdoor. Activities: exercise room. Guest Services: valet and coin laundry.

**AAA Benefit:** Members save 5% or more!

CALL 🆎M 🛏 BIZ HS 🛜 ✖ 🖥 🖼 🖥

## JASPER pop. 14,352

### HOLIDAY INN EXPRESS HOTEL & SUITES
205/302-6400

 Hotel. Rates not provided. Address: 202 Oakhill Rd 35504 Location: On SR 118, 3 mi w of jct SR 69. Facility: 64 units. 3 stories, interior corridors. Parking: winter plug-ins. Pool(s): outdoor. Activities: limited exercise equipment. Guest Services: valet and coin laundry.

 CALL 🆎M 🛏 BIZ 🛜 🖥 🖼 🖥

### QUALITY INN
(205)387-7710

 Motel $74-$84 Address: 1100 Hwy 78/118 E 35501 Location: SR 118, 1.8 mi w of jct SR 69. Facility: 59 units. 2 stories (no elevator), exterior corridors. Pool(s): outdoor. Activities: exercise room. (See ad this page.)

 CALL 🆎M 🛏 🛜 🖥 🖼 🖥 / SOME UNITS 🍳

▼ See AAA listing this page ▼

**WHERE TO EAT**

PERICO'S AUTHENTIC MEXICAN RESTAURANT 205/387-8800

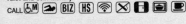 Mexican. Casual Dining. $8-$12 **AAA Inspector Notes:** This locally-owned restaurant boasts a fine happy hour and quick traditional Mexican meals. Homemade tortillas and tamales spice things up. **Features:** full bar. **Address:** 2201 Hwy 78 E 35501 **Location:** Just n of jct SR 69. [L] [D] [⊠]

## LANETT pop. 6,468

HAMPTON INN & SUITES-LANETT/WEST POINT
(334)576-5400

 **Hotel** $99-$119 **Address:** 4210 Phillips Rd 36863 **Location:** I-85 exit 77, just nw. **Facility:** 111 units. 5 stories, interior corridors. **Terms:** 1-7 night minimum stay, cancellation fee imposed. **Pool(s):** heated indoor. **Activities:** exercise room. **Guest Services:** valet and coin laundry.

**AAA Benefit:**
Members save 5% or more!

CALL [♿M] [≋] [BIZ] [HS] [🛜] [⊠] [🍴] [🖥] [💻]

## LEEDS pop. 11,773, elev. 622'
• Part of Birmingham area — see map p. 43

COMFORT INN & SUITES (205)640-6600

 **Hotel** $85-$270 **Address:** 1951 Village Dr 35094 **Location:** I-20 exit 144A westbound; exit 144B eastbound, just ne. **Facility:** 45 units. 2 stories (no elevator), interior corridors. **Pool(s):** outdoor. **Activities:** limited exercise equipment.

[🍴] [≋] [BIZ] [HS] [🛜] [🍴] [🖥] [💻]

DAYS INN OF LEEDS (205)699-9833

 **Motel** $80-$256 **Address:** 1838 Ashville Rd 35094 **Location:** I-20 exit 144A eastbound; exit 144B westbound, just s. **Facility:** 51 units. 2 stories (no elevator), exterior corridors. **Pool(s):** outdoor. **Guest Services:** coin laundry.

[🍴] [≋] [🛜] [🍴] [🖥] [💻] / SOME UNITS [≋]

**WHERE TO EAT**

RUSTY'S BAR-B-Q 205/699-4766

 Barbecue. Family Dining. $8-$20 **AAA Inspector Notes:** In addition to the famous barbecue, this local favorite also serves fresh burgers and homemade dessert. Whatever you do, do not leave without a slice of peanut butter pie, which some say tastes like heaven! **Address:** 7484 Parkway Dr 35094 **Location:** I-20 exit 140, 2.3 mi e. [L] [D] CALL [♿M]

## LINCOLN pop. 6,266

COMFORT INN (205)763-9777

 Hotel $74-$299

**Address:** 850/A Speedway Industrial Dr 35096 **Location:** I-20 exit 168, just se. **Facility:** 60 units. 3 stories, interior corridors. **Pool(s):** outdoor. **Activities:** exercise room. **Guest Services:** coin laundry. **Featured Amenity:** full hot breakfast.

[SAVE] [🍴] CALL [♿M] [≋] [BIZ] [HS] [🛜] [🍴] [🖥] [💻] / SOME UNITS [≋]

**WHERE TO EAT**

MONTANA SALOON & GRILL 205/763-1225

 Burgers Steak. Casual Dining. $6-$19 **AAA Inspector Notes:** This log cabin building, with its stained-glass doors featuring buffaloes, gives a sense of what to expect inside. Natural wood paneled walls, antler chandeliers and a wall-mounted deer head add to the mountain hunting lodge feel. Burgers, both beef and buffalo, along with grilled steaks are the signature menu selections. **Features:** full bar, happy hour. **Address:** 75023 Hwy 77 35096 **Location:** I-20 exit 168, 0.5 mi s. [L] [D] CALL [♿M] [⊠]

## LUVERNE pop. 2,800

GUESTHOUSE INN & SUITES (334)335-3050

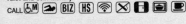 Hotel $65-$75 **Address:** 1701 Montgomery Hwy 36049 **Location:** Jct US 331 and SR 10. Behind Hook's BBQ. **Facility:** 49 units. 2 stories, interior corridors. **Pool(s):** outdoor. **Activities:** exercise room.

[🍴] CALL [♿M] [≋] [BIZ] [HS] [🛜] [🍴] [💻] / SOME UNITS [≋] [🖥]

**WHERE TO EAT**

HOOK'S BBQ 334/335-2807

 Barbecue. Casual Dining. $5-$15 **AAA Inspector Notes:** Enter into this rustic roadside cabin, and the aroma of smoke permeates the air, which is the tell-tale sign that all the meats are smoked on the premises. You can eat on site in the basic, no-frills dining area or take your meal to go. **Address:** 1703 Montgomery Hwy 36049 **Location:** Jct US 331 and SR 10. [B] [L] [D]

KINFOLK'S 334/535-3663

 Southern Comfort Food. Casual Dining. $6-$8 **AAA Inspector Notes:** Dining at this cozy, family-operated dinette is just like going to eat at grandma's house. A limited rotating menu lists one hot meat or fish with pre-set sides and dessert. Be sure to call ahead to find out what's being served that day to make sure it's to your liking. Only lunch is served on Sunday. **Address:** 1374 S Forest Ave 36049 **Location:** Jct US 331 and 29, 1.4 mi s on SR 9. [L] [D]

## MADISON pop. 42,938
• Restaurants p. 102

BAYMONT INN & SUITES MADISON/HUNTSVILLE AIRPORT
(256)258-0800

 Hotel $69-$89 **Address:** 122 Cleghorn Blvd 35758 **Location:** I-565 exit 9, just sw. **Facility:** 55 units. 3 stories, interior corridors. **Pool(s):** outdoor. **Activities:** exercise room. **Guest Services:** coin laundry.

[🍴] CALL [♿M] [≋] [BIZ] [HS] [🛜] [⊠] [🍴] [🖥] [💻]

BEST WESTERN PLUS MADISON-HUNTSVILLE HOTEL
(256)772-7170

 Hotel $77-$110

Best Western PLUS

**AAA Benefit:** Members save up to 20%!

**Address:** 9035 Madison Blvd 35758 **Location:** I-565 exit 9, just nw. **Facility:** 164 units. 2 stories, interior/exterior corridors. **Amenities:** video games. **Dining:** Port of Madison Restaurant, see separate listing. **Pool(s):** outdoor. **Activities:** hot tub, exercise room. **Guest Services:** valet and coin laundry, area transportation. **Featured Amenity:** continental breakfast.

[SAVE] [✈] [🍴] [🛁] [Y] [≋] [BIZ] [HS] [🛜] [🎥] [🍴] [🖥] [💻]

**COUNTRY INN & SUITES BY CARLSON/HUNTSVILLE AIRPORT**                              (256)325-0007

WWW Hotel $75-$200 Address: 101 Westchester Dr 35758 Location: I-565 exit 9, just n to jct Madison Blvd and SR 20, then just w. Facility: 64 units. 3 stories, interior corridors. Terms: cancellation fee imposed. Pool(s): heated indoor. Activities: hot tub, exercise room. Guest Services: complimentary laundry.

[icons]

**HAMPTON INN-HUNTSVILLE/MADISON**          (256)464-8999

WWWW Hotel $99-$129 Address: 9225 Madison Blvd 35758 Location: I-565 exit 9, just n to SR 20, then 0.6 mi w. Facility: 140 units. 3 stories, interior corridors. Terms: 1-7 night minimum stay, cancellation fee imposed. Amenities: video games. Pool(s): heated outdoor. Activities: hot tub, exercise room. Guest Services: valet and coin laundry, area transportation.

**AAA Benefit:**
Members save 5% or more!

[icons]

**RADISSON HOTEL HUNTSVILLE AIRPORT**          (256)772-8855

WWW Hotel $88-$109 Address: 8721 Madison Blvd 35758 Location: I-565 exit 9, just n to jct SR 20, then 0.4 mi e. Facility: 136 units. 2 stories (no elevator), interior corridors. Terms: 45 day cancellation notice. Amenities: Some: safes. Pool(s): outdoor. Activities: picnic facilities, exercise room. Guest Services: valet laundry, area transportation.

[icons]

## WHERE TO EAT

**BISON'S BAR & GRILL**          256/772-4477

WW WW American. Casual Dining. $6-$15 AAA Inspector Notes: Known for wings and burgers, this relaxed Southwestern-style cantina offers steak, chicken and fish dishes, as well as sandwiches and wraps. Features: full bar. Address: 8020 Madison Blvd 35758 Location: I-565 exit 8, 2 mi ne; in Madison Centre Plaza.

[L] [D] CALL [icons]

**GREENBRIER BAR-B-QUE**          256/355-6062

WW WW Southern Barbecue. Casual Dining. $7-$14 AAA Inspector Notes: A local favorite featuring Southern-style entrées and sides, this establishment has been "the original" since 1957. Enjoy barbecue pork, ham, and chicken; seafood also is available. Not to be confused with another similarly named eatery nearby, Greenbrier's Bar-B-Que is easy to find and conveniently parallel to the highway. Inside, you'll find a simply-set dining room and a very friendly wait staff. There's also a large dining room perfect for parties and group functions. Features: senior menu. Reservations: required. Address: 15050 Hwy 20 W 35758 Location: I-565 exit 3, just n to N Service Rd (SR 20), then 0.5 mi w. [L] [D] CALL [icons]

**GUADALAJARA JALISCO**          256/774-1401

WW WW Mexican. Casual Dining. $5-$12 AAA Inspector Notes: Authentic and delicious traditional Mexican meals are found here, served up by a friendly team. Features: full bar, happy hour. Address: 8572 Madison Blvd 35758 Location: I-565 exit 8, 0.3 mi n on Wall Triana Hwy, then 0.8 mi e; in Walmart Plaza. [L] [D]

**PORT OF MADISON RESTAURANT**          256/772-7170

WW WW American. Casual Dining. $9-$28 AAA Inspector Notes: Hearty American fare is offered for breakfast and dinner at this popular and conveniently located establishment. Features: full bar, patio dining, happy hour. Address: 9035 Madison Blvd 35758 Location: I-565 exit 9, just nw; in BEST WESTERN PLUS Madison-Huntsville Hotel. [B] [D] CALL [icons]

**SAIGON VIETNAMESE RESTAURANT**          256/772-0202

WW WW Vietnamese. Casual Dining. $7-$32 AAA Inspector Notes: Native Vietnamese chefs prepare delicious specialties such as seafood hot clay pots, mango rolls, and noodle soups. Features: beer only. Address: 8760 Madison Blvd, Suites P & Q 35758 Location: I-565 exit 8, just n, then just e; in Spencer Square Center Plaza. [L] [D]

## MARBURY (E-4) pop. 1,418, elev. 520'

**CONFEDERATE MEMORIAL PARK,** 437 CR 63, contains two cemeteries dedicated exclusively to Confederate soldiers. The Old Soldiers Home operated here 1902-39, giving care to elderly Confederate Civil War veterans. A museum displays Confederate uniforms, equipment and Soldiers Home artifacts. Nature trails traverse the 102-acre park.

Time: Allow 30 minutes minimum. Hours: Grounds daily 6 a.m.-dusk. Museum daily 9-5. Closed major holidays. Cost: $4; $3 (ages 62+, students with ID and active military with ID); $1 (ages 6-18 with adult). Phone: (205) 755-1990. [icon]

## McCALLA (D-3) elev. 475'
• Part of Birmingham area — see map p. 43

**TANNEHILL IRONWORKS HISTORICAL STATE PARK** is at 12632 Confederate Pkwy. These 1,500 acres of wooded hills preserve ironworks that operated 1829-65. A major Confederate munitions supplier during the Civil War, the ironworks was destroyed by Union forces in 1865. The Alabama Iron and Steel Museum displays artifacts of the industry. Walking trails trace historic roadways. Olde Tyme Educational Crafts demonstrations are held weekends March through November.

Hours: Park daily 7 a.m.-dusk. Museum Mon.-Sat. 8:30-4:30, Sun. 12:30-4. A gristmill operates the third weekend of the month. Cost: Park $3; $2 (ages 62+); $1 (ages 6-11). Museum $2; $1 (ages 6-11 and 62+). Train $2. Phone: (205) 477-5711. [icons]

## MILLBROOK pop. 14,640

**COUNTRY INN & SUITES BY CARLSON, PRATTVILLE**                              334/495-3000

WWWW Hotel. Rates not provided. Address: 1925 Cobbs Ford Rd 36054 Location: I-65 exit 179, just e. Facility: 63 units. 3 stories, interior corridors. Pool(s): heated indoor. Activities: exercise room. Guest Services: valet and coin laundry.

[icons]

**KEY WEST INN**          334/309-2004

WWW Motel. Rates not provided. Address: 2275 Cobbs Ford Rd 36054 Location: I-65 exit 179, just e. Facility: 41 units. 2 stories (no elevator), exterior corridors. Pool(s): outdoor. Activities: limited exercise equipment. Guest Services: coin laundry.

[icons]

**SLEEP INN & SUITES**          (334)532-0500

WWW Hotel $78-$90 Address: 2295 Cobbs Ford Rd 36054 Location: I-65 exit 179, just e. Facility: 58 units. 3 stories, interior corridors. Pool(s): heated indoor. Activities: hot tub, exercise room. Guest Services: valet and coin laundry.

[icons]

Use travel time to share driving tips and rules of the road with your teens

## WHERE TO EAT

**CATFISH HOUSE**    334/285-7225

▼▼ Seafood. Casual Dining. $10-$18 **AAA Inspector Notes:** Since 1974, seafood lovers have enjoyed this establishment's traditional seafood entrées of shrimp, oysters, scallops, crab and catfish. Popular among landlubbers are several chicken dishes. Decorated with nostalgic memorabilia, the eatery offers a rustic yet relaxed ambience. **Features:** senior menu. **Address:** 3011 Cobbs Ford Rd 36054 **Location:** I-65 exit 179, 1 mi e. [D]

**FANTAIL**    334/285-7255

▼ Southern Seafood. Quick Serve. $16 **AAA Inspector Notes:** Diners can tell this is a popular venue from the full parking lot, however, the multiple dining areas can seat a sizable crowd. Typical Southern fare is offered such as fried oysters and shrimp, shrimp Creole, hush puppies, fried okra, seafood gumbo with some chicken and barbecue for meat lovers. Be aware that buffet items consist primarily of fried items with a few exceptions. **Features:** beer & wine. **Address:** 2060 Downing St 36054 **Location:** I-65 exit 179, 0.5 mi w on service road. [D] CALL [ĠM]

**JOE MAMA'S AMERICAN GRILL**    334/285-1881

▼ Burgers Sandwiches. Quick Serve. $4-$8 **AAA Inspector Notes:** Scrumptious hamburgers, plus hot dogs and sandwiches, are enjoyed at this very popular hometown eatery. **Address:** 63 Wisteria Pl 36054 **Location:** I-65 exit 181, 2.1 mi ne on SR 14.
[L] [D]

## MOBILE (H-1) pop. 195,111, elev. 8'

Mobile was founded in 1702 by Jean Bienville le Moyne and was named after the Mauvilla Indians, who had a settlement on the site. A much-coveted port throughout its history, Mobile was particularly important to the Confederacy.

In 1864 the Union captured the CSS *Tennessee* in the Battle of Mobile Bay but lost the monitor *Tecumseh.* The subsequent surrender of Fort Gaines *(see Dauphin Island p. 70)* and Fort Morgan *(see Gulf Shores p. 85)* on Mobile Point, coupled with the siege of Fort Blakely and Spanish Fort on the east side of the bay 6 months later, wore down the Confederates' resistance. Federal forces occupied Mobile on April 12, 1865. Relics of the battles are still evident.

Alabama's only seaport, Mobile is on the west side of the Mobile River near the mouth of Mobile Bay. The city's river channel, only 10 feet deep in 1826, has been dredged over the years to accommodate oceangoing vessels of 40-foot draft. The discovery of large natural gas deposits also has brought drilling rigs to the bay.

Meetings, conventions and cultural activities take place in the Mobile Civic Center, a huge waterfront facility and entertainment complex.

The ▼ Mobile Mardi Gras, though smaller in size than the celebration in New Orleans, is said to be the original American pre-Lenten carnival. First observed in 1703 and suspended during the Civil War, the festivities have been held continually since 1866. On the Sunday before Mardi Gras day, several thousand revelers turn out to celebrate Joe Cain Day, named for the man who revived Mardi Gras in Mobile after the Civil War.

A premier flower and garden event, ▼ Festival of Flowers showcases and celebrates the beauty of nature. Highlights include landscaped gardens and flowers from around the world. The festival spans 4 days in late March and is held on the Providence Hospital campus. For 3 days in early October, the ▼ Bayfest Music Festival plays host to top-name performers of classic rock, country, alternative, gospel, blues and jazz music.

Mobile also is the site of the Senior Bowl football game in January, played by the nation's best senior collegiate football players, and the ▼ GoDaddy.com Bowl, held the first week in January at the Ladd-Peebles Stadium with teams from the Sun Belt and Mid-American conferences. Teenage girls from throughout the nation compete for scholarships and awards at the Distinguished Young Women Scholarship Program in June.

A moderate climate allows for year-round golfing at an array of championship golf courses with scenic views. Part of Alabama's Robert Trent Jones Golf Trail, Magnolia Grove Golf Course, 7001 Magnolia Grove Pkwy., offers 54 holes on contoured greens.

Mobile Greyhound Park is 10 miles west off I-10 at the Dawes Theodore Road exit; racing season runs from January to mid-December; phone (251) 653-5000.

**Note:** Policies concerning admittance of children to pari-mutuel betting facilities vary. Phone for information.

(See map & index p. 109.)

**Mobile Bay Convention & Visitors Bureau:** 150 S. Royal St., Mobile, AL 36602. **Phone:** (251) 208-2000 or (800) 566-2453. *(See ad this page.)*

**Self-guiding tours:** Mobile is most beautiful during azalea season, mid-March through early April. The Site of Historic Fort Condé Welcome Center provides maps that show where visitors can best see azaleas in bloom as well as brochures for self-guiding walking and driving tours of Mobile. The city's historic districts also can be seen on walking and driving tours *(see attraction listing p. 107)*.

**Shopping areas:** Bel Air Mall at Airport Boulevard and I-65 (3299 Bel Air Mall) has Belk, Dillard's, JCPenney and Sears.

## INSIDER INFO:
### Robert Trent Jones Golf Trail

Alabama's Robert Trent Jones Golf Trail features a network of 468 holes at 11 facilities stretching from north Alabama to the Gulf of Mexico. All the courses along the golf trail were designed by golf course architect Robert Trent Jones Sr., and each was intended to give golfers a challenging experience in country-club elegance at public course prices.

Most facilities include two 18-hole championship courses or three nine-hole championship courses, in addition to an 18- or nine-hole (respectively) short course. The course at Capitol Hill has three championship 18-hole courses, while the Ross Bridge in Hoover has one 18-hole course covering 330 acres, making it the third longest course in the world.

Sites include Oxmoor Valley in Birmingham, (205) 942-1177; Ross Bridge in Hoover, (205) 949-3085; Hampton Cove in Huntsville, (256) 551-1818; Magnolia Grove in Mobile, (251) 645-0075; The Shoals in Muscle Shoals, (256) 446-5111; Grand National in Auburn/Opelika, (334) 749-9042; Lakewood in Point Clear, (251) 928-9201; Highland Oaks in Dothan, (334) 712-2820; Cambrian Ridge in Greenville, (334) 382-9787; Capitol Hill in Prattville, (334) 285-1114; and Silver Lakes in Calhoun County, (256) 892-3268.

Fees at each course range $45-$136 for 18 holes ($15 for the 18-hole short course), or $7.50 for the nine-hole short course. Cart rentals are $15 per person for regular courses and $10 per person for short courses.

For additional information, to verify rates or to reserve a tee time phone (800) 949-4444.

---

**AFRICAN-AMERICAN ARCHIVES & MULTICULTURAL MUSEUM** is at 564 Dr. Martin Luther King, Jr. Ave., in the Davis Ave. branch of the Mobile Public Library. This small museum houses biographies of African-Americans who made significant

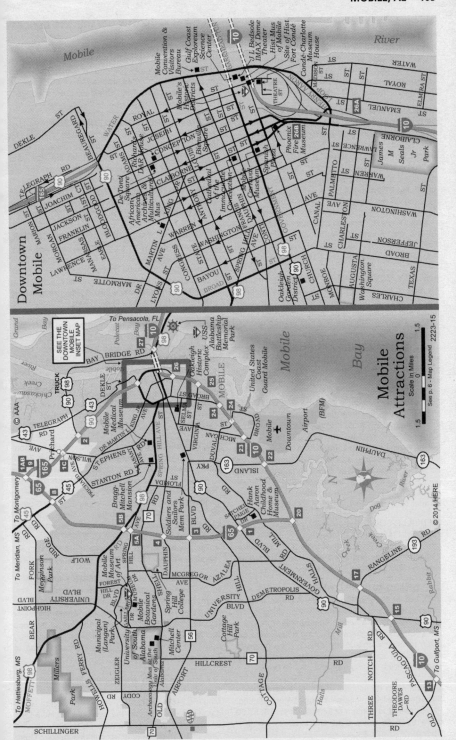

## Downtown Mobile

## Mobile Attractions

Scale in Miles

See p. 6 · Map Legend   2223-15

© AAA

© 2014 HERE

(See map & index p. 109.)

contributions to the history of the nation, such as Rosa Parks and Willie Mays. Artifacts include slavery and Civil War memorabilia. **Time:** Allow 1 hour minimum. **Hours:** Mon.-Fri. 8-4, Sat. 10-2, Sun. by appointment. Closed major holidays. **Cost:** Donations. **Phone:** (251) 433-8511.

## ARCHAEOLOGY MUSEUM AT THE UNIVERSITY OF SOUTH ALABAMA, off University Blvd. on USA South Dr. in Delchamps Archaeology Building, relates 12,000 years of local history through archeological artifacts and life-size displays featuring realistic mannequins. A botanical garden with native plants is on the grounds. Museum visitors should park in the P2 lot and obtain a parking pass from the museum on weekdays.

**Time:** Allow 45 minutes minimum. **Hours:** Tues.-Fri. 9-4, Sat. noon-4. Closed major holidays. **Cost:** Free. Guided tour $3; reservations are required. **Phone:** (251) 460-6106 or (251) 460-6911. GT

## BAY CITY CONVENTION & TOURS departs from the Site of Historic Fort Condé welcome center at 150 S. Royal St. The company offers 1-hour historical and ghost tours of the historic districts. On the historical tour, a guide shares insights into the history, antebellum architecture and customs of Mobile. The ghost tour features stories about local residents who may still reside in Mobile in spirit form. A 3-hour tour of USS *Alabama* Battleship Memorial Park also is offered.

**Hours:** Historic Mobile and USS *Alabama* Battleship Memorial Park tours depart Mon.-Sat. at 10:30 and 2, Sun. at 2. Ghost tour departs Mon.-Fri. at 7. **Cost:** Historic Mobile tour $16 per person (two people minimum or one person for a $32 fee). Ghost tour $20 per person (six people minimum). USS *Alabama* Battleship Memorial Park tour (includes transportation and attraction admission) $22 per person (two people minimum). Reservations are required. **Phone:** (251) 479-9970 or (800) 338-5597.

## BIENVILLE SQUARE, bounded by Dauphin, St. Joseph, St. Francis and Conception sts. in the business district, is a park featuring a wrought-iron fountain, benches and many live oaks and azaleas. **Hours:** Daily 24 hours. **Cost:** Free.

SAVE **BRAGG-MITCHELL MANSION** is 2.4 mi. e. of I-65 at 1906 Spring Hill Ave. A combination of Greek Revival and Italianate architectural styles, it is said to be one of Mobile's finest antebellum mansions. Stately oaks surrounding the house were cut down to allow Confederate artillery free range to shell Federal troops. The owner, Judge John Bragg, replanted using acorns from the original trees.

**Time:** Allow 45 minutes minimum. **Hours:** Tues.-Fri. 10-4. Last tour begins 1 hour before closing. Phone ahead to confirm schedule. **Cost:** $8; $7.50 (ages 65+); $5 (ages 3-12 and students with ID). **Phone:** (251) 471-6364. GT

## CATHEDRAL OF THE IMMACULATE CONCEPTION, 2 S. Claiborne St. between Conti and Dauphin sts., is one of the oldest churches in the city. Built 1835-50, it occupies the site used by Mobile's first settlers as a burial ground. Shamrocks and fleurs-de-lis emblems adorn the vaulted ceiling. **Hours:** Daily 8:30-4:30. **Cost:** Free. **Phone:** (251) 434-1565.

## CONDÉ-CHARLOTTE MUSEUM HOUSE, 104 Theatre St., is in an 1822 building that was Mobile's first jail and courthouse. The museum displays European and American furnishings from the 18th- and 19th centuries. A walled Spanish garden and an authentically equipped kitchen complement the house. **Time:** Allow 30 minutes minimum. **Hours:** Tues.-Sat. 11-3:30. Closed major holidays. **Cost:** $5; $2 (ages 6-18). **Phone:** (251) 432-4722. GT

## GULF COAST EXPLOREUM SCIENCE CENTER, 65 Government St. at jct. Water St., features more than 150 interactive activities in three permanent exhibit halls. Internationally recognized traveling exhibits, updated several times each year, explore scientific themes. Science-based films are shown at the J.L. Bedsole IMAX Dome Theater.

**Time:** Allow 2 hours minimum. **Hours:** Tues.-Sat. 9-5, Sun. noon-5. Hours may vary with featured exhibits; phone ahead. Closed major holidays. **Cost:** Science center $12; $10.50 (ages 13-18 and 60+); $10 (ages 2-12). Combination ticket with J.L. Bedsole IMAX Dome Theater $16; $15 (ages 13-18 and 60+); $13.50 (ages 2-12). Rates may increase for special exhibits. Reservations are recommended for the theater. **Phone:** (251) 208-6873 or (877) 625-4386.

## J.L. Bedsole IMAX Dome Theater, 65 Government St. at Gulf Coast Exploreum Science Center, presents large-format science films. **Time:** Allow 1 hour minimum. **Hours:** Shows are given on the hour Tues.-Fri. 9-5, Sat. 10-5, Sun. noon-5. Closed major holidays. **Cost:** $8.75; $7.25 (ages 13-18 and 60+); $6.50 (ages 2-12). Combination ticket with Gulf Coast Exploreum Science Center $16; $15 (ages 13-18 and 60+); $13.50 (ages 2-12). Prices may vary; phone ahead. Reservations are recommended. **Phone:** (251) 208-6873 or (877) 625-4386.

## HANK AARON CHILDHOOD HOME & MUSEUM is at 755 Bolling Brothers Blvd. at Hank Aaron Stadium. Baseball great Hank Aaron's Mobile childhood home has been moved to the site where the minor league Mobile BayBears play. The house includes family items and baseball memorabilia, including items on loan from the National Baseball Hall of Fame and Museum.

Admission tickets are available in the administrative office. **Time:** Allow 1 hour minimum. **Hours:** Mon.-Fri. 10-4, Sat. 10-2. Also open during home games. Hours may vary the week of Christmas-Dec. 31. Closed Jan. 1, Easter, Thanksgiving and Christmas. Phone ahead to confirm schedule. **Cost:**

(See map & index p. 109.)

$5; $3 (ages 0-12). Free with BayBear admission ticket on day of game. **Phone:** (251) 479-2327.

**HISTORY MUSEUM OF MOBILE** is in the historic district at 111 S. Royal St. at jct. Church St. Housed in the 1857 Southern Market/Old City Hall, this museum presents more than 300 years of local history and culture. Exhibits chronologically detail Mobile's development from early French settlement to modern times. Areas are dedicated to showcasing the lives of native inhabitants, enslaved people and Civil War soldiers.

Time: Allow 1 hour minimum. **Hours:** Tues.-Sat. 9-5, Sun. 1-5. Closed major holidays. **Cost:** $7; $6 (ages 55+); $5 (students with ID); free (ages 0-6, military with ID and to all first Sun. of the month). **Phone:** (251) 208-7508. GT

**MOBILE BOTANICAL GARDENS** is off I-65 exit 5A, 1.5 mi. w. on Springhill Ave., just s. on Pfc. John New St., then .6 mi. w. to 5151 Museum Dr. next to Langan Park. This 100-acre site contains seven distinct areas in a woodland setting: The Herb Garden, The Founders Fragrance & Texture Garden, The Rhododendron Garden, The John Allen Smith Japanese Maple Garden, The Fern Glade, the 35-acre Longleaf Pine Forest with hiking and biking trails and The Kosaku Sawada Winter Garden. **Time:** Allow 1 hour minimum. **Hours:** Daily dawn-dusk. **Cost:** $5; free (ages 0-12). **Phone:** (251) 342-0555. 🅰️

SAVE **MOBILE CARNIVAL MUSEUM** is at 355 Government St. This museum presents the history of Mobile's Mardi Gras celebration through memorabilia and interactive exhibits, including a children's area and a float. The showpiece is the extensive collection of elaborate gowns, trains, crowns and scepters of carnival royalty dating from 1921. **Time:** Allow 1 hour minimum. **Hours:** Mon., Wed. and Fri.-Sat. 9-4. Last tour begins 1 hour before closing. Closed Jan. 1 and Christmas. **Cost:** $5; $2 (ages 0-12). **Phone:** (251) 432-3324. GT

**MOBILE MEDICAL MUSEUM** is at 1664 Springhill Ave. The museum houses a large collection of medical artifacts dating from the late 1700s to the present. Exhibits include an iron lung, quackery devices, Civil War-era surgical instruments and bloodletting implements. **Time:** Allow 1 hour minimum. **Hours:** Open by appointment only Tues.-Fri. 10-3. Closed major holidays. **Cost:** $5; $4 (students with ID and senior citizens); $3 (ages 0-11). **Phone:** (251) 415-1109. GT

GEM **MOBILE MUSEUM OF ART** is off Springhill Ave. in Langan Park at 4850 Museum Dr. This art museum, one of the Gulf Coast's largest, has a permanent collection of more than 6,000 works spanning more than 2,000 years of cultural history. Exhibits include 19th-century American landscape paintings; mid-20th-century American Scene paintings; Southern decorative arts and furniture; African, Asian and European art; and contemporary crafts, particularly ceramics and wood art. The Haverty Collection of International Studio Glass is displayed as well. Touring exhibitions from other prestigious museums and collections also are presented.

Time: Allow 1 hour minimum. **Hours:** Tues.-Sun. 10-5 (also Thurs. 5-9). Closed Jan. 1, Memorial Day, July 4, Thanksgiving and Christmas. **Cost:** $10; $8 (ages 50+ and military with ID); $6 (students with ID); free (ages 0-6). Additional fees may be charged for special exhibits. **Phone:** (251) 208-5200.

GEM **MOBILE'S HISTORIC DISTRICTS** are within a 2-mi. radius of the Oakleigh Historic Complex *(see attraction listing p. 108)* at 300 Oakleigh Pl. The districts are a cross section of the city's architectural heritage and can be explored on self-guiding walking or driving tours designed by the Mobile Historic Development Commission. Brochures are available at most downtown hotels or the Site of Historic Fort Condé Welcome Center, 150 S. Royal St. at Church Street. **Phone:** (251) 208-7281.

**Church Street East,** extending from Water St. to Broad St., is the city's most diverse historic district. The original structures built during Mobile's Colonial French, Spanish and English eras were destroyed by fires in 1827 and 1839. Present buildings, dating from the early 19th century, represent Greek Revival, Italianate, Queen Anne and Victorian architectural styles. The district contains several museums and the city's welcome center at the Site of Historic Fort Condé.

**De Tonti Square,** 5 blks. n. of the central business area, is characterized by dignified brick townhouses, iron-lace fences, antique gaslights and flagstone sidewalks. Many of these residences, built in the 1850s and '60s, reflect the city's prosperity as a cotton-shipping port. The resulting affluence gave rise to fashionable houses constructed in the Greek Revival, Italianate, Victorian and Gulf Coast Cottage styles.

**Lower Dauphin Street Commercial District,** Dauphin St. between Water and Broad sts., is the only predominantly 19th-century commercial district in Mobile. It is characterized by a high concentration of closely spaced, two- and three-story brick structures built in the Greek Revival, Italianate, Victorian and 20th-century Revival styles. The district's eastern end features early skyscrapers and buildings dating from the 1920s and '30s. It serves as the entertainment, legal and financial center of Mobile.

**Oakleigh Garden District,** surrounding Oakleigh House Museum and Washington Sq., contains some of the city's finest late 19th-century residences. The district is characterized by architectural details that followed individual tastes rather than an

(See map & index p. 109.)

adherence to strict stylistic designs. The result is a mix of early 20th-century mansions set amid modest cottages and simple houses. The district is known for its canopy of oaks.

**Old Dauphin Way,** which lies w. of downtown, roughly between Broad St., Houston St., US 98 (Springhill Ave.) and Government St., is the largest historic district in Mobile. Its buildings range from early cottages to 19th-and 20th-century mansions. Many of the Gulf Coast cottages and Victorian-style structures housed middle-class merchants and clerks. The smaller cottages were the homes of servants who worked in the grand houses along Government Street or on the docks. There are numerous bungalows of various sizes and a variety of revival styles scattered through the neighborhood.

**Spring Hill,** off I-65 exit 5A to Springhill Avenue, about 6.5 miles w. of the waterfront, was founded in the 1820s as a wooded summer retreat far from the inner city, which was ravaged by yellow fever. Greek Revival houses dating from the 1850s can be seen. Also in this area is Spring Hill College, established in 1830 and said to be the first institution of higher learning in Alabama.

SAVE **OAKLEIGH HISTORIC COMPLEX,** 300 Oakleigh Pl., features two museums. Cox-Deasy Cottage is a raised Gulf Coast cottage typical of Mobile's 19th-century middle class. The Oakleigh Period House Museum is in an 1833 Greek Revival ,mansion furnished with antiques of the Empire, Regency and early Victorian periods. Among its fine portrait collection is the Thomas Sully painting of Madame Le Vert, the queen of Mobile's social and literary circle in the mid-19th century. The mansion also displays silver, china and jewelry.

**Time:** Allow 30 minutes minimum. **Hours:** Tues.-Sat. 10-4. Last tour begins 1 hour before closing. Closed Jan. 1, Easter, Memorial Day, July 4, Labor Day, Thanksgiving and Christmas. **Cost:** $10; $5 (ages 5-12). **Phone:** (251) 432-1281. GT

**PHOENIX FIRE MUSEUM,** 203 S. Claiborne St., is in the restored home of the Phoenix Volunteer Fire Company No. 6. This building houses turn-of-the-20th-century horse-drawn steam engines and early motorized vehicles. The upstairs gallery recounts the history of the volunteer fire companies of Mobile from their organization in 1819. **Time:** Allow 30 minutes minimum. **Hours:** Tues. and Thurs. 9-5. Closed city holidays. **Cost:** Free. **Phone:** (251) 208-7508. GT

**RICHARDS DAR HOUSE,** 256 N. Joachim St. in De Tonti Sq., is a restored townhouse built in 1860 by

Charles G. Richards, a steamboat captain. The Italianate house features iron-lace trim and lavish early Victorian and Empire furnishings. A formal garden is on the grounds.

**Time:** Allow 30 minutes minimum. **Hours:** Mon.-Fri. 11-3:30, Sat. 10-4, Sun. 1-4. Last tour begins at 3. Closed Jan. 1, weekend before Mardi Gras, Easter, July 4, Thanksgiving, day after Thanksgiving, Dec. 23, Christmas Eve, Christmas, day after Christmas and Dec. 31. **Cost:** $10; $5 (ages 6-11). **Phone:** (251) 208-7320. GT

**SITE OF HISTORIC FORT CONDÉ,** 150 S. Royal St. at jct. Church St., served as an administrative and military center of the Louisiana Territory. The re-created fort, a four-fifths-scale model of its 1702 appearance, was occupied successively by French, English and Spanish troops. A museum displays artifacts recovered from on-site archeological excavations. Exhibit rooms contain equipment once necessary for the fort's operation. Fort Condé also is the official welcome center for the city of Mobile. **Time:** Allow 1 hour minimum. **Hours:** Daily 8:30-4:30. Closed major holidays. **Cost:** Free. **Phone:** (251) 208-7304. GT

**SOLDIERS AND SAILORS MEMORIAL PARK,** 1850 Government St., was created in memory of men killed in World War I. The half-acre park contains an azalea-bordered pool that mirrors a memorial arch. **Hours:** Daily dawn-dusk. **Cost:** Free.

GEM SAVE **USS *ALABAMA* BATTLESHIP MEMORIAL PARK,** 2703 Battleship Pkwy., is a 175-acre park dedicated to the Alabamians who served in the armed forces during World War II, the Korean War, the Vietnam War, Operation Desert Storm, Operation Iraqi Freedom and Afghanistan. On-site are World War II heroes the USS *Alabama,* a battleship that earned its nine battle stars while part of a strike force in the Pacific, and the submarine USS *Drum,* which earned 12 battle stars undertaking 13 missions in the Pacific theater.

The USS *Alabama's* decks, turrets, mess, berth compartments, bridge, wardroom and captain's cabin are open for tours, as are the USS *Drum's* torpedo rooms and the crew's quarters. The park also displays 28 historic aircraft.

The battleship's military service was highlighted by its dominant role in the occupation of the Yokosuka-Tokyo area at the close of World War II. Decommissioned in 1947, the ship was towed 5,600 miles from Bremerton, Wash., and was established as a floating shrine in 1965.

**Time:** Allow 1 hour, 30 minutes minimum. **Hours:** Daily 8-6, Apr.-Sept.; 8-4, rest of year. Closed Christmas. **Cost:** (includes both vessels) $15; $6 (ages 6-11). **Parking:** $2. **Phone:** (251) 433-2703 or (251) 432-5951.

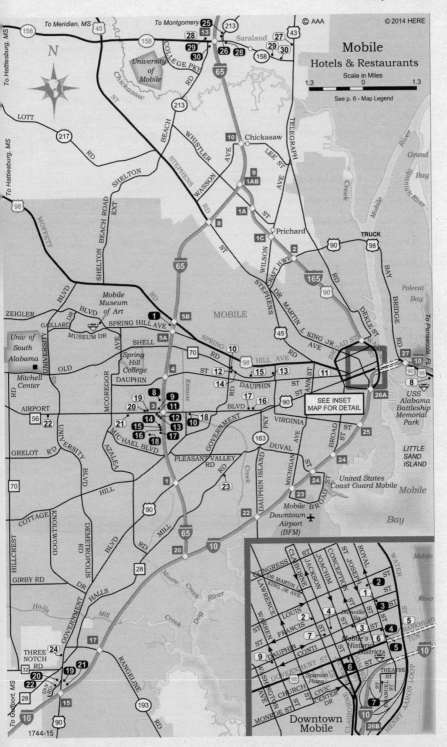

Mobile
Hotels & Restaurants
Scale in Miles
1.3    0    1.3
See p. 6 - Map Legend

© AAA
© 2014 HERE

Downtown Mobile

1744-15

# Mobile

This index helps you "spot" where approved hotels and restaurants are located on the corresponding detailed maps. Hotel dail rate range is for comparison only. Restaurant price range is a combination of lunch and/or dinner. Turn to the listing page fo more detailed rate and price information and consult display ads for special promotions.

## MOBILE

| Map Page | Hotels | Diamond Rated | Rate Range | Page |
|---|---|---|---|---|
| **1** p. 109 | Wingate by Wyndham Mobile | ◆◆◆ | $119-$139 | 114 |
| **2** p. 109 | Candlewood Suites Downtown | ◆◆◆ | $119-$139 | 111 |
| **3** p. 109 | Renaissance-The Battle House Mobile Hotel & Spa | ◆◆◆◆ | $189-$263 SAVE | 114 |
| **4** p. 109 | Hampton Inn & Suites Mobile/Downtown Historic District | ◆◆◆ | $139-$189 | 112 |
| **5** p. 109 | Renaissance Mobile Riverview Plaza Hotel | ◆◆◆◆ | $131-$219 SAVE | 113 |
| **6** p. 109 | Admiral Semmes Hotel | ◆◆◆ | Rates not provided | 111 |
| **7** p. 109 | Fort Conde Inn | ◆◆◆◆ | Rates not provided SAVE | 112 |
| **8** p. 109 | Holiday Inn Mobile-Airport | ◆◆◆ | $89-$149 | 112 |
| **9** p. 109 | Ashbury Hotel & Suites | ◆◆ | Rates not provided | 111 |
| **10** p. 109 | Mobile Marriott | ◆◆◆ | $119-$199 SAVE | 113 |
| **11** p. 109 | La Quinta Inn Mobile | ◆◆ | $72-$195 | 113 |
| **12** p. 109 | Drury Inn-Mobile | ◆◆◆ | $103-$159 | 112 |
| **13** p. 109 | Hilton Garden Inn Mobile West | ◆◆◆ | $99-$169 | 112 |
| **14** p. 109 | Fairfield Inn & Suites by Marriott Mobile | ◆◆◆ | $79-$109 | 112 |
| **15** p. 109 | Residence Inn by Marriott Mobile | ◆◆◆ | $116-$129 | 114 |
| **16** p. 109 | Courtyard by Marriott Mobile | ◆◆◆ | $99-$129 | 112 |
| **17** p. 109 | Hampton Inn & Suites-Mobile I-65 at Airport Blvd | ◆◆◆ | $119-$189 | 112 |
| **18** p. 109 | TownePlace Suites by Marriott Mobile | ◆◆◆ | $89-$119 | 114 |
| **19** p. 109 | Holiday Inn Mobile West I-10 (See ad p. 113.) | ◆◆◆ | $109-$139 SAVE | 112 |
| **20** p. 109 | Tillman's Corner Comfort Suites | ◆◆◆ | $89-$129 | 114 |
| **21** p. 109 | Wingate by Wyndham I-10 West | ◆◆◆ | $99-$140 SAVE | 114 |
| **22** p. 109 | Hampton Inn I-10 West/Bellingrath Gardens (Tillman's Corner) | ◆◆◆ | $119-$139 | 112 |

| Map Page | Restaurants | Diamond Rated | Cuisine | Price Range | Page |
|---|---|---|---|---|---|
| ① p. 109 | **The Trellis Room** | ◆◆◆◆ | Southern American | $22-$40 | 116 |
| ② p. 109 | The Blind Mule Restaurant & Bar | ◆◆ | American | $9-$15 | 114 |
| ③ p. 109 | Busaba's Thai Cuisine | ◆◆ | Thai | $8-$14 | 115 |
| ④ p. 109 | NoJa | ◆◆◆ | Fusion | $29-$36 | 115 |
| ⑤ p. 109 | The Harbor Room | ◆◆◆ | Seafood | $9-$35 | 115 |
| ⑥ p. 109 | The Royal Scam | ◆◆ | American | $9-$30 | 116 |
| ⑦ p. 109 | Spot of Tea | ◆◆ | Continental | $8-$10 | 116 |
| ⑧ p. 109 | John Word's Restaurant & Jazz Cafe | ◆◆ | Southern American | $8-$32 | 115 |
| ⑨ p. 109 | The Bull Restaurant | ◆◆◆ | New Southwestern | $17-$40 | 115 |
| ⑩ p. 109 | Shrimp Basket | ◆◆ | Seafood | $7-$15 | 116 |
| ⑪ p. 109 | True Midtown Kitchen | ◆◆◆ | Southern American | $9-$29 | 116 |

| Map Page | Restaurants (cont'd) | Diamond Rated | Cuisine | Price Range | Page |
|---|---|---|---|---|---|
| ⑫ p. 109 | Butch Cassidy's | ▽▽ | Burgers Sandwiches | $7-$10 | 115 |
| ⑬ p. 109 | Dew Drop Inn | ▽ | American | $7-$15 | 115 |
| ⑭ p. 109 | Ashland Midtown Pub | ▽▽ | Pizza Sandwiches | $6-$25 | 114 |
| ⑮ p. 109 | Fuego Coastal Mexican Eatery | ▽▽ | Mexican | $11-$24 | 115 |
| ⑯ p. 109 | Ruth's Chris Steak House | ▽▽▽ | Steak | $21-$85 | 116 |
| ⑰ p. 109 | Benjamin's | ▽▽ | Regional Comfort Food | $8-$23 | 114 |
| ⑱ p. 109 | Sage Restaurant | ▽▽▽ | American | $10-$32 | 116 |
| ⑲ p. 109 | Bamboo Bistro | ▽▽ | Asian | $10-$30 | 114 |
| ⑳ p. 109 | Momma Goldberg's Deli | ▽ | American | $6-$10 | 115 |
| ㉑ p. 109 | Bangkok Thai Cuisine | ▽▽ | Thai | $8-$15 | 114 |
| ㉒ p. 109 | Jerusalem Cafe | ▽▽ | Middle Eastern | $6-$17 | 115 |
| ㉓ p. 109 | Osman's Restaurant | ▽▽▽ | American | $19-$33 | 115 |
| ㉔ p. 109 | Dick Russell's | ▽ | Barbecue | $4-$22 | 115 |

### SARALAND

| Map Page | Hotels | Diamond Rated | Rate Range | Page |
|---|---|---|---|---|
| ㉕ p. 109 | **BEST WESTERN Motorsports Inn & Suites** | ▽▽▽ | $60-$150 SAVE | 139 |
| ㉖ p. 109 | Microtel Inn & Suites by Wyndham Saraland/North Mobile | ▽▽ | $70-$90 | 139 |
| ㉘ p. 109 | Quality Inn | ▽▽ | $60-$120 | 139 |
| ㉙ p. 109 | Hampton Inn Saraland/ North Mobile | ▽▽▽ | $99-$124 | 139 |
| ㉚ p. 109 | **Holiday Inn Express & Suites** | ▽▽▽ | $113-$132 SAVE | 139 |

| Map Page | Restaurants | Diamond Rated | Cuisine | Price Range | Page |
|---|---|---|---|---|---|
| ㉗ p. 109 | Ming's Buffet & Bar | ▽ | Asian | $6-$13 | 140 |
| ㉘ p. 109 | J. Rodgers BBQ | ▽ | Barbecue | $5-$15 | 140 |
| ㉙ p. 109 | Catfish Junction | ▽▽ | Southern Seafood | $7-$21 | 139 |
| ㉚ p. 109 | Something Special Deli | ▽▽ | Deli | $7-$9 | 140 |

**ADMIRAL SEMMES HOTEL**          251/432-8000  **6**

▽▽▽ **Classic Historic Hotel.** Rates not provided. **Address:** 251 Government St 36602 **Location:** I-10 exit 26B, just w of Water St; in downtown historic district. **Facility:** Dating from 1940, this historic downtown hotel offers an elegant period lobby and large rooms. 170 units. 12 stories, interior corridors. **Parking:** on-site (fee). **Pool(s):** outdoor. **Activities:** hot tub. **Guest Services:** valet and coin laundry. 🍴 🍸 🛳 📶 🔌 📷 💻

**ASHBURY HOTEL & SUITES**          251/344-8030  **9**

▽▽ **Hotel.** Rates not provided. **Address:** 600 W I-65 Service Rd S 36608 **Location:** I-65 exit 3 (Airport Blvd), just w, then just n on service road. **Facility:** 200 units. 2-4 stories, interior/exterior corridors. **Pool(s):** outdoor, heated indoor. **Activities:** tennis, game room. **Guest Services:** valet and coin laundry. 🍸 🛳 BIZ 📶 🔌 📷 💻 / SOME UNITS HS

---

Plan complete trip routings
with the online and mobile
TripTik® Travel Planner

**BEST WESTERN MOFFETT ROAD INN**     (251)645-1275

Hotel
$90-$111

 **AAA Benefit:**
Members save up to 20%!

**Address:** 7688 Moffett Rd 36618 **Location:** On US 98, just e of jct CR 31. **Facility:** 50 units. 3 stories, interior corridors. **Pool(s):** outdoor. **Activities:** exercise room. **Guest Services:** coin laundry. **Featured Amenity:** breakfast buffet.

SAVE CALL 📶M 🛳 BIZ HS 📶
🔌 📷 💻

**CANDLEWOOD SUITES DOWNTOWN**     (251)690-7818  **2**

▽▽▽ **Extended Stay Hotel** $119-$139 **Address:** 121 N Royal St 36602 **Location:** Corner of St. Louis St; downtown; parking and rear entrance on St. Joseph St. **Facility:** 81 efficiencies. 4 stories, interior corridors. **Pool(s):** outdoor. **Activities:** exercise room. **Guest Services:** valet and coin laundry.

🍴+ 🛳 BIZ HS 📶 ✖ 🔌 📷 💻
/ SOME UNITS 🐾

(See map & index p. 109.)

### COURTYARD BY MARRIOTT MOBILE   (251)344-5200   **16**

▼▼▼▼ Hotel $99-$129 **Address:**
1000 W I-65 Service Rd S 36609 **Loca-**
**tion:** I-65 exit 3 (Airport Blvd), just w,
then 0.4 mi s. **Facility:** 78 units, some efficiencies. 3 stories, interior corridors.
**Pool(s):** heated indoor. **Activities:** hot tub, exercise room. **Guest**
**Services:** valet and coin laundry, boarding pass kiosk.

**AAA Benefit:**
Members save 5%
or more!

  BIZ 🛜 ✕ ▣ /SOME UNITS (HS) 🔋 🖼

### DRURY INN-MOBILE   (251)344-7700   **12**

▼▼▼▼ Hotel $103-$159 **Address:** 824 W I-65 Service Rd S
36609 **Location:** I-65 exit 3 (Airport Blvd), just s. **Facility:**
103 units. 4 stories, interior corridors. **Terms:** cancellation fee imposed. **Pool(s):** outdoor. **Activities:** hot tub, exercise room. **Guest**
**Services:** valet and coin laundry.

🍴 🛄 BIZ (HS) 🛜 ✕ 🔋 🖼 ▣
/SOME UNITS 🆂

### FAIRFIELD INN & SUITES BY MARRIOTT MOBILE
(251)316-0029   **14**

▼▼▼▼ Hotel $79-$109 **Address:**
950A W I-65 Service Rd S 36609 **Loca-**
**tion:** I-65 exit 3 (Airport Blvd), just w,
then 0.4 mi s. **Facility:** 80 units. 3 stories, interior corridors. **Pool(s):** heated
indoor. **Activities:** exercise room. **Guest Services:** valet and coin
laundry. 🛄 🛜 ✕ ▣ /SOME UNITS 🔋 🖼

**AAA Benefit:**
Members save 5%
or more!

### FORT CONDE INN   251/405-5040   **7**

▼▼▼ ▼▼▼
**Historic Bed**
**& Breakfast**
Rates not provided

**Address:** 165 St Emanuel St 36602 **Lo-**
**cation:** Corner of Monroe St; downtown.
**Facility:** A beautifully restored historic
home offers large, well-appointed rooms
in its main house. This quaint vintage
neighborhood includes a variety of
accommodations—choose from suites,
cottages and some modest units. 19
units, some cottages. 1-3 stories, interior
corridors. **Parking:** on-site and street.
**Terms:** age restrictions may apply. **Activ-**
**ities:** kids club, massage. **Guest Ser-**
**vices:** valet laundry, area transportation.

SAVE CALL 🛄 (HS) 🛜 ✕ 📹
▣ /SOME UNITS 🔋 🖼

### HAMPTON INN & SUITES MOBILE/DOWNTOWN HISTORIC
DISTRICT   (251)436-8787   **4**

▼▼▼▼ Hotel $139-$189 **Address:**
62 S Royal St 36602 **Location:** Corner
of Conti St; downtown. **Facility:** 149
units. 7 stories, interior corridors.
**Parking:** on-site (fee). **Terms:** check-in

**AAA Benefit:**
Members save 5%
or more!

4 pm, 1-7 night minimum stay, cancellation fee imposed. **Pool(s):**
outdoor. **Activities:** exercise room. **Guest Services:** valet and coin
laundry.

🍴 CALL 🛄 🛄 BIZ (HS) 🛜 ✕ 🔋 🖼 ▣

### HAMPTON INN & SUITES-MOBILE I-65 AT AIRPORT BLVD
(251)343-4007   **17**

▼▼▼▼ Hotel $119-$189 **Address:**
1028 W I-65 Service Rd S 36609 **Loca-**
**tion:** I-65 exit 3 (Airport Blvd), just w,
then 0.5 mi s. **Facility:** 101 units. 4 stories, interior corridors. **Terms:** 1-7 night
minimum stay, cancellation fee imposed. **Amenities:** video games.
**Pool(s):** outdoor. **Activities:** exercise room. **Guest Services:** valet
and coin laundry.

**AAA Benefit:**
Members save 5%
or more!

CALL 🛄 🛄 BIZ (HS) 🛜 📹 🔋 🖼 ▣

### HAMPTON INN I-10 WEST/BELLINGRATH GARDENS
(TILLMAN'S CORNER)   (251)660-9202   **22**

▼▼▼▼ Hotel $119-$139 **Address:**
5478 Inn Rd 36619 **Location:** I-10 exit
15B, just e on US 90, then just n. **Fa-**
**cility:** 80 units. 3 stories, interior corridors. **Terms:** 1-7 night minimum stay,
cancellation fee imposed. **Pool(s):** outdoor. **Activities:** exercise
room. **Guest Services:** valet and coin laundry.

**AAA Benefit:**
Members save 5%
or more!

🍴 🛄 BIZ 🛜 🔋 🖼 ▣

### HILTON GARDEN INN MOBILE WEST   (251)544-6000   **13**

▼▼▼▼ Hotel $99-$169 **Address:**
828 W I-65 Service Rd S 36609 **Loca-**
**tion:** I-65 exit 3 (Airport Blvd), just w,
then just s. **Facility:** 101 units. 5 stories,
interior corridors. **Terms:** 1-7 night
minimum stay, cancellation fee imposed. **Amenities:** video games.
**Pool(s):** outdoor. **Activities:** hot tub, exercise room. **Guest Ser-**
**vices:** valet and coin laundry.

**AAA Benefit:**
Members save 5%
or more!

🍴 🍸 CALL 🛄 🛄 BIZ (HS) 🛜 ✕ 📹 🔋
🖼 ▣

### HOLIDAY INN MOBILE-AIRPORT   (251)344-7446   **8**

▼▼▼▼ Hotel $89-$149 **Address:** 3630 Springhill Memorial Dr S
36608 **Location:** I-65 exit 3 (Airport Blvd), just n on frontage service
road, then just w. **Facility:** 97 units. 4 stories, interior corridors.
**Pool(s):** heated indoor. **Activities:** exercise room. **Guest Services:**
valet and coin laundry.

🚹 🍴 🛄 🍸 CALL 🛄 🛄 BIZ (HS) 🛜 ✕
🔋 ▣

### HOLIDAY INN MOBILE WEST I-10
(251)666-5600   **19**

▼▼▼
Hotel
$109-$139

**Address:** 5465 Hwy 90 W 36619 **Loca-**
**tion:** I-10 exit 15B, just e on US 90,
then just s on Coca Cola Rd. **Facility:**
159 units. 5 stories, interior corridors.
**Pool(s):** outdoor. **Activities:** exercise
room. **Guest Services:** valet and coin
laundry, area transportation. *(See ad*
*p. 113.)*

SAVE 🚹 🍴 🛄 🍸 🛄
BIZ 🛜 ✕ 🔋 🖼 ▣
/SOME UNITS 🐾

---

(See map & index p. 109.)

**HOMEWOOD SUITES MOBILE**        (251)634-8664

 Extended Stay Hotel $109-$209 **Address:** 530 Providence Park Dr E 36695 **Location:** I-65 exit 3 (Airport Blvd), 4.5 mi w. Located near Providence Hospital. **Facility:** 86 efficiencies, some two bedrooms. 3 stories, interior corridors. **Terms:** 1-7 night minimum stay, cancellation fee imposed. **Pool(s):** outdoor. **Activities:** exercise room. **Guest Services:** valet and coin laundry, area transportation.

**AAA Benefit:** Members save 5% or more!

**LA QUINTA INN MOBILE**        (251)343-4051  **11**

 Motel $72-$195 **Address:** 816 W I-65 Service Rd S 36609 **Location:** I-65 exit 3 (Airport Blvd), just w, then just s. **Facility:** 122 units. 2 stories (no elevator), interior/exterior corridors. **Pool(s):** outdoor. **Guest Services:** coin laundry.

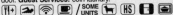

**MOBILE MARRIOTT**        (251)476-6400  **10**

 Hotel $119-$199

MARRIOTT

**AAA Benefit:** Members save 5% or more!

**Address:** 3101 Airport Blvd 36606 **Location:** I-65 exit 3 (Airport Blvd), 0.5 mi e. **Facility:** 251 units. 20 stories, interior corridors. **Amenities:** safes. **Dining:** Sage Restaurant, see separate listing. **Pool(s):** outdoor. **Activities:** exercise room. **Guest Services:** valet laundry.

---

**RENAISSANCE MOBILE RIVERVIEW PLAZA HOTEL**
(251)438-4000  **5**

 Contemporary Hotel $131-$219

**AAA Benefit:** Members save 5% or more!

**Address:** 64 S Water St 36602 **Location:** I-10 exit 26B, just ne. **Facility:** Jutting above the city skyline, this well-appointed, contemporary high-rise property is easily identified. On the bay and in the historic downtown district, it affords scenic views from any vantage point. 373 units. 28 stories, interior corridors. **Parking:** on-site (fee) and valet. **Amenities:** safes. **Dining:** The Harbor Room, see separate listing. **Pool(s):** heated outdoor. **Activities:** hot tub, regulation golf, exercise room, massage. **Guest Services:** valet laundry, rental car service.

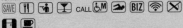

R
**RENAISSANCE**
HOTELS

**Located in downtown Mobile, next to the entertainment district & within walking distance to museums.**

---

▼ See AAA listing p. 112 ▼

Holiday Inn

Holiday Inn Mobile West I-10
5465 Hwy 90 W • Mobile, AL 36619
(251)666-5600
www.holidayinn.com/mobile-i10

- 5th Avenue Restaurant and Lounge
- Swimming Pool
- Free Wireless Internet
- Kids Eat & Stay Free
- In-room Microwave/ Fridge
- 2400 Sq Ft of Meeting Space
- Pets Allowed

---

AAA Vacations® packages ...

unforgettable experiences and unrivaled value

(See map & index p. 109.)

## RENAISSANCE-THE BATTLE HOUSE MOBILE HOTEL & SPA
(251)338-2000 **3**

**Historic Hotel**
$189-$263

**AAA Benefit:**
Members save 5% or more!

**Address:** 26 N Royal St 36602 **Location:** I-10 exit 26B (Water St) eastbound, w on Government St, then just n. **Facility:** Originally built in 1852, this beautifully renovated historical hotel in downtown Mobile exudes old Southern charm alongside modern amenities. 238 units. 6-8 stories, interior corridors. **Parking:** on-site (fee) and valet. **Terms:** check-in 4 pm. **Amenities:** safes. **Dining:** The Trellis Room, see separate listing, entertainment. **Pool(s):** heated outdoor. **Activities:** hot tub, regulation golf, tennis, exercise room, spa. **Guest Services:** valet laundry.

SAVE 🍴 👤 Y CALL 👤M 🏊 BIZ HS 📶
✕ 📷 🔒 🖥 🖨 / SOME UNITS 🐾

## R
### RENAISSANCE®
HOTELS
**Located in downtown Mobile and within walking distance to the entertainment district and museums.**

## RESIDENCE INN BY MARRIOTT MOBILE
(251)304-0570 **15**

🔷🔷🔷 **Extended Stay Hotel**
$116-$129 **Address:** 950 W I-65 Service Rd S 36609 **Location:** I-65 exit 3 (Airport Blvd), just w, then 0.4 mi s. **Facility:** 66 units, some two bedrooms, efficiencies and kitchens. 3 stories, interior corridors. **Terms:** check-in 4 pm. **Pool(s):** heated indoor. **Activities:** exercise room. **Guest Services:** valet and coin laundry.

**AAA Benefit:**
Members save 5% or more!

CALL 👤M 🏊 📶 ✕ 🔒 🖥 🖨 / SOME UNITS 🐾

## TILLMAN'S CORNER COMFORT SUITES
(251)665-0161 **20**

🔷🔷🔷 **Hotel** $89-$129 **Address:** 5660 Tillman's Corner Pkwy 36619 **Location:** I-10 exit 15B, just e on US 90, then just n. **Facility:** 65 units. 3 stories, interior corridors. **Pool(s):** outdoor. **Activities:** exercise room. **Guest Services:** coin laundry.

🍴 CALL 👤M 🏊 BIZ HS 📶 ✕ 🔒 🖥 🖨

## TOWNEPLACE SUITES BY MARRIOTT MOBILE
(251)345-9588 **18**

🔷🔷🔷 **Extended Stay Hotel**
$89-$119 **Address:** 1075 Montlimar Dr 36609 **Location:** I-65 exit 3 (Airport Blvd), 0.5 mi w, then 0.5 mi s. Located in a commercial area. **Facility:** 95 kitchen units, some two bedrooms. 3 stories, interior corridors. **Terms:** check-in 4 pm. **Pool(s):** outdoor. **Activities:** exercise room. **Guest Services:** valet and coin laundry.

**AAA Benefit:**
Members save 5% or more!

🍴 🏊 📶 ✕ 🔒 🖥 🖨 / SOME UNITS 🐾 HS

## WINGATE BY WYNDHAM I-10 WEST
(251)661-9099 **21**

🔷🔷🔷 **Hotel**
$99-$140

**Address:** 5190 Motel Ct 36619 **Location:** I-10 exit 15B, just ne. **Facility:** 100 units. 4 stories, interior corridors. **Amenities:** safes. **Pool(s):** outdoor. **Activities:** exercise room. **Guest Services:** valet and coin laundry.

SAVE CALL 👤M 🏊 BIZ HS 📶
✕ 🔒 🖥 🖨

## WINGATE BY WYNDHAM MOBILE
(251)441-1979 **1**

🔷🔷🔷 **Hotel** $119-$139 **Address:** 516 Spring Hill Plaza Ct 36608 **Location:** I-65 exit 5A, just w, then just n. **Facility:** 3 stories, interior corridors. **Terms:** cancellation fee imposed. **Amenities:** safes. **Pool(s):** outdoor. **Activities:** exercise room. **Guest Services:** valet and coin laundry.

✈ CALL 👤M 🏊 BIZ HS 📶 ✕ 🔒 🖥 🖨

## WHERE TO EAT

## ASHLAND MIDTOWN PUB
251/479-3278 **14**

🔷🔷 Pizza Sandwiches. Casual Dining. $6-$25 **AAA Inspector Notes:** On the fringes of a residential area, this small neighborhood pub is best known for its crispy, thin-crust pizza. Other menu options include pasta dishes, po' boys and a few seafood selections. Live music is presented during Wednesday Ladies Night and on Saturday evening. **Features:** full bar, Sunday brunch, happy hour. **Address:** 2453-A Old Shell Rd 36607 **Location:** I-65 exit 5A, just s on service road, then 1.6 mi e on SR 70. L D

## BAMBOO BISTRO
251/378-5466 **19**

🔷🔷 Asian. Casual Dining. $10-$30 **AAA Inspector Notes:** Whether you're in the mood for hibachi, sushi or stir-fry, it's all available in this relaxed setting. Watch the skilled chef create his artistic rolls at the sushi bar; be entertained by the antics of the hibachi chef at the grill; or sit at a table or booth for a casual, quiet meal. **Features:** full bar. **Address:** 3662 Airport Blvd, Suite A 36608 **Location:** I-65 exit 3 (Airport Blvd), just w. L D CALL 👤M

## BANGKOK THAI CUISINE
251/344-9995 **21**

🔷🔷 Thai. Casual Dining. $8-$15 **AAA Inspector Notes:** This restaurant offers not only a palatable but visual taste of Thai culture. Intricately carved wood furniture and adornment fill the dining room along with ethnic artwork and crafts. A wide variety of Thai, Asian and sushi dishes is offered. The food is prepared with no additives or preservatives. **Address:** 3821 Airport Blvd 36608 **Location:** I-65 exit 3 (Airport Blvd), 0.8 mi w. L D CALL 👤M

## BENJAMIN'S
251/450-9377 **17**

🔷🔷🔷 Regional Comfort Food. Casual Dining. $8-$23 **AAA Inspector Notes:** A nice selection of Southern home-style cooking—such as red beans and rice, shrimp and grits and shepherd's pie—can be found at this informal café. Also available are burgers, sandwiches and some Southern-style appetizers with an added kick. **Features:** full bar, patio dining, Sunday brunch, happy hour. **Address:** 2101 Airport Blvd 36606 **Location:** I-65 exit 3 (Airport Blvd), 2 mi e. L D

## THE BLIND MULE RESTAURANT & BAR
251/694-6853 **2**

🔷🔷 American. Casual Dining. $9-$15 **AAA Inspector Notes:** A quaint New Orleans-style courtyard, complete with a flowing fountain, is available for outdoor dining at this restaurant. The upstairs space, known as The Attic, presents area bands on weekends. **Features:** full bar, patio dining, Sunday brunch. **Address:** 57 N Claiborne St 36602 **Location:** Between St Francis and St Michael sts; downtown. L D

(See map & index p. 109.)

**THE BULL RESTAURANT**   251/378-5091   ⑨

▽▽▽▽ New Southwestern. Fine Dining. $17-$40 **AAA Inspector Notes:** This chic, intimate café serves an eclectic menu, which changes seasonally to ensure the fresh ingredients. Rich dark wood accents and an exposed brick wall, along with subdued, soft lighting, creates a soothing atmosphere. This is a popular venue with the area's professional crowd. Lunch is served only on Friday. **Features:** full bar. **Reservations:** suggested. **Address:** 609 Dauphin St 36602 **Location:** Between Warren and Dearborn sts; downtown. **Parking:** on-site and street. [D] CALL [&M]

**BUSABA'S THAI CUISINE**   251/405-0044   ③

▽▽ Thai. Casual Dining. $8-$14 **AAA Inspector Notes:** Find this ethnic eatery in a restored red brick Victorian structure built in 1893 in historic downtown. The place has been treating the Mobile metro area to spicy, authentic dishes since 2001. **Features:** beer & wine. **Address:** 203 Dauphin St 36602 **Location:** Corner of Conception St; in historic downtown; diagonally across from Bienville Square. **Parking:** street only. [L] [D]

**BUTCH CASSIDY'S**   251/450-0690   ⑫

▽▽ Burgers Sandwiches. Casual Dining. $7-$10 **AAA Inspector Notes:** Established in 1993, this laid-back neighborhood bar and grill is the home of the Butch burger, their signature sandwich that is cooked to order and dressed with bacon, cheese, lettuce, tomato, onion and pickles. Other menu items include a variety of sandwiches, salads, chili and a daily rotating hot entrée special. **Features:** full bar, happy hour. **Address:** 60 N Florida St 36607 **Location:** I-65 exit 4, 1.4 mi e on Dauphin St, then just n. [L] [D]

**DEW DROP INN**   251/473-7872   ⑬

▽ American. Casual Dining. $7-$15 **AAA Inspector Notes:** *Classic Historic.* In business since 1924, this inn holds the honor of being the longest operating restaurant in Mobile. Its signature hamburgers and hot dogs have developed a loyal following including singer, Jimmy Buffett, who acknowledges in the Parrot Head Handbook of developing his burger lust at this establishment. Closes at 3 pm on Monday and Saturday. **Features:** beer only. **Address:** 1808 Old Shell Rd 36607 **Location:** I-65 exit 5A (Springhill Ave), 2.6 mi e, just s on Mobile Infirmary Blvd, then just w. [L] [D]

**DICK RUSSELL'S**   251/661-6090   ㉔

▽ Barbecue. Casual Dining. $4-$22 **AAA Inspector Notes:** Offering good home-style food, this restaurant is a popular stop along the I-10 corridor. **Features:** beer & wine. **Address:** 5360 Hwy 90 W 36619 **Location:** I-10 exit 17, 0.4 mi w on SR 193, then just w. [B] [L] [D]

**DREAMLAND BAR-B-QUE**   251/479-9898

▽ Barbecue. Casual Dining. $6-$13 **AAA Inspector Notes:** "Ain't nothing like 'em nowhere" is the motto at this barbecue cafe. The menu is small, but that is okay because everybody comes for one thing: the ribs. Barbecue dishes come with white bread and a kicking sauce. Friendly Southern hospitality and a casual backdrop help make this place a favorite. **Features:** beer only. **Address:** 3314 Old Shell Rd 36607 **Location:** I-65 exit 5A (Springhill Ave), just e to service road, then just s. [L] [D] [✎]

**FUEGO COASTAL MEXICAN EATERY**   251/378-8621   ⑮

▽▽ Mexican. Casual Dining. $11-$24 **AAA Inspector Notes:** The upscale, contemporary south-of-the-border decor serves as a precursor to ethnic cuisine with a twist at this casual spot. Menu highlights include fried snapper with a citrus jalapeno reduction and baked mahi mahi in banana leaves covered in a citrus orange sauce. Embellished traditional dishes such as fajitas, burritos and enchiladas are not forgotten and available for the less adventurous. **Features:** full bar, happy hour. **Address:** 2066 Old Shell Rd 36607 **Location:** I-65 exit 5A (Springhill Ave), 2 mi e on US 98, just s on Upham St, then just e. [L] [D] CALL [&M]

**THE HARBOR ROOM**   251/438-4000   ⑤

▽▽▽ Seafood. Fine Dining. $9-$35 **AAA Inspector Notes:** Patrons at this upscale, sophisticated restaurant enjoy spectacular views of the harbor. **Features:** full bar. **Reservations:** suggested. **Address:** 64 S Water St 36602 **Location:** I-10 exit 26B, just ne; in Renaissance Mobile Riverview Plaza Hotel. **Parking:** on-site (fee) and valet. [B] [L] [D] CALL [&M]

**THE HUNGRY OWL**   251/633-4479

▽ Southern Creole. Casual Dining. $9-$30 **AAA Inspector Notes:** Diversity is key at this eatery where diners can choose from such specialties as alligator pot pie, Creole barbecue Gulf shrimp, Asian-style chicken, stuffed Tony burger, flatbread pizza and gourmet wraps. Chef Tony Nicholas prepares affordable, slow-cooked food as fast as it can be served. **Address:** 7899 Cottage Hill Rd 36695 **Location:** Corner of Schillinger Rd S; in Schillinger Place Plaza. [L] [D] CALL [&M]

**JERUSALEM CAFE**   251/304-1155   ㉒

▽▽ Middle Eastern. Casual Dining. $6-$17 **AAA Inspector Notes:** This intimate bistro displays the sights, sounds and taste of the Holy Land. Middle Eastern music plays softly in the background, ethnic costumes and landscape photos adorn the walls, and pungent aromas of Mediterranean food embrace you upon arrival. **Features:** patio dining, Sunday brunch. **Address:** 4715 Airport Blvd, Suite 330 36608 **Location:** I-65 exit 3 (Airport Blvd), 3 mi w; in Regency Square Shopping Center; behind Applebee's. [L] [D] [🛒]

**JOHN WORD'S RESTAURANT & JAZZ CAFE**   251/433-3790   ⑧

▽▽ Southern American. Casual Dining. $8-$32 **AAA Inspector Notes:** This restaurant, located on Mobile Bay next to the USS Alabama Memorial Park, is open 365 days a year and offers a wide range of menu options. Live jazz is featured in the lounge Thursday, Friday and Saturday evenings. **Features:** full bar. **Address:** 2701 Battleship Pkwy 36602 **Location:** I-10 exit 27, just e; in Battleship Inn Resort. [B] [L] [D] CALL [&M]

**MOMMA GOLDBERG'S DELI**   251/344-9500   ⑳

▽ American. Quick Serve. $6-$10 **AAA Inspector Notes:** An ideal place for a quick bite, this eatery offers freshly-made signature sandwiches and salads. Call ahead as they do not serve dinner on Sunday evening. **Features:** beer only, patio dining. **Address:** 3696B Airport Blvd 36608 **Location:** I-65 exit 3 (Airport Blvd), just w; in Yester Oaks Shopping Center. [L] [D] CALL [&M]

**NOJA**   251/433-0377   ④

▽▽▽▽ Fusion. Fine Dining. $29-$36 **AAA Inspector Notes:** A former townhouse built in the 1840s, this bistro incorporates a New Orleans-style charm with a private enclosed open-air courtyard. Its interior displays a bright red floor, lime green accent wall and pumpkin-orange trim adding a funky, Bohemian flair. The menu is categorized as Mediterrasian, a fusion of Mediterranean and Asian cuisine. A large portion of the menu changes daily, sometimes even twice in one night due to the small quantities purchased to ensure absolute freshness of ingredients. **Features:** full bar, patio dining. **Reservations:** suggested. **Address:** 6 N Jackson St 36602 **Location:** Between St Francis and Dauphin sts; downtown. **Parking:** street only. [D]

**ORIGINAL OYSTER HOUSE**   251/626-2188

▽▽ ▽▽
Seafood
Casual Dining
$8-$28

**AAA Inspector Notes:** This family-oriented restaurant is popular with locals and visitors alike, and it is easy to see why. Fresh seafood is served in generous portions by the friendliest servers around. Expect knowledgeable, casual, friendly service provided by a staff that genuinely cares. **Features:** full bar. **Address:** 3733 Battleship Pkwy 36527 **Location:** I-10 exit 30, 1 mi nw on US 90. [L] [D] [✎]

**OSMAN'S RESTAURANT**   251/479-0006   ㉓

▽▽▽ American. Fine Dining. $19-$33 **AAA Inspector Notes:** On a side road in an industrial section guests can find this hidden treasure offering dining pleasures. The cozy, intimate bistro offers a mixture of Italian, German and American fare. It is wise to call ahead to reserve a table due to the limited seating. **Features:** full bar. **Reservations:** suggested. **Address:** 2579 Halls Mill Rd 36606 **Location:** I-65 exit 1 (Government Blvd), just ne on US 90, 0.6 mi s on N McVay Dr, then 0.6 mi ne. [D]

(See map & index p. 109.)

### THE ROYAL SCAM  251/432-7226  6

▼▼ American. Casual Dining. $9-$30 **AAA Inspector Notes:** Dine in the intimate, contemporary lounge featuring portraits of jazz greats or outdoors in the enclosed courtyard. **Features:** full bar, patio dining, happy hour. **Address:** 72 S Royal St 36602 **Location:** I-10 exit 26B, just e on Government St, then just n. **Parking:** street only.

L D CALL 占M ◢

### RUTH'S CHRIS STEAK HOUSE  251/476-0516  16

▼▼▼ Steak. Fine Dining. $21-$85 **AAA Inspector Notes:** The main fare is steak, which is prepared from several cuts of Prime beef and cooked to perfection, but the menu also lists lamb, chicken and seafood dishes. Guests should come hungry because the side dishes, which are among the a la carte offerings, could make a meal in themselves. **Features:** full bar. **Reservations:** suggested. **Address:** 2058 Airport Blvd 36606 **Location:** I-65 exit 3 (Airport Blvd), 2.1 mi e. D

### SAGE RESTAURANT  251/476-6400  18

▼▼▼ American. Casual Dining. $10-$32 **AAA Inspector Notes:** Steaks, chicken, seafood and pasta offerings are presented in an upscale manner. An enhanced ambience characterizes the open dining area. Guests also can choose from a selection of lighter fare. **Features:** full bar. **Address:** 3101 Airport Blvd 36606 **Location:** I-65 exit 3 (Airport Blvd), 0.5 mi e; in Mobile Marriott.

B L D CALL 占M

### SHRIMP BASKET  251/471-0191  10

▼▼ Seafood. Family Dining. $7-$15 **AAA Inspector Notes:** A casual, nautical atmosphere can be found in this spot where seafood abounds. Shrimp, oysters and fish can be steamed, grilled or fried. Burgers and chicken are available for meat lovers. Rotating nightly all-you-can-eat specials are offered. **Features:** full bar. **Address:** 2540 Old Shell Rd 36607 **Location:** I-65 exit 4, 1.4 mi e on Dauphin St, then just n on Florida St. L D CALL 占M

### SONNY'S REAL PIT BAR-B-Q  251/634-0999

▼ Barbecue. Family Dining. $8-$15 **AAA Inspector Notes:** Bearing the name after its founder, Floyd "Sonny" Tillman, this barbecue restaurant first opened its doors circa 1968 in Gainesville, Florida and has since spawned over 150 more throughout the Southeast. The menu is steeped in finger lickin' favorites such as ribs, pulled pork, beef brisket, burgers, catfish, shrimp and char-grilled chicken. Let's not forget about the fried okra, which is the perfect starter dish, and their homemade baked beans. **Features:** beer only. **Address:** 770 Schillinger Rd S 36695 **Location:** I-65 exit 3 (Airport Blvd), 6.1 mi w, then 0.6 mi s. L D

### SPOT OF TEA  251/433-9009  7

▼▼ Continental. Casual Dining. $8-$10 **AAA Inspector Notes:** As the name suggests, this popular breakfast and lunch spot is an ideal place for a spot of tea, particularly the signature strawberry iced tea. A Victorian influence is evident in the dining room, where patrons savor an excellent selection of omelets and sandwiches. The folks at this popular restaurant pride themselves on super-fast service, no matter how busy the place is. **Features:** wine only, Sunday brunch. **Address:** 310 Dauphin St 36602 **Location:** Between Jackson and Claiborne sts; downtown; in historic district. **Parking:** on-site (fee) and street. B L

### THE TRELLIS ROOM  251/338-5493  1

▼▼▼▼

Southern American Fine Dining $22-$40

**AAA Inspector Notes:** *Historic.* Guests find elegant, contemporary dining in a historical setting. The high, two-story, arched stained-glass ceiling is a focal point of the dining room. It allows a soft, natural light to brighten the rich, dark wood interior. The seasonally changing menu offers delicious and distinctive creations using fresh ingredients, including many organically raised items. **Features:** full bar, Sunday brunch. **Reservations:** suggested. **Address:** 26 N Royal St 36602 **Location:** I-10 exit 26B (Water St) eastbound, w on Government St, then just n; in Renaissance-The Battle House Mobile Hotel & Spa. **Parking:** valet and street only. B D CALL 占M

### TRUE MIDTOWN KITCHEN  251/434-2002  11

▼▼▼ Southern American. Casual Dining. $9-$29 **AAA Inspector Notes:** An inviting open space offering country charm, this kitchen features high, open rafter ceilings, exposed brick walls, large bright red barn-like doors, an exhibition kitchen, simplistic Americana-style artwork and hardy thick-legged wood tables. The relaxed, laid-back atmosphere supports a frequently changing menu which reflects a home-style selection but with some added twists to regional favorites. Utilizing local purveyors ensures the freshest of ingredients. **Features:** full bar, patio dining. **Address:** 1104 Dauphin St 36604 **Location:** Jct N Hallett St, just w. L D CALL 占M

### WINTZELL'S OYSTER HOUSE  251/341-1111

▼▼ Southern Seafood. Casual Dining. $9-$24 **AAA Inspector Notes:** Diners can request their oysters fried, stewed or nude at this eatery which has been preparing them 10 different ways since 1938. The menu also lists an exceptional variety of seafood. **Features:** full bar. **Address:** 6700 Airport Blvd 36608 **Location:** I-65 exit 3 (Airport Blvd), 4.5 mi w. L D ◢

## MONROEVILLE (G-3) pop. 6,519, elev. 413'

Monroeville cherishes its connection to the Pulitzer Prize-winning novel "To Kill a Mockingbird." Its author, Nelle Harper Lee, was born here in 1926, and many elements of the book are rooted in her upbringing in this small town. A mural at Lyle Salter Park on South Alabama Avenue features a scene from the book.

Fellow author Truman Capote was born in New Orleans, La., in 1924 and soon after was sent to live in Monroeville with his mother's cousins, the Faulks, who lived next to the Lee family. He attended school here until 1933, when he moved to New York City to live with his mother and stepfather, but he returned every summer and for holidays. The future literary sensations were good childhood friends, and their friendship lasted throughout Capote's life. A marker commemorating Capote stands outside the site where the Faulk house once stood on Alabama Avenue.

Monroeville has been home to other successful writers in addition to Lee and Capote, and to celebrate that fact, it was declared "The Literary Capital of Alabama" in 1997.

**Monroeville/Monroe County Chamber of Commerce:** 86 N. Alabama Ave., P.O. Box 214, Monroeville, AL 36461. **Phone:** (251) 743-2879.

**Self-guiding tours:** A self-guiding audio tour (with Quick Response signage for scanning) is available from the chamber of commerce and pinpoints some 24 noteworthy sites from the Historic Downtown Commercial District (Alabama Avenue, Pineville Road and South Mount Pleasant Street). Among the sites on the route are the 1903 courthouse; the courthouse square; a 1937 post office with a WPA mural; and the Monroe County Public Library, which used to be the hotel where Gregory Peck stayed on his visit to Monroeville prior to filming "To Kill a Mockingbird."

**OLD COURTHOUSE MUSEUM** is on the town square at 31 N. Alabama Ave. The courtroom of this 1903 courthouse was used as a model for the movie "To Kill a Mockingbird," based on the book by Monroeville author Harper Lee. Exhibits focus on the courthouse, Harper Lee and Truman Capote's childhood in

Monroeville. A 45-minute video about the book and the film may be seen. "To Kill a Mockingbird" performances are held select days in late April and May.

**Hours:** Tues.-Fri. 10-4, Sat.10-2, Mar.-Nov.; Tues.-Fri. 10-4, Sat. 9-noon, rest of year. Closed Jan. 1, Martin Luther King Jr. Day, Memorial Day, July 4, Labor Day, Veterans Day, Thanksgiving and Christmas. **Cost:** Free. **Phone:** (251) 575-7433.

---

**BEST WESTERN INN** (251)575-9999

Motel
$72-$80

**AAA Benefit:**
Members save up to 20%!

**Address:** 4419 S Alabama Ave 36460 **Location:** On SR 21, 0.5 mi n of jct US 84. **Facility:** 42 units. 2 stories (no elevator), exterior corridors. **Terms:** cancellation fee imposed. **Pool(s):** outdoor. **Activities:** exercise room. **Guest Services:** valet laundry.

---

**COUNTRY INN & SUITES BY CARLSON** (251)743-3333

Hotel $77-$139 **Address:** 120 Hwy 21 S 36460 **Location:** On SR 21, just s of jct US 84. **Facility:** 42 units. 2 stories (no elevator), interior corridors. **Terms:** cancellation fee imposed, resort fee. **Pool(s):** outdoor. **Activities:** exercise room.

---

**MOCKINGBIRD INN & SUITES** (251)743-3297

Motel $75-$140 **Address:** 4389 S Alabama Ave 36460 **Location:** On SR 21, 0.5 mi n of jct US 84. **Facility:** 62 units. 2 stories (no elevator), exterior corridors. **Terms:** 3 day cancellation notice, resort fee. **Pool(s):** outdoor. **Activities:** exercise room.

---

## WHERE TO EAT

**A. J.'S FAMILY RESTAURANT** 251/575-2276

Southern American. Family Dining. $3-$18 **AAA Inspector Notes:** The large, bright red A.J.'s sign above the door makes it easy to spot this plain structure. Order off the menu for a variety of simply prepared sandwiches, steak, chicken and seafood or take advantage of the daily rotating buffet selections. Only breakfast and lunch are served on Saturday and Sunday. **Address:** 214 Hwy 21 S 36460 **Location:** Jct US 84 and SR 21, just sw.

---

**COURT HOUSE CAFE** 251/743-3663

American. Casual Dining. $5-$15 **AAA Inspector Notes:** Just down the block from the old courthouse immortalized in the film "To Kill A Mockingbird" patrons can dine on simple, no frills cooking in a small town atmosphere. The luncheon menu primarily consists of sandwiches and burgers, while hot entrées are offered for dinner. **Address:** 27 W Claiborne St 36460 **Location:** Between Mt. Pleasant and Johnson aves; downtown. **Parking:** street only.

---

**RADLEY'S FOUNTAIN GRILLE** 251/743-2345

American. Casual Dining. $7-$21 **AAA Inspector Notes:** This cozy, casual bistro serves soup, salad and sandwiches for lunch and generous portions of beef, pasta, seafood and poultry for after 5 dining. Homemade cakes are a must try. **Features:** beer & wine. **Address:** 1559 S Alabama Ave 36460 **Location:** Jct SR 47 and 41, 0.7 mi s.

---

**MONTEVALLO** (D-3) pop. 6,323, elev. 430'
• Part of Birmingham area — see map p. 43

**THE AMERICAN VILLAGE,** 3727 SR 119, showcases the ideals of American liberty and self-government. The site features a Colonial garden as well as replicas of the White House Oval Office and East Room, Bruton Parish Church of Williamsburg, a Colonial chapel and the Concord Bridge. Washington Hall is patterned after George Washington's Mount Vernon. The Pettus Randall Miniature Museum of American History presents some 35 historical dioramas populated by figurines that depict notable events. The National Veterans Shrine and Register of Honor presents stories of service and sacrifice by America's veterans.

The "Liberty!" program (offered September through May) presents costumed interpreters reenacting Colonial times and events that shaped American history. Interpreters assuming the roles of George Washington, Patrick Henry, Abigail Adams and other historical figures interact with guests. The summer "Celebrate America" program involves interactive experiences like drilling with the Continental Army and playing 18th-century games. Special celebrations are held on Washington's Birthday, Memorial Day and Veterans Day, and on July 4 an Independence Day 1776 celebration is held, concluding with fireworks at twilight.

**Time:** Allow 1 hour, 30 minutes minimum. **Hours:** Mon.-Fri. 10-4. Programs may vary. Phone ahead to confirm schedule. **Cost:** $10; $9 (ages 5-17 and 60+); free (veterans and active military with ID). Independence Day 1776 event $5; free (veterans and active military with ID). **Phone:** (205) 665-3535 or (877) 811-1776.

---

**MONTGOMERY** (E-4) pop. 205,764, elev. 191'
• Hotels p. 124 • Restaurants p. 126
• Attractions map p. 118
• Hotels & Restaurants map & index p. 122

Montgomery was chartered in 1817 and named after Gen. Richard Montgomery, a Revolutionary War hero who died in 1775 during the battle of Québec. Prior to the Civil War, it flourished as a cotton market and transportation center. The town's volume of commerce and its central location led to the transfer of the state government from Tuscaloosa in 1846.

In February 1861, Jefferson Davis arrived in Montgomery and was sworn in as president of the Confederate States of America. On April 11, 1861, he sent a telegraph commanding troops to remove Northern aggressors from Fort Sumter in South Carolina, culminating in the first shots of the Civil War.

Montgomery's status as capital of the Confederacy was short-lived; within months the Confederate government moved to more strategically located Richmond, Va. Montgomery was spared devastation during the war, although prosperity ended abruptly when the town was surrendered to Union troops. Recovery began when railroad lines

**(See map & index p. 122.)**

came through in the 1880s. Union Station was completed in 1898 and served as the city's rail station until the late 1970s; it is now the Montgomery Area Visitor Center.

Montgomery was the nation's first city to introduce an electric streetcar system to local travel; the Lightning Route operated 1886-1936. Today's trolleys travel through the downtown Montgomery area, providing transportation to government buildings; historical sites; the Riverfront Amphitheatre; and Riverwalk Stadium, home to baseball's Class AA Montgomery Biscuits. The trolleys run continually Mon.-Sat. 9-4 at 1-hour intervals.

Maxwell Air Force Base, where the Wright Brothers' Flight School once stood, is the site of the Air University, the Air Force's center of professional military education. The Air Force Senior NCO Academy and the Extension Course Institute are at nearby Gunter Annex to Maxwell Air Force Base.

The Hank Williams Memorial honors the country singer, who is perhaps best known for his lovesick ballad, "Your Cheatin' Heart." The memorial is downtown at 1305 Upper Wetumpka Rd. in the Oakwood Cemetery Annex and is open daily dawn-dusk; phone (334) 262-3200. You can also see a statue of Williams, guitar in hand, at Lister Hill Plaza on N. Perry Street.

Weekdays the W.A. Gayle Planetarium, 1010 Forest Ave., presents sky shows and science programs; phone (334) 241-4799.

Every second Saturday of the month from April through September, a fun-filled family event takes place at Riverfront Park where live music, games and fireworks are offered.

**Montgomery Area Visitor Center in Historic Union Station:** 300 Water St., Montgomery, AL 36104. **Phone:** (334) 262-0013 or (800) 240-9452.

**Self-guiding tours:** The 54-mile Selma to Montgomery National Historic Trail runs from the Brown Chapel AME Church in Selma to the state capitol in Montgomery. The Montgomery Area Visitor Center in Historic Union Station offers a 31-page brochure about this trail and the state's other important civil rights sites.

**Shopping areas:** Eastdale Mall, at the intersection of US 231 and US 80 Bus. Rte., has Dillard's, JCPenney, Sears and more than 90 other stores and restaurants. The Shoppes at EastChase, off I-85 between Taylor Road and Chantilly Parkway, includes such upscale retailers as Dillard's, Banana Republic and Williams-Sonoma. The Mulberry District, off I-85N exit 2, offers boutique shopping and casual restaurants in a neighborhood setting.

**ALABAMA STATE CAPITOL,** on Capitol (Goat) Hill at 600 Dexter Ave., is a Greek Revival-style structure with a 119-foot white dome. The 1851 building

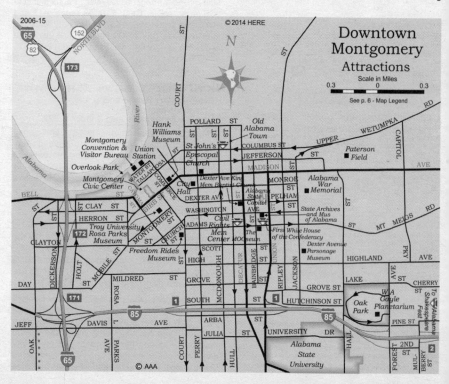

**(See map & index p. 122.)**

served as the capitol of the Confederacy during the first 3 months of the Civil War. Twin three-story spiral stairways and murals depicting Alabama history adorn the interior; a Confederate monument is on the north lawn. The Confederate Constitution was drafted in the Senate chamber.

A bronze star on the west portico marks the spot where Jefferson Davis took the oath of office. In March 1965, the Selma to Montgomery Voting Rights March, led by Martin Luther King Jr., ended on the street in front of the Capitol. **Hours:** Self-guiding tours are available Mon.-Fri. 9-4. Guided 45-minute tours are given Sat. at 9, 11, 1 and 3. Closed state holidays. **Cost:** Free. **Phone:** (334) 242-3935. GT

**ALABAMA WAR MEMORIAL,** at 120 N. Jackson St. at jct. Monroe St., commemorates the Alabamians who fought in all wars. **Hours:** Daily 24 hours. Closed major holidays. **Cost:** Free. **Phone:** (334) 262-6638.

**CIVIL RIGHTS MEMORIAL CENTER,** 400 Washington Ave., features background information about civil rights movement participants, exhibits about social justice and a 56-seat theater. Visitors who make a pledge to stand up for justice, equality and human rights can add their names to The Wall of Tolerance.

The Civil Rights Memorial stands adjacent to the center as a monument to those who died in the struggle for racial equality. The memorial features a round black granite table covered with a thin sheet of flowing water and inscribed with dates of key events and names of people involved in the civil rights movement. It is set against a 40-foot curved waterfall flowing over inscribed words from Martin Luther King Jr.'s "I Have a Dream" speech.

**Time:** Allow 1 hour minimum. **Hours:** Memorial center open Mon.-Fri. 9-4:30, Sat. 10-4; closed major holidays. Memorial open daily 24 hours. **Cost:** Memorial center $2; free (ages 0-17). Memorial free. **Phone:** (334) 956-8439.

**DEXTER AVENUE KING MEMORIAL BAPTIST CHURCH** is at 454 Dexter Ave. The Rev. Dr. Martin Luther King Jr. was its pastor 1954-60. It was in this church that the leaders of the desegregation movement met for the first time in 1955 and decided to institute a bus boycott as a form of peaceful protest. The church contains a detailed mural chronicling Dr. King's nonviolent crusade against racial oppression as well as Dr. King's pulpit and pastoral office.

**Hours:** Guided tours depart on the hour Tues.-Fri. 10-4, Sat. 10-2. Closed major holidays. **Cost:** $5.50; $3.30 (ages 4-11). Combination ticket with Dexter Avenue Parsonage Museum $11; $5.50 (ages 4-11). **Phone:** (334) 263-3970. GT

**DEXTER AVENUE PARSONAGE MUSEUM** is at 309 S. Jackson St. Several ministers of Dexter Avenue King Memorial Baptist Church made this 1920s parsonage their home. The house was the residence of the Rev. Dr. Martin Luther King Jr. and his family 1954-60 while Dr. King led the Montgomery Bus Boycott. An interpretive center and the King-Johns Garden of Reflection are on the property.

Tours begin at the interpretive center. **Time:** Allow 1 hour minimum. **Hours:** Tues.-Fri. 10-4, Sat. 10-2. Closed major holidays. **Cost:** Museum $5.50; $3.30 (ages 4-11). Garden free. Combination ticket with Dexter Avenue King Memorial Baptist Church $11 $5.50 (ages 4-11). Reservations are recommended. **Phone:** (334) 261-3270. GT

**FIRST WHITE HOUSE OF THE CONFEDERACY,** at 644 Washington Ave. across from the south side of the capitol, was the home of Jefferson Davis and his family when Montgomery was the Confederate capital. Designed in the Italianate style, the two-story wooden house, built 1832-35, was moved 10 blocks to its present site in the early 20th century.

Period furnishings, war relics and some of Davis' personal property are displayed. The restored house features reception halls, double parlors and a library. **Hours:** Mon.-Fri. 8-4:30, Sat. 9-4. Closed state and federal holidays. **Cost:** Free. **Phone:** (334) 242-1861.

**FREEDOM RIDES MUSEUM** is at 210 S. Court St. at jct. Adams Ave., behind the courthouse. This museum is housed in the Greyhound bus station where 21 youths, all under age 22, arrived by bus May 20, 1961, to peacefully protest racial segregation on public transportation. Despite their nonviolent approach, they were met with violence. The museum showcases their bravery with photographs, artworks, quotes and outdoor exhibit panels. A video booth plays interviews with many of the Freedom Riders who have visited the museum.

The building has been preserved to its 1968 appearance as much as possible, and the separate entrance for African-American passengers can still be seen as well as the waiting room and restaurant areas designated for white passengers only. Guides are available to share information, but visitors may also tour the museum on their own.

**Time:** Allow 1 hour minimum. **Hours:** Fri.-Sat. noon-4. Closed state holidays. **Cost:** $5; $4 (ages 65+ and college students and military with ID); $3 (ages 6-18); $12 (family). **Phone:** (334) 242-3935. GT

**HANK WILLIAMS MUSEUM,** downtown across from the convention center at 118 Commerce St., honors the country music legend. The acclaimed singer and songwriter is remembered through an extensive collection that includes his 1952 baby blue Cadillac, custom-made boots, hats, a tie collection, awards, furniture, portraits, records, record contracts, a horse saddle, a piano, rare film footage and family history.

**Time:** Allow 1 hour minimum. **Hours:** Mon.-Fri. 9-4:30, Sat. 10-4, Sun. 1-4; phone for holiday

(See map & index p. 122.)

schedules. **Cost:** $10; $8 (military with ID); $3 (ages 3-14). **Phone:** (334) 262-3600.

SAVE **MANN WILDLIFE LEARNING MUSEUM** is at 325 Vandiver Blvd., next to the Montgomery Zoo. Conservation is the theme of this natural history museum, which features mounted native North American animals and aquatic creatures. Hands-on displays allow visitors to touch and feel the furs of some of the animals, including bears and deer. Detailed fossil exhibits include woolly mammoth bones and mastodon tusks.

**Hours:** Daily 9-5:30. Last admission 1 hour before closing. Closed Jan. 1, Thanksgiving and Christmas. **Cost:** $6; $4 (ages 3-12 and 65+). Combination ticket with Montgomery Zoo $16; $11 (ages 3-12 and 65+). **Phone:** (334) 240-4900.

SAVE **MONTGOMERY ZOO,** 2301 Coliseum Pkwy., next to the Mann Wildlife Learning Museum, contains approximately 900 birds, mammals and reptiles from around the world, including rare and endangered species. The animals are grouped geographically in outdoor, barrier-free settings. Visitors can feed birds, river otters and fish as well as giraffes. A skylift ride is available. Zoo Weekend, held in late March or early April, features stage shows and activities for all.

**Time:** Allow 1 hour minimum. **Hours:** Daily 9-5:30. Last admission 1 hour before closing. Closed Jan. 1, Thanksgiving and Christmas. **Cost:** $12; $10 (ages 65+); $7 (ages 3-12). Train ride $3. Skylift $4. Combination ticket with Mann Wildlife Learning Museum $16; $11 (ages 3-12 and 65+). **Phone:** (334) 240-4900.

**THE MOOSEUM** is at 201 S. Bainbridge St. Geared for children, the MOOseum educates guests about the past, present and future of the beef cattle industry in Alabama. **Time:** Allow 30 minutes minimum. **Hours:** Mon.-Fri. 8-noon and 1-4:30. Closed major holidays. **Cost:** Donations. **Phone:** (334) 265-1867 or (888) 276-3362.

GEM SAVE **OLD ALABAMA TOWN,** downtown at 301 Columbus St., is a collection of 50 restored buildings representing life in 19th- and early 20th-century central Alabama. The village depicts living and working conditions ranging from the simple existence of rural pioneers to the elegant surroundings of the urban gentry.

Included are a three-story 1850 Italianate townhouse that retains its original kitchen, slave quarters and well; a country doctor's office, with period medical equipment and implements; an 1892 corner grocery whose shelves are stocked with goods common to that time; a log cabin; a cotton gin; a blacksmith shop; a gristmill; and shotgun and dog-trot houses. Drugstore and print shop museums depict those occupations.

**Time:** Allow 2 hours minimum. **Hours:** Mon.-Fri. 9-4, Sat. 9-3. Last admission 1 hour, 30 minutes before closing. Closed Jan. 1, Thanksgiving and Christmas. **Cost:** $10; $5 (ages 6-18). **Phone:** (334) 240-4500.

**ST. JOHN'S EPISCOPAL CHURCH,** 113 Madison Ave. at N. Perry St., was built in 1834 and is the oldest Episcopal church in the city. The pew in which Jefferson Davis sat is marked. **Hours:** Mon.-Fri. 9-4. **Cost:** Free. **Phone:** (334) 262-1937.

**SCOTT AND ZELDA FITZGERALD MUSEUM,** 919 Felder Ave., is in the house the Fitzgeralds occupied during the 1930s while Scott worked on "Tender is the Night" and Zelda completed "Save Me the Waltz." The noted couple's lives are featured in a video presentation.

Photographs, letters and other memorabilia—including a complete collection of first editions of their works—are displayed. Many exhibits pertain to Zelda Fitzgerald, who was born and raised in Montgomery. **Time:** Allow 1 hour minimum. **Hours:** Wed.-Fri. 10-2, Sat.-Sun. 1-5. Closed major holidays. **Cost:** $5; $3 (ages 65+); $2 (students with ID). **Phone:** (334) 264-4222.

**STATE ARCHIVES AND MUSEUM OF ALABAMA,** in the Alabama Department of Archives and History at 624 Washington Ave., explores the development of Alabama through Native American, pioneer and military artifacts; portrait galleries; and a children's gallery. An exhibit about 19th-century life features the official state Bible used by Jefferson Davis when he took the oath of office. A photograph display traces the Selma-to-Montgomery Civil Rights March and the voting-rights struggle of the 1960s. Alabama Voices unfolds the history of Alabama from the 1700s to the present through some 800 artifacts and hundreds of images and documents.

**Hours:** Museum Mon.-Sat. 8:30-4:30. Reference room Tues.-Fri. (also second Sat. of the month) 8:30-4:30. Closed federal and state holidays. **Cost:** Free. **Phone:** (334) 242-4364, or (334) 242-4435 for the reference room.

SAVE **TROY UNIVERSITY ROSA PARKS MUSEUM** is at 252 Montgomery St., on the Troy University campus. This interactive museum honors Rosa Parks, whose 1955 arrest for refusing to give up her seat on a public bus led to the Montgomery Bus Boycott. The protest precipitated the U.S. Supreme Court decision that banned bus segregation. Exhibits tell the story of the struggle for civil rights in the 1950s. **Time:** Allow 1 hour minimum. **Hours:** Mon.-Fri. 9-5, Sat. 9-3. Closed major holidays. **Cost:** $7.50; $5.50 (ages 4-12). **Phone:** (334) 241-8616. GT

**WYNTON M. BLOUNT CULTURAL PARK,** 6055 Vaughn Rd., encompasses 350 acres and is home to Alabama Shakespeare Festival, Montgomery Museum of Fine Arts and The Shakespeare Garden. The scenic park has ponds, walking trails and a dog park. **Hours:** Park grounds open daily dawn-dusk. Attraction schedules vary. **Cost:** Park, Montgomery Museum of Fine Arts and The Shakespeare Garden free. **Phone:** (334) 625-2300. ♿

(See map & index p. 122.)

**Alabama Shakespeare Festival,** in the Carolyn Blount Theatre at 1 Festival Dr., within Wynton M. Blount Cultural Park, presents classical and contemporary plays. The professional repertory company performs in two theaters: the 792-seat Festival Stage and the 262-seat Octagon. Meet-the-cast parties, pre-show and after-theater discussions, and a landscaped park are additional features.

**Hours:** Performances are given Tues.-Sat. at 7:30 p.m. Matinees are given Sat.-Sun. at 2. Schedule may vary; phone ahead. **Cost:** Tickets $24-$54. **Phone:** (334) 271-5353 or (800) 841-4273.

**Montgomery Museum of Fine Arts,** at 1 Museum Dr. within Wynton M. Blount Cultural Park, has a permanent collection noted for American paintings and sculpture, Old Master prints, Southern regional art and 19th-century American decorative arts. Such artists as Robert Henri, John Singer Sargent, James McNeill Whistler, Rembrandt and Edward Hopper are represented. The hands-on ARTWORKS gallery encourages creativity while educating children of all ages about the elements of art.

A sculpture garden is expected to open in early spring 2016. **Hours:** Tues.-Sat. 10-5 (also Thurs. 5-9), Sun. noon-5. Guided tours are offered Sun. at 1. Closed Jan. 1, Thanksgiving and Christmas. **Cost:** Free. **Phone:** (334) 240-4333.

**The Shakespeare Garden,** 1 Festival Dr. within Wynton M. Blount Cultural Park, contains flowers and greenery found in Shakespeare's plays. Highlights include rosemary, honeysuckle, Asiatic lilies, narcissus and roses. Shade trees create a canopy over garden paths. The thatched-roof stone Shakespearean-style amphitheater seats 200 guests. **Time:** Allow 15 minutes minimum. **Hours:** Mon.-Fri. 9-5, Sat.-Sun. 1-5. Closed major holidays. **Cost:** Free. **Phone:** (334) 625-2300.

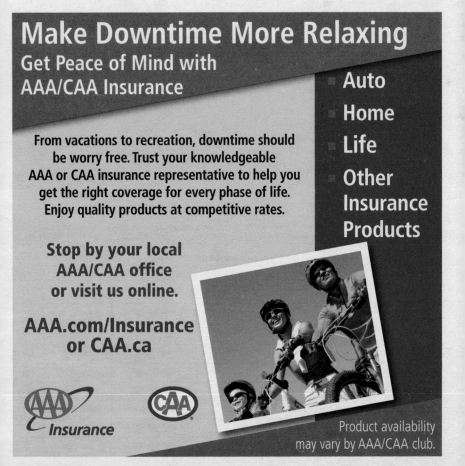

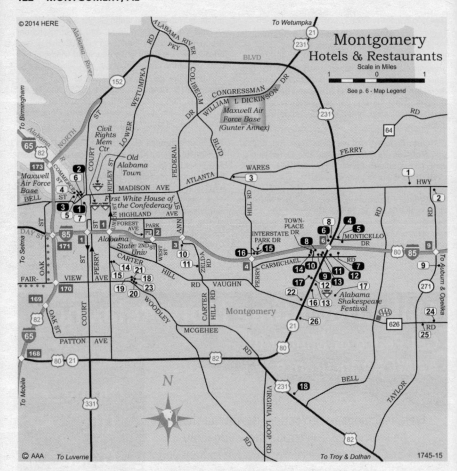

© 2014 HERE

## Montgomery
### Hotels & Restaurants

Scale in Miles

See p. 6 - Map Legend

© AAA   To Luverne

1745-15

## Montgomery

This index helps you "spot" where approved hotels and restaurants are located on the corresponding detailed maps. Hotel daily rate range is for comparison only. Restaurant price range is a combination of lunch and/or dinner. Turn to the listing page for more detailed rate and price information and consult display ads for special promotions.

### MONTGOMERY

| Map Page | Hotels | Diamond Rated | Rate Range | Page |
|---|---|---|---|---|
| **1** this page | **Renaissance Montgomery Hotel & Spa at the Convention Center** | ▽▽▽▽ | $119-$219 SAVE | 125 |
| **2** this page | Hampton Inn & Suites Downtown | ▽▽▽ | $99-$159 | 124 |
| **3** this page | Embassy Suites Montgomery-Hotel & Conference Center | ▽▽▽ | $119-$199 | 124 |
| **4** this page | Baymont Inn & Suites | ▽▽ | $49-$69 | 124 |
| **5** this page | Comfort Suites | ▽▽▽ | $80-$150 | 124 |
| **6** this page | Drury Inn & Suites-Montgomery | ▽▽▽ | $110-$184 | 124 |
| **7** this page | **Residence Inn by Marriott Montgomery** | ▽▽▽ | $89-$139 SAVE | 125 |
| **8** this page | SpringHill Suites by Marriott Montgomery | ▽▽▽ | $89-$99 | 125 |
| **9** this page | Country Inn & Suites By Carlson East | ▽▽▽ | $89-$159 | 124 |

**MONTGOMERY (cont'd)**

| Map Page | Hotels (cont'd) | Diamond Rated | Rate Range | Page |
|---|---|---|---|---|
| **10** p. 122 | Value Place Montgomery | ◆ | Rates not provided | 126 |
| **11** p. 122 | La Quinta Inn Montgomery Eastern Bypass | ◆◆ | $59-$149 | 125 |
| **12** p. 122 | Courtyard by Marriott Montgomery | ◆◆◆ | $69-$89 | 124 |
| **13** p. 122 | La Quinta Inn & Suites Montgomery Carmichael Road | ◆◆ | $65-$185 | 125 |
| **14** p. 122 | Sleep Inn & Suites | ◆◆◆ | $67-$94 | 125 |
| **15** p. 122 | Homewood Suites by Hilton | ◆◆◆ | $89-$189 | 125 |
| **16** p. 122 | Hilton Garden Inn Montgomery East | ◆◆◆ | $89-$189 | 125 |
| **17** p. 122 | Wingate Inn by Wyndham | ◆◆◆ | $74-$179 | 126 |
| **18** p. 122 | Holiday Inn Express Hotel & Suites | ◆◆◆ | $81 | 125 |

| Map Page | Restaurants | Diamond Rated | Cuisine | Price Range | Page |
|---|---|---|---|---|---|
| ① p. 122 | Eastside Grille | ◆◆ | American | $7-$20 | 126 |
| ② p. 122 | Wishbone Cafe | ◆◆ | Cajun | $7-$18 | 128 |
| ③ p. 122 | Lek's Taste of Thailand | ◆◆ | Thai | $7-$20 | 127 |
| ④ p. 122 | Lek's Railroad Thai | ◆◆◆ | Thai | $8-$18 | 127 |
| ⑤ p. 122 | **The House** | ◆◆◆ | American | $9-$38 | 126 |
| ⑥ p. 122 | Sa Za Serious Italian Food | ◆◆◆ | Italian | $9-$26 | 127 |
| ⑦ p. 122 | Cool Beans at the Cafe d'Art | ◆◆ | Sandwiches | $9-$15 | 126 |
| ⑧ p. 122 | Saigon Bistro | ◆◆ | Vietnamese | $6-$9 | 127 |
| ⑨ p. 122 | La Jolla | ◆◆◆ | American | $9-$33 | 127 |
| ⑩ p. 122 | Country's Barbecue | ◆◆ | Barbecue | $6-$14 | 126 |
| ⑪ p. 122 | Michael's Table | ◆◆◆ | International | $10-$30 | 127 |
| ⑫ p. 122 | Sushi Yama | ◆◆ | Japanese Sushi | $8-$27 | 127 |
| ⑬ p. 122 | Los Vaqueros Mexican Restaurant | ◆◆ | Mexican | $5-$15 | 127 |
| ⑭ p. 122 | Filet & Vine | ◆ | Deli Sandwiches | $9-$13 | 126 |
| ⑮ p. 122 | The Chop House Vintage Year | ◆◆◆ | Steak | $16-$35 | 126 |
| ⑯ p. 122 | Baumhowers Restaurant | ◆◆ | American | $6-$22 | 126 |
| ⑰ p. 122 | Sinclair's Eastside | ◆◆ | American | $7-$25 | 127 |
| ⑱ p. 122 | Sinclair's Cloverdale | ◆◆ | American | $8-$26 | 127 |
| ⑲ p. 122 | El Rey Burrito Lounge | ◆◆ | Mexican | $10-$19 | 126 |
| ⑳ p. 122 | Tomatinos Pizza & Bake Shop | ◆◆ | Pizza | $8-$26 | 128 |
| ㉑ p. 122 | Cafe Louisa | ◆◆ | Sandwiches | $6-$9 | 126 |
| ㉒ p. 122 | Willow Tree Korean/Japanese Restaurant | ◆◆ | Asian | $8-$30 | 128 |
| ㉓ p. 122 | Jubilee Seafood | ◆◆ | Seafood | $18-$31 | 127 |
| ㉔ p. 122 | Chappy's Deli | ◆◆ | Deli Sandwiches | $5-$8 | 126 |
| ㉕ p. 122 | Sommer's Place | ◆◆ | American | $7-$23 | 127 |
| ㉖ p. 122 | Woo Ga Korean BBQ Restaurant | ◆◆ | Korean | $8-$30 | 128 |

(See map & index p. 122.)

### BAYMONT INN & SUITES (334)277-4442 **4**

▼▼ ▼▼ Motel $49-$69 **Address:** 5837 Monticello Dr 36117 **Location:** I-85 exit 6, just n, then just e. **Facility:** 47 units. 2 stories (no elevator), exterior corridors. **Pool(s):** outdoor. **Activities:** limited exercise equipment. **Guest Services:** coin laundry.

🍴⁺ 🏊 📶 🔲 🖼 💻 / SOME UNITS 🛎 HS

### BEST WESTERN HOPE HULL INN (334)280-0306

▼▼ ▼▼
Hotel
$72-$80

**AAA Benefit:**
Members save up to 20%!

**Address:** 7731 Slade Plaza Blvd 36105 **Location:** I-65 exit 164, just s. **Facility:** 46 units. 2 stories, interior corridors. **Pool(s):** outdoor. **Guest Services:** coin laundry.

SAVE 🏊 BIZ 📶 🔲 🖼 💻 / SOME UNITS 🛎

### CANDLEWOOD SUITES AT EASTCHASE (334)277-0677

▼▼ ▼▼ ▼ **Extended Stay Hotel** $90-$109 **Address:** 9151 Boyd Cooper Pkwy 36117 **Location:** I-85 exit 11, just sw. **Facility:** 101 efficiencies. 3 stories, interior corridors. **Activities:** picnic facilities, exercise room. **Guest Services:** valet and coin laundry.

🍴⁺ CALL 👤M BIZ HS 📶 ✖ 🔲 🖼 💻 / SOME UNITS 🛎

### COMFORT INN & SUITES (334)532-4444

▼▼ ▼▼ Hotel $85-$149 **Address:** 10015 Chantilly Pkwy 36117 **Location:** I-85 exit 11, just e. **Facility:** 71 units. 4 stories, interior corridors. **Amenities:** safes. **Pool(s):** heated indoor. **Activities:** limited exercise equipment. **Guest Services:** valet and coin laundry.

🍴⁺ 🏊 BIZ HS 📶 ✖ 🔲 🖼 💻

### COMFORT SUITES (334)387-2585 **5**

▼▼ ▼▼ ▼ Hotel $80-$150 **Address:** 5918 Monticello Dr 36117 **Location:** I-85 exit 6, just n, then just e. **Facility:** 60 units. 3 stories, interior corridors. **Pool(s):** outdoor. **Activities:** hot tub, exercise room. **Guest Services:** valet and coin laundry.

🍴⁺ 🏊 BIZ HS 📶 ✖ 🔲 🖼 💻

### COMFORT SUITES MONTGOMERY AIRPORT (334)613-9843

▼▼ ▼▼ ▼ Hotel $72 **Address:** 110 Folmar Pkwy 36105 **Location:** I-65 exit 164, just w. **Facility:** 69 units. 3 stories, interior corridors. **Pool(s):** outdoor. **Activities:** exercise room. **Guest Services:** coin laundry.

✈ 🍴⁺ CALL 👤M 🏊 BIZ HS 📶 ✖ 🔲 🖼 💻

### COUNTRY INN & SUITES BY CARLSON 334/277-4142

▼▼ ▼▼ ▼ Hotel. Rates not provided. **Address:** 10095 Chantilly Pkwy 36117 **Location:** I-85 exit 11, just se. **Facility:** 80 units. 4 stories, interior corridors. **Amenities:** safes. **Pool(s):** heated indoor. **Activities:** exercise room. **Guest Services:** valet and coin laundry.

CALL 👤M 🏊 BIZ HS 📶 ✖ 🔲 🖼 💻

### COUNTRY INN & SUITES BY CARLSON EAST (334)270-3223 **9**

▼▼ ▼▼ ▼ Hotel $89-$159 **Address:** 5155 Carmichael Rd 36106 **Location:** I-85 exit 6, just s on Eastern Blvd, then just w. **Facility:** 108 units. 3 stories, interior corridors. **Terms:** cancellation fee imposed. **Pool(s):** heated indoor. **Activities:** hot tub, exercise room. **Guest Services:** valet and coin laundry.

🍴⁺ CALL 👤M 🏊 BIZ 📶 🔲 🖼 💻

### COURTYARD BY MARRIOTT MONTGOMERY (334)272-5533 **12**

▼▼ ▼▼ ▼ Hotel $69-$89 **Address:** 5555 Carmichael Rd 36117 **Location:** I-85 exit 6, just s on Eastern Blvd, then just e. **Facility:** 146 units. 3 stories, interior corridors. **Pool(s):** outdoor. **Activities:** exercise room. **Guest Services:** valet and coin laundry.

**AAA Benefit:**
Members save 5%
or more!

🍴 CALL 👤M 🏊 BIZ HS 📶 ✖ 🔲 💻 / SOME UNITS 🖼

### DRURY INN & SUITES-MONTGOMERY (334)273-1101 **6**

▼▼ ▼▼ ▼ Hotel $110-$184 **Address:** 1124 Eastern Blvd 36117 **Location:** I-85 exit 6, just n. **Facility:** 180 units. 7 stories, interior corridors. **Terms:** cancellation fee imposed. **Pool(s):** heated outdoor, heated indoor. **Activities:** hot tub, exercise room. **Guest Services:** valet and coin laundry.

🍴⁺ CALL 👤M 🏊 BIZ 📶 🔲 🖼 💻 / SOME UNITS 🛏

### EMBASSY SUITES MONTGOMERY-HOTEL & CONFERENCE CENTER (334)269-5055 **3**

▼▼ ▼▼ ▼ Hotel $119-$199 **Address:** 300 Tallapoosa St 36104 **Location:** Between Molton and Commerce sts; downtown. **Facility:** 237 units. 8 stories, interior corridors. **Parking:** on-site (fee) and valet. **Terms:** 1-7 night minimum stay, cancellation fee imposed. **Dining:** 2 restaurants. **Pool(s):** heated indoor. **Activities:** hot tub, exercise room. **Guest Services:** valet and coin laundry, area transportation.

**AAA Benefit:**
Members save 5%
or more!

➕ 🍴 🛗 🍸 CALL 👤M 🏊 BIZ 📶 🎥 🔲 🖼 💻 / SOME UNITS 🛎 SHS

### FAIRFIELD INN & SUITES BY MARRIOTT MONTGOMERY-EASTCHASE PARKWAY (334)260-8650

▼▼ ▼▼ ▼ Hotel $109-$175 **Address:** 8970 EastChase Pkwy 36117 **Location:** I-85 exit 11, just s, then just w. **Facility:** 105 units. 3 stories, interior corridors. **Pool(s):** heated indoor. **Activities:** hot tub, exercise room. **Guest Services:** valet and coin laundry.

**AAA Benefit:**
Members save 5%
or more!

🍴⁺ CALL 👤M 🏊 BIZ HS 📶 ✖ 🔲 🖼 💻

### HAMPTON INN & SUITES DOWNTOWN (334)265-1010 **2**

▼▼ ▼▼ ▼ **Historic Hotel** $99-$159 **Address:** 100 Commerce St 36104 **Location:** Corner of Bibb St. Located in historic district. **Facility:** Originally built as a hotel in the 1920s, this beautiful building was also a former bank. Original architecture and layout delight at every turn, as do the contemporary furnishings and modern conveniences. 86 units. 10 stories, interior corridors. **Parking:** on-site (fee) and valet. **Terms:** 1-7 night minimum stay, cancellation fee imposed. **Activities:** exercise room. **Guest Services:** valet laundry.

**AAA Benefit:**
Members save 5%
or more!

🍴⁺ CALL 👤M BIZ HS 📶 💻 / SOME UNITS 🔲 🖼

### HAMPTON INN & SUITES MONTGOMERY-EASTCHASE (334)277-1818

▼▼ ▼▼ ▼ Hotel $134-$154 **Address:** 7651 EastChase Pkwy 36117 **Location:** I-85 exit 9 (Taylor Rd), just s, then 0.9 mi e; in The Shoppes of EastChase. **Facility:** 102 units. 4 stories, interior corridors. **Terms:** cancellation fee imposed. **Pool(s):** heated outdoor. **Activities:** exercise room. **Guest Services:** valet laundry.

**AAA Benefit:**
Members save 5%
or more!

🍴⁺ 🏊 BIZ HS 📶 🔲 🖼 💻

Get AAA/CAA travel information in the digital and printed formats you prefer

(See map & index p. 122.)

### HILTON GARDEN INN MONTGOMERY EAST
(334)272-2225

▼▼▼▼ **Hotel** $89-$189 **Address:** 1600 Interstate Park Dr 36109 **Location:** I-85 exit 4, just n on Perry Hill, then just e. **Facility:** 97 units. 4 stories, interior corridors. **Terms:** 1-7 night minimum stay, cancellation fee imposed. **Pool(s):** outdoor. **Activities:** hot tub, exercise room. **Guest Services:** valet and coin laundry.

**AAA Benefit:** Members save 5% or more!

🍴 🛎 CALL 🅼 �'🏊 BIZ HS 🛜 🛏 🖥 🖵

### HOLIDAY INN EXPRESS
334/271-5516

▼▼▼ **Hotel.** Rates not provided. **Address:** 9250 Boyd-Cooper Pkwy 36117 **Location:** I-85 exit 11, just w. **Facility:** 106 units. 4 stories, interior corridors. **Pool(s):** outdoor. **Activities:** exercise room. **Guest Services:** valet and coin laundry.

🍴 CALL 🅼 🚌 BIZ HS 🛜 ✕ 🛏 🖥 🖵

### HOLIDAY INN EXPRESS HOTEL & SUITES
(334)288-8844

▼▼▼ **Hotel** $81 **Address:** 4273 Troy Hwy 36116 **Location:** 1 mi s of jct US 80 and 231 (Troy Hwy). **Facility:** 59 units. 3 stories, interior corridors. **Pool(s):** outdoor. **Activities:** limited exercise equipment. **Guest Services:** valet and coin laundry.

🚌 BIZ HS 🛜 ✕ 🛏 🖥 🖵 / SOME UNITS 🐾

### HOLIDAY INN-MONTGOMERY AIRPORT SOUTH
(334)288-3858

▼▼▼ **Hotel** $79-$134 **Address:** 96 Folmar Pkwy 36105 **Location:** I-65 exit 164, just sw. **Facility:** 90 units. 4 stories, interior corridors. **Dining:** Magnolia's, see separate listing. **Pool(s):** heated indoor. **Activities:** limited exercise equipment. **Guest Services:** valet and coin laundry.

🛬 🍴 🛋 🍷 CALL 🅼 🚌 BIZ HS 🛜 🛏 🖵

### HOMEWOOD SUITES BY HILTON
(334)272-3010

▼▼▼ **Extended Stay Hotel** $89-$189 **Address:** 1800 Interstate Park Dr 36109 **Location:** I-85 exit 4, just n on Perry Hill Rd, then just e. **Facility:** 91 efficiencies, some two bedrooms. 4 stories, interior corridors. **Terms:** 1-7 night minimum stay, cancellation fee imposed. **Pool(s):** outdoor. **Activities:** exercise room. **Guest Services:** valet and coin laundry.

**AAA Benefit:** Members save 5% or more!

CALL 🅼 🚌 BIZ HS 🛜 🛏 🖥 🖵 / SOME UNITS 🐾

### LA QUINTA INN & SUITES MONTGOMERY CARMICHAEL ROAD
(334)277-6000

▼▼ ▼ **Hotel** $65-$185 **Address:** 5225 Carmichael Rd 36106 **Location:** I-85 exit 6, just s on Eastern Blvd, then just w. **Facility:** 100 units. 3 stories, interior corridors. **Pool(s):** outdoor. **Guest Services:** valet and coin laundry.

🍴 🚌 🛜 🖵 / SOME UNITS 🐾 🛏 🖥

### LA QUINTA INN MONTGOMERY EASTERN BYPASS
(334)271-1620

▼▼ ▼ **Motel** $59-$149 **Address:** 1280 Eastern Blvd 36117 **Location:** I-85 exit 6, just s. **Facility:** 131 units. 2 stories (no elevator), exterior corridors. **Pool(s):** outdoor.

🍴 🚌 🛜 🖵 / SOME UNITS 🐾 🛏 🖥

### MICROTEL INN & SUITES BY WYNDHAM MONTGOMERY
(334)649-4465

▼▼▼ **Hotel** $60-$80 **Address:** 100 Gibbons Dr 36117 **Location:** I-85 exit 11, just nw. **Facility:** 58 units. 3 stories, interior corridors. **Terms:** check-in 4 pm. **Amenities:** safes. **Guest Services:** coin laundry.

CALL 🅼 BIZ HS 🛜 / SOME UNITS 🐾 🛏 🖥 🖵

### MOTEL 6 MONTGOMERY AIRPORT-HOPE HULL
(334)280-1866

▼▼ ▼ **Motel** $46-$60 **Address:** 7760 Slade Plaza Blvd 36105 **Location:** I-65 exit 164, just s. **Facility:** 63 units. 3 stories, interior corridors. **Terms:** cancellation fee imposed. **Pool(s):** outdoor. **Guest Services:** coin laundry.

CALL 🅼 🚌 HS 🛜 🛏 🖥 / SOME UNITS 🐾

### RENAISSANCE MONTGOMERY HOTEL & SPA AT THE CONVENTION CENTER
(334)481-5000

▼▼▼▼ **Hotel** $119-$219

**R** RENAISSANCE® HOTELS

**AAA Benefit:** Members save 5% or more!

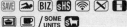

**Address:** 201 Tallapoosa St 36104 **Location:** I-65 exit 172, 0.8 mi ne; corner of Commerce and Bibb sts. Located in historic downtown district. **Facility:** With a beacon of light radiating from its peaked central tower, this property can't be missed. Enjoy the city's skyline while relaxing at the rooftop pool and spa. 342 units. 12 stories, interior corridors. **Parking:** on-site (fee) and valet. **Terms:** check-in 4 pm. **Amenities:** safes. **Dining:** The House, see separate listing, nightclub, entertainment. **Pool(s):** heated outdoor. **Activities:** hot tub, steamroom, exercise room, spa. **Guest Services:** valet and coin laundry.

SAVE 🍴 💆 🍷 CALL 🅼 🚌 BIZ SHS 🛜 ✕ 🛏 🖥 / SOME UNITS 🖨

### RESIDENCE INN BY MARRIOTT MONTGOMERY
(334)270-3300

▼▼▼ **Extended Stay Hotel** $89-$139

**Residence** Inn® **Marriott.**

**AAA Benefit:** Members save 5% or more!

**Address:** 1200 Hilmar Ct 36117 **Location:** I-85 exit 6, just s on Eastern Blvd, then just e. **Facility:** 94 units, some two bedrooms, efficiencies and kitchens. 2 stories (no elevator), exterior corridors. **Pool(s):** outdoor. **Activities:** picnic facilities, exercise room. **Guest Services:** valet and coin laundry.

SAVE 🚌 BIZ SHS 🛜 ✕ 🛏 🖨 🖵 / SOME UNITS 🐾

### SLEEP INN & SUITES
(334)387-1004

▼▼▼ **Hotel** $67-$94 **Address:** 5005 Carmichael Rd 36106 **Location:** I-85 exit 6, just s. **Facility:** 58 units. 3 stories, interior corridors. **Pool(s):** heated indoor. **Activities:** hot tub, exercise room. **Guest Services:** valet and coin laundry.

🍴 🚌 BIZ HS 🛜 🛏 🖥 🖵 / SOME UNITS 🐾

### SPRINGHILL SUITES BY MARRIOTT MONTGOMERY
(334)409-9999

▼▼▼ **Hotel** $89-$99 **Address:** 1201 Towneplace Dr 36106 **Location:** I-85 exit 6, just s, then 0.4 mi w on Carmichael Rd. **Facility:** 79 units. 3 stories, interior corridors. **Pool(s):** heated indoor. **Activities:** hot tub, limited exercise equipment. **Guest Services:** valet and coin laundry.

**AAA Benefit:** Members save 5% or more!

🍴 CALL 🅼 🚌 BIZ 🛜 ✕ 🛏 🖥 🖵

(See map & index p. 122.)

**STAYBRIDGE SUITES-EASTCHASE** (334)277-9383

▼▼▼▼ **Extended Stay Hotel** $119-$149 **Address:** 7800 East-Chase Pkwy 36117 **Location:** I-85 exit 9 (Taylor Rd), just s, then 1 mi e; in The Shoppes of EastChase. **Facility:** 92 efficiencies, some two bedrooms. 4 stories, interior corridors. **Terms:** 3 day cancellation notice-fee imposed. **Pool(s):** heated outdoor. **Activities:** exercise room. **Guest Services:** valet and coin laundry.

[icons]
/ SOME UNITS [icon]

**VALUE PLACE MONTGOMERY** 334/396-3505 ⑩

▼ **Extended Stay Hotel.** Rates not provided. **Address:** 5031 Woods Crossing Dr 36106 **Location:** I-85 exit 6, just s. **Facility:** 105 efficiencies. 4 stories, interior corridors. **Guest Services:** coin laundry. [icons]

**WINGATE INN BY WYNDHAM** (334)244-7880 ⑰

▼▼▼▼ **Hotel** $74-$179 **Address:** 2060 Eastern Blvd 36117 **Location:** I-85 exit 6, 0.7 mi s. Next to Lowe's. **Facility:** 84 units. 3 stories, interior corridors. **Amenities:** safes. **Pool(s):** outdoor. **Activities:** hot tub, exercise room. **Guest Services:** complimentary and valet laundry.

[icons]

---

### WHERE TO EAT

**BAUMHOWERS RESTAURANT** 334/271-1831 ⑯

▼▼▼ American. Family Dining. $6-$22 **AAA Inspector Notes:** Enjoy hearty portions, legendary food and plenty of sports on multiple TVs at this eatery. Friendly staff members make everyone feel right at home. **Features:** full bar, happy hour. **Address:** 2265 Eastern Blvd 36117 **Location:** I-85 exit 6, 1 mi s. [L] [D] CALL [icon]

**CAFE LOUISA** 334/264-4241 ㉑

▼▼ Sandwiches. Quick Serve. $6-$9 **AAA Inspector Notes:** Located on a busy street near Huntingdon College, in an unassuming storefront, this quaint bistro offers wholesome, nutritious selections including a grilled portobello sandwich on fresh baked multi-grain or rye bread, homemade daily soup and quiche of the day. The wide variety of organic coffees will satisfy java cravings or guests can chill with a brewed herbal tea. **Address:** 1034 E Fairview Ave 36106 **Location:** I-65 exit 70, 1.8 mi e towards Huntingdon College; next to Tomatinos Pizza & Bake Shop. **Parking:** street only. [B] [L] [D]

**CHAPPY'S DELI** 334/279-1226 ㉔

▼▼ Deli Sandwiches. Casual Dining. $5-$8 **AAA Inspector Notes:** Since 1989, this New York-style deli has offered burgers, salads and specialty sandwiches. Customers also can create their own sandwiches. Save room for the rich and delicious desserts. **Features:** beer only, patio dining. **Address:** 8141 Vaughn Rd 36116 **Location:** I-85 exit 9 (Taylor Rd), 1.5 mi s, then just e; in Peppertree Shopping Center. [B] [L] [D] CALL [icon] [icon]

**CHARLES ANTHONY'S RESTAURANT AT THE PUB**
334/281-3911

▼▼ Seafood Steak. Casual Dining. $15-$29 **AAA Inspector Notes:** Reminiscent of an old English countryside home, this restaurant serves well-prepared selections of steak, chicken, pork, shrimp and fish. Guests may choose to sit in the charming dining room or on the fully enclosed outdoor patio. **Features:** full bar, patio dining. **Address:** 10044 Chantilly Pkwy 36117 **Location:** I-85 exit 11, just s. [D]

**THE CHOP HOUSE VINTAGE YEAR** 334/264-8463 ⑮

▼▼▼ Steak. Fine Dining. $16-$35 **AAA Inspector Notes:** Warm, contemporary décor provides an ideal setting for a relaxing, elegant dinner. Although known for steaks, the kitchen offers superbly prepared seafood, lamb, veal and chicken. **Features:** full bar. **Address:** 405 Cloverdale Rd 36106 **Location:** I-85 exit 1, 0.5 mi s, then just e. **Parking:** street only. [D]

**COOL BEANS AT THE CAFE D'ART** 334/269-3302 ⑦

▼▼ Sandwiches. Casual Dining. $9-$15 **AAA Inspector Notes:** This eatery is an avant-garde bistro serving healthful, imaginative breakfast and lunches. Sandwiches and entrées are named after such Hollywood elite as Tim Burton, Grace Kelly and John Huston. Fresh bagels from New York and organic and fair-trade gourmet coffees also are offered. Rotating exhibitions of artwork by local artisans are on display and for sale. **Address:** 115 Montgomery St 36104 **Location:** Between Lee and S Court sts; downtown. **Parking:** street only. [B] [L]

**COUNTRY'S BARBECUE** 334/262-6211 ⑩

▼▼ Barbecue. Family Dining. $6-$14 **AAA Inspector Notes:** Pulled pork, beef, barbecue ribs, chicken, Brunswick stew and barbecue coleslaw are some of the tasty treats offered at this eatery. **Features:** beer only. **Address:** 2610 Zelda Rd 36107 **Location:** I-85 exit 3, just e. [L] [D]

**DREAMLAND BAR-B-QUE** 334/273-7427

▼ Barbecue. Casual Dining. $8-$20 **AAA Inspector Notes:** "Ain't nothing like 'em nowhere" is the motto at this barbecue cafe. The menu is small, but that is okay because everybody comes for one thing: the ribs. Barbecue dishes come with white bread and a kicking sauce. Friendly Southern hospitality and a casual backdrop help make this place a favorite. **Features:** beer only. **Address:** 101 Tallapoosa St 36104 **Location:** Between Commerce and Coosa sts; downtown; in The Alley. **Parking:** street only. [L] [D] CALL [icon]

**EASTSIDE GRILLE** 334/274-1200 ①

▼▼ American. Casual Dining. $7-$20 **AAA Inspector Notes:** This eatery offers a variety of good food at a good price including burgers, steak, gourmet pizza, sandwiches, seafood and pasta. Lunch specials are available between 10:30 am and 2 pm and an early bird menu is offered from 3 to 6 pm. Dinner is not served on Sunday. **Features:** full bar, patio dining, early bird specials, Sunday brunch. **Address:** 6667 Atlanta Hwy 36117 **Location:** Jct Atlanta Hwy and McLemore Dr; in Walmart Plaza. [L] [D]

**EL REY BURRITO LOUNGE** 334/832-9688 ⑲

▼▼ Mexican. Casual Dining. $10-$19 **AAA Inspector Notes:** A cool, mellow atmosphere enhances a delicious dining experience. Overstuffed burritos, freshly made guacamole and a delicious array of salsas make this one hot spot. **Features:** full bar. **Address:** 1031 E Fairview Ave 36106 **Location:** I-85 exit 1, 1.1 mi s, then 1 mi e; between Boultier St and Cloverdale Rd. **Parking:** street only. [D]

**FILET & VINE** 334/262-8463 ⑭

▼ Deli Sandwiches. Quick Serve. $9-$13 **AAA Inspector Notes:** Sharing space with a gourmet market and bottle shoppe, this deli-style café offers a rotating daily menu of hot entrées, sandwiches, soups and salad bar...all for dining in or take out. More than a 150 brands of beer/ale and 1,250 types of wine are for sale. Wine tasting is offered every Thursday from 5-6:30 pm. Breakfast is available on Saturday only. **Features:** beer & wine, patio dining. **Address:** 431 Cloverdale Rd 36106 **Location:** I-85 exit 1, 0.5 mi s, then just e. **Parking:** street only. [L] [D] CALL [icon]

**GARRETT'S** 334/396-9950

▼▼▼ American. Fine Dining. $17-$35 **AAA Inspector Notes:** Treat yourself to a finely prepared meal at this upscale, contemporary restaurant. Succulent meats and seafood are complemented by savory sauces. Dessert lovers should try the chocolate soufflé, which is superb. Nightly early dining specials can be enjoyed from 5-6:30 pm, or make it an elegant affair while listening to live piano, offered Friday and Saturday, 6-9 pm. **Features:** full bar, early bird specials, happy hour. **Address:** 7780 Atlanta Hwy 36117 **Location:** Jct SR 27; 0.7 mi e on US 80 and SR 8. [L] [D] CALL [icon]

**THE HOUSE** 334/481-5166 ⑤

▼▼▼
American
Fine Dining
$9-$38

**AAA Inspector Notes:** This downtown spot welcomes guests to a fine-dining experience in a sophisticated atmosphere. Specialty items include well-prepared duck, Kobe beef, foie gras, venison, quail, fish and other seafood dishes. **Features:** full bar. **Reservations:** suggested. **Address:** 201 Tallapoosa St 36104 **Location:** I-65 exit 172, 0.8 mi ne; corner of Commerce St; in historic downtown; in Renaissance Montgomery Hotel & Spa at the Convention Center. **Parking:** on-site and valet.
[B] [L] [D] CALL [icon]

**(See map & index p. 122.)**

**IXTAPA BAR & GRILL**     334/277-7600

▼▼ Mexican. Casual Dining. $6-$14 **AAA Inspector Notes:** Since 1986, this family-owned and -operated cantina has served traditional recipes to the community. **Features:** full bar. **Address:** 7157 EastChase Pkwy 36117 **Location:** I-85 exit 9 (Taylor Rd), just s, then 0.6 mi e; in The Shoppes of EastChase. [L] [D] CALL [&M]

**JUBILEE SEAFOOD**     334/262-6224  (23)

▼▼ Seafood. Casual Dining. $18-$31 **AAA Inspector Notes:** Enjoy what many rave is the best and freshest seafood this side of the Gulf. You can begin with a succulent West Indies salad, then sample any number of daily fish specials and finally delve into a mouth-watering slice of Key lime pie. **Features:** full bar. **Address:** 1057 Woodley Rd 36106 **Location:** Jct Woodley Rd and Fairview Ave; in Historic Old Cloverdale. [D]

**LA JOLLA**     334/356-2600  (9)

▼▼▼ American. Fine Dining. $9-$33 **AAA Inspector Notes:** Smart and hip, this restaurant is located in the middle of the best shops Montgomery has to offer. The food is distinctive and attractively presented. The modern and upscale décor reinforces the sophisticated, adult (over age 18) atmosphere. **Features:** full bar, happy hour. **Address:** 6854 EastChase Pkwy 36117 **Location:** I-85 exit 9 (Taylor Rd), just s; in The Shoppes of EastChase. **Parking:** street only. [L] [D] CALL [&M] [✎]

**LEK'S RAILROAD THAI**     334/269-0708  (4)

▼▼▼ Thai. Casual Dining. $8-$18 **AAA Inspector Notes:** History, character and ethnic charm create a delightful dining experience in a unique atmosphere. Located inside the restored downtown Union Train Station, the kitchen presents savory Thai cuisine as well as such Asian dishes as sushi, plus vegetarian and American choices. Be sure to try the original mango sticky rice for dessert. **Features:** full bar, patio dining. **Address:** 300-B Water St 36104 **Location:** Between Molton and Commerce sts; in historic downtown; in Union Train Station. **Parking:** street only. [L] [D] CALL [&M]

**LEK'S TASTE OF THAILAND**     334/244-8994  (3)

▼▼ Thai. Casual Dining. $7-$20 **AAA Inspector Notes:** Just as its name indicates, this ethnic restaurant truly offers the savory delights of Thai cuisine. The restaurant offers friendly service and a huge menu of dishes served in large portions. Even though meals leave bellies full, it is a good idea to leave a little room for homemade green tea or seasonal mangoes. **Features:** full bar. **Address:** 5421 Atlanta Hwy 36109 **Location:** I-85 exit 6, 1.4 mi n; in Montgomery East Plaza. [L] [D]

**LOS VAQUEROS MEXICAN RESTAURANT**
    334/277-8339  (13)

▼▼ Mexican. Casual Dining. $5-$15 **AAA Inspector Notes:** Ride on down (no horses, please) to Los Vaqueros (in English, the Cowboys) for freshly-prepared Mexican fare. Select from the "Ten Most Wanted Burritos" as well as typical south-of-the-border dishes, including quesadillas, fajitas and tacos, to name a few. Vegetarian and combo platters are available. Lunch specials are offered 11 am-3 pm from the express menu. **Features:** full bar, early bird specials, happy hour. **Address:** 2195 Eastern Blvd 36117 **Location:** I-85 exit 6, 1 mi s. [L] [D]

**MAGNOLIA'S**     334/288-3858

▼▼ American. Casual Dining. $8-$25 **AAA Inspector Notes:** Although the menu is limited at this conveniently located, in-hotel restaurant, it covers a good variety of standard options, including burgers, wings, steaks, chicken, fish, pasta and sandwiches. **Features:** full bar, happy hour. **Address:** 96 Folmar Pkwy 36105 **Location:** I-65 exit 164, just sw; in Holiday Inn-Montgomery Airport South. [B] [D] CALL [&M]

**MICHAEL'S TABLE**     334/272-2500  (11)

▼▼▼ International. Casual Dining. $10-$30 **AAA Inspector Notes:** Chef Michael Hochhalter's upscale, intimate bistro offers a creative and eclectic menu, which is revised monthly. Although menu selections are unpredictable, a delicious, satisfying meal is assured. Only dinner is served on Saturday, and on Sunday, only brunch. **Features:** full bar, patio dining, Sunday brunch. **Reservations:** suggested. **Address:** 2960 Zelda Rd, Suite A 36106 **Location:** I-85 exit 3, 0.8 mi se. [L] [D] [🐾]

**NO WAY JOSE GRILL AND CANTINA**     334/819-7363

▼▼ Mexican. Casual Dining. $5-$11 **AAA Inspector Notes:** Along with standard south-of-the-border fare, the menu at this cantina offers Caribbean-inspired entrées such as Dominican chicken and pescado Caribbean style to name a few. Outdoor patio dining is available in warm weather. **Features:** full bar. **Address:** 8844 Minnie Brown Rd 36117 **Location:** I-85 exit 11, just s, then just w on EastChase Pkwy; in Chantilly Corners Plaza. [L] [D] CALL [&M]

**SAIGON BISTRO**     334/279-5921  (8)

▼▼ Vietnamese. Casual Dining. $6-$9 **AAA Inspector Notes:** A good selection of traditional dishes is offered in this simple, yet comfortable, setting. **Address:** 1060 East Blvd 36117 **Location:** I-85 exit 6, just n. [L] [D] CALL [&M]

**SA ZA SERIOUS ITALIAN FOOD**     334/495-7292  (6)

▼▼▼ Italian. Casual Dining. $9-$26 **AAA Inspector Notes:** Creator and chef Joe DiMaggio, Jr. (a distant cousin of the baseball great) achieves his vision of offering extreme peasant cuisine at this innovative café with a casual and relaxed setting. Even though he studied with many master chefs around the world, including Italy, France, Japan, Austria, Belgium, Canada and New York, Joe goes back to his roots by utilizing his grandmother's recipes in most of the menu selections. **Features:** full bar. **Address:** 130 Commerce St 36104 **Location:** Between Tallapoosa and Bibb sts; downtown; in Alley Station. **Parking:** street only. [L] [D] CALL [&M]

**SINCLAIR'S CLOVERDALE**     334/834-7462  (18)

▼▼ American. Casual Dining. $8-$26 **AAA Inspector Notes:** Patrons can enjoy great food while waxing nostalgic about the past. Pictures of Hollywood legends, such as Clark Gable, James Dean, Marilyn Monroe and Greta Garbo, line the walls of the retro-style eatery. **Features:** full bar, patio dining, Sunday brunch. **Address:** 1051 E Fairview Ave 36106 **Location:** I-65 exit 170, 1.7 mi e; corner of Boultier Ave. **Parking:** on-site and street. [L] [D] [🐾]

**SINCLAIR'S EASTSIDE**     334/271-7654  (17)

▼▼ American. Casual Dining. $7-$25 **AAA Inspector Notes:** Artistic renditions of such classic Hollywood stars as Clark Gable, James Dean, Marilyn Monroe and Greta Garbo line the walls of this local favorite. Menu offerings range from pasta and seafood to burgers and entrée-size salads. **Features:** full bar, Sunday brunch, happy hour. **Address:** 7847 Vaughn Rd 36116 **Location:** I-85 exit 9 (Taylor Rd), 1.7 mi s, then just w; in Halcyon Village Plaza. [L] [D] [✎]

**SOMMER'S PLACE**     334/279-5401  (25)

▼▼ American. Casual Dining. $7-$23 **AAA Inspector Notes:** This family-operated establishment has been in business for decades. Serving the community for generations, its walls are filled with caricatures of local patrons dating back to the 1990s. Only lunch is served on Sunday. **Features:** full bar. **Address:** 7972 Vaughn Rd 36116 **Location:** I-85 exit 9, 1.5 mi s on US 80/231, then just e on CR 626. [L] [D] CALL [&M]

**SUSHI YAMA**     334/612-7800  (12)

▼▼ Japanese Sushi. Casual Dining. $8-$27 **AAA Inspector Notes:** The menu at this casual spot offers a wide selection of sushi as well as hibachi, steak and seafood platters. All-inclusive special lunch combos are available at economical prices. **Features:** full bar. **Address:** 2070 Eastern Blvd 36117 **Location:** I-85 exit 6, just s. [L] [D] CALL [&M]

**TASTE OF INDIA**     334/356-4533

▼▼ Indian. Casual Dining. $10-$18 **AAA Inspector Notes:** A wide variety of authentic ethnic dishes is available on the menu. At lunchtime, a buffet is an option. **Features:** beer & wine, happy hour. **Address:** 8868 Minnie Brown Rd 36117 **Location:** I-85 exit 11, just s, then just w; in Chantilly Plaza. [L] [D] CALL [&M]

**(See map & index p. 122.)**

TOMATINOS PIZZA & BAKE SHOP     334/264-4241   20
▼▼ ▼▼ Pizza. Casual Dining. $8-$26 **AAA Inspector Notes:** Popular with locals and nearby college students alike, dine here and enjoy a pizza or stuffed calzones made with organic dough, then add traditional or gourmet toppings, including fresh Alabama produce. Daily wine specials and a variety of imported beers also is available. **Features:** beer & wine. **Address:** 1036 E Fairview Ave 36106 **Location:** I-65 exit 170, 1.8 mi e; just w of Huntingdon College. **Parking:** street only.   L   D

WILLOW TREE KOREAN/JAPANESE RESTAURANT
    334/271-9600   22
▼▼ ▼▼ Asian. Casual Dining. $8-$30 **AAA Inspector Notes:** This is a stylish, contemporary designed place with an Asian flair. Dine in the open dining area, at the sushi bar or in semi-private cubicles for an intimate meal. Choose from a nice blend of Japanese, Chinese and Korean menu options. **Address:** 2690 Eastern Blvd 36117 **Location:** I-85 exit 6, 1.4 mi s on US 80/SR 21.
L   D   CALL  M

WISHBONE CAFE     334/244-7270   2
▼▼ ▼▼ Cajun. Casual Dining. $7-$18 **AAA Inspector Notes:** What this former sandwich shop, which the owner has designated as a no fry zone, lacks in space it makes up for in New Orleans-style flavor. Along with multiple spicy entrées (some created with a Jamaican influence), the homemade soups are wholesome and satisfying. Although the recipe for their signature sweet tea is secret, a hint of pineapple could be detected. With limited seating capacity, a worthwhile wait may be necessary for service. **Address:** 7028 Atlanta Hwy 36117 **Location:** I-85 exit 11, 2.3 mi n; in Taylor Junction Shopping Center.   L   D

WOO GA KOREAN BBQ RESTAURANT     334/649-4815   26
▼▼ ▼▼ Korean. Casual Dining. $8-$30 **AAA Inspector Notes:** This relaxed café serves authentic native fare. Unfamiliar with the cuisine? The staff is helpful in explaining the various dishes and willing to make recommendations for first-timers. **Features:** full bar. **Address:** 2911 Eastern Blvd 36116 **Location:** I-85 exit 6, 1.8 mi s on US 80/SR 21.   L   D   CALL  M

MARTIN'S RESTAURANT     334/265-1767
fyi Not evaluated. Family owned and operated since the 1930s, this very basic no-frills family-style restaurant has been an area staple with its Southern comfort food. Their specialties include fried chicken, catfish, meatloaf, chopped steak and fried chicken livers, to name but just a few. Sides include pickled beets, collard greens, fried okra, sweet potato casserole and homemade cornbread. Save room for dessert. The portions are large, so bring your appetite. **Address:** 1796 Carter Hill Rd 36106

## MOUNDVILLE (D-2) pop. 2,427, elev. 164'

One of the country's best preserved prehistoric mound groups lies on the south bank of the Black Warrior River in Moundville. The agrarian Native American culture, which built the mounds, developed from A.D. 1000 to 1500 into what is considered one of the most advanced prehistoric civilizations north of Mexico.

Possessing considerable artistic skill, the people advanced pottery making, copper working and stone carving to high levels of refinement. Moundville served as the civic and cultural center for many small villages up and down the river.

SAVE **MOUNDVILLE ARCHAEOLOGICAL PARK,** 634 Mound State Pkwy., preserves the ceremonial center of Moundville Indian culture. Remnants of this 300-acre city, dating from A.D. 1100, consist of 28 mounds once used as platforms for lodges and temples. Steps lead to the summit of the largest, which stands 60 feet high. The Jones Archaeological Museum's impressive artifact collection as well as multimedia, special effects and re-created scenes are used to illustrate ancient Moundville culture. Models of aboriginal dwellings and earthworks also are presented.

**Time:** Allow 1 hour minimum. **Hours:** Park daily 9-dusk. Museum daily 9-5. Closed Jan. 1, Easter, Thanksgiving, Christmas Eve, Christmas and Dec. 31. **Cost:** $8; $7 (senior citizens); $6 (students with ID). **Phone:** (205) 371-2234. 🏕 🚻

## MOUNTAIN BROOK pop. 20,413

- **Hotels & Restaurants map & index p. 54**
- **Part of Birmingham area — see map p. 43**

HAMPTON INN-MOUNTAIN BROOK     (205)870-7822   37
▼▼ ▼▼ Hotel $99-$159 **Address:** 2731 US Hwy 280 35223 **Location:** Jct US 31, just e. **Facility:** 129 units. 5 stories, interior corridors. **Terms:** 7 night minimum stay, cancellation fee imposed.

| **AAA Benefit:** Members save 5% or more! |

**Pool(s):** outdoor. **Activities:** limited exercise equipment. **Guest Services:** valet laundry.
🍴 🛎 BIZ 📶 ✕ 🖥 /SOME UNITS 🛗 🧳

**WHERE TO EAT**

ANOTHER BROKEN EGG CAFE     205/871-7849
▼▼ ▼▼ Breakfast Sandwiches. Casual Dining. $5-$16 **AAA Inspector Notes:** Enjoy a breakfast experience you will not soon forget; huge cinnamon buns, Popeye's omelet and fruit and nut pancakes or french toast are some of the menu specialties. **Features:** Sunday brunch. **Address:** 2418 Montevallo Rd 35223 **Location:** I-459 exit 19, 4.1 mi w on US 280, then just e on Hollywood Blvd.   B   L

AVO     205/871-8212   49
▼▼▼ ▼▼ Northern American. Fine Dining. $9-$38 **AAA Inspector Notes:** The clean, crisp environment embellishes this social gathering area along with an eclectic menu featuring fresh and organic ingredients. This is a popular rendezvous spot with the young professional crowd. **Features:** full bar, patio dining, Sunday brunch. **Address:** 2721 Cahaba Rd 35223 **Location:** Jct Montevallo Rd; downtown circle. **Parking:** street only.   D   CALL  M   ✎

CHEZ LULU & CONTINENTAL BAKERY     205/870-7011   48
▼▼ ▼▼ French. Casual Dining. $10-$35 **AAA Inspector Notes:** In the quaint and charming area of shops known as Olde English Village, the bistro-style restaurant presents a French-themed menu that lists tartes, salads, sandwiches and soups. Imported cheeses and homemade spreads go into such interesting choices as pan bagna, goat cheese with fresh pear, organic lettuce and roasted walnuts on sourdough and French brie with roasted red pepper, organic lettuces and kalamata olives on focaccia. The bakery turns out homemade European-style breads and pastries. **Features:** full bar. **Address:** 1909 Cahaba Rd 35223 **Location:** Jct 20th Ave S. **Parking:** street only.   L   D

---

## Upgrade to Plus or Premier membership
### for *more* of the benefits you need most

(See map & index p. 54.)

DANIEL GEORGE RESTAURANT & BAR   205/871-3266   (50)
▼▼▼ American. Fine Dining. $10-$36 **AAA Inspector Notes:** Diners sit down to creative American cuisine in a casually elegant setting. Representative of seafood, wild and domestic game, meats and poultry prepared with flair are such entrees as bourbon-molasses pork tenderloin and pan-seared black tuna. The wine list is extensive. They are closed for lunch on Monday. **Features:** full bar, patio dining. **Reservations:** suggested. **Address:** 2837 Culver Rd 35223 **Location:** US 280 exit Hollywood Blvd, just ne on Montevallo Rd, just s on Cahaba Rd, then just nw. **Parking:** street only. [L] [D]

LA PAZ RESTAURANT   205/879-2225   (46)
▼▼ Mexican. Casual Dining. $7-$17 **AAA Inspector Notes:** Traditional Mexican and Southwestern dishes--including seafood choices, stuffed peppers, great margaritas and fresh salsa made on the premises daily--are served in a casual and lively dining area decorated with Mexican handicrafts. **Features:** full bar, patio dining, happy hour. **Address:** 99 Euclid Ave 35213 **Location:** Just w of Church St. **Parking:** street only. [L] [D] [🖐]

OLEXA'S   205/871-2060   (51)
▼▼ American. Casual Dining. $8-$14 **AAA Inspector Notes:** Enjoy a taste of heaven when you order the wedding cake by the slice at this wonderfully cute lunch spot. Delicious salads and light sandwiches round out the menu. The grilled cheese is the perfect combination of gooey cheeses and crunchy bread, and best when dipped in the rich tomato soup. **Features:** beer & wine. **Address:** 2838 Culver Rd 35223 **Location:** US 280 exit Mountain Brook, 0.4 mi e, then just s; in Mountain Brook Village. **Parking:** street only. [L]

SURIN OF THAILAND   205/871-4531   (47)
▼▼ Thai Sushi. Casual Dining. $7-$22 **AAA Inspector Notes:** The menu at this casual spot is a bit on the eclectic side, offering such popular Thai dishes as stir-fries and Thai noodles with chicken and shrimp, as well as sushi. Menu highlights include roasted duck marinated in a red curry sauce served with tomatoes, pineapple and kaffir leaf, or pork tenderloin in a spicy onion, garlic and pepper sauce. **Features:** full bar. **Address:** 64 Church St 35213 **Location:** Downtown. **Parking:** street only. [L] [D] CALL [🖐M]

## MUSCLE SHOALS AREA (A-2)

The region known as Muscle Shoals in northwestern Alabama includes the Quad-Cities of Muscle Shoals *(see place listing)*, Florence *(see place listing p. 78)*, Sheffield *(see place listing p. 142)* and Tuscumbia *(see place listing p. 149)*; two dams on the Tennessee River; and more than 1,200 miles of scenic lakeshore.

A 650-mile navigation channel and the hydroelectric-generating facilities created by a system of Tennessee Valley Authority (TVA) dams ensure economic potential for the Muscle Shoals area and the Tennessee River Valley. Industries include the International Fertilizer Development Center featuring a free lobby display. Across Wheeler Dam in Rogersville is Joe Wheeler State Park *(see Recreation Areas Chart)*.

In 1965 a local disc jockey set up a recording studio in the small community of Muscle Shoals. When local singer Percy Sledge recorded "When a Man Loves a Woman," which sold more than a million copies, the soulful Muscle Shoals sound began. Other artists followed, including Aretha Franklin, Peggy Lee, Liza Minnelli, Bob Seger and the Rolling Stones.

## MUSCLE SHOALS (A-2) pop. 13,146

Muscle Shoals and three other cities make up the Muscle Shoals Area *(see place listing)*.

## NATURAL BRIDGE (C-2) pop. 37, elev. 761'

**NATURAL BRIDGE** is on US 278, 1 mi. w. of jct. SRs 5 and 13, in a scenic area. Formed some 200 million years ago, the rock arch is 148 feet long and towers 60 feet above winding pathways. The natural gardens are adorned with mountain laurel, snowball bushes and giant magnolias. **Time:** Allow 30 minutes minimum. **Hours:** Daily 8 a.m.-dusk. **Cost:** $2.50; $1.50 (ages 6-12). **Phone:** (205) 486-5330.

# NORTHPORT pop. 23,330

## BEST WESTERN CATALINA INN (205)339-5200

Motel
$80-$300

**AAA Benefit:**
Members save up to 20%!

**Address:** 2015 McFarland Blvd 35476 **Location:** On US 82, just nw of jct US 43/SR 69. **Facility:** 36 units. 1 story, exterior corridors. **Terms:** 2 night minimum stay - seasonal. **Pool(s):** outdoor.

## WHERE TO EAT

**CITY CAFE** 205/758-9171

Southern. Casual Dining. $4-$10 **AAA Inspector Notes:** Guests can retreat to the good old days at the cafe, where customers are treated like family but the dishes are better than mom's. **Address:** 408 Main Ave 35476 **Location:** SR 69 N, just w to Robert Cardinal Airport Rd, just s; in historic downtown. **Parking:** street only. B L

# ONEONTA pop. 6,567
• Part of Birmingham area — see map p. 43

**CAFE ON MAIN** 205/274-4050

Comfort Food. Cafeteria. $7-$9 **AAA Inspector Notes:** Coming home for lunch in Mom's kitchen replicates the ambience of this quaint café. A daily limited, rotating menu of Southern home-cooked meals is offered cafeteria-style. On Thursday a Southern Thanksgiving-style meal provides mid-day comfort. **Address:** 110 2nd Ave W 35121 **Location:** Jct US 231 and SR 75, just s; corner of A St N. L

**CHINA WOK BUFFET** 205/625-6668

Chinese. Casual Dining. $6-$10 **AAA Inspector Notes:** This cozy restaurant prepares typical Chinese selections, and its buffet lunch specials are a steal. **Address:** 410 2nd Ave E 35121 **Location:** Just s of jct US 231. L D

# OPELIKA (E-6) pop. 26,477, elev. 822'

Opelika was established in the mid-1800s and has a mixture of fine Greek Revival and Victorian houses. From late March through early April the Azalea/Dogwood Trail, a self-guiding driving tour, leads visitors past many of these houses during the peak blooming season of these perennials. A different kind of driving tour can be taken on the 54 holes of the Grand National, a course on the Robert Trent Jones Golf Trail. Handmade figures adorn the porches and lawns of dozens of houses in the North Opelika Historic Neighborhood during the Victorian Front Porch Tour Christmas event in early December.

**Shopping areas:** Downtown Opelika offers shops, galleries and antique stores. USA Town Center at 1220 Fox Run Pkwy. offers major-brand bargains in more than 20 establishments.

**MUSEUM OF EAST ALABAMA** is downtown at 121 S. 9th St. The museum contains more than 10,000 pieces from the 19th- and 20th centuries. Exhibits focus on east Alabama, Opelika and state history as well as sound recording technology, agriculture and firefighting. Also on display are musical instruments, World War II POW camp artifacts and household items. **Time:** Allow 1 hour minimum. **Hours:** Tues.-Fri. 10-4, Sat. 2-4. Closed major holidays. **Cost:** Donations. **Phone:** (334) 749-2751.

## BEST WESTERN AUBURN/OPELIKA INN (334)745-6293

Hotel
$70-$275

**AAA Benefit:**
Members save up to 20%!

**Address:** 205 N 21st St 36801 **Location:** I-85 exit 58, 1.5 mi w. **Facility:** 56 units. 2 stories (no elevator), interior corridors. **Terms:** 2 night minimum stay - seasonal. **Pool(s):** outdoor. **Activities:** picnic facilities, exercise room. **Guest Services:** coin laundry.

## COMFORT INN (334)741-9977

[fyi] Hotel $75-$226 Under major renovation, scheduled to be completed August 2014. **Last Rated:** Address: 811 Fox Run Pkwy 36801 **Location:** I-85 exit 62, just w. **Facility:** 59 units. 3 stories, interior corridors. **Pool(s):** outdoor. **Activities:** exercise room. **Guest Services:** valet laundry.

## FAIRFIELD INN & SUITES BY MARRIOTT AUBURN OPELIKA (334)742-2590

Hotel $89-$199 **Address:** 2257 Interstate Dr 36801 **Location:** I-85 exit 58, just w to Interstate Dr, then just s; in Tiger Town. **Facility:** 74 units. 3 stories, interior corridors. **Pool(s):** heated indoor. **Activities:** hot tub, exercise room. **Guest Services:** valet and coin laundry.

**AAA Benefit:**
Members save 5% or more!

## HAMPTON INN & SUITES (334)745-4311

Hotel $109-$299 **Address:** 3000 Capps Way 36804 **Location:** I-85 exit 58, just e, then just s. **Facility:** 83 units. 3 stories, interior corridors. **Terms:** 1-7 night minimum stay, cancellation fee imposed. **Pool(s):** outdoor. **Activities:** exercise room. **Guest Services:** valet laundry.

**AAA Benefit:**
Members save 5% or more!

## MARRIOTT AUBURN OPELIKA HOTEL & CONFERENCE CENTER AT GRAND NATIONAL (334)741-9292

Hotel $159-$230 **Address:** 3700 Robert Trent Jones Tr 36801 **Location:** I-85 exit 58, 4.1 mi n on US 280, then 2.5 mi e on CR 97 (Grand National Pkwy). **Facility:** 129 units, some efficiencies. 4 stories, interior/exterior corridors. **Parking:** on-site and valet. **Terms:** check-in 4 pm. **Amenities:** video games. **Dining:** 3 restaurants. **Pool(s):** outdoor, heated indoor. **Activities:** sauna, hot tub, regulation golf, tennis, bicycles, picnic facilities, trails, exercise room. **Guest Services:** valet laundry, area transportation.

**AAA Benefit:**
Members save 5% or more!

## MICROTEL INN & SUITES BY WYNDHAM OPELIKA
(334)745-0415

Hotel
$59-$199

**Address:** 1651 Parker Way 36801 **Location:** I-85 exit 58, just ne. **Facility:** 77 units. 4 stories, interior corridors. **Pool(s):** outdoor. **Activities:** exercise room. **Guest Services:** valet and coin laundry. **Featured Amenity:** continental breakfast.

[SAVE] CALL [&M] [≈] [HS] [≈] [X]
[▤] [▤] [▤]

### WHERE TO EAT

### CAFE ONE-TWENTY-THREE
334/737-0069

American. Fine Dining. $14-$31 **AAA Inspector Notes:** Expect fine dining without the formality at this eatery offering both Southern and continental food. The menu changes frequently. Warm, knowledgeable and relaxed servers work the very handsome dining room. Crab-stuffed avocado and brown sugar-rubbed rib-eye are two examples of the excellent cuisine. **Features:** full bar. **Reservations:** suggested, weekends. **Address:** 123 S 8th St 36801 **Location:** Historic downtown. **Parking:** street only. [D]

### CHUCK'S BAR-B-QUE
334/749-4043

Barbecue. Family Dining. $3-$18 **AAA Inspector Notes:** This casual eatery near Auburn University offers delicious barbecue chicken, pork and ribs. In a hurry? Try the daily, weekend or game-day specials. Friendly, straightforward service ensures that you're in and out without delay. A breakfast menu offers mostly biscuit sandwiches. **Address:** 905 Short Ave 36801 **Location:** I-85 exit 60, 0.8 mi n. [B] [L] [D] CALL [&M]

### COCK OF THE WALK
334/705-0004

Seafood. Casual Dining. $10-$20 **AAA Inspector Notes:** Fried catfish is the house specialty at this distinctive eatery, which is built around a river keelboat theme and set in the midst of a pleasant wooded site. The menu features such dishes as oysters, shrimp, chicken, crab claws and fried dill pickles. **Features:** beer & wine. **Address:** 1702 Frederick Rd 36801 **Location:** I-85 exit 58, just w to Frederick Rd, then 0.3 mi n. [D]

### DURANGO MEXICAN RESTAURANT
334/742-0149

Mexican. Casual Dining. $6-$13 **AAA Inspector Notes:** Great drink specials pair with plates of Mexican favorites at this lively restaurant. **Features:** full bar. **Address:** 1107 Columbus Pkwy 36801 **Location:** I-85 exit 62, just e. [L] [D]

### JIMMY'S
334/745-2155

Creole. Fine Dining. $7-$24 **AAA Inspector Notes:** Enter into this intimate dining room where the ambience of muted lights, soft music, wrought iron and subtle Mardi Gras decorative adornments creates the setting for a relaxed feast. New Orleans-style cuisine is the mainstay of the weekly changing menu. **Features:** full bar. **Address:** 104 S 8th St 36801 **Location:** Corner of S Railroad Ave; downtown. **Parking:** street only. [L] [D] CALL [&M]

### MA FIA'S RISTORANTE & PIZZERIA
334/745-6266

Italian. Casual Dining. $9-$28 **AAA Inspector Notes:** In the center of an alcove of eclectic boutiques and cafés, this quaint, intimate bistro offers stucco walls, distressed wood wainscot, shutters and window panes tastefully arranged to give an Old World ambience. Portion size choices are a welcome option of menu selections which include a variety of traditional pasta dishes, salads, antipasti, specialty pizza and meat, seafood and vegetarian entrées. **Features:** full bar, patio dining. **Address:** 811 S Railroad Ave 36801 **Location:** Between 8th and 9th sts; downtown. **Parking:** street only.

[L] [D] CALL [&M]

### SARA JAY'S
334/749-7272

Southern. Family Dining. $3-$11 **AAA Inspector Notes:** The simple café serving such Southern favorites as fried chicken and catfish, turnip greens, mashed potatoes and cornbread. Expect very congenial service. **Address:** 1801 2nd Ave 36801 **Location:** Jct Five Points. [B] [L]

### WOK 'N ROLL RESTAURANT AND BAR
334/745-3338

Asian. Casual Dining. $5-$15 **AAA Inspector Notes:** Chinese, Japanese (including hibachi), Thai and wings are all found on one delicious menu at this eatery. Enjoy handsome Asian decor, a creative bar menu, and gracious service. **Features:** full bar, patio dining. **Address:** 1703 Columbus Pkwy 36802 **Location:** I-85 exit 62, 0.4 mi e. [L] [D]

## OPP pop. 6,659

### BEST WESTERN PLUS OPP INN
(334)493-9000

Hotel
$80-$160

**AAA Benefit:**
Members save up to 20%!

**Address:** 7084 Veterans Memorial Pkwy 36467 **Location:** 0.5 mi e of jct US 84 and 331. **Facility:** 43 units. 2 stories, interior corridors. **Pool(s):** outdoor. **Activities:** exercise room. **Guest Services:** valet and coin laundry.

[SAVE] CALL [&M] [≈] [BIZ] [HS] [≈]
[X] [▤] [▤] [▤]

### EXECUTIVE INN
334/493-6399

Motel. Rates not provided. **Address:** 812 Florala Hwy/US 331 S Business 36467 **Location:** On US Business Rt 331, 1.9 mi n of jct US 84, through town center. **Facility:** 42 units. 2 stories (no elevator), exterior corridors. **Pool(s):** outdoor.

[▥] [≈] [▤] [▤] [▤]

## ORANGE BEACH pop. 5,441
• Restaurants p. 132

### HAMPTON INN & SUITES ORANGE BEACH
(251)923-4400

Hotel $99-$449 **Address:** 25518 Perdido Beach Blvd 36561 **Location:** Oceanfront. On SR 182, just sw of jct SR 161. **Facility:** 160 units. 9 stories, interior corridors. **Terms:** check-in 4 pm, 1-7 night minimum stay, cancellation fee imposed. **Pool(s):** heated outdoor, heated indoor. **Activities:** hot tub, exercise room. **Guest Services:** valet and coin laundry.

**AAA Benefit:**
Members save 5% or more!

[▥+] [Y] CALL [&M] [≈] [BIZ] [HS] [≈] [X] [▤]
[/SOME UNITS] [▤] [▤]

### HILTON GARDEN INN ORANGE BEACH BEACHFRONT
(251)974-1600

Hotel $89-$399 **Address:** 23092 Perdido Beach Blvd 36561 **Location:** Oceanfront. On SR 182, 2.7 mi w of jct SR 161. **Facility:** 137 units. 6 stories, interior corridors. **Terms:** check-in 4 pm, 1-7 night minimum stay, cancellation fee imposed. **Pool(s):** heated indoor. **Activities:** hot tub, exercise room. **Guest Services:** valet and coin laundry.

**AAA Benefit:**
Members save 5% or more!

[▥+] CALL [&M] [≈] [BIZ] [HS] [≈] [X] [▤] [▤] [▤]

### THE ISLAND HOUSE HOTEL
(251)981-6100

Hotel $119-$399 **Address:** 26650 Perdido Beach Blvd 36561 **Location:** Oceanfront. On SR 182, 1.1 mi e of jct SR 161. **Facility:** 161 units. 10 stories, interior corridors. **Terms:** 2 night minimum stay - seasonal and/or weekends, 3 day cancellation notice-fee imposed. **Amenities:** safes. **Pool(s):** heated outdoor. **Activities:** exercise room. **Guest Services:** coin laundry.

[▥] [▥] [Y] [≈] [≈] [X] [▤] [/SOME UNITS] [▤] [▤]

**PERDIDO BEACH RESORT**                     (251)981-9811

▼▼▼▼ **Resort Hotel** $129-$299 **Address:** 27200 Perdido Beach Blvd 36561 **Location:** Oceanfront. On SR 182, 1.5 mi e of jct SR 161. **Facility:** The beach is steps away and a view of the water comes with every room at this resort which fronts the Gulf of Mexico. 346 units. 8 stories, interior corridors. **Parking:** on-site and valet. **Terms:** check-in 4 pm, 5 day cancellation notice-fee imposed. **Amenities:** safes. **Dining:** 3 restaurants, also, Voyagers Restaurant, see separate listing, entertainment. **Pool(s):** heated outdoor, heated indoor. **Activities:** hot tub, fishing, tennis, game room. **Guest Services:** valet laundry.

[icons]

**PHOENIX ON THE BAY I**                      251/980-5700

▼▼▼▼ **Vacation Rental Condominium.** Rates not provided. **Address:** 27580 Canal Rd 36561 **Location:** Waterfront. Foley Beach Expwy to SR 180, 4.6 mi e. **Facility:** This sleek, sophisticated high-rise condo offers breathtaking Gulf views. Choose from one-, two- and three-bedroom units. Many activities are on site, including a waterslide, lazy river and putting green. 70 condominiums. 5 stories, exterior corridors. **Pool(s):** outdoor, heated indoor. **Activities:** sauna, hot tub, marina, fishing, tennis, exercise room. **Guest Services:** complimentary laundry.

[icons]

**WHERE TO EAT**

**CAFE GRAZIE**                               251/981-7278

▼▼ **Italian.** Casual Dining. $12-$31 **AAA Inspector Notes:** You will "thank" this eatery for offering a nice change of pace from this seafood-loaded coastal area. From the antipasto to the house specialties, the kitchen pleases with such offerings as toasted ravioli, margherita pizza, linguine with clams and grouper piccata. The menu has good variety, and the whimsical décor provides a casual but inviting experience. **Features:** full bar, patio dining, happy hour. **Address:** 27267 Perdido Beach Blvd, Suite 302 36561 **Location:** On SR 182, 1.5 mi e of jct SR 161; at SanRoc Cay Marina.

**COBALT THE RESTAURANT**                     251/923-5300

▼▼▼ **American.** Casual Dining. $8-$35 **AAA Inspector Notes:** This chic, bay-side bistro is tucked away under the east side of the Alabama Point Bridge, next to the Caribe Resort. A relaxing, breathtaking view of Terry Cove can be enjoyed while dining inside or outside the expansive patio. Slips are available for docking if arriving by boat. The eclectic menu includes pizza, free-range chicken, Gulf shrimp, oysters, fish, bison rib-eye, pasta, sandwiches and salads. **Features:** full bar, patio dining, Sunday brunch, happy hour. **Address:** 28099 Perdido Beach Blvd 36561 **Location:** Jct SR 59 and 182, 8.7 mi e, just w on access road under east side of bridge.

[icons]

**COSMO'S RESTAURANT**                        251/948-9663

▼▼▼ **Seafood.** Casual Dining. $8-$28 **AAA Inspector Notes:** The rustic wood walls, adorned with nautically-themed artwork, are appropriate for the location and cuisine at this eatery. A seasonal patio courtyard offers outdoor dining. The website lists daily specials along with additional weekly regionally themed menus. **Features:** full bar, patio dining, happy hour. **Address:** 25753 Canal Rd 36561 **Location:** On SR 180, just w of jct SR 161.

[icons]

**COTTON'S**                                  251/981-9268

▼▼▼ **Seafood Steak.** Casual Dining. $14-$30 **AAA Inspector Notes:** Across from the Gulf and on the main beach thoroughfare is an elevated rustic wood structure with distinctive red neon lights edging the roofline. Known for its seafood, this casual eatery has been serving the coast for more than 25 years. **Features:** full bar. **Address:** 26009 Perdido Beach Blvd 36561 **Location:** On SR 182, 6.5 mi e of jct SR 59.

---

Enjoy great member rates and

benefits at AAA/CAA Preferred Hotels

**LOUISIANA LAGNIAPPE**                       251/981-2258

▼▼▼ **Creole Seafood.** Fine Dining. $15-$39 **AAA Inspector Notes:** Whimsical tropical décor and a view of the docked boats in the marina may reinforce your appetite for some ultra-fresh seafood, all prepared with Southern Creole flair. **Features:** full bar, Sunday brunch. **Address:** 27267 Perdido Beach Blvd, #201 36561 **Location:** On SR 182, 1.5 mi e of jct SR 161; at SanRoc Cay Marina.

[icons]

**VOYAGERS RESTAURANT**                       251/981-9811

▼▼▼ **Seafood.** Fine Dining. $11-$42 **AAA Inspector Notes:** This wonderful restaurant's elegant dining room overlooks the Gulf of Mexico. Examples of the light Gulf Coast Creole cuisine are the highly recommended oysters Rockefeller, turtle soup and rack of lamb. Casual resort attire is acceptable. **Features:** full bar. **Reservations:** suggested. **Address:** 27200 Perdido Beach Blvd 36561 **Location:** On SR 182, 1.5 mi e of jct SR 161; in Perdido Beach Resort. **Parking:** on-site and valet.

[icons]

**WINTZELL'S OYSTER HOUSE**                   251/974-2122

▼▼ **Southern Seafood.** Casual Dining. $9-$24 **AAA Inspector Notes:** Established in 1938, this eatery offers an exceptional variety of seafood. Ten different ways to prepare oysters, the trademark of this casual eatery. They are offered as stated in their logo: fried, stewed and nude. **Features:** full bar, happy hour. **Address:** 24131 Perdido Beach Blvd 36561 **Location:** On SR 182, 4.6 mi e of jct SR 59.

[icons]

# ORRVILLE (F-3) pop. 204

**OLD CAHAWBA ARCHAEOLOGICAL PARK** is 6.8 mi. e. on SR 22, 3.4 mi. s. on CR 9, then 1.4 mi. e. to 9518 Cahaba Rd., at the confluence of the Cahaba and Alabama rivers. Once a thriving antebellum river town, the site served as the state capital 1820-26. The town was an important prison site during the Civil War, but all that remains today are a one-story frame townhouse, a two-story brick slave building and some ruins. Streets and building sites are marked with interpretive signs. **Hours:** Park daily 9-5. Welcome center daily noon-5. Closed Jan. 1, Thanksgiving and Christmas. **Cost:** Free. **Phone:** (334) 872-8058.

# OXFORD pop. 21,348

**COMFORT INN**                               (256)831-0860

▼▼▼ **Motel** $60-$250 **Address:** 138 Elm St 36203 **Location:** I-20 exit 185, just s. **Facility:** 62 units. 2 stories (no elevator), exterior corridors. **Pool(s):** outdoor. **Guest Services:** valet and coin laundry.

[icons]

**COMFORT SUITES**                            (256)835-8873

▼▼▼ **Hotel** $79-$80 **Address:** 125 Davis Loop Rd 36203 **Location:** I-20 exit 188, just n, then w. **Facility:** 63 units. 3 stories, interior corridors. **Pool(s):** outdoor. **Activities:** exercise room. **Guest Services:** valet and coin laundry.

[icons]

**FAIRFIELD INN & SUITES BY MARRIOTT ANNISTON OXFORD**
(256)831-1921

▼▼▼▼ **Hotel** $104-$120 **Address:** 143 Colonial Dr 36203 **Location:** I-20 exit 188, just n, then w. **Facility:** 81 units. 4 stories, interior corridors. **Amenities:** safes. **Pool(s):** outdoor. **Activities:** exercise room. **Guest Services:** valet and coin laundry.

**AAA Benefit:**
Members save 5% or more!

[icons]

## HAMPTON INN & SUITES                    (256)831-8958

Hotel
$99-$129

**AAA Benefit:**
Members save 5% or
more!

**Address:** 210 Colonial Dr 36203 **Location:** I-20 exit 188, just n, then w. **Facility:** 101 units. 4 stories, interior corridors. **Terms:** 1-7 night minimum stay, cancellation fee imposed. **Pool(s):** outdoor. **Activities:** hot tub, exercise room. **Guest Services:** valet and coin laundry.

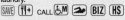

### HILTON GARDEN INN OXFORD/ANNISTON        (256)831-0083

Hotel $89-$169 **Address:** 280 Colonial Dr 36203 **Location:** I-20 exit 188, just n, then w. **Facility:** 125 units. 4 stories, interior corridors. **Terms:** 1-7 night minimum stay, cancellation fee imposed. **Pool(s):** heated indoor. **Activities:** hot tub, exercise room. **Guest Services:** valet and coin laundry.

**AAA Benefit:**
Members save 5% or more!

### HOLIDAY INN EXPRESS & SUITES ANNISTON/OXFORD
256/835-8768

Hotel
Rates not provided

**Address:** 160 Colonial Dr 36203 **Location:** I-20 exit 188, just n, then w. **Facility:** 80 units. 3 stories, interior corridors. **Pool(s):** heated indoor. **Activities:** hot tub, exercise room. **Guest Services:** valet and coin laundry.

## LA QUINTA INN & SUITES OXFORD           (256)241-0950

Hotel
$75-$300

**Address:** 100 Colonial Dr 36203 **Location:** I-20 exit 188, just n, then w. **Facility:** 64 units. 3 stories, interior corridors. **Pool(s):** heated indoor. **Activities:** hot tub, exercise room. **Guest Services:** valet and coin laundry. **Featured Amenity:** full hot breakfast.

### QUALITY INN                              (256)835-2170

Motel $59-$64 **Address:** 161 Colonial Dr 36203 **Location:** I-20 exit 188, just n, then w. **Facility:** 62 units. 2 stories (no elevator), exterior corridors. **Pool(s):** outdoor. **Activities:** limited exercise equipment. **Guest Services:** valet laundry. *(See ad this page.)*

### WHERE TO EAT

### FRONTERA MEXICAN RESTAURANT            256/835-9905

Mexican. Casual Dining. $5-$15 **AAA Inspector Notes:** The south-of-the-border atmosphere begins as guests approach this hacienda-style structure. The interior is nicely appointed with ethnic handiwork including ornately carved wood tables and chairs, pottery and original artwork. A covered, semi-enclosed open-air patio is another seating option to enjoy favorite Mexican cuisine. **Features:** full bar, patio dining. **Address:** 1750 E Hamric Dr 36203 **Location:** I-20 exit 185, just n on SR 21, then 1.4 mi e.

### FUJI JAPANESE CUISINE                   256/835-8788

Japanese. Casual Dining. $7-$33 **AAA Inspector Notes:** Talented chefs entertain and prepare meals at hibachi tables, or guests can opt for a seat in the dining room's more relaxing, intimate atmosphere. The menu offers multiple selections of Asian cuisine, including sushi. **Features:** full bar, happy hour. **Address:** 218 Davis Loop 36203 **Location:** I-20 exit 188, just n, then just w.

▼ See AAA listing this page ▼

**GARFRERICK'S CAFE** 256/831-0044

▼▼▼ Natural/Organic. Casual Dining. $6-$32 **AAA Inspector Notes:** The perfect place for health conscious eaters, this contemporary bistro serves organic vegetables, hormone-free chicken and grain-fed natural beef. They take pride in the fact that there is no fryer on the premises. On Saturday only dinner is served. **Features:** full bar, Sunday brunch. **Address:** 655 Creekside Dr, Suite C 36203 **Location:** I-20 exit 185, 0.8 mi n on US 431/SR 21; in plaza behind Red Lobster. L D CALL ⑤M

**JEFFERSON'S RESTAURANT** 256/835-5858

▼▼ Wings Burgers. Casual Dining. $6-$13 **AAA Inspector Notes:** Known for burgers, oysters and wings, this relaxed establishment is a great place to watch the game on one of the many flatscreen TVs. **Features:** full bar, patio dining. **Address:** 230 Spring Branch Dr 36203 **Location:** I-20 exit 185, just s on SR 21, just w on Elm St, then just nw. L D CALL ⑤M

**LOS MEXICANOS** 256/835-8700

▼ Tex-Mex. Casual Dining. $6-$12 **AAA Inspector Notes:** An evening here offers a wide variety of classic Tex-Mex cuisine such as tacos, enchiladas, burritos and fajitas. Diners enjoy the contemporary Mexican-theme atmosphere and efficient service. **Features:** full bar. **Address:** 1936 Hwy 78 E 36203 **Location:** I-20 exit 188, 0.3 mi n to US 78, then just w. L D CALL ⑤M

**STRUTS** 256/835-8102

▼ Burgers Wings. Casual Dining. $6-$20 **AAA Inspector Notes:** Can't decide if you want a burger or wings? Well, here you can have the best of both with a combo slider/wings basket. Root for your favorite team while watching the game on one of the many wall-mounted, flat-screen TVs. **Features:** beer only, happy hour. **Address:** 88 Ali Way 36203 **Location:** I-20 exit 185, just n on SR 21, just e on US 78, then just s; behind Logan's Roadhouse. L D CALL ⑤M

**YUME JAPANESE & ASIAN CUISINE** 256/241-0142

▼▼ Asian. Casual Dining. $8-$22 **AAA Inspector Notes:** Behind the sushi bar, a black granite wall with bright pink blossoms is an attention grabber for guests as they dine on Japanese, Chinese, Thai and Korean favorites. **Features:** full bar. **Address:** 301 Colonial Dr 36203 **Location:** I-20 exit 188, just n, then 1 mi w. L D CALL ⑤M

## OZARK pop. 14,907

**BAYMONT INN & SUITES OZARK** (334)774-0233

▼▼ Motel $59-$99 **Address:** 1360 S US Hwy 231 36360 **Location:** 0.3 mi s of jct SR 249. **Facility:** 40 units. 2 stories (no elevator), exterior corridors. **Pool(s):** outdoor. **Activities:** exercise room. **Guest Services:** valet laundry. *(See ad this page.)*
CALL ⑤M ➤ 🛜 🔲 🖼 🖵 / SOME UNITS 🔊

**HAMPTON INN OZARK** (334)443-6669

▼▼▼ Hotel $109-$159 **Address:** 235 N US Hwy 231 36360 **Location:** Jct SR 27. **Facility:** 62 units. 3 stories, interior corridors. **Terms:** 1-7 night minimum stay, cancellation fee imposed. **Pool(s):** outdoor. **Activities:** exercise room. **Guest Services:** valet and coin laundry.

**AAA Benefit:** Members save 5% or more!

CALL ⑤M ➤ BIZ HS 🛜 🔲 🖼 🖵

**MICROTEL INN & SUITES BY WYNDHAM OZARK** (334)774-2771

▼▼ Hotel $65-$115 **Address:** 1140 US Hwy 231 N 36360 **Location:** Jct SR 27, 1 mi n. **Facility:** 58 units. 3 stories, interior corridors. **Pool(s):** outdoor. **Activities:** playground, exercise room. **Guest Services:** coin laundry.
➤ BIZ HS 🛜 ✖ / SOME UNITS 🔲 🖼 🖵

**WHERE TO EAT**

**COLBY'S PLACE** 334/774-4404

▼ Southern Comfort Food. Casual Dining. $7-$8 **AAA Inspector Notes:** Locally-owned and -operated by a husband and wife team, this all-you-can-eat buffet restaurant is named in memory of their late son. Serving a daily rotating menu of Southern comfort foods such as fried chicken, catfish and meatloaf, traditional sides include macaroni and cheese, turnip and collard greens, okra and fried green tomatoes. Open daily for lunch and also for dinner on Friday. **Address:** 129 S East Ave 36360 **Location:** Corner of Broad St; downtown. L CALL ⑤M

Visit the AAA and CAA senior driving websites for valuable resources

▼ *See AAA listing this page* ▼

## PELHAM (D-3) pop. 21,352, elev. 460'
- Hotels & Restaurants map & index p. 54
- Part of Birmingham area — see map p. 43

**OAK MOUNTAIN STATE PARK,** about .5 mi. from jct. State Park Rd. and John Findlay III Dr., comprises 9,940 acres at the southernmost part of the Appalachian chain and features a scenic drive to the top of Double Oak Mountain. The site also offers an 18-hole golf course, a beach, nature and hiking trails, horseback riding, a BMX track, kayaks, pedal boats, canoes and a wildlife rehabilitation center where visitors can see the more than 2,000 animals from behind a glass window. *See Recreation Areas Chart.* **Hours:** Daily 7 a.m.-dusk. **Cost:** $3; $1 (ages 6-11 and 62+). **Phone:** (205) 620-2524 or (800) 252-7275.

### BEST WESTERN PLUS OAK MOUNTAIN INN
(205)982-1113  68

Hotel
$100-$200

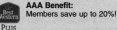
**AAA Benefit:** Members save up to 20%!

**Address:** 100 Bishop Cir 35124 **Location:** I-65 exit 246, just s. **Facility:** 60 units. 3 stories, interior corridors. **Pool(s):** outdoor. **Featured Amenity:** breakfast buffet.

### FAIRFIELD INN & SUITES BY MARRIOTT BIRMINGHAM PELHAM/I-65
(205)987-9879  71

Hotel $104-$175 **Address:** 230 Cahaba Valley Rd 35124 **Location:** I-65 exit 246, 0.6 mi w on SR 119. **Facility:** 93 units. 4 stories, interior corridors. **Pool(s):** heated indoor. **Activities:** hot tub, exercise room. **Guest Services:** valet and coin laundry.

**AAA Benefit:** Members save 5% or more!

### HAMPTON INN & SUITES PELHAM
(205)313-9500  70

Hotel $89-$175 **Address:** 232 Cahaba Valley Rd 35124 **Location:** I-65 exit 246, just w. **Facility:** 86 units. 3 stories, interior corridors. **Terms:** 1-7 night minimum stay, cancellation fee imposed. **Pool(s):** outdoor. **Activities:** exercise room. **Guest Services:** valet and coin laundry.

**AAA Benefit:** Members save 5% or more!

### HOLIDAY INN EXPRESS
205/987-8888  69

Hotel. Rates not provided. **Address:** 260 Cahaba Valley Rd 35124 **Location:** I-65 exit 246, just w; behind Pelham Civic Complex. **Facility:** 81 units. 3 stories, interior corridors. **Pool(s):** heated indoor. **Activities:** limited exercise equipment. **Guest Services:** valet and coin laundry.

### RAMADA INN
(205)987-0444  66

Hotel $60-$236 **Address:** 113 Cahaba Valley Park E 35124 **Location:** I-65 exit 246, just nw. **Facility:** 47 units. 2 stories (no elevator), exterior corridors. **Terms:** cancellation fee imposed. **Pool(s):** outdoor. **Activities:** limited exercise equipment. **Guest Services:** valet and coin laundry.

### SLEEP INN
(205)982-9800  67

Hotel $75-$276 **Address:** 200 Southgate Dr 35124 **Location:** I-65 exit 246, 0.4 mi w on SR 119. **Facility:** 80 units. 3 stories, interior corridors. **Pool(s):** outdoor. **Guest Services:** valet laundry.

## WHERE TO EAT

### 2 PESOS MEXICAN CAFE
205/987-3800  83

Mexican. Casual Dining. $6-$21 **AAA Inspector Notes:** Enjoy hearty portions in this hacienda-style dining room or on the covered outdoor patio. Attentive staff guarantees customer satisfaction. **Features:** full bar, patio dining. **Address:** 201 Southgate Dr 35124 **Location:** I-65 exit 246, 0.3 mi w on SR 119.

### CAFE TRENTUNO
205/664-7887

Italian. Casual Dining. $7-$18 **AAA Inspector Notes:** With its red-and-white checkered covered tables and Tuscan Valley vineyard wall mural, this neighborhood ristorante creates the illusion of dining in the Italian countryside. Along with its signature pizza selection, a variety of pasta dishes is on the menu along with daily weekday specials. **Features:** beer & wine. **Address:** 3018 Pelham Pkwy, Suite 102 35124 **Location:** I-65 exit 242, 0.7 mi w on CR 52, then 0.7 mi n on US 31; in Pelham Plaza.

### NINO'S ITALIAN RESTAURANT
205/620-1116

Italian. Casual Dining. $7-$15 **AAA Inspector Notes:** Nosh on authentic Italian favorites prepared by two native New Yorkers. Luscious pasta dishes, pizza, calzones and subs all are made from scratch. Traditional desserts include tiramisu, cannoli, creme wedding cake and Nino's exclusive—Ca Nino—a cannoli shell filled with praline cheesecake and covered in caramel chocolate. **Features:** beer & wine, patio dining. **Address:** 2698 Pelham Pkwy 35124 **Location:** I-65 exit 246, 0.7 mi w on SR 119, then 1.3 mi s on US 31.

## PELL CITY pop. 12,695
- Restaurants p. 136
- Part of Birmingham area — see map p. 43

### COMFORT SUITES
(205)338-5570

Hotel $79-$119 **Address:** 270 Vaughan Ln 35125 **Location:** I-20 exit 158 eastbound; exit 158A westbound, just ne. **Facility:** 63 units. 3 stories, interior corridors. **Pool(s):** outdoor. **Activities:** exercise room. **Guest Services:** coin laundry.

### HAMPTON INN
(205)814-3000

Hotel $89-$119 **Address:** 220 Vaughan Ln 35125 **Location:** I-20 exit 158 eastbound; exit 158A westbound, just ne. **Facility:** 75 units. 4 stories, interior corridors. **Terms:** 1-7 night minimum stay, cancellation fee imposed. **Pool(s):** outdoor. **Activities:** exercise room. **Guest Services:** valet and coin laundry.

**AAA Benefit:** Members save 5% or more!

### HOLIDAY INN EXPRESS PELL CITY
205/884-0047

Hotel. Rates not provided. **Address:** 240 Vaughan Ln 35125 **Location:** I-20 exit 158 eastbound; exit 158A westbound, just ne. **Facility:** 91 units. 3 stories, interior corridors. **Pool(s):** outdoor. **Activities:** exercise room. **Guest Services:** valet and coin laundry.

Keep your focus safely
on the road when driving

## WHERE TO EAT

**EL CAZADOR MEXICAN GRILL**      205/338-4801

Mexican. Casual Dining. $5-$13 **AAA Inspector Notes:** Located right off the interstate, this spacious café offers a nice selection of Mexican fare and quick service. The cozy outdoor seating area is great when weather permits. Multiple hotels are within walking distance. **Features:** full bar, patio dining. **Address:** 200 Vaughan Ln 35125 **Location:** I-20 exit 158 eastbound; exit 158A westbound, just ne. L D CALL M

**GOLDEN RULE BAR-B-Q AND GRILL**      205/338-1443

Barbecue. Family Dining. $5-$15 **AAA Inspector Notes:** The Golden Rule claims to be the South's most famous barbecue. Since 1891, Alabamians have enjoyed the delicious flavors of real pit barbecue. Now a local chain, the eatery cooks up a variety of Southern favorites. **Features:** beer only, patio dining, Sunday brunch. **Address:** 1700 Martin St N 35125 **Location:** I-20 exit 158, just n. L D

# PHENIX CITY pop. 32,822

**HAMPTON INN & SUITES PHENIX CITY/COLUMBUS AREA**
(334)664-0776

Hotel $109-$159 **Address:** 620 Martin Luther King Jr Pkwy 36869 **Location:** US 280 exit US 431, just s. **Facility:** 81 units. 4 stories, interior corridors. **Terms:** 1-7 night minimum stay, cancellation fee imposed. **Pool(s):** outdoor. **Activities:** hot tub, exercise room. **Guest Services:** valet and coin laundry.

> **AAA Benefit:**
> Members save 5% or more!

CALL M BIZ HS X /SOME UNITS

**HOLIDAY INN EXPRESS HOTEL & SUITES PHENIX CITY-FT. BENNING AREA**      334/298-9404

Hotel. Rates not provided. **Address:** 1702 US 280 Bypass 36867 **Location:** Jct US 280 and 431, 0.7 mi ne. **Facility:** 82 units. 4 stories, interior corridors. **Pool(s):** outdoor. **Activities:** exercise room. **Guest Services:** valet and coin laundry.

CALL M BIZ HS X

## WHERE TO EAT

**MIKE & ED'S BAR-B-Q**      334/297-1012

Barbecue. Quick Serve. $3-$15 **AAA Inspector Notes:** The meat plate, cool coleslaw, baked beans, Brunswick stew and some tempting desserts are some examples of the tasty treats found at this no-frills barbecue house. **Address:** 2001 Crawford Rd 36867 **Location:** 0.5 mi n of jct US 280. L D

**SHARK'S FISH & CHICKEN CHICAGO STYLE**      334/480-9700

Fish & Chips Chicken. Quick Serve. $6-$17 **AAA Inspector Notes:** Your meal is freshly prepared once your order is placed. Large orders may need additional preparation time. **Address:** 2001 US Hwy 280 36867 **Location:** Jct US 80 and 280, 2 mi nw. L D CALL M

# PICKENSVILLE (D-1) pop. 608, elev. 232'

**TENN-TOM WATERWAY/TOM BEVILL VISITOR CENTER** is .5 mi. s. of SR 86 on SR 14 at the Tom Bevill Lock and Dam; the visitor center is at 1382 Lock and Dam Rd. By connecting the Tennessee and Tombigbee rivers with a system of locks, this 234-mile canal provides a shortcut to the Gulf of Mexico. The visitor center, built in 19th-century Greek Revival style and furnished in period, features displays about river travel and wildlife. Photographs, models and audiovisual presentations also are presented. A 19th-century cast-iron fountain dominates the garden.

**Hours:** Tues.-Sat. 9-5, Mar.-Oct.; Mon.-Fri. 8-4, rest of year. Visitor center closed holidays except Memorial Day, July 4 and Labor Day. Phone ahead to confirm schedule. **Cost:** Free. **Phone:** (205) 373-8705.

**U.S. Snagboat Montgomery,** at the Tom Bevill Visitor Center at 1382 Lock and Dam Rd., is one of the last steam-powered stern-wheelers used in the South. The snag boat, which for nearly 60 years removed debris from nearby rivers, has exhibits that chronicle maintenance operations on the South's major waterways. **Hours:** Tues.-Sat. 9-5, Mar.-Oct.; Mon.-Fri. 8-4, rest of year. Closed holidays except Memorial Day, July 4 and Labor Day. **Cost:** Free. **Phone:** (205) 373-8705.

# POINT CLEAR pop. 2,125

**GRAND HOTEL MARRIOTT RESORT, GOLF CLUB & SPA**
(251)928-9201

Historic Resort Hotel $189-$360 **Address:** One Grand Blvd 36564 **Location:** Waterfront. On US Scenic 98, 1.2 mi n of jct CR 32. **Facility:**

> **AAA Benefit:**
> Members save 5% or more!

On Mobile Bay, the public areas reflect a bygone era of elegance and are sprinkled with historical mementos. The spacious grounds are beautifully landscaped and change seasonally. 405 units. 2-4 stories, interior corridors. **Parking:** on-site and valet. **Terms:** check-in 4 pm, 5 day cancellation notice, resort fee. **Amenities:** safes. **Dining:** Grand Steakhouse, Saltwater Grill, see separate listings, entertainment. **Pool(s):** outdoor, heated outdoor, heated indoor. **Activities:** sauna, hot tub, steamroom, marina, fishing, regulation golf, tennis, recreation programs, bicycles, playground, game room, spa. **Guest Services:** valet laundry, area transportation.

BIZ HS

## WHERE TO EAT

**GRAND STEAKHOUSE**      251/928-9201

New American Fine Dining $21-$36

**AAA Inspector Notes:** An outstanding dining experience with exceptional service in a relaxing, elegant atmosphere is what you can expect at this establishment. The intimate dining room was built in the 1940s. The curved picture windows offer an extraordinary view of the bay and twinkling lights of Mobile. A seasonally changing menu offers the bounty of the chef's garden and fresh seafood from the gulf, as well as meats and poultry raised on natural farms. **Features:** full bar. **Reservations:** suggested. **Address:** One Grand Blvd 36564 **Location:** On US Scenic 98, 1.2 mi n of jct CR 32; in Grand Hotel Marriott Resort, Golf Club & Spa. **Parking:** on-site and valet. D CALL M

**SALTWATER GRILL**      251/928-9201

Seafood Fine Dining $11-$36

**AAA Inspector Notes:** A breathtaking sunset over Mobile Bay can be relished while savoring a luscious feast of such Gulf delicacies as shrimp, flounder, oysters, grouper and red snapper. **Features:** full bar. **Reservations:** suggested. **Address:** One Grand Blvd 36564 **Location:** On US Scenic 98, 1.2 mi n of jct CR 32; in Grand Hotel Marriott Resort, Golf Club & Spa. **Parking:** on-site and valet.  D CALL M

## PRATTVILLE (E-4) pop. 33,960, elev. 193'
• Restaurants p. 138

Established in the late 1830s by Daniel Pratt of New Hampshire, Prattville has the feel of its founder's native New England. The town's historic district has more than 150 buildings, many predating the Civil War.

**Prattville Area Chamber of Commerce:** 131 N. Court St., Prattville, AL 36067. **Phone:** (334) 365-7392.

**PRATTAUGAN MUSEUM AND HERITAGE CENTER,** 102 E. Main St. at jct. Chestnut St., is in the 1848 McWilliams-Smith-Rice house. Displays highlight town founder Daniel Pratt and his pilgrimage to Alabama as well as Civil War and World War II history pertaining to Autauga County, including bomb casings that were manufactured in the Gin Shop, the manufacturing history of cotton gins, a medical room and early American living displays.

The museum also houses an extensive archive containing genealogical, church and cemetery histories that includes documents and photographs. **Hours:** Tues.-Fri. 10-4, Sat. 10-2. Closed major holidays. **Cost:** Free. **Phone:** (334) 361-0961.

BAYMONT INN & SUITES PRATTVILLE          (334)361-6463
〰️〰️ **Hotel** $59-$79 **Address:** 104 Jameson Ct 36067 **Location:** I-65 exit 179, 1.4 mi w. **Facility:** 60 units. 2 stories (no elevator), exterior corridors. **Pool(s):** outdoor. **Activities:** exercise room. *(See ad this page.)*

COURTYARD BY MARRIOTT MONTGOMERY PRATTVILLE
(334)290-1270
〰️〰️〰️ **Hotel** $104-$189 **Address:** 2620 Legends Pkwy 36066 **Location:** I-65 exit 179, 0.8 mi sw. **Facility:** 84 units. 3 stories, interior corridors. **Pool(s):** outdoor. **Activities:** hot tub, exercise room. **Guest Services:** valet and coin laundry.

**AAA Benefit:** Members save 5% or more!

DAYS INN & SUITES                          (334)285-5312
〰️〰️ **Hotel** $65-$100 **Address:** 600 Old Farm Ln S 36066 **Location:** I-65 exit 179, 0.8 mi w. Located in a busy commercial area. **Facility:** 52 units. 3 stories, interior corridors. **Pool(s):** outdoor. **Guest Services:** valet and coin laundry.

**ECONO LODGE**                             (334)361-2007
〰️ 〰️
Motel
$64-$74

**Address:** 798 Business Park Dr 36066 **Location:** I-65 exit 181, just sw, then just n. **Facility:** 52 units. 2 stories (no elevator), interior/exterior corridors. **Pool(s):** outdoor. **Featured Amenity:** continental breakfast.

HAMPTON INN & SUITES PRATTVILLE          (334)285-6767
〰️〰️〰️ **Hotel** $109-$169 **Address:** 2590 Cobbs Ford Rd 36066 **Location:** I-65 exit 179, just nw. **Facility:** 101 units. 4 stories, interior corridors. **Terms:** 1-7 night minimum stay, cancellation fee imposed. **Pool(s):** outdoor. **Activities:** exercise room. **Guest Services:** valet and coin laundry.

**AAA Benefit:** Members save 5% or more!

## HOWARD JOHNSON
(334)285-3420

▼▼ ▼▼ Hotel $83-$125 Address: 2585 Cobbs Hill Pl 36066 Location: I-65 exit 179, just nw. Facility: 112 units. 2-3 stories, interior/exterior corridors. Terms: 1-7 night minimum stay, cancellation fee imposed. Pool(s): outdoor. Guest Services: valet laundry.

[symbols]

## LA QUINTA INN & SUITES
(334)358-5454

▼▼▼▼ Hotel $81-$184 Address: 261 Interstate Commercial Park Loop 36066 Location: I-65 exit 181, just w. Facility: 62 units. 3 stories, interior corridors. Pool(s): outdoor. Activities: hot tub, exercise room. Guest Services: valet and coin laundry.

[symbols] / SOME UNITS

## MONTGOMERY MARRIOTT PRATTVILLE HOTEL & CONFERENCE CENTER AT CAPITOL HILL
(334)290-1235

▼▼▼ Hotel $140-$230 Address: 2500 Legends Cir 36066 Location: I-65 exit 179, 1.3 mi w on SR 6. Facility: 96 units, some two bedrooms and kitchens. 3 stories, interior corridors. Dining: Oak Tavern, see separate listing. Pool(s): outdoor. Activities: hot tub, regulation golf, tennis, exercise room. Guest Services: valet laundry, boarding pass kiosk, area transportation.

**AAA Benefit:**
Members save 5% or more!

[symbols] / SOME UNITS

## QUALITY INN
(334)365-6003

▼▼◆ Hotel $70-$77 Address: 797 Business Park Dr 36067 Location: I-65 exit 181, just sw, then just n. Facility: 53 units. 2 stories (no elevator), interior corridors. Pool(s): outdoor. Guest Services: valet and coin laundry.

[symbols] / SOME UNITS

### WHERE TO EAT

## CHAPPY'S DELI
334/290-3313

▼▼ ▼▼ Sandwiches. Family Dining. $5-$8 AAA Inspector Notes: Montgomery's favorite sandwich place has finally come to Prattville! Located at the top of the new High Point Town Center, it's the perfect place to rest your feet and look over all those great purchases. Enjoy the outdoor patio when the weather's agreeable, or book the party room for a special event. Wrap up your day with a fresh wrap, salad or burger. Features: patio dining. Address: 585 Pinnacle Pl 36066 Location: I-65 exit 179, just w. Parking: on-site and street.

[symbols]

## FANCI FREE BOUTIQUE & GARDEN CAFE
334/358-1524

▼▼ Sandwiches. Casual Dining. $3-$10 AAA Inspector Notes: This quaint luncheonette offers a quick bite while shopping the eclectic shops in the historic downtown area. It is located inside the Fanci Free Boutique, which features distinctive gifts made by local artisans. Address: 146 W Main St 36067 Location: Between Chestnut and Bridge sts; downtown. Parking: street only. [symbols]

## HOUSE OF JAVA
334/491-5282

▼▼ Coffee/Tea. Quick Serve. $2-$8 AAA Inspector Notes: Baked goods and sandwiches accompany various specialty brews at this Wi-Fi hot spot. The intimate cafe houses an indoor playground for the little tykes. Address: 2132 Cobbs Ford Rd 36066 Location: I-65 exit 179, 1.4 mi w. [symbols]

## JIM 'N NICK'S BAR-B-Q
334/290-1000

▼▼ ▼▼ Barbecue. Casual Dining. $8-$25 AAA Inspector Notes: Southern hospitality reigns at Jim 'N Nick's, where diners get neighborly treatment as they dig into huge portions of tasty lean sausage, fresh chili, juicy smoked beef and pork. A slice of sublime homemade pie ends the meal on a high note. Features: full bar. Address: 2550 Cobbs Ford Rd 36066 Location: I-65 exit 179, just sw.

[symbols]

## JIM'S RESTAURANT
334/365-7231

▼▼ ▼▼ Southern Comfort Food. Family Dining. $3-$12 AAA Inspector Notes: Serving up "meat-and-three" every day of the year except Christmas, this family-owned establishment has been welcoming diners since 1958. Simple but delicious dinner specials change daily and desserts are made from scratch. Come in, sit down and feel like family. Features: senior menu, Sunday brunch. Address: 1504 S Memorial Dr 36067 Location: Jct US 82 and 31, just se. [symbols]

## MEXICO TIPICO
334/365-8677

▼▼ ▼▼ Mexican. Casual Dining. $5-$25 AAA Inspector Notes: This popular establishment offers fresh, authentic Mexican food served in a festive environment. A large dining facility easily accommodates large parties. Features: full bar. Address: 1870 E Main St, Suite 3 36066 Location: I-65 exit 179, 1.5 mi w; in Kmart Shopping Center. [symbols]

## OAK TAVERN
334/290-1235

▼▼▼▼ Southern American. Casual Dining. $10-$32 AAA Inspector Notes: The spectacular view of the manicured golf greens adds to the relaxed atmosphere of this café. A large breakfast buffet is offered in the morning. Features: full bar. Address: 2500 Legends Cir 36066 Location: I-65 exit 179, 1.3 mi w on SR 6; in Montgomery Marriott Prattville Hotel & Conference Center at Capitol Hill. [symbols]

## TOKYO JAPANESE STEAK HOUSE & SUSHI BAR
334/285-7088

▼▼ ▼▼ Japanese Sushi. Casual Dining. $8-$30 AAA Inspector Notes: A wide variety of Asian dishes is offered in this contemporary atmosphere. Menu offerings include hibachi, sushi, sashimi, noodles, hot pots and curry dishes. Features: full bar. Address: 594 Pinnacle Pl 36066 Location: I-65 exit 179, just w, then just n; in High Point Town Center. [symbols]

# PRICEVILLE pop. 2,658

## COMFORT INN
(256)355-1037

▼▼ ▼▼ Hotel $79-$99 Address: 3239 Point Mallard Pkwy 35603 Location: I-65 exit 334, just w. Facility: 58 units, some efficiencies. 3 stories, interior corridors. Amenities: safes. Pool(s): heated indoor. Activities: exercise room. Guest Services: coin laundry.

[symbols] / SOME UNITS

## SUPER 8 - DECATUR
(256)355-2525

▼▼ Motel $60-$70 Address: 70 Marco Dr 35603 Location: I-65 exit 334, just e. Facility: 55 units. 2 stories (no elevator), exterior corridors. Terms: cancellation fee imposed. Pool(s): outdoor. Guest Services: coin laundry.

[symbols] / SOME UNITS

### WHERE TO EAT

## JW STEAKHOUSE
256/355-5560

▼▼ ▼▼ Steak. Casual Dining. $8-$22 AAA Inspector Notes: Set in a relaxed atmosphere, this steakhouse serves a variety of steak, fish, shrimp and chicken entrées as well as burgers and sandwiches. Little tykes have a nice selection of food on the kids' menu. Features: full bar. Address: 45 Marco Dr 35603 Location: I-65 exit 334, just e. [symbols]

# RAINSVILLE  pop. 4,948

## SUPER 8 RAINSVILLE                    (256)638-1640

WWW
Hotel
$41-$69

**Address:** 46 Roy Sanderson Ave 35986 **Location:** I-59 exit 218, 5.9 mi nw. **Facility:** 38 units. 2 stories, interior corridors. **Pool(s):** outdoor. **Activities:** limited exercise equipment. **Guest Services:** coin laundry. **Featured Amenity:** continental breakfast.

[SAVE] [YI+] [▨] [BIZ] [HS] [📶] [🔌]
[▣] [💻] / SOME UNITS [🐾]

# RUSSELL CAVE NATIONAL MONUMENT  (A-4)

Eight miles northwest of Bridgeport via CRs 75 and 98, Russell Cave National Monument is a 310-acre archeological site first investigated in 1953. The focal point of the site is a cave shelter where the Tennessee River Valley traverses the Cumberland Plateau. This cave, continuously occupied by various cultures for 10,000 years, is part of a larger cavern that extends about 7 miles into the side of a limestone mountain.

Excavations have uncovered, layer by layer, the story of the people who inhabited the cave from approximately 10,000 B.C. to A.D. 1650. Artifacts found in the area chart societal progress from the Paleo period through the Mississippian period when residents used pottery and more sophisticated weapons and tools, buried their dead in mounds and developed a primitive form of agriculture.

Using objects recovered from the excavations, the visitor center portrays these prehistoric people. Guided tours are available to the nearby shelter, where visitors can see exposed cave wall rock layers. Nature trails wind through the site. Interpreters demonstrate the prehistoric people's tools and weapons. Audiovisual programs are presented in the visitor center. Daily 8-4:30. Closed Jan. 1, Thanksgiving and Christmas. Free. Phone (256) 495-2672.

# RUSSELLVILLE  pop. 9,830

## BEST WESTERN PLUS RUSSELLVILLE HOTEL & SUITES                         (256)332-1002

WWW
Hotel
$85-$95

**AAA Benefit:**
Members save up to 20%!

**Address:** 13770 Hwy 43 35653 **Location:** 0.4 mi n of jct SR 24. **Facility:** 60 units. 3 stories, interior corridors. **Pool(s):** outdoor. **Activities:** exercise room. **Guest Services:** valet and coin laundry. **Featured Amenity:** full hot breakfast.

[SAVE] CALL [M] [▨] [BIZ] [HS] [📶]
[🔌] [▣] [💻]

# SARALAND  pop. 13,405
• Hotels & Restaurants map & index p. 109

## BEST WESTERN MOTORSPORTS INN & SUITES
(251)675-4446  **25**

WWWW
Hotel
$60-$150

**AAA Benefit:**
Members save up to 20%!

**Address:** 1118 Shelton Beach Rd 36571 **Location:** I-65 exit 13, just e, then just n. **Facility:** 73 units. 4 stories, interior corridors. **Pool(s):** heated indoor. **Activities:** exercise room. **Guest Services:** valet and coin laundry.

[SAVE] [YI+] CALL [M] [▨] [BIZ] [HS]
[📶] [🔌] [▣] [💻]

## HAMPTON INN SARALAND/ NORTH MOBILE
(251)679-7953  **29**

WWW **Hotel** $99-$124 **Address:** 1320 Industrial Pkwy 36571 **Location:** I-65 exit 13, just w. **Facility:** 58 units. 3 stories, interior corridors. **Terms:** 1-7 night minimum stay, cancellation fee imposed. **Pool(s):** outdoor. **Activities:** exercise room. **Guest Services:** valet and coin laundry.

**AAA Benefit:**
Members save 5% or more!

CALL [M] [▨] [BIZ] [HS] [📶] [✕] [🔌] [▣] [💻]

## HOLIDAY INN EXPRESS & SUITES   (251)378-6300  **30**

WWW
Hotel
$113-$132

**Address:** 1401 Industrial Pkwy 36571 **Location:** I-65 exit 13, just w. **Facility:** 103 units. 4 stories, interior corridors. **Pool(s):** outdoor. **Activities:** hot tub, exercise room. **Guest Services:** valet and coin laundry.

[SAVE] CALL [M] [▨] [BIZ] [HS] [📶]
[✕] [🔌] [▣] [💻]

## MICROTEL INN & SUITES BY WYNDHAM SARALAND/NORTH MOBILE
(251)675-5045  **26**

WW [WW] **Hotel** $70-$90 **Address:** 1124 Shelton Beach Rd 36571 **Location:** I-65 exit 13, then just n. **Facility:** 70 units. 4 stories, interior corridors. **Amenities:** safes. **Activities:** exercise room. **Guest Services:** valet and coin laundry.

[YI+] CALL [M] [HS] [📶] [💻] / SOME UNITS [🐾] [🔌] [▣]

## QUALITY INN                           (251)679-8880  **28**

WW [WW] **Hotel** $60-$120 **Address:** 1111 Industrial Pkwy 36571 **Location:** I-65 exit 13, just e on SR 158. **Facility:** 59 units. 2 stories, interior corridors. **Amenities:** safes. **Pool(s):** outdoor. **Activities:** exercise room. **Guest Services:** valet and coin laundry.

[▨] [BIZ] [📶] [🔌] [▣] [💻]

### WHERE TO EAT

## BENZI'S PIZZA                          251/675-9600

WW [WW] Pizza. Casual Dining. $8-$15 **AAA Inspector Notes:** This locally owned pizzeria is situated in a residential area. Although most of its business is take-out orders, the café has a small dining area in front enhanced by a painted wall mural of the Tuscan countryside and Roman columns. Some pasta dishes and calzones are available. **Address:** 311 Shelton Beach Rd 36571 **Location:** I-65 exit 13, just e, then 1.8 mi n. [L] [D]

## CATFISH JUNCTION                       251/679-6666  **29**

WW [WW] Southern Seafood. Casual Dining. $7-$21 **AAA Inspector Notes:** Use of fresh, local seafood at this spot guarantees a tasteful meal along with friendly service. **Address:** 300 Industrial Pkwy 36571 **Location:** I-65 exit 13, 1.3 mi e on SR 158. [L] [D] CALL [M]

(See map & index p. 109.)

### J. RODGERS BBQ
251/675-3282  (28)

Barbecue. Quick Serve. $5-$15 **AAA Inspector Notes:** What appears to be an industrial corrugated metal building actually houses this classic rib joint. You can help yourself to the daily buffet or order off the menu. Either way, you're in for a treat of tender meats, which are "smoked low and slow." **Address:** 1444 Industrial Pkwy 36571 **Location:** I-65 exit 13, just w.  L  D

### MING'S BUFFET & BAR
251/675-9868  (27)

Asian. Casual Dining. $6-$13 **AAA Inspector Notes:** This restaurant offers an expansive buffet featuring Japanese, Chinese, hibachi, sushi and some American fare, which is replenished frequently. Whether guests decide to help themselves to the all-you-can-eat option or order off the menu, both offer an economical value. **Features:** full bar, happy hour. **Address:** 929 Saraland Blvd 36571 **Location:** I-65 exit 13, 2.1 mi e on SR 158, then just n on US 43.

L  D  CALL ⌂M

### SOMETHING SPECIAL DELI
251/675-3023  (30)

Deli. Casual Dining. $7-$9 **AAA Inspector Notes:** For a quarter of a century, this locally owned luncheonette has served salads, sandwiches and weekly blue plate special options. Save room for a slice of one of the homemade pies and cakes. Open until 8 p.m. Wed.-Fri. **Address:** 128 Industrial Pkwy 36571 **Location:** I-65 exit 13, 2.2 mi e on SR 158.  L

### WINTZELL'S OYSTER HOUSE
251/442-3335

Southern Seafood. Casual Dining. $7-$24 **AAA Inspector Notes:** Diners can request their oysters fried, stewed or nude, as this eatery's been preparing them 10 different ways since 1938, but if oysters aren't your thing, the menu also lists burgers, steaks and chicken for meat-lovers. **Features:** full bar, patio dining, happy hour. **Address:** 1208 Shelton Beach Rd 36571 **Location:** I-65 exit 13, just e, then just n.  L  D

## SATSUMA pop. 6,168

### PINTOLI'S ITALIAN CAFE
251/675-0607

Italian. Casual Dining. $6-$24 **AAA Inspector Notes:** Enjoy such traditional Italian fare as lasagna, spaghetti, chicken parmigiana, pizza and calzones along with sandwiches, salads and a child's menu in an intimate, romantic setting. An outdoor patio, perfect for star gazing, adds to the overall alluring atmosphere. **Features:** beer & wine, patio dining, Sunday brunch. **Address:** 5573 Hwy 43 36572 **Location:** I-65 exit 19, 2 mi s.  L  D  ⊠

## SCOTTSBORO (B-4) pop. 14,770, elev. 643'

**Shopping areas:** The merchandise at the Unclaimed Baggage Center, 509 W. Willow St., consists of unclaimed cargo and the contents of unclaimed luggage, including nearly everything that can be packed in baggage or shipped by air. The building covers a city block.

### COMFORT INN & SUITES
(256)259-8700

Hotel $89-$119 **Address:** 25775 John T Reid Pkwy 35768 **Location:** Jct US 72 and SR 35/279, 1.2 mi ne, just e on CR 33. Located in a quiet area. **Facility:** 77 units. 4 stories, interior corridors. **Pool(s):** heated indoor. **Activities:** hot tub, exercise room. **Guest Services:** valet and coin laundry.

CALL ⌂M  ⊇  BIZ  HS  🛜  🖥  🗔  📺  / SOME UNITS  🐾

### HAMPTON INN & SUITES - SCOTTSBORO
(256)259-5200

Hotel $89-$129 **Address:** 24747 John T Reid Pkwy 35768 **Location:** Jct US 72 and SR 35/279, just ne. **Facility:** 81 units. 4 stories, interior corridors. **Terms:** 1-7 night minimum stay, cancellation fee imposed. **Pool(s):** outdoor. **Activities:** exercise room. **Guest Services:** coin laundry.

> **AAA Benefit:** Members save 5% or more!

🍴 CALL ⌂M  ⊇  BIZ  HS  🛜  ⊠  🖥  🗔  📺

### QUALITY INN
(256)574-6666

Hotel $69-$129 **Address:** 208 Micah Way 35769 **Location:** On US 72, just s of jct SR 35. Adjacent to Parkway Plaza. **Facility:** 60 units. 2 stories (no elevator), exterior corridors. **Pool(s):** outdoor. **Activities:** exercise room. *(See ad this page.)*

🍴 ⊇ BIZ 🛜 🖥 🗔 📺 / SOME UNITS 🐾

---

## Add AAA or CAA Associate Members to bring home the benefits of membership

▼ See AAA listing this page ▼

## WHERE TO EAT

### BUENA VISTA MEXICAN RESTAURANT
256/574-3543

▼▼ Mexican. Casual Dining. $5-$17 **AAA Inspector Notes:** Enjoy piping hot, traditional Mexican cuisine served promptly by friendly staff, amid "South of the border" ambience. Festive super-size décor and custom mural-size paintings brighten the atmosphere. **Features:** full bar, patio dining, happy hour. **Address:** 24663 John T Reid Pkwy 35768 **Location:** Jct US 72 and SR 35/279, just ne on Frontage Rd; in front of Hampton Inn & Suites - Scottsboro and Home Depot. (L) (D) CALL (M)

### CARLILE'S RESTAURANT
256/574-5629

▼▼ American. Family Dining. $5-$20 **AAA Inspector Notes:** The third generation now runs this family-operated restaurant which has been in business since 1976. Tomato pie, the signature dish, can be ordered as an appetizer or entrée. Diners can order off the menu with a nice mix of meat, seafood, sandwiches and pasta dishes, or enjoy the buffet which is served daily except Saturday evening when a prime rib special is offered. On Sunday only lunch is served. **Features:** beer only, patio dining, senior menu. **Address:** 23730 John T Reid Pkwy 35768 **Location:** On US 72, 0.6 mi s of jct SR 35/279.

(L) (D) CALL (M)

### GENO'S PIZZA & GRILL
256/574-1533

▼▼ Pizza. Family Dining. $5-$17 **AAA Inspector Notes:** Anything goes at this family restaurant, where patrons can watch sports, chow down on pizza and play video games. **Features:** full bar, happy hour. **Address:** 102 Micah Way 35769 **Location:** On US 72, just s of jct SR 35. (L) (D) CALL (M)

### STEVARINOS
256/259-5420

▼▼ Italian. Casual Dining. $5-$18 **AAA Inspector Notes:** Delicioso! Italian cuisine includes traditional spaghetti, lasagna, manicotti, Marsala and scampi. Of course you'll find pizza and calzones as well. Be sure to save room for a piece of tiramisu or maybe a cannoli. Yum! **Features:** full bar, patio dining, happy hour. **Address:** 3509 S Broad St 35769 **Location:** Jct US 72 and SR 279, 1.5 mi sw; in The Village on Broad St Plaza. (L) (D) (◣)

### TRIPLE R BBQ
256/574-1620

▼▼ Barbecue. Casual Dining. $5-$20 **AAA Inspector Notes:** Antique and rustic decor is everywhere in this family-owned restaurant, including part of a 175-year-old cabin. Mouthwatering barbecue choices—chicken, ribs, pork, and catfish—are pleasing in sandwiches or on filling platters. Find limited dining on Sundays, open until 3 p.m. **Address:** 2940 Veterans Dr 35769 **Location:** Jct SR 35/US 72, 1.8 mi s. (L) (D)

## SELMA (E-3) pop. 20,756, elev. 139'
• Hotels p. 142 • Restaurants p. 142

Selma first drew national attention during the Civil War when it was second only to Richmond as an arsenal of the Confederacy. The Selma Ordnance Works manufactured one of the most powerful muzzle-loading cannons ever built as well as iron-clad ships, including the CSS *Tennessee,* remembered for its historic role in the Battle of Mobile Bay *(see Mobile p. 103).*

The destruction of Selma's shot and shell foundry, powder mill and navy yard became a Union imperative that was fulfilled when Gen. J.H. Wilson and his Union forces destroyed nearly two-thirds of the city during the Battle of Selma in April 1865. A monument to those who fought and died stands in the historic Old Live Oak Cemetery.

The five blocks of Water Avenue that survived the Civil War constitute one of the few remaining antebellum riverfront business districts in the South. Built

in 1837, the St. James Hotel at 1200 Water Ave. is a rare example of an early riverfront hotel. It served as quarters for Confederate officers as well as arsenal and foundry personnel. Later it hosted outlaw brothers Frank and Jesse James.

Selma's Old Town Historic District includes more than 1,250 historic structures. Among its notable residences is the two-story frame home of Sen. John Tyler Morgan, one of Alabama's most honored political and military leaders. In late March several private homes are opened to the public during The Historic Selma Pilgrimage.

In the 1960s battles of another sort took place in Selma, including a watershed event that forever linked its name to the civil rights struggle. On March 21, 1965, Martin Luther King Jr. began his legendary voting rights march at the Brown Chapel AME Church, 410 Martin Luther King Jr. St. Five days later, he and thousands of marchers arrived in the state capital to demand equal voting rights. The Selma to Montgomery National Historic Trail memorializes the 54-mile walk; it includes the Edmund Pettus Bridge and other landmarks that figured prominently in the demonstration.

A commemoration of the Selma-to-Montgomery march, the ▼▼ Bridge Crossing Jubilee is a festival of music, art, dancing and storytelling. The event attracts 30,000 people each year and takes place in early March.

**Selma-Dallas County Tourism and Convention Bureau:** 912 Selma Ave., Selma, AL 36701. **Phone:** (334) 875-7241 or (800) 457-3562.

**Self-guiding tours:** The Selma Windshield Tour leads drivers through a historic district that includes the Old Town and Water Avenue districts as well as Martin Luther King Jr. Street and Old Live Oak Cemetery. Brochures for this and other tours, including the 54-mile Selma to Montgomery National Historic Trail running between Selma's Brown Chapel AME Church and the state capitol in Montgomery, can be obtained at the Selma-Dallas County Tourism and Convention Bureau or at the visitor center, 132 Broad St.

**NATIONAL VOTING RIGHTS MUSEUM AND INSTITUTE,** 6 US 80E, is w. of the Edmund Pettus Bridge, a historic landmark from the Selma-to-Montgomery voting-rights march. The museum houses a variety of displays depicting the struggles and accomplishments of the voting-rights movement. **Time:** Allow 1 hour minimum. **Hours:** Mon.-Thurs. 10-4, Fri.-Sun. by appointment. Closed major holidays. **Cost:** $6.50; $4.50 (age 55+ and students with ID); free (ages 0-5). **Phone:** (334) 418-0800.

**OLD DEPOT MUSEUM,** 4 Martin Luther King St. at jct. Water Ave., is a restored brick railroad depot. Displays depict local history and include Civil War and African-American history exhibits. A railcar and caboose contain railroad exhibits, and a museum houses antique fire trucks. An archive reference room is available. **Time:** Allow 1 hour minimum.

**Hours:** Mon.-Fri. 10-4, Sat. by appointment. Closed major holidays. **Cost:** $5; $4 (ages 65+); $2 (students). **Phone:** (334) 874-2197.

**SELMA INTERPRETIVE CENTER,** 2 Broad St., is part of the Selma to Montgomery National Historic Trail and is located at the foot of the Edmund Pettus Bridge. Exhibits and a 25-minute film chronicle Selma's role in the civil rights movement. Pets are permitted on the trail only. **Hours:** Center open Tues.-Sat. 9-4:30; closed Jan. 1, Thanksgiving and Christmas. Trail open daily, year-round. Phone ahead to confirm schedule. **Cost:** Free. **Phone:** (334) 872-0509.

**STURDIVANT HALL,** 713 Mabry St., is a restored 1852 mansion that exemplifies neoclassic architecture. Furnished with period antiques, the building epitomizes the South's golden age of the 1850s. A display of antique dolls is noteworthy. **Hours:** Tues.-Sat. 10-4. Closed major holidays. **Cost:** $5; $2 (ages 6-18). **Phone:** (334) 872-5626. GT

**VAUGHAN-SMITHERMAN MUSEUM,** 109 Union St., is a 19th-century antebellum structure that has served as a Confederate hospital, a courthouse and a military school. The three-story Greek revival building houses Civil War artifacts, antique furniture, exhibits about local hospitals and politics, and various displays depicting Selma's history. **Hours:** Tues.-Sat. 9-4. Closed major holidays. **Cost:** $3; free (ages 0-11). **Phone:** (334) 874-2174.

COMFORT INN                              (334)875-5700
▼▼ Hotel $61-$91 **Address:** 1812 Hwy 14 E 36703 **Location:** Jct SR 14 and US 80 Bypass. **Facility:** 51 units, some efficiencies. 2 stories (no elevator), interior corridors. **Pool(s):** outdoor. **Activities:** limited exercise equipment.

HAMPTON INN                              (334)876-9995
▼▼▼ Hotel $99-$159 **Address:** 2200 Highland Ave 36701 **Location:** On US 80, jct SR 14. **Facility:** 60 units. 3 stories, interior corridors. **Terms:** 1-7 night minimum stay, cancellation fee imposed. **Pool(s):** heated indoor. **Activities:** hot tub, exercise room. **Guest Services:** valet and coin laundry.

> **AAA Benefit:** Members save 5% or more!

**WHERE TO EAT**

TALLY-HO RESTAURANT                      334/872-1390
▼▼▼ American. Fine Dining. $14-$30 **AAA Inspector Notes:** *Historic.* Dating from the early 1920s, the original log cabin was first a private residence, then a tea room and finally a hunting lodge. Now, the cabin serves as the entrance and half of the dining area of this eatery. Tremendous efforts have been made to preserve its history; look for original exposed beams and a collection of historic menus pinned to a wall. After savoring a choice from the excellent steak and seafood selection, consider the homemade zucchini bread or chocolate cheesecake. **Features:** full bar, happy hour. **Reservations:** required. **Address:** 509 Mangum Ave 36701 **Location:** 0.5 mi n on Summerfield Rd from jct US 80, just e, follow signs; in residential area.

**SHEFFIELD** (A-2) pop. 9,039

Sheffield is one of four cities making up the Muscle Shoals Area *(see place listing p. 129).*

**SOUTHSIDE** pop. 8,412

THE FISHERMAN                            256/442-5252
▼▼ Seafood. Casual Dining. $7-$19 **AAA Inspector Notes:** A ship crow's nest perched in the center of the dining room, surrounded by fish nets, lobster pots and nautical maps, will put you in the right mood for the various seafood selections on the menu. **Features:** full bar. **Address:** 1873 Hwy 77 35907 **Location:** I-59 exit 181, 6.5 mi s.

**SPANISH FORT** (H-2) pop. 6,798, elev. 158'

Spanish Fort sits on a hill directly opposite the bay from Mobile. True to its name, the site served as an active fort during the Revolutionary War, the War of 1812 and the Civil War. Preserved Civil War breastworks still are visible throughout town.

Meaher State Park is 1,327 acres of wetlands on Mobile Bay offering a boat launch, an elevated fishing pier, a nature trail and limited overnight camping facilities. The park is 2 miles west on US 90/98 (Battleship Parkway); phone (251) 626-5529. *See Recreation Areas Chart.*

**HISTORIC BLAKELEY STATE PARK** is 1.2 mi. w. on US 31, 1.2 mi. n. on Blakeley Way, then 3.2 mi. n. to 34745 SR 225. This 3,800-acre site was the scene of the last major battle of the Civil War; the engagement ended hours after the surrender by Gen. Robert E. Lee at Appomattox Courthouse in Virginia, April 9, 1865. Every other April (odd-numbered years), the battle is reenacted.

More than 10 miles of nature trails are offered. Bicycling, camping, fishing, hiking and horseback riding are permitted. **Hours:** Daily 9 a.m.-dusk. Closed Christmas Eve and Christmas. **Cost:** $3; $2 (ages 6-12). **Phone:** (251) 626-5581.

COURTYARD BY MARRIOTT MOBILE SPANISH
FORT/EASTERN SHORE                       (251)370-1161
▼▼▼ Hotel $89-$129 **Address:** 13000 Cypress Way 36527 **Location:** I-10 exit 35, just n, just e on Bass Pro Dr, then just n. **Facility:** 91 units. 3 stories, interior corridors. **Pool(s):** heated indoor. **Activities:** hot tub, exercise room. **Guest Services:** valet and coin laundry, boarding pass kiosk.

> **AAA Benefit:** Members save 5% or more!

FAIRFIELD INN & SUITES BY MARRIOTT MOBILE SPANISH
FORT/EASTERN SHORE                       (251)370-1160
▼▼▼ Hotel $79-$119 **Address:** 12000 Cypress Way 36527 **Location:** I-10 exit 35, just n, just e on Bass Pro Dr, then just n. **Facility:** 83 units. 3 stories, interior corridors. **Pool(s):** heated indoor. **Activities:** hot tub, exercise room. **Guest Services:** valet and coin laundry.

> **AAA Benefit:** Members save 5% or more!

## WHERE TO EAT

**BLUEGILL RESTAURANT**                    251/625-1998

▼▼ Seafood. Casual Dining. $6-$18 **AAA Inspector Notes:** *Historic.* A beloved local tradition for more than 50 years, this restaurant is noted for serving delicious regional seafood dishes. Located on the causeway, patrons will enjoy great waterfront views. Live music on weekends is an added bonus. **Features:** full bar, patio dining. **Address:** 3775 Battleship Pkwy 36527 **Location:** I-10 exit 30, 1.6 mi e on US 90. [L] [D] CALL [&M] [\]

**CALIFORNIA DREAMING**                    251/626-9942

▼▼ American. Casual Dining. $9-$30 **AAA Inspector Notes:** This full-service restaurant appeals to adults, particularly those with an appetite for innovative concepts in food. Revised weekly, the menu consistently incorporates sophisticated, cutting-edge California dishes with Pacific Rim influences throughout. Among house specialties are flatbread appetizers baked in a brick oven, sushi, sashimi and some vegetarian dishes. The wine list focuses primarily on California vintages. **Features:** full bar, patio dining. **Address:** 30500 State Hwy 181 36527 **Location:** I-10 exit 38, just ne; in Eastern Shore Centre. [L] [D] CALL [&M]

**FELIX'S FISH CAMP**                    251/626-6710

▼▼ Southern Seafood. Casual Dining. $11-$27 **AAA Inspector Notes:** Copious selections of fresh fish as well as some steak entrées are the order of the day at this weathered bayside restaurant. Be on the lookout for a possible gator appearance in the marshland. Advance reservations usually are needed for waterside window tables. **Features:** full bar. **Address:** 1530 Battleship Pkwy 36527 **Location:** I-10 exit 30 westbound, 0.8 mi w; exit 27 eastbound, 2 mi e. [L] [D] CALL [&M] [\]

**LAP'S GROCERY & GRILL**                    251/626-0045

▼▼ Seafood. Casual Dining. $8-$25 **AAA Inspector Notes:** Located on the causeway connecting Mobile and the east bay, this building is perched 20 feet up on wood poles. The establishment houses not only a restaurant but also a gift and convenience store, meat and seafood market, as well as a bait shop. Boat docking is available so whether you travel by land or water come enjoy the bayside view along with your meal. **Features:** full bar, patio dining. **Address:** 1595 Battleship Pkwy 36527 **Location:** I-10 exit 30, 0.5 mi w. [B] [L] [D] CALL [&M]

**POOR MEXICAN**                    251/621-7433

▼▼ Mexican. Casual Dining. $6-$15 **AAA Inspector Notes:** Traditional south-of-the-border fare is served in a bright and festive atmosphere. Daily lunch specials are offered. **Features:** full bar, patio dining, happy hour. **Address:** 30500 State Hwy 181, Suite 134 36527 **Location:** I-10 exit 38, just ne; in Eastern Shore Centre. [L] [D] CALL [&M]

## STEVENSON  (A-5) pop. 2,046, elev. 628'

**STEVENSON RAILROAD DEPOT MUSEUM,** 207 W. Main St. (SR 117), displays photographs, memorabilia and Civil War relics. During the Civil War this railroad junction and its depot were strategically vital to the South. **Time:** Allow 30 minutes minimum. **Hours:** Mon.-Fri. 8-3:30. Closed state holidays. **Cost:** Free. **Phone:** (256) 437-3012.

## SUMMERDALE  (I-2) pop. 862, elev. 112'

**ALLIGATOR ALLEY** is off I-10 exit 44, s. on SR 59, then e. on Couch Plant Rd., crossing over CR 71 to the entrance at 19500 CR 71. More than 400 alligators that were removed from the wild roam freely at this alligator farm. Visitors walk on an elevated boardwalk above 20 acres of swampland and may watch gators at feeding time. Captain Crunch is a

13-foot gator weighing more than 800 pounds. Also on view are ospreys, turtles, owls and other reptiles and amphibians.

**Time:** Allow 1 hour minimum. **Hours:** Daily 10-5, with feedings at 11, 1 and 4. Closed major holidays. Phone ahead to confirm schedule. **Cost:** $10; $8 (ages 4-12 and 65+). **Phone:** (251) 946-2483 or (866) 994-2867. [Ⅱ] [A]

## SYLACAUGA  (D-4) pop. 12,749, elev. 600'

Sylacauga (sil-a-COG-a), known as the Marble City, is built on a foundation of solid marble. This translucent white stone, in some places only 12 feet below the surface, has been used since the 1840s to construct notable buildings, one of which is the U.S. Supreme Court Building in Washington, D.C. Sylacauga's quarries also produce crushed and ground marble.

**Sylacauga Chamber of Commerce:** 17 W. Fort Williams St., P.O. Box 185, Sylacauga, AL 35150. **Phone:** (256) 249-0308.

**ISABEL ANDERSON COMER MUSEUM & ARTS CENTER,** 711 N. Broadway Ave., displays local archeological finds and historical artifacts as well as changing exhibits of works by Southeastern artists. **Hours:** Tues.-Fri. 10-5. Closed major holidays. **Cost:** Free. **Phone:** (256) 245-4016.

**QUALITY INN**                    (256)245-4141

▼▼ Motel $80-$180 **Address:** 89 Gene Stewart Blvd 35151 **Location:** Jct US 280, just s. **Facility:** 62 units. 2 stories (no elevator), exterior corridors. **Pool(s):** outdoor. **Activities:** exercise room.

[Ⅱ+] [🚲] [BIZ] [📶] [🔌] [🖥] [💳] / SOME UNITS [S🔒]

## TALLADEGA  (D-4) pop. 15,676, elev. 553'
• Hotels p. 144

In November 1813 Andrew Jackson led his men to the aid of a besieged pioneer fort and in the ensuing Battle of Talladega (tal-ah-DIG-ah) defeated a large band of Creek Indians. His route, the Jackson Trace, is designated by a marker 5 miles south of Talladega on SR 77.

Talladega was founded along the Appalachian foothills in 1834 and is one of the state's oldest inland towns. The city is home to the Alabama Institute for the Deaf and Blind and to Talladega College. Some of the largest motor sports events in Alabama are held at the Talladega Superspeedway *(see attraction listing).*

Six miles southeast of the city is the Waldo Covered Bridge, one of the state's oldest. The 115-foot bridge was built in the 1850s of a Howe and Queenspost combination design.

**Greater Talladega Area Chamber of Commerce:** 210 East St. S., Talladega, AL 35160. **Phone:** (256) 362-9075.

SAVE **INTERNATIONAL MOTORSPORTS HALL OF FAME AND MUSEUM,** off I-20 exit 173 or 168, at 3198 Speedway Blvd., next to the Talladega Superspeedway. This five-building complex houses more than 100 racing vehicles as well as racing-related memorabilia and a research library. **Time:** Allow 1 hour minimum. **Hours:** Daily 9-4. Closed Jan. 1, Easter, Thanksgiving and Christmas. **Cost:** $12; $8 (ages 7-17). Combination ticket with Talladega Superspeedway tour $16; $8 (ages 6-12). **Phone:** (256) 362-5002.

**TALLADEGA SUPERSPEEDWAY** is at 3366 Speedway Blvd. The stands of this 2.66-mile tri-oval track seat more than 108,000 and the 212-acre in-field accommodates thousands more. The 45-minute bus tour includes the pit area. The two major events at Talladega are the Aaron's 499 NASCAR Sprint Cup Race in May and the GEICO 500 NASCAR Sprint Cup Race in October.

**Hours:** Track tour daily 9-4; no tours race week and the week following race week. Closed major holidays. **Cost:** Tour $12; $5 (ages 6-17). Combination ticket with International Motorsports Hall of Fame and Museum $16; $8 (ages 6-12). **Phone:** (256) 362-2261, (877) 462-3342 or TTY (866) 472-8725. GT

---

HOLIDAY INN EXPRESS & SUITES          (256)362-7780
▼▼▼▼ Hotel $89-$119 **Address:** 240 Haynes St 35160 **Location:** Jct SR 77 and 21, just s. **Facility:** 73 units. 3 stories, interior corridors. **Pool(s):** outdoor. **Activities:** exercise room. **Guest Services:** coin laundry.
[◎↑] CALL [&M] [🛁] [BIZ] [HS] [📶] [🔌] [🖥] [▭]

## TALLADEGA NATIONAL FOREST  (C-5)

Elevations in the forest range from 578 ft. at Big Wills Lake to 2,407 ft. at Cheaha Mountain. Refer to AAA maps for additional elevation information.

---

Divided into two sections, Talladega National Forest consists of the Talladega division (235,000 acres) in eastern Alabama near the Georgia border and the Oakmulgee division (154,000 acres) just southeast of Tuscaloosa in west-central Alabama. Within the Oakmulgee Division is the 45,000-acre Oakmulgee Wildlife Management Area surrounding Payne Lake.

The Talladega Division contains two wildlife management areas: 39,320-acre Choccolocco in the northern portion and 31,943-acre Hollins in the southern portion. Also in the Talladega Division is the Pinhoti Trail system, which traverses the highest terrain in Alabama, providing a 145-mile hike through rugged but scenic country between the towns of Piedmont and Sylacauga. The trail connects through Georgia to the Appalachian trail by way of a road walk. Several miles of marked side trips and loop trails branch off the main trail. Also within this division is the Cheaha Wilderness, comprising 7,245 acres and the

9,200-acre Dugger Mountain Wilderness. Warden Station Horse Camp offers 30 miles of scenic trails. The 23-mile Kentuck ORV Trail is used by ATV enthusiasts. The Sylaward Mountain Bike Trail, near Sylacauga, provides 14 miles of hills and thrills.

The Talladega Scenic Drive runs through 23 miles of the forest, following the crest of Horseblock Mountain along SR 281. For more information contact the Talladega National Forest, Forest Service Office, 1001 North St. (SR 21N), Talladega, AL 35160; phone (256) 362-2909. *See Recreation Areas Chart.*

## THEODORE  (H-1) pop. 6,130, elev. 50'

GEM **BELLINGRATH GARDENS AND HOME** is e. off CR 59 at 12401 Bellingrath Gardens Rd. The 65 acres of cultivated and landscaped gardens that surround the 1935 mansion were first opened to the public in 1932 and patterned after the grand gardens of Italy, France and England by Walter D. Bellingrath, a pioneer in the Coca-Cola bottling industry. The Asian garden melds cultural concepts of landscape art. A grotto, conservatory and lake are nearby. The grounds bloom with more than 3 million lights and animated displays during ▼ Magic Christmas in Lights, held late November through late December.

The brick and wrought-iron mansion contains Bessie Morse Bellingrath's collection of furniture; Dresden, Meissen, Royal Doulton and Sèvres porcelain; china; crystal; sterling silver; and Oriental rugs. The Delchamps Gallery of Boehm Porcelain, in the center of the gardens, houses one of the largest public exhibits of Boehm porcelain in existence.

Daffodils and tulips blossom in February; azaleas flower mid-March to early April. Lilies, hydrangeas, fuchsia and delphinium bloom in the spring while tropical annuals dominate in summer. Cascading chrysanthemums appear in November and poinsettias highlight the gardens during the holiday season. Camellias, the state flower, bloom late November through March. More than 2,000 rose bushes bloom mid-April to November.

**Time:** Allow 1 hour, 30 minutes minimum. **Hours:** Gardens daily 8-5 (also 5-9, day after Thanksgiving-Dec. 31). House daily 9-4 (also 4-8, day after Thanksgiving-Dec. 31). Closed Jan. 1, Thanksgiving and Christmas. **Cost:** House and gardens $20; $12 (ages 5-12). Gardens only $12; $6.50 (ages 5-12). **Phone:** (251) 973-2217 or (800) 247-8420. GT [🍴]

## THOMASVILLE  pop. 4,209

COMFORT INN          (334)636-2000
▼▼ Hotel $89-$120 **Address:** 571 N Park Dr 36784 **Location:** On US 43, 0.6 mi s of jct SR 5. **Facility:** 50 units. 2 stories (no elevator), interior corridors. **Pool(s):** outdoor. **Guest Services:** coin laundry.
[◎↑] CALL [&M] [🛁] [BIZ] [HS] [📶] [🔌] [🖥] [▭]
/ SOME UNITS [S🛏]

# TROY (F-5) pop. 18,033, elev. 581'

**PIONEER MUSEUM OF ALABAMA,** 248 US 231N, is a multibuilding village depicting rural 19th- and early 20th-century Southern life. More than 18,000 artifacts are presented in the main building. Set on 35 acres are a corn crib and barn, a re-created covered bridge, a working smokehouse, an 1881 locomotive and 1894 depot, log cabins, a tenant house, a gristmill and general stores.

**Time:** Allow 1 hour minimum. **Hours:** Tues.-Sat. 9-5. Closed Easter, Thanksgiving and Christmas. **Cost:** $6; $5 (senior citizens); $4 (students in grades K-12). **Phone:** (334) 566-3597.

## BEST WESTERN TROY INN                (334)566-1585

Hotel
$80-$110

**AAA Benefit:**
Members save up to 20%!

**Address:** 100 Hunters Mountain Pkwy 36079 **Location:** On US 231, 0.5 mi s of jct US 29. **Facility:** 53 units. 2 stories, interior corridors. **Terms:** 2 night minimum stay - seasonal. **Pool(s):** indoor. **Activities:** exercise room. **Featured Amenity: full hot breakfast.**

## COURTYARD BY MARRIOTT TROY            (334)566-0540

Hotel $113-$128 **Address:** 115 Troy Plaza Loop 36081 **Location:** On US 231, 2 mi s of jct US 29. **Facility:** 90 units. 3 stories, interior corridors. **Pool(s):** outdoor. **Activities:** exercise room. **Guest Services:** coin laundry, boarding pass kiosk.

**AAA Benefit:**
Members save 5% or more!

## HAMPTON INN                          (334)807-5900

Hotel $109-$179 **Address:** 103 Troy Plaza Loop 36081 **Location:** On US 231, 2 mi s of jct US 29. **Facility:** 82 units. 3 stories, interior corridors. **Terms:** 1-7 night minimum stay, cancellation fee imposed. **Pool(s):** outdoor. **Activities:** exercise room.

**AAA Benefit:**
Members save 5% or more!

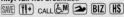
### WHERE TO EAT

## THE BRICK SPORTS GRILL               334/566-5382

American. Casual Dining. $5-$23 **AAA Inspector Notes:** Seek out the Vincent van Gogh reproduction wall mural at this local favorite in the heart of downtown. The cafe offers a nice variety of meat, poultry, seafood and pasta dishes to dine in or take out. A lighter lunch menu is offered on weekdays. **Features:** full bar. **Address:** 100 Emma Dr 36081 **Location:** 1.3 mi se of jct US 231/SR 10 and SR 87/167. **Parking:** street only.

## COUNTRY'S BARBECUE                    334/566-9940

Barbecue. Casual Dining. $6-$14 **AAA Inspector Notes:** Pulled pork, beef ribs, chicken, Brunswick stew and barbecue coleslaw represent some of the savory favorites offered at this eatery. **Features:** beer only, senior menu. **Address:** 100 Southland Village, US Hwy 231 36079 **Location:** Jct US 231/167; in Southland Village.

## HALF SHELL OYSTER BAR & GRILL         334/566-1254

Seafood. Casual Dining. $7-$18 **AAA Inspector Notes:** For more than two decades, this popular eatery with rustic décor offers a variety of seafood selections as well as beef, chicken and pasta. Live entertainment is generally scheduled for Thursday and Friday evenings. **Features:** full bar. **Address:** 119 Southland Village, Suite C 36081 **Location:** Jct US 231 and SR 87, just s.

## JULIA'S RESTAURANT                    334/566-5440

Southern. Casual Dining. $8-$17 **AAA Inspector Notes:** Feast on a bountiful buffet of Southern favorites at lunch, then come back to try the Thursday evening buffet and Friday night seafood offerings. Don't forget breakfast, either—the place opens at 6 am. **Features:** Sunday brunch. **Address:** 809 US Hwy 231 S 36081 **Location:** 1.3 mi s of jct US 29.

## MIKATA JAPANESE STEAK HOUSE & SUSHI BAR
334/566-1500

Japanese. Casual Dining. $11-$33 **AAA Inspector Notes:** The contemporary, simplistic Oriental décor and the demure, hospitable servers costumed in native attire embellish your Asian dining experience at this steakhouse and sushi bar. **Features:** full bar. **Address:** 1663 Hwy 231 S 36079 **Location:** On US 231, 3.1 mi s of jct US 29.

## MONARCAS MEXICAN RESTAURANT           334/808-9424

Mexican. Casual Dining. $7-$21 **AAA Inspector Notes:** All of the favorite south-of-the-border dishes are offered at this café with ethnic décor. Multiple wall-mounted TVs are found throughout for viewing while dining. **Features:** full bar. **Address:** 107 Hwy 231 N 36081 **Location:** 0.9 mi s of jct US 29, on access road.

## MOSSY GROVE SCHOOL HOUSE RESTAURANT
334/566-4921

Southern American. Casual Dining. $8-$21 **AAA Inspector Notes:** *Classic Historic.* Dating back to the 1850s, this former schoolhouse is shaded by large Spanish moss-covered trees that add Southern charm as well as explain the restaurant's name. Greetings are written on a large chalkboard, and antique tools are mounted on the rustic walls. Every table is automatically served hush puppies and a bowl of Great Northern beans. The simple menu lists seafood, steak, chicken and pork. **Features:** full bar. **Address:** 184 AL Hwy (SR 87) 36079 **Location:** Jct US 231 and SR 87, 2 mi s on Elba Hwy.

## RODEO MEXICAN RESTAURANT              334/770-0400

Mexican. Casual Dining. $5-$15 **AAA Inspector Notes:** This intimate family-run operation offers friendly service and typical south-of-the-border fare. **Features:** full bar. **Address:** 106 Troy Plaza St 36081 **Location:** On US 231, 2 mi s of jct US 29.

## SISTERS' RESTAURANT                   334/566-0064

Southern American. Casual Dining. $8-$17 **AAA Inspector Notes:** A daily rotating menu of Southern comfort foods is available for lunch. Thursday dinner is buffet-style, and guests will find a seafood buffet on Friday evenings. **Features:** Sunday brunch. **Address:** 13153 US Hwy 231 36081 **Location:** 5.5 mi s of jct US 29.

# TRUSSVILLE pop. 19,933

## COMFORT INN & SUITES                  205/661-3636

Hotel. Rates not provided. **Address:** 4740 Norrell Dr 35173 **Location:** I-59 exit 141, just e on Chalkville Rd, then just n. **Facility:** 66 units. 3 stories, interior corridors. **Pool(s):** outdoor. **Activities:** exercise room. **Guest Services:** valet and coin laundry.

(See map & index p. 54.)

HAMPTON INN BIRMINGHAM/TRUSSVILLE
(205)655-9777  **16**

WWWW **Hotel** $104-$109 **Address:**
1940 Edwards Lake Rd 35235 **Location:** I-459 exit 32, just e on US 11, then
just n. **Facility:** 78 units. 4 stories, interior corridors. **Terms:** 1-7 night minimum
stay, cancellation fee imposed. **Amenities:** video games. **Pool(s):**
outdoor. **Activities:** exercise room. **Guest Services:** valet laundry,
area transportation.

| **AAA Benefit:** |
| Members save 5% |
| or more! |

HOLIDAY INN EXPRESS HOTEL & SUITES     205/655-2700

WWW **Hotel.** Rates not provided. **Address:** 5911 Valley Rd
35173 **Location:** I-59 exit 141, just e on CR 10, then just s. **Facility:**
64 units. 3 stories, interior corridors. **Pool(s):** outdoor. **Activities:** exercise room. **Guest Services:** valet and coin laundry.

QUALITY INN     (205)661-9323

WWW **Hotel** $82-$87 **Address:** 4730 Norrell Dr 35173 **Location:**
I-59 exit 141, just e on Chalkville Rd, then just n. **Facility:** 60 units. 2
stories (no elevator), exterior corridors. **Pool(s):** outdoor. **Activities:**
exercise room. *(See ad p. 60.)*

## WHERE TO EAT

COSTA'S MEDITERRANEAN CAFE     205/655-9779

WW **Mediterranean. Casual Dining.** $9-$23 **AAA Inspector
Notes:** This popular Greek and Italian dishes up Mediterranean standards in huge portions. Fresh, warm garlic loaves accompany each entree. Among Italian offerings are baked ziti, baked
lasagna and veal parmigiana. Greek selections range from moussaka
and pastitsio to preparations of lamb, chicken and pork. Homemade
sauces are incomparable. **Features:** full bar. **Address:** 5891 Trussville Crossing Pkwy 35235 **Location:** I-59 exit 141, 0.5 mi w; in
plaza.  L  D

EL CAZADOR MEXICAN RESTAURANT     205/661-0904  **22**

WW **Mexican. Casual Dining.** $5-$13 **AAA Inspector Notes:**
Inexpensive lunch specials entice groups small and large to congregate at this popular, busy restaurant. The large bar area is great for
relaxing, while the dining room fills with the tempting aromas of traditional burritos, tacos and fajitas. **Features:** full bar. **Address:** 1930
Edwards Lake Rd 35235 **Location:** I-459 exit 32, just e on US 11,
then just n.  L  D

## TUSCALOOSA (D-2) pop. 90,468, elev. 225'
• Restaurants p. 148

In the Choctaw language *tusko* means "warrior"
and *loosa* means "black." By permission of the U.S.
Government, Creek Indians established the Black
Warrior Town in 1809; 4 years later it was burned
after a revolt. Defeated, these Native Americans
were forced to move westward, and new settlers
who came from South Carolina called their community Tuscaloosa (tus-ka-LOO-sa).

Tuscaloosa was the state capital 1826-46. Although the University of Alabama was established in
1831, it was not until 1896 that the efforts of educator Julia Strudwick Tutwiler resulted in the admission of women. Stillman College, founded in 1876,
offers liberal arts studies to 1,200 students.

Today's Tuscaloosa offers an array of cultural and
historic attractions, year-round events and many opportunities for shopping and dining. Several of the

city's graceful antebellum houses still stand, especially in the Druid City District near Queen City Avenue. The Mildred Warner House on Eighth Street is
a Georgian residence occupied 1820-1962.

Holt Lake *(see Recreation Areas Chart)* offers
many water sports, as does Lake Lurleen State Park
*(see Recreation Areas Chart).* Outdoor enthusiasts
and bird-watchers enjoy walking trails along the
Warrior River.

**Tuscaloosa Tourism & Sports Commission:** 1900
Jack Warner Pkwy., P.O. Box 3167, Tuscaloosa, AL
35403. **Phone:** (205) 391-9200 or (800) 538-8696.

**Shopping areas:** Tuscaloosa's major shopping
center is University Mall at McFarland Boulevard and
15th Street. It includes Belk, JCPenney and Sears.

**BATTLE-FRIEDMAN HOUSE,** 1010 Greensboro
Ave., is a Greek Revival mansion built in 1835. Late
19th-century chandeliers grace the parlor while other
furnishings date from the early 1800s. Plaster stucco
made to look like Italian pink marble distinguishes the
mansion's facade. **Time:** Allow 30 minutes minimum.
**Hours:** Tues.-Sat. 10-noon and 1-4. Closed major
holidays. **Cost:** $5. **Phone:** (205) 758-6138.

**CHILDREN'S HANDS-ON MUSEUM,** 2213 University Blvd., is in a three-story building containing a variety of participatory exhibits for children ages 2-12.
The interactive programs are designed to stimulate
children's curiosity and promote an understanding of
their world. Among the highlights are the Choctaw
Indian Village; Beaver's Bend, a developmental
center for preschoolers; a hospital; farmers market
and general store.

**Time:** Allow 1 hour, 30 minutes minimum. **Hours:**
Mon.-Fri. 9-5 (also Fri. 5-7:30), Sat. 10-4. Closed
major holidays. **Cost:** $9; $7 (ages 60+); $6 (ages
1-2). **Phone:** (205) 349-4235.

**TUSCALOOSA MUSEUM OF ART, HOME OF THE
WESTERVELT COLLECTION** is at 1400 Jack
Warner Pkwy. The museum celebrates American
history with its collection of more than 400 paintings
and sculptures by such American artists as Winslow
Homer, Hiram Powers, John Singer Sargent, James
Whistler and Andrew Wyeth; portraits of Thomas
Jefferson, the Marquis de Lafayette and George
Washington; Paul Revere silver; and Duncan Phyfe
furniture.

**Time:** Allow 1 hour minimum. **Hours:** Tues.-Sat.
10-6, Sun. 1-6. Closed Jan. 1, July 4, Thanksgiving
and Christmas. **Cost:** Donations. **Phone:** (205)
562-5280.

**UNIVERSITY OF ALABAMA** is at 801 Campus Dr.,
just w. of US 82; University Blvd. runs through the
campus. The college offers art galleries and a 50-acre
arboretum featuring native woodland, walking trails and
several themed gardens. The campus also contains the
Alabama Museum of Natural History, the Gorgas
House and the Paul W. Bryant Museum. An information
desk is in the Ferguson Center/Student Union.

Arboretum maps are available on-site. **Hours:** Arboretum open daily 8-dusk; closed Jan. 1, Thanksgiving and Christmas. Guided tours of the campus depart from the Welcome Center in the south end of the football stadium Mon.-Fri. at 8:15, 9:45 and 12:45 and from Room 203 of the Student Services Center Sat. at 8:15. **Cost:** Arboretum and guided tours free. Reservations are recommended. **Phone:** (205) 348-5666 or (800) 933-2262, ext. 3. GT

**Alabama Museum of Natural History** is in Smith Hall at jct. 6th Ave. and Capstone Dr., at the n.e. corner of the University of Alabama campus quadrangle. Exhibits include fossils and minerals from the Coal Age, Dinosaur Age and ice ages. Of special interest is the Hodges meteorite, which gained distinction in 1954 when it crashed through the roof of a Sylacauga house and struck the napping occupant, thus making it the only known meteorite to have hit a human. **Hours:** Mon.-Sat. 10-4:30. Closed major holidays. **Cost:** $2; $1 (ages 5-18 and 55+). **Phone:** (205) 348-7550.

**Gorgas House** is at 810 Capstone Dr. on the n.w. corner of the University of Alabama campus quadrangle. Built in 1829, the house was designed as a student dining hall. It is one of only four structures to have survived the burning of the university during the Civil War. In 1879 the house became the residence of Gen. Josiah B. Gorgas, Chief of Ordnance for the Confederacy and later president of the university. Now open for self-guiding and guided tours, the house contains some of Gorgas' personal effects. **Hours:** Mon.-Fri. 9-noon and 1-4:30. Closed university holidays. **Cost:** $2. **Phone:** (205) 348-5906. GT

**Paul W. Bryant Museum** is at 300 Paul W. Bryant Dr. across from the Coleman Coliseum on the University of Alabama campus. The museum illustrates the University of Alabama football tradition from its 1892 beginning to the present. There is a special exhibit about coach Paul "Bear" Bryant as well as photographs, audiovisual displays, a research library and a games film library. **Time:** Allow 1 hour minimum. **Hours:** Daily 9-4. Closed major holidays. **Cost:** $2; $1 (ages 6-17 and 60+). **Phone:** (205) 348-4668.

**CENTERSTONE INN** (205)556-3232
 Hotel $70-$300 **Address:** 4700 Doris Pate Dr 35405 **Location:** I-59/20 exit 76, just n. **Facility:** 59 units. 2 stories, interior corridors. **Terms:** cancellation fee imposed. **Amenities:** safes. **Pool(s):** outdoor. **Guest Services:** valet and coin laundry.

**COMFORT SUITES** (205)553-4343
Hotel $90-$130 **Address:** 3916 McFarland Blvd E 35405 **Location:** I-59/20 exit 73, just n. **Facility:** 75 units. 4 stories, interior corridors. **Pool(s):** heated indoor. **Activities:** exercise room. **Guest Services:** valet and coin laundry.
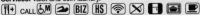    

▼ *See AAA listing this page* ▼

## COUNTRY INN & SUITES BY CARLSON
205/345-9999

▼▼▼▼ **Hotel.** Rates not provided. **Address:** 4801 McFarland Blvd E 35405 **Location:** I-59/20 exit 73, 0.5 mi se on US 82. **Facility:** 62 units. 3 stories, interior corridors. **Pool(s):** outdoor. **Activities:** exercise room. **Guest Services:** valet and coin laundry.

---

## DAYS INN SUITES OF TUSCALOOSA
(205)759-5000

▼▼ ▼▼ **Hotel** $65-$140 **Address:** 1201 Skyland Blvd E 35405 **Location:** I-59/20 exit 73, just e on US 82, then just n. **Facility:** 59 units. 2 stories (no elevator), exterior corridors. **Terms:** cancellation fee imposed. **Activities:** exercise room.

---

## FAIRFIELD INN BY MARRIOTT TUSCALOOSA
(205)366-0900

▼▼ ▼▼ **Hotel** $99-$129 **Address:** 4101 Courtney Dr 35405 **Location:** I-59/20 exit 71A, just s on SR 69; just e on Skyland Blvd; then just n. **Facility:** 63 units. 3 stories, interior corridors. **Pool(s):** heated indoor. **Activities:** limited exercise equipment. **Guest Services:** valet laundry.

**AAA Benefit:**
Members save 5% or more!

---

## HAMPTON INN TUSCALOOSA EAST
(205)562-9000

▼▼▼ ▼▼ **Hotel** $99-$169 **Address:** 6400 Interstate Dr 35453 **Location:** I-59/20 exit 77, just nw. **Facility:** 80 units. 3 stories, interior corridors. **Terms:** 1-7 night minimum stay, cancellation fee imposed. **Pool(s):** outdoor. **Activities:** exercise room. **Guest Services:** valet and coin laundry.

**AAA Benefit:**
Members save 5% or more!

---

## HAMPTON INN-UNIVERSITY
(205)553-9800

▼▼▼ ▼▼ **Hotel** $119-$169 **Address:** 600 Harper Lee Dr 35404 **Location:** I-59/20 exit 73, 2.8 mi nw on US 82 to Campus Dr exit. **Facility:** 101 units. 3 stories, interior corridors. **Terms:** 1-7 night minimum stay, cancellation fee imposed. **Pool(s):** outdoor. **Activities:** exercise room. **Guest Services:** valet laundry.

**AAA Benefit:**
Members save 5% or more!

---

## HILTON GARDEN INN TUSCALOOSA
(205)722-0360

▼▼▼ ▼▼ **Hotel** $129-$199 **Address:** 800 Hollywood Blvd 35405 **Location:** I-59/20 exit 71A, just s on SR 69, just e on Skyland Blvd, then just n. **Facility:** 122 units. 6 stories, interior corridors. **Terms:** 1-7 night minimum stay, cancellation fee imposed. **Amenities:** video games. **Pool(s):** heated indoor. **Activities:** hot tub, exercise room. **Guest Services:** valet and coin laundry.

**AAA Benefit:**
Members save 5% or more!

---

## HOLIDAY INN EXPRESS HOTEL & SUITES UNIVERSITY
(205)464-4000

▼▼▼ ▼▼ **Hotel** $134-$144 **Address:** 1120 Veterans Memorial Pkwy 35404 **Location:** I-59/20 exit 73, 1.8 mi n on US 82, then just e. **Facility:** 109 units. 4 stories, interior corridors. **Terms:** check-in 4 pm. **Pool(s):** outdoor. **Activities:** exercise room. **Guest Services:** valet laundry.

---

Keep a current AAA/CAA
Road Atlas in every vehicle

---

## HOTEL CAPSTONE
205/752-3200

▼▼▼ ▼▼ **Hotel.** Rates not provided. **Address:** 320 Paul Bryant Dr 35401 **Location:** I-59/20 exit 73, 2.6 mi w on US 82 to University Blvd E, just s on SR 215, then 1 mi n. Located on University of Alabama campus. **Facility:** 150 units. 3 stories, interior corridors. **Amenities:** safes. **Pool(s):** outdoor. **Activities:** exercise room. **Guest Services:** valet laundry, area transportation.

---

## LA QUINTA INN TUSCALOOSA
(205)349-3270

▼▼ ▼▼ **Motel** $55-$315 **Address:** 4122 McFarland Blvd E 35405 **Location:** I-59/20 exit 73, just sw on US 82. **Facility:** 122 units. 2 stories (no elevator), exterior corridors. **Pool(s):** outdoor.

---

## MICROTEL INN & SUITES BY WYNDHAM TUSCALOOSA
(205)553-4095

▼▼ ▼▼ **Hotel** $70-$150 **Address:** 1417 Veterans Memorial Pkwy 35404 **Location:** I-59/20 exit 73, 1.8 mi n on US 82 W, then 0.5 mi e. Located near University of Alabama. **Facility:** 59 units. 4 stories, interior corridors. **Amenities:** Some: safes. **Activities:** limited exercise equipment.

---

## SUPER 8
(205)758-8878

▼▼ ▼▼ **Hotel** $56-$250 **Address:** 4125 McFarland Blvd E 35405 **Location:** I-59/20 exit 73, just se on US 82. **Facility:** 58 units. 3 stories (no elevator), interior corridors.

---

## WINGATE BY WYNDHAM TUSCALOOSA
(205)553-5400

▼▼▼ ▼▼ **Hotel** $79-$289 **Address:** 4918 Skyland Blvd E 35405 **Location:** I-59/20 exit 76, just n. **Facility:** 91 units. 5 stories, interior corridors. **Amenities:** safes. **Pool(s):** outdoor. **Activities:** hot tub, exercise room.

---

## WHERE TO EAT

## BAUMHOWER'S OF TUSCALOOSA
205/556-5658

▼▼▼ Wings Burgers. Gastropub. $7-$10 **AAA Inspector Notes:** Hearty portions, good food and fun for the entire family can be found at this eatery. The friendly staff makes you feel right at home and the multitude of games helps keep everyone entertained. **Features:** full bar. **Address:** 500 Harper Lee Dr 35404 **Location:** I-59/20 exit 73, 2.8 mi nw on US 82, then exit Campus Dr.

---

## CHUCK'S FISH
205/248-9370

▼▼ ▼▼ Southern American. Casual Dining. $12-$30 **AAA Inspector Notes:** Popular with locals and college students for its premiere seafood and chic, relaxed ambience, this eatery offers hook-and-line caught fish entrées, sushi, steak and pizza. There is something for everyone's tastes. **Features:** full bar, patio dining. **Address:** 508 Greensboro Ave 35401 **Location:** Between University Blvd and 6th St; downtown. **Parking:** street only.

---

## THE CYPRESS INN
205/345-6963

▼▼ ▼▼ Seafood. Casual Dining. $12-$26 **AAA Inspector Notes:** This sprawling cypress wood lodge overlooks the Black Warrior River and has been a "must-visit" since 1984. Family recipes contribute heavily to the Southern-style menu, offering traditional items like fried green tomatoes, award-winning Alabama catfish, shrimp and grits, and the specialty, smoked chicken with white barbecue sauce. End your meal on a heavenly note with a slice of rich, smooth, peanut butter pie. It's so divine you'll want one now and another later! **Features:** full bar, patio dining, happy hour. **Address:** 501 Rice Mine Rd N 35406 **Location:** I-59/20 exit 73, 4 mi w on US 82 to Rice Mine Rd, then 1.3 mi s.

## DEPALMA'S ITALIAN CAFE                    205/759-1879

▼▼ Italian. Casual Dining. $6-$26 **AAA Inspector Notes:** Authentic Italian meals are served in a unique downtown setting. Watch as your New York-style pizza is hand tossed, or feast on one of numerous fresh pasta dishes. Inquire about the lasagna of the day, and leave room for the fabulous tiramisu. The white chocolate bread pudding is sure to elicit a wow! Closed Thanksgiving weekend. **Features:** beer & wine. **Address:** 2300 University Blvd 35401 **Location:** Corner of 23rd Ave and University Blvd; downtown. **Parking:** street only.

L   D

## DREAMLAND BAR-B-QUE                       205/758-8135

▼ Barbecue. Quick Serve. $7-$20 **AAA Inspector Notes:** *Classic.* "Ain't nothing like 'em nowhere" is the motto at this barbecue cafe. The menu is small, but that is okay because everybody comes for one thing: the ribs. Barbecue dishes come with white bread and a kicking sauce. Friendly Southern hospitality and a casual backdrop help make this place a favorite. **Features:** beer only, patio dining. **Address:** 5535 15th Ave E 35405 **Location:** I-59/20 exit 73, 0.5 mi e on US 82, then 0.8 mi n on Jug Factory Rd, follow signs.

L   D

## EPIPHANY FARM-TO-FORK                     205/344-5583

▼▼ Southern American. Fine Dining. $14-$25 **AAA Inspector Notes:** Owner and executive chef Tres Jackson regularly changes his eclectic farm-to-fork menu offerings so that diners have fresh seasonal foods from which to choose. **Features:** full bar, patio dining, happy hour. **Reservations:** suggested. **Address:** 519 Greensboro Ave 35401 **Location:** Between University Blvd and 6th St; downtown. **Parking:** street only.   D   🛍

## FIG                                        205/345-8888

▼▼ American. Casual Dining. $7-$11 **AAA Inspector Notes:** This casual café was named for the acronym "Food Is Good" and it definitely lives up to its name. The sandwiches on gourmet breads are yummy as are the soups and salads. **Features:** full bar, Sunday brunch. **Address:** 1351 McFarland Blvd NE 35406 **Location:** I-59/20 exit 73, 4.3 mi nw on US 82.   L

## FIVE BAR                                   205/345-6089

▼▼ American. Casual Dining. $12-$28 **AAA Inspector Notes:** This popular café is situated in the heart of the block between art galleries and quaint boutiques. The five concept is reflected in the menu, offering five entrées, five appetizers, five red and five white wines, and five signature cocktails. When the door opens at 5 pm enter into an open, airy space with exposed brick walls, dark wood floors, a wall-length mahogany bar, numerous chandeliers and stained-glass windows suspended from the ceiling. **Features:** full bar, patio dining, Sunday brunch. **Address:** 2324 6th St 35401 **Location:** Between Greensboro and 23rd aves; downtown. **Parking:** street only.

D   CALL 🛍M

## JIMMY JOHN'S GOURMET SANDWICHES            205/722-2268

▼ Sandwiches. Quick Serve. $4-$8 **AAA Inspector Notes:** Serving quickly-made, fresh sandwiches since 1983, this spot is a great place for an economical meal in a hurry. Dine in, take out or have it delivered. **Features:** patio dining. **Address:** 815 Lurleen Wallace Blvd S 35401 **Location:** Between Stillman Blvd and 8th St; downtown.   L   D   LATE CALL 🛍M

## KOZY'S                                     205/556-4112

▼▼▼ American. Fine Dining. $18-$33 **AAA Inspector Notes:** In what appears to be an unassuming white Cape Cod residential home, diners will find a fine dining bistro which has been touted as the best kept secret in Tuscaloosa. Although a bit off the beaten path, it is definitely worth the trip. The seasonally changing menu guarantees the freshest ingredients. **Features:** full bar, patio dining, Sunday brunch, happy hour. **Reservations:** suggested. **Address:** 3510 Loop Rd 35404 **Location:** I-59/20 exit 73, 1.1 mi n on US 82, then 2 mi e.   D   CALL 🛍M

## PEPITO'S GRILL                             205/391-4861

▼▼ Mexican. Casual Dining. $6-$16 **AAA Inspector Notes:** Diners can enjoy good Mexican food, festive décor, authentic music and friendly service at this popular eatery. **Features:** full bar, patio dining, happy hour. **Address:** 1301 McFarland Blvd NE 35406 **Location:** On US 82; 1.2 mi nw of Campus Dr exit.   L   D

## THE TIN TOP RESTAURANT & OYSTER BAR        205/462-3399

▼▼ Southern Seafood. Casual Dining. $11-$38 **AAA Inspector Notes:** This family-operated establishment offers fresh seafood prepared a variety of ways including dishes with a Cajun flair. Try the duck gumbo as it is the proprietor's signature creation. **Features:** full bar, patio dining, happy hour. **Address:** 2330 4th St 35401 **Location:** I-359 exit 2, 1.1 mi e.   L   D   CALL 🛍M

# TUSCUMBIA (A-2) pop. 8,423, elev. 453'
• Hotels p. 150

Tuscumbia is one of the four cities making up the Muscle Shoals Area *(see place listing p. 129).* During the 1830s a canal was built around the rapids of the Tennessee River, and the first railway west of the Alleghenies connected the canal landing to Tuscumbia. Big Spring, for which the town was originally named, is in a park at the south end of S. Main Street and produces 55 million gallons of cold spring water daily.

An unusual nearby attraction is the Key Underwood Coon Dog Memorial Graveyard, about 21 miles southwest of town off SR 247. In the Freedom Hills, a popular hunting area of the Cumberland Mountain Range, lie graves bearing touching epitaphs to prized coonhounds. A small park with picnic facilities adjoins the cemetery; phone (256) 383-0783.

▼ Plantation Christmas echoes the Old South through its late 1800s Christmas music and decorations as well as vintage ballroom dancing. The event takes place in early December at Belle Mont Mansion and refreshments also are offered; phone (256) 381-5052.

**Colbert County Tourism:** 719 US 72W, P.O. Box 740425, Tuscumbia, AL 35674. **Phone:** (256) 383-0783 or (800) 344-0783.

SAVE **ALABAMA MUSIC HALL OF FAME,** 617 US 72W, displays clothing, contracts and memorabilia associated with noted Alabama musicians. Included in the collection are Elvis Presley's original contract with Sun Records, the tour bus that belonged to the group Alabama and wax figures depicting Nat King Cole and Hank Williams.

**Time:** Allow 1 hour minimum. **Hours:** Tues.-Sat. 9-5. Phone ahead to confirm schedule. **Cost:** $8; $7 (students and senior citizens); $5 (ages 6-12). **Phone:** (256) 381-4417 or (800) 239-2643.

**BELLE MONT MANSION** is about 3.5 mi. s. on US 43 from jct. US 72, then just w. to 1569 Cook Ln. (CR 52). One of Alabama's first plantation houses, Belle Mont is highly reminiscent of Thomas Jefferson's Palladian style of architecture. Built about 1830, the U-shaped brick house is constructed around a courtyard. **Time:** Allow 1 hour minimum. **Hours:** Thurs.-Sat. 9-4, Sun. 1-5. Closed major holidays. **Cost:** $6; $5 (ages 65+ and military with ID); $3 (ages 6-18). **Phone:** (256) 381-5052.

SAVE **HELEN KELLER BIRTHPLACE AND SHRINE,** 300 N. Commons St. W., is a 10-acre site that includes Helen Keller's early home. Deaf and blind from the age of 19 months, Keller succeeded in graduating cum laude from Radcliffe College in 1904 and became a world-renowned author and lecturer. Keller's indomitable spirit led Mark Twain to liken her to Joan of Arc. The biographical play "The Miracle Worker" is presented mid-summer.

Also featured is the well pump where teacher Annie Sullivan taught Keller her first word, "water." The site's International Gardens feature gifts from 25 countries and a bronze bust of Keller. The Clearing contains native trees and shrubs, a log cabin and a gazebo. Surrounding the main buildings are magnolia and mimosa trees, roses, ivy, honeysuckle and 150-year-old English boxwoods. **Time:** Allow 30 minutes minimum. **Hours:** Mon.-Sat. 8:30-4. **Cost:** $6; $5 (senior citizens); $2 (ages 5-18). **Phone:** (256) 383-4066 or (888) 329-2124.

COMFORT INN & SUITES MUSCLE SHOALS/TUSCUMBIA
(256)248-0850
▼▼▼▼ **Hotel** $82-$119 **Address:** 5101 Hwy 43 S 35674 **Location:** Just n of jct US 72/SR 157 and US 43. **Facility:** 62 units. 3 stories, interior corridors. **Pool(s):** outdoor. **Activities:** limited exercise equipment. **Guest Services:** coin laundry.

MICROTEL INN & SUITES BY WYNDHAM TUSCUMBIA/
MUSCLE SHOALS
(256)248-0055
▼▼ ▼▼ **Hotel** $62-$150 **Address:** 1852 Hwy 72 E 35674 **Location:** Just w of jct US 72 and 43. **Facility:** 55 units. 4 stories, interior corridors. **Parking:** winter plug-ins. **Pool(s):** outdoor. **Activities:** exercise room. **Guest Services:** coin laundry.

# TUSKEGEE (E-5) pop. 9,865, elev. 459'

Named for the Creek Indian village Taskigi, Tuskegee was settled by the French, who built a fort nearby. The fort changed hands in 1763 when France surrendered the territory to England. It assumed a significant role when Andrew Jackson's troops used it to launch a campaign against the Creek Confederacy, ultimately leading to the tribe's defeat.

The seat of Macon County, Tuskegee is the home of Tuskegee University, formerly known as Tuskegee Institute. The school was designated a national historic landmark in 1965 for its great contributions in education for African-Americans. As head of the school's agricultural department, George Washington Carver's accomplishments helped the South's economic recovery after boll weevil infestations destroyed cotton farming. Today Tuskegee University enrolls some 3,000 students in liberal arts, education, business and engineering degree programs. Campus tours are available; phone (334) 727-8347.

**Tuskegee Area Chamber of Commerce:** 121 S. Main St., Tuskegee, AL 36083. **Phone:** (334) 727-6619.

**Self-guiding tours:** The Black Heritage Trail features many sites that figure prominently in African-American history. Brochures featuring a map and descriptions of the sites are available from the chamber of commerce.

**TUSKEGEE AIRMEN NATIONAL HISTORIC SITE** is at 1616 Chappie James Ave. The site honors the Tuskegee Airmen, the nation's first African-American military pilots, trained to serve in the Army Air Corps during World War II. A visitor center houses exhibits as well as a theater in which historical films documenting the history of the "Tuskegee Experience" are shown. Now a museum, the historic Hangar No. 1 also can be toured. There are wayside exhibits on the grounds and a scenic overlook. **Time:** Allow 30 minutes minimum. **Hours:** Daily 9-4:30. Closed Jan. 1, Thanksgiving and Christmas. **Cost:** Donations. **Phone:** (334) 724-0922. 🚻

**TUSKEGEE INSTITUTE NATIONAL HISTORIC SITE,** 1200 W. Montgomery Rd. (SR 126), on the Tuskegee University campus, honors Booker T. Washington, the school's first president. Originally established to train African-American teachers, the institute gained prominence in the early 1900s thanks to agricultural innovations developed by George Washington Carver. A walking tour includes the Booker T. Washington Monument and the Tuskegee University Chapel.

In the early years many students at what was then called Tuskegee Normal and Industrial Institute earned part or all of their educational expenses by helping to erect the school's first buildings. The present-day campus consists of more than 160 buildings on 1,500 acres.

**Note:** Walking tour maps are available at the Carver Museum and the National Park Service Headquarters at 1212 W. Montgomery Rd. **Hours:** Mon.-Sat. 9-4:30. Closed Jan. 1, Thanksgiving and Christmas. **Cost:** Free. **Phone:** (334) 727-3200.

**Carver Museum** is near the entrance to Tuskegee University (1200 W. Montgomery Rd.), part of Tuskegee Institute National Historic Site. It follows George Washington Carver's careers as an artist, teacher and scientist. His preserved laboratory depicts experiments that resulted in more than 300 extractions from peanuts and more than 100 by-products from sweet potatoes. Among his inventions were a paint formulated from Alabama clay and a synthetic marble made from wood pulp. The museum also has exhibits about the history of Tuskegee Institute. **Hours:** Mon.-Sat. 9-4:30. Closed Jan. 1, Thanksgiving and Christmas. **Cost:** Free. **Phone:** (334) 727-3200.

**The Oaks** is on W. Montgomery Rd. at Tuskegee University, part of Tuskegee Institute National Historic Site (1200 W. Montgomery Rd.); tours begin from the Carver Museum. This is the former home of Booker T. Washington, who lived here from 1900 until his death in 1915. Dignitaries who visited the home included presidents Howard Taft and Theodore Roosevelt as well as philanthropist Andrew

Carnegie. The restored 1899 Queen Anne-style house is furnished with period items and contains his study.

**Time:** Allow 30 minutes minimum. **Hours:** Guided tours are offered Sat. at 10, 11, 1 and 3. Closed Jan. 1, Thanksgiving and Christmas. Phone ahead to confirm schedule. **Cost:** Free. Reservations are required. **Phone:** (334) 727-3200. GT

## TUSKEGEE NATIONAL FOREST (E-5)

Elevations in the forest range from 260 ft. to 510 ft. Refer to AAA maps for additional elevation information.

Northeast of Tuskegee, the 11,255-acre Tuskegee National Forest permits hunting in season with an Alabama state license. The Bartram National Recreation Trail offers hiking through an 8.5-mile section and mountain biking through the 4-mile northern half of the trail in mostly secluded woodland. The forest also has a 14-mile loop horse and hiking trail and rustic primitive campsites. At the Taska Recreation Area located on US 29/80 a kiosk depicts Alabama's Black Belt Heritage Trail.

The district headquarters, off SR 186 near Tuskegee, is open Mon.-Fri. 8-4:30; closed federal holidays. For more information contact Tuskegee National Forest District Office at 125 National Forest Rd. 949; phone (334) 727-2652. *See Recreation Areas Chart.*

## VALLEY HEAD (B-5) pop. 558, elev. 1,026'

In the early 19th century Dr. John S. Gardner, a Methodist minister, attempted to transform the Valley Head region into a silk-producing center. He planted mulberry trees and imported silkworms, but the valley's unsuitable climate doomed the project to failure.

Gardner's home, Winston House, served as headquarters in 1863 for Union colonel Jefferson C. Davis from Kentucky, a cousin of the Confederate president. Local legend recalls a faux pas made by an old-timer who stumbled on the Union encampment. Upon hearing that the commander was Jeff Davis, the befuddled man cornered the colonel and asked, "Which pays you the most? Colonelin' the Bluecoats or Presidentin' the Confederates?" The home is now a bed and breakfast inn.

## VANCE (D-3) pop. 1,529, elev. 516'

**THE MERCEDES-BENZ VISITOR CENTER,** just e. off I-59 exit 89 at 11 Mercedes Dr., traces the German company's earliest days as a motorcycle manufacturer in the 1880s to its current standing as a world-renowned automaker. Vehicle displays include vintage automobiles, 1950s racing and sports cars, and concept models. Engineering techniques are highlighted with video presentations and exhibits.

The visitor center is located on the grounds of the company's only U.S. manufacturing plant. A 90-minute factory tour showing the assembly of M-Class sport-utility vehicles is available.

**Note:** The factory tour covers about 2 miles. **Hours:** Visitor center/museum Mon.-Fri. 8:30-4. Factory tours depart Tues. and Thurs. at 9, 9:15, 12:30 and 12:45. Closed major holidays. **Cost:** Visitor center/museum free. Factory tour $5. Ages 0-11 are not permitted on the factory tour, for which reservations are required. **Phone:** (205) 507-2252 or (888) 286-8762. GT

GREYSTONE INN & SUITES                (205)556-3606
▼▼▼ Hotel $68-$88 **Address:** 11170 Will Walker Rd 35490 **Location:** I-59/20 exit 89 northbound, 0.8 mi n on Mercedes Dr, 0.3 mi w, then just s; exit southbound, just s. **Facility:** 65 units, some efficiencies. 3 stories, interior corridors. **Activities:** exercise room. **Guest Services:** coin laundry.
CALL 👤M BIZ HS 📶 ✕ 🛏 📺 ▯ / SOME UNITS 🐾

## VESTAVIA HILLS  pop. 34,033

- **Hotels & Restaurants map & index p. 54**
- **Part of Birmingham area — see map p. 43**

DIPLOMAT DELI                     205/979-1515  58
▼▼ Sandwiches Deli. Quick Serve. $6-$20 **AAA Inspector Notes:** Locals come in for a hot sandwich, like a Reuben, muffuletta, or a New York double deli of hot pastrami and corned beef. Other favorites include the New York sub or a sausage sub. Soups are made fresh daily, along with famous Italian or chicken salad. Yummy desserts include roulage (a chocolate cake roll), chocolate silk pie, and homemade lemon ice box pie—mmm! On Sundays, only lunch is available. **Features:** beer & wine, patio dining. **Address:** 1425 Montgomery Hwy 35216 **Location:** I-65 exit 252, 1 mi n; in Park South Plaza. L D CALL 👤M 🐾

KLINGLER'S EUROPEAN BAKERY AND CAFE
205/823-4560  57
▼▼ German. Casual Dining. $6-$21 **AAA Inspector Notes:** The intimate bistro displays Old World charm with photos of Bavarian castles, a cupboard full of novelty beer steins and strains of oompa band music playing in the background. Traditional sausage platters offer bratwurst or knackwurst with German potato salad, sauerkraut and a brotchen (roll). A number of signature sandwiches include pecan chicken salad and homemade grilled pimiento cheese, both served on freshly baked breads. Display cases are full of luscious desserts baked on site. **Address:** 621 Montgomery Hwy 35216 **Location:** On US 31; between Kentucky Ave and Tyson Dr.
B L D

MISS MYRA'S PIT BAR-B-Q              205/967-6004  55
▼ Southern Barbecue. Quick Serve. $5-$12 **AAA Inspector Notes:** Miss Myra brings her Mississippi barbecue style to Alabama. She infuses her sauce with a bit of both states. Inside the store-like atmosphere, patrons need not be bashful about ordering, and she will come right out and ask how much they want. **Address:** 3278 Cahaba Heights Rd 35243 **Location:** I-459 exit 19 (US 280), just w, 0.8 mi n on Summit Blvd, then w; corner of Cahaba Heights Rd and White Oak Dr. L D CALL 👤M

MUDTOWN EAT & DRINK                 205/967-3300  54
▼▼ American. Casual Dining. $9-$29 **AAA Inspector Notes:** A visit to Mudtown is worth traveling off the beaten path to experience creative cuisine in a warm and cozy environment. Enjoy grilled fish with fried green tomatoes, or a BLT iceberg salad with bleu cheese crumbles and toasted pecans. The menu offers something for everyone. Limited seating may mean you have to wait, but it will be worth it. We'll be the first to tell you the parking is a bit of an adventure here, too. **Features:** full bar, patio dining, Sunday brunch, happy hour. **Address:** 3144 Green Valley Rd 35243 **Location:** Just e of US 280. L D 🐾

(See map & index p. 54.)

SATTERFIELD'S                              205/969-9690  56
▼▼▼▼ Continental. Fine Dining. $26-$40 **AAA Inspector Notes:** In the heart of historic Cahaba Heights, the loud, fun European bistro invites fine dining. Locally grown vegetables and nightly specials are built around the fresh seafood factor on a constantly changing menu. **Features:** full bar, patio dining, happy hour. **Reservations:** suggested. **Address:** 3161 Cahaba Heights Rd 35243 **Location:** US 280 exit Cahaba Heights Rd, 0.8 mi e. **Parking:** valet only. D

SEKISUI                                    205/978-7775
▼▼ ▼▼ Japanese Sushi. Casual Dining. $8-$31 **AAA Inspector Notes:** This contemporary restaurant presents a Japanese-themed menu with such items as chicken or beef teriyaki, lamb and strip loin, fried squid legs, baked green mussels, sauteed lobster and grilled stuffed trout, as well as combination entrees, tempura, kushiyaki and box dishes. The sushi bar turns out an extensive variety of seafood rolls, nigiri, sashimi and raw fish. **Features:** full bar, early bird specials. **Address:** 700 Montgomery Hwy, Suite 178 35216 **Location:** Just w of US 31 on Canyon Rd. L D CALL M

## WARRIOR (C-3) pop. 3,176, elev. 504'
• Part of Birmingham area — see map p. 43
RICKWOOD CAVERNS STATE PARK is at 370 Rickwood Caverns Rd. The caverns contain an interesting display of 260 million-year-old stalactites and stalagmites. Swimming is permitted. *See Recreation Areas Chart.*

Hours: Grounds daily 8 a.m.-dusk. Park facilities daily 10-6, Memorial Day-Labor Day. Cave tours daily 10-5, Memorial Day-early Aug.; Sat.-Sun. 10-5, Mar. 1-day before Memorial Day and early Aug.-Oct. 31. Last cave tour begins at closing. **Cost:** Park $1; free (ages 0-5). Cave tour $15; $6 (ages 5-11). Swimming $5; free (ages 0-3). **Phone:** (205) 647-9692. GT

## WETUMPKA (E-4) pop. 6,528, elev. 191'
The Coosa River flows through the middle of Wetumpka, creating opportunities for tourism and outdoor recreation. Nature trails, including the Swayback Ridge Trail, wind through the nearby Appalachian foothills, and Lake Martin—one of the world's largest man-made lakes—and Lake Jordan attract fishing and boating enthusiasts. These attributes help explain why Wetumpka also is known as "The City of Natural Beauty."

Upriver are remnants of the western rim of the Wetumpka Meteor Impact Crater, unusual rock formations rising out of the water. The 4-mile-wide crater was formed some 83 million years ago when a meteor more than 1,100 feet in diameter crashed into the Earth's surface; today's city sits right on the bull's-eye of what is said to be the greatest natural disaster in Alabama history.

Crossing the Coosa is the Bibb Graves Bridge, built in 1937 and one of only two known bridges south of the Mason-Dixon line that are suspended by reinforced concrete arches. Wetumpka also abounds in antebellum churches, historic homes and landmarks such as the Greek Renaissance-style Elmore County Courthouse. Annual events include the Coosa River Whitewater Festival in early June, Riverfest in mid-August and ▼▼ Christmas on the Coosa in December.

**Wetumpka Area Chamber of Commerce:** 110 East Bridge St., Wetumpka, AL 36092. **Phone:** (334) 567-4811.

AL HOLMES WILDLIFE MUSEUM is 5 mi. s. on US 231, 1.5 mi. e. on Redland Rd., then 1.5 mi. s.e. to 1759 Rifle Range Rd. The museum exhibits more than 1,200 species of mounted wildlife and offers a touch-and-feel board that allows visitors to feel different animal skins. **Time:** Allow 30 minutes minimum. **Hours:** Mon.-Fri. 9-4:30. **Cost:** $5; $3 (ages 2-12). **Phone:** (334) 567-7966.

FORT TOULOUSE-JACKSON PARK, 3 mi. w. of US 231 at 2521 W. Fort Toulouse Rd., is a wildlife sanctuary. Archeological excavations provided information for the reconstruction of forts Toulouse and Jackson. The 1825 Graves House Museum serves as an interpretive center. Nature trails, an arboretum, a Mississippian Native American mound and a boat ramp are featured. From April through November, living-history demonstrations are offered the first and third weekends of the month.

Hours: Grounds daily dawn-dusk. Graves House Museum daily 8-5. Closed Jan. 1, Thanksgiving and Christmas. **Cost:** $2; $1 (ages 6-12 and 65+). Camping fees $11-$14. **Phone:** (334) 567-3002. GT

JASMINE HILL GARDENS AND OUTDOOR MUSEUM is 4.5 mi. n. on US 231, then 2.5 mi. n. to  3001 Jasmine Hill Rd., following signs. The 20-acre garden is adorned with statues, fountains and other art objects from Greece and Italy. Of particular interest is a copy of the Temple of Hera in Olympia, Greece. Marble and bronze statues include replicas of "The Discus Thrower" and "Venus de Milo." Azaleas, Japanese cherry trees, magnolias, crepe myrtles, daylilies, dahlias, dogwoods and camellias are among the many plantings that provide bursts of color.

Time: Allow 1 hour minimum. **Hours:** Fri.-Sat. 9-5, Sun. noon-5, mid-Mar. to late June; Sat. 9-5, July-Oct. **Cost:** $10; $6 (ages 3-12). **Phone:** (334) 567-6463 for the gardens, or (334) 263-5713 for the office.

## WIND CREEK CASINO & HOTEL WETUMPKA
(866)946-3360

Contemporary
Resort Hotel
$109-$429

**Address:** 100 River Oaks Dr 36092 **Location:** I-85 exit 6, 13 mi n on US 231. **Facility:** Upon approach, one can easily spot the unique curved roof of this high rise structure. Luxurious contemporary appointments are found throughout. All rooms offer serene views of the natural riverside setting. 283 units, some two bedrooms and kitchens. 19 stories, interior corridors. **Parking:** valet and street only. **Terms:** check-in 4 pm, cancellation fee imposed. **Amenities:** safes. **Dining:** 4 restaurants. **Pool(s):** outdoor. **Activities:** hot tub, exercise room. **Guest Services:** complimentary laundry.

## WHITE HALL (F-3) pop. 858

**LOWNDES INTERPRETIVE CENTER,** 7002 US 80W, is part of the Selma to Montgomery National Historic Trail. It features exhibits honoring the men and women who participated in the March from Selma to Montgomery in 1965 during the civil rights movement. Recordings from participants and eye witnesses add to the experience. **Time:** Allow 1 hour minimum. **Hours:** Mon.-Sat. 9-4:30. Closed Jan. 1, Thanksgiving and Christmas. Phone ahead to confirm schedule. **Cost:** Free. **Phone:** (334) 877-1984.

## WILLIAM B. BANKHEAD NATIONAL FOREST (B-3)

Elevations in the forest range from 510 ft. at Lewis Smith Lake to 1,074 ft. at Penitentiary Mountain. Refer to AAA maps for additional elevation information.

In northwestern Alabama, the 180,000-acre William B. Bankhead National Forest encompasses lakes, limestone canyons and a natural bridge as well as the 25,986-acre Sipsey Wilderness Area. Recreation areas within the forest include Brushy Lake, Clear Creek, Corinth, Houston and Sipsey River. Hunting for deer, wild turkeys, squirrels and quails is permitted in season. The office in Double Springs is open Mon.-Fri. 7:30-4.

For more information contact William B. Bankhead National Forest, District Office, P.O. Box 278, Double Springs, AL 35553; phone (205) 489-5111. *See Recreation Areas Chart.*

## WINFIELD pop. 4,717

### HAMPTON INN WINFIELD
(205)487-1270

**Hotel** $109-$129 **Address:** 7005 State Hwy 129 35594 **Location:** US 78 exit 30, just s. Located in a quiet rural area. **Facility:** 63 units. 3 stories, interior corridors. **Parking:** winter plug-ins. **Terms:** 1-7 night minimum stay, cancellation fee imposed. **Pool(s):** outdoor. **Activities:** exercise room. **Guest Services:** coin laundry.

**AAA Benefit:** Members save 5% or more!

CALL

---

Pensacola beach

# Florida Panhandle

**Close your eyes and picture a sublime tropical setting. Visualize bottlenose dolphins leaping gleefully from frothy waves toward a glowing citrine sun. Imagine clusters of elegant sea oats bowing gracefully in the subtropical breeze, sprouting from sand dunes that guard alabaster-sand beaches. Envision walking into pillowy sand that gives way with each step and then into balmy aquamarine water that laps invitingly at your toes.**

Sounds quite idyllic, doesn't it? Open your eyes—you've just discovered Northern Florida, a place that evokes images of paradise. This is a part of Florida that doesn't contain crowded theme parks or high-energy nightlife, a Florida that many might not think of when planning a vacation to the Sunshine State.

## Nature's Theme Park

Miles upon miles of exquisite beaches are the main draw for North Florida. However,

St. Marks Lighthouse, St. Marks

you'll be delighted to find that the northernmost section of the state has a myriad of enjoyable attractions—museums devoted to art, science and Florida and African-American history; historic houses and buildings; parks, gardens, and even a cavern or two; and quaint historic districts—all topped off with a heaping spoonful of good, old-fashioned Southern hospitality and charm.

Southern accents ring out from such northern enclaves as Pensacola and Tallahassee. Tallahassee, Florida's state capital, was once populated by cotton and tobacco plantations; today it's home to state legislators and college students. The city boasts two state capitol buildings: the 1845 Greek Revival Historic Capitol, fronted by jaunty red-and-white-striped awnings, and the modern 22-story State Capitol built in 1977. Downtown's historic districts preserve the city's southern flavor with a wide variety of architectural styles, from early 19th-century Greek Revival and Federal to late 1800s Queen Anne and Gothic Revival to early 20th-century Art Deco and bungalows. Tallahassee's two large universities, Florida A&M University, founded in 1887, and Florida State University, established in 1851, lend an air of exuberance to the city, especially during football season.

Pensacola houses the Naval Air Station Pensacola, where visitors are inspired at the National Naval Aviation Museum, also home to the Blue Angels precision flying team. The Blue Angels engage in practice sessions at the museum most Tuesday and Wednesday mornings at 8:30 a.m. March through November; guests gaze upward in awe as these daredevils perform spellbinding maneuvers. Back on land and sea, Pensacola's beaches also awe with their talcum-soft sand and jade-green waters.

In March and April, students on spring break storm the shores in Panama City Beach for the college-goers' annual rite of passage. Slathered in sunblock, they toss Frisbees in skimpy beachwear among a crazy quilt of beach towels. Families can enjoy the sun and sea here, too, as well as attractions like Zoo World or a dolphin encounter cruise aboard the *Capt. Anderson III*. Pods of bottlenose dolphins are a common sight in Gulf waters.

If your meal anywhere in the state of Florida includes oysters, chances are those oysters came from North Florida. Apalachicola, to be exact, billed as the Oyster Capital of the World, is where 90 percent of the state's oysters are harvested. This little fishing town on the Forgotten Coast lies on the waterfront, where you'll also find charming Victorian inns, quaint antique and gift shops and plenty of fishing.

## Recreation

North Florida's polished white-quartz sand beaches and emerald-green waters invite lovers of the sand and ocean to swim, sun, build sand castles and toss volleyballs and Frisbees. But if you're not the beachgoer type, or simply want to explore the rest of the Panhandle's al fresco offerings, you'll find this part of Florida an outdoorsman's dream.

At the 571,088-acre Apalachicola National Forest, towering pine trees and sturdy oaks rise from dense thickets of palmettos, accented by myriad rivers, lakes, streams and ponds. Fresh-air activities include kayaking, boating, fishing, swimming, hiking, cycling, camping, horseback riding and hunting. Take a leisurely canoe trip on Kennedy Creek into a picturesque cypress swamp or cast for trophy-size largemouth bass as well as catfish, crappie and sunfish in the forest's lakes and rivers.

A large portion of Gulf Islands National Seashore resides in Florida. Spend a tranquil day at the seashore or go bicycle riding, primitive camping, snorkeling, swimming, fishing, hiking, beachcombing, bird-watching, wildlife viewing and boating. Pack a picnic and pedal one of nine hiking trails at Naval Live Oaks, including a 40-mile bike loop.

The beach at Santa Rosa Sound with its calm, shallow waters is a relaxing option for families with young children. The water at the seashore is fine for swimmers, especially at beaches specially designated for swimming, including Johnson Beach, Langdon Beach and Opal Beach. Perdido Key has everything you need for a day at the beach, including a lifeguard, boardwalk trails and picnic tables. The national seashore also is famous for its numerous fishing possibilities. A license is required for most types of fishing in Florida; phone (888) 347-4356 to apply.

Panama City Beach is another hot spot for anglers, with blue marlin, cobia, red snapper, pompano and trout readily chomping at the bait. Or don scuba gear and dive into the Gulf several miles offshore, where you can ogle exotic sea life in the area's 50 artificial reefs.

If you prefer your exertion on the easy to moderate end of the spectrum, catch a breeze while bicycling on the relatively flat Florida terrain. The town of White Springs is near 15 trails, including the looping Gar Pond Trail and the Big Shoals Trail, which passes one of the state's scant white-water stretches on the Suwannee River. Looking for another lazy way to pass the day? Grab a tube and go river floating at Coldwater Creek in Blackwater River State Forest.

**Apalachicola National Forest**

# Historic Timeline

| 1513 | Juan Ponce de León, searching for the Fountain of Youth, sails around Florida and lands near the future site of St. Augustine. |
| 1565 | Spanish explorer Pedro Menéndez de Aviles destroys a French Huguenot colony and establishes St. Augustine. |
| 1763 | The First Treaty of Paris cedes Florida to England; the 1783 Second Treaty of Paris returns Florida to Spain. |
| 1817 | Gen. Andrew Jackson comes to punish the Native Americans for attacking the settlers, thus instigating the First Seminole War. |
| 1819 | Spain sells Florida to the United States. |
| 1845 | Florida achieves statehood. |
| 1958 | The first U.S. satellite launches from Cape Canaveral; the National Aeronautics and Space Administration is created. |
| 1971 | Walt Disney World Resort opens, leading the way for new attractions and drawing millions of tourists to central Florida. |
| 1986 | The space shuttle *Challenger* explodes seconds after liftoff, killing all seven aboard. |
| 2004 | In an unprecedented hurricane season, four storms ranging from Category 2 to Category 4 strike Florida within 6 weeks. |
| 2011 | The space shuttle *Atlantis* launches from Kennedy Space Center, ending the space shuttle program. |

# What To Pack

| Temperature Averages Maximum/Minimum | JANUARY | FEBRUARY | MARCH | APRIL | MAY | JUNE | JULY | AUGUST | SEPTEMBER | OCTOBER | NOVEMBER | DECEMBER |
|---|---|---|---|---|---|---|---|---|---|---|---|---|
| **Apalachicola** | 62/43 | 65/46 | 70/51 | 76/58 | 83/65 | 88/72 | 90/74 | 89/74 | 87/71 | 80/61 | 72/52 | 65/45 |
| **Fort Walton Beach** | 61/37 | 65/40 | 71/46 | 78/51 | 84/60 | 90/68 | 91/71 | 91/71 | 88/66 | 80/54 | 72/46 | 64/39 |
| **Panama City Beach** | 62/39 | 65/41 | 71/47 | 77/53 | 83/61 | 88/68 | 89/71 | 89/71 | 87/67 | 79/55 | 71/47 | 64/40 |
| **Pensacola** | 61/43 | 64/45 | 70/52 | 76/58 | 83/66 | 89/72 | 91/75 | 90/74 | 87/70 | 79/60 | 70/51 | 63/45 |
| **Perry** | 67/40 | 70/44 | 76/48 | 81/53 | 86/61 | 89/68 | 90/70 | 90/70 | 87/67 | 81/57 | 75/50 | 68/42 |
| **Tallahassee** | 64/40 | 67/42 | 74/48 | 80/53 | 87/62 | 91/70 | 92/73 | 92/73 | 89/69 | 81/57 | 73/48 | 66/42 |

From the records of The Weather Channel Interactive, Inc.

# Good Facts To Know

## ABOUT THE STATE

**POPULATION:** 18,801,310.

**AREA:** 65,758 square miles; ranks 22nd.

**CAPITAL:** Tallahassee.

**HIGHEST POINT:** 345 ft., Walton County.

**LOWEST POINT:** Sea level, Atlantic Ocean.

**TIME ZONE(S):** Eastern/Central. DST.

## GAMBLING

**MINIMUM AGE FOR GAMBLING:** 18 for pari-mutuel betting; 21 for casino gambling.

## REGULATIONS

**TEEN DRIVING LAWS:** There are no passenger restrictions. Driving is not permitted 11 p.m.-6 a.m. for age 16 and 1 a.m.-5 a.m. for age 17. The minimum age for an unrestricted driver's license is 18. For more information about Florida driver's license regulations phone (850) 617-2000.

**SEAT BELT/CHILD RESTRAINT LAWS:** Seat belts are required for driver and front-seat passengers ages 18 and over. Seat belt or child restraint is required for children ages 6-17. Appropriate child restraints are required for children under age 6. AAA recommends seat belts/child restraints for driver and all passengers.

**CELL PHONE RESTRICTIONS:** Text messaging is prohibited for all drivers.

**HELMETS FOR MOTORCYCLISTS:** Required for riders under 21. Persons 21 and over may ride without helmets only if they can show proof they are covered by a medical insurance policy.

**RADAR DETECTORS:** Permitted.

**MOVE OVER LAW:** Driver is required to slow down and vacate the lane nearest stopped police, fire and rescue vehicles using audible or flashing signals. Law also requires drivers to move over for tow truck drivers assisting motorists.

**FIREARMS LAWS:** Vary by state and/or county. Contact the Florida Department of Agriculture, Division of Licensing, P.O. Box 6687, Tallahassee, FL 32314-6687; phone (850) 245-5691.

**SPECIAL REGULATIONS:** All motorists who drive trucks or pull trailers must stop at road guard agricultural inspection stations. Recreational vehicles and private passenger vehicles without trailers are not required to stop at these stations.

Permanently disabled persons with "handicapped" license plates from any state receive special parking privileges in Florida.

## HOLIDAYS

**HOLIDAYS:** Jan. 1 ▪ Martin Luther King Jr. Day, Jan. (3rd Mon.) ▪ Memorial Day, May (4th Mon.) ▪ July 4 ▪ Labor Day, Sept. (1st Mon.) ▪ Veterans Day, Nov. 11 ▪ Thanksgiving, Nov. (4th Thurs.), and following Fri. ▪ Christmas, Dec. 25.

## MONEY

**TAXES:** Florida's statewide sales tax is 6 percent, with counties allowed to impose additional levies. There is a tax on accommodations and meals, and counties have the option to add a tourist impact tax and a tourist development tax of varying levels.

## VISITOR INFORMATION

**INFORMATION CENTERS:** State welcome centers can be found just south of the Florida/Alabama border on US 231 at Campbellton ▪ south of the Florida/Georgia border off I-75 near Jennings ▪ near the Florida/Alabama border off I-10, 16 miles west of Pensacola ▪ south of the Florida/Georgia border off I-95 near Yulee ▪ and in Tallahassee at the Florida State Capitol.

**SPECIAL NOTE:** Lovebugs are very sticky insects that swarm during the day in April, May, September and October, clogging car radiators, smearing windshields and corroding a car's finish.

**FURTHER INFORMATION FOR VISITORS:**
Visit Florida Inc.
2540 W. Executive Center Cir., Suite 200
Tallahassee, FL 32301
(850) 488-5607 (Main Office)
(866) 972-5280 (Information specialist)
(850) 488-6167 (Florida Capital Welcome Center)

**NATIONAL FOREST INFORMATION:**
National Forests in Florida
325 John Knox Rd., Suite F-100
Tallahassee, FL 32303-4160
(850) 523-8500 (Main Office)
(877) 444-6777 (Reservations)
(850) 523-8503 (Receptionist)

**FISHING AND HUNTING REGULATIONS:**
Florida Fish and Wildlife Conservation Commission
620 S. Meridian St.
Tallahassee, FL 32399-1600
(850) 488-4676 (Main Office)
(888) 347-4356 (fishing licenses)
(850) 488-3641, ext. 7 (hunting licenses)
(850) 488-3641 (fishing and hunting licenses)

**RECREATION INFORMATION:**
Florida Department of Environmental Protection
3900 Commonwealth Blvd., Mail Station 535
Tallahassee, FL 32399-3000
(850) 245-2157

# Florida Panhandle Annual Events

Please call ahead to confirm event details.

## JANUARY

- Apalachicola Oyster Cook-Off / Apalachicola 850-653-9419
- Polar Bear Plunge Pensacola Beach 850-932-1500
- Tallahassee Fitness Festival Tallahassee 850-222-0200

## FEBRUARY

- Steinhatchee Fiddler Crab Festival / Steinhatchee 352-356-8185
- Battle of Olustee Re-enactment / Sanderson 386-397-4478
- Seven Days of Opening Nights / Tallahassee 850-644-6500

## MARCH

- Smokin' in the Square BBQ Cookoff / Pensacola 850-995-0060
- Gulf Coast Renaissance Faire / Pensacola 877-429-8462
- Natural Bridge Battle Re-enactment Tallahassee 850-922-6007

## APRIL

- Musical Echoes Flute Festival / Fort Walton Beach 850-243-4405
- Seabreeze Jazz Festival Panama City Beach 800-595-4849
- Wakulla Wildlife Festival Wakulla Springs 850-561-7286

## MAY

- Fiesta of Five Flags Celebration and Boat Parade / Pensacola 850-433-6512
- Florida Folk Festival White Springs 877-635-3655
- Historic Apalachicola Home and Garden Tour Apalachicola 850-653-9419

## JUNE

- Panhandle Watermelon Festival / Chipley 850-638-4157
- Emerald Coast Blue Marlin Classic / Destin 850-267-6168
- Bands on the Blackwater Milton 850-983-5466

## JULY

- Salute to Freedom Panama City 850-235-1159
- Pensacola Beach Air Show Pensacola Beach 800-635-4803
- Celebrate America Tallahassee 800-628-2866

## AUGUST

- FAMU Grape Harvest Festival / Tallahassee 850-599-3996
- Bushwacker Festival and 5K Gulf Breeze 850-434-1234
- Emerald Coast Boat Week Fort Walton Beach 850-651-7131

## SEPTEMBER

- Emerald Coast Beer Festival / Pensacola 850-438-1781
- Navarre Beach Sand Sculpting Festival / Navarre 239-634-4564
- Pensacola Seafood Festival / Pensacola 850-433-6512

## OCTOBER

- Boggy Bayou Mullet Festival / Niceville 850-279-6436
- Stephen Foster Quilt Show and Sale / White Springs 386-397-7009
- Pensacola Interstate Fair Pensacola 850-944-4500

## NOVEMBER

- Florida Seafood Festival Apalachicola 888-653-8100
- Great Gulfcoast Arts Festival / Pensacola 850-434-1234
- Emerald Coast Cruizin' Panama City Beach 662-587-9572

## DECEMBER

- Holiday on the Harbor Destin Boat Parade Destin / 850-837-6611
- Winter Festival--A Celebration of Lights, Music and the Arts Tallahassee 850-891-3866
- Grand Lagoon Christmas Boat Parade / Panama City Beach / 850-628-1740

Florida State University,
Tallahassee

Big Lagoon State Park,
Pensacola

Gulf World Marine Park,
Panama City Beach

Welcome to
FLORIDA
THE SUNSHINE STATE

Florida welcome sign

St. Andrews State Park, Panama City Beach

Index: **Great Experience for Members**

AAA editor's picks of exceptional note

National Naval
Aviation Museum

Alfred B. Maclay
Gardens State Park

Edward Ball Wakulla
Springs State Park

See Orientation map on p. 168 for corresponding grid coordinates, if applicable.

**Pensacola (B-2)**
National Naval Aviation Museum *(See p. 196.)*

**Tallahassee (B-5)**
Alfred B. Maclay Gardens State Park
*(See p. 206.)*

**Wakulla Springs (C-5)**
Edward Ball Wakulla Springs State Park
*(See p. 214.)*

# Keep Your Children Safe in the Car

AAA has teamed up with two beloved HarperCollins Children's Books characters,

 and  ,

to promote child passenger safety.

For car seat guidelines, visit
**SafeSeats4Kids.AAA.com**
and go to SeatCheck.org
or call 866-SEAT-CHECK (732-8243)
for installation information.

In Canada, visit the Child Safety section
of Transport Canada's website: tc.gc.ca

 **Remember—car seats, booster seats
and seat belts save lives**

FANCY NANCY © 2014 by J. O'Connor and R.P. Glasser. FLAT STANLEY ® is
a registered trademark of the Trust u/w/o Richard C. Brown f/b/o Duncan Brown.

# Florida Panhandle
## Atlas Section

**FLORIDA PANHANDLE**

Tallahassee

### ROADS/HIGHWAYS

| | |
|---|---|
| | INTERSTATE |
| | CONTROLLED ACCESS |
| | CONTROLLED ACCESS TOLL |
| | TOLL ROAD |
| | PRIMARY DIVIDED |
| | PRIMARY UNDIVIDED |
| | SECONDARY DIVIDED |
| | SECONDARY UNDIVIDED |
| | LOCAL DIVIDED |
| | LOCAL UNDIVIDED |
| | UNPAVED ROAD |
| | UNDER CONSTRUCTION |
| | TUNNEL |
| | PEDESTRIAN ONLY |
| | AUTO FERRY |
| | PASSENGER FERRY |
| | SCENIC BYWAY |
| 10 | DISTANCE BETWEEN MARKERS |
| | EXIT NUMBER–FREE/TOLL |
| | INTERCHANGE FULL/PARTIAL |
| | WELCOME CENTER |
| | REST AREA/ SERVICE CENTER |

### BOUNDARIES

| | |
|---|---|
| | INTERNATIONAL |
| | STATE |
| | COUNTY |
| | TIME ZONE |
| | CONTINENTAL DIVIDE |

### ROAD SHIELDS

| | |
|---|---|
| 95 95 | INTERSTATE/BUSINESS |
| 22 22 22 | U.S./STATE/COUNTY |
| 227 | FOREST/INDIAN |
| | TRANS- CANADA |
| 1 | PROVINCIAL AUTOROUTE |
| 1 | MEXICO |
| | HISTORIC ROUTE 66 |
| VT 41 | REFERENCE PAGE INDICATOR |

### AREAS OF INTEREST

| | |
|---|---|
| | INDIAN |
| | MILITARY |
| | PARK |
| | FOREST |
| | GRASSLANDS |
| | HISTORIC |
| ✈ | INT'L./REGIONAL AIRPORT |
| | INCORPORATED CITY |

### POINTS OF INTEREST

| | |
|---|---|
| ○ | TOWN |
| ⊛ | NATIONAL CAPITAL |
| ⊛ | STATE/PROVINCIAL CAPITAL |
| ▣ | AAA/CAA CLUB LOCATION |
| ■ | FEATURE OF INTEREST |
| ⌂ | COLLEGE/UNIVERSITY |
| ⚐ | CAMPGROUND INFORMATION PROVIDED BY WOODALL'S® |
| ⊚ | CUSTOMS STATION |
| | HISTORIC |
| ⚓ | LIGHTHOUSE |
| ⛪ | MONUMENT/MEMORIAL |
| ⚑ | STATE/PROVINCIAL PARK |
| ⚓ | NATIONAL WILDLIFE REFUGE |
| ⛷ | SKI AREA |
| ○ | SPORTS COMPLEX |
| | DAM |

**CITIES/TOWNS** are color-coded by size, showing where to find AAA Approved and Diamond rated lodgings or restaurants listed in the AAA TourBook guides and on AAA.com:

- ● Red - major destinations and capitals; many listings
- ● Black - destinations; some listings
- ● Grey - no listings

Use driving maps from the AAA Road Atlas to plan your itinerary and route. Purchase the complete 2015 AAA Road Atlas at participating AAA/CAA offices, retail stores and online booksellers.

ROAD
Atlas
2015
AAA
Travel With Someone You Trust
CANADA
UNITED STATES
MEXICO

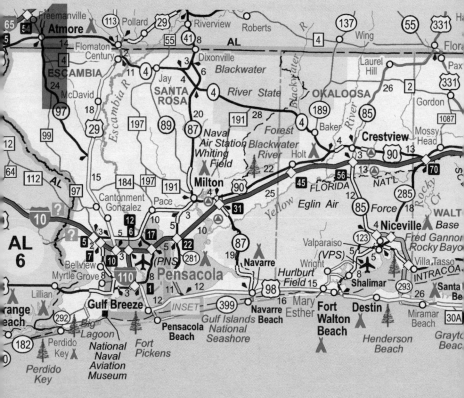

*of*

*Gulf*

# FLORIDA
# PANHANDL

# FLORIDA

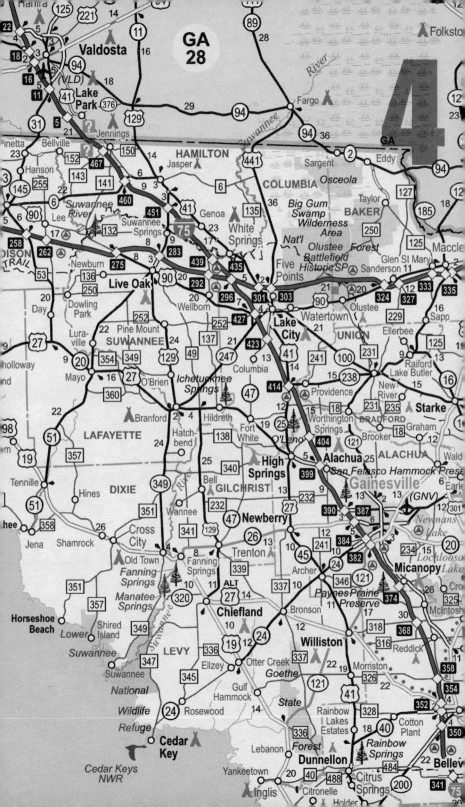

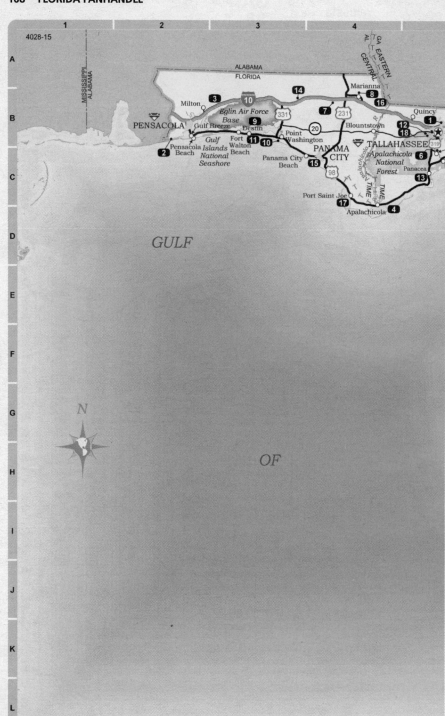

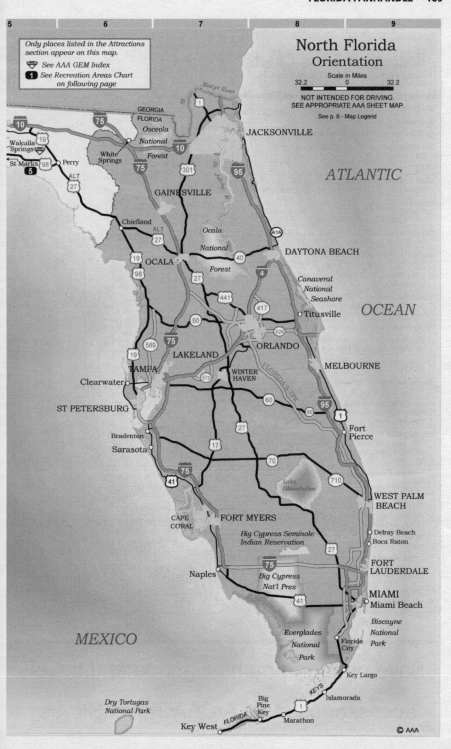

5   6   7   8   9

Only places listed in the Attractions
section appear on this map.
See AAA GEM Index
1   See Recreation Areas Chart
on following page

# North Florida
## Orientation

Scale in Miles
32.2      0      32.2

NOT INTENDED FOR DRIVING.
SEE APPROPRIATE AAA SHEET MAP.

See p. 6 - Map Legend

*Marys River*

GEORGIA
FLORIDA
*Osceola*

**JACKSONVILLE**

10

*ATLANTIC*

Wakulla
Springs
19
St Marks
5
98   Perry
ALT
27

White
Springs

*National*

*Forest*

St. Johns R.

301

95

**GAINESVILLE**

Chiefland

ALT
27

*Ocala*

*National*

A1A

**DAYTONA BEACH**

19
OCALA
98

27

*Forest*

40

4

*Canaveral
National
Seashore*

441

417

• Titusville

*OCEAN*

50

528

75
589

**LAKELAND**

**ORLANDO**

**MELBOURNE**

19

**TAMPA**

Clearwater

570

WINTER
HAVEN

FLORIDA'S TPK.

**ST PETERSBURG**

60

95

60

Bradenton

27

1

Sarasota

17

70

Fort
Pierce

75
41

*Lake
Okeechobee*

710

**WEST PALM
BEACH**

CAPE
CORAL

**FORT MYERS**

*Big Cypress Seminole
Indian Reservation*

• Delray Beach
• Boca Raton

27

**FORT
LAUDERDALE**

75

Naples

*Big Cypress
Nat'l Pres*

41

**MIAMI**
Miami Beach

*Biscayne
National*

*MEXICO*

*Everglades*

*National*

*Park*

Florida
City

*Park*

Key Largo

*Dry Tortugas
National Park*

Big
Pine
Key

KEYS

1   Islamorada

Key West

FLORIDA

Marathon

© AAA

# Recreation Areas Chart

The map location numerals in column 2 show an area's location on the preceding map.

| | MAP LOCATION | CAMPING | PICNICKING | HIKING TRAILS | BOATING | BOAT RAMP | BOAT RENTAL | FISHING | SWIMMING | PETS ON LEASH | BICYCLE TRAILS | SKIN/SCUBA | VISITOR CENTER | LODGE/CABINS | FOOD SERVICE |
|---|---|---|---|---|---|---|---|---|---|---|---|---|---|---|---|
| **NATIONAL FORESTS** *(See place listings.)* | | | | | | | | | | | | | | | |
| **Apalachicola (C-4)** 571,088 acres. Northwestern Florida. | | • | • | • | • | • | | • | • | • | • | | | | |
| **NATIONAL SEASHORES** *(See place listings.)* | | | | | | | | | | | | | | | |
| **Gulf Islands (B-3)** 135,607 acres. Northwestern Florida. Bird-watching. | | • | • | • | • | • | • | | • | • | | | • | • | • |
| **STATE** | | | | | | | | | | | | | | | |
| **Alfred B. Maclay Gardens (B-5)** 1,176 acres 5 mi. n.e. of Tallahassee on US 319. Scenic. Horse trails. *(See Tallahassee p. 206.)* | ❶ | | • | • | • | • | • | • | • | • | • | | • | | |
| **Big Lagoon (C-2)** 655 acres 10 mi. s.w. of Pensacola on SR 292A. Amphitheater, observation tower. | ❷ | • | • | • | • | • | • | • | • | • | • | | | | |
| **Blackwater River (B-3)** 635 acres 15 mi. n.e. of Milton off US 90. Historic. Tubing; guided walks. | ❸ | • | • | • | • | | | • | • | • | | | | | |
| **Dr. Julian G. Bruce St. George Island (D-4)** 2,023 acres off US 98 via CRs G1A and 300 on St. George Island. Bird-watching. | ❹ | • | • | • | • | • | | • | • | • | | | | | |
| **Econfina River (C-5)** 4,528 acres s. of Lamont at the end of CR 14. Horse trails. | ❺ | | • | • | • | | | • | | • | • | | | • | • |
| **Edward Ball Wakulla Springs (C-5)** 5,882 acres .5 mi. e. of Wakulla Springs at jct. SRs 61 and 267. Bird-watching; boat tours. *(See Wakulla Springs p. 214.)* | ❻ | | • | • | | | | • | | • | • | | | • | • |
| **Falling Waters (B-4)** 173 acres 3 mi. s. of Chipley off SR 77. | ❼ | • | • | • | | | | | • | | | | | | |
| **Florida Caverns (B-4)** 1,280 acres 3 mi. n. of Marianna on SR 166. Bird-watching; horse trails. *(See Marianna p. 182.)* | ❽ | • | • | • | • | • | | • | • | • | | | | | • |
| **Fred Gannon Rocky Bayou (B-3)** 362 acres 3.5 mi. e. of Niceville on SR 20. | ❾ | • | • | • | • | • | | • | | • | | | | | |
| **Grayton Beach (B-3)** 2,127 acres adjacent to Grayton Beach on SR 30A. | ❿ | • | • | • | • | • | | • | • | • | | | | • | • |
| **Henderson Beach (B-3)** 208 acres just e. of Destin on US 98. Wildlife viewing; boardwalks, nature trails, pavilions, playground. *(See Destin p. 174.)* | ⓫ | • | • | • | | | | • | • | • | | | | | |
| **Lake Talquin (B-5)** 526 acres (land), 10,000 acres (lake) n. of SR 20 at 14850 Jack Vause Landing Rd. in Tallahassee. Bird-watching, canoeing, kayaking, wildlife viewing; boardwalk, nature trail. | ⓬ | | • | • | • | | | • | | • | | | | | |
| **Ochlockonee River (C-5)** 385 acres 4 mi. s. of Sopchoppy on US 319. | ⓭ | • | • | • | • | • | | • | • | • | | | | | |
| **Ponce De Leon Springs (B-3)** 382 acres .5 mi. s. of US 90 on CR 181A. | ⓮ | | • | • | • | | | • | • | | | | • | • | |
| **St. Andrews (C-4)** 1,168 acres 3 mi. e. of Panama City Beach via SR 392. *(See Panama City Beach p. 191.)* | ⓯ | • | • | • | • | • | | • | • | • | | | | | • |
| **Three Rivers (B-4)** 667 acres 2 mi. n. of Sneads on SR 271 (River Rd.). | ⓰ | • | • | • | • | • | | • | | • | | | | • | |
| **T.H. Stone Memorial St. Joseph Peninsula (C-4)** 2,600 acres 20 mi. s.w. of Port St. Joe. Bird-watching, canoeing, kayaking; wilderness preserve. | ⓱ | • | • | • | • | • | • | • | • | • | | | | • | |
| **OTHER** | | | | | | | | | | | | | | | |
| **Silver Lake (B-5)** 25 acres 8 mi. w. of Tallahassee off SR 20. | ⓲ | • | • | • | • | | | • | • | | | | • | | |

Save on brand-name luggage and travel

accessories at AAA/CAA Travel Stores

## APALACHICOLA (C-4) pop. 2,231, elev. 17'
• Restaurants p. 172

Apalachicola is a Hitchiti Indian word meaning "people on the other side." Ninety percent of the state's oyster crop (10 percent of the nation's total) is cultivated in Apalachicola's more than 7,000 acres of oyster beds.

**Apalachicola Bay Chamber of Commerce:** 122 Commerce St., Apalachicola, FL 32320-1776. **Phone:** (850) 653-9419.

**Shopping areas:** Apalachicola has boutiques, antique shops and art galleries. The Grady Market houses more than a dozen shopping venues in the historical Grady Building.

**JOHN GORRIE MUSEUM STATE PARK** is 1 blk. e. of US 98 on Gorrie Square at 46 Sixth St. at jct. Ave. D. The museum is named for Dr. John Gorrie, recipient of the first U.S. patent for mechanical refrigeration in 1851. A replica of Gorrie's ice-making machine and area history exhibits are featured. **Time:** Allow 30 minutes minimum. **Hours:** Thurs.-Mon. 9-5. Closed Jan. 1, Thanksgiving and Christmas. **Cost:** $2; free (ages 0-5). **Phone:** (850) 653-9347 or (850) 245-2157.

---

**BEST WESTERN APALACH INN**          (850)653-9131

Hotel
$99-$115

 **AAA Benefit:** Members save up to 20%!

**Address:** 249 US 98 W 32320 **Location:** On US 98, 1.5 mi w. **Facility:** 42 units. 2 stories (no elevator), exterior corridors. **Terms:** 2 night minimum stay - seasonal and/or weekends, 3 day cancellation notice-fee imposed. **Pool(s):** outdoor. **Activities:** exercise room. **Guest Services:** coin laundry. **Featured Amenity:** full hot breakfast.

---

**COOMBS HOUSE INN** 850/653-9199

▼▼▼▼ **Historic Bed & Breakfast.** Rates not provided. **Address:** 80 Sixth St 32320 **Location:** US 98 (Market St) and Ave E. **Facility:** Built in 1905, this historic inn consists of three Victorian homes that have been lovingly restored for the enjoyment of its guests. Antiques abound in the furniture and artwork. 23 units. 2-3 stories (no elevator), interior corridors. **Activities:** bicycles, massage.

🛗➔ 🛜 ✕ 🖵 / SOME UNITS 🛏 🍴 🖾

**WATER STREET HOTEL & MARINA** (850)653-3700

▼▼▼▼ **Vacation Rental Condominium** $109-$450 **Address:** 329 Water St 32320 **Location:** Waterfront. Jct Ave I. **Facility:** Located at a small marina on the Apalachicola River, these upscale units have hardwood floors, stainless steel appliances, two or three bedrooms and fully enclosed, screened-in patios. 30 condominiums. 3 stories, exterior corridors. **Terms:** check-in 4 pm, 2 night minimum stay - seasonal and/or weekends, cancellation fee imposed. **Amenities:** safes. **Pool(s):** outdoor. **Activities:** marina, fishing, bicycles. **Guest Services:** complimentary laundry.

CALL 🛗ⓜ 🏊 HS 🛜 ✕ 🍴 🖾 🖵 / SOME UNITS 🛏

### WHERE TO EAT

**TAMARA'S CAFE** 850/653-4111

▼▼ Latin American. Casual Dining. $8-$29 **AAA Inspector Notes:** This is a charming place to stop for a bite while shopping amid the quaint shops found in the heart of this bay town. The menu specializes in Latin dishes with influences from South America and the Caribbean. **Features:** full bar. **Address:** 71 Market St 32320 **Location:** Jct Ave D; downtown. **Parking:** street only.

Ⓑ Ⓛ Ⓓ CALL 🛗ⓜ

## APALACHICOLA NATIONAL FOREST
(C-4)

Elevations in the forest range from 10 ft. to 100 ft.

Stretching across four northwestern counties, the Apalachicola National Forest is the largest of Florida's three national forests. Its 571,088 acres of varied terrain include pine flatwoods, hardwood hammocks, swamp, rivers, lakes and two wilderness areas: Bradwell Bay and Mud Swamp/New River. Other sites include Leon Sinks, an unusual geological area of caverns and sinkholes, and Fort Gadsden, an outpost along the Apalachicola River dating to the War of 1812. The fort vanished more than a century ago, but interpretive information and artifacts present the colorful history of this strategic location. The first fort on this site was built by the British with help from the Seminole Indians and runaway slaves; it was destroyed in 1816.

Secluded lakes and streams and canoe trails on the Sopchoppy and lower Ochlockonee rivers are popular with canoeists. Several lake areas have campgrounds and hiking trails. Hunting and fishing also are popular activities.

A portion of the 1,300-mile Florida National Scenic Trail passes through the forest, showcasing a wide variety of plants and wildlife native to the area. Hikers may catch glimpses of alligators and such rare and endangered species as the red-cockaded woodpecker, indigo snake and bald eagle.

Further information about the forest can be obtained at the district headquarters offices in Crawfordville,

(850) 926-3561, and in Bristol, (850) 643-2282. *See Recreation Areas Chart.*

## BLOUNTSTOWN (B-4) pop. 2,514, elev. 66'

**PANHANDLE PIONEER SETTLEMENT,** 17869 N.W. Pioneer Settlement Rd. in Sam B. Atkins Park, features 18 historical buildings that have been moved here from various Calhoun County locales. The restored structures were built between the 1820s and 1940s and contain historical furnishings and collections. Monthly events and festivals are held where old-time chores and skills like blacksmithing, woodstove cooking and quilting are demonstrated.

The concession stand is only open during events. Guided tours depart from the Post Office and General Store. **Time:** Allow 1 hour, 30 minutes minimum. **Hours:** Tues. and Thurs.-Sat. 10-2. Last tour begins 1 hour before closing. Closed major holidays. **Cost:** $6; $3.50 (ages 56+); $3 (ages 5-12). **Phone:** (850) 674-2777. GT 🍴 🎁 🌳

## BONIFAY pop. 2,793

**HOLIDAY INN EXPRESS & SUITES** (850)844-0600

▼▼▼▼ Hotel $90-$120 **Address:** 115 Washington Dr 32425 **Location:** I-10 exit 112, just n on SR 79. **Facility:** 64 units. 3 stories, interior corridors. **Pool(s):** outdoor. **Activities:** exercise room. **Guest Services:** coin laundry.

🛗➔ CALL 🛗ⓜ 🏊 BIZ HS 🛜 🍴 🖾 🖵

### WHERE TO EAT

**CASTAWAY OYSTER BAR & SEAFOOD RESTAURANT** 850/547-2112

▼▼▼ Seafood. Casual Dining. $6-$15 **AAA Inspector Notes:** Right off the interstate, this cozy café specializes in regional seafood catches such as oysters, shrimp, catfish and grouper. **Features:** patio dining. **Address:** 425 St. Johns Rd 32425 **Location:** I-10 exit 112, just nw. Ⓛ Ⓓ CALL 🛗ⓜ

**HOLIDAY RESTAURANT** 850/547-2212

▼▼▼ American. Casual Dining. $4-$18 **AAA Inspector Notes:** A long time fixture in this small town, the casual, family-operated establishment is a place where the clientèle greet one another on a first-name basis. Daily lunch specials are offered in addition to the limited menu. **Address:** 116 W Hwy 90 32425 **Location:** I-10 exit 112, 2 mi n on SR 79, then just w. Ⓑ Ⓛ Ⓓ CALL 🛗ⓜ

## CALLAWAY pop. 14,405
• **Hotels & Restaurants map & index p. 186**

**COMFORT SUITES CALLAWAY/PANAMA CITY** (850)215-5551 **36**

▼▼▼▼ Hotel $90-$265 **Address:** 264 N Tyndall Pkwy 32404 **Location:** On US 98; jct SR 22. **Facility:** 68 units, some two bedrooms. 3 stories, interior corridors. **Pool(s):** heated indoor. **Activities:** hot tub, exercise room. **Guest Services:** valet and coin laundry.

🛗➔ CALL 🛗ⓜ 🏊 BIZ HS 🛜 ✕ 🍴 🖾 🖵

**DAYS INN & SUITES-TYNDALL** (850)769-7400 **35**

▼▼ Motel $69-$149 **Address:** 435 N Tyndall Pkwy 32404 **Location:** On US 98, just n of jct SR 22. **Facility:** 52 units. 2 stories, interior corridors. **Terms:** cancellation fee imposed. **Pool(s):** outdoor.

🛗➔ CALL 🛗ⓜ 🏊 HS 🛜 🍴 🖾 🖵

## CRAWFORDVILLE pop. 3,702

### BEST WESTERN PLUS WAKULLA INN & SUITES
(850)926-3737

 Hotel $100-$185

 **AAA Benefit:** Members save up to 20%!

**Address:** 3292 Coastal Hwy 98 32327 **Location:** On US 98, 0.4 mi e of jct US 319. **Facility:** 57 units. 2 stories, interior corridors. **Terms:** 2 night minimum stay - seasonal, 3 day cancellation notice-fee imposed. **Pool(s):** outdoor. **Activities:** exercise room. **Guest Services:** coin laundry. **Featured Amenity:** full hot breakfast.

## CRESTVIEW pop. 20,978
• Restaurants p. 174

### COUNTRY INN & SUITES BY CARLSON
(850)306-2020

Hotel $80-$200 **Address:** 235 Rasberry Rd 32536 **Location:** I-10 exit 56, just nw on SR 85. **Facility:** 65 units. 3 stories, interior corridors. **Terms:** cancellation fee imposed. **Pool(s):** outdoor. **Activities:** exercise room. **Guest Services:** coin laundry.

### ECONO LODGE
(850)682-6255

Motel $70-$85 **Address:** 3101 S Ferdon Blvd 32536 **Location:** I-10 exit 56, 0.3 mi n on SR 85. **Facility:** 84 units. 2 stories, exterior corridors.

### HAMPTON INN
(850)689-2378

Hotel $84-$124 **Address:** 3709 S Ferdon Blvd 32536 **Location:** I-10 exit 56, just s on SR 85. **Facility:** 70 units. 3 stories, exterior corridors. **Terms:** 1-7 night minimum stay, cancellation fee imposed. **Pool(s):** outdoor. **Activities:** hot tub. **Guest Services:** coin laundry.

**AAA Benefit:** Members save 5% or more!

### HOLIDAY INN EXPRESS & SUITES
(850)398-8100

Hotel $105-$180 **Address:** 125 Cracker Barrel Dr 32536 **Location:** I-10 exit 56, just s on SR 85. **Facility:** 77 units, some kitchens. 4 stories, interior corridors. **Terms:** cancellation fee imposed. **Pool(s):** heated indoor. **Activities:** hot tub, exercise room. **Guest Services:** coin laundry.

### QUALITY INN
(850)683-1778

Hotel $71-$89 **Address:** 151 Cracker Barrel Dr 32536 **Location:** I-10 exit 56, just s on SR 85. **Facility:** 55 units. 3 stories, interior corridors. **Activities:** exercise room. *(See ad this page.)*

▼ See AAA listing this page ▼

Access trusted AAA/CAA services on the

go with the AAA and CAA Mobile apps

**BAMBOO SUSHI BAR & HIBACHI EXPRESS**        850/689-1391

Japanese Sushi. Quick Serve. $7-$23 **AAA Inspector Notes:** This quick serve eatery delivers quality Japanese cuisine in a flash. Highlights include both sushi and hibachi. **Features:** beer & wine. **Address:** 2511 S Ferdon Blvd 32539 **Location:** I-10 exit 56, 0.7 mi n; in Crestview Corners Plaza. L D CALL M

**COACH 'N' FOUR STEAKHOUSE**        850/423-1003

Steak. Family Dining. $10-$35 **AAA Inspector Notes:** Along with various cuts of steaks, this Western cowboy-themed eatery offers a nice selection of seafood along with chicken and ribs. **Features:** full bar. **Address:** 114 John King Rd 32539 **Location:** I-10 exit 56, just s, then just ne. D CALL M

**EMERALD ISLE SEAFOOD**        850/683-1418

Seafood. Casual Dining. $6-$23 **AAA Inspector Notes:** Both a market and cozy restaurant share this family-owned-and-operated business. The daily catch, displayed on ice in glass cases, show diners how fresh their meal will be. Rotating specials feature seasonal fare. **Features:** beer & wine. **Address:** 1260 S Ferdon Blvd 32536 **Location:** I-10 exit 56, 1.5 mi n on SR 85. L D CALL M

**LA RUMBA**        850/683-0208

Mexican. Casual Dining. $6-$14 **AAA Inspector Notes:** Enter this festive cantina where your eyes will automatically focus on two colorful wall murals depicting city and country life south of the border. All the standard favorites are on the menu. **Features:** full bar, patio dining. **Address:** 100 John King Rd 32539 **Location:** I-10 exit 56, just s, then just ne. L D CALL M

**THE WILD OLIVE**        850/682-4455

American. Casual Dining. $9-$29 **AAA Inspector Notes:** Situated in a former residential home, the eatery gives the feel of dining at a friend's house. An eclectic menu of savory dishes is offered along with daily specials. Between courses, enjoy the whimsical decor or gaze at the starry night if you're dining on the outdoor patio. Only lunch is served on Monday, and only dinner is served on Saturday. **Features:** patio dining. **Address:** 797 N Pearl St 32536 **Location:** Corner of Hickory Ave; downtown. L D CALL M

## DE FUNIAK SPRINGS pop. 5,177

**BEST WESTERN CROSSROADS INN**        (850)892-5111

Motel
$90-$100

**AAA Benefit:** Members save up to 20%!

**Address:** 2343 US Hwy 331 S 32435 **Location:** I-10 exit 85, just s. **Facility:** 100 units. 2 stories (no elevator), interior/exterior corridors. **Pool(s):** outdoor. **Guest Services:** coin laundry. **Featured Amenity:** full hot breakfast.

## DESTIN (B-3) pop. 12,305, elev. 26'
• Restaurants p. 177

With its quartz properties, the crystalline sand sparkles with a white luster and feels soft to the touch on Destin's share of the 24-mile Emerald Coast. The whiteness, in turn, intensifies the bluish-green hue of the Gulf of Mexico. Public beach access is available at intervals along US 98 and in Henderson Beach State Park *(see Recreation Areas Chart)*.

Harborwalk Village features a cluster of restaurants, bars and water sports outfitters and is a haven for a large fleet of charter fishing craft. Sport fishing is extremely popular here due to Destin's close proximity to the 100 fathom curve—the edge of the continental shelf—where deep-sea fishing for billfish is at its finest. Record catches have earned Destin the title World's Luckiest Fishing Village. Stop by the Destin History and Fishing Museum, 108 Stahlman Ave., for more information; phone (850) 837-6611.

**Shopping areas:** Pick up a Destin souvenir at the SAVE Hard Rock Cafe, 4260 Legendary Dr.

**BIG KAHUNA'S WATER AND ADVENTURE PARK,** 1007 US 98E, offers a variety of slides, pools, water activities and children's areas. **Note:** Guests under 48 inches tall are required to wear a life jacket and be accompanied by an adult in the wave pool. Complimentary life jacket and locker rentals are available.

**Time:** Allow 2 hours minimum. **Hours:** Water park daily 10-6, early June-early Aug.; daily 10-5, mid-May to late May and early Aug. to mid-Aug.; Sat.-Sun. 10-5, in early May and late Aug.-early Sept. Adventure Park daily 2-10, early June-early Aug.; 2-9, mid-May to early June and early Aug. to mid-Aug.; Sat.-Sun. 2-9, early May to mid-May and in late Aug. Phone ahead to confirm schedule. **Cost:** $38.99; $32.99 (military with ID); $29.99 (ages 60+ and under 48 inches tall). Reduced admission is available 3 hours prior to closing. **Phone:** (850) 837-8319. 🍴

**SOUTHERN STAR DOLPHIN CRUISES** departs from Harborwalk Village Marina Level at 100 Harbor Blvd. Narrated tours cruise the Emerald Coast for dolphin sightings. The captain teaches children how to steer, and mates provide instruction on bird-feeding. **Time:** Allow 2 hours minimum. **Hours:** Cruises Mon.-Sat.; departure times vary. Phone ahead to confirm schedule. **Cost:** $29; $25 (ages 60+); $15.50 (ages 4-14). Reservations are recommended. **Phone:** (850) 837-7741 or (888) 424-7217.

**BAY CLUB OF SANDESTIN** (850)837-8866

Vacation Rental Condominium
$155-$225

**Address:** 120 N Sandestin Blvd 32550 **Location:** Just n of jct US 98. **Facility:** The complex is located within a gated community and most units offer bay views. For a fee, facility privileges at Sandestin Resort are available, including golf, a spa, health club and restaurants. 44 condominiums. 6 stories, interior corridors. **Terms:** 3 night minimum stay, 3 day cancellation notice-fee imposed. **Pool(s):** outdoor. **Activities:** bicycles, exercise room. **Guest Services:** complimentary and valet laundry, area transportation.

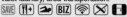

**COURTYARD BY MARRIOTT SANDESTIN AT GRAND BOULEVARD** (850)650-7411

Hotel
$129-$299

COURTYARD Marriott.

**AAA Benefit:** Members save 5% or more!

**Address:** 100 Grand Blvd 32550 **Location:** On US 98; jct Baytowne Ln. **Facility:** 174 units. 5 stories, interior corridors. **Terms:** check-in 4 pm. **Pool(s):** outdoor. **Activities:** hot tub, exercise room. **Guest Services:** valet and coin laundry, boarding pass kiosk. *(See ad this page.)*

/SOME UNITS

---

▼ See AAA listing this page ▼

**EMBASSY SUITES DESTIN-MIRAMAR BEACH**     (850)337-7000

 **Hotel** $99-$369 **Address:** 570 Scenic Gulf Dr 32550 **Location:** Just w of US 98 on Poinciana Blvd, 0.3 mi s. **Facility:** 155 units. 4 stories, interior corridors. **Terms:** check-in 4 pm, 1-7 night minimum stay, cancellation fee imposed. **Amenities:** safes. **Pool(s):** heated outdoor. **Activities:** hot tub, beach access, exercise room. **Guest Services:** valet and coin laundry.

**AAA Benefit:** Members save 5% or more!

     BIZ HS   🖥 📠 📋

**FAIRFIELD INN & SUITES BY MARRIOTT DESTIN**
(850)654-8611

 **Hotel** $144-$279 **Address:** 19001 Emerald Coast Pkwy 32541 **Location:** On US 98, jct Henderson Beach Rd. **Facility:** 100 units. 4 stories, interior corridors. **Terms:** check-in 4 pm, cancellation fee imposed. **Pool(s):** outdoor, heated indoor. **Activities:** exercise room. **Guest Services:** valet and coin laundry.

**AAA Benefit:** Members save 5% or more!

  BIZ  📠 🖥 📠 📋

**HAMPTON INN & SUITES DESTIN/SANDESTIN AREA**
(850)837-7889

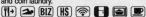 **Hotel** $89-$259 **Address:** 10861 Hwy 98 32550 **Location:** Jct South Shore Dr. **Facility:** 74 units. 4 stories, interior corridors. **Terms:** 1-7 night minimum stay, cancellation fee imposed. **Pool(s):** outdoor. **Activities:** exercise room. **Guest Services:** valet and coin laundry.

**AAA Benefit:** Members save 5% or more!

 🚣 BIZ HS 📶 🖥 📠 📋

**HILTON SANDESTIN BEACH GOLF RESORT & SPA**
(850)267-9500

 **Resort Hotel** $149-$419

**Hilton** HOTELS & RESORTS

**AAA Benefit:** Members save 5% or more!

**Address:** 4000 S Sandestin Blvd 32550 **Location:** Oceanfront. Just s of jct US 98. **Facility:** This beachfront hotel offers rooms with Gulf views and family units with bunk beds. A wide range of leisure activities and food outlets are on-site. There is a huge pool deck that overlooks the beach. 602 units. 15 stories, interior corridors. **Terms:** check-in 4 pm, 1-7 night minimum stay, cancellation fee imposed. **Amenities:** video games, safes. **Dining:** 5 restaurants, also, Seagar's Prime Steaks and Seafood, see separate listing. **Pool(s):** heated outdoor, heated indoor. **Activities:** sauna, hot tub, regulation golf, miniature golf, tennis, recreation programs in summer, bicycles, playground, game room, spa. **Guest Services:** valet and coin laundry, area transportation. *(See ad this page.)*

SAVE ECO  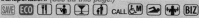  CALL    BIZ
sHS  ✕ 📷 🖥 📠 📋

▼ *See AAA listing this page* ▼

THIS IS
THATPLACE

Where the kids had as much fun jumping into the waves as they did jumping into their bunk beds.

+1 800 367 1271 | +1 850 267 9500
HiltonSandestinBeach.com
#HiltonSandestinBeach #ThatPlace

**Hilton**
SANDESTIN BEACH
GOLF RESORT & SPA

30 YEARS

## HOLIDAY INN EXPRESS HOTEL & SUITES

(850)654-9383

Hotel
$119-$300

**Address:** 108 Hutchinson St 32541 **Location:** On SR 293, just se of jct US 98. **Facility:** 74 units. 3 stories, interior corridors. **Terms:** check-in 4 pm, 2-3 night minimum stay - seasonal and/or weekends, cancellation fee imposed. **Pool(s):** outdoor. **Activities:** exercise room. **Guest Services:** valet laundry. **Featured Amenity:** full hot breakfast.

[SAVE] [†↑] [≥] [BIZ] [HS] [↗] [✕]
[🔲] [▦] [▣]

---

## RESIDENCE INN BY MARRIOTT SANDESTIN AT GRAND BOULEVARD

(850)650-7811

Extended Stay
Hotel
$149-$399

**AAA Benefit:**
Members save 5% or more!

**Address:** 300 Grand Blvd 32550 **Location:** On US 98, jct Baytowne Ln. **Facility:** 120 units, some two bedrooms, efficiencies and kitchens. 4 stories, interior corridors. **Terms:** check-in 4 pm. **Pool(s):** outdoor. **Activities:** hot tub, exercise room. **Guest Services:** valet and coin laundry.

[SAVE] [ECO] [†↑] CALL [&M] [≥]
[BIZ] [HS] [↗] [✕] [🔲] [▦] [▣] / SOME UNITS [⬛] [📶]

**Residence Inn® Marriott**

**Unique retreat for vacationers looking for a home away from home. Pet friendly.**

---

## SANDESTIN GOLF AND BEACH RESORT

(850)267-8000

Resort Hotel
$139-$329

**Address:** 9300 Emerald Coast Pkwy W 32550 **Location:** Oceanfront. On US 98; jct Sandestin Dr, follow signs to The Village. **Facility:** This 2,400-acre resort flanks both sides of US 98 and offers an extensive variety of facilities, including high-rise condos, waterfront housekeeping villas, designer-decorated homes and modest rooms. 1200 units, some two bedrooms, three bedrooms, efficiencies, kitchens, houses and condominiums. 1-22 stories, interior/exterior corridors. **Terms:** check-in 4 pm, 7 day cancellation notice-fee imposed, resort fee. **Dining:** 23 restaurants, also, Another Broken Egg Cafe, see separate listing. **Pool(s):** outdoor, heated outdoor. **Activities:** sauna, hot tub, marina, fishing, regulation golf, miniature golf, tennis, recreation programs, bicycles, playground, game room, spa. **Guest Services:** valet and coin laundry, area transportation. (See ad opposite table of contents.)

[SAVE] [†] [Y] [♿] [≥] [👨‍👩‍👧] [BIZ] [↗] [✕] [🔲]
[▦] [▣] / SOME UNITS [⬛] [📶] [HS]

---

## SUMMERPLACE INN

(850)650-8003

Hotel
$70-$289

**Address:** 14047 Emerald Coast Pkwy 32541 **Location:** On US 98, 2.5 mi w at jct SR 293. **Facility:** 72 units. 4 stories, interior corridors. **Terms:** check-in 4 pm, 2-4 night minimum stay - seasonal and/or weekends, 3 day cancellation notice-fee imposed. **Pool(s):** outdoor, heated indoor. **Activities:** hot tub, limited exercise equipment. **Guest Services:** coin laundry. **Featured Amenity:** continental breakfast.

[SAVE] [†↑] [≥] [BIZ] [↗] [✕] [▣]
[▦] [▣] / SOME UNITS [⬛]

---

## WHERE TO EAT

### ANOTHER BROKEN EGG CAFE

Breakfast Sandwiches. Casual Dining. $5-$16 **AAA Inspector Notes:** Enjoy a breakfast experience you will not soon forget; huge cinnamon buns, Popeye's omelet and fruit and nut pancakes or french toast are some of the menu specialties.

[B] [L] CALL [&M]

*For additional information, visit AAA.com*

**LOCATIONS:**
**Address:** 9300 Emerald Coast Pkwy W 32550 **Location:** On US 98; jct Sandestin Dr, follow signs to The Village; in Sandestin Golf and Beach Resort. **Phone:** 850/622-2050

**Address:** 9300 Emerald Coast Pkwy W 32550 **Location:** On US 98; jct Sandestin Dr, follow signs to Bayside; in Linkside Conference Center; in Sandestin Golf and Beach Resort. **Phone:** 850/267-7108

**Address:** 979 Hwy 98, Suite F 32541 **Location:** Jct US 98, SR 30 and 293, 3.2 mi w; in 98 Palms Shopping Center. **Phone:** 850/650-0499

### THE BACK PORCH

850/837-2022

Seafood. Casual Dining. $11-$36 **AAA Inspector Notes:** Dominating the extensive five-page menu at this multi-story, beachfront eatery is fresh Gulf seafood including the signature dish, chargrilled amberjack. Everyone is sure to find just the right dish to fulfill their craving. While waiting to be served, the kids can frolic at the restaurant's playground, located on the beach. Afterward, everyone will enjoy a quick perusal through the gift shop. **Features:** full bar, patio dining, happy hour. **Address:** 1740 Old Scenic Hwy 98 E 32541 **Location:** Just se of jct US 98/SR 30 (Emerald Coast Pkwy).

[L] [D]

### BONEFISH GRILL

850/650-3161

Seafood. Fine Dining. $10-$27 **AAA Inspector Notes:** Fish is the house specialty, and the menu and nightly specials offer a variety of choices. Well-prepared food is cooked to perfection. Service is casual in nature, and the staff is skilled and attentive. **Features:** full bar, Sunday brunch. **Address:** 4447 Commons Dr E, Suite 105 32541 **Location:** Jct US 98 and SR 293; in shopping plaza.

[D] CALL [&M]

### CALLAHAN'S RESTAURANT & DELI

850/837-6328

American. Casual Dining. $5-$23 **AAA Inspector Notes:** This is the neighborhood eatery everyone heads to when they want authentic deli sandwiches: pastrami, corned beef, roast beef, Reuben, BLT, Philly cheesesteak, turkey breast or Italian subs—or choose from a variety of burgers. The deli also has an extensive dinner menu that features soups, salads, chicken, pork chops, chicken-fried steak, chicken-fried chicken, liver and onions and blackened or grilled mahi mahi as well as many Italian choices. A display case holds tempting desserts. **Features:** beer & wine, Sunday brunch. **Address:** 791 Harbor Blvd 32541 **Location:** On US 98, 3.5 mi w of jct SR 293, just n. [L] [D]

---

## CANTINA LAREDO
850/654-5649

▼▼▼ ▼▼▼
Mexican
Casual Dining
$10-$25

**AAA Inspector Notes:** Sophisticated yet relaxed, this eatery features authentic Mexican fare with a creative twist. A great starter is the top-shelf guacamole, which is prepared tableside and primes the palate for the entree. The menu features traditional favorites such as tacos, enchiladas, fajitas, carnitas and chiles rellenos. Also featured are vegetarian and gluten-free dishes. **Features:** full bar, patio dining, Sunday brunch, happy hour. **Address:** 585 Grand Blvd, Suite N-106 32550 **Location:** Jct US 331, 6 mi w on US 98. ⬜L ⬜D

### Gourmet Mexican food, fresh-squeezed lime margaritas

---

THE CRAB TRAP SEAFOOD & OYSTER BAR    850/654-2722
▼▼▼ Seafood. Casual Dining. $11-$55 **AAA Inspector Notes:** This restaurant is located directly on the Gulf of Mexico and offers great views of the beach and sunsets. Indoor and outdoor dining along with a beachside bar area makes for a popular dining spot. The menu offers a variety of seafood specialties such as mahi mahi, yellowfin tuna, Gulf grouper, Alaskan snow crabs, Dungeness crab clusters, shrimp and blue crab. For landlubbers, there are chicken and beef dishes. **Features:** full bar, patio dining. **Address:** 3500 Old Hwy 98 32541 **Location:** On US 98; at James Lee Park. ⬜L ⬜D

THE DONUT HOLE    850/837-8824
▼ Breads/Pastries Sandwiches. Casual Dining. $6-$10 **AAA Inspector Notes:** Across from Destin Harbor sits this popular eatery known for its breakfasts and fresh donuts. You'll also find sandwiches, burgers and salads. Expect a long wait in season. **Address:** 635 Hwy 98 E 32541 **Location:** US 98, 2.3 mi w.
⬜B ⬜L ⬜D

GRAFFITI    850/424-7514
▼▼ Mediterranean. Casual Dining. $9-$29 **AAA Inspector Notes:** The walls and ceiling of this spot are embellished with an eclectic collection of artwork that keeps guests occupied between courses. This place is one of the locals' best-kept secrets. Fresh seafood creations are the chef's specialties. Patio dining is available when the weather permits. **Features:** full bar, patio dining, happy hour. **Address:** 707 Harbor Blvd 32541 **Location:** On US 98, 2.9 mi w of bridge. ⬜D 🐾

GRAFFITI    850/424-6650
▼▼ Mediterranean. Casual Dining. $9-$29 **AAA Inspector Notes:** While awaiting your meal, enjoy the eclectic collection of artwork adorning the walls and ceilings at this Baytowne Wharf restaurant. The chef specializes in crafting delicious fresh seafood creations, including chowder made with pancetta. Patio dining overlooking the marina and bay is available when the weather is nice. **Features:** full bar, patio dining. **Location:** On US 98, 10 mi e; in Sandestin Golf and Beach Resort's Village of Baytowne Wharf. **Parking:** on-site and valet. ⬜D

HARD ROCK CAFE    850/654-3310
▼▼ American. Casual Dining. $10-$23 **AAA Inspector Notes:** Rock 'n' roll memorabilia decorates the walls of the popular theme restaurant. Live music on the weekends contributes to the bustling atmosphere. On the menu is a wide variety of American cuisine—from burgers and sandwiches to seafood, steaks and pasta. **Features:** full bar. **Reservations:** suggested. **Address:** 4260 Legendary Dr 32541 **Location:** Jct US 98 and SR 293. ⬜SAVE ⬜L ⬜D

HOG'S BREATH SALOON & CAFE    850/837-5991
▼▼ American. Casual Dining. $7-$22 **AAA Inspector Notes:** A casual, no-frills beach atmosphere exists inside the well-known saloon. Live bands play Wednesday through Sunday starting at 9 pm. House specialties include smoked loin-back ribs, the beef brisket plate, smoked barbecue chicken and the popular hogzilla platter - half a rack of dry rub ribs, smoked chicken and pulled pork. The menu also offers numerous sandwiches and sliders. Key lime pie is a popular dessert. **Features:** full bar, patio dining, happy hour. **Address:** 541 Harbor Blvd 32541 **Location:** On US 98, 1 mi e of Destin Bridge. ⬜L ⬜D 🐾

---

JIM 'N NICK'S BAR-B-Q    850/424-5895
▼▼ Barbecue. Casual Dining. $8-$25 **AAA Inspector Notes:** Southern hospitality reigns at Jim 'N Nick's, where diners get neighborly treatment as they dig into huge portions of tasty lean sausage, fresh chili, juicy smoked beef and pork. A slice of sublime homemade pie ends the meal on a high note. **Features:** full bar. **Address:** 14073 Emerald Coast Pkwy 32541 **Location:** On US 98, 0.5 mi w of Mid Bay Bridge (SR 293). ⬜L ⬜D

THE LIGHTHOUSE RESTAURANT    850/654-2828
▼▼▼ Seafood. Casual Dining. $8-$30 **AAA Inspector Notes:** Bring the whole family to enjoy a relaxed atmosphere at this spot, which offers an extensive menu. A wide selection of entrées has its emphasis on seafood. The prime rib is popular as are seafood combination dishes, and an authentic Key lime pie offers a taste of the tropics. **Features:** full bar, happy hour. **Address:** 757 Harbor Blvd 32541 **Location:** On US 98, 3.6 mi w of jct SR 293; downtown; in Downtown Destin Shopping Center. ⬜L ⬜D

LOUISIANA LAGNIAPPE    850/837-0881
▼▼▼ Cajun. Fine Dining. $18-$39 **AAA Inspector Notes:** This restaurant is located in a gated community and is situated on the water offering fabulous views of the marina. A local favorite since 1984, the menu offers Louisiana favorites such as shrimp and grits, Louisiana crab cakes, grouper amandine, lobster tail and shrimp etouffée, jambalaya, red beans and rice and Louisiana oysters. The service is very professional and a cozy fine dining experience awaits. This is a great place for special occasions. **Features:** full bar, patio dining. **Address:** 775 Gulf Shore Dr 32541 **Location:** Just w of jct US 98. ⬜D

MARLIN GRILL    850/351-1990
▼▼▼ Seafood. Fine Dining. $14-$52 **AAA Inspector Notes:** In the heart of Baytowne Wharf, this fine dining establishment presents chef's creations that look too good to eat, but patrons do not seem to have a problem cleaning their plates. The warm rolls offered before the meal are scrumptious and filling. Fresh seafood is always a menu favorite. **Features:** full bar, patio dining. **Reservations:** suggested. **Address:** 9100 Baytowne Wharf Blvd, Suite B2 32550 **Location:** On US 98, 10 mi e; in The Village of Baytowne Wharf. ⬜D

MCGUIRE'S IRISH PUB OF DESTIN    850/650-0000
▼▼ Steak. Casual Dining. $8-$30 **AAA Inspector Notes:** A pleasant experience, the restaurant features steaks, seafood and tasty, oversize burgers. Sing along to nostalgic music or watch the action on the Gulf and bay from an open upper deck. Do not forget to leave your dollar bill on the wall, ceiling or on the moose head. **Features:** full bar, patio dining. **Address:** 33 E Hwy 98 32541 **Location:** On US 98; at east end of Destin Pass Bridge.
⬜L ⬜D ⬜LATE

MITCHELL'S FISH MARKET    850/650-2484
▼▼▼ Seafood. Casual Dining. $10-$30 **AAA Inspector Notes:** A variety of fresh, never-frozen fish is flown in daily, and market availability determines the daily specials. Diners may order fish grilled, broiled, blackened or steamed in the Shanghai-style with ginger, spinach and sticky rice. Among other choices are steak, pasta and chicken selections. **Features:** full bar, patio dining, happy hour. **Reservations:** suggested. **Address:** 500 Grand Blvd, Suite K-100 32550 **Location:** Jct US 331, 6 mi w on US 98; in Grand Boulevard at Sandestin. ⬜L ⬜D

POMPANO JOE'S SEAFOOD HOUSE    850/837-2224
▼▼ Seafood. Casual Dining. $11-$31 **AAA Inspector Notes:** Serving fresh, local seafood prepared with a Caribbean flair, this restaurant offers tables overlooking the surf, some perched on a deck. Adding to the casual feel, the waitstaff is dressed in colorful Caribbean shirts. Call-ahead seating is offered. **Features:** full bar, patio dining, happy hour. **Address:** 2237 Scenic Gulf Hwy 32550 **Location:** 6.5 mi e on US 98, just s on Miramar Beach Dr, just w.
⬜L ⬜D

### RUTH'S CHRIS STEAK HOUSE
850/337-5108

▼▼▼ Steak. Fine Dining. $25-$83 **AAA Inspector Notes:** The main fare is steak, which is prepared from several cuts of Prime beef and cooked to perfection, but the menu also lists lamb, chicken and seafood dishes. Guests should come hungry because the side dishes, which are among the a la carte offerings, could make a meal in themselves. **Features:** full bar. **Reservations:** suggested. **Address:** 15000 Emerald Coast Pkwy 32541 **Location:** In Silver Shells Resort. [D]

### SEAGAR'S PRIME STEAKS AND SEAFOOD
850/267-9500

Steak
Fine Dining
$30-$55

**AAA Inspector Notes:** A sophisticated setting features lavish appointments and implements an upscale dress code. The open kitchen offers USDA Prime steaks and excellent seafood with an innovative use of fresh ingredients. Sample delicacies include osetra caviar and foie gras. Enjoy an impressive, often dramatic, tableside preparation with the steak Diane. Seafood lovers can choose from the fresh selections of the day. For dessert, try the delightful chocolate soufflé. **Features:** full bar. **Reservations:** suggested. Semiformal attire. **Address:** 4000 S Sandestin Blvd 32550 **Location:** Just s of jct US 98; in Hilton Sandestin Beach Golf Resort & Spa. **Parking:** on-site and valet. *Menu on AAA.com*

[D] CALL [&M]

### THAI ELEPHANT
850/837-5344

▼▼ Thai. Casual Dining. $7-$13 **AAA Inspector Notes:** Tempting smells lingering in the parking lot lure patrons in for delicious Thai cuisine. Such entrées as eggplant with basil and chicken, are spiced to diner's preference by the owner/chef. The decor is airy with Thai memorabilia accents. The service is friendly and knowledgeable. **Features:** beer & wine. **Address:** 12889 Emerald Coast Pkwy, Suite 105-B 32550 **Location:** On US 98, 5 mi e; in Miramar Plaza. [L] [D]

### TOMMY BAHAMA'S RESTAURANT & BAR
850/654-1743

▼▼▼ Caribbean. Casual Dining. $14-$38 **AAA Inspector Notes:** Step through the door, hear the live reggae music complete with a steel drum, and walk into paradise. Wood floors and rattan paddle fans contribute to a sophisticated atmosphere great for gathering with friends or family. Start with the famous coconut shrimp or ahi tuna. Main courses include the Sanibel stuffed chicken and the Shoal Bay sea bass. Save room for dessert, as the piña colada cake and the pineapple créme brûlée should not be ignored. **Features:** full bar, patio dining, happy hour. **Address:** 525 Grand Blvd 32550 **Location:** Jct US 331, 6 mi w on US 98; in Grand Boulevard at Sandestin. [L] [D]

### (VIN'TIJ) WINE BOUTIQUE MARKET BAR BISTRO
850/650-9820

▼▼▼ Continental. Fine Dining. $9-$32 **AAA Inspector Notes:** Decorated in striking primary colors, the eclectic market and restaurant extends its eccentricities to the menu. It offers a variety of tasty choices such as cumin-seared tuna, molasses barbecue roasted Atlantic salmon, pecan roasted chicken breast, pasta alla bolognese as well as "pizzettes" and sandwiches for lighter choices. To complement your dinner, the wine bar offers 40 vintages that can be sampled in 2-ounce portions, by the glass, or by the bottle. **Features:** full bar. **Reservations:** suggested, for dinner. **Address:** 10859 Emerald Coast Pkwy E 32550 **Location:** On US 98; jct S Shore Dr.

[L] [D]

## EGLIN AIR FORCE BASE (B-3) elev. 98'

Eglin Air Force Base is where Gen. Jimmy Doolittle's "Raiders" secretly trained after the attack on Pearl Harbor and is the headquarters of the McKinley Climatic Laboratory. The 96th Test Wing is the installation's host to many units, including some 10,000 military, civilian and contract employees.

**AIR FORCE ARMAMENT MUSEUM** is at 100 Museum Dr., near SR 189 and Eglin Air Force Base's west gate. The museum exhibits 29 aircraft, including B-52 and B-17 bombers, an SR-71A Blackbird spy plane, an F-16 jet fighter, a Soviet MiG 21 and a MOAB (Mother Of All Bombs/Massive Ordnance Air Blast) as well as hundreds of other displays. The armament collection features missiles, bombs, rockets, a small arms gun vault and other artifacts depicting the heritage of the base and its mission regarding the development and fielding of air-to-air and air-to-ground non-nuclear munitions. A 20-minute film depicts the history of Eglin Air Force Base from 1935 to the present. **Hours:** Mon.-Sat. 9:30-4:30. Closed major holidays. **Cost:** Free. **Phone:** (850) 882-4062.

## FORT WALTON BEACH (B-3) pop. 19,507, elev. 18'
• Hotels p. 180 • Restaurants p. 180

Warm Gulf waters and a wide variety of recreational activities make Fort Walton Beach a popular area for family vacations. The sugary white sand beaches cover 24 miles of coast.

Emerald Coast Science Center, 139 Brooks St., offers interactive science exhibits for children; phone (850) 664-1261.

William Augustus Bowles (Capt. Billy Bowlegs), an 18th-century pirate, is remembered with pirate-themed revelry, treasure hunts, fireworks and a parade in late May or early June at the 🚩 Billy Bowlegs Pirate Festival at Fort Walton Landing.

**Emerald Coast Convention & Visitors Bureau:** 1540 Miracle Strip Pkwy. S.E., Fort Walton Beach, FL 32548. **Phone:** (850) 651-7131 or (800) 322-3319.

**CITY OF FORT WALTON BEACH HERITAGE PARK & CULTURAL CENTER,** 139 Miracle Strip Pkwy. S.E., encompasses four museums. Indian Temple Mound Museum explores 12,000 years of Native American occupation of the northwest Florida coast as well as European exploration and settlement through one of the largest collections of prehistoric ceramics in the Southeast. The temple mound, constructed around A.D. 1400, is topped with a replica temple. Camp Walton Schoolhouse and Garnier Post Office Museum depict life in the early 20th century while the Civil War Exhibit features Florida Civil War history.

**Time:** Allow 1 hour minimum. **Hours:** Indian Temple Mound Museum open Mon.-Sat. 10-4:30, June-Aug.; Mon.-Fri. noon-4:30, Sat. 10-4:30, rest of year. Historic buildings open Mon.-Sat. noon-4, June-Aug; Mon.-Sat. 1-3, rest of year. Closed major holidays. **Cost:** (includes all facilities) $5; $4.50 (ages 55+ and military with ID); $3 (ages 4-17). **Phone:** (850) 833-9595.

**GULFARIUM MARINE ADVENTURE PARK,** 1010 Miracle Strip Pkwy. S.E. (US 98), features natural habitats for otters, sharks and stingrays. Visitors can interact directly with the animals, and live shows present the antics of dolphins and sea lions. **Hours:** Daily 9-4:30. Shows are given throughout the day. Phone ahead to confirm schedule. **Cost:** $19.95; $18.95 (ages 62+ and military with ID); $11.95 (ages 3-12). **Phone:** (850) 243-9046 or (800) 247-8575.

## BEST WESTERN FT. WALTON BEACHFRONT
(850)243-9444

Hotel
$85-$235

 **AAA Benefit:** Members save up to 20%!

**Address:** 380 Santa Rosa Blvd 32548 **Location:** Oceanfront. Just sw of jct US 98; on Okaloosa Island. **Facility:** 99 units. 6 stories, exterior corridors. **Terms:** 3 day cancellation notice. **Dining:** entertainment. **Pool(s):** heated outdoor. **Guest Services:** valet and coin laundry.

## COMFORT INN & SUITES FORT WALTON
(850)362-6700

Hotel $89-$209 **Address:** 137 Miracle Strip Pkwy 32548 **Location:** On US 98, 0.6 mi w of jct SR 189. **Facility:** 75 units, some efficiencies. 4 stories, interior corridors. **Amenities:** safes. **Pool(s):** heated indoor. **Activities:** hot tub, exercise room. **Guest Services:** valet and coin laundry.

## FOUR POINTS BY SHERATON DESTIN FORT WALTON BEACH
(850)243-8116

Hotel
$89-$275

**FOUR POINTS** BY SHERATON **AAA Benefit:** Members save up to 15%, plus Starwood Preferred Guest® benefits!

**Address:** 1325 Miracle Strip Pkwy 32548 **Location:** Oceanfront. On US 98, 0.7 mi e. **Facility:** 216 units. 2-7 stories (no elevator), interior/exterior corridors. **Terms:** check-in 4 pm, 3 day cancellation notice-fee imposed. **Dining:** 2 restaurants. **Pool(s):** heated outdoor. **Activities:** hot tub, exercise room. **Guest Services:** valet and coin laundry.

## HAMPTON INN FORT WALTON BEACH
(850)301-0906

Hotel $99-$309 **Address:** 1112 Santa Rosa Blvd 32548 **Location:** Oceanfront. Just sw of jct US 98; on Okaloosa Island. **Facility:** 100 units. 2 stories, interior corridors. **Terms:** check-in 4 pm, 1-7 night minimum stay, cancellation fee imposed. **Amenities:** Some: safes. **Pool(s):** heated outdoor. **Activities:** exercise room.

**AAA Benefit:** Members save 5% or more!

## LA QUINTA INN & SUITES FORT WALTON BEACH
(850)244-1500

Hotel $89-$394 **Address:** 3 SW Miracle Strip Pkwy 32548 **Location:** On US 98; jct SR 189. **Facility:** 68 units. 4 stories, interior corridors. **Pool(s):** outdoor. **Activities:** hot tub, exercise room. **Guest Services:** valet and coin laundry.

## NAUTILUS CONDOMINIUM
850-244-9860

**Vacation Rental Condominium.** Rates not provided. **Address:** 660 Nautilus Ct 32548 **Location:** Oceanfront. 1.1 mi w of US 98 on Santa Rosa Blvd, just s. **Facility:** This condominium complex is located on the Gulf of Mexico and offers one- to three-bedroom units with all of the amenities of home. Individualized décor is found throughout. 47 condominiums. 7 stories, exterior corridors. **Terms:** check-in 4 pm. **Pool(s):** heated outdoor. **Guest Services:** complimentary laundry.

## RAMADA PLAZA BEACH RESORT
(850)243-9161

Hotel $109-$279 **Address:** 1500 Miracle Strip Pkwy SE 32548 **Location:** Oceanfront. On US 98, 1 mi e. **Facility:** 335 units. 2-6 stories, interior/exterior corridors. **Terms:** 3 day cancellation notice-fee imposed. **Amenities:** safes. **Pool(s):** outdoor, heated outdoor. **Activities:** hot tub, exercise room. **Guest Services:** valet and coin laundry.

## VALUE PLACE FT. WALTON BEACH
850/315-0383

**Extended Stay Hotel.** Rates not provided. **Address:** 915 Harrelson Dr 32547 **Location:** 2.7 mi n on SR 85 from jct US 98. **Facility:** 121 efficiencies. 4 stories, interior corridors. **Guest Services:** coin laundry.

## WYNDHAM GARDEN FORT WALTON BEACH
(850)244-8686

Hotel $89-$199 **Address:** 573 Santa Rosa Blvd 32548 **Location:** Oceanfront. 1 mi w of US 98. **Facility:** 195 units, some two bedrooms and kitchens. 7 stories, interior/exterior corridors. **Terms:** check-in 4 pm. **Amenities:** safes. **Pool(s):** heated outdoor. **Activities:** hot tub, recreation programs, game room, exercise room. **Guest Services:** valet and coin laundry.

---

**WHERE TO EAT**

## BANGKOK HOUSE THAI RESTAURANT
850/243-6911

**Thai.** Casual Dining. $9-$30 **AAA Inspector Notes:** Carved in Thailand from a 200 year old tree, a life-size wooden baby elephant is the focal point at this ethnic restaurant. Along with the native gilded headdresses, masks and sculptures, the scents and flavors of traditional dishes such as curry and pad thai make for an exotic dining experience. A lunch buffet is offered weekday afternoons. **Features:** full bar. **Address:** 201 Ferry Ave 32548 **Location:** Corner of 1st St; downtown.

## CAFFÉ ITALIA ONE89
850/664-0035

**Italian.** Casual Dining. $8-$32 **AAA Inspector Notes:** This establishment, located in a former residential house, maintains the right-at-home quality with its mix and match décor along with wafts of delicious aromas. A waterfront view can be enjoyed while dining on the extended covered deck. **Features:** full bar, patio dining, Sunday brunch. **Address:** 189 Brooks St SE 32548 **Location:** Jct US 98 and west side of Brooks Bridge, just s.

## LOS RANCHEROS MEXICAN RESTAURANT
850/862-2007

**Mexican.** Casual Dining. $7-$16 **AAA Inspector Notes:** Fajitas are a specialty at this inexpensive Mexican eatery. **Features:** full bar. **Address:** 300 Eglin Pkwy NE 32547 **Location:** 0.5 mi n of US 98.

## OLD BAY STEAMER
850/664-2795

**Seafood.** Casual Dining. $14-$38 **AAA Inspector Notes:** What more can guests ask for than a warm, welcoming atmosphere and fresh, tasty seafood? The menu includes shrimp, king crab, oysters, blue crab claws, crawfish, Maine lobster tails, fresh fish catch of the day, as well as gumbo, smoked barbecue ribs, chicken and pastas. The steamer platters are outstanding. **Features:** full bar. **Address:** 102 Santa Rosa Blvd 32548 **Location:** Just s of jct US 98; on Okaloosa Island.

## PANDORA'S STEAKHOUSE & LOUNGE 850/244-8669

▼▼▼ Steak Seafood. Fine Dining. $25-$60 **AAA Inspector Notes:** The deep, rich wood paneling and display of 1960s and sports memorabilia offers a strong masculine essence at this steakhouse. The privacy booths are perfect for an intimate dinner for two. Grilling on an oak wood-burning pit is the specialty of the house. **Features:** full bar, happy hour. **Reservations:** suggested. **Address:** 1226 Santa Rosa Blvd 32548 **Location:** Just n of US 98.

D CALL 🅰🅼

## PRANZO ITALIAN RISTORANTE 850/244-9955

▼▼ Italian Seafood. Casual Dining. $12-$27 **AAA Inspector Notes:** This restaurant nurtures an Italian atmosphere with themed artwork, cozy booths and tables and subdued lighting. Authentic cuisine is served with ample portions. Desserts are delicious. **Features:** full bar, happy hour. **Address:** 1225 Santa Rosa Blvd 32548 **Location:** Just n of jct US 98. D

## SEALAND 850/244-0044

▼▼ Seafood. Casual Dining. $13-$50 **AAA Inspector Notes:** The owner/chef is a Vietnamese refugee who was rescued by the Sealand cargo ship when he and his family were adrift at sea. He subsequently named his restaurant after this vessel as a tribute and reminder of new beginnings. A wide range of seafood, steak and pasta dishes are offered on the menu along with a few Asian selections. **Features:** beer & wine. **Address:** 47 Miracle Strip Pkwy 32548 **Location:** Just e of Beal Pkwy on US 98; downtown. D

## SHRIMP BASKET 850/362-6906

▼▼ Seafood. Casual Dining. $7-$15 **AAA Inspector Notes:** Seafood abounds in this casual, nautical atmosphere. Shrimp, oysters and fish can be steamed, grilled or fried, and meat lovers will find burgers and chicken on the menu as well. All-you-can-eat specials change nightly. **Features:** full bar. **Address:** 560 Mary Esther Cut Blvd 32548 **Location:** Jct US 98 and SR 393, 0.8 mi n.

L D CALL 🅰🅼 ◣

## SONNY'S REAL PIT BAR-B-Q 850/314-0717

▼▼ Barbecue. Family Dining. $7-$16 **AAA Inspector Notes:** Bearing the name after its founder, Floyd "Sonny" Tillman, this barbecue restaurant first opened its doors circa 1968 in Gainesville, Florida and has since spawned over 150 more throughout the Southeast. The menu is steeped in finger lickin' favorites such as ribs, pulled pork, beef brisket, burgers, catfish, shrimp and char-grilled chicken. Let's not forget about the fried okra, which is the perfect starter dish, and their homemade baked beans. **Features:** beer only. **Address:** 925 N Beal Pkwy 32547 **Location:** Jct US 98 and SR 189 (Beal Pkwy), 4.5 mi n. L D

## TIJUANA FLATS 850/301-0002

▼ Tex-Mex. Quick Serve. $6-$10 **AAA Inspector Notes:** The first one of these restaurants opened in Central Florida way back in 1995 and has since spawned over sixty more locations! The menu specializes in Tex-Mex with some all-time favorites such as burritos, chimichangas, quesadillas, tacos, enchiladas and nachos. Well known for their hot sauce bar, this eatery has a slew of them from which to choose. Careful, some are really hot! Although the restaurant is considered quick serve, the food is cooked to order. **Features:** beer & wine. **Address:** 39 Eglin Pkwy NE 32548 **Location:** Jct US 98, 0.6 mi n on SR 85. L D CALL 🅰🅼

## GULF BREEZE (B-2) pop. 5,763, elev. 16'
• Hotels & Restaurants map & index p. 197

**Gulf Breeze Area Chamber of Commerce:** 409 Gulf Breeze Pkwy., Gulf Breeze, FL 32561. **Phone:** (850) 932-7888.

**GULF BREEZE ZOO,** 8 mi. e. on US 98 at 5701 Gulf Breeze Pkwy., is home to more than 700 animals and 400 different species in naturalistic habitats. Highlights of the 50-acre zoo include a kangaroo exhibit, chimpanzee and gorilla islands, a children's petting zoo, a giraffe feeding station and interactive animal encounters every hour. Visitors ride the Safari Line train through a 20-acre wildlife preserve featuring free-roaming animals, including antelope, deer, hippos and zebras.

**Time:** Allow 1 hour, 30 minutes minimum. **Hours:** Daily 9-6, Mar.-Sept.; 9-4, rest of year. Last admission 1 hour before closing. Closed Jan. 1, Thanksgiving and Christmas. **Cost:** $14.95; $13.95 (ages 65+); $10.95 (ages 2-12). Train fare $3. Animal feed $3. **Phone:** (850) 932-2229. 🍴 🛝

## AEGEAN BREEZE 850/916-0430 32

▼▼ Greek. Casual Dining. $7-$25 **AAA Inspector Notes:** This popular local favorite sports a casual atmosphere in which to dine on ethnic and American dishes. Closed for lunch on Saturday. **Features:** beer & wine, patio dining. **Address:** 913 Gulf Breeze Pkwy, Unit 20 32561 **Location:** Just e of jct SR 399; in Harbour Town Village Plaza. L D 🛍

# GULF ISLANDS NATIONAL SEASHORE
(B-3)

Stretching west 160 miles from Fort Walton Beach to Cat Island off Gulfport, Miss., Gulf Islands National Seashore covers more than 135,000 acres, 80 percent of which are submerged lands. Most of Florida's portion is accessible by car and includes Naval Live Oaks Reservation; part of Perdido Key; Fort Barrancas *(see attraction listing p. 196)* and the Advanced Redoubt on the Naval Air Station Pensacola; the Okaloosa area near Fort Walton Beach; and portions of Santa Rosa Island including the Fort Pickens area.

Guided tours of Fort Barrancas are offered daily and tours of the restored Advanced Redoubt are offered Saturdays. A visitor center at Naval Live Oaks Reservation features an orientation film and exhibits.

Recreation opportunities include biking, boating, camping, fishing, hiking, picnicking, swimming and snorkeling. Contact the park for snorkeling regulations. The area is also a good bird-watching site. For further information contact Gulf Islands National Seashore, 1801 Gulf Breeze Pkwy., Gulf Breeze, FL 32563; phone (850) 934-2600. *See Recreation Areas Chart.*

# HORSESHOE BEACH pop. 169

## HORSESHOE BEACH CAFE 352/498-7061

▼▼ Seafood. Casual Dining. $6-$19 **AAA Inspector Notes:** On the edge of town along the Gulf, this café serves fresh seafood prepared from the owner's personal recipes. Fresh catfish, mullet, shrimp, clams, salmon, crab cakes as well as chicken and steak entrées are served up by a very friendly and polite staff. **Features:** beer & wine. **Address:** 534 Main St 32648 **Location:** Just s on CR 351; south side of town. L D

## INLET BEACH

**SPICY NOODLE**                                    850/231-0955

▼▼▼ Italian. Casual Dining. $7-$18 **AAA Inspector Notes:** A casual yet rustic Italian sports pub, locals congregate at this spot for the pizza as well as the homemade meatballs. **Features:** beer & wine, patio dining, happy hour. **Address:** 13667 E Emerald Coast Pkwy 32413 **Location:** 1 mi e of Rosemary Beach, just w of Phillips Inlet Bridge. L D

## LYNN HAVEN pop. 18,493

• **Hotels & Restaurants map & index p. 186**

**WINGATE BY WYNDHAM LYNN HAVEN**

(850)248-8080   **32**

Hotel
$95-$136

**Address:** 2610 Lynn Haven Pkwy 32444 **Location:** On SR 77, 1.8 mi n of jct SR 368. **Facility:** 68 units. 4 stories, interior corridors. **Amenities:** safes. **Pool(s):** heated indoor. **Activities:** sauna, hot tub, exercise room. **Guest Services:** valet and coin laundry. **Featured Amenity:** full hot breakfast.

SAVE 🛜 CALL 🗄M 🕹 BIZ HS 🛜 ✕ 🔲 🖳 🖳 / SOME UNITS 🛏

### WHERE TO EAT

**SONNY'S REAL PIT BAR-B-Q**                        850/763-5114

▼▼ Barbecue. Family Dining. $8-$15 **AAA Inspector Notes:** Bearing the name after its founder, Floyd "Sonny" Tillman, this barbecue restaurant first opened its doors circa 1968 in Gainesville, Florida and has since spawned over 150 more throughout the Southeast. The menu is steeped in finger lickin' favorites such as ribs, pulled pork, beef brisket, burgers, catfish, shrimp and char-grilled chicken. Let's not forget about the fried okra, which is the perfect starter dish, and their homemade baked beans. **Features:** beer only. **Address:** 2240 S Hwy 77 32444 **Location:** Just s of SR 390 (14th St). L D

## MADISON pop. 2,843

**BEST WESTERN PLUS MADISON INN**   (850)973-2020

Hotel
$99-$169

Best Western PLUS

**AAA Benefit:**
Members save up to 20%!

**Address:** 167 SE Bandit St 32340 **Location:** I-10 exit 258, just n. **Facility:** 58 units. 3 stories, interior corridors. **Terms:** cancellation fee imposed. **Pool(s):** outdoor. **Activities:** exercise room. **Guest Services:** coin laundry.

SAVE 🛜 CALL 🗄M 🕹 BIZ HS 🛜 ✕ 🔲 🖳 🖳 / SOME UNITS 🛏

## MARIANNA (B-4) pop. 6,102, elev. 89'

**FLORIDA CAVERNS STATE PARK,** 3 mi. n. on SR 166 to 3345 Caverns Rd., has extensive limestone caverns with calcite formations, a museum, natural rock gardens and a horse trail (no horse rental). The Chipola River Canoe Trail, part of the Florida Canoe Trail System, begins here. Guided 45-minute cavern tours explore a lighted passageway. *See Recreation Areas Chart.*

**Hours:** Park open daily 8-dusk. Cavern tours depart Thurs.-Mon. 9-4:30. Closed Thanksgiving and Christmas. **Cost:** $5 (per private vehicle with two to eight people); $4 (per single-occupant vehicle); $2 (per person arriving by bicycle or on foot). Cavern tour $8; $5 (ages 3-12). Canoe rental $15 per half-day, $20 per full day. **Phone:** (850) 482-9598 for recorded information, or (850) 482-1228 for cave tour information.

GT 🏔 🍴 🗙 🎣 🎪

**COMFORT INN & SUITES**                            (850)482-7112

▼▼▼ Hotel $89-$160 **Address:** 2214 Hwy 71 32448 **Location:** I-10 exit 142, just n. **Facility:** 67 units. 3 stories, interior corridors. **Pool(s):** outdoor. **Activities:** exercise room. **Guest Services:** coin laundry. 🍴 🕹 BIZ HS 🛜 🔲 🖳 🖳

**FAIRFIELD INN & SUITES BY MARRIOTT MARIANNA**
(850)482-0012

Hotel
$98-$109

FAIRFIELD INN & SUITES Marriott

**AAA Benefit:**
Members save 5% or more!

**Address:** 4966 Whitetail Dr 32448 **Location:** I-10 exit 142, just ne. **Facility:** 76 units. 3 stories, interior corridors. **Pool(s):** outdoor. **Activities:** hot tub, exercise room. **Guest Services:** valet and coin laundry.

SAVE 🍴 CALL 🗄M 🕹 BIZ HS 🛜 ✕ 🔲 🖳 🖳

**MICROTEL INN & SUITES BY WYNDHAM MARIANNA**
(850)526-5005

▼▼▼ Hotel $80-$110 **Address:** 4959 Whitetail Dr 32448 **Location:** I-10 exit 142, just n on SR 71. **Facility:** 64 units. 3 stories, interior corridors. **Amenities:** safes. **Pool(s):** outdoor. **Guest Services:** coin laundry.

🍴 CALL 🗄M 🕹 🛜 🖳 / SOME UNITS 🛏 🔲 🖳

### WHERE TO EAT

**BISTRO PALMS**                                    850/526-2226

▼▼ Sandwiches. Casual Dining. $5-$7 **AAA Inspector Notes:** The colorful, whimsical decor and lively jazz music in the background offer an upbeat setting for a light lunch at this popular bistro. **Features:** patio dining. **Address:** 2865 McPherson St 32448 **Location:** Jct US 90 (Lafayette St) and Caledonia St, just s; downtown. **Parking:** street only. L CALL 🗄M

**GAZEBO COFFEE SHOPPE & DELI**                     850/526-1276

▼ Deli. Casual Dining. $4-$8 **AAA Inspector Notes:** Located in the heart of the city, this is a great place for a hearty breakfast and quick lunch to fuel a busy day. **Address:** 4412 Lafayette St 32446 **Location:** Between Green and Caledonia sts; downtown. **Parking:** street only. B L

**MADISON'S WAREHOUSE**                             850/526-4000

▼▼ Steak. Casual Dining. $8-$20 **AAA Inspector Notes:** In a rustic warehouse once occupied by Coca-Cola Bottling Company, this steakhouse offers comfort food at a good price. **Features:** beer & wine. **Address:** 2881 Madison St 32446 **Location:** Downtown. **Parking:** street only. L D

**THE OAKS RESTAURANT** 850/526-1114

 American. Casual Dining. $6-$25 **AAA Inspector Notes:** A limited menu of steak, chicken, shrimp and catfish are cooked to order in this busy, no-frills establishment. **Address:** 4727 Hwy 90, Suite 120 32446 **Location:** I-10 exit 142, 1.8 mi n on SR 71, then 1.1 mi e; in Oak Station Plaza. L D CALL M

**SAN MARCOS MEXICAN RESTAURANT** 850/482-0062

Mexican. Casual Dining. $6-$17 **AAA Inspector Notes:** This small, colorful downtown cantina hands patrons a good-size menu of authentic Mexican cuisine and ice-cold cervezas. **Features:** beer only. **Address:** 4867 Westside Plaza 32448 **Location:** I-10 exit 142, just n. L D

**SONNY'S REAL PIT BAR-B-Q** 850/526-7274

Barbecue. Family Dining. $8-$16 **AAA Inspector Notes:** Bearing the name after its founder, Floyd "Sonny" Tillman, this barbecue restaurant first opened its doors circa 1968 in Gainesville, Florida and has since spawned over 150 more throughout the Southeast. The menu is steeped in finger lickin' favorites such as ribs, pulled pork, beef brisket, burgers, catfish, shrimp and char-grilled chicken. Let's not forget about the fried okra, which is the perfect starter dish, and their homemade baked beans. **Features:** beer only. **Address:** 2250 Hwy 71 32448 **Location:** I-10 exit 142, 0.5 mi n. L D

## MIDWAY pop. 3,004

**BEST WESTERN PLUS PANHANDLE CAPITAL INN & SUITES** (850)514-2222

Hotel
$100-$129

**AAA Benefit:**
Members save up to 20%!

**Address:** 85 River Park Dr 32343 **Location:** I-10 exit 192, just s. **Facility:** 52 units. 2 stories, interior corridors. **Pool(s):** outdoor. **Activities:** exercise room. **Guest Services:** coin laundry.

SAVE BIZ HS X / SOME UNITS

**COMFORT INN & SUITES TALLAHASSEE/MIDWAY** (850)576-7300

Hotel
$70-$100

**Address:** 215 Commerce Blvd 32343 **Location:** I-10 exit 192, just n. **Facility:** 67 units. 3 stories, interior corridors. **Amenities:** safes. **Pool(s):** outdoor. **Activities:** limited exercise equipment. **Guest Services:** coin laundry.

SAVE BIZ HS

**HOWARD JOHNSON EXPRESS INN** (850)574-8888

Motel $65-$189 **Address:** 81 Commerce Blvd 32343 **Location:** I-10 exit 192, just n. **Facility:** 49 units. 2 stories, exterior corridors. **Amenities:** safes. **Activities:** limited exercise equipment.
BIZ / SOME UNITS

## MILTON (B-2) pop. 8,826, elev. 15'
• Hotels & Restaurants map & index p. 197

A heavy growth of briars along the Blackwater River elicited Milton's early name, Scratch Ankle. The Blackwater, one of the state's most pristine rivers, has retained its importance to modern Milton as a carrier of recreational canoeists rather than commerce; canoes and tubes can be rented in the area. Blackwater River State Park *(see Recreation Areas Chart)* and Blackwater River State Forest are northeast. Historic old homes date back to the Civil War days. Whiting Field Naval Air Station is north on SR 87.

**Santa Rosa County Chamber of Commerce and Tourist Information Center:** 5247 Stewart St., Milton, FL 32570. **Phone:** (850) 623-2339.

## RECREATIONAL ACTIVITIES
### Canoeing
• **Adventures Unlimited** is 12 mi. n. on SR 87, then 4 mi. e. to 8974 Tomahawk Landing Rd. In addition to canoeing, other activities, including a zipline canopy tour, are offered. **Hours:** Daily 8-4. **Phone:** (850) 623-6197 or (800) 239-6864.

**COMFORT INN** (850)623-1511

Motel
$99-$135

**Address:** 8936 Hwy 87 S 32583 **Location:** I-10 exit 31, just s. **Facility:** 66 units. 2 stories, interior corridors. **Amenities:** safes. **Pool(s):** outdoor. **Activities:** exercise room. **Guest Services:** coin laundry.

SAVE CALL M BIZ HS
 / SOME UNITS

**HOLIDAY INN EXPRESS HOTEL & SUITES** (850)626-9060

Hotel $99-$139 **Address:** 8510 Keshav Taylor Dr 32583 **Location:** I-10 exit 31, just n on SR 87, then just w. **Facility:** 64 units. 3 stories, interior corridors. **Pool(s):** outdoor. **Activities:** exercise room. **Guest Services:** valet and coin laundry.

BIZ HS

**RED ROOF INN & SUITES-PENSACOLA EAST MILTON** (850)995-6100 24

Hotel
$70-$104

**Address:** 2672 Avalon Blvd 32583 **Location:** I-10 exit 22, just s on SR 281. **Facility:** 70 units. 3 stories, interior corridors. **Pool(s):** outdoor. **Guest Services:** coin laundry. **Featured Amenity:** continental breakfast.

SAVE CALL M X
 / SOME UNITS

### WHERE TO EAT

**BLACKWATER BISTRO** 850/623-1105

American. Casual Dining. $9-$24 **AAA Inspector Notes:** Located in a restored historic home, this establishment maintains the integrity of the era with outdoor seating on the front veranda and an inside furnished with an antique décor. **Features:** full bar, patio dining, early bird specials, happy hour. **Address:** 5147 Elmira St 32570 **Location:** Jct US 90 (Caroline St), just s; in historic downtown district. L D CALL M

## MONTICELLO pop. 2,506

**DAYS INN** (850)997-5988

 Motel $78-$105 **Address:** 44 Woodworth Dr 32336 **Location:** I-10 exit 225, just s on US 19. **Facility:** 35 units. 2 stories (no elevator), exterior corridors. **Pool(s):** outdoor.

## NAVARRE pop. 31,378

### BEST WESTERN NAVARRE WATERFRONT

(850)939-9400

Hotel
$90-$219

 **AAA Benefit:**
Members save up to 20%!

**Address:** 8697 Navarre Pkwy 32566 **Location:** Waterfront. On US 98, just e of Navarre Beach Bridge. **Facility:** 68 units. 3 stories, exterior corridors. **Pool(s):** heated outdoor. **Activities:** exercise room. **Guest Services:** coin laundry. **Featured Amenity:** full hot breakfast.

### HAMPTON INN & SUITES NAVARRE

(850)939-4848

Hotel
$89-$199

 **AAA Benefit:**
Members save 5% or more!

**Address:** 7710 Navarre Pkwy 32566 **Location:** On US 98, 0.5 mi w of Navarre Beach Bridge. **Facility:** 102 units. 4 stories, interior corridors. **Terms:** 1-7 night minimum stay, cancellation fee imposed. **Pool(s):** outdoor. **Activities:** exercise room. **Guest Services:** coin laundry. **Featured Amenity:** full hot breakfast.

### WHERE TO EAT

**CACTUS FLOWER CAFE** 850/936-4111

Mexican. Casual Dining. $8-$17 **AAA Inspector Notes:** Every dish is fresh and made-to-order so diners must not be in a hurry to eat at this cafe. Seating is limited and weekends are very busy. **Features:** beer & wine. **Address:** 8725 Ortega Park Dr 32566 **Location:** On US 98, 0.4 mi e of Navarre Beach Bridge.

## EAST BAY CRAB HOUSE

850/939-5543

▼▼▼ Seafood. Casual Dining. $15-$24 **AAA Inspector Notes:** Seafood abounds plenty, both on the menu and amid the surrounding décor, with walls filled with fishing nets, crabs, seashells and mounted fish. Along with fried, broiled or grilled preparations, the menu features house favorites like mai Thai grouper and ragin' Cajun grouper. There are several pasta plates as well as steak and chicken for the meat lovers. Love it all and can't decide? Not to worry—combo plates are a great solution. **Features:** full bar. **Address:** 9250 Navarre Pkwy 32566 **Location:** On US 98, 1.8 mi e of Navarre Beach Bridge.

D CALL &M

## VINNIE R'S ITALIAN RESTAURANT

850/936-4811

▼▼▼ Italian. Casual Dining. $8-$17 **AAA Inspector Notes:** The locally-owned-and-operated ristorante specializes in a variety of pasta dishes, pizza, stromboli, calzones and subs. All sauces and dressings are prepared from scratch in house using fine ingredients, including olive oil and pasta noodles imported from Italy. **Features:** beer & wine. **Address:** 7552 Navarre Pkwy, Suite 14 32566 **Location:** On US 98, 2.4 mi w of Navarre Beach Bridge (SR 399); in Harvest Village complex. L D CALL &M

# NAVARRE BEACH

### THE INN AT SUMMERWIND RESORT

(850)936-1312

▼▼▼ △△△
Vacation Rental
Condominium
$99-$320

**Address:** 8577 Gulf Blvd 32566 **Location:** Oceanfront. Just w of Navarre Beach Bridge; on Santa Rosa Island. **Facility:** White sandy beach and clear blue surf is the view from all units at this gulf-shore resort. Each unit offers all of the comforts of home. 40 condominiums. 16 stories, interior corridors. **Terms:** 3 night minimum stay - seasonal and/or weekends, cancellation fee imposed, resort fee. **Pool(s):** outdoor, heated outdoor. **Activities:** hot tub, exercise room. **Guest Services:** complimentary laundry.

SAVE ❙❙+ ⚓ 📶 ✕ 🛏 🖨 🖵

# NICEVILLE pop. 12,749

### COMFORT SUITES

(850)279-6547

▼▼▼ Hotel $79-$169 **Address:** 148 John Sims Pkwy W 32578 **Location:** On SR 85, just sw of jct SR 20. **Facility:** 75 units. 3 stories, interior corridors. **Pool(s):** outdoor. **Activities:** exercise room. **Guest Services:** coin laundry.

CALL &M ⚓ BIZ HS 📶 ✕ 🛏 🖨 🖵

### HAMPTON INN-NICEVILLE/EGLIN AFB

(850)897-4675

▼▼▼ Hotel $100-$209 **Address:** 4400 Ansley Dr 32578 **Location:** On SR 20, 2 mi e. **Facility:** 56 units. 3 stories, interior corridors. **Terms:** 1-7 night minimum stay, cancellation fee imposed. **Pool(s):** outdoor. **Activities:** exercise room.

**AAA Benefit:** Members save 5% or more!

CALL &M ⚓ BIZ HS 📶 ✕ 🛏 🖨 🖵

### HOLIDAY INN EXPRESS

(850)678-9131

▼▼▼ Hotel $99-$179 **Address:** 106 Bayshore Dr 32578 **Location:** On SR 20, just se of jct SR 85. **Facility:** 87 units, some kitchens. 2 stories, interior corridors. **Terms:** 3 day cancellation notice. **Pool(s):** outdoor. **Guest Services:** valet and coin laundry.

❙❙+ ⚓ BIZ HS 📶 ✕ 🛏 🖨 🖵

---

## PANACEA (C-5) pop. 816, elev. 5'

**GULF SPECIMEN MARINE LABORATORY,** just s. of US 98, following signs to 222 Clark Dr., features a 25,000-gallon marine aquarium and touch tanks housing sea horses, crabs, rays, sponges, starfish and small sharks. **Time:** Allow 1 hour minimum. **Hours:** Mon.-Fri. 9-5, Sat. 10-4, Sun. noon-4. Closed Jan. 1, Thanksgiving and Christmas. **Cost:** $9.50; $8.50 (ages 65+); $7.50 (ages 3-11). **Phone:** (850) 984-5297.

## PANAMA CITY (C-4) pop. 36,484, elev. 33'

• Hotels p. 188 • Restaurants p. 189
• Hotels & Restaurants map & index p. 186

Panama City, county seat of Bay County, is a leading port on St. Andrew Bay off the Gulf of Mexico and is the midpoint along the scenic panhandle portion of US 98 extending 98 miles to Gulf Breeze (just south of Pensacola) and eastward around the Big Bend area. Spanish expeditions visited this site 1516-40, but it was not until 1765 that an English settlement was made at St. Andrew, now part of Panama City.

Panama City is known for its sugar-white beaches and various waterways. There are numerous marinas, including the downtown marina at the foot of Harrison Avenue with berths for about 400 boats. Fishing boats can be chartered on St. Andrew Bay. The area also is home to Tyndall Air Force Base and Naval Support Activity Panama City.

**Bay County Chamber of Commerce:** 235 W. Fifth St., P.O. Box 1850, Panama City, FL 32402-1850. **Phone:** (850) 785-5206.

**Self-guiding tours:** A brochure featuring a walking tour of the historic downtown can be picked up from the Downtown Improvement Board at 413 Harrison Ave. and from the local history room in the Bay County Public Library at 898 W. 11th St.

**SCIENCE & DISCOVERY CENTER OF NORTHWEST FLORIDA,** 308 Airport Rd., offers family-oriented hands-on exhibits related to the human body, nature and the sciences. Highlights include the Pioneer Homestead, a re-created farm from the late 1800s, and a boardwalk nature trail through a swamp and forest area.

**Time:** Allow 30 minutes minimum. **Hours:** Tues.-Sat. 10-5. Science Through Stories program (ages 0-4) Tues.-Wed. at 10:30. Reptile Encounters Thurs. at 3:30. Closed major holidays. **Cost:** $7; $6 (ages 1-16, ages 65+ and military with ID). **Phone:** (850) 769-6128.

---

Get AAA/CAA travel information in the

digital and printed formats you prefer

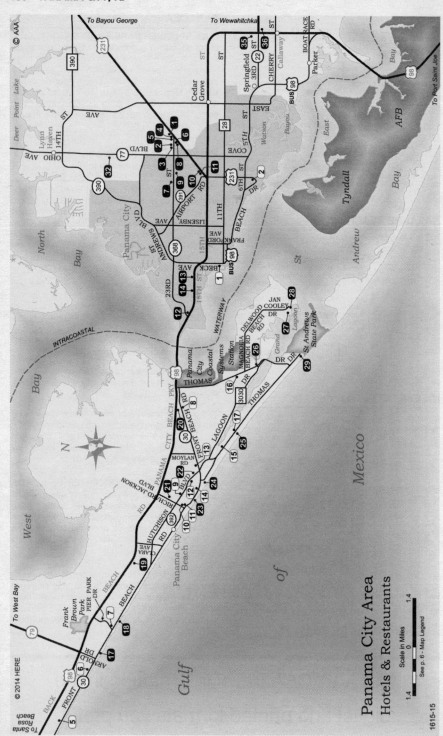

Panama City Area
Hotels & Restaurants

Scale in Miles

See p. 6 · Map Legend

1615-15

© AAA

© 2014 HERE

# Panama City

This index helps you "spot" where approved hotels and restaurants are located on the corresponding detailed maps. Hotel daily rate range is for comparison only. Restaurant price range is a combination of lunch and/or dinner. Turn to the listing page for more detailed rate and price information and consult display ads for special promotions.

## PANAMA CITY

| Map Page | Hotels | Diamond Rated | Rate Range | Page |
|---|---|---|---|---|
| 1 p. 186 | Microtel Inn & Suites by Wyndham Panama City | ▽▽ | $47-$97 | 189 |
| 2 p. 186 | Courtyard by Marriott Panama City | ▽▽ | $129-$199 | 188 |
| 3 p. 186 | TownePlace Suites by Marriott Panama City | ▽▽▽ | $99-$199 | 189 |
| 4 p. 186 | **Hampton Inn Panama City Mall** | ▽▽▽ | $109-$169 [SAVE] | 188 |
| 5 p. 186 | **BEST WESTERN Suites** | ▽▽ | $70-$130 [SAVE] | 188 |
| 6 p. 186 | La Quinta Inn & Suites | ▽▽▽ | $69-$199 | 189 |
| 7 p. 186 | Sleep Inn & Suites | ▽▽▽ | $60-$120 | 189 |
| 8 p. 186 | Hilton Garden Inn Panama City | ▽▽▽ | $79-$229 | 189 |
| 9 p. 186 | **Country Inn & Suites By Carlson Panama City** | ▽▽▽ | $75-$150 [SAVE] | 188 |
| 10 p. 186 | Red Roof Inn-Panama City | ▽▽ | $59-$199 | 189 |
| 11 p. 186 | Super 8-Panama City | ▽▽ | $52-$100 | 189 |
| 12 p. 186 | Hathaway Inn | ▽▽ | Rates not provided | 188 |
| 13 p. 186 | Comfort Inn & Suites | ▽▽▽ | $80-$200 | 188 |
| 14 p. 186 | Quality Inn & Suites | ▽▽ | $66-$130 | 189 |

| Map Page | Restaurants | Diamond Rated | Cuisine | Price Range | Page |
|---|---|---|---|---|---|
| 1 p. 186 | Uncle Ernie's Bayfront Grill & Brew House | ▽▽ | Seafood | $13-$30 | 189 |
| 2 p. 186 | Ferrucci Ristorante | ▽▽ | Italian | $8-$23 | 189 |

## PANAMA CITY BEACH

| Map Page | Hotels | Diamond Rated | Rate Range | Page |
|---|---|---|---|---|
| 17 p. 186 | Holiday Inn Club Vacations Panama City Beach Resort | ▽▽▽ | Rates not provided | 192 |
| 18 p. 186 | Osprey Motel On The Gulf | ▽▽ | $75-$325 | 192 |
| 19 p. 186 | Hampton Inn & Suites Panama City Beach Pier Park Area | ▽▽▽ | $109-$279 | 192 |
| 20 p. 186 | Hawthorn Suites by Wyndham | ▽▽▽ | $68-$156 | 192 |
| 21 p. 186 | Comfort Suites Panama City Beach | ▽▽▽ | $79-$229 | 191 |
| 22 p. 186 | Country Inn & Suites By Carlson | ▽▽▽ | Rates not provided | 192 |
| 23 p. 186 | Majestic Beach Resort | ▽▽▽ | Rates not provided | 192 |
| 24 p. 186 | Shores of Panama Beach Resort | ▽▽▽ | Rates not provided | 192 |
| 25 p. 186 | **Sunset Inn** | ▽▽ | $60-$250 [SAVE] | 192 |
| 26 p. 186 | Hampton Inn Panama City Beach | ▽▽▽ | $89-$204 | 192 |
| 27 p. 186 | Holiday Inn Club Vacations at Bay Point Resort | ▽▽▽ | Rates not provided | 192 |
| 28 p. 186 | Bay Point Wyndham Resort | ▽▽▽ | $99-$219 | 191 |
| 29 p. 186 | Moonspinner Condominium | ▽▽▽ | $130-$365 | 192 |

| Map Page | Restaurants | Diamond Rated | Cuisine | Price Range | Page |
|---|---|---|---|---|---|
| 5 p. 186 | Thomas' Donut & Snack Shop | ▽ | Sandwiches Pizza | $3-$14 | 193 |
| 6 p. 186 | Boar's Head Restaurant | ▽▽ | Steak Seafood | $14-$36 | 192 |

| Map Page | Restaurants (cont'd) | Diamond Rated | Cuisine | Price Range | Page |
|---|---|---|---|---|---|
| ⑦ p. 186 | Hofbrau Beer Garden | ▼▼ | German | $8-$18 | 193 |
| ⑧ p. 186 | Fishale Taphouse & Grill | ▼▼ | Seafood | $9-$22 | 193 |
| ⑨ p. 186 | Saltwater Grill | ▼▼ | Seafood | $15-$43 | 193 |
| ⑩ p. 186 | Firefly | ▼▼▼ | New American | $9-$42 | 193 |
| ⑪ p. 186 | Sweet Basils | ▼▼ | Italian | $7-$17 | 193 |
| ⑫ p. 186 | Wicked Wheel Bar & Grill | ▼▼ | American | $8-$15 | 193 |
| ⑬ p. 186 | Dirty Dick's Crab House | ▼▼ | Seafood | $7-$17 | 193 |
| ⑭ p. 186 | All American Diner | ▼ | American | $5-$12 | 192 |
| ⑮ p. 186 | Guadalajara Mexican Grill | ▼▼ | Mexican | $6-$13 | 193 |
| ⑯ p. 186 | Triple "J" Steak & Seafood | ▼▼ | Steak Seafood | $7-$32 | 193 |
| ⑰ p. 186 | Hognose Snapper | ▼▼ | Seafood | $8-$19 | 193 |

**LYNN HAVEN**

| Map Page | Hotel | Diamond Rated | Rate Range | Page |
|---|---|---|---|---|
| ㉜ p. 186 | **Wingate by Wyndham Lynn Haven** | ▼▼▼ | $95-$136 [SAVE] | 182 |

**CALLAWAY**

| Map Page | Hotels | Diamond Rated | Rate Range | Page |
|---|---|---|---|---|
| ㉟ p. 186 | Days Inn & Suites-Tyndall | ▼▼ | $69-$149 | 172 |
| ㊱ p. 186 | Comfort Suites Callaway/Panama City | ▼▼▼ | $90-$265 | 172 |

**BEST WESTERN SUITES**      (850)784-7700  **5**

Motel
$70-$130

**AAA Benefit:**
Members save up to 20%!

**Address:** 1035 E 23rd St 32405 **Location:** On SR 368 (23rd St), just w of jct US 231. **Facility:** 50 units. 2 stories (no elevator), interior corridors. **Pool(s):** outdoor. **Activities:** exercise room. **Guest Services:** valet laundry.

**COMFORT INN & SUITES**      (850)522-5200  **13**
▼▼▼ Hotel $80-$200 **Address:** 3602 W US 98 32401 **Location:** On US 98, 2.3 mi e of Hathaway Bridge. **Facility:** 56 units, some kitchens. 4 stories, interior corridors. **Pool(s):** outdoor. **Activities:** exercise room. **Guest Services:** valet and coin laundry.

**COUNTRY INN & SUITES BY CARLSON PANAMA CITY**
(850)913-0074  **9**

▼▼▼ Hotel
$75-$150

**Address:** 2203 Harrison Ave 32405 **Location:** 0.5 mi w of US 231; just s of SR 368 (23rd St). **Facility:** 53 units. 2 stories, interior corridors. **Terms:** cancellation fee imposed. **Pool(s):** outdoor. **Activities:** exercise room. **Guest Services:** valet laundry.

**COURTYARD BY MARRIOTT PANAMA CITY**
(850)763-6525  **2**

▼▼▼ Hotel $129-$199 **Address:** 905 E 23rd Pl 32405 **Location:** Just e of jct SR 77 (Martin Luther King Jr Blvd), just w of jct US 231 on SR 368 (23rd St), then just n on Palo Alto Ave. **Facility:** 84 units. 3 stories, interior corridors. **Pool(s):** outdoor. **Activities:** hot tub, exercise room. **Guest Services:** valet and coin laundry.

**AAA Benefit:**
Members save 5% or more!

**HAMPTON INN PANAMA CITY MALL**
(850)872-6969  **4**

Hotel
$109-$169

**AAA Benefit:**
Members save 5% or more!

**Address:** 2338 Mercedes Ave 32405 **Location:** Just w of jct US 231 on SR 368 (23rd St). **Facility:** 60 units. 3 stories, interior corridors. **Terms:** 1-7 night minimum stay, cancellation fee imposed. **Pool(s):** outdoor. **Activities:** hot tub, exercise room. **Guest Services:** coin laundry. **Featured Amenity:** full hot breakfast.

**HATHAWAY INN**      850/763-7777  **12**
▼▼ Motel. Rates not provided. **Address:** 5126 W US 98 32401 **Location:** Jct SR 368 (23rd St), 0.5 mi e of Hathaway Bridge. **Facility:** 82 units. 2 stories, interior corridors. *Bath:* shower only. **Pool(s):** outdoor. **Activities:** exercise room. **Guest Services:** valet and coin laundry.

(See map & index p. 186.)

### HILTON GARDEN INN PANAMA CITY    (850)392-1093    8

▼▼▼▼ **Hotel** $79-$229 **Address:**
1101 N Hwy 231 32405 **Location:** Just s
of jct SR 368 (23rd St). **Facility:** 111
units. 4 stories, interior corridors. **Terms:**
1-7 night minimum stay, cancellation fee
imposed. **Pool(s):** outdoor. **Activities:** hot tub, exercise room. **Guest
Services:** valet and coin laundry, area transportation.

**AAA Benefit:**
Members save 5%
or more!

ECO 🚬 🍽 🍸 CALL 🔛 🏊 BIZ HS 🛜 📹
🔲 🖥 🖨

---

### LA QUINTA INN & SUITES    (850)914-0022    6

▼▼▼▼ **Hotel** $69-$199 **Address:** 1030 E 23rd St 32405 **Location:** On SR 368 (23rd St), jct US 231. **Facility:** 119 units. 6 stories, interior corridors. **Pool(s):** heated outdoor. **Activities:** hot tub, exercise room. **Guest Services:** coin laundry.

CALL 🔛 🏊 HS 🛜 🖥 / SOME UNITS 🐾 🔲 🖨

---

### MICROTEL INN & SUITES BY WYNDHAM PANAMA CITY    (850)522-1166    1

▼▼ ▼▼ **Hotel** $47-$97 **Address:** 1110 E 24th St 32405 **Location:** Just nw of jct US 231 and SR 368 (23rd St). **Facility:** 63 units. 3 stories, interior corridors. **Pool(s):** outdoor.

CALL 🔛 🏊 HS 🛜 🖥 / SOME UNITS 🔲 🖨

---

### QUALITY INN & SUITES    (850)763-0101    14

▼▼ ▼ **Motel** $66-$130 **Address:** 4128 W Hwy 98 32401 **Location:** On US 98, 3.2 mi w of jct US 231. **Facility:** 40 units. 2 stories, exterior corridors. **Terms:** 3 day cancellation notice. **Pool(s):** outdoor. **Guest Services:** coin laundry.

🍽+ 🏊 BIZ HS 🛜 🔲 🖨 🖥

---

### RED ROOF INN-PANAMA CITY    (850)215-2727    10

▼▼▼ **Hotel** $59-$199 **Address:** 217 Hwy 231 32405 **Location:** On US 231, just ne of jct US 98. **Facility:** 73 units, some efficiencies. 3 stories, interior corridors. **Terms:** 3 day cancellation notice-fee imposed. **Pool(s):** outdoor. **Activities:** exercise room. **Guest Services:** coin laundry.

🏊 BIZ HS 🛜 🔲 🖨 🖥 / SOME UNITS 🆂

---

### SLEEP INN & SUITES    (850)215-4040    7

▼▼▼ **Hotel** $60-$120 **Address:** 2317 Jenks Ave 32405 **Location:** 0.7 mi w of jct SR 77 on SR 368 (23rd St), just n on CR 2341. **Facility:** 69 units. 3 stories, interior corridors. **Pool(s):** outdoor. **Activities:** exercise room. **Guest Services:** valet and coin laundry.

🍽+ CALL 🔛 🏊 BIZ HS 🛜 🔲 🖨 🖥

---

### SUPER 8-PANAMA CITY    (850)784-1988    11

▼▼ ▼ **Motel** $52-$100 **Address:** 207 Hwy 231 32405 **Location:** On US 231, just ne of jct US 98. **Facility:** 60 units. 2 stories (no elevator), interior/exterior corridors. **Terms:** cancellation fee imposed. **Pool(s):** outdoor.

🍽+ 🏊 HS 🛜 🔲 🖨 🖥 / SOME UNITS 🆂

---

### TOWNEPLACE SUITES BY MARRIOTT PANAMA CITY    (850)747-0609    3

▼▼▼▼ **Extended Stay Hotel**
$99-$199 **Address:** 903 E 23rd Pl
32405 **Location:** Just e of jct SR 77, w
of jct US 231 on SR 368 (23rd St), then
n on Palo Alto Ave. **Facility:** 103 units,

**AAA Benefit:**
Members save 5%
or more!

some two bedrooms, efficiencies and kitchens. 3 stories, interior corridors. **Terms:** check-in 4 pm. **Pool(s):** outdoor. **Activities:** exercise room. **Guest Services:** valet and coin laundry.

🍽+ CALL 🔛 🏊 BIZ HS 🛜 ❌ 🔲 🖨 🖥
/ SOME UNITS 🆂

---

### FERRUCCI RISTORANTE    850/913-9131    2

▼▼ ▼▼ Italian. Casual Dining. $8-$23 **AAA Inspector Notes:** This quaint intimate bistro located in the heart of town serves delicious Italian favorites. **Features:** full bar. **Address:** 301 Harrison Ave 32401 **Location:** Between E 4th St and Oak Ave; downtown. **Parking:** street only. L D CALL 🔛

---

### UNCLE ERNIE'S BAYFRONT GRILL & BREW HOUSE    850/763-8427    1

▼▼ ▼ Seafood. Casual Dining. $13-$30 **AAA Inspector Notes:** Specializing in inexpensive to moderately priced steaks, seafood and pasta, this restaurant affords nice views of the bay and marina area, particularly from the outdoor patio. Varied beers are made in the on-site brewery. **Features:** full bar, patio dining. **Address:** 1151 Bayview Ave 32401 **Location:** 0.5 mi w of jct US 98 on Business Rt 98, then just e on 12th St; in St. Andrews historic area. **Parking:** on-site and street. L D

---

## PANAMA CITY BEACH (C-4) pop. 12,018, elev. 7'

• Hotels p. 191 • Restaurants p. 192
• Hotels & Restaurants map & index p. 186

Once a collection of quaint beach cottages and small motels scattered along the coast, Panama City Beach now boasts a skyline of towering waterfront hotels and vacation condominiums with more luxury resorts being added all the time. What's the attraction? Simply put: sand and water—some of the most beautiful sand and water to be found anywhere in Florida.

The sand here owes its distinctive white, powdery appearance to quartz crystals that were carried to the coast by streams from the distant Appalachian Mountains and then pulverized by the relentless surf and bleached by the sun. The nearly 30 miles of fine, sugary sand took centuries to accumulate, and the result is soft to the touch and dazzling to the eyes.

And then there's the sea. The Gulf of Mexico's warm, green-tinted water gives this portion of the Florida Panhandle its Emerald Coast nickname. The Yucatan Current, part of the Gulf Stream, runs close to the shores of Panama City Beach, bringing with it nutrient-rich Caribbean water and a variety of marine life. Visitors strolling among the dunes are likely to spy the arched backs of dolphins breaking the sparkling water's surface just a few yards away.

While many vacationers are content simply relaxing on the sand, others take advantage of the various recreational activities Panama City Beach offers: pleasure boating, sailing, jet skiing, wind surfing and parasailing. Dozens of shipwrecks and almost 50 artificial reefs provide plenty of scuba diving options, and with nearly 320 days of sunny skies and a temperate climate, Panama City Beach is known for its "golfability" factor. Five championship golf courses are close to the beaches.

**Panama City Beach Convention and Visitors Bureau:** 17001 Panama City Beach Pkwy., Panama City Beach, FL 32413. **Phone:** (850) 233-5070, (800) 553-1330 within Canada or (800) 722-3224. *(See ad p. 190.)*

(See map & index p. 186.)

**Shopping areas:** Pier Park, at Front Beach Road and Pier Park Drive, is a large open-air shopping village with more than 100 stores, including Dillard's and JCPenney.

***CAPT. ANDERSON III,*** at Capt. Anderson's Marina, 5550 N. Lagoon Dr. at jct. Thomas Dr., offers 3-hour sightseeing cruises to Shell Island, Beach Seafari cruises and a 75-minute sunset Dolphin Encounter.

**Hours:** Beach Seafari cruise departs daily at 9 and 11:30. Shell Island cruise departs daily at 2, Apr.-Oct. Dolphin Encounter cruise departs daily at 5:30, Apr.-Oct. Phone for schedules of other cruises. **Cost:**

Beach Seafari cruise $20; $10 (ages 2-11). Shell Island cruise $23; $12 (ages 2-11). Dolphin Encounter cruise $12; $6 (ages 2-11). Phone for fares of other cruises. **Phone:** (850) 234-3435 or (800) 874-2415.

SAVE **GULF WORLD MARINE PARK** is at 15412 Front Beach Rd. Separate exhibit areas house dolphins, sea lions, stingrays, alligators, penguins, reptiles, sharks and tropical birds. Check the daily entertainment schedule for a list of shows featuring some of the park's inhabitants, or make reservations in advance for the Swim with the Dolphins program.

**Time:** Allow 2 hours minimum. **Hours:** Open daily at 9:30, day after Christmas-Nov. 28. Closing times

▼ *See AAA listing p. 189* ▼

(See map & index p. 186.)

vary, phone to confirm. Closed Thanksgiving. Phone ahead to confirm schedule. **Cost:** $28; $23 (ages 55+); $18 (ages 5-11). Swim with the Dolphins $175; ages 0-4 not permitted. **Phone:** (850) 234-5271.

**MAN IN THE SEA MUSEUM,** .25 mi. w. of jct. SR 79 at 17314 Panama City Beach Pkwy. (US 98), illustrates the history of undersea exploration using dioramas and written records. Highlights include rare and antique diving equipment and related displays. Changing exhibits are featured. **Time:** Allow 1 hour minimum. **Hours:** Wed.-Sat. 10-5. **Cost:** $5; $4.50 (ages 65+); free (ages 0-6). **Phone:** (850) 235-4101.

**RIPLEY'S BELIEVE IT OR NOT!** is at 9907 Front Beach Rd. Oddities and surprises abound within a museum shaped like a giant steamship. More than 500 exhibits include two-headed animals, a car covered in gold coins and a diminutive matchstick replica of the Eiffel Tower. A 4-D theater with moving seats features several action-packed films.

Time: Allow 1 hour minimum. **Hours:** Open daily at 10. Closing times vary. Closed major holidays. Phone ahead to confirm schedule. **Cost:** Museum $15.99; $10.99 (ages 6-12). Theater $10.99; $9.99 (ages 6-12). Combination admission $19.99; $15.99 (ages 6-12). **Phone:** (850) 230-6113.

**ST. ANDREWS STATE PARK,** 3 mi. e. off SR 392 to 4607 State Park Ln., flanks the pass separating Panama City Beach from Shell Island, the barrier isle guarding the mouth of St. Andrews Bay. The mainland portion of the park contains a restored turpentine still. The Shell Island segment, an excellent spot for swimming, snorkeling and shell gathering, is accessible only by boat. Shuttles depart from the end of Thomas Drive in the recreation area daily every 30 minutes 9-5, Memorial Day weekend through Labor Day. *See Recreation Areas Chart.*

Time: Allow 1 hour minimum. **Hours:** Daily 8 a.m.-dusk. **Cost:** $8 (per vehicle with two to eight people); $4 (per single-occupancy vehicle); $2 (per person arriving by bicycle or on foot). **Phone:** (850) 233-5140.

**SEA DRAGON PIRATE CRUISE** departs from 5325 N. Lagoon Dr. Activities such as sword fights, treasure hunting, dancing and swabbing the deck pirate-style keep children entertained while adults may enjoy a 2-hour narrated sightseeing cruise that might include dolphin sightings.

Time: Allow 2 hours minimum. **Hours:** Cruises depart daily at 3 and 6 (also at 9 and noon on selected dates), June-July; schedule varies mid-Mar. through May 31 and Aug. 1- late Oct. **Cost:** Morning or afternoon cruise $24; $20 (ages 60+); $18 (ages 3-14); $12 (ages 1-2). Sunset cruise $26; $22 (ages 60+); $20 (ages 3-14); $14 (ages 1-2). Reservations are recommended. **Phone:** (850) 234-7400.

**SHIPWRECK ISLAND WATERPARK,** 12201 Hutchison Blvd. (CR 392A), features waterslides, children's water activities, a lazy river, a wave pool and a family activity pool. Rental lockers are available. **Time:** Allow 2 hours minimum. **Hours:** Daily 10:30-5, early June-early Aug.; daily 10:30-4:30, late May-early June; Sat. 10:30-4:30 (also Labor Day weekend), late Apr.-Memorial Day and mid-Aug. to late Aug. Phone ahead to confirm schedule. **Cost:** $33; $28 (children 35-50 inches tall); $22 (ages 62+). **Phone:** (850) 234-3333 or (800) 538-7395.

**WONDERWORKS,** 9910 Front Beach Rd. at jct. Thomas Dr., features more than 100 interactive science exhibits in a building designed to appear like it landed upside down on top of a surf shop. The lobby continues the upside-down theme as guests go through an inversion tunnel to begin their adventure. The interior of the building features vibrant colors throughout, creating optical illusions.

Simulators and virtual attractions allow visitors to experience a hurricane, piloting a fighter jet and landing the space shuttle. Visitors can play trivia games and virtual sports games as well as design and ride virtual roller coasters. There also is a laser tag arena and an indoor three-story ropes course.

Note: Closed shoes are required for the ropes course. **Hours:** Opens daily at 9; phone for closing times. Hours vary by season; phone ahead to confirm schedule. Attraction is open half-days Thanksgiving and Christmas. **Cost:** $23.99; $18.99 (ages 5-12 and 55+). **Phone:** (850) 249-7000.

**ZOO WORLD** is at 9008 Front Beach Rd. The zoo is home to more than 250 animals, many of which are endangered and come from several continents. Shows, feedings, and photo and encounter opportunities are available. **Time:** Allow 1 hour minimum. **Hours:** Mon.-Sat. 9:30-5, Sun. 11-5, Memorial Day weekend-Labor Day; Mon.-Sat. 9:30-4, Sun. 11-4, rest of year. Last admission 1 hour before closing. Closed Jan. 1, Thanksgiving and Christmas. **Cost:** $16; $12 (ages 65+); $10 (ages 4-11). **Phone:** (850) 230-1243.

BAY POINT WYNDHAM RESORT            (850)236-6000  **28**
▼▼▼ **Resort Hotel** $99-$219 **Address:** 4114 Jan Cooley Dr 32408 **Location:** Waterfront. Jct CR 3031 (Thomas Dr), 1.9 mi e on Magnolia Beach Rd, 0.8 mi se. **Facility:** A bay and wildlife sanctuary provide pleasant views from the guest rooms at this 1,100-acre resort. Each unit has a patio or balcony. Shopping areas and a marina are on the grounds. 319 units, some two and three bedrooms. 6 stories, interior/exterior corridors. **Terms:** check-in 4 pm. **Amenities:** safes. **Dining:** 3 restaurants. **Pool(s):** outdoor, heated outdoor, heated indoor. **Activities:** marina, fishing, scuba diving, regulation golf, tennis, recreation programs, bicycles, playground, spa. **Guest Services:** valet and coin laundry, rental car service.

COMFORT SUITES PANAMA CITY BEACH
                                      (850)249-1234  **21**
▼▼▼ **Hotel** $79-$229 **Address:** 225 R Jackson Blvd 32407 **Location:** Just n of jct CR 392A (Hutchison Blvd). **Facility:** 74 units. 3 stories, interior corridors. **Terms:** check-in 4 pm, 3 day cancellation notice. **Pool(s):** outdoor. **Activities:** exercise room. **Guest Services:** valet and coin laundry.

**(See map & index p. 186.)**

## COUNTRY INN & SUITES BY CARLSON   850/249-4747   22

▼▼▼▼ **Hotel. Rates not provided. Address:** 10241 Clarence St 32407 **Location:** Just e of jct CR 392A (Hutchison Blvd). **Facility:** 82 units. 4 stories, interior corridors. **Terms:** check-in 4 pm. **Pool(s):** outdoor. **Activities:** exercise room. **Guest Services:** coin laundry.

[¶+] CALL [&M] [≈] [BIZ] [HS] [◉] [✕] [🔓] [📷] [🖥]

## HAMPTON INN & SUITES PANAMA CITY BEACH PIER PARK AREA   (850)230-9080   19

▼▼▼▼ **Hotel** $109-$279 **Address:** 13505 Panama City Beach Pkwy 32407 **Location:** On US 98 (Back Beach Rd), 1.8 mi e of Pier Park Dr; jct Lantana St. **Facility:** 95 units. 5 stories, interior corridors. **Terms:** 1-7 night minimum stay, cancellation fee imposed. **Pool(s):** outdoor. **Activities:** exercise room. **Guest Services:** valet and coin laundry.

| **AAA Benefit:** Members save 5% or more! |

[≈] [BIZ] [HS] [◉] [🖥] / SOME UNITS [🔓] [📷]

## HAMPTON INN PANAMA CITY BEACH   (850)236-8988   26

▼▼▼▼ **Hotel** $89-$204 **Address:** 2909 Thomas Dr 32408 **Location:** On CR 3031 (Thomas Dr), 2.5 mi s of jct US 98. **Facility:** 89 units. 3 stories, interior corridors. **Terms:** 1-7 night minimum stay, cancellation fee imposed. **Pool(s):** outdoor. **Activities:** hot tub, exercise room. **Guest Services:** valet laundry.

| **AAA Benefit:** Members save 5% or more! |

[¶+] [≈] [BIZ] [HS] [◉] [🔓] [📷] [🖥]

## HAWTHORN SUITES BY WYNDHAM   (850)233-7829   20

▼▼▼▼ **Extended Stay Hotel** $68-$156 **Address:** 7909 Panama City Beach Pkwy 32407 **Location:** Jct US 98 and SR 30. **Facility:** 78 efficiencies. 4 stories, interior corridors. **Terms:** check-in 4 pm. **Pool(s):** outdoor. **Activities:** exercise room. **Guest Services:** valet and coin laundry.

CALL [&M] [≈] [BIZ] [◉] [✕] [🔓] [📷] [🖥] / SOME UNITS [📶] [HS]

## HOLIDAY INN CLUB VACATIONS AT BAY POINT RESORT   850/236-6190   27

▼▼▼ **Vacation Rental Condominium. Rates not provided. Address:** 4100 Marriott Dr 32408 **Location:** Jct CR 3031 (Thomas Dr), 1.9 mi e on Magnolia Beach Rd, 0.7 mi se, then just nw; in Bay Point Wyndham Resort. **Facility:** This property is part of a large resort where the well-equipped facilities are shared by both the individual unit owners and renters. 36 condominiums. 4 stories, interior corridors. **Terms:** check-in 4 pm. **Amenities:** *Some:* safes. **Pool(s):** heated outdoor, indoor. **Activities:** hot tub, regulation golf, tennis, playground, exercise room, spa. **Guest Services:** complimentary laundry. [≈] [◉] [✕] [🔓] [📷] [🖥]

## HOLIDAY INN CLUB VACATIONS PANAMA CITY BEACH RESORT   850/233-8830   17

▼▼▼ **Vacation Rental Condominium. Rates not provided. Address:** 17001 Front Beach Rd 32413 **Location:** Oceanfront. Just e of jct SR 79 and US 98. **Facility:** Stylish units have gulf-view balconies and there's beach volleyball and a splash pad for the kids. 37 condominiums. 5 stories, exterior corridors. **Terms:** check-in 4 pm. **Amenities:** safes. **Pool(s):** heated outdoor. **Activities:** hot tub, limited beach access, exercise room. **Guest Services:** complimentary laundry.
CALL [&M] [≈] [BIZ] [◉] [✕] [🔓] [📷] [🖥]

## MAJESTIC BEACH RESORT   850/563-1000   23

▼▼▼ **Vacation Rental Condominium. Rates not provided. Address:** 10901 Front Beach Rd 32407 **Location:** Oceanfront. On US 98A, 0.5 mi w of jct CR 392. **Facility:** Located on the Gulf Of Mexico, these one-, two- and three-bedroom condominiums have spectacular views as well as fully equipped kitchens, waterfront balconies and are nicely appointed. 170 condominiums. 23 stories, exterior corridors. **Terms:** check-in 4 pm. **Dining:** 2 restaurants. **Pool(s):** outdoor, heated indoor. **Activities:** sauna, hot tub, steamroom, tennis, game room, exercise room. **Guest Services:** complimentary laundry.

[¶] [⛰] [≈] [◉] [✕] [🔓] [📷] [🖥]

## MOONSPINNER CONDOMINIUM   850/234-8900   29

▼▼▼▼ **Vacation Rental Condominium** $130-$365 **Address:** 4425 Thomas Dr 32408 **Location:** Oceanfront. On CR 3031 (Thomas Dr), 3.8 mi s of US 98. **Facility:** This beachfront property offers individually decorated two- and three-bedroom units. All have a full kitchen, living room, dining room and a balcony that overlooks the Gulf of Mexico and beach. 101 condominiums. 8 stories, exterior corridors. **Terms:** check-in 4 pm, 3 night minimum stay - seasonal and/or weekends, 14 day cancellation notice-fee imposed. **Pool(s):** heated outdoor. **Activities:** hot tub, tennis, exercise room. **Guest Services:** complimentary laundry.

[¶+] [≈] [BIZ] [HS] [◉] [🔓] [📷] [🖥]

## OSPREY MOTEL ON THE GULF   850/234-0303   18

▼▼ **Extended Stay Hotel** $75-$325 **Address:** 15801 Front Beach Rd 32413 **Location:** Oceanfront. 1.3 mi e of jct SR 79 and US 98. **Facility:** 70 kitchen units. 6 stories, exterior corridors. **Terms:** check-in 4 pm, 3-5 night minimum stay - seasonal and/or weekends, 14 day cancellation notice-fee imposed. **Pool(s):** heated outdoor. **Activities:** hot tub, playground. **Guest Services:** coin laundry.

[¶+] [≈] [BIZ] [HS] [◉] [✕] [🔓] [📷] [🖥]

## SHORES OF PANAMA BEACH RESORT   850/235-4044   24

▼▼▼ **Vacation Rental Condominium. Rates not provided. Address:** 9900 S Thomas Dr 32408 **Location:** Oceanfront. Just s of jct Front Beach Rd. **Facility:** This property is located on the Gulf of Mexico. Each unit has a wonderful view and offers all of the amenities of home. 187 condominiums. 23 stories, interior/exterior corridors. **Terms:** check-in 4 pm. **Pool(s):** heated outdoor, heated indoor. **Activities:** hot tub, recreation programs, kids club, game room, exercise room, spa. **Guest Services:** valet laundry.

[¶] [⛰] CALL [&M] [≈] [HS] [◉] [✕] [🔓] [📷] [🖥]

## SUNSET INN   850/234-7370   25

▼▼▼
Motel
$60-$250

**Address:** 8109 Surf Dr 32408 **Location:** Oceanfront. Jct SR 30, 0.9 mi s on Joan Ave, 0.5 mi se on CR 392, then just s on Snapper St. **Facility:** 86 units, some two bedrooms, three bedrooms, efficiencies, kitchens and condominiums. 2-3 stories (no elevator), exterior corridors. **Terms:** 3 night minimum stay - seasonal and/or weekends, 7 day cancellation notice-fee imposed. **Pool(s):** heated outdoor. **Guest Services:** coin laundry.

[SAVE] [≈] [◉] [✕] [🔓] [📷] [🖥]

## WHERE TO EAT

## ALL AMERICAN DINER   850/235-2443   14

▼ American. Casual Dining. $5-$12 **AAA Inspector Notes:** Located across the street from the beach, this 1960s-style diner is a great spot for families to grab a quick burger, sandwich, fries or milkshake. For a classic breakfast, try the pancakes, waffles, omelettes or steak and eggs. **Address:** 10590 Front Beach Rd 32407 **Location:** 3 mi w of jct US 98. [B] [L] [D]

## ANOTHER BROKEN EGG CAFE   850/249-2007

▼▼ Breakfast Sandwiches. Casual Dining. $5-$15 **AAA Inspector Notes:** Enjoy a breakfast experience you will not soon forget; huge cinnamon buns, Popeye's omelet and fruit and nut pancakes or french toast are some of the menu specialties. **Features:** patio dining, Sunday brunch. **Address:** 11535 Hutchison Blvd, Suite 100 32408 **Location:** On SR 392A, just e of Alf Coleman Rd, just w of Emerald Coast Club Blvd. [B] [L] CALL [&M]

## BOAR'S HEAD RESTAURANT   850/234-6628   6

▼▼ Steak Seafood. Casual Dining. $14-$36 **AAA Inspector Notes:** Reminiscent of a Swiss chalet with its wood-panel walls, a high, vaulted ceiling with exposed beams and multiple roaring fireplaces, this restaurant has been serving the community for nearly four decades. The menu offers many seafood and steak entrées, as well as some specialties like venison and quail. **Features:** full bar, early bird specials, happy hour. **Address:** 17290 Front Beach Rd 32413 **Location:** 0.3 mi w of jct SR 79, on US 98. [D]

(See map & index p. 186.)

**DIRTY DICK'S CRAB HOUSE**    850/230-3425  13
▼▼▼ Seafood. Casual Dining. $7-$17 **AAA Inspector Notes:** A favorite for families, this joint is a hit with kids as well as adults. The menu is varied with seafood being their main focus. Other menu choices include blackened or smoked barbecue chicken, steak kebabs, chicken étouffée, red beans and rice and various sandwiches. Specials include all you can eat snow crab legs, spiced shrimp or Dungeness crabs. **Features:** full bar. **Address:** 9800 Front Beach Rd 32407 **Location:** On SR 30, just ne of jct CR 392A (Hutchison Blvd) and 3031 (Thomas Dr). L  D

**FIREFLY**    850/249-3359  10
▼▼▼▼ New American. Fine Dining. $9-$42 **AAA Inspector Notes:** This establishment offers various dining experiences depending on seating location and menu selection. An array of dining choices include Gulf seafood, succulent meats, pasta, gourmet pizza and sushi. The main dining room re-creates an outdoor piazza complete with a central faux oak tree whose canopy is covered in twinkling "firefly" lights. The lounge area's rich dark wood, bookcases, easy chairs and one 10-inch TV screen offers a casual ambience. **Features:** full bar. **Reservations:** suggested. **Address:** 535 Richard Jackson Blvd 32407 **Location:** Just sw of jct CR 392A (Hutchison Blvd); in Shoppes at Edgewater Plaza. D  CALL  M

**FISHALE TAPHOUSE & GRILL**    850/640-1410  8
▼▼ Seafood. Gastropub. $9-$22 **AAA Inspector Notes:** With more than 65 craft brews from across the country featured on tap, this is the place for beer connoisseurs. A well-rounded menu offers such typical pub fare as wings, burgers, steak and, of course, the fresh catch from the gulf. Check the website for special events and entertainment. **Features:** full bar, happy hour. **Address:** 7715 Front Beach Rd 32407 **Location:** Jct US 98 and SR 30, just w.
L  D  CALL  M

**GUADALAJARA MEXICAN GRILL**    850/235-3300  15
▼▼ Mexican. Casual Dining. $6-$13 **AAA Inspector Notes:** This festive cantina offers interior and al fresco dining, mariachi entertainers and huge margaritas. Wall-mounted TVs and regional poster and memorabilia fill the colorful dining room, where patrons sit down to well-prepared food from a lengthy menu of standards and an unusual selection of soups that are meals in themselves. The friendly staff carries out flawless service. **Features:** full bar. **Address:** 8730 Thomas Dr, Suite 1108 32408 **Location:** On US 98A; jct Joan Ave; in St. Thomas Square. L  D

**HOFBRAU BEER GARDEN**    850/235-4632  7
▼▼ German. Casual Dining. $8-$18 **AAA Inspector Notes:** Wilkommen to this Bavarian beer garden, where you can enjoy Octoberfest year-round. Dine on traditional Fatherland specialties—bratwurst, schnitzel or kasespatzle—at long, communal tables and benches in a large hall. Food is served by a waitstaff garbed in festive native costumes. The delicious beer cheese soup is a perfect way to warm up on a chilly day. Of course you can't forget to sample the various imported Hofbrau brews. **Features:** full bar, patio dining. **Address:** 701 Pier Park Dr, Suite 155 32413 **Location:** 1.2 mi e of jct SR 79 and 30, just n. L  D  CALL  M

**HOGNOSE SNAPPER**    850/234-6673  17
▼▼ Seafood. Casual Dining. $8-$19 **AAA Inspector Notes:** This cheery café, with its bright yellow walls, mismatched wood tables and chairs and whimsical décor, emanates a homey feel. The grouper imperial is the chef's signature dish, but a nice selection of other seafood, steak and chicken is available. **Features:** full bar, patio dining. **Address:** 8100 Thomas Dr 32408 **Location:** Jct SR 30, 0.9 mi s on Joan Ave, 0.6 mi se on CR 392. L  D  CALL  M

**SALTWATER GRILL**    850/230-2739  9
▼▼▼ Seafood. Casual Dining. $15-$43 **AAA Inspector Notes:** The great ocean-themed décor at this grill includes a large 23,000-gallon saltwater aquarium behind the bar. The menu offers hickory-wood grilled seafood, steak and prime rib as well as lobster flown in fresh twice a week. Save room for the signature dessert: crème brûlée, served with dark chocolate or white chocolate vanilla beans. **Features:** full bar, early bird specials, happy hour. **Address:** 11040 Hutchison Blvd 32407 **Location:** 1.5 mi w of Front Beach Rd.
D  CALL  M

**SONNY'S REAL PIT BAR-B-Q**    850/230-4742
▼▼ Barbecue. Family Dining. $8-$15 **AAA Inspector Notes:** Bearing the name after its founder, Floyd "Sonny" Tillman, this barbecue restaurant first opened its doors circa 1968 in Gainesville, Florida and has since spawned over 150 more throughout the Southeast. The menu is steeped in finger lickin' favorites such as ribs, pulled pork, beef brisket, burgers, catfish, shrimp and char-grilled chicken. Let's not forget about the fried okra, which is the perfect starter dish, and their homemade baked beans. **Features:** beer only. **Address:** 11341 Panama City Beach Pkwy 32407 **Location:** On US 98, 5 mi e of jct SR 79. L  D

**SWEET BASILS**    850/234-2855  11
▼▼▼ Italian. Casual Dining. $7-$17 **AAA Inspector Notes:** Just right for families, this bistro's menu is chock-full of Italian favorites for every palate. Kids will love the fried cheese sticks, pizza and lasagna, while mom and dad can order the shrimp fettuccine or Cajun-fried shrimp. The half-pound meatball smothered in homemade marinara sauce and melted mozzarella cheese attracts those with a big appetite. **Features:** full bar. **Address:** 11208 Front Beach Rd 32407 **Location:** On US 98A, 1.3 mi sw of jct CR 392; jct R Jackson Blvd; in The Shoppes at Edgewater. L  D

**THOMAS' DONUT & SNACK SHOP**    850/234-8039  5
▼ Sandwiches Pizza. Casual Dining. $3-$14 **AAA Inspector Notes:** More than a doughnut shop, this self-serve beachfront eatery has been a local attraction since 1977. Locals and tourists flock here mostly for the doughnuts, most notably the Key lime doughnut, which is so popular that it is almost (but not quite) more of a souvenir than a treat. Also offered are simple breakfasts, pizza, burgers, hot dogs and lunch boxes of fried shrimp, fried oysters, chicken and fish and chips. **Features:** patio dining. **Address:** 19208 Front Beach Rd 32413 **Location:** On US 98A; jct El Reposo Pl; in Laguna Beach.
B  L

**TRIPLE "J" STEAK & SEAFOOD**    850/233-9514  16
▼▼ Steak Seafood. Casual Dining. $7-$32 **AAA Inspector Notes:** This fun, western themed steakhouse, displaying various murals and cowboy decor, offers very hearty portions of delicious homemade food. A friendly staff full of Southern hospitality will make guests feel right at home. The delicious country fried steak is a good choice as is the prime rib. Make sure to check out the homemade desserts. **Features:** full bar, patio dining, early bird specials, happy hour. **Address:** 2218 Thomas Dr 32408 **Location:** 1 mi s of US 98.
L  D

**WICKED WHEEL BAR & GRILL**    850/988-7947  12
▼▼ American. Casual Dining. $8-$15 **AAA Inspector Notes:** A classic car and motorcycle theme is obvious throughout the café. Several custom-built choppers and hot rods are on display along with illuminated old-fashioned gas pumps and signs. You can even straddle one of the bikes parked at the bar. The limited menu offers simple yet well prepared items like fried chicken, shrimp or catfish, a variety of burgers and sandwiches with home-style sides like mac 'n' cheese, cheese grits and collard greens. Kids' meals are served in cute cardboard car boxes. **Features:** full bar, patio dining, happy hour. **Address:** 10025 Hutchison Blvd 32407 **Location:** Jct SR 30 (Front Beach Rd), just nw on CR 392A (Hutchison Blvd).
L  D  CALL  M

## PENSACOLA (B-2) pop. 51,923, elev. 39'

• Hotels p. 199 • Restaurants p. 200
• Hotels & Restaurants map & index p. 197

Although an attempt was made in 1559 by Don Tristan de Luna, permanent settlement at Pensacola was not established until 1698. The City of Five Flags has flown the flags of Spain, France, England, the Confederate States and the United States, and its government has changed hands 13 times.

In 1814 the British used the harbor as a base in their war with the United States but withdrew when the city was attacked by Gen. Andrew Jackson. Here Jackson completed the transaction by which

**(See map & index p. 197.)**

Spain sold Florida to the United States in 1821. In the city's historic downtown at Plaza Ferdinand VII is the site where the Spanish flag was lowered for the last time. Pensacola was the territorial capital until 1822, and Andrew Jackson was a resident while governor of Florida.

The Seville Square historic district, bounded on the north by Government Street and on the east by Alcaniz Street, is an area of restored 19th-century buildings that now houses shops, restaurants, museums and art galleries.

Pensacola's Naval Air Station is a center for electronic warfare and cartographic training as well as headquarters for the Blue Angels precision flying team. The station is home to the National Naval Aviation Museum, one of the largest aviation museums in the world *(see attraction listing).*

Gulf Islands National Seashore *(see place listing p. 181 and Recreation Areas Chart)* offers miles of unspoiled sugar-white beaches and emerald waters. Recreational activities include boating, swimming, nature walks, bird-watching and exploring pre-Civil War forts. Other outdoor activities can be enjoyed on the area's numerous waterways, including the Blackwater and Perdido rivers and Coldwater and Sweetwater-Juniper creeks *(see Milton p. 183).* The USS *Oriskany,* a scuttled aircraft carrier and one of the world's largest artificial reefs, affords scuba divers an opportunity for underwater exploration.

The Wildlife Sanctuary of Northwest Florida, 105 N. S St., cares for injured and orphaned wildlife, including foxes, deer, eagles, egrets, herons, owls, pelicans and hawks; for information phone (850) 433-9453.

West of the city on Dog Track Road, Pensacola Greyhound Track presents dog races; phone (800) 345-3997.

**Note:** Policies vary concerning admittance of children to pari-mutuel betting facilities. Phone for information.

Pensacola throws several major festivals each year. ☙ Fiesta of Five Flags Celebration and Boat Parade in late May marks the city's founding and the five entities that have governed it—Spain, France, Britain, the Confederacy and the United States. Late September's ☙ Pensacola Seafood Festival transforms the Seville Square area into a destination for seafood dishes, entertainment, and arts and crafts vendors. The ☙ Pensacola Interstate Fair's rides, exhibits and music last 11 days in late October at the Pensacola Interstate Fairgrounds. The ☙ Great Gulfcoast Arts Festival is a 3-day event at Seville Square in early November and offers a perfect opportunity to begin your holiday shopping.

**Visit Pensacola/Pensacola Bay Area Convention and Visitors Bureau:** 1401 E. Gregory St., Pensacola, FL 32502. **Phone:** (850) 434-1234 or (800) 874-1234.

**Self-guiding tours:** The Pensacola Bay Convention and Visitors Bureau offers free information about tours of the city.

**Shopping areas:** Cordova Mall, 5100 N. Ninth Ave., contains more than 140 stores, including Belk and Dillard's. University Mall, 7171 N. Davis Hwy., features Belk, JCPenney and Sears among its 80 stores. Historic buildings have been transformed into specialty shops on downtown's Palafox Place.

**HISTORIC PENSACOLA VILLAGE,** bounded north by Government St., south by Main St., east by Seville Square and west by Plaza Ferdinand, is a complex of museum buildings reflecting 450 years of Pensacola's history. Guided tours lasting 1.5-2 hours visit the Dorr, Lavalle and Lear-Rocheblave houses as well as Old Christ Church. The other buildings open to the public are Julee Cottage, Manuel Barrios Cottage, Margaret McMillan Cottage, Museum of Commerce, Museum of Industry and Pensacola Children's Museum. Tivoli House, which features a handful of artifacts, serves as the ticket center. A tour of Barkley House—which was built around 1825 but is not part of the village—starts from Tivoli House and includes several blocks along Zaragoza Street.

**Time:** Allow 1 hour minimum. **Hours:** Houses and museums open Tues.-Sat. 10-4. Old Christ Church only open during guided tours. Guided tours depart at 11, 1 and 2:30. Barkley House tour departs Tues.-Sat. at 2. Closed state holidays and day after Christmas-Dec. 31. **Cost:** $6; $5 (ages 65+ and active military with ID); $3 (ages 4-16). Pensacola Children's Museum admission (valid for 1 year) $3; free (under 1). **Phone:** (850) 595-5985. GT

**Dorr House,** 311 S. Adams St. at Historic Pensacola Village, is an example of Greek Revival architecture built in 1871 by Clara Barkley Dorr. Furnishings represent the late Victorian period. Guided tours lasting 1.5-2 hours are available and include three other village buildings.

**Hours:** Tues.-Sat. 10-4. Guided tours depart from Tivoli House store at 11, 1 and 2:30. Closed state holidays and day after Christmas-Dec. 31. **Cost:** (includes all Historic Pensacola Village buildings except Pensacola Children's Museum) $6; $5 (ages 65+ and military with ID); $3 (ages 4-16). **Phone:** (850) 595-5985. GT

**Julee Cottage,** 210 E. Zaragoza St. at Historic Pensacola Village, was built in 1805 and once belonged to Julee Panton, a free African-American woman. The exhibits tell the story of African-Americans living in northwest Florida through the 19th century. **Hours:** Tues.-Sat. 10-4. Closed state holidays and day after Christmas-Dec. 31. **Cost:** (includes all Historic Pensacola Village buildings except Pensacola Children's Museum) $6; $5 (ages 65+ and active military with ID); $3 (ages 4-16). **Phone:** (850) 595-5985.

**Lavalle House,** 205 E. Church St. at Historic Pensacola Village, was built by Carlos Lavalle and Marianna Bonifay in 1805 during Florida's second

(See map & index p. 197.)

Spanish period. A rare example of French Creole Colonial architecture, the house is furnished to reflect the Pensacola frontier. Guided tours lasting 1.5-2 hours are available and include three other village buildings.

**Hours:** Tues.-Sat. 10-4. Guided tours depart Tivoli House store at 11, 1 and 2:30. Closed state holidays and day after Christmas-Dec. 31. **Cost:** (includes all Historic Pensacola Village buildings except Pensacola Children's Museum) $6; $5 (ages 65+ and active military with ID); $3 (ages 4-16). **Phone:** (850) 595-5985. [GT]

**Lear-Rocheblave House,** 214 E. Zaragoza St. at Historic Pensacola Village, was built in 1890 by John and Kate Lear but was home to the Capt. Benito Rocheblave family during the turn of the 20th century. The house reflects on Pensacola's seafaring tradition and the transitioning home life resulting from industry and innovation 1890-1910. Guided tours lasting 1.5-2 hours are available and include three other village buildings.

**Hours:** Tues.-Sat. 10-4. Guided tours depart from Tivoli House store at 11, 1 and 2:30. Closed state holidays and day after Christmas-Dec. 31. **Cost:** (includes all Historic Pensacola Village buildings except Pensacola Children's Museum) $6; $5 (ages 65+ and active military with ID); $3 (ages 4-16). **Phone:** (850) 595-5985. [GT]

**Manuel Barrios Cottage,** 209 E. Zaragoza St. at Historic Pensacola Village, displays a kitchen and living room vignette that looks back on the Roaring '20s, when the city was growing and embracing new technology. **Hours:** Tues.-Sat. 10-4. Closed state holidays and day after Christmas-Dec. 31. **Cost:** (includes all Historic Pensacola Village buildings except Pensacola Children's Museum) $6; $5 (ages 65+ and active military with ID); $3 (ages 4-16). **Phone:** (850) 595-5985.

**Margaret McMillan Cottage,** 213 E. Zaragoza St. at Historic Pensacola Village, showcases life on the home front and Northwest Florida's military expansion during World War II. **Hours:** Tues.-Sat. 10-4.

(See map & index p. 197.)

Closed state holidays and day after Christmas-Dec. 31. **Cost:** (includes all Historic Pensacola Village buildings except Pensacola Children's Museum) $6; $5 (ages 65+ and active military with ID); $3 (ages 4-16). **Phone:** (850) 595-5985.

**Museum of Commerce,** 201 E. Zaragoza St. at Historic Pensacola Village, features a full-scale replica of an 1890s Pensacola street inside a 19th-century warehouse. Printing presses, a hardware store, a toy shop and a horse-drawn buggy collection are among the exhibits. **Hours:** Tues.-Sat. 10-4. Closed state holidays and day after Christmas-Dec. 31. **Cost:** (includes all Historic Pensacola Village buildings except Pensacola Children's Museum) $6; $5 (ages 65+ and active military with ID); $3 (ages 4-16). **Phone:** (850) 595-5985.

**Museum of Industry,** 200 E. Zaragoza St. at Historic Pensacola Village, displays photographs, tools and equipment related to the 19th-century industrial boom in west Florida. Exhibits focus on Pensacola's fishing, brickmaking, railroad and lumber industries. **Hours:** Tues.-Sat. 10-4. Closed state holidays and day after Christmas-Dec. 31. **Cost:** (includes all Historic Pensacola Village buildings except Pensacola Children's Museum) $6; $5 (ages 65+ and active military with ID); $3 (ages 4-16). **Phone:** (850) 595-5985.

**Pensacola Children's Museum,** in the historic district at 115 E. Zaragoza St., covers 450 years of Pensacola military, multicultural and Native American history as well as its industries in two floors with themed play areas. A train set and reading nook are some of the attributes. Most of the exhibits are geared toward children under 9 years old, but there are some artifacts that would be of interest to older children and adults. Adults must be accompanied by a child to enter. **Time:** Allow 1 hour minimum. **Hours:** Tues.-Sat. 10-4. **Cost:** (valid for 1 year) $3; free (under 1). **Phone:** (850) 595-1559 or (850) 595-5985.

**NATIONAL NAVAL AVIATION MUSEUM,** on the Naval Air Station Pensacola at 1750 Radford Blvd., traces the development of American naval aviation from its beginnings to the present through more than 150 restored historic aircraft representing Navy, Marine Corps and Coast Guard aviation. Highlights include the NC-4 Flying Boat, which in 1919 became the first plane to cross the Atlantic; the only surviving SBD Dauntless from the Battle of Midway; and the Skylab Command Module.

Four A-4 Skyhawks are suspended from the ceiling in formation in the Blue Angels Atrium. Bus tours of the flight line feature additional aircraft. Walk-through displays portray a World War II carrier hangar bay, a South Pacific Sea Island forward Marine base and the wartime home front. Exhibits range from pre-World War I memorabilia to a replica of a World War II aircraft carrier island and flight deck to an interactive Top Gun flight simulator.

Hangar Bay One displays some 35 aircraft from the post-World War II era, including Vietnam aircraft, Coast Guard aircraft, presidential helicopter Marine One and the Apollo 17 lunar module space exhibit. Two flight simulators take visitors on a 3-D HD or a 2-D adventure while a 4-D motion simulator lets guests fly with the Blue Angels or take off from an aircraft carrier and battle over the Iraqi desert.

**Time:** Allow 1 hour, 30 minutes minimum. **Hours:** Daily 9-5. Closed Jan. 1, Thanksgiving and Christmas. **Cost:** Museum free. Flight simulators $6-$25. **Phone:** (850) 453-2389 or (800) 327-5002. GT □

**Fort Barrancas,** on the Naval Air Station Pensacola and part of the National Naval Aviation Museum, is one of several U.S. forts built by the U.S. Corps of Engineers in the 19th century along northwestern Florida's coastline. A dry moat surrounds the inner walls and makes access to the fort possible only by way of a drawbridge.

**Time:** Allow 45 minutes minimum. **Hours:** Daily 9:30-4:45, Mar.-Oct.; 8:30-3:45, rest of year. Fort tours are given daily at 2. Tours of the Advanced Redoubt are given Sat. at 11. Phone ahead to confirm schedule. **Cost:** Free. **Phone:** (850) 455-5167.

**IMAX Naval Aviation Memorial Theatre** is on the Naval Air Station Pensacola at the National Naval Aviation Museum at 1750 Radford Blvd. Seven stories high with a 12,000-watt digital sound, the Giant Screen Theater presents "The Magic of Flight" and other changing feature films. **Hours:** Show times are on the hour 10-4. **Cost:** $8.75; $8.25 (ages 5-12, ages 62+ and military with ID). **Phone:** (850) 453-2025 or (888) 627-4629.

**PENSACOLA VETERANS MEMORIAL PARK,** jct. Bayfront Pkwy. and Ninth Ave., contains a replica of the Vietnam Veterans Memorial in Washington, D.C., and memorials to veterans of World War I, World War II, the Korean War, the Vietnam War and the Global War on Terrorism as well as members of the Submarine Lifeguard League. **Hours:** Daily 24 hours. **Cost:** Free. **Phone:** (850) 450-5598.

**PLAZA FERDINAND VII,** S. Palafox St. between E. Government and Zaragoza sts., was part of Pensacola's original Spanish settlement. The site offers a garden, fountain and park as well as a bust of Andrew Jackson, which commemorates the transfer of Florida from Spain to the United States on July 17, 1821. **Hours:** Daily 24 hours. **Cost:** Free.

**T.T. WENTWORTH JR. FLORIDA STATE MUSEUM,** 330 S. Jefferson St., was built in the Renaissance Revival style in 1907 as Pensacola's city hall. The elaborate building houses three floors of changing exhibits about the region's history, architecture and archeology. One gallery is usually dedicated to showcasing the Civil War; the themes portrayed change in order to rotate collection pieces. The "Cabinet of Curiosities Series" honors the museum's namesake and his many collections. **Hours:** Tues.-Sat. 10-4. Closed state holidays. **Cost:** Free. **Phone:** (850) 595-5990.

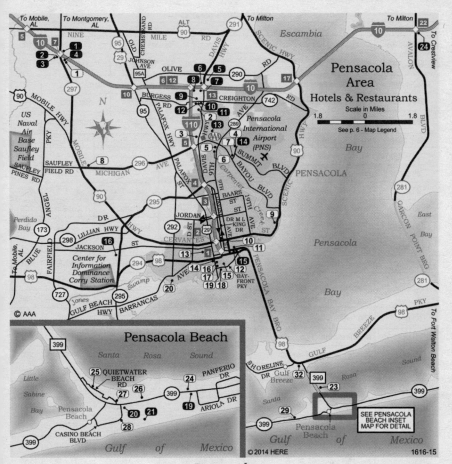

# Pensacola

This index helps you "spot" where approved hotels and restaurants are located on the corresponding detailed maps. Hotel daily rate range is for comparison only. Restaurant price range is a combination of lunch and/or dinner. Turn to the listing page for more detailed rate and price information and consult display ads for special promotions.

## PENSACOLA

| Map Page | Hotels | Diamond Rated | Rate Range | Page |
|---|---|---|---|---|
| **1** this page | **BEST WESTERN PLUS Blue Angel Inn** | ▼▼▼ | $85-$179 SAVE | 199 |
| **2** this page | Red Roof Inn Pensacola West | ▼▼ | $55-$90 | 200 |
| **3** this page | Country Inn & Suites By Carlson West | ▼▼ | $89-$145 | 199 |
| **4** this page | Holiday Inn Express Hotel & Suites | ▼▼▼ | Rates not provided | 199 |
| **5** this page | Comfort Inn | ▼▼ | $79-$169 | 199 |
| **6** this page | **Holiday Inn Pensacola** | ▼▼▼ | $89-$209 SAVE | 199 |
| **7** this page | Fairfield Inn by Marriott Pensacola | ▼▼ | $99-$139 | 199 |
| **8** this page | MainStay Suites | ▼▼▼ | $79-$159 | 200 |
| **9** this page | Hampton Inn & Suites Pensacola | ▼▼▼ | $99-$139 | 199 |
| **10** this page | SpringHill Suites by Marriott Pensacola | ▼▼▼ | $129-$169 | 200 |
| **11** this page | TownePlace Suites by Marriott Pensacola | ▼▼▼ | $129-$169 | 200 |

## PENSACOLA (cont'd)

| Map Page | Hotels (cont'd) | Diamond Rated | Rate Range | Page |
|---|---|---|---|---|
| **12** p. 197 | Courtyard by Marriott Pensacola | ◇◇◇ | $99-$139 | 199 |
| **13** p. 197 | Hilton Garden Inn Pensacola Airport/Medical Center | ◇◇◇ | $119-$169 | 199 |
| **14** p. 197 | **Hyatt Place Pensacola Airport** | ◇◇◇ | $109-$239 [SAVE] | 200 |
| **15** p. 197 | Courtyard by Marriott Pensacola Downtown | ◇◇◇ | $99-$239 | 199 |
| **16** p. 197 | Holiday Inn Express & Suites Pensacola-West Navy Base | ◇◇◇ | $109-$189 | 199 |

| Map Page | Restaurants | Diamond Rated | Cuisine | Price Range | Page |
|---|---|---|---|---|---|
| ① p. 197 | Wayne's Family Diner | ◇◇ | American | $4-$16 | 201 |
| ② p. 197 | Shrimp Basket | ◇◇ | Seafood | $5-$14 | 201 |
| ③ p. 197 | Italy's Finest Pizzeria | ◇◇ | Italian Pizza | $7-$29 | 201 |
| ④ p. 197 | Bonefish Grill | ◇◇◇ | Seafood | $10-$27 | 200 |
| ⑤ p. 197 | Jordan Valley Mediterranean Restaurant | ◇◇ | Mediterranean | $6-$14 | 201 |
| ⑥ p. 197 | The Tuscan Oven Pizzeria | ◇◇ | Pizza | $8-$24 | 201 |
| ⑦ p. 197 | O'Briens Bistro | ◇◇◇ | American | $9-$25 | 201 |
| ⑧ p. 197 | Garrett's Grill | ◇ | American | $7-$15 | 200 |
| ⑨ p. 197 | Angus | ◇◇ | Steak Seafood | $10-$39 | 200 |
| ⑩ p. 197 | The Coffee Cup | ◇ | Breakfast Sandwiches | $5-$7 | 200 |
| ⑪ p. 197 | **McGuire's Irish Pub** | ◇◇ | Irish | $8-$33 | 201 |
| ⑫ p. 197 | Franco's Italian Restaurant | ◇◇ | Italian | $8-$25 | 200 |
| ⑬ p. 197 | Five Sisters Blues Cafe | ◇◇ | Soul Food | $9-$17 | 200 |
| ⑭ p. 197 | The Global Grill | ◇◇◇ | Small Plates | $10-$45 | 201 |
| ⑮ p. 197 | Dharma Blue | ◇◇ | Seafood Sushi | $10-$30 | 200 |
| ⑯ p. 197 | The Leisure Club | ◇◇ | Coffee/Tea Small Plates | $6-$9 | 201 |
| ⑰ p. 197 | Jackson's | ◇◇◇ | American | $8-$40 | 201 |
| ⑱ p. 197 | The Fish House | ◇◇◇ | Seafood | $11-$28 | 200 |
| ⑲ p. 197 | Atlas Oyster House | ◇◇ | Seafood | $10-$32 | 200 |
| ⑳ p. 197 | The Oar House on Bayou Chico | ◇◇ | American | $8-$23 | 201 |

## PENSACOLA BEACH

| Map Page | Hotels | Diamond Rated | Rate Range | Page |
|---|---|---|---|---|
| **19** p. 197 | SpringHill Suites by Marriott Pensacola Beach | ◇◇◇ | $109-$299 | 202 |
| **20** p. 197 | Hampton Inn Pensacola Beach | ◇◇◇ | $89-$569 | 202 |
| **21** p. 197 | **Hilton Pensacola Beach Gulf Front** | ◇◇◇ | Rates not provided [SAVE] | 202 |

| Map Page | Restaurants | Diamond Rated | Cuisine | Price Range | Page |
|---|---|---|---|---|---|
| ㉓ p. 197 | The Grand Marlin Restaurant & Oyster Bar | ◇◇◇ | Seafood | $10-$35 | 202 |
| ㉔ p. 197 | Native Cafe | ◇◇ | American | $7-$11 | 202 |
| ㉕ p. 197 | Hemingway's Island Grill | ◇◇ | American | $8-$34 | 202 |
| ㉖ p. 197 | Lillo's Tuscan Grille | ◇◇ | Italian | $5-$20 | 202 |
| ㉗ p. 197 | Flounders Chowder House | ◇◇ | Seafood | $10-$24 | 202 |
| ㉘ p. 197 | Crabs we got 'em | ◇◇ | Seafood | $10-$36 | 202 |
| ㉙ p. 197 | Peg Leg Pete's Oyster Bar | ◇◇ | Seafood | $8-$30 | 202 |

## MILTON

| Map Page | Hotel | Diamond Rated | Rate Range | Page |
|---|---|---|---|---|
| **24** p. 197 | Red Roof Inn & Suites-Pensacola East Milton | ▽▽ | $70-$104 [SAVE] | 183 |

## GULF BREEZE

| Map Page | Restaurant | Diamond Rated | Cuisine | Price Range | Page |
|---|---|---|---|---|---|
| **32** p. 197 | Aegean Breeze | ▽▽ | Greek | $7-$25 | 181 |

### BEST WESTERN PLUS BLUE ANGEL INN
(850)477-7474 **1**

▽▽▽ Hotel $85-$179

**AAA Benefit:** Members save up to 20%!

**Address:** 2390 W Detroit Blvd 32534 **Location:** I-10 exit 7, just n on SR 297 (Pine Forest Rd), then just e. **Facility:** 55 units. 3 stories, interior corridors. **Pool(s):** outdoor. **Activities:** exercise room. **Guest Services:** coin laundry. **Featured Amenity:** breakfast buffet.

[SAVE] CALL [&M] [≈] [BIZ] [HS] [🅗] [✕] [🛈] [🖥] [💻]

### COMFORT INN
(850)484-8070 **5**

▽▽ Hotel $79-$169 **Address:** 8080 N Davis Hwy 32514 **Location:** I-10 exit 13, just n on SR 291. **Facility:** 115 units. 5 stories, interior corridors. **Pool(s):** outdoor. **Activities:** limited exercise equipment. **Guest Services:** valet and coin laundry.

[🍴] [≈] [BIZ] [🅗] [🛈] [🖥] [💻]

### COUNTRY INN & SUITES BY CARLSON WEST
(850)944-7653 **3**

▽▽▽ Hotel $89-$145 **Address:** 2607 Wilde Lake Blvd 32526 **Location:** I-10 exit 7, just s on SR 297, then just w. **Facility:** 63 units. 4 stories, interior corridors. **Pool(s):** heated indoor. **Activities:** hot tub, exercise room. **Guest Services:** coin laundry.

[🍴] CALL [&M] [≈] [BIZ] [HS] [🅗] [✕] [🛈] [🖥] [💻]

### COURTYARD BY MARRIOTT PENSACOLA
(850)857-7744 **12**

▽▽▽ Hotel $99-$139 **Address:** 451 Creighton Rd 32504 **Location:** I-10 exit 13, 0.5 mi s on SR 291, then just w. **Facility:** 90 units. 3 stories, interior corridors. **Pool(s):** heated indoor. **Activities:**

**AAA Benefit:** Members save 5% or more!

hot tub, exercise room. **Guest Services:** valet and coin laundry, boarding pass kiosk.

[🍴] [≈] [BIZ] [🅗] [✕] [🛈] [🖥] [💻]

### COURTYARD BY MARRIOTT PENSACOLA DOWNTOWN
(850)439-3330 **15**

▽▽▽ Hotel $99-$239 **Address:** 700 E Chase St 32502 **Location:** Jct E Gregory St and N 12th Ave; downtown. **Facility:** 120 units. 5 stories, interior corridors. **Pool(s):** heated outdoor. **Activities:** hot tub, exercise room. **Guest**

**AAA Benefit:** Members save 5% or more!

**Services:** valet and coin laundry. [🌂] [≈] [BIZ] [🅗] [🅗] [✕] [🛈] [🖥]

### FAIRFIELD INN BY MARRIOTT PENSACOLA
(850)484-8001 **7**

▽▽ Hotel $99-$139 **Address:** 7325 N Davis Hwy 32504 **Location:** I-10 exit 13, just s on SR 291. **Facility:** 63 units. 3 stories, interior corridors. **Pool(s):** heated indoor.

**AAA Benefit:** Members save 5% or more!

[🍴] [≈] [BIZ] [🅗] [✕] [💻] / SOME UNITS [HS] [🛈] [🖥]

### HAMPTON INN & SUITES PENSACOLA
(850)505-7500 **9**

▽▽▽ Hotel $99-$139 **Address:** 7050 Plantation Rd 32504 **Location:** I-10 exit 13, just s on SR 291, then just w on Creighton Rd. **Facility:** 85 units. 3 stories, interior corridors. **Terms:** 1-7 night minimum stay, cancellation fee imposed. **Pool(s):** outdoor.

**AAA Benefit:** Members save 5% or more!

**Guest Services:** valet and coin laundry.

[≈] [☗] [BIZ] [🅗] [💻] / SOME UNITS [🛈] [🖥] [💻]

### HILTON GARDEN INN PENSACOLA AIRPORT/MEDICAL CENTER
(850)479-8900 **13**

▽▽▽ Hotel $119-$169 **Address:** 1144 Airport Blvd 32504 **Location:** I-110 exit 5, 1.5 mi ne on SR 750. **Facility:** 137 units. 5 stories, interior corridors. **Terms:** 1-7 night minimum stay, cancel-

**AAA Benefit:** Members save 5% or more!

lation fee imposed. **Pool(s):** outdoor. **Activities:** hot tub, exercise room. **Guest Services:** valet and coin laundry, area transportation.

[✈] [🍴] [🍷] CALL [&M] [≈] [BIZ] [HS] [🅗] [✕] [🛈] [🖥] [💻]

### HOLIDAY INN EXPRESS & SUITES PENSACOLA-WEST NAVY BASE
(850)696-2800 **16**

▽▽▽ Hotel $109-$189 **Address:** 307 N New Warrington Rd 32506 **Location:** On SR 295, 1.2 mi s of jct US 90 (Mobile Hwy). **Facility:** 73 units. 4 stories, interior corridors. **Pool(s):** outdoor. **Activities:** hot tub, exercise room. **Guest Services:** valet and coin laundry. [≈] [BIZ] [HS] [🅗] [✕] [🛈] [🖥] [💻]

### HOLIDAY INN EXPRESS HOTEL & SUITES
850/944-8442 **4**

▽▽▽ Hotel. Rates not provided. **Address:** 130 Loblolly Ln 32526 **Location:** I-10 exit 7, just s on SR 297. **Facility:** 64 units. 3 stories, interior corridors. **Pool(s):** heated indoor. **Activities:** exercise room. **Guest Services:** valet and coin laundry.

[🍴] CALL [&M] [≈] [BIZ] [HS] [🅗] [✕] [🛈] [🖥] [💻]

### HOLIDAY INN PENSACOLA
(850)472-1400 **6**

▽▽▽ Hotel $89-$209

**Address:** 7813 N Davis Hwy 32514 **Location:** I-10 exit 13, just n on SR 291. **Facility:** 114 units. 5 stories, interior corridors. **Terms:** cancellation fee imposed. **Pool(s):** heated outdoor. **Activities:** hot tub, exercise room. **Guest Services:** valet and coin laundry.

[SAVE] [🍴] [🍷] CALL [&M] [≈] [BIZ] [HS] [🅗] [✕] [🛈] [💻] / SOME UNITS [🖥]

---

Upgrade to Plus or Premier membership for more of the benefits you need most

(See map & index p. 197.)

## HYATT PLACE PENSACOLA AIRPORT
(850)483-5599  **14**

Hotel
$109-$239

**AAA Benefit:** Members save 10%!

**Address:** 161 Airport Ln 32504 **Location:** I-110 exit 5, 2.7 mi e on SR 750, just n on 12th Ave, then just e. **Facility:** 127 units. 6 stories, interior corridors. **Terms:** cancellation fee imposed. **Pool(s):** heated indoor. **Activities:** exercise room. **Guest Services:** valet and coin laundry, boarding pass kiosk, area transportation. **Featured Amenity: breakfast buffet.**

## MAINSTAY SUITES
(850)479-1000  **8**

**Extended Stay Hotel** $79-$159 **Address:** 7230 Plantation Rd 32504 **Location:** I-10 exit 13, just s on SR 291, then 0.3 mi w. **Facility:** 64 kitchen units. 2 stories (no elevator), exterior corridors. **Pool(s):** outdoor. **Activities:** hot tub, exercise room. **Guest Services:** coin laundry.

## RED ROOF INN PENSACOLA WEST
(850)941-0908  **2**

**Hotel** $55-$90 **Address:** 2591 Wilde Lake Blvd 32526 **Location:** I-10 exit 7, just s on SR 297, then just w. **Facility:** 73 units. 3 stories, interior corridors. **Pool(s):** outdoor. **Guest Services:** coin laundry.

## SPRINGHILL SUITES BY MARRIOTT PENSACOLA
(850)475-0055  **10**

**Hotel** $129-$169 **Address:** 487 Creighton Rd 32504 **Location:** I-10 exit 13, 0.3 mi s on SR 291, then just w. **Facility:** 106 units. 4 stories, interior corridors. **Pool(s):** outdoor. **Activities:** exercise room. **Guest Services:** valet and coin laundry.

**AAA Benefit:** Members save 5% or more!

## TOWNEPLACE SUITES BY MARRIOTT PENSACOLA
(850)484-7022  **11**

**Extended Stay Hotel** $129-$169 **Address:** 481 Creighton Rd 32504 **Location:** I-10 exit 13, 0.3 mi s on SR 291, then just w. **Facility:** 98 units, some two bedrooms, efficiencies and kitchens. 4 stories, interior corridors. **Terms:** check-in 4 pm. **Pool(s):** outdoor. **Guest Services:** valet and coin laundry.

**AAA Benefit:** Members save 5% or more!

---

**WHERE TO EAT**

---

## ANGUS
850/432-0539  **9**

Steak Seafood. Casual Dining. $10-$39 **AAA Inspector Notes:** For nearly a half century, this family-run restaurant has been offering delicious steak and seafood all served in a casual atmosphere. **Features:** full bar, patio dining, happy hour. **Address:** 1101 Scenic Hwy 32503 **Location:** On US 90; between E Moreno and E Blount sts.

## ATLAS OYSTER HOUSE
850/470-0003  **19**

Seafood. Casual Dining. $10-$32 **AAA Inspector Notes:** This casual port-side eatery shares a wood clapboard building with its adjacent casual sister restaurant. Oysters are prepared multiple ways along with other fish and shellfish options. A large deck provides outdoor dining with a waterfront view. **Features:** full bar, patio dining, Sunday brunch. **Address:** 600 S Barracks St 32502 **Location:** At Port of Pensacola.

## BONEFISH GRILL
850/471-2324  **4**

Seafood. Fine Dining. $10-$27 **AAA Inspector Notes:** Fish is the house specialty, and the menu and nightly specials offer a variety of choices. Well-prepared food is cooked to perfection. Service is casual in nature, and the staff is skilled and attentive. **Features:** full bar, Sunday brunch. **Address:** 5025 N 12th Ave 32504 **Location:** Jct Airport Rd, just s.

## THE COFFEE CUP
850/432-7060  **10**

Breakfast Sandwiches. Casual Dining. $5-$7 **AAA Inspector Notes:** *Classic.* This traditional diner has been a local landmark since 1945. They offer inexpensive breakfast and lunch fare served by a friendly, cheerful staff in a classic diner setting. **Address:** 520 E Cervantes St 32501 **Location:** I-110 exit 2, 0.5 mi e on US 90/98.

## DHARMA BLUE
850/433-1275  **15**

Seafood Sushi. Casual Dining. $10-$30 **AAA Inspector Notes:** In historic downtown, across from the town square, sits a quaint pink cottage with a white picket fence. On a nice sunny day, its porch and front yard are full of people enjoying a meal and conversation. Lunch offers a variety of salads, sandwiches, light entrées and a quiche of the day. An expanded evening menu includes crab cakes, blackened fish, sautéed shrimp, paneed chicken, vegetarian paella as well as sushi. **Features:** full bar. **Address:** 300 S Alcaniz St 32501 **Location:** Corner of Government St. **Parking:** street only.

## THE FISH HOUSE
850/470-0003  **18**

Seafood. Fine Dining. $11-$28 **AAA Inspector Notes:** This popular, upscale restaurant is located at the Port of Pensacola in a large clapboard wood structure with its more casual sister eatery alongside. The menu offers an extensive variety of fish and shellfish, which can be savored while enjoying the waterside view. **Features:** full bar, patio dining, Sunday brunch. **Address:** 600 S Barracks St 32502 **Location:** At Port of Pensacola.

## FIVE SISTERS BLUES CAFE
850/912-4856  **13**

Soul Food. Casual Dining. $9-$17 **AAA Inspector Notes:** Food and music are paid tribute here, where the owner/chef attempts to recapture the fondest memories of his youth via taste and sound. Such Southern standards as fried chicken, red rice and beans and country fried steak can be accompanied by fried okra, collard greens or cheese grits, to name a few options. Walls are adorned with portraits of blues legends created by local artists. Live music is presented Thursday through Saturday nights. **Features:** full bar, patio dining, Sunday brunch. **Address:** 421 W Belmont St 32501 **Location:** Corner of DeVilliers St; in historic downtown.

## FRANCO'S ITALIAN RESTAURANT
850/433-9200  **12**

Italian. Family Dining. $8-$25 **AAA Inspector Notes:** If pasta is what you are craving, than this is the place to get your fix. Cannelloni, tortellini, fettuccine, penne, ziti or the old stand by, spaghetti, are staples on the menu. Numerous chicken, veal and seafood dishes also are offered. The cozy and comforting atmosphere is perfect for a casual gathering for a hungry crowd. **Features:** beer & wine. **Address:** 523 E Gregory St 32501 **Location:** 0.4 mi e of civic center; downtown.

## GARRETT'S GRILL
850/944-3444  **8**

American. Casual Dining. $7-$15 **AAA Inspector Notes:** The locals assemble here for the food value and quality. While the menu may be simple, the burgers and hot dogs are mouthwatering delicious. **Features:** beer only, patio dining. **Address:** 3110 W Michigan Ave 32526 **Location:** Jct US 90 and Saufley Field Rd, just e.

(See map & index p. 197.)

### THE GLOBAL GRILL   850/469-9966   (14)

▼▼ Small Plates. Fine Dining. $10-$45 **AAA Inspector Notes:** In the midst of a bustling, rejuvenated area featuring fashionable boutique shops, restaurants, bars and theaters, this upscale tapas bistro occupies two former storefronts. The eclectic menu changes bi-weekly, always ensuring a distinctive dining experience. The global menu is reflected not only in the décor but in the menu and wine list. **Features:** full bar. **Address:** 27 Palafox Pl 32501 **Location:** Between Romana and Garden sts; downtown. **Parking:** street only. (D) CALL (&M)

### ITALY'S FINEST PIZZERIA   850/607-8575   (3)

▼▼ Italian Pizza. Casual Dining. $7-$29 **AAA Inspector Notes:** This popular café is run by an Italian husband, wife and sons. Specializing in both thin and thick crust they also serve traditional ethnic fare prepared from family recipes. **Features:** full bar. **Address:** 5555 N Davis Hwy, Suite A 32503 **Location:** I-110 exit 5, 0.5 mi e on Airport Blvd, then just s on SR 291. (L) (D) CALL (&M)

### JACKSON'S   850/469-9898   (17)

▼▼▼ American. Fine Dining. $8-$40 **AAA Inspector Notes:** This historic downtown restaurant provides a selection of Prime aged meats as well as fresh, local and Pan-American seafood. An extensive selection of wine is available. **Features:** full bar. **Reservations:** suggested. **Address:** 400 S Palafox St 32501 **Location:** Downtown. **Parking:** street only. (L) (D)

### JORDAN VALLEY MEDITERRANEAN RESTAURANT
850/832-7328   (5)

▼▼ Mediterranean. Casual Dining. $6-$14 **AAA Inspector Notes:** Dine on standard favorites while the ethnic background music helps to create a Middle Eastern atmosphere. Bring your own bottle of wine to enjoy with dinner. **Address:** 5045 N 9th Ave 32504 **Location:** I-110 exit 5, 1.1 mi e on SR 296, then just s. (L) (D) CALL (&M) (✎)

### LEGENDS BAR & GRILLE   850/492-1223

▼▼ American. Casual Dining. $7-$16 **AAA Inspector Notes:** Located in Perdido Bay Golf Club, the menu at this casual spot features burgers, hot dogs and deli sandwiches. On Friday the dinner menu is set, but any other night choose something you're hungry for. **Features:** full bar, patio dining, Sunday brunch, happy hour. **Address:** 1 Doug Ford Rd 32507 **Location:** Jct US 98 and Blue Angel Pkwy, s to Sorrento Dr, 4.3 mi w. (B) (L) (D)

### THE LEISURE CLUB   850/912-4229   (16)

▼▼ Coffee/Tea Small Plates. Casual Dining. $6-$9 **AAA Inspector Notes:** This intimate storefront coffee shop is a great place for socialization. Along with specialty sandwiches and a few entrées, the menu offers handcrafted boards of gourmet finger foods in various sizes. Located steps away from the Saeger Theatre, this is the perfect spot for a quick bite before or after a performance. **Features:** beer & wine, patio dining. **Address:** 126 Palafox Pl 32502 **Location:** Between Intendencia and Romana sts; downtown. **Parking:** street only. (B) (L) (D)

### MCGUIRE'S IRISH PUB   850/433-6789   (11)

Irish
Casual Dining
$8-$33

**AAA Inspector Notes:** True to their ethnic heritage, this establishment's décor has the look of a European pub as well as the standard fare to match, such as corned beef and cabbage, shepherd's pie and authentic Irish stew. Steaks, chops, seafood and a variety of burgers are also offered. The best bargain on the Florida panhandle is the Senate bean soup which costs only 18 cents. Beer, ale, porter and stout are brewed on site as well as the expansive world-renowned wine cellar which will make deciding on a wine a difficult choice. Be aware they serve stiff mixed drinks using 1.5 ounce shots. **Features:** full bar. **Address:** 600 E Gregory St 32502 **Location:** 0.3 mi e of civic center; downtown.

(L) (D) (LATE)

### THE OAR HOUSE ON BAYOU CHICO   850/549-4444   (20)

▼▼ ▼▼ American. Casual Dining. $8-$23 **AAA Inspector Notes:** A fun, happening joint overlooking Bahia Mar Marina, diners can watch the boats and wildlife while dining on the multi-tiered decks or from under the shaded comfort of the tiki open-air cabana. Live bands are scheduled during the season and even some volleyball courts keep things lively. Of course there is seafood aplenty with fresh catches served numerous ways. **Features:** full bar, patio dining, senior menu, happy hour. **Address:** 1000 S Pace Blvd 32502 **Location:** I-110 exit 4, 1.1 mi w on SR 295 (Fairfield Dr), then 3 mi s on SR 292. (L) (D) (LATE) CALL (&M) (✗) (🐕)

### O'BRIENS BISTRO   850/477-9120   (7)

▼▼▼▼ American. Casual Dining. $9-$25 **AAA Inspector Notes:** The wine theme decor of this intimate café reinforces the owner's motto of pairing great wine with great food. Only brunch is offered on Sundays until 2 pm. **Features:** beer & wine, patio dining, Sunday brunch. **Address:** 4350 Bayou Blvd, Suite 8 32503 **Location:** Jct N 12th Ave and SR 296, just n. (L) (D) CALL (&M) (🐕)

### SHRIMP BASKET   850/476-1041   (2)

▼▼ Seafood. Casual Dining. $5-$14 **AAA Inspector Notes:** This casual restaurant is known for their fresh seafood. Fried baskets include popcorn shrimp, crayfish, oysters, scallops, white fish, catfish and crab claws. They also offer po' boys, sandwiches, salads and steamed platters. **Features:** full bar, patio dining. **Address:** 6501 N Davis Hwy 32504 **Location:** I-110 exit 5, just ne on SR 296 (Brent Ln), then 1.2 mi n. (L) (D)

### SONNY'S REAL PIT BAR-B-Q

▼▼ Barbecue. Family Dining. $8-$15 **AAA Inspector Notes:** Bearing the name after its founder, Floyd "Sonny" Tillman, this barbecue restaurant first opened its doors circa 1968 in Gainesville, Florida and has since spawned over 150 more throughout the Southeast. The menu is steeped in finger lickin' favorites such as ribs, pulled pork, beef brisket, burgers, catfish, shrimp and char-grilled chicken. Let's not forget about the fried okra, which is the perfect starter dish, and their homemade baked beans. **Bar:** beer only. (L) (D)

*For additional information, visit AAA.com*
**LOCATIONS:**
**Address:** 630 N Navy Blvd 32507 **Location:** 3.3 mi w of downtown on US 98.
**Address:** 6702 N 9th Ave 32504 **Location:** 1.3 mi e on Airport Blvd, 1.4 mi n. **Phone:** 850/476-7618
**Address:** 8313 Chellie Rd 32526 **Location:** I-10 exit 7 (SR 297), just se on Pine Forest Rd, then just s. **Phone:** 850/944-6633

### TIJUANA FLATS   850/476-2200

▼▼ Tex-Mex. Quick Serve. $6-$10 **AAA Inspector Notes:** The first one of these restaurants opened in Central Florida way back in 1995 and has since spawned over sixty more locations! The menu specializes in Tex-Mex with some all-time favorites such as burritos, chimichangas, quesadillas, tacos, enchiladas and nachos. Well known for their hot sauce bar, this eatery has a slew of them from which to choose. Careful, some are really hot! Although the restaurant is considered quick serve, the food is cooked to order. **Features:** beer & wine. **Address:** 4970 Bayou Blvd 32503 **Location:** Jct N 9th Ave, just e. (L) (D)

### THE TUSCAN OVEN PIZZERIA   850/484-6836   (6)

▼▼ Pizza. Casual Dining. $8-$24 **AAA Inspector Notes:** Occupying a yellow brick residential-style building, this family-operated pizza parlor has been in business since 2004. The focal point inside is the huge wood-fired oven which was imported from Italy and made of brick, clay and pumice. Sandwiches and pasta dishes also are available. **Features:** beer & wine, patio dining. **Address:** 4801 N 9th Ave 32503 **Location:** I-110 exit 5, 1.1 mi e on SR 296, then just s; corner of Royce St. (L) (D) CALL (&M)

### WAYNE'S FAMILY DINER   850/944-5354   (1)

▼▼ American. Casual Dining. $4-$16 **AAA Inspector Notes:** The menu at this roadside diner spotlights such traditional favorites as patty melts, Philly cheesesteaks, flounder, catfish, steak, liver and onions, fried chicken, burgers and hot dogs. If nothing else, stop for the homemade pies and cakes. **Address:** 100 Loblolly Ln 32526 **Location:** I-10 exit 7, just s on Pine Forest Rd. (L) (D)

## PENSACOLA BEACH (B-2) elev. 7'
• Hotels & Restaurants map & index p. 197

Snow-white sand and aquamarine water make Pensacola Beach one of Florida's most beautiful beaches. Bordered by two preserved seashores, the area offers more than 20 miles of beachfront covered in sugary sand composed of 99 percent pure quartz. Visitors have access to plenty of undeveloped oceanfront.

Sun-and-fun seekers can choose from sailing, sailboarding, parasailing, swimming, snorkeling and other aquatic recreation. For fishing enthusiasts there is a large selection of charter boats or a 1,470-foot fishing pier.

The Blue Angels and civilian performers grace the skies with their flight demonstrations at the 2-day ✈ Pensacola Beach Air Show in mid-July.

**Pensacola Beach Chamber of Commerce Visitor Information Center:** 735 Pensacola Beach Blvd., Pensacola Beach, FL 32561. **Phone:** (850) 932-1500 or (800) 635-4803.

### HAMPTON INN PENSACOLA BEACH
(850)932-6800  **20**

▼▼▼ Hotel $89-$569 **Address:** 2 Via De Luna Dr 32561 **Location:** Oceanfront. SR 399; center. **Facility:** 181 units, some kitchens. 4 stories, interior corridors. **Terms:** 1-7 night minimum stay, cancellation fee imposed. **Pool(s):** heated outdoor. **Activities:** exercise room. **Guest Services:** valet and coin laundry.

**AAA Benefit:** Members save 5% or more!

### HILTON PENSACOLA BEACH GULF FRONT
850/916-2999  **21**

▼▼▼ Hotel
Rates not provided

**AAA Benefit:** Members save 5% or more!

**Address:** 12 Via De Luna Dr 32561 **Location:** Oceanfront. Just e on SR 399. **Facility:** 275 units, some two bedrooms, three bedrooms and kitchens. 7-17 stories, interior/exterior corridors. **Parking:** on-site and valet. **Amenities:** video games. **Pool(s):** outdoor, heated indoor. **Activities:** hot tub, exercise room, spa. **Guest Services:** valet and coin laundry.

### SPRINGHILL SUITES BY MARRIOTT PENSACOLA BEACH
(850)932-6000  **19**

▼▼▼ Hotel $109-$299 **Address:** 24 Via De Luna Dr 32561 **Location:** Oceanfront. 0.5 mi e on SR 399. **Facility:** 117 units, some two bedrooms. 5 stories, interior corridors. **Terms:** check-in 4 pm. **Pool(s):** heated outdoor. **Activities:** hot tub, exercise room. **Guest Services:** valet and coin laundry.

**AAA Benefit:** Members save 5% or more!

### CRABS WE GOT 'EM
850/932-0700  **28**

▼▼ Seafood. Casual Dining. $10-$36 **AAA Inspector Notes:** If you fancy crab, this is the place for you. Located right on the beach, the lively location has an indoor dining area, as well as a terrace, a canopied beach dining area and a children's beach play area. The menu boasts an impressive choice of crab—Alaskan snow crab clusters, king crab legs, Dungeness crab, Maryland soft-shell crab and crab cakes. Combo platters, surf and turf and mixed seafood platters round out the options. **Features:** full bar, patio dining, Sunday brunch. **Address:** 6 Casino Beach Blvd 32561 **Location:** Just s of jct SR 399. L D

### FLOUNDERS CHOWDER HOUSE
850/932-2003  **27**

▼▼ Seafood. Casual Dining. $10-$24 **AAA Inspector Notes:** On Santa Rosa Sound, this restaurant is known for its friendly service and generous portions of such dishes as blackened tuna, stuffed flounder and mouth-watering barbecue shrimp. The three-layer Key lime pie will satisfy any sweet tooth. Live entertainment is offered daily in season. **Features:** full bar. **Address:** 800 Quietwater Beach Rd 32561 **Location:** Just e of Quietwater Beach boardwalk. L D

### THE GRAND MARLIN RESTAURANT & OYSTER BAR
850/677-9153  **23**

▼▼▼ Seafood. Casual Dining. $10-$35 **AAA Inspector Notes:** This upscale restaurant, located on Santa Rosa Sound and Pensacola Bay, offers great sunset views and wonderful food artfully presented. The outdoor dining area features live entertainment. **Features:** full bar, patio dining, Sunday brunch, happy hour. **Address:** 400 Pensacola Beach Blvd 32561 **Location:** On SR 399, just e. L D CALL

### HEMINGWAY'S ISLAND GRILL
850/934-4747  **25**

▼▼ American. Casual Dining. $8-$34 **AAA Inspector Notes:** This laid-back restaurant creates an island feel with distressed wood walls and floor, nautical-style lighting, rattan leaf-shaped ceiling fans, a terrace and lively bar area. Vintage black-and-white photos and a full-size marlin fish adorn the walls. Steak, fresh seafood, burgers, grilled sandwiches, salads and thin-crust pizzas make up the menu. The frequently updated wine list has an impressive selection of wines by the glass. The indoor dining area offers comfortable booths for added privacy. **Features:** full bar, patio dining, Sunday brunch, happy hour. **Address:** 400 Quietwater Beach, Suite 16 32561 **Location:** On Quietwater Beach boardwalk. L D

### LILLO'S TUSCAN GRILLE
850/934-5456  **26**

▼▼ Italian. Casual Dining. $5-$20 **AAA Inspector Notes:** Traditional Italian favorites are offered in a cozy atmosphere at this eatery. **Features:** full bar, early bird specials. **Address:** 5 Via De Luna Dr 32561 **Location:** SR 399; center. L D

### NATIVE CAFE
850/934-4848  **24**

▼▼ American. Casual Dining. $7-$11 **AAA Inspector Notes:** This popular beach stop features simple, fresh and delicious food. The fish tacos are mouth-watering and the homemade desserts are worth the splurge. Seating is limited. **Features:** full bar. **Address:** 45A Via De Luna Dr 32561 **Location:** 0.5 mi e on SR 399. B L

### PEG LEG PETE'S OYSTER BAR
850/932-4139  **29**

▼▼ Seafood. Casual Dining. $8-$30 **AAA Inspector Notes:** Located in the inlet, this popular gathering spot has received many local awards for best beach dining. The staff is friendly and the seafood is fresh. **Features:** full bar, patio dining, happy hour. **Address:** 1010 Fort Pickens Rd 32561 **Location:** Just off SR 399. L D

## PERRY (C-6) pop. 7,017, elev. 30'

**FOREST CAPITAL MUSEUM STATE PARK,** 1 mi. s. on US 19 at 204 Forest Park Dr., depicts the development of the forest industry in north Florida. Exhibits illustrate the history of forestry and highlight turpentine production, regional wildlife and the cutting of virgin forests, cypress swamps and hardwood hammocks. The adjacent North Florida Cracker Homestead, built in the 1860s, interprets the lifestyle of early settlers. A visitor center, playground and pavilions also are on-site.

**Time:** Allow 30 minutes minimum. **Hours:** Thurs.-Mon. 9-noon and 1-5. Last tour departs 40 minutes before closing. Closed Jan. 1, Thanksgiving and Christmas. **Cost:** $2; free (ages 0-5). **Phone:** (850) 584-3227. GT 🎦 🅰

**HOLIDAY INN EXPRESS & SUITES**          (850)584-3200

Hotel
$99-$199

**Address:** 601 Everett Way 32348 **Location:** On Alternate Rt US 19/27/98, 1.3 mi s of jct US 221. **Facility:** 78 units, some two bedrooms. 3 stories, interior corridors. **Pool(s):** outdoor. **Activities:** exercise room. **Guest Services:** coin laundry. **Featured Amenity:** full hot breakfast.

SAVE 🍽+ CALL ♿M 🚭 BIZ HS 🛜 ✕ 🕿 📷 🖥

### WHERE TO EAT

**MAMA'S ITALIAN FAMILY RESTAURANT**          850/223-1109

🔻🔻 Italian. Casual Dining. $7-$22 **AAA Inspector Notes:** Expect to be pleasantly surprised at the classic Italian recipes served in this small Southern town eatery. The menu is loaded with traditional favorites such as lasagna, stuffed manicotti, rigatoni, spaghetti and meatballs and ravioli. They also serve wraps, submarine sandwiches and panini. **Features:** beer & wine. **Address:** 2275 S Byron Butler Pkwy 32348 **Location:** 0.7 mi s of jct US 221. L D

## POINT WASHINGTON (B-3) elev. 16'

**EDEN GARDENS STATE PARK AND WESLEY HOUSE** is at 181 Eden Gardens Rd. Magnolias, colorful camellias and azaleas, a historic rose garden and live oaks draped in Spanish moss surround an 1897 antebellum mansion filled with Colonial, Empire and Victorian furnishings. The house was built on the site of a lumber mill owned by William H. Wesley. A Civil War encampment is held in late January. Forty-five-minute guided tours of the mansion are offered.

**Hours:** Grounds open daily 8-dusk. Mansion tours Thurs.-Mon. on the hour 10-3. Holiday candlelight tours also are offered. **Cost:** $4 (per private vehicle with two to eight people); $2 (per person arriving by bicycle or on foot). Mansion tour $4; $2 (ages 0-12). **Phone:** (850) 267-8320. GT 🅰

## PORT ST. JOE (C-4) pop. 3,445, elev. 5'

**CONSTITUTION CONVENTION MUSEUM STATE PARK,** 200 Allen Memorial Way, preserves the site of Florida's first constitutional convention. Exhibits pertain to this event and other local history. Animated talking mannequins provide 2 minutes of closing remarks at the end of the tour. **Time:** Allow 30 minutes minimum. **Hours:** Thurs.-Mon. 9-noon and 1-5 Eastern Time. **Cost:** $2; free (ages 0-5). **Phone:** (850) 229-8029.

## QUINCY (B-5) pop. 7,972, elev. 187'
• Restaurants p. 204

Established in 1828, the agricultural town of Quincy owed its early prosperity to the tobacco industry. The Quincy State Bank eventually persuaded its patrons to invest in the fledgling Coca-Cola Co., resulting in economic fortune for both the town and its citizens.

Soldiers from the battles of Natural Bridge and Olustee were treated in Quincy, a medical center during the Civil War. The town also served as a supply commissary for the Confederate Army. In 1868 a fire destroyed more than half the town, leading to an ordinance requiring that all new buildings be constructed of brick.

The 36-block historic district features landscaping, period lighting and Victorian-style buildings. Most structures were built in the late 1880s, although several houses date back to the 1840s.

**Gadsden County Chamber of Commerce:** 208 N. Adams St., P.O. Box 389, Quincy, FL 32353. **Phone:** (850) 627-9231.

**Self-guiding tours:** A brochure outlining a tour of the historic district is available from the chamber of commerce.

**ALLISON HOUSE INN**          (850)875-2511

🔻🔻🔻 Historic Bed & Breakfast $85-$175 **Address:** 215 N Madison St 32351 **Location:** Just n of town center; in historic district. **Facility:** This 1843 English country-style home offers comfortable, distinctively decorated rooms. Enjoy granola and biscotti among the homemade foods served to guests. Breakfast is served on an enclosed upper front porch. 6 units. 2 stories (no elevator), interior corridors. **Terms:** 21 day cancellation notice-fee imposed.
🛜 ✕ 🕿 / SOME UNITS 🐾

**HAMPTON INN QUINCY**          (850)627-7555

Hotel
$99-$319

**AAA Benefit:** Members save 5% or more!

**Address:** 165 Spooner Rd 32351 **Location:** I-10 exit 181, just s on SR 267. **Facility:** 63 units. 3 stories, interior corridors. **Terms:** 1-7 night minimum stay, cancellation fee imposed. **Pool(s):** outdoor. **Activities:** exercise room. **Guest Services:** coin laundry.
SAVE 🚭 BIZ HS 🛜 🕿 📷 🖥

**HOLIDAY INN EXPRESS HOTEL & SUITES**    850/875-2500

▼▼▼▼ **Hotel.** Rates not provided. **Address:** 101 Spooner Rd 32351 **Location:** I-10 exit 181, just s on SR 267. **Facility:** 56 units. 3 stories, interior corridors. **Pool(s):** outdoor. **Activities:** exercise room. **Guest Services:** valet and coin laundry.

⊃ BIZ HS 🛜 ✕ 🖥 🖨 💻

---

**MCFARLIN HOUSE BED & BREAKFAST INN**    850/875-2526

▼▼▼▼ **Historic Bed & Breakfast** $109-$249 **Address:** 305 E King St 32351 **Location:** On SR 12, jct N Love St; in historic district. **Facility:** This 1895 Queen Anne Victorian features dramatic woodwork and a grand stairway in the public areas, which are beautifully decorated with authentic period pieces. 9 units. 4 stories (no elevator), interior corridors. **Terms:** check-in 4 pm, 2 night minimum stay - weekends, 30 day cancellation notice-fee imposed. **Activities:** hot tub. **Guest Services:** area transportation.

🕂 🍴 🛜 ✕

---

### WHERE TO EAT

**THE WHIP WATERFRONT PUB & GRUB**    850/875-2605

▼▼ **Seafood Steak. Casual Dining.** $8-$24 **AAA Inspector Notes:** On Lake Talquin at the Whippoorwill Sportsman's Lodge and Campground, the rustic, fishing-themed restaurant affords great views of the lake and sunsets. This place glibly boasts "great view, good food and lousy service." The latter isn't exactly true, but the service is relaxed, as is the atmosphere. Good simple fare includes hand-cut steaks, chops, comfort food and seafood. On Friday nights a low country shrimp boil is the highlight. **Features:** beer & wine, patio dining, happy hour. **Address:** 3129 Cooks Landing Rd 32351 **Location:** 3 mi se of jct SR 267.   L  D  🛍

---

## ST. MARKS (C-5) pop. 293, elev. 7'

In 1836 a railroad was built to connect Tallahassee with St. Marks. Now dismantled, the Tallahassee-St. Marks Historic Railroad State Trail offers a 16-mile paved trail for bicyclists, hikers, horseback riders and skaters. For additional information phone (850) 245-2052.

**ST. MARKS NATIONAL WILDLIFE REFUGE** covers approximately 68,000 acres along the Gulf of Mexico; the visitor center is at 1255 Lighthouse Rd. The refuge borders Apalachee Bay and extends from the Aucilla River west to the Ochlockonee River. Forty-nine miles of the Florida Trail pass through the refuge. Wintering whooping cranes and other birds are among wildlife that can be observed. Fishing, hiking and photography opportunities abound. The refuge is home to St. Marks Lighthouse, built in 1831, and several other historic sites.

**Hours:** Daily dawn-dusk. Visitor center open Mon.-Fri. 8-4, Sat.-Sun. 10-5. Closed major holidays. **Cost:** $5 (per private vehicle); $1 (per person arriving by bicycle or on foot). **Phone:** (850) 925-6121.

**SAN MARCOS DE APALACHE HISTORIC STATE PARK,** off SR 363, 1 mi. s.w. to 148 Old Fort Rd., displays Native American, Spanish and Civil War artifacts. The interpretive center is on the site of a fort built by the Spanish in 1679 at the confluence of the Wakulla and St. Marks rivers and later occupied by English, Confederate and Federal troops. Outside are a military cemetery and the remains of the fort and earthworks.

**Time:** Allow 30 minutes minimum. **Hours:** Thurs.-Mon. 9-5. Closed Jan. 1, Thanksgiving and Christmas. **Cost:** Free. Museum $2; free (ages 0-5). **Phone:** (850) 925-6216. 🎢

---

**SWEET MAGNOLIA INN**    850/925-7670

▼▼▼▼ **Bed & Breakfast** $125-$225 **Address:** 803 Port Leon Dr 32355 **Location:** On CR 363; center. **Facility:** Built in 1916, this cozy structure sits a stone's throw from the water and is a restful retreat. Most rooms have queen-size poster beds. The property is just a short ride from the capital city. 6 units. 2 stories, interior corridors. **Terms:** 2 night minimum stay - weekends, 5 day cancellation notice-fee imposed. **Activities:** bicycles. 🛜 ✕ 🌀

---

# SANTA ROSA BEACH

**WATERCOLOR INN & RESORT**    (850)534-5000

▼▼▼▼ ▼▼▼▼
**Boutique Resort Hotel**
$275-$545

**Address:** 34 Goldenrod Cir 32459 **Location:** Oceanfront. 6.1 mi e on CR 30A, just s; 0.9 mi w of jct CR 395, just w of Seaside. **Facility:** This boutique-style hotel is located on the Gulf of Mexico and offers gorgeous sunset, beach and dune views as well as a multitude of wildlife viewing. 60 units. 2-4 stories, interior corridors. *Bath:* shower only. **Parking:** on-site and valet. **Terms:** check-in 4 pm, 2-3 night minimum stay - seasonal and/or weekends, 7 day cancellation notice-fee imposed, resort fee. **Amenities:** safes. **Dining:** 2 restaurants, also, Fish Out of Water, see separate listing. **Pool(s):** outdoor, heated outdoor. **Activities:** tennis, recreation programs in summer, bicycles, spa. **Guest Services:** valet laundry, area transportation.

SAVE ECO 🍴 🧒 🍽 ⊃ 🧖 BIZ HS 🛜 ✕ 🖥 💻

---

### WHERE TO EAT

**ANOTHER BROKEN EGG CAFE**    850/231-7835

▼▼▼ **Breakfast Sandwiches. Casual Dining.** $5-$15 **AAA Inspector Notes:** Enjoy a breakfast experience you will not soon forget; huge cinnamon buns, Popeye's omelet and fruit and nut pancakes or french toast are some of the menu specialties. **Features:** Sunday brunch. **Address:** 51 Grayton Uptown Cir 32459 **Location:** Just s of jct E CR 30A.   B  L  CALL 📶

---

**THE DONUT HOLE**    850/267-3239

▼▼▼ **Breakfast Sandwiches. Casual Dining.** $6-$12 **AAA Inspector Notes:** This popular spot offers yummy breakfasts, fresh doughnuts, sandwiches, burgers and salads. Although pleasant servers keep up a frenetic diner-style pace, patrons still can expect long waits in season. **Address:** 6745 Hwy 98 W 32459 **Location:** Just e of jct CR 30A.   B  L  D

---

**FISH OUT OF WATER**    850/534-5050

▼▼▼▼ ▼▼▼▼
**Seafood Fine Dining**
$8-$40

**AAA Inspector Notes:** Save this fish out of water for a special occasion. The menu changes daily as the local catches and other specialty items are made available. The servers are attentive and knowledgeable of preparations as well as familiar with the extensive wine offerings. Feast on Blue crab claws, Apalachicola bay oysters, Florida hopper shrimp, Gulf tuna, Gulf grouper or Amish chicken. The raw bar is a popular offering in season. **Features:** full bar, patio dining. **Reservations:** suggested. **Address:** 34 Goldenrod Cir 32459 **Location:** 6.1 mi e on CR 30A, just s; 0.9 mi w of jct CR 395, just w of Seaside; in WaterColor Inn & Resort. **Parking:** on-site and valet.   B  D  CALL 📶

**MISS LUCILLE'S GOSSIP PARLOR**          850/267-2522

American. Quick Serve. $3-$10 **AAA Inspector Notes:** Guests come by for a bakery treat and snuggle on the sofa with a warm cup of tea, or stop in for lunch and enjoy a bowl of soup or a panini to order. Traveling without a laptop? Miss Lucille allows guests to gossip on the Internet for free on one of two computers reserved for diners. **Features:** beer & wine, patio dining. **Address:** 45 Town Center Loop, Suite C7 32459 **Location:** Jct CR 393, 3 mi e of US 98, on CR 30A; in Gulf Place Shopping Village. B L

**PANDORA'S OF GRAYTON BEACH**          850/231-4102

Steak Seafood. Casual Dining. $22-$55 **AAA Inspector Notes:** This family-owned and -operated restaurant has been in the area since 1978. They are known for fresh seafood and steaks which are cooked on an oak wood-burning grill. Bacon-wrapped yellowfin tuna, broiled rock lobster tail, baby back ribs and the steak with shrimp combo are popular items. **Features:** full bar, early bird specials. **Address:** 63 Defuniak St 32459 **Location:** Jct US 98, 1.7 mi s on CR 283; jct CR 30A. D

# SEAGROVE BEACH

### ANGELINA'S PIZZERIA & PASTA          850/231-2500

Italian
Casual Dining
$7-$20

**AAA Inspector Notes:** This West Florida landmark, known for its homelike atmosphere and homemade lasagna, has been around for as long as any local can remember. Diners feel as if they are dining at a friend's house while enjoying such Italian favorites as pizza, calzones, stromboli and their specialty pasta dishes-eggplant parmigiana, baked ravioli, linguine with clam sauce, fettuccine primavera, chicken Marsala, shrimp scampi and lobster ravioli. **Features:** beer & wine. **Address:** 4005 E County Hwy 30A 32459 **Location:** On CR 30A, just e. L D

# SHALIMAR pop. 717

**FAIRFIELD INN & SUITES BY MARRIOTT FORT WALTON BEACH-EGLIN AFB**          (850)651-9999

Hotel $137-$218 **Address:** 1280 Eglin Pkwy N 32579 **Location:** On SR 85, jct Richbourg Ave. **Facility:** 92 units. 4 stories, interior corridors. Pool(s): heated outdoor. **Activities:** hot tub, exercise room. **Guest Services:** valet and coin laundry.

**AAA Benefit:** Members save 5% or more!

# STEINHATCHEE pop. 1,047

**ROY'S RESTAURANT**          352/498-5000

Steak Seafood. Casual Dining. $5-$28 **AAA Inspector Notes:** A lovely Gulf view and superbly prepared food help explain why this restaurant has been serving happy customers for 30 years. Guests argue that this spot serves the tastiest shrimp in the region, along with other ocean fare that patrons can request fried, broiled or steamed. All meals come with the eatery's great hushpuppies. **Features:** beer & wine. **Address:** 100 1st Ave SW 32359 **Location:** Just w of town center. L D

# TALLAHASSEE (B-5) pop. 181,376, elev. 216'

In 1823 two explorers set out to find a permanent seat of government for the newly formed territory of Florida. The site they chose—midway between St. Augustine and Pensacola—was called "tallahassee" (tal-a-HASS-ee) by the Creek and Seminole Indians, a name meaning "old town." The rendezvous point became the state capital.

A convention in 1861 declared Florida an independent nation and a member of the Confederate States of America. In 1865 during the Civil War, Confederate Floridian soldiers repelled Union forces at the Battle of Natural Bridge *(see attraction listing)* to protect Tallahassee, making it the only uncaptured Confederate capital east of the Mississippi River.

Tallahassee's first state house was a log cabin; two more impressive structures were constructed in later years. The Historic Capitol, built in 1845, is now The Florida Historic Capitol Museum and an elegant centerpiece to the Florida State Capitol complex, which was completed in 1977. *See attraction listings.*

The oldest building in the city is the Columns, begun in 1830 by wealthy banker William "Money" Williams. It served as the focal point of financial, political and social development in the state's early history and was saved from demolition by being moved to 100 N. Duval St. in 1971.

Another historic landmark is Mission San Luis *(see attraction listing)*, an archeological site where the Spanish and Appalachia Indians lived and worked in harmony.

Letchworth-Love Mounds Archaeological State Park, 4500 Sunray Rd., features a 46-foot-tall ceremonial mound that was likely built 1,100 to 1,800 years ago. The park also offers hiking trails and a covered picnic area.

Artists and artisans create, display and sell their works in more than 50 working studios at Railroad Square Art Park, a 10-acre cultural hub in downtown Tallahassee's historic warehouse district. Noteworthy is 621 Art Gallery, which features quality contemporary works by local, national and international artists while offering a variety of interactive experiences. The art park's Friday Gallery Hop occurs at 6 p.m. on the first Friday of the month; phone (850) 224-6163.

In a region of rolling hills, live oak forests and rivers, Tallahassee has beautiful landscapes and large lakes, some of which can be enjoyed on the Big Bend Scenic Highway, a 220-mile cross-county trail accessible via SR 263 near Tallahassee Regional Airport. The city also is noted for its many canopy roads, southern gardens and historic homes.

Tallahassee and surrounds provide numerous recreational opportunities and the Gulf of Mexico is only a half-hour away. Biking, camping, exploring, picnicking and swimming are among the activities that can be enjoyed. Lake Talquin *(see Recreation Areas Chart)* is popular for fishing and Wakulla Springs, one of the world's largest and deepest freshwater springs, offers boat tours, kayaking and swimming. Wildlife areas such as St. Marks National Wildlife Refuge *(see attraction listing p. 204)* and Apalachicola National Forest *(see attraction listing p. 172)* provide habitat for birds and monarch butterflies.

In 1836 a railroad was built to connect Tallahassee with St. Marks. Now dismantled, the Tallahassee-St. Marks Historic Railroad State Trail

(See map & index p. 208.)

offers a 16-mile paved trail for bicyclists, hikers, horseback riders and skaters. For additional information phone (850) 245-2052.

Two major universities, both centrally located, provide cultural programs, sports events and other activities. The 422-acre campus of Florida A&M University stands on one of Tallahassee's highest hills, and Florida State University is on a 463-acre campus slightly west of downtown.

🌱 Springtime Tallahassee Festival is a 1-day festival held downtown in either late March or early April and features arts and crafts, a parade, a seafood festival, children's activities and music. Holiday shoppers will want to visit 🌱 Market Days at the North Florida Fairgrounds in early December to peruse the arts and crafts of more than 300 vendors. Also in early December is 'Just one More' Invitational Art Festival, a celebration of the arts held at Bloxham and Ponce de Leon parks.

**Tallahassee Area Visitor Information Center:** 106 E. Jefferson St., Tallahassee, FL 32301. **Phone:** (850) 606-2305 or (800) 628-2866.

**Self-guiding tours:** Brochures for a downtown walking tour can be picked up from the Tallahassee Area Visitor Information Center. The route features historical and architecturally significant buildings and sites. Maps of the canopy roads also are available.

**Shopping areas:** The Midtown District and Market District (Timberlane Road and Market Street) both offer a variety of shops. Among the 120 stores at Governor's Square Mall, 1500 Apalachee Pkwy., are Dillard's, JCPenney, Macy's and Sears. Antique stores and art galleries line Main Street in downtown Havana, a small town 13 miles north of Tallahassee.

◆ **ALFRED B. MACLAY GARDENS STATE PARK,** at 3540 Thomasville Rd., .5 mi. n. of I-10 exit 203 on US 319, consists of more than 1,100 acres, including 28 acres of ornamental gardens that are the focal point of the park. New York businessman Alfred B. Maclay and his wife, Louise, began the gardens in 1923. Colorful azaleas, camellias and Oriental magnolias as well as many native plants bloom January through April. The Maclay House has restored living and dining rooms and serves as a center for information about the Maclays, camellias and the gardens.

Nearly 8 miles of hiking, biking and horse trails run through the park, which also features a picturesque picnic/recreation area with covered shelters, a swimming area, a paddleboat launch, rental kayak and a playground. Audio tours of the gardens are available. *See Recreation Areas Chart.*

**Time:** Allow 1 hour minimum. **Hours:** Park open daily 8-dusk. Gardens open daily 9-5. House open daily 9-5, Jan.-Apr. **Cost:** Park $6 (per private vehicle with two to eight people); $4 (per single-occupancy vehicle); $2 (per person arriving by bicycle or on foot). Garden admission (including house) Jan.-Apr. $6; $3 (ages 2-12); free rest of year with paid park admission. **Phone:** (850) 487-4556. 🗙 🛖

**CARRIE MEEK-JAMES N. EATON SR. SOUTH-EASTERN REGIONAL BLACK ARCHIVES RESEARCH CENTER AND MUSEUM** is on the Florida A&M University campus at 445 Campbell St. Housed in the 1907 Carnegie Library and Meek-Eaton facility, the museum contains artifacts, photographs, manuscripts, art works, oral history tapes and rare maps that document the history and culture of Africans and African-Americans, including their institutions and organizations.

A visitor parking permit is available at the campus parking services on Wahnish Way. **Time:** Allow 1 hour minimum. **Hours:** Mon.-Fri. 9-5. Closed major holidays. **Cost:** Free. **Phone:** (850) 599-3020, or (850) 561-2203 for parking information.

**THE FLORIDA HISTORIC CAPITOL MUSEUM,** 400 S. Monroe St., has been restored to its 1902 appearance. Self-guiding tours of the building cover the House and Senate chambers, the Governor's suite, the supreme court and the rotunda. The political history museum explores the political process and individuals who have played important roles in Florida's colorful history.

**Time:** Allow 30 minutes minimum. **Hours:** Mon.-Fri. 9-4:30, Sat. 10-4:30, Sun. and holidays noon-4:30. Closed Thanksgiving and Christmas. **Cost:** Donations. **Phone:** (850) 487-1902.

**FLORIDA STATE CAPITOL,** 400 S. Monroe St., is a 22-story tower with House and Senate chambers on either side, both with public viewing galleries. There is an observation deck on the top floor and a Florida information center just inside the west plaza entrance. Florida's legislature is in session from March through April. **Time:** Allow 1 hour minimum. **Hours:** Mon.-Fri. 8-5. Closed major holidays. **Cost:** Free. **Phone:** (850) 488-6167 for guided tour information. 🄶🅃

**GOODWOOD MUSEUM AND GARDENS** is at 1600 Miccosukee Rd. The restored antebellum house is appointed with marble fireplaces, mahogany staircases and a fresco depicting Aesop's Fables. Originally a composite of Greek Revival, Federal and Italianate architectural styles, the house was modified with the addition of columns in the early 1900s. The estate was home to several prominent Floridians, including Sen. William C. Hodges.

**Time:** Allow 1 hour minimum. **Hours:** Gardens open Mon.-Fri. 9-5, Sat. 10-2. Guided house tours are given Tues.-Fri. at 10, 11:30, 1 and 2:30, Sat. at 10, 11:30 and 1. Closed major holidays. **Cost:** Gardens free. Guided house tour $12; $10 (ages 65+); $6 (ages 6-12). Reservations are recommended. **Phone:** (850) 877-4202. 🄶🅃 🍽

(See map & index p. 208.)

## JOHN G. RILEY CENTER AND MUSEUM OF AFRICAN AMERICAN HISTORY & CULTURE is at
419 E. Jefferson St. Exhibits of documents, artifacts, photographs and personal memorabilia in the restored 1890 house of John G. Riley highlight African-American history and the life of the self-taught businessman and educator. **Time:** Allow 30 minutes minimum. **Hours:** Mon.-Thurs. 10-4, Fri.-Sat. 10-2. Closed major holidays. **Cost:** $2; $1 (ages 0-11). **Phone:** (850) 681-7881.

**THE KNOTT HOUSE MUSEUM,** 301 E. Park Ave., was built in 1843 as a private home. Restored to its 1930s appearance, this stately house has been restored and is fully furnished with the Victorian pieces acquired by the Knott family when they bought the house in 1928. Colorful stories of William Knott, career politician, and his wife Luella, a poet, musician and community activist, are recounted.

**Hours:** Narrated tours are given Wed.-Fri. on the hour 1-3, Sat. 10-3, Sept.-July. Closed Thanksgiving and Christmas. Phone ahead to confirm schedule. **Cost:** Free. **Phone:** (850) 922-2459.

**LAKE JACKSON MOUNDS ARCHAEOLOGICAL STATE PARK** is at 3600 Indian Mounds Rd., at the s. tip of Lake Jackson. The mounds are remains of a ceremonial center that existed A.D. 1100-1200. Four earth temple mounds are within the site. **Hours:** Daily 8-dusk. **Cost:** $3 (per private vehicle with maximum 8 people); $2 (per person arriving by bicycle or on foot). **Phone:** (850) 922-6007. 🏕

**MISSION SAN LUIS,** at 2100 W. Tennessee St., is a National Historic Landmark comprised of a reconstructed fort, Spanish dwelling, Franciscan church and friary and Native American council house on a hilly, oak-shaded site, which was home to an Apalachee-Spanish village 1656-1704. Costumed interpreters demonstrate 17th-century life. A visitor center has exhibits and a 125-seat orientation theater.

**Time:** Allow 1 hour minimum. **Hours:** Tues.-Sun. 10-4. Closed Jan. 1, Easter, July 4, Thanksgiving, Christmas Eve and Christmas. **Cost:** $5; $3 (ages 65+); $2 (ages 6-17); free (active military with ID). **Phone:** (850) 245-6406.

**MUSEUM OF FLORIDA HISTORY,** in the R.A. Gray Building at 500 S. Bronough St., has exhibits depicting Florida's vibrant history. Visitors can view a variety of artifacts, including a mastodon skeleton and a giant armadillo mannequin from the Pleistocene era, gold and silver from Spanish shipwrecks, flags flown during the Civil War, a partial replica of a Florida steamboat, memorabilia reflecting Florida's role in World War II and various artifacts from the changing gallery. Touring exhibits and educational programs also are featured.

**Time:** Allow 30 minutes minimum. **Hours:** Mon.-Fri. 9-4:30 (also third Thurs. of the month 4:30-8), Sat. 10-4:30, Sun. and holidays noon-4:30. **Cost:** Donations. **Phone:** (850) 245-6400. 🍴

**NATURAL BRIDGE BATTLEFIELD HISTORIC STATE PARK,** 7502 Natural Bridge Rd., is the 6-acre site where the Battle of Natural Bridge was fought Mar. 5, 1865, to prevent Union troops from capturing the Capitol at Tallahassee. **Hours:** Daily 8-dusk. **Cost:** $3 (per private vehicle with maximum eight people); $2 (per person arriving by bicycle or on foot). **Phone:** (850) 922-6007. 🏕

**TALLAHASSEE AUTOMOBILE MUSEUM** is at 6800 Mahan Dr. Among the vehicles in this collection are a 1948 Tucker Torpedo, three Batmobiles used in Batman movies and the hearse that carried Abraham Lincoln's body. Automotive collectibles and related memorabilia also are displayed. **Time:** Allow 1 hour minimum. **Hours:** Mon.-Fri. 8-5, Sat. 10-5, Sun. noon-5. **Cost:** $16; $13.50 (senior citizens); $10.75 (students with ID); $7.50 (ages 5-9). **Phone:** (850) 942-0137.

**TALLAHASSEE MUSEUM,** 6.5 mi. s.w. on Lake Bradford at 3945 Museum Dr., depicts north Florida's natural and human history. A nature trail winds through 52 acres of scenic lakeshore woodlands, which are home to Florida panthers, red wolves, otters, deer and bears. Also on the grounds are a restored 1880s farm complex; Bellevue Plantation, the antebellum home of the great-grandniece of George Washington; a one-room schoolhouse; a church and a caboose.

The museum's Tallahassee Tree to Tree Adventures features an adventure course and ziplines. Visitors move among the trees with tightropes, crab walks, jungle bridges, nets and ziplines; a children's course, an intermediate course and a 2-hour course for the truly adventurous are offered.

**Note:** Closed, secured athletic footwear is required for the ziplines and adventure course. **Time:** Allow 2 hours minimum. **Hours:** Mon.-Sat. 9-5, Sun. 11-5. Tallahassee Tree to Tree Adventures hours vary. Closed Jan. 1, Thanksgiving, Christmas Eve and Christmas. **Cost:** $9; $8.50 (ages 65+ and college students with ID); $6 (ages 4-15). Tallahassee Tree to Tree Adventures $15-$40. **Phone:** (850) 575-8684 or (850) 576-1636.

# Recommend places you'd like us to inspect
# at AAA.com/TourBookComments

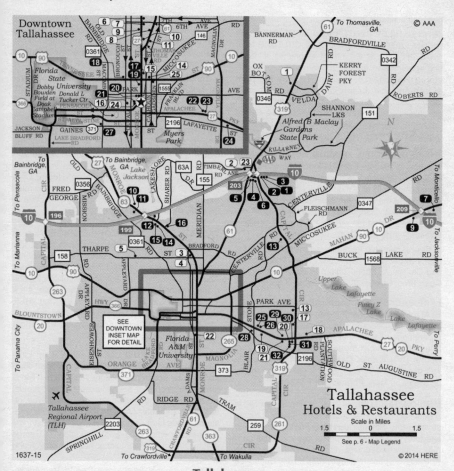

Downtown Tallahassee

Florida State
Bobby Bowden
Field at Doak
Campbell
Stadium

© AAA

To Thomasville, GA

BANNERMAN RD

BRADFORDVILLE

KERRY FOREST PKY

SHANNON LKS

Alfred B Maclay Gardens State Park

KILLARNEY WAY

Florida A&M University

Tallahassee Regional Airport (TLH)

SEE DOWNTOWN INSET MAP FOR DETAIL

To Panama City

To Crawfordville        To Wakulla

# Tallahassee
## Hotels & Restaurants

Scale in Miles
1.5    0    1.5

See p. 6 - Map Legend

1637-15

© 2014 HERE

# Tallahassee

This index helps you "spot" where approved hotels and restaurants are located on the corresponding detailed maps. Hotel daily rate range is for comparison only. Restaurant price range is a combination of lunch and/or dinner. Turn to the listing page for more detailed rate and price information and consult display ads for special promotions.

## TALLAHASSEE

| Map Page | Hotels | Diamond Rated | Rate Range | Page |
|---|---|---|---|---|
| **1** this page | Extended Stay America Tallahassee-Killearn | ◇◇ | $60-$225 | 211 |
| **2** this page | Residence Inn by Marriott Tallahassee North I-10 Capital Circle | ◇◇◇ | $76-$299 | 212 |
| **3** this page | Courtyard by Marriott Tallahassee North/I-10 Capital Circle | ◇◇◇ | $67-$199 | 210 |
| **4** this page | Cabot Lodge-Thomasville Rd | fyi | $109-$499 | 210 |
| **5** this page | Hilton Garden Inn Tallahassee | ◇◇◇ | $119-$189 | 211 |
| **6** this page | Hampton Inn & Suites I-10/Thomasville Rd | ◇◇◇ | $119-$309 | 211 |
| **7** this page | Staybridge Suites Tallahassee | ◇◇◇ | Rates not provided | 212 |
| **9** this page | BEST WESTERN Seminole Inn | ◇◇ | $70-$250 SAVE | 210 |
| **10** this page | Fairfield Inn by Marriott Tallahassee North/I-10 | ◇◇ | $98-$115 | 211 |
| **11** this page | Country Inn & Suites By Carlson | ◇◇◇ | Rates not provided | 210 |

**TALLAHASSEE (cont'd)**

| Map Page | Hotels (cont'd) | Diamond Rated | Rate Range | Page |
|---|---|---|---|---|
| 12 p. 208 | La Quinta Inn Tallahassee (North) | ◆◆ | $59-$309 | 212 |
| 13 p. 208 | TownePlace Suites by Marriott Tallahassee Northeast/Capital Circle | ◆◆ | $85-$375 | 212 |
| 14 p. 208 | Howard Johnson Express Inn | ◆◆ | $70-$230 | 212 |
| 15 p. 208 | Wingate by Wyndham | ◆◆◆ | $89-$279 | 212 |
| 16 p. 208 | **Econo Lodge** | ◆◆ | $55-$85 [SAVE] | 211 |
| 17 p. 208 | Hotel Duval | ◆◆◆ | Rates not provided | 212 |
| 18 p. 208 | **Four Points by Sheraton Tallahassee Downtown** | ◆◆◆ | $99-$549 [SAVE] | 211 |
| 19 p. 208 | **Aloft Tallahassee Downtown** | ◆◆◆ | $99-$269 [SAVE] | 210 |
| 20 p. 208 | DoubleTree by Hilton Hotel Tallahassee | ◆◆◆ | $109-$279 | 211 |
| 21 p. 208 | Governors Inn | ◆◆ | $109-$229 | 211 |
| 22 p. 208 | **Courtyard by Marriott Tallahassee** | ◆◆◆ | $89-$269 [SAVE] | 210 |
| 23 p. 208 | Comfort Suites | ◆◆◆ | $69-$169 | 210 |
| 24 p. 208 | Ramada Plaza | ◆◆ | $62-$71 | 212 |
| 25 p. 208 | **BEST WESTERN Pride Inn & Suites** | ◆◆ | $70-$400 [SAVE] | 210 |
| 26 p. 208 | **Quality Inn & Suites** | ◆◆ | $75-$159 [SAVE] | 212 |
| 27 p. 208 | **Residence Inn by Marriott Tallahassee Universities at the Capitol** | ◆◆◆ | $119-$299 [SAVE] | 212 |
| 28 p. 208 | Hilton Garden Inn Tallahassee Central | ◆◆◆ | $109-$269 | 211 |
| 29 p. 208 | Baymont Inn & Suites Tallahassee Central | ◆◆ | Rates not provided | 210 |
| 30 p. 208 | Fairfield Inn & Suites by Marriott Tallahassee Central | ◆◆◆ | $89-$299 | 211 |
| 31 p. 208 | Hampton Inn Tallahassee Central | ◆◆◆ | $109-$249 | 211 |
| 32 p. 208 | Homewood Suites by Hilton | ◆◆◆ | $119-$299 | 212 |

| Map Page | Restaurants | Diamond Rated | Cuisine | Price Range | Page |
|---|---|---|---|---|---|
| 1 p. 208 | Rummy's Pizza, Pasta & Grill | ◆◆ | Pizza | $7-$19 | 214 |
| 2 p. 208 | A La Provence | ◆◆◆ | French | $10-$35 | 212 |
| 3 p. 208 | Milano Pizzeria | ◆◆ | Pizza | $6-$25 | 214 |
| 4 p. 208 | **Barnacle Bill's** | ◆◆ | Seafood | $8-$19 | 213 |
| 5 p. 208 | Wells Brothers Bar and Grill | ◆◆ | Burgers | $8-$11 | 214 |
| 6 p. 208 | Joe Mama's Wood Fired Pizza | ◆◆◆ | Pizza | $7-$19 | 214 |
| 7 p. 208 | The Mockingbird Cafe | ◆◆◆ | American | $7-$25 | 214 |
| 8 p. 208 | Midtown Filling Station | ◆◆ | American | $6-$12 | 214 |
| 9 p. 208 | Bella Bella | ◆◆ | Italian | $9-$19 | 213 |
| 10 p. 208 | Masa | ◆◆◆ | Asian | $8-$29 | 214 |
| 11 p. 208 | Kool Beanz Cafe | ◆◆◆ | American | $7-$25 | 214 |
| 13 p. 208 | Hobbit American Grill | ◆ | Wings Burgers | $8-$10 | 213 |
| 14 p. 208 | Cypress Restaurant | ◆◆◆ | Southern American | $12-$34 | 213 |
| 15 p. 208 | Avenue Eat and Drink | ◆◆◆ | Southern Fusion | $8-$46 | 213 |
| 16 p. 208 | Harry's Seafood Bar and Grille | ◆◆◆ | Southern Seafood | $8-$21 | 213 |
| 17 p. 208 | Pepper's Mexican Grill & Cantina | ◆◆ | Mexican | $5-$14 | 214 |

| Map Page | Restaurants (cont'd) | Diamond Rated | Cuisine | Price Range | Page |
|---|---|---|---|---|---|
| ⑱ p. 208 | Azu Lucy Ho's | ▽▽ | Chinese | $7-$36 | 213 |
| ⑲ p. 208 | The Black Bean Cuban Cafe | ▽ | Cuban | $5-$10 | 213 |
| ⑳ p. 208 | Georgio's Fine Food & Spirits | ▽▽ | Continental | $15-$40 | 213 |
| ㉑ p. 208 | Marie Livingston's Steak House | ▽▽▽ | Steak | $6-$35 | 214 |
| ㉒ p. 208 | Dog Et Al | ▽ | Hot Dogs | $2-$10 | 213 |
| ㉓ p. 208 | Momo's Pizza | ▽▽ | Pizza | $6-$24 | 214 |
| ㉔ p. 208 | Andrews 228 Restaurant | ▽▽▽ | New American | $14-$42 | 212 |
| ㉕ p. 208 | Backwoods Bistro | ▽▽ | American | $9-$18 | 213 |

## ALOFT TALLAHASSEE DOWNTOWN

(850)513-0313　**19**

▽▽▽ Hotel $99-$269

**AAA Benefit:** Members save up to 15%, plus Starwood Preferred Guest® benefits!

**Address:** 200 N Monroe St 32301 **Location:** 0.4 mi n of Capitol. **Facility:** 162 units. 7 stories, interior corridors. *Bath:* shower only. **Amenities:** safes. **Pool(s):** outdoor. **Activities:** exercise room. **Guest Services:** valet laundry, area transportation.

SAVE ⌸ 🏊 BIZ HS 🛜 ✕ 🔌 🖥 / SOME UNITS 🐾

## BAYMONT INN & SUITES TALLAHASSEE CENTRAL

850/878-5099　**29**

▽▽ **Hotel.** Rates not provided. **Address:** 2850 Apalachee Pkwy 32301 **Location:** 3 mi se on US 27. **Facility:** 134 units. 3-4 stories, exterior corridors. **Pool(s):** outdoor.

⌸ CALL &M 🏊 🛜 🖥 / SOME UNITS 🐾 🔌 🖨

## BEST WESTERN PRIDE INN & SUITES

(850)656-6312　**25**

▽▽▽ Motel $70-$400

**AAA Benefit:** Members save up to 20%!

**Address:** 2016 Apalachee Pkwy 32301 **Location:** 1 mi se on US 27. **Facility:** 78 units. 2 stories (no elevator), exterior corridors. **Pool(s):** outdoor. **Guest Services:** valet and coin laundry. **Featured Amenity:** breakfast buffet.

SAVE ⌸ 🏊 HS 🛜 🔌 🖨 🖥 / SOME UNITS S⌐

## BEST WESTERN SEMINOLE INN

(850)656-2938　**9**

▽▽ Motel $70-$250

**AAA Benefit:** Members save up to 20%!

**Address:** 6737 Mahan Dr 32308 **Location:** I-10 exit 209A, just w on US 90. Located in a quiet rural area. **Facility:** 59 units. 2 stories, exterior corridors. **Terms:** cancellation fee imposed. **Pool(s):** outdoor. **Guest Services:** coin laundry.

SAVE ⌸ 🏊 🛜 🔌 🖨 🖥 / SOME UNITS S⌐ HS

## CABOT LODGE-THOMASVILLE RD

(850)386-7500　**4**

[fyi] **Hotel** $109-$499 Under major renovation, scheduled to be completed October 2014. **Last Rated:** ▽▽ **Address:** 1653 Raymond Diehl Rd 32308 **Location:** I-10 exit 203, 0.4 mi se. **Facility:** 135 units. 5 stories, interior corridors. **Terms:** 7 day cancellation notice-fee imposed. **Pool(s):** outdoor. **Guest Services:** coin laundry.

ECO ⌸ CALL &M 🏊 BIZ 🛜 ✕ 🔌 🖨 🖥

## COMFORT SUITES

(850)224-3200　**23**

▽▽▽ **Hotel** $69-$169 **Address:** 1026 Apalachee Pkwy 32301 **Location:** 1 mi se on US 27. **Facility:** 64 units. 3 stories, interior corridors. **Amenities:** safes. **Pool(s):** outdoor. **Activities:** exercise room. **Guest Services:** valet and coin laundry.

⌸ CALL &M 🏊 BIZ HS 🛜 ✕ 🔌 🖨 🖥

## COUNTRY INN & SUITES BY CARLSON

850/701-2850　**11**

▽▽▽ **Hotel.** Rates not provided. **Address:** 3096 N Monroe St 32303 **Location:** I-10 exit 199, just n. **Facility:** 65 units. 4 stories, interior corridors. **Pool(s):** outdoor. **Activities:** limited exercise equipment. **Guest Services:** valet and coin laundry.

🏊 BIZ HS 🛜 ✕ 🔌 🖨 🖥

## COURTYARD BY MARRIOTT TALLAHASSEE

(850)222-8822　**22**

▽▽▽ Hotel $89-$269

COURTYARD Marriott

**AAA Benefit:** Members save 5% or more!

**Address:** 1018 Apalachee Pkwy 32301 **Location:** 1 mi se on US 27. **Facility:** 154 units. 3-4 stories, interior corridors. **Pool(s):** outdoor. **Activities:** exercise room. **Guest Services:** valet and coin laundry, boarding pass kiosk.

SAVE ECO ⌸ 🍽 🏊 BIZ 🛜 ✕ 🔌 / SOME UNITS 🔌 🖨

## COURTYARD BY MARRIOTT TALLAHASSEE NORTH/I-10 CAPITAL CIRCLE

(850)422-0600　**3**

▽▽▽ **Hotel** $67-$199 **Address:** 1972 Raymond Diehl Rd 32308 **Location:** I-10 exit 203 (US 319), just s on Thomasville Rd, then just e. **Facility:** 93 units. 3 stories, interior corridors. **Pool(s):** heated indoor. **Activities:** hot tub, exercise room. **Guest Services:** valet and coin laundry, boarding pass kiosk.

**AAA Benefit:** Members save 5% or more!

ECO ⌸ 🍽 🍸 CALL &M 🏊 BIZ HS 🛜 ✕ 🔌 🖥 / SOME UNITS 🖨

(See map & index p. 208.)

## DOUBLETREE BY HILTON HOTEL TALLAHASSEE
(850)224-5000  **20**

▼▼▼ Hotel $109–$279 **Address:** 101 S Adams St 32301 **Location:** Jct Adams St and Park Ave; downtown. Opposite courthouse. **Facility:** 243 units. 16 stories, interior corridors. **Parking:** on-site (fee) and valet. **Terms:** 1-7 night minimum stay, cancellation fee imposed. **Pool(s):** outdoor. **Activities:** exercise room. **Guest Services:** valet laundry.

**AAA Benefit:** Members save 5% or more!

[ECO] [↔] [¶↑] [🐾] [Y] CALL [&M] [≈] [BIZ] [📶] [✕]
[📷] [💻] / SOME UNITS [🛏]

---

## ECONO LODGE
(850)385-6155  **16**

▼▼▼ Motel $55–$85

**Address:** 2681 N Monroe St 32303 **Location:** I-10 exit 199, 0.5 mi s. **Facility:** 81 units. 2 stories, exterior corridors. **Guest Services:** coin laundry. **Featured Amenity:** continental breakfast.

[SAVE] [¶↑] [📶] [🛏] [🖼] [💻]
/ SOME UNITS [🛏]

---

## EXTENDED STAY AMERICA TALLAHASSEE-KILLEARN
(850)383-1700  **1**

▼▼ Extended Stay Hotel $60–$225 **Address:** 1950 Raymond Diehl Rd 32308 **Location:** I-10 exit 203, 2.4 mi s, then just n. **Facility:** 59 kitchen units. 3 stories, interior corridors. **Terms:** cancellation fee imposed. **Pool(s):** outdoor. **Activities:** limited exercise equipment. **Guest Services:** coin laundry.

[¶↑] CALL [&M] [≈] [📶] [🖼] [🖼] [💻] / SOME UNITS [🛏]

---

## FAIRFIELD INN & SUITES BY MARRIOTT TALLAHASSEE CENTRAL
(850)210-1210  **30**

▼▼▼ Hotel $89–$299 **Address:** 2997 Apalachee Pkwy 32301 **Location:** Jct US 27 and 319, just w. **Facility:** 97 units. 4 stories, interior corridors. **Pool(s):** indoor. **Activities:** exercise room. **Guest Services:** valet and coin laundry.

**AAA Benefit:** Members save 5% or more!

[¶↑] [≈] [BIZ] [HS] [📶] [✕] [🖼] [🖼] [💻]

---

## FAIRFIELD INN BY MARRIOTT TALLAHASSEE NORTH/I-10
(850)562-8766  **10**

▼▼ Hotel $98–$115 **Address:** 3219 N Monroe St 32303 **Location:** I-10 exit 199, just n. **Facility:** 79 units. 3 stories, interior corridors. **Pool(s):** heated indoor. **Activities:** limited exercise equipment.

**AAA Benefit:** Members save 5% or more!

CALL [&M] [≈] [📶] [✕] [💻] / SOME UNITS [🖼] [🖼]

---

Enjoy great member

rates and benefits at

AAA/CAA Preferred Hotels

---

## FOUR POINTS BY SHERATON TALLAHASSEE DOWNTOWN
(850)422-0071  **18**

▼▼▼ Hotel $99–$549

FOUR POINTS BY SHERATON

**AAA Benefit:** Members save up to 15%, plus Starwood Preferred Guest® benefits!

**Address:** 316 W Tennessee St 32301 **Location:** Just w of US 27; downtown. **Facility:** 164 units. 12 stories, interior corridors. **Terms:** cancellation fee imposed. **Amenities:** safes. **Pool(s):** heated outdoor. **Activities:** exercise room. **Guest Services:** valet laundry, area transportation.

[SAVE] [↔] [¶↑] [🐾] [Y] [≈] [BIZ]
[HS] [📶] [✕] [💻]

/ SOME UNITS [🛏] [🖼] [🖼]

---

## GOVERNORS INN
(850)681-6855  **21**

▼▼ Historic Boutique Hotel $109–$229 **Address:** 209 S Adams St 32301 **Location:** Just n of state Capitol; center. **Facility:** This boutique hotel features pine paneling and an antique mahogany bar. Named after a past state governor, rooms have unique décor and include a posted biography of the featured governor. 41 units. 3 stories (no elevator), interior corridors. **Parking:** valet and street only. **Terms:** cancellation fee imposed. **Guest Services:** valet laundry.

[ECO] [¶↑] [📶] [✕] [💻] / SOME UNITS [🖼]

---

## HAMPTON INN & SUITES I-10/THOMASVILLE RD
(850)574-4900  **6**

▼▼▼ Hotel $119–$309 **Address:** 3388 Lonnbladh Rd 32308 **Location:** I-10 exit 203, 0.3 mi e on Raymond Diehl Rd. **Facility:** 122 units. 5 stories, interior corridors. **Terms:** 1-7 night minimum stay, cancellation fee imposed. **Pool(s):** outdoor. **Activities:** exercise room. **Guest Services:** valet and coin laundry.

**AAA Benefit:** Members save 5% or more!

[ECO] [¶↑] [≈] [BIZ] [HS] [📶] [✕] [🖼]
/ SOME UNITS [🖼] [🖼]

---

## HAMPTON INN TALLAHASSEE CENTRAL
(850)309-1300  **31**

▼▼▼ Hotel $109–$249 **Address:** 2979 Apalachee Pkwy 32301 **Location:** US 27, 3.5 mi s. **Facility:** 78 units. 4 stories, interior corridors. **Terms:** 1-7 night minimum stay, cancellation fee imposed. **Pool(s):** outdoor. **Activities:** exercise room. **Guest Services:** valet laundry.

**AAA Benefit:** Members save 5% or more!

[ECO] [¶↑] CALL [&M] [≈] [BIZ] [📶] [✕] [🖼] [🖼] [💻]

---

## HILTON GARDEN INN TALLAHASSEE
(850)385-3553  **5**

▼▼▼ Hotel $119–$189 **Address:** 3333 Thomasville Rd 32308 **Location:** I-10 exit 203, just s. **Facility:** 99 units. 4 stories, interior corridors. **Terms:** 1-7 night minimum stay, cancellation fee imposed. **Pool(s):** outdoor. **Activities:** hot tub. **Guest Services:** valet and coin laundry.

**AAA Benefit:** Members save 5% or more!

[ECO] [¶↑] [Y] [≈] [🐾] [BIZ] [HS] [📶] [🖼] [🖼] [💻]

---

## HILTON GARDEN INN TALLAHASSEE CENTRAL
(850)893-8300  **28**

▼▼▼ Hotel $109–$269 **Address:** 1330 S Blairstone Rd 32301 **Location:** Just s of Apalachee Pkwy. **Facility:** 85 units. 5 stories, interior corridors. **Terms:** 1-7 night minimum stay, cancellation fee imposed. **Amenities:** safes. **Pool(s):** outdoor. **Activities:** exercise room. **Guest Services:** valet and coin laundry.

**AAA Benefit:** Members save 5% or more!

[¶↑] [Y] CALL [&M] [≈] [BIZ] [HS] [📶] [✕] [🖼] [🖼]
[💻]

(See map & index p. 208.)

## HOMEWOOD SUITES BY HILTON     (850)402-9400   32

WWW **Extended Stay Hotel** $119-$299 **Address:** 2987 Apalachee Pkwy 32301 **Location:** US 27, 3.5 mi s. **Facility:** 94 efficiencies, some two bedrooms. 5 stories, interior corridors. **Terms:** 1-7 night minimum stay, cancellation fee imposed. **Pool(s):** outdoor. **Activities:** exercise room. **Guest Services:** valet and coin laundry.

**AAA Benefit:**
Members save 5% or more!

ECO ‖ ↦ ⚲ BIZ 📶 🗄 🖨 🖥 / SOME UNITS 🐾

## HOTEL DUVAL     850/224-6000   17

WWW **Boutique Contemporary Hotel.** Rates not provided. **Address:** 415 N Monroe St 32301 **Location:** 0.5 mi n of Capitol. **Facility:** The upscale hotel sits within walking distance of the government district and downtown. The chic, top-level bar has rooftop, open-air balcony seating offering a bird's-eye view of downtown. 117 units. 7 stories, interior corridors. *Bath:* shower only. **Parking:** on-site (fee) and valet. **Dining:** 3 restaurants. **Activities:** exercise room. **Guest Services:** valet laundry.

ECO ↦ ‖ ⬙ ⚲ BIZ 📶 🗄 🖨 🖥

## HOWARD JOHNSON EXPRESS INN     (850)386-5000   14

WW **Motel** $70-$230 **Address:** 2726 N Monroe St 32303 **Location:** I-10 exit 199, 0.5 mi s. **Facility:** 51 units. 2 stories, exterior corridors. **Amenities:** safes. **Pool(s):** outdoor. **Guest Services:** coin laundry. ‖ ⚲ 📶 🗄 🖨 🖥

## LA QUINTA INN TALLAHASSEE (NORTH)     (850)385-7172   12

WW **Hotel** $59-$309 **Address:** 2905 N Monroe St 32303 **Location:** I-10 exit 199, just s on US 27. **Facility:** 154 units. 2-3 stories, exterior corridors. **Pool(s):** outdoor.

‖ ⚲ 📶 🖥 / SOME UNITS 🐾 🗄 🖨

## QUALITY INN & SUITES     (850)877-4437   26

Hotel
$75-$159

**Address:** 2020 Apalachee Pkwy 32301 **Location:** 2.2 mi s on US 27. **Facility:** 90 units. 3 stories, interior corridors. **Amenities:** safes. **Pool(s):** outdoor. **Guest Services:** coin laundry. **Featured Amenity:** full hot breakfast.

SAVE ECO ‖ ⚲ BIZ 📶 🗙
🗄 🖥 / SOME UNITS 🐾 🖨

## RAMADA PLAZA     (850)877-3171   24

WW **Hotel** $62-$71 **Address:** 1355 Apalachee Pkwy 32301 **Location:** 1.3 mi se on US 27. **Facility:** 148 units. 4 stories, interior corridors. **Pool(s):** outdoor. **Activities:** exercise room. **Guest Services:** valet laundry.

‖ ⬙ ⬙ ⚲ BIZ 📶 🗙 🖥
/ SOME UNITS 🐾 🗄 🖨

## RESIDENCE INN BY MARRIOTT TALLAHASSEE NORTH I-10 CAPITAL CIRCLE     (850)422-0093   2

WWW **Extended Stay Hotel** $76-$299 **Address:** 1880 Raymond Diehl Rd 32308 **Location:** I-10 exit 203, just s. **Facility:** 78 units, some two bedrooms, efficiencies and kitchens. 3 stories, interior corridors. **Pool(s):** heated indoor. **Activities:** hot tub, exercise room. **Guest Services:** valet and coin laundry.

**AAA Benefit:**
Members save 5% or more!

ECO ‖ CALL 🔊M ⚲ BIZ 📶 🗙 🗄 🖨 🖥
/ SOME UNITS 🐾

## RESIDENCE INN BY MARRIOTT TALLAHASSEE UNIVERSITIES AT THE CAPITOL     (850)329-9080   27

Extended Stay Hotel
$119-$299

Residence Inn Marriott

**AAA Benefit:**
Members save 5% or more!

**Address:** 600 W Gaines St 32304 **Location:** 0.5 mi w of S Monroe St; downtown. **Facility:** 135 efficiencies, some two bedrooms. 5 stories, interior corridors. **Terms:** check-in 4 pm. **Pool(s):** outdoor. **Activities:** hot tub, exercise room. **Guest Services:** valet and coin laundry, area transportation. **Featured Amenity:** breakfast buffet.

SAVE ECO ↦ CALL 🔊M ⚲ BIZ
📶 🗙 🎥 🗄 🖨 🖥 / SOME UNITS 🐾

## STAYBRIDGE SUITES TALLAHASSEE     850/219-7000   7

WWW **Extended Stay Hotel.** Rates not provided. **Address:** 1600 Summit Lake Dr 32317 **Location:** I-10 exit 209B, just n. **Facility:** 104 efficiencies, some two bedrooms. 4 stories, interior corridors. **Amenities:** safes. **Pool(s):** outdoor. **Activities:** exercise room. **Guest Services:** valet and coin laundry.

ECO ⚲ BIZ HS 📶 🗙 🗄 🖨 🖥
/ SOME UNITS 🐾

## TOWNEPLACE SUITES BY MARRIOTT TALLAHASSEE NORTHEAST/CAPITAL CIRCLE     (850)219-0122   13

WWW **Extended Stay Hotel** $85-$375 **Address:** 1876 Capital Cir NE 32308 **Location:** I-10 exit 203, just e to US 319, then 2.1 mi s. **Facility:** 94 kitchen units, some two bedrooms. 3 stories, interior corridors. **Terms:** check-in 4 pm. **Pool(s):** outdoor. **Activities:** exercise room. **Guest Services:** valet and coin laundry.

**AAA Benefit:**
Members save 5% or more!

ECO CALL 🔊M ⚲ 📶 🗙 🗄 🖨 🖥 / SOME UNITS 🐾

## WINGATE BY WYNDHAM     (850)553-4400   15

WWW **Hotel** $89-$279 **Address:** 2516 W Lakeshore Dr 32312 **Location:** I-10 exit 199, 0.4 mi s. **Facility:** 116 units. 4 stories, interior corridors. **Terms:** check-in 4 pm. **Pool(s):** outdoor. **Activities:** hot tub, exercise room. **Guest Services:** valet and coin laundry.

‖ CALL 🔊M ⚲ BIZ HS 📶 🗙 🗄 🖨 🖥

## WHERE TO EAT

## A LA PROVENCE     850/329-6870   2

WWW French. Fine Dining. $10-$35 **AAA Inspector Notes:** This intimate restaurant offers a seasonally changing menu using fresh ingredients. Diners are delighted with the lobster bisque, and locals rave over the crab cakes a l'aubergine. Choose from a wide variety of wines, many available by the glass. Always leave room to make a selection from the dessert offerings. For those wishing a more casual experience, sit at the café de artiste to the rear of the dining room. **Features:** full bar, patio dining. **Address:** 1415 Timberlane Rd 32312 **Location:** I-10 exit 203, 0.3 mi n, then w; in Market Square. L D

## ANDREWS 228 RESTAURANT     850/222-3444   24

WWW New American. Fine Dining. $14-$42 **AAA Inspector Notes:** With a presence of over 40 years in the downtown area, this is considered by many as "the place to go" in the capital city. Over the years many famous celebrities have graced the restaurant such as Jay Leno and Bill Clinton. Patrons will find a diverse selection of dishes on the seasonally changing menu which features fresh food from local sustainable farms. **Features:** full bar, patio dining. **Address:** 228 S Adams St 32301 **Location:** Between W College and W Jefferson sts; downtown. **Parking:** street only. D

**(See map & index p. 208.)**

## AVENUE EAT AND DRINK
850/224-0115 ⑮

◆◆◆ Southern Fusion. Casual Dining. $8-$46 **AAA Inspector Notes:** This downtown eatery sports an after-five vibe. Exposed brick, deep purple walls, and unique lighting sources support an atmosphere that is cozy and intimate. This is a popular gathering place for the Capitol and college crowd. There is an emphasis on using local vendors for veggies, beef, poultry and seafood. Some samples include braised boneless short ribs, farm-raised semi-boneless quail, wahoo steak, and seared duck breast. **Features:** full bar, Sunday brunch, happy hour. **Reservations:** suggested. **Address:** 115 E Park Ave 32301 **Location:** Jct Adams St and Park Ave; downtown. **Parking:** on-site (fee). Ⓛ Ⓓ 🐾

## AZU LUCY HO'S
850/893-4112 ⑱

◆ Chinese. Casual Dining. $7-$36 **AAA Inspector Notes:** In business for more than 40 years, this restaurant is often considered the best in the area for Asian cuisine. A professional staff will gladly help you select from the many entrées featured on its extensive menu. The crab Rangoon is delicious, with huge pieces of crab prepared with a light peanut oil. Large, heaping portions and a sushi bar will please every appetite. **Features:** beer & wine, Sunday brunch, happy hour. **Address:** 3220 Apalachee Pkwy 32311 **Location:** Jct US 319, just e on US 27; in Big Oak Plaza. Ⓛ Ⓓ

## BACKWOODS BISTRO
850/320-6345 ㉕

◆◆ American. Casual Dining. $9-$18 **AAA Inspector Notes:** Locally-owned and -operated, this restaurant and lounge has a relaxed atmosphere featuring a menu with a little something for everyone. Basics such as sandwiches, burgers and wings along with some meat, seafood, vegetarian and pasta dishes make up the menu. The bar remains open long after food service ends. Live music is often presented on the weekend. **Features:** full bar, Sunday brunch, happy hour. **Address:** 401 E Tennessee St 32301 **Location:** Jct N Gadsden St; downtown. Ⓛ Ⓓ CALL 📶

## BARNACLE BILL'S
850/385-8734 ④

◆◆◆

Seafood
Casual Dining

$8-$19

**AAA Inspector Notes:** A popular local gathering spot, this spot features Florida seafood, pasta and a oyster bar with seasonal outdoor seating. The efficient waitstaff excels at keeping guests happy. A close cousin of jambalaya, the shrimp skillet is a nice mix of rice and sausage. **Features:** full bar, patio dining, happy hour. **Address:** 1830 N Monroe St 32303 **Location:** I-10 exit 199, 2 mi s.

Ⓓ CALL 📶 🐾

## BELLA BELLA
850/412-1114 ⑨

◆ Italian. Casual Dining. $9-$19 **AAA Inspector Notes:** Located on a busy main street, this eatery is easy to overlook as is nestled among other downtown businesses—but look for the painted murals on the exterior. Two dining areas offer a variety of seating. The front room offers space for large parties of four to eight as well as a small lounge. The Back has tables that are closer together and less private. Along with the standard menu a wide variety of specials change daily. Dessert is a must. **Features:** full bar, patio dining, happy hour. **Address:** 123 E 5th Ave 32303 **Location:** I-10 exit 199, 3.7 mi s; jct Monroe St and W 5th Ave. Ⓛ Ⓓ

## THE BLACK BEAN CUBAN CAFE
850/656-7848 ⑲

◆ Cuban. Family Dining. $5-$10 **AAA Inspector Notes:** Great Cuban traditional fare is served in a compact modest setting. Papa rellena, empanadas, Cuban sandwiches, masitas (chunks of pork lightly fried), palomilla steak and house specialties of black bean gumbo and habanero barbecue pork are all made in house. The popularity of this café may make getting a table during peak meal hours a little rough. Delivery is available. **Features:** beer only, patio dining. **Address:** 2205 Apalachee Pkwy 32301 **Location:** 1 mi se on US 27. Ⓛ Ⓓ 🐾

---

## CODY'S ORIGINAL ROADHOUSE
850/402-3014

◆◆ American. Casual Dining. $9-$23 **AAA Inspector Notes:** One can't help but notice this roadside establishment with an orange antique truck parked by an old-fashion gas pump out front and the vintage signs plastered all over the building. The rustic interior filled with old-time memorabilia continues the theme. You may step on some peanut shells, which are strewn about the floor as patrons deposit them there when munching from the full bucket on every table. American favorites on the menu include steaks, seafood, ribs and burgers. **Features:** full bar, patio dining, happy hour. **Address:** 1926 Capital Cir NE 32308 **Location:** I-10 exit 203, just e to US 319, then 1.9 mi s. Ⓛ Ⓓ CALL 📶

## CRISPERS
850/656-4222

◆ Sandwiches Soup. Quick Serve. $5-$11 **AAA Inspector Notes:** A healthy alternative for lunch or dinner, the restaurant prepares towering specialty sandwiches on warm, fresh homemade bread. Salad selections with combinations of meats, fruit and cheese are just as tempting. Varied coffees go well with freshly baked cakes and brownies. **Address:** 1241 Apalachee Pkwy 32301 **Location:** Just w of Magnolia Dr. Ⓛ Ⓓ

## CYPRESS RESTAURANT
850/513-1100 ⑭

◆◆◆ Southern American. Fine Dining. $12-$34 **AAA Inspector Notes:** Try pulled pork on top of corn cakes, dolloped with slaw and decorated in peach barbecue sauce—and that's just the appetizer. The menu has limited entrée selections presented in a fun and inspired way, with creative sauces and accompaniments. A cheese menu consisting of eight to 10 cheeses is offered with a pick-three or pick-five tasting flight. Attention to detail in both food and service comes together nicely. A casual and relaxed menu is offered at the bar. Brunch is the only offering on Sunday. **Features:** full bar, Sunday brunch, happy hour. **Reservations:** suggested. **Address:** 320 E Tennessee St 32301 **Location:** Between N Gadsden and N Calhoun sts; downtown. Ⓓ

## DOG ET AL
850/222-4099 ㉒

◆ Hot Dogs. Quick Serve. $2-$10 **AAA Inspector Notes:** In business for nearly three decades, this hot dog joint serves beef and turkey franks, corn dogs, bratwurst, and smoked Southern, Polish and Italian sausages in a variety of sizes, ranging from little to "Bigfoot." Numerous toppings are available to allow you to have your wiener the way you like it. The combo meal includes a hot dog, drink, homemade chips or fries and fried apple pie. The place is especially busy during lunchtime so you may have to wait for a seat. **Address:** 1456 S Monroe St 32301 **Location:** On SR 61/373, between E Pershing and E Jennings sts. Ⓛ Ⓓ

## GEORGIO'S FINE FOOD & SPIRITS
850/877-3211 ⑳

◆◆◆ Continental. Casual Dining. $15-$40 **AAA Inspector Notes:** The family that owns this restaurant has been a staple on the restaurant scene in Tallahassee for many years, bringing a level of sophistication to Italian comfort food. Large portions fill each plate, and leaving hungry will never happen. The escargot, crab cakes, and jumbo shrimp are savory appetizers, while the chicken Rockefeller, salmon fettuccine, filet au poivre, and stuffed grouper add substance with large portions. A variety of after-dinner coffees and sinful desserts are offered. **Features:** full bar. **Reservations:** suggested. **Address:** 2971 Apalachee Pkwy 32301 **Location:** US 27, 3.5 mi s. Ⓓ

## HARRY'S SEAFOOD BAR AND GRILLE
850/222-3976 ⑯

◆◆◆ Southern Seafood. Casual Dining. $8-$21 **AAA Inspector Notes:** Both the menu and the décor are inspired by New Orleans at this popular downtown eatery. Bright Mardi Gras posters and artwork depicting Bourbon Street and jazz add to the festive atmosphere. Parking is in the garage under Kleman Plaza. **Features:** full bar, patio dining, happy hour. **Address:** 301 S Bronough St 32301 **Location:** Jct W College Ave; downtown; entrance in Kleman Plaza. **Parking:** on-site (fee). Ⓛ Ⓓ CALL 📶

## HOBBIT AMERICAN GRILL
850/402-2900 ⑬

◆ Wings Burgers. Casual Dining. $8-$10 **AAA Inspector Notes:** Serving the capital city for more than 30 years, this establishment offers typical sports bar fare. Fourteen TVs throughout give every table an unobstructed view of the featured game. **Features:** full bar, patio dining, happy hour. **Address:** 400 Capital Cir SE, Suite 16 32308 **Location:** Jct US 319/SR 261 and 265, just s; in plaza. Ⓛ Ⓓ LATE CALL 📶

**(See map & index p. 208.)**

### JOE MAMA'S WOOD FIRED PIZZA    850/577-1231   ⑥
▼▼▼ Pizza. Casual Dining. $7-$19 **AAA Inspector Notes:** A sleek, stylish décor in a relaxed and friendly atmosphere can be found here. Artisan pizza with gourmet toppings are baked quickly and to perfection in an 800-degree brick oven. Add a healthy selection of craft beers and imported wines and you have the recipe for a delicious meal. **Features:** beer & wine. **Address:** 1307 N Monroe St 32303 **Location:** I-10 exit 199, 2.4 mi s. **Parking:** on-site and street. D CALL ⑤M

### KOOL BEANZ CAFE    850/224-2466   ⑪
▼▼▼ American. Casual Dining. $7-$25 **AAA Inspector Notes:** A fun gathering spot where talking loud and gathering with friends is encouraged. Wine and beer menus can be found on empty bottles left on the table. The menu, presented on a clipboard, is exciting and changes daily. Fresh seafood is brought to the location daily and delicious entrées include blackened cobia, sesame-seed-crusted tuna, bacon-wrapped grouper and walnut-floured flounder. Desserts are made onsite. Be prepared to wait. **Features:** beer & wine, patio dining, Sunday brunch. **Address:** 921 Thomasville Rd 32303 **Location:** Between Johnston and Williams sts; downtown. L D

### MARIE LIVINGSTON'S STEAK HOUSE    850/562-2525   ㉑
▼▼▼ Steak. Casual Dining. $6-$35 **AAA Inspector Notes:** The owner proudly put her name on this upscale establishment to indicate her personal touch on the food and service. The succulent, cooked-to-order steaks are flavored with a secret special sauce. For two decades, this family-operated restaurant has secured a loyal clientèle. **Features:** full bar, patio dining. **Address:** 2705 Apalachee Pkwy 32303 **Location:** Jct US 27 and 319, 0.5 mi w. L D CALL ⑤M

### MASA    850/847-0003   ⑩
▼▼▼ Asian. Casual Dining. $8-$29 **AAA Inspector Notes:** This cozy, mid-town Asian bistro offers not only traditional dishes but some signature entrées which merge Western and Eastern cuisines. **Features:** beer & wine. **Address:** 1001 N Monroe St 32303 **Location:** I-10 exit 199, 2.8 mi s; jct Third Ave. L D CALL ⑤M

### MIDTOWN FILLING STATION    850/329-7981   ⑧
▼▼ American. Gastropub. $6-$12 **AAA Inspector Notes:** Fun names on classic favorites can be found here. Try the drunken tater tot with New Castle fondue cheese and scallions; the train wreck with smoked turkey, roast beef, bacon, sharp cheddar and Swiss; or the Goliath burger with bacon, leeks, potatoes, blue cheese and homemade blackened tomato ketchup. Some menu items change daily, including the boiled nut, hummus and quesadilla of the day. There is an expanded craft beer menu. **Features:** full bar, patio dining, happy hour. **Address:** 1122 Thomasville Rd 32303 **Location:** Between E 5th and Williams sts; downtown. L D 🐄

### MILANO PIZZERIA    850/270-9100   ③
▼▼ ▼ Pizza. Casual Dining. $6-$25 **AAA Inspector Notes:** This family-run neighborhood pizza house also serves a variety of pasta dishes. A large covered patio offers an alternative seating option in warm weather. **Features:** beer only, patio dining. **Address:** 1940 N Monroe St 32303 **Location:** I-10 exit 199, 2.1 mi s on US 27, then just w on SR 158; on south side of Northwood Centre Mall. L D CALL ⑤M

### THE MOCKINGBIRD CAFE    850/222-4956   ⑦
▼▼▼ American. Casual Dining. $7-$25 **AAA Inspector Notes:** Choose from two places to dine once inside—the fun, upbeat music room, or the quieter, more reserved dining room. Music changes nightly, so consult the website for appearing artists. The menu changes weekly and often offers such tantalizing selections as bison, duck and crab. I chose the farfalle pasta with butternut squash, Brussels sprouts, seared ham, broccoli and shaved Parmesan cheese; it was earthy and delicious. **Features:** full bar, patio dining, Sunday brunch, happy hour. **Address:** 1225 N Monroe St 32303 **Location:** Just n of downtown. L D LATE 🐄

### MOMO'S PIZZA    850/412-0222   ㉓
▼▼ ▼ Pizza. Casual Dining. $6-$24 **AAA Inspector Notes:** Slices as big as your head is the promise here. And what goes best with pizza? Why beer of course. This place offers the best of both with hand tossed New York style pies along with fresh on-site brewed beer with seasonally changing flavors. Have your own favorite craft beer? The wide selection offered almost guarantees that they have it. If you are lucky, you'll also hear live music. **Features:** beer only, patio dining. **Address:** 1410 Market St 32312 **Location:** I-10 exit 203, just n on US 319, then just w; in shopping plaza. L D CALL ⑤M

### PEPPER'S MEXICAN GRILL & CANTINA    850/877-2020   ⑰
▼▼ ▼ Mexican. Casual Dining. $5-$14 **AAA Inspector Notes:** This cozy family-operated café serves all the traditional favorites. **Features:** full bar, patio dining. **Address:** 1140 Capital Cir SE, Suite 15 32301 **Location:** Jct US 27 and 319, 0.5 mi n; in Governor's Court Plaza. L D CALL ⑤M

### RUMMY'S PIZZA, PASTA & GRILL    850/878-8669   ①
▼▼ ▼ Pizza. Casual Dining. $7-$19 **AAA Inspector Notes:** This casual pizzeria offers a family-friendly atmosphere with games and specials for the kids, plus plenty of TVs for the sports fan. A selection of specialty pizzas is offered, as well as sandwiches, salads, burgers and some Italian entrées. **Features:** full bar, patio dining, senior menu, happy hour. **Address:** 2887 Kerry Forest Pkwy 32312 **Location:** 3 mi n on Thomasville Rd. L D CALL ⑤M 🐄

### SONNY'S REAL PIT BAR-B-Q
▼▼ ▼ Barbecue. Family Dining. $8-$16 **AAA Inspector Notes:** Bearing the name after its founder, Floyd "Sonny" Tillman, this barbecue restaurant first opened its doors circa 1968 in Gainesville, Florida and has since spawned over 150 more throughout the Southeast. The menu is steeped in finger lickin' favorites such as ribs, pulled pork, beef brisket, burgers, catfish, shrimp and char-grilled chicken. Let's not forget about the fried okra, which is the perfect starter dish, and their homemade baked beans. **Bar:** beer only. L D

*For additional information, visit AAA.com*
**LOCATIONS:**
**Address:** 2707 N Monroe St 32303 **Location:** I-10 exit 199, 1.2 mi s. **Phone:** 850/385-2167
**Address:** 1460 Timberlane Rd 32312 **Location:** I-10 exit 203, 0.3 mi n, then w; at Market Square. **Phone:** 850/906-9996

### WELLS BROTHERS BAR AND GRILL    850/942-6665   ⑤
▼▼ ▼ Burgers. Casual Dining. $8-$11 **AAA Inspector Notes:** This simple brick structure has become synonymous with hamburgers to the local community. Formerly known as Monk's, this burger joint also serves sandwiches and pizza. Multiple napkins are required while devouring the juicy, cooked-to-order specialty. **Features:** full bar, patio dining, happy hour. **Address:** 1710 W Tharpe St 32303 **Location:** I-10 exit 199, 2.1 mi s on US 27 (N Monroe St), then 1.8 mi w on SR 158. L D

### LOFTY PURSUITS    850/521-0091
fyi Not evaluated. Dairy sodas, handmade sodas, egg creams, French sodas, fizzy sodas, rickeys, ades, floats, freezes, yips, shakes, malts, and more than 52 combinations of ice cream sundaes are offered on this menu. The sushi sundae, baklava sundae, Key lime pie sundae and pound cake sundae are some tempting confections, but the kitchen sink sundae beats them all, with 26 scoops of ice cream and every possible topping in the store. If you eat in 2 hours, you'll earn a spot on the wall of fame. **Address:** 1415 Timberlane Rd, #410 32312 **Location:** I-10 exit 203, just n, then w.

## WAKULLA SPRINGS (C-5)

◄ EDWARD BALL WAKULLA SPRINGS STATE PARK, 465 Wakulla Park Dr., was known to early Native Americans for its plentiful wildlife. The main spring, with a water temperature of 69 F, is considered one of the state's deepest, having been explored to a depth of 350 feet. The maximum flow was recorded in 1973 at 1.2 billion gallons a day; in 1931 the minimum flow was measured at 20 million gallons. The average is 252 million gallons of water daily.

A popular "birding mecca," the park offers swimming and hiking opportunities, and a bicycle and nature trail. Narrated river cruises provide glimpses of animals in their native habitats. *See Recreation Areas Chart.*

**Time:** Allow 2 hours minimum. **Hours:** Park daily 8-dusk. River cruises depart daily every hour 9:30-5, during DST; 9:15-4:30, rest of year (weather permitting). **Cost:** $6 (per private vehicle with two to eight people); $4 (per single-occupancy vehicle); $2 (per person arriving by bicycle or on foot). River cruise $8; $5 (ages 3-12). **Phone:** (850) 561-7276. ⓘ ⓧ ⓐ

---

WAKULLA SPRINGS LODGE                    850/421-2000

♦♦ **Historic Country Inn.** Rates not provided. **Address:** 550 Wakulla Park Dr 32327 **Location:** Waterfront. Jct CR 61 and SR 267; in Edward Ball Wakulla Springs State Park. **Facility:** This historic lodge is set within a 6,000-acre wildlife sanctuary and is a haven for those desiring a nature retreat. The park has many areas to explore, including the Wakulla Springs and River. 27 units. 2 stories, interior corridors. **Dining:** The Ball Room, see separate listing. **Activities:** recreation programs, playground. ⓘ 🛜 ⓧ ⓦ

### WHERE TO EAT

THE BALL ROOM                            850/926-0700

♦♦ Regional Comfort Food. Casual Dining. $7-$27 **AAA Inspector Notes:** Freshly prepared meals with a strong Southern accent include fried chicken, pan-fried beef liver and fried seafood. They also offer a variety of sandwiches. Appetizers include fried green tomatoes. Gaze out over lovely and scenic Wakulla Springs as you dine. **Reservations:** suggested, for dinner. **Address:** 550 Wakulla Park Dr 32327 **Location:** Jct CR 61 and SR 267; in Edward Ball Wakulla Springs State Park; in Wakulla Springs Lodge.

ⓑ ⓛ ⓓ

## WHITE SPRINGS (B-6) pop. 777, elev. 125'

Once a health resort, White Springs is built around sulfur springs. Seminole and Timucuan Indians considered the springs sacred and believed their warriors were impervious to attack while recuperating.

**STEPHEN FOSTER FOLK CULTURE CENTER STATE PARK,** 11016 Lillian Saunders Dr., covers 888 wooded acres beside the Suwannee River, which the composer immortalized in his song "Old Folks At Home." The museum displays animated dioramas depicting Foster's songs, and the 200-foot carillon tower houses one of the largest set of tubular bells in the world. The Crafts Square features Florida Cracker-style buildings with craft studios. Hiking and bicycling trails, horseback riding, a canoe launch and a playground are available. The Florida Folk Festival is held here over the Memorial Day weekend.

**Time:** Allow 4 hours minimum. **Hours:** Daily 9-dusk. **Cost:** $5 (per private vehicle with two to eight people); $4 (per single-occupant vehicle); $2 (per person arriving by bicycle or on foot). Some events have varying admission charges. **Phone:** (386) 397-2733. ⓐ ⓘ ⓧ 🎁 ⓐ

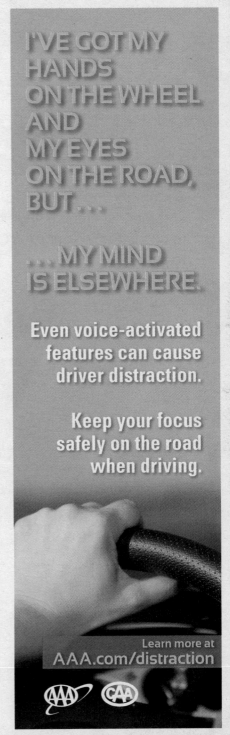

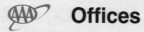

# Offices

Main office listings are shown in **BOLD TYPE** and toll-free member service numbers appear in *ITALIC TYPE*.
All are closed Saturdays, Sundays and holidays unless otherwise indicated.
The addresses, phone numbers and hours for any AAA/CAA office are subject to change.
The type of service provided is designated below the name of the city where the office is located:

✛ Auto travel services, including books and maps, and on-demand TripTik® routings.
● Auto travel services, including selected books and maps, and on-demand TripTik® routings.
■ Books/maps only, no marked maps or on-demand TripTik® routings.
▲ Travel Agency Services, cruise, tour, air, car and rail reservations; domestic and international hotel reservations; passport photo services; international and domestic travel guides and maps; travel money products; and International Driving Permits. In addition, assistance with travel related insurance products including trip cancellation, travel accident, lost luggage, trip delay and assistance products.
⚙ Insurance services provided. If only this icon appears, only insurance services are provided at that office.
◗ Car Care Plus Facility provides car care services.
⬛ Electric vehicle charging station on premises.

---

**AAA NATIONAL OFFICE:** 1000 AAA DRIVE, HEATHROW, FLORIDA 32746-5063, (407) 444-7000

## ALABAMA

**BIRMINGHAM**—AAA-ALABAMA, 2400 ACTON RD, 35243. WEEKDAYS (M-F) 8:00-6:00, SAT 9:00-2:00. (205) 978-7000, *(800) 521-8124.* ✛▲⚙

**DECATUR**—AAA-ALABAMA, 1605 BELTLINE RD SW #D-9, 35603. WEEKDAYS (M-F) 8:30-5:00. (256) 353-4924, *(800) 521-8124.* ✛▲⚙

**DOTHAN**—AAA-ALABAMA, 3850 W MAIN ST, 36305. WEEKDAYS (M-F) 8:30-5:00. (334) 793-6080, *(800) 521-8124.* ✛▲⚙

**FLORENCE**—AAA-ALABAMA, 102 S PINE ST, 35630. WEEKDAYS (M-F) 8:30-5:00. (256) 764-9173, *(800) 521-8124.* ✛▲⚙

**FULTONDALE**—AAA-ALABAMA, 3345 LOWERY PKWY STE 115, 35068. WEEKDAYS (M-F) 9:30-6:00, SAT 10:00-3:00. (205) 841-2374, *(800) 521-8124.* ✛▲⚙

**HUNTSVILLE**—AAA-ALABAMA, 2625 MEMORIAL PKWY SW, 35801. WEEKDAYS (M-F) 8:30-5:00, SAT 9:00-2:00. (256) 539-7493, *(800) 521-8124.* ✛▲⚙

**MOBILE**—AAA-ALABAMA, 720 SCHILLINGER RD S #5, 36695. WEEKDAYS (M-F) 9:00-6:00, SAT 9:00-2:00. (251) 639-3510, *(800) 521-8124.* ✛▲⚙

**MONTGOMERY**—AAA-ALABAMA, 6901 VAUGHN RD, 36116. WEEKDAYS (M-F) 8:30-5:00. (334) 272-1650, *(800) 521-8124.* ✛▲⚙

**OXFORD**—AAA-ALABAMA, 119 COMMONS WAY #101, 36203. WEEKDAYS (M-F) 8:30-5:00. (256) 832-3101, *(800) 521-8124.* ✛▲⚙

**TUSCALOOSA**—AAA-ALABAMA, 312 MERCHANTS WALK #5A, 35406. WEEKDAYS (M-F) 8:30-5:00. (205) 759-1202, *(800) 521-8124.* ✛▲⚙

## NORTHERN PANHANDLE FLORIDA

**PENSACOLA**—AAA AUTO CLUB GROUP, 540 BRENT LN, 32503. WEEKDAYS (M-F) 8:30-5:30. (850) 477-6860 ✛▲⚙

**TALLAHASSEE**—AAA AUTO CLUB GROUP, 3491 THOMASVILLE RD #26, 32309. WEEKDAYS (M-F) 9:00-6:00. (850) 907-1000 ✛▲⚙

---

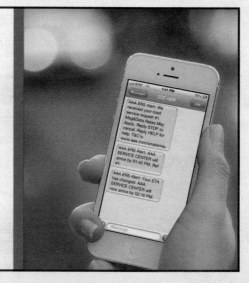

# Metric Equivalents Chart

## TEMPERATURE

To convert Fahrenheit to Celsius, subtract 32 from the Fahrenheit temperature, multiply by 5 and divide by 9.
To convert Celsius to Fahrenheit, multiply by 9, divide by 5 and add 32.

## ACRES

1 acre = 0.4 hectare (ha)      1 hectare = 2.47 acres

## MILES AND KILOMETERS

**Note:** A kilometer is approximately 5/8 or 0.6 of a mile.
To convert kilometers to miles multiply by 0.6.

| Miles/Kilometers | | Kilometers/Miles | |
|---|---|---|---|
| 15 | 24.1 | 30 | 18.6 |
| 20 | 32.2 | 35 | 21.7 |
| 25 | 40.2 | 40 | 24.8 |
| 30 | 48.3 | 45 | 27.9 |
| 35 | 56.3 | 50 | 31.0 |
| 40 | 64.4 | 55 | 34.1 |
| 45 | 72.4 | 60 | 37.2 |
| 50 | 80.5 | 65 | 40.3 |
| 55 | 88.5 | 70 | 43.4 |
| 60 | 96.6 | 75 | 46.6 |
| 65 | 104.6 | 80 | 49.7 |
| 70 | 112.7 | 85 | 52.8 |
| 75 | 120.7 | 90 | 55.9 |
| 80 | 128.7 | 95 | 59.0 |
| 85 | 136.8 | 100 | 62.1 |
| 90 | 144.8 | 105 | 65.2 |
| 95 | 152.9 | 110 | 68.3 |
| 100 | 160.9 | 115 | 71.4 |

## LINEAR MEASURE

| Customary | Metric |
|---|---|
| 1 inch = 2.54 centimeters | 1 centimeter = 0.4 inches |
| 1 foot = 30 centimeters | 1 meter = 3.3 feet |
| 1 yard = 0.91 meters | 1 meter = 1.09 yards |
| 1 mile = 1.6 kilometers | 1 kilometer = .62 miles |

## LIQUID MEASURE

| Customary | Metric |
|---|---|
| 1 fluid ounce = 30 milliliters | 1 milliliter = .03 fluid ounces |
| 1 cup = .24 liters | 1 liter = 2.1 pints |
| 1 pint = .47 liters | 1 liter = 1.06 quarts |
| 1 quart = .95 liters | 1 liter = .26 gallons |
| 1 gallon = 3.8 liters | |

## Celsius ° / Fahrenheit °

| Celsius ° | | Fahrenheit ° |
|---|---|---|
| 100 | BOILING | 212 |
| 37 | | 100 |
| 35 | | 95 |
| 32 | | 90 |
| 29 | | 85 |
| 27 | | 80 |
| 24 | | 75 |
| 21 | | 70 |
| 18 | | 65 |
| 16 | | 60 |
| 13 | | 55 |
| 10 | | 50 |
| 7 | | 45 |
| 4 | | 40 |
| 2 | | 35 |
| 0 | FREEZING | 32 |
| -4 | | 25 |
| -7 | | 20 |
| -9 | | 15 |
| -12 | | 10 |
| -15 | | 5 |
| -18 | | 0 |
| -21 | | -5 |
| -24 | | -10 |
| -27 | | -15 |

## WEIGHT

| If You Know: | Multiply By: | To Find: |
|---|---|---|
| Ounces | 28 | Grams |
| Pounds | 0.45 | Kilograms |
| Grams | 0.035 | Ounces |
| Kilograms | 2.2 | Pounds |

## PRESSURE

Air pressure in automobile tires is expressed in kilopascals. Multiply pound-force per square inch (psi) by 6.89 to find kilopascals (kPa).

| | |
|---|---|
| 24 psi = 165 kPa | 28 psi = 193 kPa |
| 26 psi = 179 kPa | 30 psi = 207 kPa |

## GALLONS AND LITERS

| Gallons/Liters | | Liters/Gallons | |
|---|---|---|---|
| 5 | 19.0 | 10 | 2.6 |
| 6 | 22.8 | 15 | 3.9 |
| 7 | 26.6 | 20 | 5.2 |
| 8 | 30.4 | 25 | 6.5 |
| 9 | 34.2 | 30 | 7.8 |
| 10 | 38.0 | 35 | 9.1 |
| 12 | 45.6 | 40 | 10.4 |
| 14 | 53.2 | 50 | 13.0 |
| 16 | 60.8 | 60 | 15.6 |
| 18 | 68.4 | 70 | 18.2 |
| 20 | 76.0 | 80 | 20.8 |
| 25 | 95.0 | 90 | 23.4 |

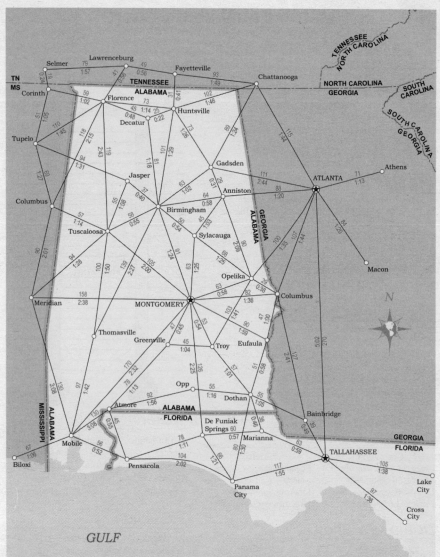

## ALABAMA-
# NORTH FLORIDA
### DRIVING DISTANCES
MILES:100 AVERAGE TIME (EXCLUDING STOPS): 2:00

© AAA

©2014 HERE

# LET YOUR VOICE BE HEARD

## We Want to Hear From You

**Property Comments/ Recommendations**

- If a AAA listed establishment doesn't meet your expectations, send us the details so we can look into it.

- Or, if you've got a favorite hotel, restaurant or attraction you'd like us to consider for AAA inspection, send us your recommendation.

## Complete an easy online form at
### AAA.COM/TOURBOOKCOMMENTS

# Points of Interest Index

 Attractions appear at the top of each category
and offer a Great Experience for Members®.

## Index Legend

| | | | |
|---|---|---|---|
| NB. | national battlefield | NR. | national river |
| NBP. | national battlefield park | NS. | national seashore |
| NC. | national cemetery | NWR. | national wildlife refuge |
| NF. | national forest | PHP. | provincial historic(al) park |
| NHM. | national historic(al) monument | PHS. | provincial historic(al) site |
| NHP. | national historic(al) park | PP. | provincial park |
| NHS. | national historic(al) site | SF. | state forest |
| NL. | national lakeshore | SHM. | state historic(al) monument |
| NME. | national memorial | SHP. | state historic(al) park |
| NMO. | national monument | SHS. | state historic(al) site |
| NMP. | national military park | SME. | state memorial |
| NP. | national park | SP. | state park |
| NRA. | national recreation area | SRA. | state recreation area |

## SHOPPING & NIGHTLIFE

## SPORTS & RECREATION

## TOURS & SIGHTSEEING

# Photo Credits

Page numbers are in bold type. Picture credit abbreviations are as follows:
- (i) numeric sequence from top to bottom, left to right ■ (AAA) AAA Travel library.

# Travel Farther With AAA

Get more travel value when you book, pack and pay using AAA:

- **BOOK** your trip with a AAA Member Rewards credit card and get triple points on qualifying travel, $500,000 travel accident insurance, lost luggage protection and much more.

- **PACK** your wallet with currency from more than 70 countries and a reloadable AAA travel money card with ATM withdrawal and emergency cash disbursement.

- **PAY** with confidence knowing you'll get the AAA benefits you expect plus low fees and easy card replacement.

*Visit us at AAA.com/financial or stop by a AAA office.*

# Maximize Your Membership

**G**et more from your AAA/CAA membership.
**Upgrade to Plus or Premier.**

With expanded roadside assistance – and a host of
other benefits – Plus or Premier is a smart choice.

To upgrade, contact your local
club office, visit **AAA.com** or
**CAA.ca**, or call **800-Join-AAA**
(564-6222).

# Plan the Joy

**When traveling with pets, planning ahead means the difference between g-r-reat and r-r-ruff!**

Know what to expect with the annually updated *AAA PetBook*:

- Policies and services at thousands of pet-friendly AAA Approved places to stay, play and eat
- Handy travel tips and resources
- Highlights of the AAA PetBook Photo Contest

Available at participating AAA/CAA offices and online booksellers.
**AAA.com/PetBook**

238

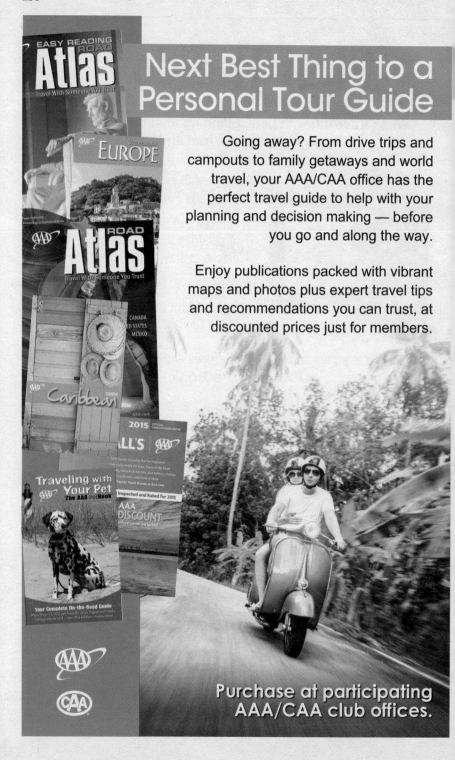